Macro Social Work Practice

WORKING FOR CHANGE IN A MULTICULTURAL SOCIETY

Michael Reisch

Bassim Hamadeh, CEO and Publisher
Leah Sheets, Associate Editor
Charlotte Andrews, Production Editor
Alia Bales, Associate Production Editor
Jess Estrella, Senior Graphic Designer
Alexa Lucido, Licensing Coordinator
Natalie Piccotti, Senior Marketing Manager
Kassie Graves, Vice President of Editorial
Jamie Giganti, Director of Academic Publishing

Printed in the United States of America

ISBN: 978-1-5165-0757-3 (pbk) / 978-1-5165-0758-0 (br)

Macro Social Work Practice

WORKING FOR CHANGE IN A MULTICULTURAL SOCIETY

BRIEF CONTENTS

DETAILED CONTENTS

Preface and Acknowledgments

One of the great liabilities of history is that all too many people fail to remain awake through great periods of social change. Every society has its protectors of the status quo and its fraternities of the indifferent who are notorious for sleeping through revolutions. Today, our very survival depends on our ability to stay awake, to adjust to new ideas, to remain vigilant and to face the challenge of change.

—**Martin Luther King Jr.**

Man [sic] is condemned to be free; because once thrown into the world, he is responsible for everything he does. It is up to you to give [life] a meaning.

—**Jean-Paul Sartre**

Within 20 short years, there will be no racial or ethnic majority in the United States. Some Americans find this fact hard to accept. Some fear and resist the consequences. Others embrace this inevitable reality. Whatever one's feelings about the changes occurring in the American social and cultural landscape, it is undeniable that they will have major implications for social workers, particularly those who practice in diverse communities and organizations, and the increasingly contentious policy-making environment, and for our clients and constituents. These effects already appear in most urban areas and states such as California, Florida, New York, and Texas. These changes have had a major effect on U.S. politics and policy, as the 2016 election campaign and its aftermath illustrate. They will reverberate in unpredictable ways in the years ahead.

I wrote this text, therefore, with eyes open wide regarding the inevitability of these changes but with limited vision to predict what they portend. Nevertheless, based on my practice experience and research, I have tried to provide readers with some of the knowledge and skills social workers will require in this rapidly transforming environment. The book emphasizes how communities, social service organizations, and advocacy groups can address the consequences of structural inequalities. The implications of the nation's increasing demographic and cultural diversity for macro social work practice are a central theme.

Matching one's knowledge and skills to a dynamic context is consistent with the conceptual focus of all first-year (foundation) MSW and BSW programs in schools of social work. It is also a prerequisite for advanced study in community organization, management and administration, policy practice, and policy advocacy. It is even valuable for students who choose to focus their careers primarily on practice with individuals and families. Whether these students recognize it now or several years from now, they will not be able to escape the effect of unprecedented population shifts on their interactions with clients. After all, nearly all social workers practice in community and organizational settings. In fact, some clinical practitioners will become advocates, administrators, and managers—often within three to five years of graduation.

With this in mind, each chapter includes brief illustrations on how the practice principles presented apply in different ways within different contexts. Through exercises, simulations, and suggested assignments, the book encourages students to engage in the critical thinking processes involved in resolving the dilemmas that social workers regularly confront. It is my intention that these exercises will stimulate class discussions about the practice issues they raise and motivate students to examine how their professional and social roles, personal backgrounds and **values**, and the context of their practice influence how they assess and act in specific situations. Exercises also emphasize that there is no single "right" approach by underscoring the multiple components involved in practice decisions. In sum, the book illustrates how macro social workers and social workers in macro settings try to make sense of the issues that arise in an increasingly heterogeneous, divided, and complex society.

In addition, the book tries to serve three complementary purposes:

- satisfy the educational and accreditation requirements standards (EPAS) of the Council on Social Work Education;
- present the material in a manner that holds the attention of students, makes the content accessible, and demonstrates the importance of practice in communities and organizations to all social workers and other health and human service professionals; and
- provide students who wish to pursue careers in macro social work practice with a strong conceptual foundation.

Instructors can use the book as a core text or as a major resource in courses that focus on macro social work practice at the MSW and advanced BSW levels.

Based on observations gleaned from my practice and teaching experience, I have become aware of the following educational issues in recent years. Most students enter social work programs today with a narrow concept of practice. They tend to define social work as practice with individuals and families, often in a "therapeutic" role. Approximately 85–90% of them "major" in the clinical concentration. As a result, they often do not see the relevance of macro social work practice content to their education or their future career. They are frequently resistant to learning this material, particularly if presented in a required course or as part of a required course sequence. Although MSW foundation-year internships and BSW placements are supposed to be "generalist" in nature, most of them provide scant opportunities for students to develop macro practice skills or to understand the ways that the community and organizational context influences practice at all levels with all populations or problems (Reisch, 2016a). As many field instructors have been educated in programs with diminished emphasis on macro practice theories and skills, they have considerable difficulty developing macro-oriented assignments even when required by their academic partners.

In addition, due to recent changes in K-12 and undergraduate education, and the effect of digital technology, students increasingly seek "cookbook" solutions to tough practice dilemmas. They are reluctant to develop the critical thinking and analytic skills needed to address complex situations, or even to read assigned material, particularly if it focuses on theoretical content, because they regard such content as disconnected from "real world" practice. Their reliance on digital technology has also diminished the attention span needed to struggle with difficult practice issues. Over the next decade, these trends will only continue. Educators will have to find creative solutions that balance acceptance of these realities with refusal to acquiesce to the lower standards they could produce.

Recognizing these issues, this book tries to combine accessibility and rigor. The primary market for the text consists of students and faculty members in MSW courses on macro social work practice (which have various titles), and as one of the core books in a generalist first-year MSW program or second-year BSW program at U.S. schools and in other English-speaking nations (e.g., Australia, Canada, India, New Zealand, Singapore, United Kingdom) whose users may also find value in this book. In addition, as many of the skills taught in this book are critical for other health and human service professions, a secondary market for this book includes schools of public health, public administration, public policy, education, and nursing, and programs or departments in counseling, gerontology, community/applied psychology, and applied anthropology or sociology. Finally, established professionals (including field instructors) who wish to reorient their work to macro social work practice issues will find this book an important resource. They may be attracted to the book's exercises and simulations for training purposes.

The book consists of 15 chapters plus a brief epilogue, some of which focus specifically on aspects of organizational practice, others on particular aspects of community or policy practice, particularly the various forms of advocacy. Although presented in a particular order, instructors can assign chapters to match the particular structure of their syllabi. As stated previously, each chapter includes exercises, simulations, discussion questions, and potential assignments. A brief epilogue discusses the personal side of macro social work practice from my perspective. At the end of the book, there is a glossary of key terms and a list of references.

In writing this book, I drew upon the wisdom acquired from many individuals, directly and indirectly. I would like to express my gratitude for their contributions to my "continuing professional education." They include my teachers and mentors when I was a MSW student at the Silberman School of Social Work at Hunter College of the City University of New York—Steve Burghardt, Bertram Gross, Harold Lewis, Robert Salmon, and Harold Weissman—and the many faculty colleagues at the various universities where I have been fortunate to work. Among my colleagues I need to give a special "shout out" to Susan Bendor, John Haynes, Steve Holloway, Sanford Kravitz, and Steve Rose at Stonybrook University; Paul Ephross, Karen Hopkins, Amanda Lehning, Megan Meyer, Susan Roll, Adam Schneider, Jeff Singer, Steve Soifer, and Stan Wenocur at the University of Maryland; Jane Isaacs Lowe at the University of Pennsylvania; Willia Gray, Felix Rivera, and Tim Sampson at San Francisco State University; Mike Austin at the University of California, Berkeley; and Barry Checkoway, Janet Finn, Larry Gant, Charles Garvin, and Lorraine Gutierrez at the University of Michigan. I am also grateful for the guidance and wisdom provided by former supervisors and professional colleagues: Jack Goldberg, Lou Levitt, Barry Morowitz, Fred Newdom, and Robert Salmon at the Child Study Association-Wel-Met Inc.; Pat Grossman and Bill Weinstein at the Mosholu-Montefiore Community Association; Margaret Brodkin at Coleman Advocates for Children and Youth in San Francisco; and Shelly Yanoff at Philadelphia Citizens for Children and Youth. Any errors of fact or judgment in the book are entirely my responsibility—the results of misinterpretation or poor memory.

Finally, I want to express my particular appreciation to Kassie Graves, an editor without parallel, for her ongoing encouragement, stimulation, and support; to reviewers of the manuscript; and to staff members at Cognella Academic Publishing who were unceasingly patient, responsive, and helpful.

CHAPTER 1

Macro Practice in a Multicultural Society: An Overview

You really can change the world if you care enough.

—Marian Wright Edelman, founder and president, Children's Defense Fund

If not us, then who? If not now, then when?

—Rep. John Lewis

Introduction

IN-CLASS EXERCISE

Imagine yourself as a social worker in one of the following settings:

1. You work in a nonprofit organization whose primary clients are new immigrants and refugees, some of whom are undocumented. The government has just instituted restrictive travel bans that affect your clients and their families. In addition to helping them acquire the psychosocial, financial, and legal supports they need, what else could you and your colleagues do? What are your ethical obligations in this setting?
2. You work in a low-income, African American urban community where gang-related violence has recently increased. Police officers have also shot numerous young men, exacerbating long-standing tensions with the community. Many formerly incarcerated people have experienced major challenges in reintegrating successfully into society. In addition to working with the victims of trauma, violence, and chronic unemployment and with their families, what steps could you take to address these environmental issues?
3. You work in the local Veterans Administration hospital where many patients exhibit the symptoms of post-traumatic stress disorder (PTSD) and are having difficulty readjusting to civilian life. Besides providing these veterans and their families with counseling, what could you and the hospital do to help them?
4. You are a social worker in a public high school in which LGBTQ students have experienced an increase in bullying, both in-person and through social media. A recent decision by the state legislature that rescinded local anti-discrimination laws affecting this population appears to have made the situation worse. In addition to working with the students, how might you address this issue?

In each of these case examples, effective social work involves moving outside of the traditional dyadic client-worker relationship into the realm of macro practice. As the chapters in this book will attempt to demonstrate, the role of macro practice and macro practice skills is more important than ever in today's fractious, multicultural, and hyper-partisan environment.

This chapter provides an overview of the history, major components, and basic features of macro social work practice with a particular emphasis on its application to our increasingly diverse, multicultural society. It emphasizes how macro practice involves translating "private troubles" into "public issues" through the development and implementation of planned and purposeful change, and working with people, individually and in groups, and not merely with abstract "systems" or institutions. One of the goals of this chapter, and the book as a whole, is to demonstrate that, contrary to frequent usage, macro social work is not a form of "indirect practice." Much as social work efforts to produce change in individuals and families, changes at the macro level require information gathering, effective problem definition, clear and consistent issue **framing**, mobilization of tangible and intangible resources, strategic planning, targeted action, and reflective **evaluation** of the interventions we attempt (a process referred to as **praxis**). The chapter also stresses that working with people in macro practice settings emphasizes relationship building, the importance of collaboration and mutual goal setting, the facilitation of task-oriented groups and meetings, and the ability to mobilize individuals and groups to create positive change. These skills are particularly important if we are to transform demographic and cultural diversity from an obstacle to change into an asset.

The chapter also demonstrates how the major forms of macro practice—community organization, administration, and policy practice—reflect the underlying values of the NASW *Code of Ethics* (2017). Finally, through case examples, this chapter illustrates how macro practice can create direct change in communities, empower people through the development of responsive services, and reorganize services specifically with structural change in mind. Macro practice also has the potential to produce structural change through the replacement of critical actors, the redistribution of social roles, changes in the reward structure, and the redistribution of rights, opportunities, and obligations. The book's chapters discuss these skills along with a critical assessment of the negative and positive forces affecting macro practice today.

The Changing Environment of Social Work Practice

Although the effects of poverty, inequality, and discrimination on human well-being have been central concerns of social work practice since the profession emerged more than a century ago, these issues have taken on a new character in the 21st century as a consequence of domestic and international political, economic, demographic, technological, and cultural developments. To put it simply, our society and the world are much more interconnected and interdependent than in the past due to economic globalization, human migration, the spread of digital technology, and increased social and cultural diversity. Public health crises, civil conflicts, and natural disasters that once affected only specific regions or clearly defined communities now cross national boundaries and give many local problems an international dimension. The increased power and influence of social media have accelerated the spread of information and disinformation. These changes provoke more rapid and often less thoughtful responses to crises, even as they create the need for increased critical analysis and careful reflection on what constitutes a "fact" or the "truth," and how to address the intended and unintended consequences of crucial decisions. In addition, the growth of social media and the spread of digital technology have intensified the privatization of social life and reinforced what Christopher Lasch (1991, 1979) referred to decades ago as the nation's "culture of narcissism."

Instant communication makes us aware of global events as soon as they occur, yet it also illuminates the persistent gulfs that exist among and within nations and cultures about the interpretation of these events. Domestic politics in the United States, for example, reflects a level of hyper-partisanship not seen since the Civil War. Serious divisions exist among the nation's regions, and within political parties, **grassroots organizations**, and nonprofit service providers. Today, we express these divisions—explicitly and implicitly—along racial, ethnic, religious, class, gender, generational, and regional lines.

Table 1.1 Negative and Positive Forces in Today's Practice Environment

Negative Forces	Positive Forces
• The growth of anti-democratic, authoritarian elements in U.S. society	• Increased awareness of socioeconomic inequality
• Political gridlock and hyper-partisanship	• Formation of new cross-cultural and trans-national coalitions
• Lingering effects of the 2007–08 recession particularly in low-income communities and communities of color	• Greater awareness of human needs (through the media)
• The effect of economic globalization on local communities and attitudes toward government intervention to address people's needs	• Empowerment of new communities
• Anti-immigrant and anti-refugee rhetoric	• Emergence of a truly multicultural society
• "Demographic panic" in response to increasing diversity	• More openness to new ideas and new solutions to longstanding issues
• A focus on fiscal costs and austerity rather than social costs	• Increased embrace of diversity and receptivity to change by younger generations
• Loss of public space	
• The effects of a 24/7 news cycle and divisive forces in the media	
• Persistence of institutional and cultural racism, sexism, homophobia	
• The effects of neoliberal ideology on the nature of services and the social work profession itself	

Table 1.1: *Updated and adapted from Robert Fisher and Howard Jacob Karger, Social Work and Community in a Private World. Copyright © 1997 by Pearson.*

Why Macro Practice Matters

The 2016 election and its aftermath have already normalized the denigration of government as a problem-solving institution and ideologically motivated attacks on social welfare policies and programs and the people they help. Both government and nonprofit agencies, which employ most social workers, are undergoing dramatic changes. As of this writing, the consequences of these changes are unpredictable but they will certainly be serious and long lasting. Mistrust in the nation's political institutions, including the Supreme Court, is at an all-time low (Gallup, 2016). The pressure to privatize public spaces and to turn over increasing aspects of our public life, such as education and health care, to market forces threatens to undermine the basic premises of social work (Reisch, 2013a).

These issues have recently acquired new urgency because of the effects of economic globalization and climate change and the consequences of the recent election. Unbridgeable divisions exist over immigrant and refugee rights; the nature of our criminal justice system; the role of labor unions; and how to respond effectively to the threats of terrorism and the effects of increasing socioeconomic inequality. Longstanding issues such as reproductive choice and Affirmative Action have acquired new urgency. Our language and discourse reflect these divisions and this confusion as well. Proponents of different ideologies, for instance, use words such as **oppression**, **privilege**, **empowerment**, and **social justice** to promote vastly different political and social goals. Groups with dramatically different visions of our society's future use "alternate facts" to rationalize diametrically opposed objectives (Reisch & Jani, 2012).

Given these circumstances, the **marginalization** of macro social work within the social work profession during the past several decades (Fisher & Corciullo, 2011) is a particularly ironic and unfortunate development. Today, less than 9% of MSW students are enrolled in all macro practice areas combined (CSWE, 2012), fewer than one-quarter of accredited MSW programs have advanced macro practice concentrations, and only 6% of the nation's 38,000 MSW students have macro-oriented internships (CSWE, 2014). The composition of the wider practice community mirrors these trends in social work education. According to a recent study, less than one in seven social workers consider themselves macro practitioners and most social workers devote scant attention on a weekly basis to community or policy-oriented work (Whitaker & Arrington, 2008). The shortage of macro social workers is particularly acute in low-income, low-power communities where many racial and ethnic minority populations live (Mott, 2008).

We cannot solve these problems easily under current circumstances. According to a study by Rothman (2013), the organizational culture and climate in many educational programs reflect considerable resistance to the integration of macro practice content into courses or field placements. As a result, students develop little understanding of what macro social work involves or of its significance in the history of the profession and U.S. society. These features also diminish students' desire to pursue macro careers or even to incorporate macro skills into their practice.

This situation is unfortunate because the structural approach at the core of macro social work practice is more urgent than ever (Hasenfeld & Garrow, 2012). Macro social work's focus on systemic and institutional changes reflects the recognition that we cannot solve people's problems by individual or family interventions alone. Solutions to these problems also require the development of new leaders, enhanced **civic participation**, and policy changes that redistribute societal resources, rights, power, opportunities, status, and obligations more equitably (Mizrahi & Morrison, 2013). By emphasizing the importance of community dynamics and the multiple processes that affect social service delivery, macro social workers strive to empower people, enhance the effectiveness of existing programs, and create new ways to improve human well-being (Homan, 2016; Burghardt, 2013). All social workers need to appreciate this connection if we are to fulfill our ethical commitment to social justice.

In sum, in today's environment the retreat of the social work profession from its historic commitment to macro practice reduces its ability to influence critical policy decisions that affect our most vulnerable clients and **constituents** at the local, state, national, and international levels. This diminished influence contributes indirectly to the shortage of critical resources these individuals and communities need to survive and thrive. Given the likelihood that the current administration will attempt to undertake a major restructuring of the nation's social welfare system, the declining role of macro practice in the social work field has portentous implications for the people with whom we work and the survival of the profession itself.

What is Macro Social Work Practice? How is it Similar? How is it Different?

Most definitions of macro social work emphasize its two distinguishing features. Macro practice involves intervention "with organizations, communities, and groups of people" (Meenaghan, Gibbons, & McNutt, 2005) in order "to bring about *planned change* in" those systems (Netting, Kettner, McMurty, & Thomas, 2011, emphasis added). Macro practice, therefore, is a *collective and collaborative* endeavor that seeks to create *purposive* change. Although macro social workers practice in a wide variety of fields—from **advocacy** for children to developing services for the aged—it possesses certain common, distinctive elements. These components often fall into discreet practice functions, as outlined in the charts below.

Table 1.2 Components of Macro Social Work Practice

Community Practice	• Neighborhood and community organizing • Organizing functional communities • Social, economic, and sustainable development • Inclusive program development • Social planning • Coalitions • Political and social action • Movements for progressive change
Management	• Developing and managing stakeholder relationships • Modeling appropriate professional behavior • Initiating and facilitating innovative change processes • Demonstrating effective cross-cultural interpersonal and communication skills • Encouraging active involvement of all staff members and stakeholders in decision making • Establishing and promoting, the vision, philosophy, goals, objectives, and values of the organization • Planning, promoting, and modeling lifelong learning • Designing and developing programs • Strategic planning • Building inter-organizational relationships to enhance service delivery
Policy Practice	• Identifying and assessing the effects of problems and issues that affect individuals, families, and communities • Analyzing the effects (positive, negative, and unintended) of existing policies • Developing alternative policy solutions • Creating and implementing strategies to achieve them • Implementing policy decisions • Evaluating policies and programs in terms of their effectiveness, efficiency, and effect

Table 1.2: *Sources: Weil, Gamble and Ohmer, 2013; Hassan and Wimpfheimer, 2014; Jansson, 2014*

Skills for Macro Practice

One set of skills, which is common to all social work practice, consists of *relationship* or *engagement skills*, including the ability to observe, listen, and hear. This skill set also includes the ability to "read between the lines" and to interpret body language and the influence of context. These skills are particularly valuable when working with communities that have different cultural histories, **norms**, and values. Of particular importance in today's climate is the ability to be genuine with the people with whom we work. Without such skills, developing trust in our work with diverse populations, already a challenging and frequently fragile enterprise, will be nearly impossible. Macro social workers must also be able to communicate to diverse individuals and groups in meaningful, direct, honest, and effective ways and be able to handle negativism, conflict, anger, resistance, and failure. Steve Burghardt (2013), an experienced organizer and leading social work educator, maintains that the cultivation of these skills requires certain personal qualities, such as the conscious use of self, innovation, independence, flexibility, and a high degree of personal responsibility.

Organizational or *group management skills* constitute a second set of skills. They include the ability to:

- identify problems, crystallize issues, and develop specific goals from sometimes vague and diffuse expressions of interest or need;
- translate broad goals into concrete program activities;
- establish and maintain group or organizational structures;
- plan and conduct a wide array of activities, such as conferences, campaigns, media events, hearings, and demonstrations;
- organize and facilitate task-oriented group meetings;
- choose from among difficult and often ethically challenging priorities; and
- balance constituents' competing concerns and demands.

Third, macro social workers must develop *skills in critical analysis*. These include the ability to study, assess, and describe a situation, problem, or issue, to identify and collect the data needed to analyze it in greater depth and breadth, and to situate their analysis in both the historical and contemporary context. In addition, macro practitioners must be able to engage in a power analysis of a particular situation and to assess the politics surrounding an issue. They must also be able to organize and systematically address alternative goals and strategies, and develop well-organized and cogent arguments for their choice of selected strategies. Finally, they must have the ability to specify the tasks required to create a desired change, and by whom, how, and in what order to implement a particular **strategy**.

These qualities require *strategic or political skills*. These skills include the ability to assess the interests, motivations, underlying assumptions, and commitments of the different individuals and groups with whom we interact as collaborators, allies, and opponents. They also include the ability to identify the sources of influence and power in an organization, group, community, or institution to enhance one's own power or appearance of power, and to minimize the threat posed by the power of adversaries. These skills need to be complemented by the ability to strengthen the cohesiveness of one's group, organization, or constituency, and to work effectively in collaborations or **coalitions**—a skill that, in turn, requires the ability to identify and use areas of actual or potential conflict and converging interest and to engage in conflict management, bargaining, mediation, and negotiation as needed. Perhaps above all, political skills involve persuasiveness in both verbal and written communication, and the ability to tailor one's arguments to the culture and interests of diverse audiences.

A fifth set of *skills in administration and management* reflect both the intellectual and pragmatic aspects of macro social work. It is both an intellectual and practical challenge, for example, to match an organization's programs to its mission and to the goals of the communities with whom it works, particularly as they relate to the development and allocation of scarce resources. This, in turn, requires considerable intellectual work to learn about a community or a complex system, to teach what you have learned to other staff or community members, to participate effectively in group decision making and planning, to establish effective working relationships with superordinates, peers, and subordinates, and to combine respect for difference with assertiveness. Lastly, as in practice with individuals and families, effective macro practice is impossible without the ability to use one's time effectively and efficiently and to maintain accurate and complete records.

The five categories summarized below reflect one way to organize these broad skill areas. As will be discussed throughout the book, each of these skills must be adapted specifically to culturally diverse communities and organizations:

KEY CONCEPT SUMMARY
FIVE SKILL AREAS OF MACRO SOCIAL WORK PRACTICE

1. **Relationship or engagement skills**
   - Ability to observe.
   - Ability to listen and to hear.
   - Ability to demonstrate interest, identification, and commitment to others.
   - Ability to communicate with diverse populations in meaningful and effective ways.

- Ability to handle negativism, conflict, anger, resistance, and failure.
- Ability to be direct and honest.

2. **Desirable Personal Characteristics**
   - Conscious use of self (Burghardt, 1982).
   - Innovation
   - Independence and responsibility
   - Flexibility
3. **Organizational or Group Management Skills**
   - Ability to identify problems, crystallize issues, and develop specific goals from sometimes vague and diffuse expressions of interest or need.
   - Ability to operationalize goals into program activities.
   - Ability to establish and maintain group or organizational structure.
   - Ability to plan and conduct conferences, campaigns, events, demonstrations.
   - Ability to plan and conduct group meetings.
   - Ability to choose priorities and balance competing concerns and demands.
4. **Analytic Skills**
   - Ability to study, assess, and describe a situation or problem, and to identify and collect the data needed to analyze it further.
   - Ability to undertake a political or power analysis of a particular situation/issue.
   - Ability to organize and systematically address alternative goals and strategies.
   - Ability to develop well-organized and cogent arguments for selected strategies.
   - Ability to specify the tasks that need to be performed, and by whom, how, and when in order to implement a particular strategy.
5. **Strategic or Political Skills**
   - Ability to assess the interests and commitments of different individuals and groups.
   - Ability to identify sources of influence and power, and to enhance one's own power or appearance of power, and to minimize the threat of adversaries.
   - Ability to strengthen the cohesiveness of one's group, organization, or constituency, including the ability to work in collaborative inter-organizational relations or diverse coalitions.
   - Ability to identify and use areas of conflict and converging interest and to engage in conflict management, bargaining, mediation, and negotiation as needed.
   - Persuasiveness in both verbal and written communication, and the ability to tailor one's arguments to the culture and interests of different audiences.

6. **Administrative/Management Skills**
   - Ability to match organizational activities to organizational/community goals (this includes skills related to resource development and allocation).
   - Skill in participation in group decision making and planning.
   - Ability to learn and to teach.
   - Ability to establish effective working relationships with superordinates, peers, and subordinates; tolerance for difference combined with assertiveness.
   - Ability to use time effectively and efficiently.
   - Ability to maintain records, minutes, reports, etc.

We can also conceive of macro social work in terms of its specific practice functions. Weil and Gamble (2013) identified eight arenas of community practice: neighborhood and community organizing; organizing functional communities; social, economic, and **sustainable** development; inclusive **program development**; **social planning**; coalition work; political and **social action** and policy practice; and movements for progressive change (p. 170). According to Warren (1978), through these various forms of practice, macro social workers help communities perform five major tasks: the production, distribution, and consumption of tangible and intangible "goods"; socialization; social control; social participation; and mutual support.

Similarly, macro practice in administration and management, while often highly specialized, includes processes that apply to all forms of macro practice. These include goal setting and leadership; the creation and maintenance of formal and informal structures; program design, implementation, and evaluation; the establishment of communication and control systems; acquiring, allocating, and assessing the effect of applied resources; hiring, supervising, training, and evaluating staff; creating motivation and reward systems; and interacting with diverse forces within the external environment (Patti, 2008).

Finally, the macro field of policy practice and advocacy involves a range of activities. These include identifying and assessing how problems and issues affect individuals, families, and communities; analyzing the effects (positive, negative, and unintended) of existing policies; developing alternative policy solutions; creating strategies to achieve them; implementing policy decisions; and evaluating policies and programs in terms of their effectiveness, efficiency, and effect (*see chapters 12–14*). In sum, macro social work practice involves the integration of all these practice areas in different combinations depending on the issues and the environmental context.

By combining all these practice functions, macro social work expands the profession's scope and influence. It promotes a more comprehensive perspective on **human rights**, human needs, and human well-being, through which *all* social workers can focus on the prevention of people's problems, not merely their amelioration. Macro practice also stresses structural solutions to the inequalities and injustices that particularly affect oppressed and marginalized communities, solutions that go beyond the enhancement of people's abilities to adapt to their environments more successfully. This represents a clear expression of the social work profession's historic commitment to social justice and social change.

As the chart below illustrates, social workers apply macro practice skills in many ways.

KEY CONCEPT SUMMARY
THE APPLICATION OF COMMON MACRO SOCIAL PRACTICE SKILLS

- Working with task-oriented groups.
- Individual and group supervision
- Resource development, mobilization, and management
- Marketing or promoting a service or cause
- Negotiation and participatory management
- Inter-organizational planning and leadership development
- Community, organizational, and policy analysis
- Program development, implementation, and evaluation
- Advocacy, lobbying, public education, and coalition building
- Media relations and public speaking
- Cultivating and exercising leadership.
- Managing planned change and conflict.
- Assessing the strengths and assets of communities and organizations.
- Facilitating the empowerment of clients, constituents, and the groups to which they belong.
- Communicating effectively across class, racial, and cultural boundaries.
- Analyzing the structure, dynamics, and culture of human service organizations and the communities in which they exist.
- Determining when and how to exert influence in communities and social service systems (Austin & Lowe, 1994).

Because many students and even some practicing social workers (including some field instructors) are unclear about the nature of macro practice, it may be useful at this point to correct some persistent misimpressions. One is that macro social work is "indirect practice." This phrase frequently appears in textbooks and official pronouncements. This oft-repeated statement overlooks the reality that virtually all social work practice occurs in a community and organizational context and that social policies, directly and indirectly, shape the practice environment. In addition, as in "micro" practice, human relationships lie at the core of macro social work. Macro practitioners engage regularly *with* people, not solely with or within impersonal "systems" (Burghardt, 2013). This direct contact with people is particularly important when working with individuals and communities from different racial, cultural, and class backgrounds.

Similar to micro practitioners, the changes macro social workers seek are purposeful; the strategic interventions they develop are based on careful assessment and planning. They are informed by research (evidence), experience (practice wisdom), and—ideally—the perspectives of clients and constituents. Macro practice similarly involves ongoing reflection on the effect of interventions, through *praxis*, and reflexivity in adapting to changing conditions. Later chapters will discuss these important processes in more detail. Finally, macro social workers attempt to produce community, organizational, and policy changes that complement the goals of practitioners who work primarily with individuals and families.

While the specific practice skills that micro and macro social workers employ may differ, both reflect the profession's core values. The NASW *Code of Ethics* reflects this shared vision:

> *Social workers should engage in social and political action* that seeks to ensure that all people have equal access to the resources, employment, services and opportunities they require to meet their basic human needs and to develop fully. *Social workers ... should advocate for changes in policy and legislation to improve social conditions in order to meet basic human needs and promote social justice* (Section 6.04, emphasis added).

Macro social workers, however, express this ethical imperative in unique ways. They emphasize the importance of shared participation by clients, constituents, colleagues, and coalition partners in the identification of human needs, the development of systemic approaches to address these needs, and the evaluation of strategies employed. They believe that people have the right and the capacity to change the institutions that shape their lives and to contribute to the creation of more responsive policies and programs. This reflects social work's longstanding **belief** in "empowerment" (Simon, 1990). (*See Chapter 2 for further discussion of the role of power and empowerment.*) Macro practitioners generally prefer a nonhierarchical approach to problem solving that requires a synthesis of scientifically acquired "expertise" (e.g., "evidence-based practice") and the unique insights of clients and constituents. They believe in an inclusive and more expansive concept of leadership; they stress the need to cultivate new, more diverse leaders and to recognize that leadership may take different forms in an increasingly diverse society. (*See Chapter 6 for a discussion of leadership.*)

As stated above, a major goal of macro practice is to transform people's "private troubles" into "public issues" (Mills, 1963). "Troubles" (or "problems") occur within the character of the individual and within the range of his or her immediate relations with others. "Issues" have to do with structural, systemic, and institutional forces that transcend these local environments of the individual and the range of a person's inner life.

IN-CLASS EXERCISE
FROM PRIVATE TROUBLE TO PUBLIC ISSUE

Think about the transformation of the following private troubles into public issues:

- unemployment;
- poverty;
- socioeconomic inequality;
- child abuse;
- domestic violence and sexual assault;
- homelessness;
- substance abuse;
- mental illness;
- health inequities/disparities;
- HIV/AIDS;
- racial profiling and mass incarceration;
- discrimination against LGBTQ persons;
- needs of undocumented youth; and
- human trafficking.

Select one or more of the problems above and address the following questions:

1. What was the original definition and explanation of the problem?
2. Who defined the problem in this manner? What purpose did this definition serve?
3. How did the transformation of this problem from a "private trouble" to a "public issue" occur?

Questions for Discussion

1. What is a problem on which you and your organization are currently working? How does the organization define the problem? Who developed this definition?
2. What are the implications of this definition for the nature of your practice?
3. How could you define the problem differently?
4. If you did, what would be the effects of this redefinition—on your clients or constituents, your practice, your agency?

The transformation of a problem from a private trouble to a public issue is important because of the need for broader structural or institutional changes to address issues that interventions at the individual or family level cannot solve by themselves. This need for structural and social change is also increasingly important as our society and its communities and organizations become both more diverse and interdependent. Macro practice attempts to produce this structural change through the replacement of critical actors; the redistribution and redefinition of social roles; and the promotion of changes in the goals and reward structures of society and its organizations, particularly how it distributes rights, benefits, opportunities, access, status, and obligations. Macro social work practitioners also strive to create change by altering the goals and dynamics of communities and organizations; empowering people through the creation of new or more responsive services; and developing programs and policies that affect people's lives, specifically with structural change in mind—a process referred to as "non-reformist reform" (Gorz, 1968).

All social work practice involves the identification of an issue of concern (e.g., ensuring the safety of a woman who is the victim of domestic violence, providing adequate in-home care for an elderly person, finding permanent shelter for a person who is experiencing homelessness). Macro social workers often work in systems that are hostile to the interests of our clients and constituents. They practice in chronically under-resourced communities and organizations. Consequently, they need to pay particular attention to the framing of an issue; the assessment of its extent or severity; the proposed target of intervention; and the analytic factors that they exclude or treat as marginal. In sum, macro practice requires us to determine both the ends of intervention (its goals) and also the means to create purposive change. In addition, in today's contentious political environment, our practice requires us to consider who determines these goals. Who initiates and controls the change effort? How are affected individuals or communities involved? When will the intervention end? How is "success" or "failure" defined? Who will evaluate the outcome of the intervention? Through what means will this evaluation occur?

An underlying assumption of macro practice, therefore, is that all reality is "socially constructed"; macro practitioners believe that most societal conditions that we accept as "givens"—as reflected, for example, in the oft-quoted statement "the poor will always be with us"—are neither "natural" nor inevitable. Rather, they are cultural reflections of the dominant forces in society that rationalize long-standing structural arrangements and perpetuate the status quo. There are many examples of this phenomenon, including our acceptance of a market-oriented economy and its definitions of work, success, and dependency; and our views of gender norms, racial characteristics, and social institutions such as marriage and the family. Perhaps of greatest importance in our increasingly multicultural society is the need to recognize how we construct social categories such as race, gender, age, and sexual orientation. Looking at the practice environment through this lens helps us recognize that the distinctions our society makes between "private troubles" and "public issues" are neither "natural" nor inevitable.

Macro social workers also question whether the damages produced by "natural disasters," such as recent hurricanes or wildfires, are, in fact, solely natural (Bates & Swan, 2010). They dare to ask: *Who* defines what constitutes a problem worthy of our attention? *What* is the explanation for their existence? *What* criteria determine what are acceptable "needs" and acceptable forms of "helping" (Green, 1998)? By posing these questions, they hope to increase the possibility of structural change (Mizrahi, 2015). Of particular importance in today's environment, macro practitioners are aware of the frequent indifference or hostility toward clients and constituents that exists in the United States, sometimes even within the systems in which social workers practice, particularly those that target excluded and marginalized populations (Reisch & Garvin, 2016).

IN-CLASS EXERCISE
EXPLORING THE DIMENSIONS OF MACRO SOCIAL WORK PRACTICE

Introduction

After you leave class today and cross the street, a hungry person approaches you. What could you do?

Figure 1.1 Begging Boy

Fig. 1.1: *Dir. David Lean, "Begging Boy," Oliver Twist. Copyright © 1948 by United Artists Corporation.*

List your possible responses. They could include:

- *give the person* food or money—provide a benefit or service;
- refer the person to get help;
- advocate—for the individual (to get help) or for new anti-hunger laws;
- organize other hungry persons—collectivize the issue; and
- build community and create new social alternatives—redefine the situation.

Now, analyze your choice(s) in terms of:

- their underlying assumptions about the nature of social change;
- the knowledge and skills you would need to implement them;
- the role(s) you would play as a social change agent; and
- the role(s) of the persons affected by your choice(s).

These potential responses not only reflect the different dimensions of macro social work practice, they also reveal their different underlying problem definitions, assumptions, and goals. Understanding the implications of these differences is particularly critical in today's socially and culturally diverse environment.

For example, the response "give the person food" (options 1 and 2) defines the problem primarily in individual terms and seeks to provide immediate relief. Potential allies in these interventions include anyone in the community who has food or access to food. This could involve generous persons, private charities, social service organizations, and government agencies. Potential "opponents" include those who would object to the provision of "handouts" to individuals in need on moral or fiscal grounds. Note, however, that this approach does not view this "private trouble" as a "public issue." It also does not regard the hungry individual as part of a community that might—potentially—have the power to take action on its own behalf.

The advocacy-oriented response (Option 3)—to fight for change on behalf of the hungry person and others in a similar situation—regards the matter as a public issue based on the assumption that all people possess the "right" to have their basic needs met. If the intervention went beyond **"case advocacy"** (on behalf of an individual) to **"class advocacy"** (on behalf of a group with a similar problem), it would link the needs of a particular individual with those of others and examine the structural sources of this need. Allies would consist of other advocates, service providers, and sympathetic members of the political establishment and the media. Opponents would most likely be those forces in the political arena that reject the "rights-based" foundation of the advocacy effort. Ironically, given this premise, while some forms of advocacy involve constituents in the change process, for the most part they remain an expert-driven activity in which the people most affected by the proposed change have little or no role.

By contrast, options 4 and 5—to collectivize the issue by organizing other people who are hungry or at risk of hunger, and/or to redefine the situation and present alternative solutions—reflect a different perspective on the nature of power and change. Instead of seeking alliances from traditional sources and implicitly emphasizing the "deficits" of people in need, these approaches emphasize the assets that all individuals and communities possess and their ability to reframe and address their issues in new ways. By presenting alternative solutions to the problem of hunger (e.g., creating community gardens and food co-ops) they attempt to empower affected individuals and communities, end their isolation, and raise people's consciousness. Ironically, this approach provokes opposition not only by the political adversaries referred to above, but also by social service providers who regard any challenge to the status quo as a threat to their professional status.

As this exercise also implies, the systems and institutions that shape the context of macro social work practice in the 21st century can be both oppressive and supportive. This illustrates the tension in a multicultural and divided society between finding common ground and respecting diversity. It also reflects the political challenges all social workers face, particularly those involved in macro practice, which often leads to their marginalization within society and even within the organizations where they work.

Social Work Values and Macro Practice

INJUSTICE BY PABLO NERUDA
(translated by Alastair Reid)

Whoever discovers the who of me will find out the who of you,
and the why, and the where.
Early on, I discovered the range of injustice.
Hunger was not just hunger,
but rather a measure of man.
Cold and wind were also measures.
The proud man racked up a hundred hungers, then fell.
Pedro was buried at the hundredth frost.
The poor house endured a single wind.
And I learned that centimeter and gram,
spoon and tongue, were measures of greed,
and that the harassed man soon fell
in a hole, and knew no more.
Nothing more. That was the setting,
the real gift, the reward, light, life.
That was it, suffering cold and hunger,
not having shoes, feeling fear
in front of the judge, in front of the other one,
the other being with his sword or his inkwell,
and so, digging and cutting,
sewing, making bread, planting wheat,
hammering every nail the wood needed,

burrowing in the earth as in intestines
to drag out, blind, the cracking coal,
and, even more, going up rivers and mountains,
riding horses, tending to ships
baking tiles, blowing glass, washing clothes
in such a way as to make that seem
a kingdom newly brought into being,
grapes shining in their clusters,
when man set his mind on being content,
and was not, and was not so. I was discovering
the laws of misery,
the throne of bloodstained gold,
the whore freedom,
the land with no overcoat,
the wounded, worn-out heart,
and the sound of the dead, tearless,
dry, like falling stones.
And then I stopped being a child
because I understood then that for my people
life was not allowed
and the grave has forbidden them.

As this powerful poem by Nobel laureate Pablo Neruda vividly expresses, injustice takes many forms. It creates and perpetuates oppression, and the marginalization and exclusion of significant portions of the population of the United States and other nations. For more than a century, the social work profession has been committed in its rhetoric and sometimes in its actions to the eradication of these injustices. Social workers who engage in macro practice have played a leading role in these efforts in the past and continue to do so today.

Today, in a value-based profession such as social work, macro practitioners must go beyond the development of specific knowledge and skills, and ask themselves several value-driven questions: Should our practice be morally neutral or should we make our values explicit? If so, what should those values be? (*See other chapters for a discussion of the value and ethical components of practice, particularly Chapter 8.*) What should we do if our values differ from those of the people and communities with whom we work? In our attempts to produce social and policy change, should we work inside or outside established institutions, or both? Under what circumstances is it acceptable to disobey laws or regulations, even those we consider unjust? What are the risks involved in either option? These are not merely abstract philosophical questions. They are as important to our practice as the acquisition of in-depth knowledge and sophisticated skills.

IN-CLASS EXERCISE
DEALING WITH VALUE CONFLICTS IN MACRO SOCIAL WORK

Imagine you work in a community-based, nonprofit social service organization. Neighborhood residents have expressed opposition to the following projects:

a. Creation of a shelter for homeless people
b. Development of a transitional program for former inmates
c. The integration of refugees from Muslim nations into the community

Questions for Discussion

1. How might community residents express their concerns?
2. How would you respond?
3. How would you reconcile the social work values of inclusion and self-determination?

As this exercise demonstrates, macro social workers, in their efforts to address these difficult issues, emphasize three complementary values that on occasion come into conflict: participation, expertise, and leadership. The value of participation assumes that people should use existing institutions as a means to achieve democratically determined ends. This value influenced the historically important concept of "empowerment" (Simon, 1990). (*See Chapter 2 for further discussion of this concept.*) Expertise reflects the belief in the efficacy and utility of "nonpartisan," scientific problem-solving processes by "objective" experts. The current emphasis on "evidence-based practice" (EBP) reflects this value. On occasion, the emphasis on EBP can conflict with the value of expanding democratic participation. Finally, the value of leadership underscores the importance of efficient decision making in community groups, social service agencies, and advocacy organizations. This value can conflict with the value of acknowledging the strengths of diverse people and communities.

A Brief History of Macro Practice

Before social work emerged as an organized profession in the United States at the turn of the 20th century, people in communities of every racial, ethnic, and religious background organized services to meet their specific needs, mobilized to fight perceived injustices, and advocated for reforms to improve their lives and make the nation more democratic and more equal (Fisher, 1994). Although the label "macro practice" is a fairly recent invention (it emerged in the mid-1980s), and although macro practitioners have always been a minority in the social work profession, they have played a significant role in defining the meaning of social justice and, through their leadership, in translating this ideal into concrete policies and programs. Its earliest practitioners recognized the inter-relationship between meeting basic human needs and creating fundamental social and political change. They were most effective in combining these goals when they responded sensitively to demographic changes and the emergence of new cultural norms and values. They had to be open to new ideas from multiple sources and recognize the connection between **social movements** and community-based services. They had to integrate research findings into their practice in a manner that genuinely reflected professional values. Finally, they had to take the risks involved in proposing innovative solutions to seemingly intractable social problems, including the use of new technology.

We therefore cannot locate the roots of macro practice merely in the soil that produced mainstream social work agencies, such as charity organization societies (COS), settlement houses, and public welfare departments. Macro social work practice emerged from multiple sources: workers' struggles to organize unions, radical political organizations and movements for racial justice, women's rights and immigrants' rights groups, and, perhaps above all, from the variety of **self-help** and **mutual aid organizations** that excluded and marginalized communities created (Reisch & Andrews, 2002; Fisher, 1994; Specht & Courtenay, 1994; Betten & Austin, 1990; Wenocur & Reisch, 1989). For more than a century, macro social work practice evolved in response to rapid societal changes, the effect of external events such as the Great Depression and world wars, and the influence of new domestic and foreign ideologies. The identity-based social movements of the 1960s and 1970s shaped macro social work practice as did the emergence of an increasingly heterogeneous U.S. society (Rothman, 1999). Today, domestic social forces continue to transform the nature of macro social work practice in the United States and around the world. These forces include the Black Lives Matter and Occupy movements, the work of "Dreamers," LGBTQ advocacy on behalf of marriage equality and the rights of transgender persons, and the development of international coalitions to address such issues as climate change, environmental justice, and human trafficking.

The earliest macro social workers emerged during the Progressive Era (~1890–1918). They included women from elite backgrounds such as Jane Addams (cofounder of Hull House in Chicago), Florence Kelley, and Lillian Wald (founder of the Henry Street Settlement and the field of public health nursing), and African American leaders such as George Edmund Haynes, Mary Church Terrell, and Forrester Washington. The earliest macro social workers developed public and nonprofit social service organizations at the local and state levels. They conducted research on poverty, child welfare, juvenile justice, factory conditions, and public health issues and trained a generation of social researchers. They helped organize labor unions, especially for women and immigrants. Through their participation in various social movements and interracial advocacy coalitions, such as the National Association for the Advancement of Colored People (NAACP) and the YWCA, macro social workers helped pass legislation that banned child labor and created mothers' pensions. They established public health standards, housing codes, and occupational safety requirements. They increased the public's awareness of racial and gender discrimination and created many features of contemporary urban life, including playgrounds, street lighting, and kindergartens. Without these efforts, the social work profession would have lacked the organizational and moral foundation it needed to develop and thrive (Carlton-LaNey, 2001; Wenocur & Reisch, 1989).

When the Progressive Movement declined after World War I, most of the social work profession turned inward in the quest for higher occupational status—a pattern often repeated to the present day. Many macro social workers, however, continued to advocate for **social reforms**, such as social insurance, which ultimately led to the passage of the landmark Social Security Act in 1935 and the foundation of the modest U.S. welfare state. They promoted greater participation of community members in decisions that affected their lives, used survey research to analyze issues such as unemployment, and modernized the nature of human services administration (Lubove, 1969; Reisch, 2008b).

During the Great Depression of the 1930s their efforts began to bear fruit. Macro practitioners such as Harry Hopkins, Frances Perkins (the first female member of the Cabinet), and Mary McLeod Bethune were key architects of the New Deal. Other macro social workers, including E. Franklin Frazier, Jacob Fisher, and Mary van Kleeck, prodded the Roosevelt administration to provide more attention to the needs of millions of Americans, particularly African Americans and Latinos (Reisch & Andrews, 2002). During this tumultuous decade, macro social workers also frequently took leadership roles in the reformist and radical movements of the era. They promoted the democratization of industry through labor unions and the creation of more active roles for clients in shaping the programs developed by public and private social service organizations (Reisch, 2008). By the end of the 1930s, the mainstream social work profession finally recognized both community practice and group work as social work methods (Wenocur & Reisch, 1989; Betten & Austin, 1990). Yet, for several decades legislative bodies and the executive branch of the government persecuted many macro practitioners who spearheaded these efforts (Reisch & Andrews, 2002).

During World War II, macro practitioners developed and administered new childcare and health care services for the burgeoning wartime work force, organized relief for war refugees fleeing fascism, and helped military personnel and their families deal with the stress of loss, separation, and readjustment to civilian life. After the war, they led the struggle to expand the programs established by the New Deal to include fair employment practices, civil rights legislation, open (i.e., nondiscriminatory) housing policies, and universal health care. The anti-communist hysteria of the McCarthy era (c. late 1940s to early 1960s), however, repressed much of this activism and, once again, redirected the focus of the social work profession away from social and community change to professionalization. Social service agencies, such as the United Way, and schools of social work also blacklisted and marginalized activist colleagues. During this period, even many macro social workers rejected conflict-oriented approaches to practice in favor of more politically appealing methods, such as top-down community planning, an emphasis on organizational efficiency and professionalism, and incremental strategies for policy change (Specht & Courtenay, 1994; Wenocur & Reisch, 1989).

The revival of social and political change efforts among macro practitioners did not occur until the advent of the "War on Poverty" and the emergence of new social movements (NSMs) during the 1960s. Throughout this decade, in alliance with neighborhood residents and activist organizations, macro practitioners developed new models of service, such as Mobilization for Youth in New York City, and developed **Community Action Programs** (CAPs) throughout the nation. Macro practitioners such as Whitney Young, director of the National Urban League, held leadership positions in NASW, the now defunct National Conference of Social Welfare (NCSW), and government agencies at the local, state, and federal levels. They helped create such cornerstones of contemporary social welfare as Medicare, Medicaid, the Older Americans Act, and the Economic Opportunity Act. Activist academics and macro practitioners such as Frances Fox Piven, Richard Cloward, and Dorothy Height helped organize and provide critical support for the National Welfare Rights Organization, the United Farm Workers, and various civil rights and anti-war groups (Reisch & Andrews, 2002).

During the last quarter of the 20th century, however, the increasingly conservative political environment required macro practitioners, particularly those in large public and nonprofit organizations, to adopt defensive strategies to protect the fragile gains of the 1930s and 1960s and to survive during a period of fiscal austerity and antisocial welfare rhetoric. Yet, even in this climate, macro practitioners continued to pursue long-standing social justice causes, such as poverty, and to raise awareness around such issues as the HIV/AIDS crisis, domestic violence, chronic homelessness, environmental racism, the needs of immigrants and refugees, criminal justice reform, health disparities, and the importance of promoting international human rights (Wronka, 2017; Reichert, 2011; Healy, 2008). They developed new forms of practice that responded to the demands of some of the identity-based organizations that appeared during these years and designed new organizational models, such as those based on feminist practice, new forms of service delivery, and new tactical approaches to community work and advocacy that made creative use of media. Macro practitioners also became increasingly involved in electoral politics, both as candidates and **campaign** staff members (Haynes & Mickelson, 2010).

In the 21st century, in response to the effect of economic globalization and the potential of new media and digital technologies, macro practitioners began to forge local-international linkages in their work, address issues such as climate change, global poverty, civil conflict, human trafficking, police violence and mass incarceration affecting communities of color, LGBTQ rights, and growing socioeconomic inequality. They have used new technologies, particularly social media, to develop new multicultural and cross-national alliances in their advocacy and community organizing efforts, and have begun to adapt to practice environments that are increasingly interdisciplinary and shaped by new demographic, fiscal, and political realities (Mizrahi & Morrison, 2013; Reisch, 2016).

As the table below illustrates, macro practitioners have played a major role in shaping the profession of social work and in achieving its stated mission and goals.

Without macro practice, social work in the United States and other nations would be a dramatically different profession. Through research and advocacy, macro practitioners have analyzed the root causes of inequality and injustice, demonstrated the conflict between market-oriented values and those of social welfare, critiqued cultural norms that stigmatized marginalized individuals and groups, raised the public's consciousness about a range of critical issues, and promoted alternative visions of society, community, and social service. They have emphasized the importance of power dynamics in practice at the micro, mezzo, and macro levels, focused on revising organizations to meet human needs, created new, more responsive and participatory forms of service, and promoted structural and institutional change. They have shaped the vocabulary of the social work field by introducing, defining, reinterpreting, and applying such concepts as social justice, empowerment, **social capital**, **community competence** and participation, consciousness-raising, oppression, marginalization, **social exclusion**, diversity, and multiculturalism. Macro practitioners have also supplied the profession with much of its leadership and, by taking considerable risks, have applied the concepts of social justice and empowerment in their practice. In the process, they have provided all social workers with the "moral cover" needed to do work that is often unpopular, unrecognized, and underfunded.

Table 1.3 Accomplishments and Future Challenges for Macro Practice

Accomplishments	Future Challenges
• Analyzed root causes of inequality and injustice	• Increasing social and political inequality
• Demonstrated conflicts between market-oriented values and those of social welfare and social work	• Persistent racism, sexism, and homophobia
• Critiqued cultural norms that stigmatized marginalized individuals and groups	• Fiscal austerity and social welfare cutbacks
• Raised public consciousness about critical issues	• Effect of privatization on social services
• Promoted alternative visions of society, community, and social services	• Competition for scarce resources
• Emphasized the importance of power dynamics at the micro, mezzo, and macro levels	• Major demographic and cultural changes
• Focused on revising existing organizations or creating new ones to meet human needs	• The effect of technology on services
• Created new, more responsive, and more participatory forms of service	• Increasingly complex client needs
• Promoted structural and institutional change	
• Shaped social work's conceptual vocabulary	
• Provided much of the profession's leadership	

Confronting the Practice Challenges in Our Multicultural Society

Social workers, including macro practitioners, consider themselves part of a "helping profession," yet we rarely consider the possibility that our attitudes toward helping and those of the people with whom we work might reflect substantial cultural differences with significant practical consequences. As James Green (1998) astutely observed, an individual or group's conceptions of need and helping are shaped by a range of contextual and cultural factors, including the community's history and current context, its underlying values and goals, the availability of suitable resources, and the relationship of the person seeking help to those providing assistance. Rivera and Erlich (1997) have also examined the implications of these differences from the perspective of community practice.

In the United States, the definition of human "needs"—and the helping interventions designed to respond to those needs—evolved from short-term, temporary aid in times of catastrophe to long-term, more or less permanent assistance (and, in some cases such as welfare policy, back again). Increasingly, the community or its representatives, not the individual, played a role in determining what constituted a "need." For the most part, however, "experts" largely controlled and continue to control this process by formulating policies and programs that reflected the interests of the dominant culture and, as a result, restrict the choices of targeted, often marginalized communities. To a considerable extent in recent decades, the gap between the needs and interests of the mainstream community and those of excluded populations has become wider, more distinct, and more antagonistic (Schram, 2006; Fisher & Fabricant, 2002; Reisch & Jani, 2012). This gap constitutes one of the underlying causes of increased political and social conflict in U.S. society and of the growing mistrust of elites of all political persuasions.

Throughout history, resources to meet people's needs have always been finite. In modern times, however, the relationship of these resources to the ultimate purposes they serve has become somewhat less clear and more complicated. Although the programs and policies funded by these resources purportedly target specific needy populations, they also serve unstated economic, political, and ideological purposes, such as social control, cultural assimilation, and the maintenance of the economic and political status quo (Margolin, 1997; Iglehart & Becerra, 2010). In implementing these policies and programs, professionals, including social workers, directly and indirectly define what constitutes help, decide which people need help, determine who will provide the help, and develop the mechanisms through which help is provided and evaluated.

In pre-industrial societies, and in some developing nations today, a closer relationship existed between the providers and receivers of assistance (with the exception of help provided to strangers). Since the Industrial Revolution of the 19th century, however, divisions in the helping process have emerged based on class, race, gender, ethnicity, religion, nationality, age, sexual orientation, ability status, and even geography. To rationalize this separation of benefactors and beneficiaries and the hierarchical structure of assistance on which it exists, those with the means and power to help had to affirm their moral, intellectual, and social superiority (Sumner, 1884). In the United States during the Progressive Era, this justified the emergence of "scientific charity" and the application of social scientific research to what became known as macro practice. Thus, what is now called "social work" evolved from a system of assistance originally based on mutual aid and shared community responsibility to a full-time occupation of professional helpers (Wenocur & Reisch, 1989).

For centuries, those who needed help were considered to be potentially productive members of their communities. The provision of assistance to the "needy," therefore, served both their interests and those of the community as a whole. Because the entire community benefited from this assistance, the amelioration of a person's temporary or permanent incapacity served both individual and collective interests. This mutuality was a core value of most major religions that reflected their conception of social justice (Reisch & Garvin, 2016).

As modern market economies evolved, however, many needy persons became superfluous to the well-being of society. In the late 18th century, even relatively enlightened observers such as Benjamin Franklin regarded individuals in need (often called paupers at the time) as a drain on society and an obstacle to prosperity and social progress (Franklin, 1766). Nevertheless, except in the most extreme circumstances, society had to strike a balance between ignoring these individuals and groups, blaming them for their plight (Ryan, 1971), and acknowledging their existence, either as a source of embarrassment or a potential social, political, or cultural threat (Brace, 1872; Sumner, 1883; Mandler, 1990). To maintain this balance, societies provided some help, for the most part at a minimal level. Thus, society neither accepted responsibility for people's plight nor encouraged them to become or remain nonproductive members of the community. Instead, policies such as the Poor Laws (the antecedent of modern social welfare) reflected either neglect, compulsion, or coercion, best embodied by the institution of the workhouse (Katz, 1996). Up to the present day, such policies are consistently applied more harshly to members of racial, ethnic, and religious minority communities (Soss, Fording, & Schram, 2011; Alexander, 2010).

Thus, the evolution of modern social welfare systems reflected the erosion of long-standing moral and social obligations to help individuals and communities in need in a manner that combined a sense of mutual responsibility based on personal connections with collective self-interest. Consequently, the spread of market-oriented institutions and values not only magnified and intensified the extent of social needs, it also alienated individuals from one another and their community and impeded the provision of social assistance.

The concurrent decline of religious motivations to help others, particularly strangers, inspired the need for other rationales. Such terms as "noblesse oblige," the "spirit of charity," "professional responsibility," and the importance of fixing the "culture of poverty" emerged in place. Many of these rationales contained code words that masked the social control function underlying many modern patterns of helping (Margolin, 1997; Schram, 2006). In recent decades, the spread of **neoliberal** ideas, which emphasize individual responsibility and resiliency rather than resistance, represents the latest version of this phenomenon (Abramovitz, 2012; Soss, Fording, & Schram, 2011; McDonald & Reisch, 2008).

As a result, macro social workers, particularly those who remain committed to the values of social justice and empowerment, practice today in an environment in which definitions of need and the meaning of giving or receiving help have significantly changed and are applied differently based on an individual or group's demographic and cultural characteristics. For the most part, people in need do not define either the nature or the extent of their needs or how to address them. Instead, professionals, who often lack political power, or policy makers, who often lack substantive expertise, largely define these needs and determine how to respond to them. Under these circumstances, the assistance provided through public policies has become increasingly insufficient, reluctantly given, and—with notable exceptions, such as Social Security and Medicare—inefficiently distributed. Finally, of greatest significance for macro social work practice in our rapidly changing 21st-century society, contemporary definitions of need and helping reflect a "universal" framework of values and standards that largely ignores the effect of culture, class, race, gender, or sexual orientation, yet continues to stigmatize those being helped and the alternative values they embrace. The challenge of overcoming these conceptual and political obstacles constitutes the core of macro social work practice in the decades ahead and is one of the central themes of this book.

Clarifying Our Terms

Throughout this book, I will attempt to clarify the meaning of oft-used but seldom understood terms such as social justice, empowerment, and oppression. What follows, by way of example, is a brief discussion of the concept of oppression and its relationship to the goals of macro social work practice.

According to Mullaly (2010), "oppression" is not merely a condition that individuals or communities experience on an interpersonal level whether through "micro-aggressions," **implicit bias**, or the discriminatory practices of individuals and organizations. It is also important to understand the concept of oppression in terms of how it affects the distribution of essential resources and the social practices that created long-standing inequities in this distribution process. **Oppression** takes different forms today from the past, yet it continues to operate through virtually all of society's structures and institutions, often in subtle and unacknowledged ways. These include the exploitation of people's labor, such as the low wages and deplorable working conditions experienced by undocumented immigrants employed as migrant farm workers, factory employees, or domestic workers. Systematic oppression also restricts the choices that low-income people, particularly racial and ethnic minorities, have in their diets, housing arrangements, environmental conditions, education, or health care.

Due to systemic oppression, major economic, political, and cultural institutions consistently marginalize and exclude significant portions of the population. Because of persistent health inequities, children perform more poorly in school and develop chronic health conditions. Because they have fewer opportunities to obtain a decent education, oppressed people are less likely to enter well-paying and higher status occupations and far more likely to be imprisoned. They are vastly underrepresented in key decision-making processes at every level of government (Bartels, 2016). They are, therefore, often powerless to shape the conditions that govern their daily lives.

Cultural imperialism is a particularly insidious form of oppression. This is a process through which the values, beliefs, customs, and worldview of dominant groups become "normal," while those of marginalized communities are frequently characterized as "deviant" (Jani & Reisch, 2011). Through this form of oppression, sometimes referred to as cultural **"hegemony"** (Gramsci, 1992), compulsory assimilation into the cultural mainstream becomes a prerequisite for individual success, sometimes even for survival. Examples of this phenomenon range from the exaltation of "traditional" family patterns to attitudes about work, leisure, gender relations, and the receipt of government assistance.

Recently, however, excluded communities have resisted this process. Often this resistance takes the form of protests over the display of the Confederate battle flag or statues of former slaveholders, and over the names of buildings on college campuses. These protests represent more than symbolic controversies. They are a response to institutional oppressions that are so deeply rooted in our society that most people in the majority culture scarcely notice them.

During the past few years, the Black Lives Matter campaign forced the American public to pay attention to an extreme form of oppression—physical violence—and the chronic threat of violence, coercion, or intimidation that exists in many communities of color. This form of oppression has not only produced the deaths of unarmed individuals while under arrest or in police custody, but persistent racial disproportionality in arrests, prosecutions, convictions, and sentencing (Alexander, 2010; Coates, 2015) and the psychological effect of this violence on the communities in which it occurs. To practice effectively in today's multicultural environment, therefore, social workers must be aware of the effects of this violence, and of *all forms* of oppression, particularly as they affect communities of color and other disenfranchised and excluded populations (Sharpe & Boyas, 2011).

As recent authors have pointed out, the long-term effects of oppression go beyond the needless loss of life. They range from the denial of a community's racial and cultural heritage to the effect of compulsory assimilation into a society that never fully accepts the "assimilated" (Coates, 2015). They also produce acts of personal rebellion—that are both inner-directed and self-destructive, such as substance abuse and gang violence—and outer-directed and creative, such as hip-hop culture, political activism, and collective resistance (Dyson, 2017). They simultaneously strengthen the "bonding social capital" of isolated communities, which enables them to survive, and diminish their "bridging social capital," which would enable them to overcome their isolation and exclusion (Reisch & Guyet, 2007). Social workers who work in communities affected by oppressive conditions must be cognizant of the historical forces that produced these conditions, their contemporary consequences at both the individual and community level, and their structural roots. The depth of this awareness will determine to what extent their practice will promote the profession's ethical imperative to work toward social justice as a recent document by NASW (2015) recognizes.

As stated previously, in today's increasingly complex and conflict-ridden environment, effective macro practice requires social workers to be knowledgeable about how to use strategic interventions to translate awareness of "private troubles" into "public issues" in the form of effective programs and policies. This requires an understanding of how social service agencies and service delivery networks operate intraorganizationally and inter-organizationally within and among the public, nonprofit, and private, for-profit sectors. Practitioners must also know the histories and contemporary dynamics of the diverse communities in which they work and how these histories affect a community's ability to shape its own destiny.

At the same time, social workers engaged in macro practice must be sensitive to the different effect that chronic issues such as poverty have on the lives and life chances of people in excluded and marginalized communities. Becoming aware of the effects of oppression necessitates the abandonment of a "one size fits all" explanation of the causes and consequences of people's issues. Social workers also need to recognize the multiple obstacles these communities face due to long-standing institutional neglect and deliberate policy choices. This awareness can help us develop targeted interventions in cooperation with the people with whom we work.

In this regard, today's social workers would benefit considerably from learning how communities of color and other excluded and marginalized populations analyze the current context and have developed, recently and in the past, alternative organizational configurations to address both new and chronic issues (Delgado, 1994). Alternative analytical frameworks based, for example, on **critical theory** (Fook, 2014) emphasize the centrality of racism as a primary mode of oppression. They also strive to enhance the capacity of young people, integrate an international component into practice, and revitalize and give new meaning to indigenous cultural practices and values (Weaver, 2014). As the Black Lives Matter and Dreamers movements demonstrate, they employ both "inside" and "outside" strategies and diverse organizational forms to promote change (Sen, 2013; Delgado, 1994). Although some observers have expressed concern that these approaches will strengthen "separatist," identity-based tendencies in U.S. society, there is also evidence of the potential progress that multiracial, crosscutting coalitions have achieved and could achieve, provided there is genuinely shared leadership and that organizations of traditionally excluded populations are able to maintain their independence. The chapters that follow will examine some of the implications of these developments in more detail.

Summary and Conclusion

As the chart below indicates, the social work profession faces many challenges today that affect all practitioners and the people with whom we work now and in the future. Social workers will have to address numerous conflicts, including the value conflicts produced by demographic diversity itself. For example, by the mid-2040s, when most of today's students will be at the peak of their careers, there will be no racial "majority" in the United States (U.S. Census Bureau, 2016). By itself, this unprecedented demographic and cultural transformation, which is already under way in California and cities such as New York, will have profound implications for the country's future and for social work's capacity to respond to that future in constructive ways. It is also a not-so-subtle cause of the "demographic panic" underlying current "nationalist" rhetoric and policy decisions in Washington and many state capitals.

Consequently, social workers will practice in an environment in which communities, organizations, and society itself will be changing in unpredictable ways. To be effective practitioners in this rapidly changing context, all social workers will need to understand the implications of the demographic, cultural, economic, and technological changes that are underway and assess how they will affect the nature of social welfare provision. This may involve acquiring the ability to reconcile the conflicting interests of multiple constituencies and forge new diverse alliances, both domestically and globally (Reisch, 2013b).

Definitions of human need and social assistance are also changing rapidly, in part because of the effects of increasing diversity. Yet, values that do not reflect the emerging character of U.S. society still largely shape our responses to these changing needs. We will have to clarify how to apply the concepts of empowerment, oppression, and social justice to our practice. As the history section previously cited indicated, macro practitioners have played and can continue to play a critical role in this regard (Rothman, 1999; Austin, Anthony, Knee, & Mathias, 2015; Rothman & Mizrahi, 2014). Understanding the macro components of practice, therefore, will be essential knowledge for *all* social workers. It is "in the … self-interest of the profession as a whole and the people with whom" we work (Reisch, 2016).

It would be misguided, however, to believe that we could apply the knowledge and skills that have worked in the past without critically assessing their relevance to the current environment. Among the many lessons we can learn from history, perhaps the most important is that nothing is permanent. The chapters that follow represent a modest attempt to identify and communicate what the knowledge and skills for future macro social workers might include.

END-OF-CHAPTER EXERCISE
YOUR UNDERLYING VALUES

Ask yourself

1. What values inspired you to become a social worker?
2. How do the issues about which you are concerned reflect these values?
3. What are the sources of these values (e.g., religious beliefs, a secular ideology, your family or community background, your personal or professional experiences)?
4. What are the positive and potentially negative implications of these values for your practice?
5. How do these values compare to the expressed values of the social work profession?

IN-CLASS EXERCISE
WARM-UP

Instructions: Find classmates who shares the same characteristics as you in as many of the following areas as possible. You **must** find a **different** classmate for each area. Have the person sign his or her initials on the appropriate line.

___ Was born in the same month

___ Has a pet

___ Lives in same neighborhood or a town similar to yours

___ Comes from a large family (has three or more siblings)

___ Has lived or studied in another country

___ Wants to practice social work in the same area

___ Shares a similar hobby

___ Likes the same type of food

___ Likes the same music

___ Had the same undergraduate major

___ Comes from a similar ethnic background

___ Went to the same high school

___ Worships at the same church

CHAPTER 2

Theories Underlying Macro Social Work Practice in a Multicultural Society

It is a capital mistake to theorize before one has data. Insensibly one begins to twist facts to suit theories, instead of theories to suit facts.

—**Arthur Conan Doyle, Sherlock Holmes**

In theory, there is no difference between theory and practice. But in practice, there is.

—**Yogi Berra**

Introduction

In recent years, three powerful social movements have captured the imagination of the public. The "Occupy Movement" that emerged in the aftermath of the Great Recession heightened public awareness of growing socioeconomic inequality, both in the United States and globally. Some of its catchwords—"the 1%" and "the 99%"—seem permanently etched in public discourse. It helped dramatize the relationship between inequalities of income and wealth and the widening inequities in education, health care, and housing, and of the role of fiscal and social policies in perpetuating these gaps. Yet, to date, the movement has produced few discernable policy changes. Although the heightened awareness the movement produced may have contributed somewhat to the electoral successes of both Senator Bernie Sanders and presidential candidate Donald Trump in 2016, it is unclear whether the movement created the structural basis for a sustained, long-term effort to address the issues it raised (Gitlin, 2012).

The "Black Lives Matter" movement, inspired by police killings of unarmed African Americans, similarly drew public attention to a long-standing problem in U.S. society. In some cities, the movement has also increased the public's consciousness of the connections between police violence and other inequalities that afflict communities of color (Rickford, 2016). Yet, this movement, too, has struggled to establish a national organization, expand its agenda to encompass a broader set of racial justice issues that could be translated into public policies, and link its concerns with those of other marginalized groups to forge a broad, diverse social justice coalition. Beyond the development of consent decrees that may produce some modest reforms in local police departments (reforms that are now threatened by the policies of the new administration), the movement has produced few tangible outcomes.

By contrast, the movement for marriage equality achieved notable successes in judicial, legislative, and executive policy formation in a relatively short period. Not only did it succeed in turning around a large swath of public opinion within a few years, it "locked in" its victories with a Supreme Court decision and the support of major U.S. corporations. Although cultural opposition to marriage equality and LGBTQ rights in general persists, the movement fundamentally changed the terms of the debate, perhaps permanently (Frank, 2017).

Overview

What accounts for the different experiences of these social justice movements? How can theoretical frameworks about power and change help answer this question? That is one of the goals of this chapter.

This chapter provides an overview of the major theoretical frameworks that underlie and have the potential to inform practice in demographically and culturally diverse communities and organizations. It attempts to complement the theoretical material students receive in foundation courses on human behavior. The chapter also includes brief critiques of the various ways scholars have conceptualized community and organizational practice, with particular attention to the role of power and its various manifestations at the community and organizational levels. It addresses the distinctions among different types of organizations, particularly as they relate to the development of strategies to effect community and societal change.

The organization of the chapter is as follows: First, it briefly discusses how theoretical frameworks derived from research influence the development of practice models and principles. Theory is critical for effective practice; practitioners must not only understand relevant conceptual frameworks, they must also be able to apply them to the essential components of socially just practice. These include: (1) critical analysis of the issues clients, constituents, and practitioners confront and their contexts; (2) development of clear practice goals and the strategies to implement them; and (3) monitoring and evaluating the effect of our practice.

Theorizing is particularly important for our work as our communities and organizations become increasingly diverse. It is one of the most important practical tools for creating effective change because it requires us to analyze situations in context and to recognize their multiple dimensions. Theorizing also provides the intellectual foundation to maintain our perspective and equilibrium throughout the difficult process of creating change. This is necessary because the combination of our own social location and the structural forces that inevitably resist change can sometimes distort our perceptions of the very situations we are trying to transform.

The act of theorizing, especially when conducted jointly with others, can help those working for change expand their sense of possibility and develop more insightful analyses and effective strategies. In addition, it helps people acquire a clearer understanding of the different—and often subtle—forces that shape their circumstances, to resist the tendency to engage in self-blame, rage, or other self-destructive responses to injustice and oppression, and to overcome the inevitable frustrations involved in practice. Finally, theories can help identify and illuminate potential practice goals and provide a lens through which people can forge innovative change strategies and anticipate the consequences of different approaches to change.

Next, to provide a broad framework for the reader, the chapter provides a brief overview of major theories about social stability and social change. These include theories that focus on different types of change (evolutionary/incremental or transformative/revolutionary), different sources of change (structural, ideological, or conflict-driven), different mechanisms of change (innovation, social reform, or social movements), and different change strategies (**consensus**, contest, or conflict). These theories attempt to explain both how change happens and also what factors maintain community, social, or organizational stability (or stagnation). The theories to be covered include those that address the issue of consciousness and people's motivation for change; theories about the roles **ideology** and values play in the change process; theories that provide critical structural analyses of the effects of race, gender, and sexuality; and theories that focus on changing complex systems.

The next section summarizes the evolution of modern concepts of social justice, different interpretations of social justice today, the underlying assumptions of their major proponents, and the implications of these approaches to social justice for practice in a diverse society. It introduces a model of social justice practice that future chapters will cover in more depth.

The chapter concludes with sections on power and empowerment. They include content on the implications of various definitions of power and empowerment for macro practice; a discussion of the sources and diverse forms of power in communities and organizations; an exploration of alternative concepts of power and their practice implications; a description of the stages in the process of empowerment; and a discussion of the factors that facilitate and hinder personal, community, and organizational empowerment. It uses examples of empowerment-oriented intervention at the community and organizational levels to illuminate ongoing issues regarding empowerment practice, with particular attention to their implications in a diverse society.

Theories of Social Change

Why and how does social change occur? Why do people who have endured oppressive conditions for years organize to alter these conditions? For centuries, scholars and activists have offered diverse explanations, including:

1. Dissatisfaction with the application of long-standing values. In other words, growing awareness of a widening gap between societal rhetoric and social reality.
2. Failure of societal institutions to respond to major environmental changes.
3. Emergence of new social or cultural conditions and new ideologies to explain or rationalize them.
4. Conditions become too oppressive to bear and people have little or nothing to lose by attempting to change these conditions (Giddens, 1977; Dahrendorf, 1959; Piven & Cloward, 1977).

Each of these explanations rests upon one or more theories—theories about human nature, about the nature of societal institutions, and about the process of change itself. It is useful to examine these theories to understand the components of social change and the roles macro social workers can play in facilitating the change process in communities, organizations, and society.

A theory is a network of interrelated hypotheses or propositions concerning a phenomenon or set of phenomena (Fook, 2014). A theory is also a way of organizing experience that enables us to go beyond the mere presentation of empirical data to determine the implications of data for our work and the relationships we need to develop. Theories can also provide a stimulus and guide for further research to confirm, challenge, modify, or refute existing hypotheses or theories (Vago, 1999). In a sense, therefore, theories are building blocks that enable us to explain and communicate our understanding of phenomena. They reflect and occasionally modify our assumptions about human nature and our understanding of how people interact with one another.

Different theories serve different purposes. The theories of purposive social change that underlie macro social work practice attempt to explain how features of social reality emerged and how targeted interventions might alter them. To effect social or political change in a socially just manner, practitioners must determine which theories are most useful to interpret the challenges they are facing and to develop strategies to achieve their specific goals. They ask the following questions: Which theories help clarify what needs to be changed and how to make these changes in a manner consistent with the goals of social justice and greater equality? Which theories best explain the origins of a particular injustice or inequality? Which theories best interpret the processes involved in social or political change and why do some change efforts succeed or fail at various points in time?

All forms of macro social work practice involve purposive change—that is, conscious, planned interventions that occur in a dynamic situation or environment. Purposive structural change occurs in three distinct ways:

- replacement of critical actors or reallocation of existing roles and statuses;
- innovation—for example, changing roles within a community or organization; and
- redistribution of rewards, rights, and obligations in a community or organization.

Macro social work practice consists of deliberate processes to achieve clearly defined outcomes that require multiple stakeholders to consider the proposed action from different perspectives. Theories are critical components of macro social work practice because macro practitioners focus on three levels of purposive change:

1. *Organizational change*: This type of change is critical to all forms of macro practice because organizations (of all sizes) play a key role in communities and society. Organizational change efforts emphasize issues of leadership development and changes in an organization's mission, goals, resource allocation patterns, culture, staffing configuration, or programs. Theories of organizational change recognize that, absent a crisis, changes within organizations occur gradually; these theories help us analyze deliberate attempts to promote change within and between organizations and assess which strategies are most likely to produce desired outcomes in different circumstances. For example, if an organization needs to address

major changes in the demographics of its client population, or an unanticipated cut in its funding, or the unexpected departure of its leader, what theories can best prepare staff members to respond effectively?

2. *Community change*: Community change involves altering the structure, distribution, and dynamics of power relations within a specific area (e.g., a neighborhood) or population (e.g., a community of identity). It involves decisions regarding how the community allocates finite resources, identifies and interprets its problems, issues, and needs, and assesses its strengths. Theories of community change emphasize the structure of group or inter-organizational relationships within a community or between a community and the public and private institutions with which it must interact. For example, macro social workers need to determine which theories best provide the conceptual foundation for the development of effective strategies to address the deterioration of police-community relations in a community, or promote adequate governmental responses to long-standing inequities in health care, education, and housing.
3. *Societal change*: Changes at this level include changes in a society's demographic composition, institutional structure, economic system, social relationships or culture, and the ideological rationales that promote or impede these transformations. Theories of societal change attempt to interpret the origins, goals, structure, strategies, **tactics**, and outcomes of social movements and social movement organizations and explain how their actions influence continuity or change in social structures and systems. For instance, why do certain social movements produce lasting changes while others do not? In what ways can individuals and groups become effective participants in large-scale social change efforts? What is the relationship between community and organizational change and changes that occur at the societal level?

From a theoretical perspective, key issues in assessing purposive change efforts include: (1) determining what is *purposive* in the change effort; (2) clarifying the relationship between formal and informal structures and systems in change efforts; and (3) understanding who controls the change process, how the process is controlled and to what extent, and what effects this exercise of control produces.

William Domhoff (2010) outlined three components of all change efforts:

1. *Analysis*: A comprehensive, overall analysis of the situation one wishes to change, which includes a detailed understanding of what it is and how it works.
2. *Alternatives:* A detailed blueprint for the future or a way of doing things better in a particular situation or environment.
3. *Action:* A strategy or program to achieve specific objectives (in other words, a "roadmap" describing how to get from Point A to Point B).

Coser (1966) identified two criteria to distinguish these types of change efforts: the speed with which change agents implement the desired change and the extent the system that is the target of change is actually changed. For example, why did it take seven decades from the Seneca Falls Convention until the passage of the 19th Amendment that gave women in the United States the right to vote, or a century between the adoption of the Civil War amendments and the passage of the Civil Rights Act and Voting Rights Act? By contrast, what accounts for the relatively rapid acceptance of marriage equality in the early 21st century? On a local level, why are some organizations and communities better able to adapt to the demographic changes produced by the influx of immigrants and refugees?

Despite significant differences, all modern theories of social change assume the following:

1. Every society and all the institutions within it are constantly subject to the processes of change—that is, *social change is ubiquitous and ongoing.*
2. Every society and its component parts constantly reflect both dissensus and conflict—that is, *social conflict is ubiquitous and inevitable.*
3. Every component in every society and its parts contributes in some ways to the process of change—that is, *everything is interconnected.*
4. The foundation of every society is the coercion of some of its members by others—that is, *power dynamics are ubiquitous.*
5. In every society, social conflict often arises because different members of a society regard this coercion as just or unjust—that is, *people's standpoints matter* (Dahrendorf, 1959).

Given these realities, a theory of social change attempts to accomplish several objectives. First, it assesses the current conditions of a society, community, or organization to determine what needs to be changed and whether such change is desirable and feasible. This is the value dimension of the theory. Second, it analyzes the root causes of these conditions. This step combines both objective empirical elements (what we commonly refer to today as "evidence") and subjective components (e.g., deciding which data to emphasize and how to interpret the data). Next, the theory explicitly or implicitly constructs or describes alternative values and an alternative vision of an organization, community, or society. The theory then prescribes or proscribes certain courses of action to create the desired change in a manner that reflects these alternative values. Finally, the theory outlines an evaluative process to determine whether the desired change has occurred and suggests ways to measure its consequences, intended and unintended.

Thus, theories of social change all attempt to understand both why change occurs and also how it occurs. As stated previously, these changes can appear in many forms, such as changes in structures, institutions, and the distribution of power and resources; changes in values, attitudes, and beliefs; changes in status and roles; and changes in people's behavior or attitudes. Practitioners need to understand when and how such changes have occurred and whether the change is permanent or temporary. They need to determine the sources of change and explain how our social position and those of the people with whom we work shape our perceptions of the change process.

Theories of change also distinguish between the arenas in which change is to occur; the issues that motivate change; the goals, purposes, and underlying assumptions of the change effort; the level of analysis and change desired; the intended beneficiaries of the change effort; the targets of change; and the type or pattern of change desired. Given the context, desired change could be gradual, incremental, or revolutionary. It could be transformative or restorative, planned or spontaneous (Warren, 1977; Piven & Cloward, 1977). Some theorists regard change as a linear process, others view it as a cycle or a pendulum. Some consider change to be a dialectical process that involves the emergence and resolution of internal contradictions within a given situation (Marx & Engels, 1848). Some practice theories promote change through consensus, others through conflict (Alinsky, 1971; Eichler, 2007; Hardcastle, 2011; Sen, 2013).

Theories also reflect different views on the evidence needed to justify and inform a change effort, the pre-conditions for change to occur (Tilly, 1978; Piven & Cloward, 1977), the barriers to change, and how strategies can overcome these barriers. They also suggest different ways in which change can be initiated, the preferred agents of change, the best means of evaluating the change effort, and the most effective methods of change (Gamson, 1990). Effective change strategies can include consciousness-raising and cultural transformation; structural modification; the introduction of new processes or material incentives; the use of disruptive activities; the diffusion of innovation or transfer of technology; the promotion of cultural challenges to deviance, marginality, and social exclusion; and the use of different types of leadership.

To a greater or lesser extent, each **theory of change** addresses various aspects of the change process itself. These include changes in structures or institutions, behaviors and attitudes, status and power, the distribution of tangible and intangible resources, and the transformation of values and beliefs. Some focus on how a specific change affects a specific segment of the population (e.g., women, people of color, the LGBTQ population).

C. Wright Mills (1963) posed several key questions in this regard:

1. How does the theory address the structure of a particular organization, community, or society as a whole? What does it regard as its essential components and their interrelationship? How do these components affect the processes of continuity and change in the society?
2. Where does the society stand in relation to its history? What are the mechanisms by which it is changing? How do the features of the contemporary environment differ from those in the past?

3. Who are the members of the dominant and subordinate group? What changes in this pattern of domination and subordination are under way? What are the reasons for these changes? What are the responses to these changes?

These questions underlie the development of all theories of change, at whatever societal level.

The Evolution of Theories of Change

Prior to the 19th century, Western theories of change treated "the people" (98% of the population in most countries) as if they were incapable of continuous, rational, calculated pursuit of their collective interests. These theories regarded the structure of society and its institutions as "givens," usually as divinely ordained phenomena. The "people" allegedly responded largely to impulses—good and bad—and to manipulation by elites (Wolff, 1997). This condescending, antidemocratic, and often paternalistic view persisted throughout the 20th century (e.g., in critics of "mass society" such as Ortega y Gasset, 1985). Perspectives today that explicitly or implicitly reflect a mistrust of democracy or assume that certain segments of the population (e.g., people of color, women, immigrants, youth, or persons with disabilities) are incapable of rational political conduct continue this conservative tradition. Their underlying assumptions support ongoing efforts to restrict voting rights, cut funding for civic education, and prevent public comment on environmental matters.

In addition, for two centuries all major Western social theorists have defined social change in terms of societal change (or "grand change"). They have developed general laws—or metanarratives—to explain past changes, interpret the current environment, and predict the future. Each of these theories takes a position as to whether a deliberate intervention—a purposive change effort—is feasible or desirable. These different positions continue to influence views of change in the 21st century and shape the contours of our politics and policies at the local and national levels. For example, should government compel people to purchase health insurance in the private market? Should government subsidize families who opt to send their children to private, religious schools? Should government policy promote assimilation into the dominant culture or allow people to maintain their own culture? What should we do if different cultural values come into conflict in our communities and organizations?

To address these persistent questions, four metatheories of change dominated Western social thought until the late 20th century. Despite critiques and revisions by contemporary authors, the work of 19th-century theorists—e.g., Karl Marx, Emile Durkheim, John Stuart Mill, and Max Weber—continue to have major implications for community, organizational, and societal change today. It is worthwhile, therefore, to review briefly their perspectives because of their influence on contemporary macro social work practice.

Marx (1959) was the first Western theorist to break with traditional approaches to social change and develop what postmodern thinkers refer to as a metanarrative—one that continues to be influential throughout the world. (The distinguished non-Marxist sociologist, Robert Merton, once commented that all sociological inquiry since the 19th century has been a **dialogue** with Marx.) Marx was the first theorist to posit that **collective action** is rational; that it results from shared material interests and reflects class conflict; that the collective consciousness of people from the same class is a critical factor in promoting collective action; and that the conflict this collective action produces is both inevitable and desirable for change to occur.

Marx's vision of change has influenced both Marxist and non-Marxist theorists and activists in several ways, including how they address contemporary issues of race, ethnicity, gender, and religion. Even without explicit **acknowledgments**, evidence of Marx's influence is widespread in contemporary macro social work practice, particularly among practitioners who rely on exchange or **conflict theory**, including Saul Alinsky (1971). Ironically, some practitioners who reject or are ignorant of Marx's ideological and political leanings embrace some of his ideas. Community practitioners, for example, focus on the material needs of their constituents, emphasize the importance of group solidarity, often use intergroup conflict as a change strategy, and attempt to instill in the people with whom they work a belief in the possibility and desirability of change (Simon, 1990; Hardcastle, 2011; Reisch, 2012).

Similarly, efforts to promote organizational change stress the dynamic relationship between organizational conditions and structural environmental forces. (*See Chapter 5 for further discussion.*) They recognize that different groups within organizations have different needs that manifest themselves in different ways and try to identify the sources of actual or potential conflict. They acknowledge that changes in one part of an organization have consequences for every other aspect of the organization, and in ways that are predictable and unforeseen, intended and unintended. Finally, they emphasize the change agent's role in intragroup and intergroup development.

Much as Marx, Durkheim (1972) analyzed the nature of change processes within society and its various components. Unlike Marx, however, he focused less on the distribution of material resources than on the effect of social conditions and social structures on individual and collective behavior. According to Durkheim, the forces of integration and disintegration in communities, organizations, and societies produced by major economic and social changes are in constant struggle. This struggle produces three types of collective action: (1) *routine conflict* (such as elections), which—ideally—renew shared beliefs on a regular basis; (2) *anomic forms of conflict* (such as radical cultural or social movements), which shake up shared beliefs; and (3) *restorative conflict* (e.g., reforms passed in response to protest), which recreate social integration after periods of disruption. The civil rights legislation of the 1960s is a good example of an attempt at the latter.

Durkheim's influence can be found in contemporary theories of change proposed both by conservatives, such as Samuel Huntington (2011), who drew a connection between so-called "deviant" behavior and nonroutine collective action (protest, social movements), and also by liberals, such as Charles Tilly, who regarded collective action as the result of a combination of rational group interest and perceived opportunity (1978). Tilly influenced scholars of community practice who emphasize the importance of seeking common ground through consensus organizing (Ohmer & DeMasi, 2009); through activities that promote community strengths and well-being (Saleeby, 2002; Kretzmann & McKnight, 1993); and in the work of researchers and activists who emphasize the importance of altering the culture and climate of communities and organizations. In addition, the contemporary focus on the importance of the **organizational life cycle** owes a great deal to Durkheim, as do theories of organizational culture and organizational development and change. (*See chapters three, four, and 15.*) Practitioners who embrace this perspective attempt to create processes that produce restorative action, connect change efforts to the original mission of the group or organization by seeking out its roots, and strive to create coherence to a group's original beliefs (Hardcastle, 2011; Mizrahi, 2015).

While Durkheim and Marx emphasized *group* interests in their analyses of collective action, Mill (2002) focused on the connection between collective action and the calculated, rational pursuit of *individual* interests. He emphasized the critical relationship between individuals and the state (government) and the **nongovernmental institutions** that shaped their lives. Although Mill provided little insight into how people's interests arise and change, and how they articulate and organize their interests, his ideas have had a strong influence on pluralist theories of change and on **rational choice theory**, particularly in the United States (Godwin, Ainsworth, & Godwin, 2013; Coleman & Fararo, 1992).

Macro social work practitioners have also incorporated Mill's ideas into contemporary practice in several ways. In community practice, the application of Mill's ideas leads to efforts to help people identify their individual interests *first* and then find ways to merge these individual interests into group action. Working from this perspective, organizers would address such questions as what makes people (in this particular community) act? What might lead them to join or leave a local community organization or a social movement (Tilly, 1978; Perlman, 1976; Paley, 2001)? They would also focus on a community's relationship to powerful external forces and on the strengthening of "bridging social capital" (Reisch & Guyet, 2007). (*See chapters 5 and 9 for further discussion of social capital.*)

At the organizational level, practitioners relying on these theories would analyze how proposed intraorganizational changes (e.g., in programs, staffing patterns, or policies.) might affect individual actors and seek ways to link purposive change efforts to the self-interest of staff members, clients, funders, supporters, and constituents. Within this framework, macro social work practitioners would examine their organization's decision-making processes and try to build intraorganizational coalitions to promote change. Such interventions require sophisticated skills in negotiation and conflict resolution, particularly in demographically and culturally diverse agencies. (*See Chapter 15 on this topic.*)

Similar to Durkheim, Weber (1946) distinguished between routine and nonroutine collective action. Yet, his approach to change differed considerably from Durkheim and other major social theorists. In Weber's view, collective action is the outgrowth of a shared ideology (worldview) that is the product of rapid social change. In "routine" collective action (i.e., action that takes place in a manner consistent with prevailing values, such as the replacement of an agency's executive director or the president of a community group), the organizational structure mediates between long-standing organizational beliefs and proposed actions. Under such circumstances, group interests play a larger, more direct role (Dahrendorf, 1959; Berger & Neuhaus, 1977). By contrast, in "nonroutine" collective action, (i.e., action in which conflicts with prevailing values come to the surface), the shared beliefs of a group have a stronger, more direct effect. The recent emergence of "nationalist" movements in Europe and the United States is an example of this phenomenon.

According to Weber and other theorists of change that he influenced, such as Talcott Parsons (1954), the structure and actions of a group, community, or organization emerge largely from its initial commitment to a particular belief system. As practical examples, think of the importance of an organization's mission and vision statements, the NASW *Code of Ethics*, or the preamble of the U.S. Constitution. Ideology alone, however, cannot produce collective action. The emergence of a charismatic leader who can articulate this ideology and give it meaning to others is also required. From this perspective, people in organizations and communities develop alliances around both common material interests and common belief systems. These formal and informal ties are critical components of "bonding social capital" (Reisch & Guyet, 2007).

According to Weber, practitioners engaged in organizational and community change efforts should emphasize the creation of new norms or the clarification of long-standing values, and connect organizational change and revitalization to the organization's original mission and goals. The development of leaders who can translate these values into concrete actions and inspire others to act collectively is critical in this regard (Patti, 2008). Weber's theories, therefore, have been particularly influential in the analysis of complex organizations and, on a practical level, in examining leadership "succession problems" in social movements and organizations (Young, 2017; Austin & Gilmore, 1993). His theories of leadership and change have also had enormous influence on our understanding of complex organizations, such as bureaucracies, and on contemporary ideas about leadership. (*See Chapter 6 for further discussion of leadership.*)

IN-CLASS EXERCISE
CLARIFYING OUR VALUES

Introduction: Underlying Assumptions

1. Our activities as social workers in community, organizational, and societal settings reflect our personal beliefs and goals and emerge from our personal experience.
2. Social work practice, therefore, can never be value-free (or "objective").
3. All social work practice—and all aspects of our social lives—is political.

Think about your vision of society—the one that shapes your personal, professional, and social goals, and affects the nature of your present and future work. Indicate where you stand in relationship to the following statement:

> "My vision of a just society can best be achieved within existing economic, social, and political institutions."

1	2	3	4
Strongly agree	Agree	Disagree	Strongly disagree

Questions of Discussion

Think about the implications of your answer, particularly regarding issues of politics and power.

1. Do you believe you have the right to impose your view of society and change on the people with whom you work in communities and organizations?
2. If so, under what circumstances?
3. If not, why not? How will you realize your vision of a just society?
4. How did issues of politics and power influence your answers?

Theories of Society and Social Structure

General theories of society and social structure also reflect ideas about power and its role in purposive change. In this regard, three major perspectives have been particularly influential on contemporary macro social work practice. One theory—***structural functionalism***—emphasizes, much as systems theory, the importance of social stability and adaptation to change. In this view, the challenge for organizations and communities is to respond constructively to environmental changes, reduce social tensions, and socialize their members into patterned social roles. Consensus models of community organizing and management, and pluralist models of policy change reflect this perspective (Ohmer & DeMasi, 2009; Eichler, 2007).

While structural functionalist theory focuses on the systematic use of social arrangements to maintain order, it does not examine the processes that create and maintain these arrangements. By contrast, ***conflict perspectives***, such as **Marxism** and **critical race theory**, analyze how some groups benefit more from prevailing social arrangements and how these arrangements reflect and perpetuate inequalities, social divisions, and injustices. ***Conflict theorists***, for example (Collins, 2009; Young, 2011), regard the societal order as the product of dominance and coercion, not the collective pursuit of harmony. Institutional arrangements, therefore, exist to maintain the power and privilege of elite individuals and groups (their "hegemony") at the expense of others (Foucault, 1995). Critical race theory, feminist theory, and queer theory are prominent contemporary examples of this perspective (Bell, 1992; Marable, 2000; Berger, 2014; Kennedy, 2017).

Symbolic interactionism reflects a third theoretical perspective on the relationship between power and social change. In contrast to theories that focus primarily on societal and institutional patterns and their consequences, this perspective examines the day-to-day personal interactions of individuals and groups. These interactions occur through symbolic communication—such as language, gestures, body position, and cultural artifacts—that historical and contemporary forces influence at the group, community, or organizational level. In other words, the objective nature of a situation (e.g., how resources, roles, and power are distributed within an organization) is not the sole determinant of people's behavior. The meanings people attach to the situation based on their subjective perspective also shapes how they respond to the situation (Shulman, 2017). This perspective leads to examination, for example, of how communities respond differently to the development of social policies such as the Affordable Care Act, or to recent presidential executive orders restricting immigration and the admission of refugees to the United States, and how they express these different perspectives through language and symbols.

Critical Theory

Critical theory, which rose to prominence during the past four decades, is a particular useful perspective for macro social work practitioners in today's multicultural society. Critical theorists assert that "reality" (including fundamental concepts such as "whiteness," "gender," and "hetero-normativity") is actually a **social construction** designed to create and recreate preferred conceptions of what is "normal" or ideal human behavior. One way in which social construction influences our worldview is by imposing binary thinking that divides fundamental concepts into two mutually exclusive categories, such as White/Black, man/woman, reason/emotion, and heterosexual/homosexual (Ortiz & Jani, 2010).

Critical theorists maintain that practitioners should avoid sweeping generalizations about any group. They argue that doing so "essentializes" a population based on the assumption that a single characteristic, such as skin color or gender, defines its behavior and values. Instead, they strive to understand the combined effect of history, structural conditions, and immediate situations on people's individual and collective behavior. They reject the tendency to regard individuals and groups as possessing inherent, unchanging characteristics rooted in biology or a self-contained culture, status, or societal role. These theoretical concepts provide the foundation for constructing macro practice principles that reflect social work's philosophical commitment to social justice.

In addition, critical theorists emphasize the range of cultural influences that affect individuals and people within the same group. They posit that each person has multiple intersecting dimensions and a single demographic variable cannot define a person. Instead of viewing race, class, gender, sexuality, ethnicity, religion, nationality, age, ability, and other identifying variables as isolated features of social organization, critical theorists analyze them as mutually constructed components that shape and that are, in turn, shaped by individuals' experiences. The concept of ***intersectionality*** reflects this perspective (Collins & Bilge, 2016).

A corollary to the notion of intersectionality is that each person's social position (e.g., class, race, gender and gender identity, religion, age, sexual orientation) influences her or his construction of reality and the interpretation of other people's constructions and behaviors. Proponents of ***standpoint theory***, from which this concept emerged, further argue that the location of an individual or group in the context of hierarchical power relationships produces common challenges for individuals similarly located. These shared challenges foster similar perspectives on history and current conditions (a "collective consciousness") that are essential for taking collective action to alter that reality (Littlejohn & Foss, 2011). The growth of the Black Lives Matter movement is an example of this phenomenon. Practitioners who apply standpoint theory focus on the importance of developing this critical awareness. In this way, their ideas are similar to Marx's emphasis on the importance of developing class-consciousness and Paulo Freire's concept of **"conscientization"** (1971).

These theories have clear implications for macro social work practice. Because individuals in groups, organizations, and communities are affected by diverse, multiple, and overlapping influences they are not isolated, whatever their material circumstances, and, hence, they do not act alone. A dynamic, interactive relationship exists between people and their environments, although this relationship is often imperceptible. Sometimes it appears through the emergence of collective consciousness about a group's social situation, the acceptance of a common interpretive framework to explain the presence of certain problems or issues, or the development of oppositional knowledge that defends an oppressed group's interests and fosters the group's collective resistance. The development of collective consciousness can also produce a counter-narrative that challenges the dominant culture's rationalization of existing patterns of domination and subordination. Through the expression of these counter-narratives, even people in desperate situations can possess a self-defining and self-determining will that enables them to maintain some sense of control over their lives. This concept is consistent with an empowerment perspective and a strengths-based approach to practice (Simon, 1990; Saleeby, 2002).

Thus, important prerequisites for people to express their agency or self-determination are the cultivation of awareness of their place and role in history, and the affirmation of their ability to produce change over time. In sum, the assumptions of critical theorists that culture is dynamic and potentially receptive to targeted change efforts, and that people contain multiple, intersectional identities, are of particular importance for today's practitioners. Because social work is unique among professions in its belief in the value and possibility of change, this concept is particularly important for practitioners to embrace in today's complex and rapidly changing environment (Collins, 2009).

Social Justice and Macro Social Work Practice

For more than a century, the pursuit of social justice has been a central tenet of the organized social work profession and one of its distinguishing philosophical characteristics (Reisch & Garvin, 2016). Yet, most of the literature in the social work field, including the literature on macro social work practice, discusses the issue of social justice primarily in terms of the eradication of injustice and oppression. The NASW *Code of Ethics* (2017) reflects this tendency:

> **A.** Social workers should promote conditions that encourage respect for cultural and social diversity within the United States and globally. Social workers should promote policies and practices that demonstrate respect for difference, support the expansion of cultural knowledge and resources, advocate for programs and institutions that demonstrate cultural competence, and promote policies that safeguard the rights and confirm equity and social justice for all people.
>
> **B.** Social workers should act to prevent and eliminate domination of, exploitation of, and discrimination against any person, group, or class on the basis of race, ethnicity, national origin, sex, sexual orientation, gender identity or expression, age, marital status, political belief, religion, immigration status, or mental or physical disability (6.04, Social and Political Action).

The meaning of social justice, however, is largely undefined. The Code and other professional documents generally discuss the concept in vague and ambiguous ways (Council on Social Work Education, 2015; International Federation of Social Workers, 2014). A recent post on the national NASW website admitted as much:

> There is no right or wrong way to engage in social and political action. The Code does not prescribe which causes or activities social workers should undertake.

This ambiguity mirrors the multiple ways in which our society defines social justice. A summary of these diverse approaches to social justice follows.

KEY CONCEPT SUMMARY
CONCEPTIONS OF SOCIAL JUSTICE

- Equality of rights and opportunities, or as Ryan (1981) termed it, "Fair Play"
- Equality or equity of outcomes, or in Ryan's phrase, "Fair Shares"
- Unequal distribution based on individual needs or capabilities
- Unequal distribution based on individual status
- Unequal distribution based on different "contracts"
- Unequal distribution based on merit/ productivity
- Unequal distribution based on compensation
- A balance of equality of rights with more equitable outcomes, especially for the least advantaged (distributive justice)

These competing interpretations of social justice reflect significant differences about preferred societal priorities. **Libertarians** such as Nozick (1974) and Hayek (1976) equate social justice with the preservation of individual liberty or freedom, the protection of private property rights, and the maintenance of social structures and cultural norms (Stoesz, 2014). Liberals such as Rawls (1999) focus on the expansion of civil rights and a more equitable distribution of society's benefits and burdens. Communitarians, such as Michael Sandel (2009) and Amitai Etzioni (2004), stress the creation of greater cooperation, trust, and mutuality in societal institutions and social relationships. The goals of social democrats and those to their political left emphasize social and political equality, social solidarity and sustainability, and enhanced civic participation (Giddens, 2013). Proponents of the **"capabilities perspective,"** such as Amartya Sen (2009) and Martha Nussbaum (2010), focus on the full inclusion of previously excluded and marginalized individuals and groups. They favor socially just processes that reflect people's different cultural and historical contexts and acknowledge multiple forms of power, oppression, and privilege. They stress the importance of restructuring societal institutions to ensure the satisfaction of people's material and nonmaterial capabilities.

This book attempts to present a synthesis of some of these perspectives. It considers the following as the key features of socially just macro practice:

- analysis of the root causes of injustice and assessment of social structures from a critical perspective;
- awareness of the effects of power in all aspects of practice;
- a critique of the role and influence of dominant ideologies and cultural norms;
- a focus on the relationship between societal institutions and basic human needs;
- promotion of sustainable structural and institutional changes, rather than participation in existing systems; and
- the articulation of an alternative vision of an organization, community, or society, and the structures and processes that would comprise it.

The lack of clarity about the meaning of social justice obscures its relationship to social work practice and practice theory (Reisch & Garvin, 2016). It leaves unresolved the important question of how to reconcile diverse and often conflicting interpretations of justice in an increasingly multicultural society and multipolar world. This makes it more difficult to develop effective change strategies in pursuit of social justice goals. In fact, some scholars and activists question whether the concept of social justice reflects a Western bias or whether it should be the philosophical basis for social welfare and social work practice (Akimoto, 2014; Weaver, 2014).

In today's complex environment, macro social work practitioners also need to apply a critical perspective to long-standing assumptions that have shaped practice for decades because several of these assumptions may no longer be valid. For example, it has become increasingly clear that the expansion of government-sponsored social welfare provisions alone cannot create a more just society. Governments, as they are *currently* constructed, may not be the most effective instrument to create a just society today. In other words, the components of 21st-century social justice may not be compatible with the 20th-century welfare state or past versions of social work practice. Finally, although social workers often celebrate diversity, the conflicts it produces may diminish support for more socially just policies and more socially responsive organizations, at least in the short term.

Adoption of a critical perspective would also help us recognize the new local and global realities that have significant consequences for communities and organizations and integrate this awareness into practice. For example, social and cultural divisions today are more complex than in the past; we can no longer analyze them solely along a "majority/minority" axis. Because of this increasing complexity, we cannot solve emerging issues in policy or programmatic "silos." For example, the U.S. population is rapidly aging concurrent to dramatic shifts in its racial, ethnic, and religious composition (U.S. Census Bureau, 2016). As a result, by mid-century, nearly two-thirds of the elderly U.S. population will still be white, while the majority of the working age population will be persons of color. Unless we confront this demographic and cultural reality, there is the likelihood of increased social and political conflict. The 2016 election and its aftermath may be just the first round in a series of critical contests.

Common Elements of Social Justice Practice

According to Reisch and Garvin (2016), the components of socially just macro social work practice parallel those of socially just practice with individuals, families, and groups. Both arenas of practice stress the importance of self and the significance of one's social location, history, and standpoint. Recognition of the importance of self requires us to broaden our conceptualization of macro social work practice beyond the attainment of specific goals to incorporate socially just processes as well, such as the centrality of relationship in practice.

Integrating the value of social justice into macro social work practice also compels us to acknowledge the educational aspects of all our work and to stress the development of **critical consciousness** in ourselves and in those with whom we work. It places an emphasis on the integration of socially excluded and marginalized groups into all phases of practice and the importance of creating diverse, multicultural, sustainable coalitions and organizations. Rather than challenging the contemporary focus on evidence-based practice (EBP) in the formulation of intervention strategies, socially just macro social work practice stresses the need to develop community-based, **participatory action research** to broaden the definition of "evidence." Finally, it expands the current emphasis on practitioners' self-care to include the development of ongoing support mechanisms for clients and constituents.

The profession's failure to resolve several ongoing conceptual issues complicates the application of social justice to macro social work practice. For example, which views of social justice should we adopt (e.g., religious or secular)? This issue is particularly important in an increasingly multicultural society. Should we institute a universal definition of social justice, or should it be culturally relative? If so, to what extent? What is the relationship of social justice to concepts such as equality and freedom?

There are also practical, strategic concerns that we need to address. Should we focus on promoting social justice for individuals or for groups? Should our work apply social justice to the promotion of social change or to the maintenance of social stability? How can we balance this ideal with ever-present fiscal and political realities?

Given the social work profession's long-standing rhetorical commitment to social justice, is socially just practice merely good social work practice? Not exactly. Social justice practice refers more broadly to *concerted social action in the context of unequal power relations.* An underlying assumption of such practice is that the pursuit of social justice is central, not an add-on or a superficial veneer. Another assumption is that our vision of social justice practice expands with our experience. Environmental changes may always recreate old injustices or produce new ones. New forms of resistance to injustice and social conflicts may arise. This requires practitioners to engage constantly in negotiations with the implications of these contextual changes across and within shifting group boundaries, and to attend to both socially just goals and also socially just processes. Acquiring awareness of our positionalities and standpoints are critically important in this regard.

Core practice competencies for socially just macro practice, therefore, include the following:

1. The creation of a personal vision of social justice goals.
2. A focus on the centrality of interpersonal relationships.
3. The ability to apply critical contextual analysis.
4. The cultivation of critical consciousness and generativity through reflecting and reflexive practices.
5. The use of praxis to integrate these competencies in an ongoing manner (Reisch & Garvin, 2016).

Awareness of our social location is a critical tool to help people achieve their aspirations, solve problems, and obtain vital resources. It also enables us to work in and across multiple group and social location boundaries. It contributes to greater recognition of the importance of mutuality and reciprocity, the promotion of true democratic participation at all levels, and our ability to address the mutually reinforcing structures of privilege and domination in all of their forms.

Another important component of socially just practice involves a modification of how we gather, construct, and use information. In addition to the traditional uses of information (evidence) in practice, a social justice approach emphasizes the importance of capturing and monitoring the processes of community or organizational change and measuring our progress to socially just goals. It also helps us illuminate new issues or reinterpret existing issues, identify potential unintended consequences, and avoid replicating or exacerbating existing injustices.

From a social justice perspective, macro social work practitioners should reflect upon:

1. What information and knowledge are possible to obtain and are useful for our work, both initially and also as our work evolves?
2. Who will define, collect, and interpret this information?
3. What assumptions underlie the measures and methods we are using to gather data?
4. How will we interpret the data and apply this interpretation in our practice?

To decenter dominant paradigms of knowledge and information, we need to acquire multiple types of information from diverse sources, and use different concepts about knowledge. Above all, we need to involve clients and constituents in all aspects of these processes.

The application of critical contextual analysis is another essential ingredient of socially just practice, particularly in a diverse environment. In both community and organizational practice, social workers should strive to know the history of key actors and be aware of their positionalities, standpoints, and perspectives on the issues they confront. This includes analyzing their underlying assumptions about their community or organization and its goals; about intragroup and intraorganizational politics, and intergroup behavior; and about the change process itself. In sum, critical contextual analysis enables social workers to identify the self-interests of actors and groups with whom we work and increase our awareness of the dynamics of power and influence.

It involves regular reflection, analysis, and theorizing across three major areas:

1. Ourselves and our multiple social locations
2. The people with whom we interact.
3. The immediate and larger historical, cultural, political, and social contexts.

The application of Freire's (1971) concept of praxis helps us develop and maintain the skills required for critical contextual analysis. Praxis involves the ongoing dialectical process of taking action in conjunction with critical analyses. As the chart below demonstrates, it applies to all phases of socially just macro practice.

KEY CONCEPT SUMMARY
APPLYING PRAXIS AND CRITICAL CONTEXTUAL ANALYSIS TO THE PHASES OF MACRO SOCIAL WORK PRACTICE

1. Exploration: Learning how people perceive the issues confronting their communities and organizations and determining their goal priorities. It requires us to assess the perception of each group within a community or organization and to determine what changes each group prioritizes.
2. Engagement: Working within and across multiple lines of identity and interest.
3. Planning: Creating shared goals in shared ways.
4. Implementation: Using multiple strategies and organizational forms.
5. Monitoring and Evaluation: Engaging in ongoing negotiation.
6. Celebration and Termination: Assessing how to sustain our efforts.

To conclude this section, here are some general implications of applying a socially just model to macro social work practice:

1. First, we must cultivate a positive vision of change and go beyond a critique of existing systemic and institutional injustices. We must stand for something and work with people to develop constructive alternatives.
2. We must strive to infuse socially just goals and processes into all aspects of our work because injustices operate in different domains and appear at all levels of society.
3. We must integrate into our analysis a recognition of the roles of history, culture, and power—and attend to our social location and that of the actors with whom we work, because they limit our ability to recognize the diverse mechanisms of injustice.
4. We must be prepared to engage constantly in the negotiation of boundaries and conflict.
5. We must be prepared intellectually and emotionally for resistance to change, from both our "opponents" and allies.
6. We must be able to apply multiple analytic frames to the complex issues we face.
7. We must be aware of how theory and knowledge can create or sustain injustices.
8. We must recognize that all systems needed to create and maintain social justice have the potential to produce injustice.
9. We must be conscious that social justice is a complex, subjective, dynamic, and conflict-laden concept.
10. Finally, we must be aware that no group achieves social justice for all time (Reisch & Garvin, 2016).

Table 2.1 Values and Ethical Principles for Community Practitioners

National codes of ethics Example: Values noted in U.S. National Association of Social Workers *Code of Ethics* or the social work code of social workers in your nation	Particular values and ethical issues critical for community practitioners
Service	Interdependence
Social justice	Empowerment practice
Dignity and worth of the person	Reciprocity
Importance of human relationships	Partnerships and mutuality in work
Integrity	Citizen and community participation
Competence	Human rights and social justice
	Structural analyses and approaches (work toward changing programs, policies and root causes, not just manifestations of problems)

Social Work, Social Justice, and Human Rights

In recent years, social workers in the West have linked the profession's historic commitment to social justice with the implementation of universal human rights. The United Nations' *Universal Declaration of Human Rights*, first adopted in 1948, has since expanded to encompass three sets of rights:

1. Negative Rights: Political freedom, civil rights
2. Positive Rights: Adequate standard of well-being
3. Collective Rights: International cooperation and respect for cultural diversity

Some scholars and activists have challenged the connection between human rights and social justice. Critics of a human rights approach have focused on its Western bias (e.g., the emphasis on individual—rather than collective—responsibility to pursue rights remedies, and the focus on political—rather than social—democracy). Other critics have pointed out how a human rights approach can become a mechanism for cultural domination and imperialism. Still others have addressed the challenge of enforcement.

Nevertheless, the role of human rights remains a central focus of social work practice, particularly in the United States. Reichert (2007) summarizes the reasons for this appeal: "Social work ... is the only profession imbued with social justice as its fundamental value and concern. But social justice is a fairness doctrine that provides civil and political leeway in deciding what is just and unjust. Human rights, on the other hand, encompass social justice, but transcend civil and political customs, in consideration of the basic life-sustaining needs of all human beings, without distinction" (p. 4).

Yet, Reichert's assertions still leave unanswered some important questions. These include:

1. What do we mean by "human rights"?
2. What are the bases of human rights?
3. What are the different categories of rights and to what extent should we apply them?
4. To whom do they apply? Who decides? How?
5. Are human rights and social justice always compatible in diverse, increasingly multicultural societies?
6. Does a universal idea of social justice exist?
7. Is social work currently a human rights profession?
8. Should social work be a human rights profession?

Murdach (2011), for instance, argues it is difficult if not impossible to operationalize human rights principles in ways that do not reinforce and reproduce the dominant order and prevailing assumptions about universal human needs, power, and privilege. If Murdach is correct, macro social workers need to go beyond the implementation of rights developed by potentially unjust institutions to create an alternative vision of society and alternative institutions. Ife suggested one possible resolution of this dilemma—the construction of "human rights from below" (Ife, 2010).

Table 2.2 Matrix of Human Rights

	Examples of rights in each category (not exhaustive lists):
Social Rights	family life; privacy; recreation/leisure; education; choice of partner, lifestyle, sexuality, housing
Economic Rights	basic living standard, earn a living, work, achieve social and economic security, accrue savings, have a choice of spending patterns
Civil/Political Rights	free speech, free assembly, vote, fair trial, run for office, join organizations, join unions, strike
Cultural Rights	cultural expression, cultural practices, clothing, religious expression, intellectual property, land rights
Environmental Rights	pollution free, poison free, wilderness, beauty, sustainability, access to land
Spiritual Rights	choice, religious expression, rituals, experience nature, personal fulfillment, sacred land/objects
Survival Rights	life, food, water, shelter, clothing, health, safety

Source: *Ife, J. (2010). Human rights from below. Reproduced with permission of Cambridge University Press.*

In sum, the application of human rights to social work practice will require us to address some still unresolved issues:

1. Who has the authority and power to define, implement, and enforce these rights? Through what means?
2. How can we resolve conflicts between universal human rights and the preservation of cultural diversity and cultural autonomy?
3. In what ways are social justice and human rights approaches compatible? In conflict?
4. What are the ethical implications of a human rights approach to social work practice?
5. Finally, how can we translate a human rights approach into day-to-day macro social work practice?

Defining Empowerment: Implications for Macro Social Work Practice

According to Simon (1990), the concept of empowerment, under various names, has been a foundational principle of social work practice since the emergence of the profession. Since Barbara Solomon (1976) first introduced the term in the late 1970s as a construct that fused the psychosocial and political-economic components of practice, the concept of empowerment has become increasingly popular. Social workers apply the concept to all aspects of practice, although its meaning and implications are not always understood.

According to one definition, empowerment is a process that enables people (individuals, organizations, communities) to develop and implement organized responses to circumstances that affect their lives (Gutierrez, Parsons, & Cox, 1998). Rivera (1997) argued, however, that scholars have rarely examined the phenomenon of citizen empowerment—a core value of macro social work practice—as an issue of human development and learning. While there is considerable scholarship on citizen participation, community organizing, and the experience of powerlessness and alienation, this scholarship often focuses on people's problems, deficiencies, disadvantages, and constraints. Consequently, the deficit models so prevalent in psychological research—also often implicit in some models of organizational and social change—have failed to provide insights into the successful cultivation of abilities, understandings, and awareness that characterize "participatory competence," a critical feature of empowerment.

This critique points out that the frequently employed concepts of powerlessness and empowerment refer to the intersection of conscious and unconscious experiences, identifiable skills, and people's perceptions of their social and political relationships. As Freire (1971) noted, "powerless" individuals (or groups) are viewed as occupying the role of "object" in the world—who are acted upon by dominant and frequently oppressive forces—rather than as "subjects" who are active in and act upon their environment—or, to use a more contemporary term, who possess "agency." Powerlessness, therefore, implies alienation from positive participation in the construction of social reality. Because vast tapestries of social and structural relations reinforce this passivity and cultural mystification—in sophisticated and often subtle ways—it is reasonable to describe the powerlessness of individuals, groups, and communities as their submersion in and perceived loss of control over those complex, interwoven relationships.

A revised definition of empowerment derived from Freire emphasizes the role of "critical consciousness" in its development. According to Freire (2013), critical consciousness is a process through which "... people develop their power to perceive critically the way they exist in the world with which and in which they find themselves." The convergence of this notion with theories of personal "competence" is important for social workers engaged in macro social work practice to comprehend.

In brief, "empowerment" incorporates three primary dimensions:

1. The development of a more positive and potent sense of self.
2. The construction of a more critical comprehension of the web of social and political relations that comprise one's experienced environment.
3. The cultivation of the resources and "functional competence" that people require for the efficacious attainment of their personal and collective sociopolitical goals.

Empowerment, therefore, represents both a state of being and a process of becoming. Individuals, groups, and communities are empowered as they become able to participate in the dynamic social relations that surround them with a personal sense of potency, critical political awareness, and practical strategic skills. In sum, empowerment is the process of developing "participatory competence."

Common themes in empowerment theory include the following:

- Empowerment is a value that infuses action on both personal and collective levels;
- Empowerment requires respectful dialogue among all participants in a change effort;
- Empowerment is a mutually reinforcing process—that is, the participants in a practice relationship are all affected by "disempowering" environmental forces and must engage in reciprocal activities to strengthen their response to these forces; and
- No one, even social workers, can give people power. Power is not a tangible commodity that exists outside of relationships.

Various issues remain unresolved, however, in the practice literature. These include how to measure the extent of a group's empowerment and who qualifies to make this assessment; how to balance the goals of individual, group, and structural change; and, of particular importance for this volume, what roles can macro social workers play in the empowerment process?

Ironically, a lack of emphasis on the actual role that power plays in groups, communities, and organizations often accompanies widespread references to the concept of empowerment. The primary point here is that power is ubiquitous in social work practice. It frequently involves the connection between a need and a means to address it. This produces a relationship characterized by influence and dependence. The degree of power that an individual, group, or community possesses can be determined by measuring these two factors. Power, therefore, is often associated with force, influence, control, and domination (Hasenfeld, 2010).

In the contexts in which macro social work practice occurs, there are multiple sources of power. They include knowledge (of policies, organizational rules, community culture) and expertise (in fund-raising or communication); tangible and intangible resources (e.g., money and interpersonal connections); legal authority (law); social status; reputation; and personal style (charisma). The failure to recognize how these attributes of power appear in different communities and cultures is a major flaw in some contemporary social work literature. This failure subtly reinforces the tendency to undervalue the potential efficacy of a group or community to initiate a constructive change process. Other chapters in this volume will examine these issues in more detail.

Summary and Conclusion

Today and in the decades ahead, macro social workers will need to respond to multiple social, cultural, economic, political, and technological changes if they are to be effective. For example, immigration and population migration are fundamentally altering the demographic composition of the United States and the character of urban areas, the workforce, and households. The recent resurgence and partial normalization of racist, misogynist, anti-Semitic, xenophobic, and homophobic beliefs produces new challenges at both the local and national levels and make it more difficult to address the widening gap in income and wealth, and the persistence of racial inequities in health and mental health care, education, housing, employment, and criminal justice. Conflicting attitudes about sexual orientation, gender roles, family, work, and retirement create new barriers to social progress. Intense political polarization threatens the survival of long-standing social policies designed to ameliorate the effects of a market economy and reduces the ability of government to respond proactively to conditions created by economic globalization, technological advances, and climate change.

The Chinese character for "crisis" is a combination of the symbols for "problem" and "opportunity." This accurately depicts the current situation confronting macro social workers. Although the problems described here are daunting and often appear insurmountable, the situation is not hopeless. Our response to social exclusion and injustice, therefore, should recognize that whatever form it takes, it is the inevitable byproduct of systems based on inequality and competition, rather than equality, mutuality, and reciprocity. The reduction or elimination of social exclusion can only occur if we challenge the structural foundations of the inequalities that produce it at the community, organizational, and societal levels.

To achieve these ambitious social justice goals, participatory inclusiveness is a necessary but insufficient condition. To develop meaningful and sustainable solutions to these problems requires more than the accumulation of practice skills. It also requires basing these skills on a solid theoretical and conceptual foundation, evidence obtained from multiple sources in diverse ways, and connecting our knowledge to our values in a manner that reflects the realities of the 21st century rather than those of a distant, often mythologized past.

END-OF-CHAPTER EXERCISE
APPLYING HUMAN RIGHTS IN THE 21ST CENTURY

1. If you updated the "U.N. Declaration of Rights," which rights would you: Include? Exclude? Revise? Add? Expand?
2. If you revised the NASW *Code of Ethics* to incorporate a human rights approach, what would you add?
3. How would you enforce these provisions?

CHAPTER 3

Human Service Organizations in a Multicultural Society

The development of organizations is the principle mechanism by which, in a highly differentiated society, it is possible to "get things done," to achieve goals beyond the reach of the individual.

—**Talcott Parsons, 1960**

Our society is an organizational society. We are born in organizations, educated by organizations, and most of us spend our lives working in organizations. We spend much of our leisure time paying, playing, and praying in organizations. Most of us will die in an organization, and when it comes time for burial, the largest organization of all—the state—must grant official permission.

—**Amitai Etzioni, 1964**

Introduction

There is growing human need in urban and rural communities throughout the United States. These needs range from chronic poverty and hunger to the ravages of opioid abuse, from the challenges of reintegrating former inmates into their communities of origin to the challenges of integrating new immigrants and refugees into new communities and a vastly different culture. How can we respond effectively and efficiently to these human needs through community-based organizations? This is a central question of macro social work practice.

Individual acts of compassion are valuable. Yet, to develop sustainable programs that respond effectively to human needs, such as those just described, organizations are necessary. Social workers largely work in and through these organizations. It is important, therefore, for practitioners—in all methods and all fields of practice—to understand the features of organizations that try to address these issues, the community context in which the issues emerge, and the relevant policies that, alternately, created or could improve the lives of community residents.

Many factors influence the ability of organizations to develop programs that effectively address individual and social problems. These include:

1. Their leadership structure, including how they use power.
2. The processes by which they make critical decisions.
3. Their vision, mission, values, goals, and objectives.
4. Their culture and climate, including how they address issues of demographic and cultural diversity.
5. How they acquire and allocate vital resources.

REFLECTION EXERCISE

Ask yourself:

1. How could we apply our knowledge of the community and the organization in which we work to address the above issues?
2. What do we know about the particular problems or issues the community is experiencing (e.g., violence, unemployment, homelessness)?
3. What do we know about the populations affected by these problems (e.g., children, women, immigrants, ex-offenders)?
4. How would we approach their problems from a community perspective?
5. How would we approach them from an organizational perspective?

It is widely acknowledged that organizations are the primary vehicle that deliver social services. They are also a critical instrument in the process of social change. This occurs in two ways. Organizations use tangible and intangible resources to create programs that change the lives of people and the communities in which they live. On occasion, they also intervene to effect change within other organizations to increase their responsiveness to community needs. They use evidence gleaned from research and best practices to guide their decisions and produce better results.

Organizations, therefore, are more or less formal structures that engage in conscious processes of need definition and assessment; resource development, allocation, and management; issue prioritization; strategic planning; program development and evaluation; and the establishment and maintenance of relationships with clients, constituents, collaborators, and community sponsors. Yet, the practices of many organizations frequently reflect a gap between their stated principles, goals, and objectives and their day-to-day practice (Hasenfeld, 2015).

The gap between organizational intentions and outcomes affects organizations in several ways. First, the programs and change strategies they create do not match the needs of the communities they purport to serve. Second, worker-client, worker-constituent, and worker-worker interactions sometimes run counter to the democratic values that the organizations espouse. Third, the organizations maintain an adversarial and hierarchical relationship with the communities they purport to serve, rather than one that is **cooperative** and egalitarian. Finally, the internal climate and culture of organizations are often not consistent with their expressed values.

These gaps between rhetoric and reality affect how the organization establishes priorities, makes decisions, and allocates resources. They influence the quality of collegial relationships and the overall interpersonal atmosphere of the organization. Consequently, in the present diverse and frequently contentious and resource scarce environment, many organizations fail to achieve their goals of empowerment and social justice in their actual practice and often inadvertently perpetuate oppressive and privileged ways of thinking and acting. This diminishes the effectiveness of their services and erodes the level of trust both within an organization and between the organization and the individuals and groups with whom it works.

To prepare students and practitioners to address these critical issues, this chapter covers the following topics:

1. *The organizational context of practice*: This includes the connection between practice in organizations and practice with individuals, families, and communities. It underscores how nearly all social work practice occurs within and/or through organizations.
2. *The organizational life cycle*: What it is, what shapes it, and what are its implications for practice.

3. *Theoretical perspectives on organizations and administration*: These include economic (rational choice), behavioral, cultural, open systems, and ecological perspectives.
4. *Patterns of organizational structure*: These include bureaucratic/hierarchical, cooperative/horizontal, and hybrid structures, their relationship to the organization's vision, mission, and goals, and the means by which they shape specific programs.
5. *Organizational vision, mission, and goals*: What they mean, how they are established, and how they influence practice.
6. *Acquiring and Allocating Resources*: What are the ways in which human service organizations obtain the resources they need? What are the implications for program development? This section includes suggestions on how to address fiscal scarcity effectively and ethically in politically contentious times.

Each section will situate these components of organizational practice in today's complex, multicultural environment.

The Organizational Context of Practice

Why do we create organizations to deliver vital services? What are the alternatives?

Organizations are "collectives of individuals gathered together to serve a particular purpose" (Netting et al., 2011, p. 213). They are also "formally structured arrangements of people, tools, and resources brought together to achieve predetermined objectives through institutionalized strategies" (Furman & Gibelman, 2012, p. 5). We use the term ***human service organization*** (HSO) to describe both public and private agencies. HSOs focus on the "prevention, amelioration, or resolution of health, mental health, social or environmental problems that afflict individuals, families, specific groups, or communities" (Furman & Gibelman, p. 2). Since the emergence of social work as a profession in the late 19th century, social workers have primarily practiced in and through such organizations (Reisch, 2008b). Unlike businesses that produce commodities, such as automobiles or clothing, the "raw materials" that human service organizations attempt to transform is people (Hasenfeld, 2010).

HSOs are not merely entities that employ social workers; they are key partners in the design and delivery of services. By ongoing interaction with community members and groups, HSOs establish the parameters of social work practice with a particular population. Understanding how organizations function—what they can and cannot do—is critical, therefore, to the development of effective and efficient programs and services.

There are five basic types of HSOs; all have both common and different features. Public sector or governmental organizations represent one major type. They exist at every level of government—city, county, state, and federal—and range from very large organizations, such as the Social Security Administration (federal), to small and mid-sized agencies, such as city or county welfare departments, child welfare programs, or public health clinics. Public sector agencies are dependent on some legislative or executive body for legal sanction (legitimacy), authority, and funding. They are statutorily required to comply with broad policy directives and specific regulations. Some public HSOs are subunits of larger organizations with which they have an administrative relationship. An example is the child welfare division of a state's department of human services. In other cases, social work departments are housed within large non-social work bureaucracies (e.g., schools, hospitals) that serve as the "host" agency that sets policy and provides fiscal support and legal sanction. In most cases, the head of major departments are appointed by the executive branch (president, governor, or mayor) and may require legislative confirmation, while the department head appoints the director of divisions or programs. These different levels of authority often create tension and conflict among different branches of government and between social service organizations and their public-sector funders. These conflicts occur more frequently when racial or ethnic differences exist among organizational and political leaders.

Although their manner of service provision and the distribution of administrative tasks may vary, these agencies tend to be highly structured bureaucracies (see below) that implement public policies in a formal, rule-driven manner. As a result, they often do not **collaborate** with the communities they purport to serve and sometimes have contentious relationships with their clients, particularly those who are seeking cash assistance or are involved with the child welfare or juvenile justice systems. Often this conflict acquires a racial and class dimension, especially when the agency's staff or the political leadership of the state, county, or municipality does not reflect the demographics of the community.

Another major type of HSO, the nonprofit organization, is, in many ways a uniquely U.S. phenomenon. Originally called **voluntary organizations** (because their staffing consisted primarily of volunteers rather than paid employees), most of the world today refers to them as nongovernmental organizations (or NGOs). This type of HSO emerged during the late 18th and 19th centuries for several purposes. They represented efforts to limit the power of government, fill in gaps in services that the government did not or would not provide, respond more effectively to the unique needs of underserved communities, and advocate for policy reforms that addressed pressing social issues, such as slavery, women's suffrage, child abuse, and alcoholism (Young, 2006; Hall, 2010). (*See Chapter 1 of this volume.*) Although members of the upper class or upper middle class initially created many of these organizations, (including organizations such as the Charity Organization Societies and settlement houses in which the social work profession began), immigrant communities and communities of color also developed their own HSOs in response to neglect, exclusion, or the provision of culturally inappropriate services (Iglehart & Becerra, 2010).

Nonprofit organizations usually operate under the general policy directives of a board of directors. (*See Chapter 7.*) Federal and state governments, however, sanction and regulate them in various ways, particularly through tax policy and limits placed on their political activities.

Nonprofit organizations have several features that distinguish them from governmental agencies and private companies. Their charters indicate that they serve some facet of the common good, such as the provision of foster care or adoption services. They are legally under the control of a board of directors, which is fiscally responsible for the organization's operations, although an executive director (or CEO) is in charge of day-to-day oversight. They also have a particular tax-exempt status in the U.S. tax code. This empowers them to hire employees to carry out their mission and engage in fund-raising to support their programs and services. It also makes them publicly accountable for their activities in order to maintain their tax-exempt status and public support. Unlike private, for-profit organizations, nonprofits must return their excess revenue (surplus) to the organization to expand or create new programs, improve its infrastructure, or establish a "rainy day fund." By law, nonprofits cannot distribute this surplus to board members in the form of a dividend or to staff members as a bonus. In fact, if a nonprofit generates too much surplus it could be subject to an IRS audit. In addition, the IRS and some states restrict nonprofits' participation in political activities and **legislative advocacy**. As discussed in Chapter 12, this has significant implications for the type of advocacy in which HSOs can engage.

In recent years, the nonprofit sector has been the fastest-growing segment of the U.S. economy; it employs more than 11 million workers and accounts for more than 10% of the nation's total private employment. This growth is primarily concentrated in several expanding service fields—health care, education, and social services, which represent 87% of nonprofit employment. Other factors include the dramatic increase in government spending on social welfare during the past half century, such as the 2009 American Reinvestment and Recovery Act, and the move to privatize many services formerly delivered by the government (Reisch, 2017; Kamerman & Kahn, 2014).

Today, there are tens of thousands of nonprofit organizations in the United States. They range from well-established multi-branch national networks such as Family Services of America (the descendant of the COS) to tiny neighborhood-based programs that operate on a shoestring budget. They are usually organized around the population they serve (e.g., the elderly), the services they provide (e.g., mental health counseling), their geographic location, or their general function (e.g., strengthening families). Not surprisingly, many of the smaller, less wealthy and less influential HSOs are situated in the communities with the greatest need.

If current trends continue, there is considerable evidence that future nonprofit organizations will be increasingly expected to provide more services, address new, more complex problems, and be increasingly accountable for the effectiveness, efficiency, and overall effect of their programs. Other emerging developments include greater reliance on volunteers, which creates the need for improved volunteer management, growing use of a social enterprise model (see below), and increased competition from for-profit organizations in several key social welfare fields.

A subgroup within the nonprofit sector consists of *sectarian* organizations. They operate under the auspices of or with the support of religious organizations. They often emerged for the primary purpose of providing services to members of a specific religious group that mainstream charities denied services to or provided with culturally inappropriate services. Examples include Catholic Charities, Lutheran Social Services, and Associated Jewish Charities. In addition, as Cnaan and Boddie point out (2002), more than 90% of all religious congregations deliver some form of social services. These services, however, are of widely varying quality. It is important, therefore, to distinguish between well-established, highly professionalized sectarian social service organizations, such as the three cited previously, and the thousands of faith-based programs operated primarily by volunteers through churches or affiliated storefront organizations.

Since the 1970s, there has been a substantial increase in the number and effect of a third HSO type—the private, for-profit organization. Although their structure is somewhat similar to that of many nonprofit agencies, for-profit organizations also bear some resemblance to private businesses and possess similar economic goals. Similar to nonprofits, they are legal entities, established as a corporation, partnership, or sole proprietary organization. They have a charter, partnership agreement or articles of association, and a constitution or bylaws. The respective mission statements of nonprofit and for-profit social service organizations generally reflect their different value orientations.

Some for-profits may engage in "good works" as a means to an end (i.e., being good for business), but not-for-profit organizations regard "being good" as an end in itself. Whatever their primary activity, for-profit organizations are established primarily for the financial benefit of their owners and/or shareholders. Their principle goal is profit for their owners or shareholders on which the organization pays taxes. As discussed previously, the mission of a nonprofit entity focuses on the "greater good" of the community, society, or the world. Because of their unique statutory status, nonprofits do not pay taxes (not even sales taxes), but they also cannot use their funds for anything other than their original mission.

In the 21st century, for-profit HSOs primarily exist in the fields of health, mental (or behavioral) health, education, and child welfare, although for-profit prisons and welfare-to-work programs have also recently proliferated (Weisbrod, 2000; Young & Salamon, 2002). Some observers have praised for-profit HSOs for introducing business practices, such as cost efficiency, into social service delivery. For-profits often have easier access to capital to develop or expand services; state and local governments frequently prefer collaborating with them, perhaps because their executives come from the same backgrounds as many government officials. Despite these advantages, some critics argue that a fundamental contradiction exists between the goals of helping people and making a profit (Guo, 2006).

A fourth type of HSO, the **social enterprise organization**, blurs the boundaries between nonprofit and for-profit agencies. These emerging organizations, often started by public-spirited individuals who have become wealthy through new technology-based companies, use profit-making activities as a means to generate funding for specific social services. Many of them work both globally and domestically. Examples include the Grameen Bank in Bangladesh; workplace-based financial wellness programs; Saravajal, which creates franchises that provide clean drinking water to people living on less than $1 a day; and Recyclebank, which rewards people for taking daily green actions (San Diego State University, 2017). To some extent, community and family foundations serve a similar purpose.

Finally, a fifth type of HSO, the self-help or **mutual aid organization**, has a long history in the United States. During the 19th and 20th centuries, people of color, immigrant groups, and women created many of these organizations to respond to the unique problems of their communities. Examples include the *Alianza Hispanico* in the Southwest, the Irish Emigrant Aid Society and the Hebrew Immigrant Aid Society on the East Coast, and local organizations developed by Chinese, Filipino, Japanese, and Korean immigrants on the West Coast (Reisch & Andrews, 2002). Many of these organizations evolved to become more formal, nonprofit agencies, such as Alcoholics Anonymous. Today, organizations in this so-called "tertiary sector" range from babysitting and food co-ops to advocacy organizations on behalf of the children of undocumented immigrants (Haedicke, 2012; Leitner & Strunk, 2014).

The following charts demonstrate the importance of HSOs, particularly nonprofit HSOs in the United States today. Figures 3.3 and 3.4 demonstrate the vital role the nonprofit sector plays in the nation's economy as one of the largest areas of employment.

Figure 3.1 The Economic Effect of the Nonprofit Sector

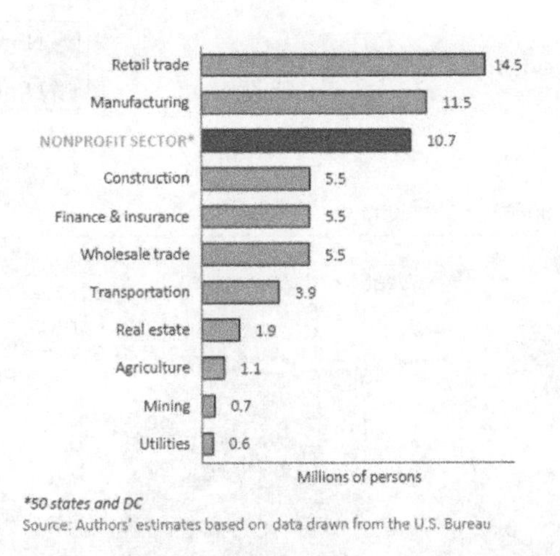

Figure 3.2 Job Growth in the Nonprofit Sector, 2000–2010

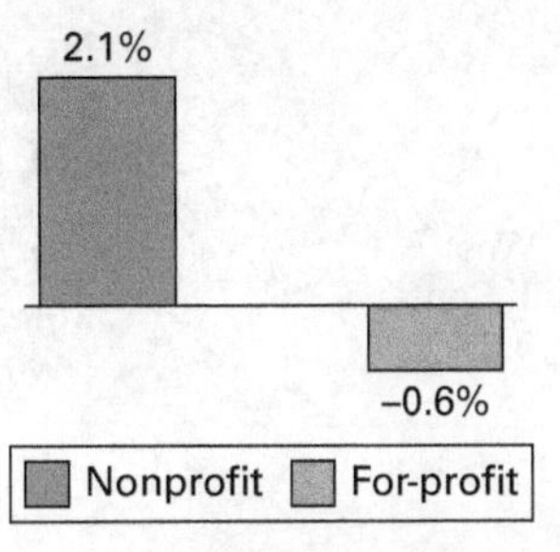

Figure 3.3 The Economic Effect of the Nonprofit Human Services

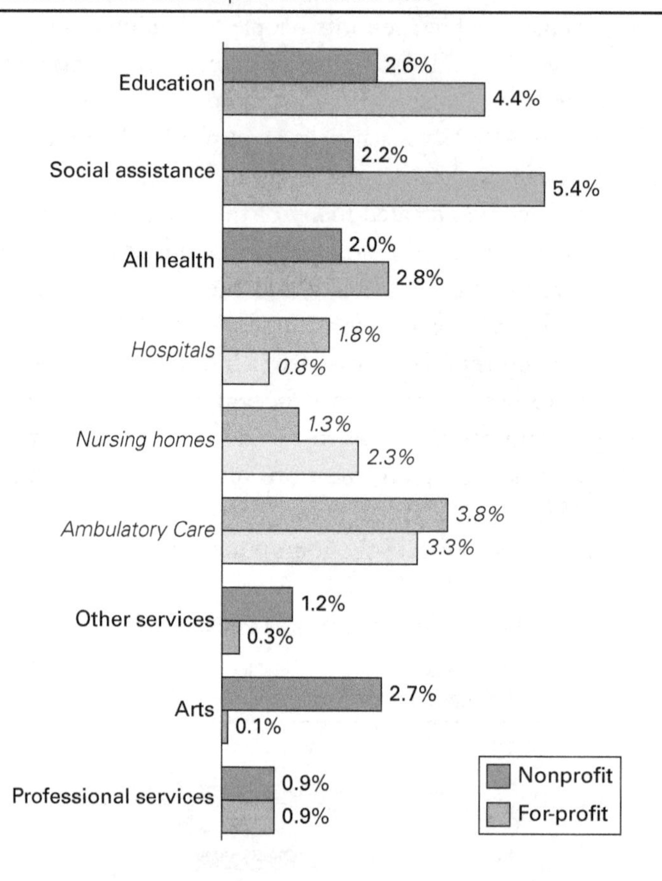

Figure 3.4 Regional Differences in the Nonprofit Sector

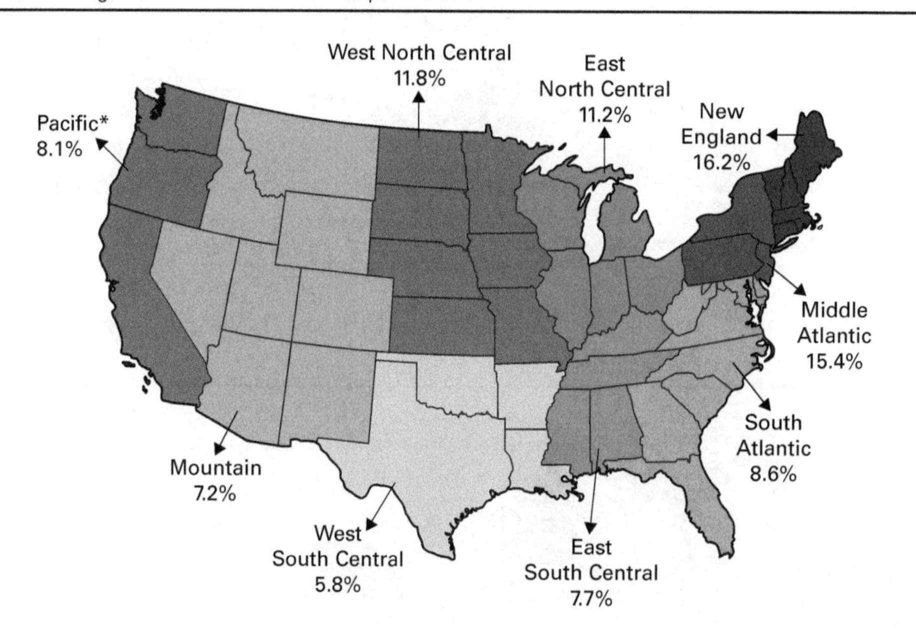

Figure 3.5 demonstrates that the human services sector plays a particular critical role in the U.S. economy. It continues to be one of the few areas of consistent employment growth, even in tough economic times such as the Great Recession. Many of the fields in which social workers practice have experienced the most consistent pattern of growth, as Figure 3.5 illustrates. The relative importance of the nonprofit sector, however, varies considerably from region to region, as Figure 3.4 reflects.

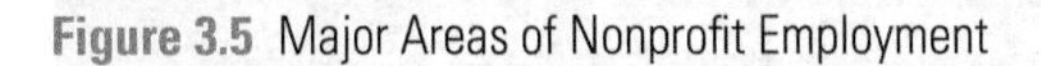

Figure 3.5 Major Areas of Nonprofit Employment

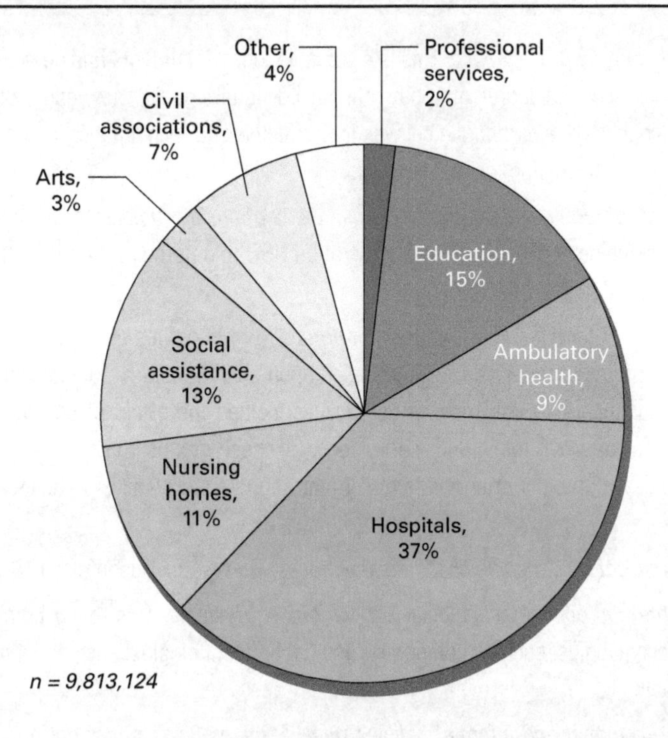

Organizations are complex, multidimensional phenomena. We can analyze them in terms of the raw materials they use, the nature of their moral and political work, and the ways in which the work they do is affected by issues of gender, race, class, and culture. As stated above, four general factors largely influence an HSO's ability to respond effectively to human needs and to develop programs that address a community's problems:

1. The organization's mission, which shapes its overall goals and program objectives.
2. The organization's structure, including the nature of its leadership, distribution and use of power, and methods of decision making.
3. The organization's culture, including how it treats its staff members and the people with whom it works.
4. The organization's financial position. This includes how it obtains the revenues it needs to fulfill its mission and how it uses these revenues to achieve this purpose.

As Lauffer (1992) points out, it is helpful to recognize the different lens through which one can view organizations, particularly HSOs. The following is a summary of the different lenses for viewing organizations and their implications for practice:

KEY CONCEPT SUMMARY
LENSES TO VIEW ORGANIZATIONS (LAUFFER, 1992)

- *As a career arena or workplace.* This is a valuable lens for students and new professionals to apply. It assesses the degree of fit between an individual's goals, knowledge, skills, roles, and values, and those of a potential employer. It also focuses on such practical concerns as income, prestige, and job satisfaction and security.
- *As a system of formal and informal roles and the relationships among them.* In this regard, it is useful to examine the organizational chart of an HSO to determine the respective boundaries and responsibilities it reflects.
- *As a system of formal and informal small groups.* Formal groups include teams and program divisions; informal groups can emerge based upon shared identity, ideological solidarity, job roles, and comparable influence. Critical issues include the effect of behavioral norms, the development of group roles, and the influence of these groups on organizational processes. This lens pays particular attention to the organization's culture and climate. (*See Chapter 4 in this volume.*)
- *As an input/output or people changing and processing system* (Hasenfeld, 1972).
- *As a context to apply "technologies" to various subsystems.* This refers both to the use of "hard" technologies, such as computers, and "soft" technologies, such as means of working with people.
- *As a set of formal and informal policies/rules.* These policies affect not only how workers function within the organization but also the extent to which and how an organization can fulfill its stated goals and objectives.
- *As a player in an environmental set.* This lens emphasizes the importance of boundaries and the effect of critical features in the task environment, such as external relationships, the political economy, and the organization's connection to the community. It also evaluates the organization's role as a collaborator in a larger community or network and as a partner in services or system coordination. In addition, it can assess the extent to which the HSO is a player within the larger community and polity. (*See Chapter 5 for further discussion of the effects of the external environment on organizations.*)
- *As a goal-seeking entity.* This perspective focuses on the assessment of the specific outcomes and **outputs** (measurable goals and objectives) the organization achieves and on their relationship to its vision, mission, and legitimacy in the eyes of the public.

- *As a locus of formal and informal power.* As discussed in Chapter 6, this approach stresses the role of power in the organization, the distinctive types of power, and the connection between power within the organization and power in the external environment. This lens can determine whether the organization is a site of social change or social control. As this book's theme emphasizes, this lens also examines whether the organization promotes multicultural progress or maintains institutionalized discrimination, and whether the organization advocates for meaningful change or engages in disempowering processes.
- Finally, one can view an organization *as a component of a nation or state.* This involves looking at its connection to social movements, state and national organizations, professional associations, etc.

All HSOs, particularly nonprofit organizations, have seven common functional arenas:

1. *Governance*: How the organization makes critical decisions.
2. *Leadership*: Who is responsible for making and enforcing critical decisions.
3. *Marketing*: How it presents itself to the outside world.
4. *Financing*: How it acquires and distributes the resources required to fulfill its stated mission.
5. *Administration*: How it survives as a legal entity.
6. *Products and Services*: How it designs, delivers, and evaluates its programs.
7. *Staffing*: How it recruits, hires, trains, supervises, evaluates, and rewards the individuals who deliver its programs and services.

These different functions produce common tasks in which all HSOs engage.

KEY CONCEPT SUMMARY
SEVEN TASKS OF HUMAN SERVICE ORGANIZATIONS

1. *Planning*: Setting goals, specifying strategies
2. *Organizing*: Structuring roles and tasks
3. *Human Resources*: Hiring, training, developing staff members
4. *Fiscal Management*: Costing out staff, capital, operations
5. *Directing*: Guiding, motivating, and supervising
6. *Evaluating*: Measuring standards and outcomes
7. *Resource Development*: Securing funds for programs. Research shows that managers spend ~two-thirds of their time running meetings and securing *funding*.

Similarly, all organizations go through a particular **life cycle**. Because of both internal and external factors, they are subject to the inevitable forces of growth and decline. Understanding the life cycle of an organization is important, therefore, to analyze all aspects of its operation—especially those factors that contribute to its effectiveness, efficiency, and effect (Quinn & Cameron, 1983).

A number of critical factors influence the life cycle of all organizations. External factors include the environmental context in which the organization is situated, changing societal priorities, and shifting political dynamics. Internal factors include its pattern of leadership and leadership succession; its structure, size, and auspice (public, nonprofit, private for-profit); and the processes by which it creates, delivers, and evaluates its services.

Hasenfeld and Schmid (1989) identified five stages of this life cycle and their respective goals:

1. *Formation*: Dream and inspire
2. *Development*: Found and frame
3. *Maturation*: Ground, grow, and sustain
4. *Elaboration*: Review and renew
5. *Decline and Dissolution*: Death or reconfiguration of the organization

During the *formation* stage, organizations reflect such features as a high degree of instability and uncertainty. They are concerned about organizational survival and what form the organization will take. At this point in their development, entrepreneurial leadership is particularly important. Staff members often lack fixed, formal roles. Many organizations rely heavily on the use of volunteers and employ a relatively simple service "technology." The key issue in this stage is whether the original dream that inspired the organization's founders can be realized.

In the *development* stage, the organization reflects greater internal stability. By this stage, it acquires formal nonprofit status and is now what the IRS calls a 501(c) (3) organization. Rather than relying exclusively on a charismatic leader, its leadership style is more cooperative. Although the distribution of organizational functions is still largely informal, some role differentiation and specialization begins to emerge—for example, between board and staff members, or between service delivery and administrative personnel. Finally, the methods of service delivery become more sophisticated as the organization further refines its objectives. As the organization's activities become routine, the key challenge is to maintain the board and staff's initial enthusiasm for the organization's mission.

In the third stage, *maturation*, the organization's external and internal environment becomes more predictable and its roles become more formally structured. Its services are now well established and recognized by the wider community. As it grows, the organization creates systems of accountability and begins to apply supplemental service technologies. This creates new resource and staffing demands that require the development of strategic plans to help sustain the organization and formal personnel policies. The goal in this stage is how to "grow" the organization and still maintain its viability.

If the organization has passed successfully through Stage 3, it reaches Stage 4, the *elaboration* stage. Now the organization is a prominent part of its **environmental set**. During this stage, a successful organization engages in periodic critical self-reflection to assess which programs to retain and strengthen, which programs to terminate, and which new programs to develop. The board of directors reassesses the organization's mission, vision, services, and structure through a strategic planning process. (*See Chapter 7.*) Because the organization has grown, its internal environment becomes more dynamic and the organization develops new services in response to new challenges. In a sense, the organization "recycles" back to an earlier stage to revitalize itself. To do this effectively, it needs transformational leaders who are intellectually astute, attuned to environmental changes, charismatic, and able to take risks. The key issue during this stage: Can the organization revitalize itself?

The fifth stage, which involves the death or reconfiguration of the organization, can occur at any point in the organization's life cycle, but the attainment of this stage is not inevitable. An organization can reach this stage for one reason or several reasons. Due to changing community needs or demographics, the demand for its services decreases; ironically, this could result from the success of the organization's programs. The organization could lose its market niche because of heightened inter-organizational competition or the presence of other organizations whose services are more sophisticated, more effective, or more in tune with the community's culture. The presence of poor leaders—due to mistakes in leadership succession—or the emergence of more rigid patterns of leadership could also contribute to the organization's decline.

When this occurs, it often produces internal tensions within the organization. Staff members feel increased pressure to "do more with less" this may lead to "burnout" among staff members who experience less job satisfaction. As a result, staff turnover increases, creating a vicious cycle. Employees begin to resist the demands of their superiors, often in passive aggressive ways, and the quality of the agency's services suffers. Program cuts lead to the dismantling of some services and a retreat to the organization's core technology, stifling efforts at necessary innovation.

Externally, the organization loses its legitimacy and experiences a cut in resources from critical funders. The organization is at a crossroads: Can it survive and maintain its original mission? If not, can the organization manage its "death" skillfully with as little damage to its clients and staff members as possible?

CASE ILLUSTRATION
THE ORGANIZATIONAL LIFE CYCLE

For a number of years, the author served as president of the board of a nonprofit crisis center and emergency shelter in a mid-Atlantic state. Initially, the organization served primarily runaway and "throwaway" (abandoned) youth, many of whom had substance abuse problems. Its staff consisted exclusively of volunteer mental health and health care professionals. The center operated on a shoestring budget. This was the formation stage in its life cycle.

When the author joined the board, the agency had acquired formal nonprofit [501(c) (3)] status, hired a few paid staff members and had a modest budget. During this development stage, its reputation in the community grew. Most of its staff members and clients, however, continued to be white.

Over the following five years, under the leadership of a dynamic executive director and several active board members, the agency grew enormously. This was the maturation stage of the agency's life cycle. Primarily due to sizable contracts with county government and a large annual grant from the United Way, its budget increased more than 500%. It added new services and paid staff members, and took on additional leadership responsibilities in the human services community. It made deliberate and largely successful efforts to diversify its paid and volunteer staff and board of directors.

By now, the agency had become an integral part of the county and region's human service network. This was its elaboration stage. Funders sought out opportunities to invest resources in its programs, staff members from diverse backgrounds moved into key program roles, and the board reflected diversity in many ways.

A crisis emerged when the longtime executive director moved to another state and her replacement proved to be an unfortunate choice whose actions to divide the board and staff along racial lines almost destroyed the agency. Fortunately, the agency's investment in organizational development and external relations, and the strong interpersonal connections it had cultivated over a number of years, enabled it to survive the crisis and the organization continued to thrive, although not without some major soul-searching.

As in the private, for-profit sector, there are three most common outcomes in this situation: (1) the organization could merge with another organization that has similar values and goals, but can contribute much needed resources, innovative programs, or political connections. This would create an entirely new organization, with a new name, and a revised mission, board, and structure; (2) a larger or better-situated organization could "acquire" the distressed HSO. In this scenario, the struggling organization's programs would be "folded into" the structure of the larger organization. Some board members could join the board of the new organization and some or all of its staff members could become employees of the new organization; and (3) the organization could undergo a process of formal dissolution. At best, this dissolution process could ensure that its clients continue to receive the services they needed and that its staff members had sufficient time and compensation to find new positions.

The following is an example of a successful dissolution.

CASE ILLUSTRATION
A SAD, BUT SUCCESSFUL DISSOLUTION

ABC Women's Crisis Center was the first of its kind in the county. It pioneered sexual assault and domestic violence programs and gained a wide reputation for its excellent and culturally competent work. Over the years, it forged successful partnerships with public and private agencies and religious institutions across the region and became a leader in various networks that provided services to women.

Because of its strong reputation, funders asked the center to take on new programs that they subsequently supported for a limited grant period. Eager to take advantage of these offers, the center's executive director expanded the agency's programs enormously. More women benefited from these services, but the long-term effects on the agency were drastic.

When the center hired a new executive director, she quickly learned that the organization's budget had relied almost exclusively on "soft" money (grants and contracts) for program expansion but that this soft money did not include resources for ongoing infrastructure expenses. When the grants and contracts expired, the center lost these critical resources but felt obligated to continue the services the soft money enabled it to provide. Essentially, the fiscal foundation of the center rested on sand, and the center was on the verge of collapse.

Fortunately, the new executive director was both resourceful and well connected. She persuaded the local United Way to provide an emergency six-month grant to enable the center to continue operating. Meanwhile, she strategically arranged the transfer of its programs to other well-regarded HSOs in the community so the center's clients maintained continuity of service. She also managed to help place most staff members in new positions. Imagine what could have occurred had the new executive director had less talent, imagination, and energy.

Hasenfeld and Schmid (1989) point out that the changes outlined here are not necessarily the result of an organization's age; they are more likely the consequence of its size and complexity. This model underscores how organizations are not fixed, static entities; they evolve in response to external and internal dynamics and reach certain crisis points because of this evolution. Using this life cycle model can help organizational leaders and managers determine what steps to take to resolve the challenges each of these stages presents. Finally, the model emphasizes that unless an organization is responsive to its changing environment and constantly involved in the process of renewal, it could decline and even die.

Table 3.1 The Life Cycle of Human Service Organizations (Hasenfeld & Schmid, 1989)

Stage	Goals	Some Characteristics	Possible Reactions
Formation	Survival	• High degree of instability and uncertainty • Entrepreneurial leadership • Personality of executive dominates • No formalization of roles • Simple service technology	• Plan, create, and market its program(s)
Development	Growth	• Leaders begin to delegate but keep basic control • Environment becomes more stable and familiar • More cooperative leadership style • Beginning role differentiation and specialization, but still informal • Service delivery becomes more sophisticated and accommodating	• Avoid over-bureaucracy and build structures for teamwork and responsiveness to clients • Create systems for renewal and change, e.g., learning systems, and respond pro-actively to the needs of clients and constituents and to environmental changes
Maturation	Stability and Expansion	• More formally structured work units and role definitions; division of labor, rules, procedures and control systems • Formal bureaucratic systems may be developed with clear hierarchies • Environment becomes more dynamic as it searches for growth • Increase of specialization/professional power; services institutionalized • Environment becomes more predictable and less competitive • Supplementary service technology developed; may replace the core	• Develop lower-level staffing and collaborations as needed • Leadership characterized by intellectual stimulation and charisma • Leadership style is "trans-actional," emphasizing exchange relations
Decline		• Decreased demand for services and changes in the "market" • Contradictory leadership styles characteristic of instability • Transformation in structure to reduced staff autonomy and staff resistance • Retreat to core technology • Protect status quo	• Respond to environmental change • Examine mission, goals, objectives within existing environment and make changes

Stage	Goals	Some Characteristics	Possible Reactions
Death		• Becomes "delegitimized" and the flow of resources stops • Rigid leadership emerges due to lack of confidence and unfamiliar situation • Shrinking workforce, operations/units are dissolved, internal tension intensifies • Services are dismantled while staff members still struggle to provide services to clients	• Seek out new organizational partners through merger or acquisition or attempt to manage dissolution of the organization

Table 3.1: *Yeheskel Hasenfeld and Hillel Schmid, "The Life Cycle of Human Service Organizations: An Administrative Perspective," Administration in Social Work, vol. 13. Copyright © 1989 by Haworth Press.*

Theoretical Perspectives on Organizations and Organizational Practice

As the multiple lenses Lauffer (1992) suggested illustrate, practitioners can analyze organizations from a variety of theoretical perspectives, each of which emphasizes different aspects of organizational life and organizational behavior. Descriptive theories focus on the organization's structure and its influence on an organization's internal processes. The most famous exponent of such theories, Max Weber (1946), was the first to provide a comprehensive framework to analyze how large-scale organizations (bureaucracies) function.

Today the term **"bureaucracy"** has largely negative connotations. Weber, however, noted its many desirable features. Bureaucracies, he wrote, possessed greater efficiency of operation and were less prone to corruption. Although they had a hierarchical structure in which the most important decisions occurred in a "top-down" fashion, Weber claimed that individual workers and the recipients of a bureaucracy's services benefited from its task specialization. Bureaucracies acknowledged the authority of workers' expertise and defined employees' roles clearly and permanently. Because workers had little discretion over rule-based decisions and could depend on a fixed merit and reward system, bureaucracies avoided the subjective and uneven results produced by older forms of organization.

In the United States, the Social Security Administration is an example of the positive features of a human services bureaucracy—it treats everyone by the same rules and applies its underlying policies equally and with considerable efficiency. The millions of Americans who receive Social Security benefits get their checks in a timely fashion and the administrative costs of its programs, such as Medicare, are approximately 10% of comparable costs incurred by private health insurance companies (Kaiser Family Foundation, 2017).

Organizational Structure

An organization's structure is the formal arrangement of its personnel, resources, and functions that are required to achieve its intended results. The organization's structure is both the product of the underlying values and assumptions that created it and a major determinant of its culture, strategic approaches, and ability to achieve its stated goals and objectives. The structure determines the organization's allocation of work roles and administrative mechanisms that, in turn, create a pattern of interrelated work activities. Structure also affects the organization's ability to provide quality services and use its resources efficiently. Under certain circumstances, organizational restructuring (e.g., of staff roles and responsibilities) can produce more effective, efficient, and culturally competent services. In sum, the structure of an organization enables it to conduct, coordinate, and control its activities (Jackson & Morgan, 1982).

The structure of most human service organizations usually falls somewhere between two poles. It varies depending on the type of agency, its ideological orientation, client or constituent population, community context, or the services it provides. On one end of a continuum are **mechanistic organizations**, such as large bureaucracies (e.g., Department of Social Services, Social Security Administration, United Way).

In these hierarchical, **bureaucratic organizations**, there is a strict division of labor and clear lines of authority. Workers have discrete, specialized, and clearly defined functions they are expected to fulfill through highly routinized procedures. They often have limited discretion in decision making because their behavior is primarily rule-driven—a product of externally imposed policies and extensive internal rules and regulations. Supervision exists at each level of the hierarchy and leadership roles are formally recognized. Power, authority, and presumed knowledge are at the top and all decisions need approval by higher-ups.

At the other end of this continuum are **organic organizations**; their structures have few or no hierarchical features. They operate on a collective or **cooperative** model, sometimes referred to as a "pancake model." In their purest form, these organizations have no formally recognized leaders, a low division of labor, and rotating work roles. There is shared responsibility for the attainment of organizational goals and objectives across all levels, and the expectation exists that each staff member will contribute to the whole and participate in a collective or consensus decision-making process. **Self-help and mutual aid organizations** are most likely to conform to this structural pattern.

Somewhere in the middle of the continuum are organizations with a hybrid structure, which incorporates features of both "pure" organizational types. These organizations display some features of a bureaucracy, particularly for activities that are required to maintain their infrastructure (resource development and management, building maintenance, supervision of staffers), and often have high specialization or differentiation of functions within their established programs. Unlike bureaucracies, however, these organizations have multiple centers of power and dispersed authority. Staff members make key decisions through a cooperative and collegial process. There is limited executive authority and workers have considerable control over their activities, including discretion regarding the interpretation and application of the agency's policies and regulations. In contrast with rule-determined decision making processes, this discretion creates greater choice for staff members (Handler, 1992) and has a significant effect on their psychological well-being. The structure of many small and mid-sized HSOs resembles this model.

Another structural variation is a mixed matrix model that organizes staff members in teams or around specific projects. Some large organizations, such as software companies and multi-service HSOs, use this model to unleash employees' innovation, give workers more control over (some) decisions, and create a more informal organizational environment. Control of major policy decisions, however, still resides in positions of formal authority. Figures 3.6 and 3.7 illustrate the varieties of organizational structure in different ways.

Figure 3.6 The Varieties of Organizational Structures

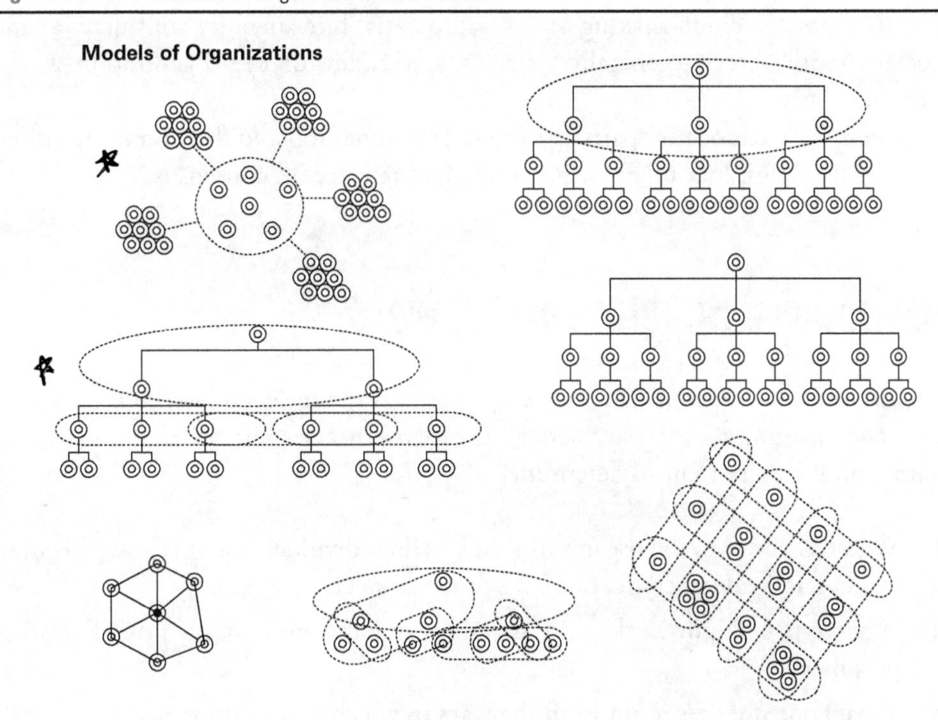

Figure 3.7 The Organizational Structure Continuum

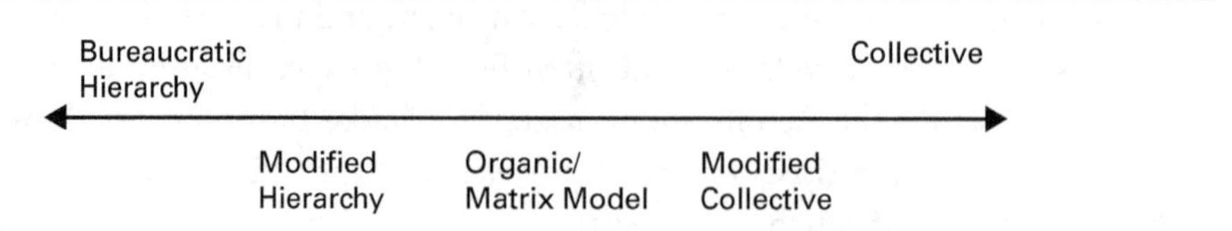

Organizational Structure and Decision Making

All organizations must make critical decisions. Some occur during an unforeseen crisis, but most arise on a routine basis. They include decisions about the organization's priorities, its allocation of resources, its staffing patterns, and its relationship to the external environment. The key elements in making effective decisions are time and information. If they exist in sufficient quantity, they enable organizational decision makers to assess a situation carefully and to determine strategically what action(s) to take. Ideally, the organization will not make a premature decision. Unfortunately, in many circumstances, organizations do not possess either sufficient time or adequate information.

What makes a good decision? First, your analysis must separate facts and values. You must be clear as to where values influence your perception of the situation. Second, wherever possible, the process itself should not predetermine the results.

The four basic decision-making styles—autocratic, bureaucratic, consultative, and democratic/participatory—generally reflect the structure of the organization as described previously.

For example, a democratic/participatory style assumes full and free communication, genuine participation (not token or nominal), and reliance on consensus.

Organizational Structure and Power

As discussed in chapters four, six, and seven, power is the means by which individuals, groups, and institutions exert influence on others. In assessing the dynamics of an organization, it is important to determine:

1. Who has power in the organization? How do individuals use this power (e.g., in an autocratic, democratic, or *laissez-faire* manner)?
2. What types of power do staff members employ most frequently? For what purposes?
3. What consequences result from the ways in which people use power?

4. What is the relationship between the organization's structure and the nature of power within it?

In addition to focusing on organizational structure, descriptive theories also analyze how organizations establish their goals and make critical decisions. Increasingly, they focus on the role that power and politics play in shaping organizational processes and outcomes. Leading contemporary examples of descriptive theories include **open systems theory** and **contingency theory**. The former regards organizations as organic entities that transform various inputs (money, nonmonetary resources, political influence, personnel) into outputs (programs and services) through a variety of internally and externally focused processes or "throughputs." Open systems theorists argue that organizations not only have permeable boundaries but are part of a larger environment that influences their behavior in an ongoing fashion through a perpetual pattern of feedback loops (Roberts, 1994). Because of this constant interaction with the environment, a change in any one part of the organization (for example, losing funds for a program) produces changes in other parts of the organization (such as another program) *and* the overall internal and external environment of the organization.

Similarly, contingency theorists adopt a systems-oriented approach to analyzing organizations. They recognize that there is no one best way of organizing agencies. The most effective way depends on the specific context of the organization and the particular circumstances (challenges, opportunities) it must address (Donaldson, 2001).

By contrast, *prescriptive theories* focus on the internal processes of organizations and the various factors that shape workers' behaviors and the outcomes they produce. These theories fall roughly into three categories based on their primary emphasis. Theories that adopt a *behavioral perspective* analyze how the actions of people in the organization determine organizational outcomes. They also focus on the subjective dimensions of this behavior—that is, they examine what people consider to be important (e.g., public appearances) rather than on what can be objectively measured as important (e.g., actual service outcomes) (Tsang, 1997; Grandori, 1984).

Prescriptive theories that adopt an *economic perspective*, such as **rational choice theory**, assume that organizations make "rational" decisions to maximize optimal outcomes. For example, they use cost/benefit analysis to produce the greatest amount of "good" that their resources permit (Coleman & Fararo, 1992). In the early 20th century, Frederick Taylor (1911) developed the first such theory based on concepts of "**scientific management**." He analyzed and synthesized the workflows that occurred in factory assembly lines with the primary objective of improving economic efficiency, especially labor productivity. His analysis complemented Weber's theory of bureaucracy in its goals of organizational stability, predictability, and maximum individual productivity.

Although scientific management may have initially reduced per unit costs of commodity production, it exacerbated the dehumanizing tendencies of factory work as best illustrated by a scene in Charlie Chaplin's classic film, *Modern Times*. The application of scientific management in human service organizations initially occurred in the Charity

Organization Societies through the development of "scientific charity" (Wenocur & Reisch, 1989). In the late 20th century, it inspired what Fabricant and Burghardt (1992) called the "industrialization of social service work" and produced results and accountability-oriented approaches to management. These trends appear, for example, in the paperwork clients must complete when they apply for benefits and in the multiple documents social workers must file when reporting an incidence of child abuse or neglect. According to some critics (Margolin, 1997; Soss, Fording, & Schram, 2011), by creating obstacles to the receipt of benefits and services, this paperwork serves as a means of social control and social exclusion, particularly for low-income and minority populations.

In addition, rational choice theory assumes that who defines a "good" and how to measure its attainment resides primarily in the hands of organizational leaders rather than service recipients or the public. This can become a particular problem when there are dramatic demographic and cultural differences between service providers and recipients. The implication for practice here is that there needs to be a balance between efforts to enhance organizational efficiency and actions designed to further the best interests of clients and constituents.

A third theoretical perspective stresses the role of **organizational culture** in shaping organizational behavior. It assumes that, as do people in all communities, organizations develop specific cultural norms, patterns, and rituals. They reflect these qualities in their underlying values and beliefs, their assumptions about people and problem causation, and the expectations imposed on their boards and staff members. An organization's culture can be strong, negative, empowering, or oppressive and conflict-producing. (*See Chapter 4 for further discussion of organizational culture.*)

A version of this theoretical perspective that focuses on human relations emerged out of the famous Hawthorne studies of the 1920s that attempted to understand the social factors of organizational life. Its authors found that workers responded well to the receipt of noneconomic rewards for their contributions rather than solely on the basis of material needs. This theory led to increased attention to the importance of organizational culture and climate and how the nature of work itself influenced employees' behavior and, ultimately, organizational outcomes.

McGregor's (2006) postulation of Theory X and Theory Y, based on Maslow's (1968) hierarchy of needs, summarizes effectively the differences in these perspectives. According to Theory X, some people dislike work. They will only "produce" if they receive clear direction and are subject to ongoing scrutiny. Proponents of Theory Y, however, believe that people in organizations are committed to their work and to the goals of the organization and respond more effectively to positive incentives rather than punishments or sanctions. Not only does each theory reflect different assumptions about human behavior, it is also subject to the biases of administrators who may interpret workers' behavior based on dominant cultural norms. (*See Chapter 4 for further discussion of the implications for diverse organizational cultures.*)

IN-CLASS EXERCISE
MANAGEMENT STYLES

1. What are some examples of management styles that reflect Theory X and Theory Y?
2. In your view, which theory is better suited for human service organizations? What are the pros and cons of each approach?
3. How would you apply the theory to practice in your agency?

Quality-oriented management is a contemporary modification of these theories. It emphasizes Theory Z. This theory assumes that workers are the key to organizational productivity. Proponents of Theory Z stress the organizational benefits of lifetime employment and treating workers as family through such structures as quality circles and the introduction of noncash benefits such as onsite child care, sabbatical leaves, and health promotion programs (Ouchi & Price, 1978). Senge (2006) outlines the features of **learning organizations** in which "people continually expand their capacity to create the results they truly desire, where new and expansive patterns of thinking are nurtured, where collective aspiration is set free, and where people are continually learning to see the whole together" (p. 3). Figure 3.8 illustrates the major principles of a learning organization. In today's "gig economy," however, the prospects of developing such organizations are uncertain. (*See Chapter 15 for more on this topic.*)

Figure 3.8 Learning Organizations

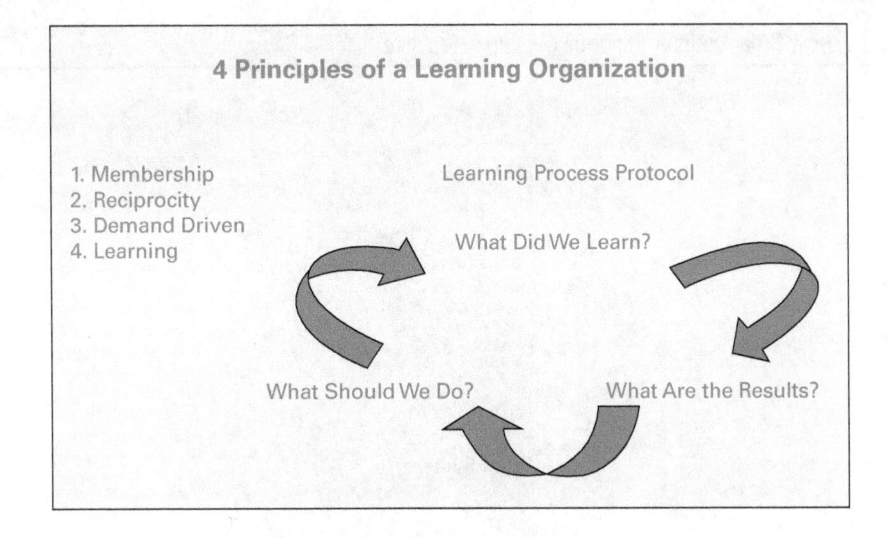

A related prescriptive theory, **total quality management** (TQM), focuses on customer satisfaction, ongoing employee training, and intraorganizational cooperation. It stresses the importance of multidirectional communication within an organization and between an organization and its various constituencies. It also emphasizes the need for ongoing evaluation not only of organizational outcomes, but also of organizational processes at every level (Dale, 2015).

By contrast, **management by objectives** (MBO), developed by Peter Drucker (2008), focuses on the relationship between program goals and outcomes. It places considerable importance on strategic planning and the ability to establish and assess measurable outcomes. **Evidence-based management** is the latest iteration of this approach.

Finally, theories derived from contemporary feminism reflect the assumption that women manage organizations differently from men. They focus on the importance of partnerships and shared leadership, rather than the maintenance of traditional hierarchies. They reflect a different conception of power and a more horizontal (pancake model) and consensus style of decision making. Feminist managers and administrators also strive to create new types of organizations based on the assumption that established agencies often replicate, intentionally or inadvertently, the oppression of the broader society. Even socially progressive entities, such as high-tech companies in Silicon Valley, resist hiring women and many minorities of color into leadership positions (Shih, 2006).

Most organizations use as a combination of these theories as the basis of their internal and external processes. Much as clinical practitioners, experienced administrators rarely adhere to one model; they create a flexible, eclectic approach that draws upon the theoretical components best suited to their organizations. Figure 3.9 illustrates the overlap.

Figure 3.9 How Organizational Theories Overlap in Practice

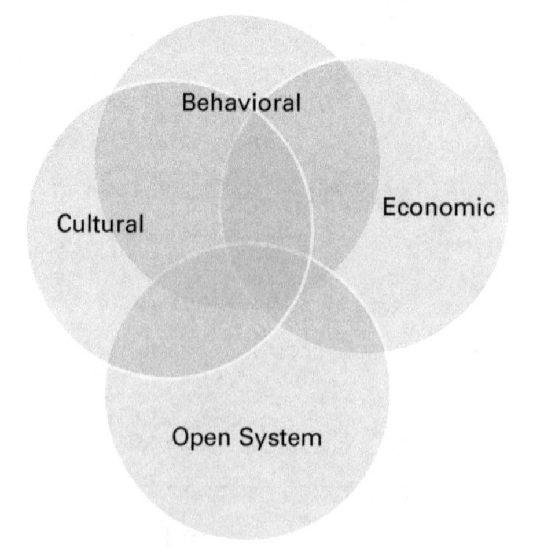

Organizational Vision, Mission, and Goals

All organizations develop a vision to guide their activities. The vision describes a desired future state that it wishes to create or to which it aspires to contribute. An example might be a "world without hunger" or an "end to violence against women." The mission statement of an organization interprets this vision to the public and all of its stakeholders and constituents by articulating clearly and concisely what the organization is about, and where, how, and why it provides its services. A mission statement gives the organization direction and motivation. It should reflect the agency's overarching values and be congruent with the services it provides or its core activities. The two most common approaches to defining an organization's missions are to review and select a mission statement drafted by similar organizations or to draft one from scratch. Because drafting a mission statement from scratch can be very difficult, the following exercise may be useful.

IN-CLASS EXERCISE
DRAFTING A MISSION STATEMENT

1. Divide the class into groups of six to eight. (In the "real world," you would convene a group of 15–18 volunteers, staffers, and community members.)
2. Provide everyone with a pad and pencil. Have two flip charts or a computer with LCD capacity.
3. Ask each person to list five to 10 key words that describe the purpose of the organization, its core values, and what it hopes to do for those who receive its services.
4. Ask each person to give one word from her or his list. Record them. Continue this recording process until all words from everyone's list have been recorded. Usually, there will be 30–40 key words identified.
5. Divide the groups into subgroups of three or four members. Ask each smaller group to review the composite list and draft a mission statement that answers the question: "What does our organization do for its clients or constituents?" Each draft should use 17 words or less from the key word list plus appropriate connecting words. Set aside 20–30 minutes for this process. When completed, record each suggested mission statement.
6. Review the various draft statements. Identify similar words each group has used and ask each group to explain why it selected certain key words. Discuss the similarities and differences in the statements.
7. Ask each of the smaller groups to write a revised statement. Stipulate that the group cannot use its first draft. Set aside 20 minutes for this process.
8. Record and compare the revised statements.
9. Continue this process until there is agreement on a single statement. Normally a group can reach consensus in the second or third round.

10. Ideally, the final mission statement should be no more than one sentence.

After completing this exercise, think about (a) how to ensure that all staff members are highly committed to the organization's mission; and (b) how to enable individual staff members from diverse demographic or cultural backgrounds to contribute to the advancement of the mission.

Figure 3.10 An Example of a Mission Statement

SAMPLE MISSION STATEMENT
HEALTH CARE FOR THE HOMELESS
BALTIMORE, MARYLAND

We work to **prevent and end homelessness**
by providing **whole-person health care**
to our neighbors without homes.

Our Mission

Health Care for the Homeless works to prevent and end homelessness for vulnerable individuals and families by providing quality, integrated health care and promoting access to affordable housing and sustainable incomes through direct service, advocacy and community engagement

Fig. 3.10: *"An Example of a Mission Statement," http://www.sbrapecrisiscenter.org/01About%20Us/about.html.*

As feminist women and men, we believe: Sexual assault is rooted in society's assumption that one segment of society needs to dominate and control another.

Sexual assault is perpetuated by institutionalized male domination and sanctioned discrimination, including racism, classism, sexism, ageism, heterosexism, and ableism as a means of oppressing women.

Sexual assault, exploitation, and discrimination are unacceptable and destructive to individuals and society. We are committed to ending these forms of oppression within our community and our society through empowerment in education and healing.

SBRCC acknowledges the political analysis and achievements of the feminist women who initially worked for societal changes. Our work is a continuation of their efforts.

KEY CONCEPT SUMMARY
COMPONENTS OF AN ORGANIZATION'S VISION, MISSION, AND VALUES

- *Vision*: Desired future state(s).
- *Mission*: Why you exist and what you seek to accomplish.
- *Values*: Principles by which the organization operates.

Organizational Goals

Based on its mission statement, an organization develops a set of formal goals, which express in broad terms what it hopes to achieve and how. Sometimes these goals are included in the introduction of an organization's bylaws; the organization periodically reviews these goals through the organization's strategic planning process. (*See Chapter 11.*) Staff members translate the organization's goals into specific, measurable program objectives that enable the organization to determine how it should allocate its finite resources (including staffers) and assess its overall success. In addition to formal stated goals, all organizations have latent, informal, and largely unstated (and less visible) goals that influence how the agency operates. These could include the image it wants to convey to the public or the atmosphere it wants to create for clients and staff.

As discussed previously, in some manner all HSOs have the goal of producing change—in people, communities, systems, policies, and/or institutions. It is important, therefore, for organizations to demonstrate in their stated mission and goals how they perceive the relationship between social change and the services they provide or the activities in which they engage. The following exercise asks you to analyze how the stated vision, mission, and goals of your organization explicitly or implicitly reflect a social change focus.

REFLECTION EXERCISE
HUMAN SERVICE ORGANIZATIONS AND SOCIAL CHANGE

1. What is your organization's stated vision? Mission? Goals?
    - Is any part of your organization's mission/vision/goals unstated? If so, what part? Why?
    - When did your organization decide upon its mission/vision/goals? How did the organization make this decision? Who was part of this decision-making process?
2. How does your organization engage with individuals, communities, and the public to achieve its stated mission/vision/goals? What types of activities (e.g., services, advocacy, organizing) does your agency undertake to achieve its goals? What are the objectives of these activities? Who benefits from them?
3. What changes would be necessary to achieve your organization's stated vision/mission/goals? What would be required to bring about these changes (e.g., different services, increased advocacy, better organizing, more resources)?
4. In what ways does your organization promote social change? In what ways does it promote social control?
5. How does the type of organization (public, nonprofit, for-profit) shape its stated vision/mission/goals, activities, and ability to seek social change?
6. At what stage of the organizational life cycle is your organization? What characteristics lead you to this assessment? How does this affect its ability to achieve its stated mission?

Because all organizations experience multiple, competing pressures and often exist in chaotic environments, they frequently encounter the problem of **goal displacement**. Goal displacement refers to the phenomenon when an organization's means to its desired ends become ends in themselves. The organization sacrifices long-standing program goals for the sake of other organizational priorities, generally having to do with organizational maintenance, such as funding, staff cutbacks, competing priorities, and shifts in the political climate.

In most instances, goal displacement also occurs when an organization places greater emphasis on its **outputs**—for example, the number of clients it serves or the number of trainings it conducts—than on its **outcomes**—such as the effect of its programs on the community it serves and the relationship of its programs to the organization's mission. Prioritizing the needs of staff members over those of clients—in the hours of service, the location of the agency, or the format of agency programs—is another form of goal displacement. Particularly in an environment of increased resource scarcity and cutbacks, organizational survival frequently becomes more important than service quality. The organization seeks grants or contracts from various funders without regard to how the programs it must create to receive these funds fit with the agency's original mission. This is an especially common form of goal displacement.

Acquiring and Allocating Resources

The problem of goal displacement reflects two increasingly critical aspects of organizational life: the need to acquire adequate resources to achieve the organization's mission and goals, and the need to allocate these resources effectively and efficiently. Adequate resources include staff members who can engage in fund-raising and resource development; a sufficient number of well-trained staffers and volunteers to deliver services; enough space and supplies to deliver services effectively; up-to-date technology; and an ample supply of leaders, supporters, allies, and members (if a membership organization).

Organizations also require a variety of intangible resources to thrive. These include:

- a sense of solidarity among staff and board members reflected in issue consensus and a sense of belonging;
- the ability of leaders and supervisors to motivate and mobilize people;
- a clear, well-articulated vision and mission;
- well-defined strategies and tactics;
- effective internal and external communication;
- good inter-organizational relationships;
- an equitable reward structure;

- public visibility, power, and influence, including credibility and an impeccable reputation; and
- possession of sufficient information or access to that information.

Sources of Funding

The source of an organization's funds depends to a considerable extent on the type of organization and the programs or services it seeks to provide. Federal organizations that provide social services or benefits, such as the Department of Veterans Affairs or the Social Security Administration, receive funding through annual congressional allocations or mandates contained within specific legislation. Increasingly, the federal government funds programs and services that state and local governments, nonprofit organizations, and even for-profit entities implement. It allocates resources via block grants to the states (as in the case of welfare reform) or matching grants (as in the case of many health care programs), or through some competitive bidding or application process.

In addition to federal support, many states fund services through their legislatures, and administer them through local (county or municipal) governments, or through some combination of the two. K-12 education is a good example of the latter. Sometimes, state agencies play a purely administrative or research function (e.g., an Area Agency on Aging) or distribute resources to private-sector agencies much as quasi-foundations. California's county-based 0–5 programs function in this manner.

Nonprofit HSOs obtain the resources they need through a variety of activities. Government grants and contracts provide a majority of nonprofits' funds. Other funding sources for nonprofits include:

- philanthropic contributions from individuals or foundations;
- fund-raising activities such as bequests, annual appeal campaigns, solicitation of support through direct requests, and events such as award luncheons or dinners;
- federated sources such as the United Way;
- corporate support such as in-kind contributions, technical support, or cause branding;
- charging fees for their services (often on a sliding scale); and
- for-profit activities, including social enterprise activities.

Funds received for general operating expenses, rather than specific programs, are the most desirable.

Proprietary (for-profit) organizations have a similar pattern of resource development. They rely heavily on fees for service, state or local government contracts, and government grants. Unlike nonprofits, they are not obligated to return their revenue surplus (profit) to the organization and may distribute a surplus to board members (as a dividend) or staff members (as a bonus).

Effective resource development depends on the adoption of several key strategies that address both resource acquisition and resource utilization. In today's fiscal environment it is particularly important not to rely on a single source of revenue. To diversify an organization's revenues, its leaders need to make a serious time commitment to fund-raising; develop a multiphase resource development plan; proactively seek new sources through donor cultivation and solicitations; and involve as many organizational actors as possible (board leadership, existing individual, foundation, staff, and corporate donors) in the process. Fund-raising is a time-consuming process that requires both patience and persistence, particularly for small and mid-size organizations whose resource development is starting from "scratch." This creates particular problems for organizations in low-income, racial minority communities.

Once an organization receives funds, it must be careful to maintain control of the revenue and monitor its cash flow. This requires an organization to demonstrate to the public and to funders that it is using its resources efficiently and effectively and is committed to long-term growth and financial stability. To maximize the ability to raise funds, organizations need to provide donors with many points of entry and show ongoing appreciation to their supporters, even those who make only modest contributions.

Figure 3.11 The Changing Environment of Resource Development

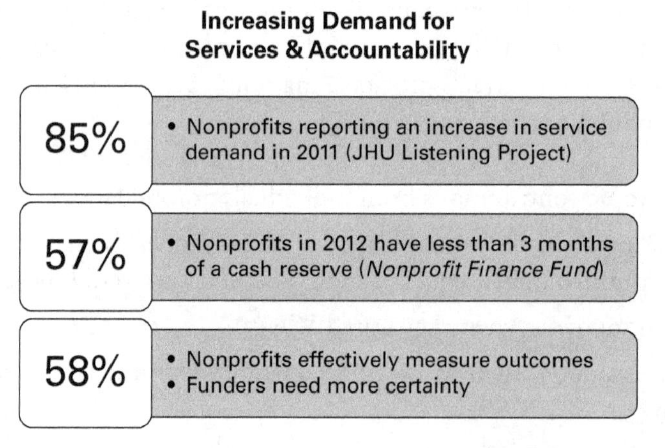

Fig. 3.11: *Based on information from the Johns Hopkins University Listening Project and the Nonprofit Finance Fund, http://www.nonprofitfinancefund.org.*

Table 3.2 illustrates the relative effectiveness of different resource development strategies.

Table 3.2 Comparison of Resource Development Approaches

Approach	Effort/Time Involved	Cost	Productivity/Results
Annual Giving	High	Variable	High
Capital Program (larger gifts)	High	Low (5–10%)	High
Deferred Giving	Low (but complex)	Minimal	High
Events	High	Variable (+/- 50%)	Variable
Grant Solicitation	High	High	Variable
Collections	Low staff involvement but high time commitment	Low	Low
Direct Mail (or online)	High	High	Variable
Merchandise Sales	Medium	Variable	Very Low
Advertising	Medium (but complex)	High	Low

Summary and Conclusion

This chapter summarized the major features of human service organizations and the theories that explain and guide their behavior and determine their essential functions and tasks. The next chapter focuses on a particular important issue in an increasingly diverse society: How the culture of an organization shapes practice and the various relationships that exist within it.

END-OF-CHAPTER EXERCISE
RESOURCE DEVELOPMENT

Use the following exercise to assess your agency's resource development strategy.

Introduction

Think about the resource situation of the agency in which you are working as a staff member, volunteer, or intern. Indicate on the chart below your assessment of the agency's current situation, using assigned course readings and lectures.

NCSO

On a scale of 1–10, rate your agency in each of the following categories:

1. Agency Mission and/or Ideology

1 2 3 4 5 6 7 8 9 10

Points ________

Think about the following issues:

- Is the agency a response to a social movement or broader change effort? N
- Does the organization serve a clearly identified oppressed group or groups? N
- Does the organization have a unique approach to the issues it addresses? N
- Does the organization have a radical or nonmainstream ideology? N

Start with 10 points and subtract 2.5 points for each affirmative answer. If only three questions are clearly relevant, subtract 3.3 points for each affirmative answer.

2. Agency Self-Definition

1 2 3 4 5 6 7 8 9 10

Alternative Model (collective) — Traditional Model (hierarchical)

Points ________

3. Locus of agency's resource development strategy and decision-making processes

1 2 3 4 5 6 7 8 9 10

Points ________

Some Guidelines:

Group decision making	1 point
Committee decision making	3 points
Majority of staff makes decisions	5 points
Board of directors makes decisions	7 points
Executive director makes decisions	10 points

4. Cleared defined division of labor regarding resource development work

1 2 3 4 5 6 7 8 9 10

Points ________

Three dimensions to consider:

Distinct responsibilities exist (each person has a different title)—3.3 points

Each position also has different duties—add 3.3 points

No overlap in duties exists—add 3.3 points

5. There are clearly defined rules about resource development

1	2	3	4	5	6	7	8	9	(10)

Points ________

Some Guidelines:

Little or no rules:	1 point
A few rules:	3 points
Some rules:	5 points
Largely rule-driven:	7 points
Totally rule-driven:	10 points

6. Stability of Funding (10 = Most Stable)

1	2	3	4	5	6	7	8	9	(10)

Points ________

From most stable (traditional) to least stable (alternative), typical funding sources include:

Government grants or contracts

Grants from major foundations

Fees for services (from clients or insurance companies)

Grants from small foundations

Membership fees/contributions

Major donor contributions

Fund-raising events

7. Extent to which resource development strategies have changed in recent years

(1)	2	3	4	5	6	7	8	9	10
No Change		Some Change			Considerable Change			A great deal	

Points ________

TOTAL POINTS 55

END-OF-CHAPTER EXERCISE
CONDUCTING AN ORGANIZATIONAL AUDIT

(Adapted from Lewis, J., Lewis, M., Packard, T., & Souflee, F. (2001). *Management of human service programs.* Belmont, CA: Brooks/Cole.)

(Note: Students may complete this exercise in pieces throughout the semester, matching the various categories to the content of the book's chapters.)

Indicate the degree to which each factor is present in your organization. Use a rating of "4" if all aspects are fully present with positive effect; use a "1" when the factor is absent or not at all effective; use a "2" or "3" to reflect relative amounts of the factor being present/effective or problematic.

Use the Following Scale in Answering the Questions Below:

1 = To little or no degree

2 = To some degree

3 = To a great degree

4 = To a very great degree

Part 1. Planning

To what degree:

1. __2__ Does the organization have and use a strategic plan?
2. __4__ Does the organization have a clearly defined mission that is well known, well understood, and well accepted by staff members?
3. __3__ Are the strategies, goals, and objectives of the organization based on the mission?
4. __4__ Are the goals and objectives complete and clear?
5. __2__ Do the objectives reflect measurable client benefits and other outcomes?
6. __3__ Are the plans of the organization used on a regular basis?

Management of the Environment

To what degree:

7. __2__ Can you identify the problems or needs the organization intends to address?
8. __4__ Can you define the target population (e.g., demographics, geographic boundaries) the organization intends to serve?
9. __2__ Are key stakeholders (funders, other agencies, regulators) satisfied with agency programs and services?

Client Relations

To what degree:

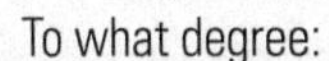

10. 4 Can you define what consumers of the service perceive their needs to be?
11. 4 Is the relationship between the organization and its clients clearly defined and communicated to both?
12. 2 Are clients satisfied with the services as delivered by the organization?

Program Design/Technology

To what degree:

13. 2 Is each service appropriate to meet identified client or community needs?
14. 3 Are service delivery technologies appropriate to achievement of the mission, strategies, and objectives?
15. 2 Does the agency base its service delivery methods on the most powerful proven models and theories?
16. 2 Is each service effective in accomplishing its stated goals and objectives?
17. 1 Are there clear program standards that describe the quality and efficiency of services expected for clients?
18. 1 Does the organization specify objectives and outcomes for each client?

Structure and Design

To what degree:

19. 2 Are all staff members' roles and performance expectations clear and agreed to?
20. 1 Are the organization's structure and reporting relationships clear to all?
21. 2 Does the organization have clear, written policies and procedures consistent with its mission and goals and that drive expected behavior?
22. 2 Is the agency's structure clearly aligned with strategy?
23. 1 Is the agency's structure flexible and minimally bureaucratic?
24. 1 Does the organization's structure facilitate cross-function collaboration, teamwork, and support?
25. 2 Does the organization have communication mechanisms or processes to keep staff members informed about current and anticipated activities or developments?

Management Information Systems

To what degree:

26. 4 Does the agency have a computerized client data collection and processing system for its demographic, services, and outcome data?

27. __1__ Does the organization have a way of identifying and aggregating client outcome data (effectiveness)?
28. __3__ Does the organization have clearly defined units of service that can be used to measure the types and amounts of services provided (efficiency)?
29. __1__ Are there clear performance standards for which aggregated client data are used in ongoing service monitoring and feedback?
30. __2__ Are data produced by the organization's management information system (MIS) considered in rewarding staff members and in making program changes?
31. __1__ Can the MIS measure productivity, cost-benefit, and cost-effectiveness?

Budget and Financial Management

To what degree:

32. __4__ Can you calculate program costs from budget data?
33. __1__ Can you calculate the cost per successful client outcome from budget data?
34. _____ Do financial reports provide managers with effective, accurate, and timely information?
35. _____ Do expenditures consistently match program budgets and actual income?
36. _____ Has an external audit been conducted within the last year, have results been shared, and have problems been corrected?
37. _____ Are administration and program budgets clearly aligned with strategies and objectives?

Staffing and Human Resources Management

To what degree:

38. _____ Is the organization staffed with people fully qualified to perform their duties?
39. _____ Is the organization staffed with people carefully oriented and supervised?
40. _____ Are there appropriate and adequate staff development opportunities for staff members?
41. _____ Does the organization recruit and select staff members whose professional ideology and training are compatible with the mission and style of the agency?
42. _____ Does the organization respect the professionalism of the staffers?
43. _____ Does the agency have a formal performance appraisal system that is appropriate and regularly used?

Program Evaluation

To what degree:

56. _____ Does the organization evaluate the outcomes of specific program activities?
57. _____ Does the organization evaluate program efficiency?
58. _____ Are less formal methods of evaluation used (for example, collection and review of staff impressions, client complaints and suggestions)?

59. _____ Does the organization compare the effect of its programs to the initial need?

60. _____ Does the organization follow up with consumers to collect data that indicate the long-term effects of its services?

61. _____ Does the organization use the results of program evaluation to make changes?

62. _____ Are all relevant accreditation, licensing, or regulatory standards currently met?

Personal Assessment

After completing the audit, based on what you have learned, answer the following questions:

1. What do you see as the agency's major assets or strengths?
2. What do you see as the areas in need of change or improvement?
3. What barriers to organizational effectiveness exist?

In a memorandum, propose a concrete plan for action that builds on the agency's strengths and addresses the agency's challenges.

CHAPTER 4

Creating a Diverse Organizational Culture

What is the point of hiring smart people if you don't empower them to fix what's broken?

—Ed Catmull, *Creativity, Inc.*

Diversity doesn't mean Black and White only.

—Henry Louis Gates

As our society becomes increasingly demographically and culturally diverse, the ability of community-based organizations to respond effectively to this diversity has become more critical. Practitioners at all levels who work with a variety of populations and problems need to be aware of the dynamic relationship between their organization's culture and the composition of its staff members, clients, and constituents. This chapter addresses these issues through coverage of the following topics:

1. Definitions of organizational culture—its tangible and intangible components, its formal and informal features, its multiple layers, and its distinction from **organizational climate**.
2. Ways in which organizational culture perpetuates itself, including explicit and implicit forms of discrimination, and the risks involved in maintaining the status quo.
3. A critique of traditional approaches to addressing the issue of diversity within organizations.
4. Models of organizational practice in multicultural settings.
5. Different styles of communication and their implications for practice in **multicultural organizations** and communities.
6. Suggested ways to overcome privilege and its consequences in organizational settings and to create a more socially just and empowering organizational culture.
7. Alternative patterns of decision making, including methods of involving clients, constituents, and staff members in the decision-making process in meaningful ways.
8. Skills for assessing, developing, and enhancing critical consciousness, self-monitoring, and praxis in oneself and throughout the organization.

What is Organizational Culture?

Every organization, no matter how large or small, regardless of its vision, mission, or goals, has an identifiable **organizational culture**. As in a community or society, this culture serves a crucial if often unstated purpose: to sustain and reinforce the organization's mission, values, and structure, and how the organization attempts to achieve its established goals. The following features of every organization reflect its organizational culture:

1. Official statements of its vision, mission, goals, and objectives
2. Methods of program development, implementation, and evaluation
3. Decision-making structures, processes, and roles

4. Formal and informal, internal and external patterns of communication
5. Methods of resource development and management
6. Personnel practices
7. External relations (including its use of social capital)

As the preceding list reflects, an organization's culture contains tangible and intangible components. Tangible components include written documents, such as the bylaws that govern how the organization makes critical decisions, its mission statement, annual reports, strategic plans, personnel policies, and materials on its website. These are largely available—if rarely read—to staff members, board members, volunteers, clients, constituents, and the public. Intangible components include the organization's preferred style of communication, the ways in which staff members interact, and its approach to diversity and inclusiveness.

The organization's formal and informal systems reflect these components in different ways. Formal systems include the organization's board of directors, program structure (e.g., through departments or committees), patterns of supervision and decision making, and methods of staff recruitment, training, and evaluation. They usually appear in written form—in bylaws, program proposals, training manuals, and meeting minutes—and, therefore, are easier to identify and analyze.

Informal systems are harder to detect and decipher. They reflect an organization's "unofficial" history, personal relationships, unspoken norms and rules, and hidden agendas. Individuals who have little power in an organization's formal structure may have considerable power and influence in its informal systems because of their expertise, experience, or personality. Key decisions might be made through informal, "behind the scenes" processes that cannot be found in any formal documents and may be unseen by strangers or newcomers to its culture. Staff members with little formal role may be informal "gatekeepers" to those who possess formal authority and power. Those who possess "institutional memory" may be more adept at negotiating complex formal systems than newcomers who appear to possess a higher position within the organization. Because an organization's culture has multiple layers that are often invisible, it takes time, patience, considerable insight, and guidance to become familiar with its nature and potential consequences.

Racial and gender diversity complicate this process. Women and minorities of color may be less familiar with the unwritten and unspoken "rules" of the dominant organizational culture. In addition, they have to cope with implicit bias and microaggressions that undermine their ability to assimilate into the established organizational culture. New staff members, therefore, benefit from having a mentor or guide who can "show them the ropes" and enable them to avoid pitfalls or traps that can ensnare those who are ignorant of unstated cultural rules. In many organizations, however, the challenge of finding a suitable mentor is particularly difficult for women and minorities of color because of a paucity of senior staff members to whom they can relate, and among those who maintain the culture a resistance to "let them in" and educate them about its subtle components.

According to Schein (1981), there are three layers of organizational culture. The "top" layer consists of "artifacts and creations" that are visible to everyone, but whose meaning and significance is often more difficult to interpret. These include the ways in which the organization uses technology, the appearance of the organization's physical space and public documents, and the manner and content of its communications. For example, do employees have private offices or do they work in an "open floor" plan? What types of logos or slogans appear in the organization's official documents? Does the organization communicate primarily through digital means or does it use a variety of methods?

The organization's values make up the second or middle layer of its culture. Although these are stated clearly in the organization's vision and mission statements—and translated in its annual reports, strategic plans, and funding proposals into specific goals—there may be a considerable discrepancy between an organization's rhetoric (which is often primarily for public consumption) and its actual behaviors. For example, an organization might trumpet the values of democratic participation and empowerment, but make most of its key decisions in a hierarchical, top-down manner. It may give the appearance of an inclusive environment, but ignore the opinions of staff members from different cultures and maintain a "glass ceiling" that blocks women and racial and ethnic minorities from positions of leadership. It is, therefore, possible to assess the congruence of an organization's values to its day-to-day activities only through careful observation of its internal and external environment and through honest communication with colleagues.

The deepest layer of an organization's culture consists of its basic assumptions; staff members often take these assumptions for granted. They are unstated and largely invisible. These include how the organization conceives of time and defines "work," its views of human nature and change, the language it employs and the specific meaning it gives to frequently used concepts and terms, and its attitudes on human relationships. How the organization relates to the multiple dimensions of its environment is the clearest example of this layer of culture (Schein, 1981).

In sum, an organization's culture is reflected in virtually every aspect of its environment, including its style of leadership and management, its staffing patterns, the ways in which communications occur and decisions are made, staff morale and staff commitment to the organization's mission, and even the physical arrangement of its space.

There is a significant difference, however, between an organization's culture and its climate. Think of the difference between an individual's personality and that individual's present mood. While they are related in many ways, they are fundamentally different in their origins and effect.

Organizational culture is a component of the social system, whereas **organizational climate** is a property of the individuals within that system. The attitudes, experiences, and values of an entire organization all reflect the organizational culture. It includes shared beliefs, values and assumptions, behavioral norms, rituals, stories, symbols, and language (including jargon). Each organization has a unique culture that constantly evolves.

An organization's climate reflects its employees' perceptions of their work environment at a specific moment in its life cycle. In particular, the psychological climate of an organization, often referred to as morale, is an indicator of how the overall atmosphere of the workplace affects employees' well-being. Unlike an organization's culture that is deeply rooted, complex, and dynamic, an organization's climate is a snapshot of the "mood" of the organization at a particular moment. We can assess an organization's climate with relative ease, but we can understand its culture only after considerable time and effort.

There are several ways to determine the relationship between an organization's culture and climate. One method involves analyzing the written documents of the organization—annual reports, grant applications, websites, and marketing materials. Another is to speak with staff members in different parts of the organization and probe their opinions about the attributes just listed. A third method is to observe the physical and interpersonal environment over time to get the "feel" of the place. Finally, one can assess how the organization translates its stated vision, mission, and values across its overall culture.

Remember, these reflect:

1. Mission: Why the organization exists and what it seeks to accomplish.
2. Vision: Desired future state(s).
3. Values: Principles by which the organization operates.

Here is an example of how an organization's culture reflects its stated purpose:

CASE ILLUSTRATION
AN ORGANIZATION'S MISSION, VISION, AND VALUES

Domestic Violence Solutions for River County [not its real name] works to end the intergenerational cycle of domestic violence by providing prevention and intervention services and by challenging society's attitudes, beliefs, and behaviors to effect social change.

Vision

1. In River County, all people will take personal responsibility in promoting zero tolerance for domestic violence within their interpersonal relationships, families, and in the community at large.
2. Community beliefs and attitudes that support domestic violence will be changed and all people will see themselves as part of the solution.
3. Domestic violence will be replaced by respect and equality for one another.

4. Dignity and hope will be restored to all those affected by domestic violence so that they are empowered to maximize the potential of their lives.

Values

1. We affirm that we live in a society with an unequal distribution of resources, power, privileges, rewards, and justice. Therefore, we hold these truths to be self-evident:
2. Domestic violence is not solely a woman's issue nor is it solely a man's issue; however, the vast majority of victims of domestic violence are women.
3. Domestic violence is about power and control.
4. Domestic violence is not a relationship problem.
5. A person using power and control over another is entirely responsible for his or her behavior and the outcome.
6. Domestic violence affects all people in our society—not only the victim and the perpetrator.
7. Domestic violence is child abuse; it is a learned behavior; it affects the whole family; and is cyclical and intergenerational.
8. Domestic violence feeds on silence.
   a. Therefore, it is our conviction that:
9. Domestic violence is preventable.
10. With effective intervention, we can replace violent and abusive behavior and attitudes with healthy behavior and attitudes that are based on equality.
11. Both men and women must work to end domestic violence.
12. Societal norms must change if we are to end domestic violence.

How would you determine whether the culture of this organization reflected its mission, vision, and values? How would you assess the extent to which paid and volunteer staff members were highly committed to the organization's mission? How would you determine in what ways individual staff members contribute to the advancement of the organization's mission?

For Reflection and Classroom Discussion

1. What are some examples of an organization's culture that you have experienced?
2. In your experience, how does race/ethnicity/gender/sexual orientation complicate an organization's culture?

Culture and Social Change

Culture structures people's commitment to change or continuity in groups and organizations. It consists of both material (physical) and nonmaterial (symbolic, value-laden) products, such as knowledge, beliefs, values, customs, **morals**, and symbols. Culture is most apparent when its assumptions are questioned or its rules are violated, or when more than one culture vies for dominance in a particular setting. This is one reason why the struggle over multiculturalism has important implications for practice.

The primary elements of culture are beliefs, values, norms, roles, expressive symbols, and collectivities or institutions. Beliefs reflect how people think the universe and its component parts operate. A unified collection of beliefs is an ideology or worldview. From a sociological perspective, values define a system of preferences regarding desirable goals and outcomes. From an ethical perspective, values indicate what we consider as good and right in our actions and those of others (Lewis, 1981). *(See Chapter 8 for further discussion of ethics and values.)*

Norms can be formal (expressed through laws or policies) or informal (expressed through customs, mores, and traditions). They provide guidance as to what is proper or necessary behavior within particular roles or settings. They define what is acceptable and what is deviant. Roles define the boundaries between and within social structures. Expressive symbols are representations of beliefs, values, and norms. Examples include language, other forms of communication, and rituals. Collectivities or institutions are structures that perform defined and important functions.

The following elements make up what Griswold (2008) referred to as the "cultural diamond":

1. **Cultural objects:** symbols, beliefs, values, and practices.
2. **Cultural creators:** individuals, organizations, and systems that produce and distribute (and enforce) cultural objects.
3. **Cultural receivers:** the people who experience culture and specific cultural objects.
4. **Cultural context (environment):** the social world in which people create and experience a culture—a social construction.

Culture performs several discrete functions in a social system. Through motivational and enforcement mechanisms, it is a primary means of socialization that shapes personality development, consciousness, identity formation, and identity maintenance. It stratifies relationships between individuals, groups, and communities, and between people and institutions. Often this stratification reflects racial, class, gender and other forms of discrimination. It constructs knowledge and ways of knowing—what is a "fact" and how it can be used (e.g., the role of "evidence" in shaping practice). It helps maintain traditions and power relationships. It shapes concepts of continuity, conflict, and change. All of these functions exist within the cultures of communities and organizations.

Different theoretical perspectives exist on the relationship between culture and social change. Structural functionalists see a close fit between culture and social change or continuity. They regard deviance from cultural norms as dysfunctional for the maintenance of social order and well-being.

In Mills' (1963) view, culture is durable and action-oriented. The features of culture—patterns of communication, values, norms, rules, and customs—constitute the glue that holds society together. They confer legitimization and collective recognition through our behaviors, language, and foundational precepts about work, social relationships, and the nature of change itself. Although the formation of culture, in general, may be an innate and inevitable aspect of all societies and human groups, the specific components of a particular culture are a conscious social construction. In this manner, ideas, values, laws, religious and secular ideologies are determined—to different extents and in different ways—by a society's material conditions and the social relationships they produce. Culture, therefore, in Marx's words, forms the "superstructure" of society. Finally, for symbolic interactionists (Geertz, 2000) culture is an historically transmitted pattern of meanings, a coherent system of inherited concepts through which people communicate, perpetuate, and develop their knowledge about and attitudes toward life.

Despite their differences, there is some consistency in these theories in terms of their implications for macro social work practice. Because it serves as a form of collective recognition and legitimization, culture is the glue that holds social groups, such as communities and organizations, together. At the same time, because the environment is dynamic, not static, culture is constantly changing in response. Culture is also important to understand because it designates the expressive side of human existence.

Functions of Cultural Values and Value Patterns

Cultural values include shared ideas about what people consider important or unimportant, fair or unfair, and ethical or unethical behavior. They define our identity, individually and collectively, and are implicitly understood and celebrated via day-to-day, often mundane communication rituals. They help guide our behavior and that of others, through explicit and implicit rewards and punishments. They also intentionally and unintentionally encourage in-group inclusion and intergroup separation.

Four Key Cultural Value Dimensions

According to Ting-Toomey and Chung (2012), there are four key dimensions of cultural values, which they term *identity*, *power distance*, *uncertainty avoidance*, and *femininity-masculinity*. If we applied their model to organizations, the first dimension would assess whether a particular organizational culture emphasized individual or collective (group or community) responsibility in its leadership style, decision-making processes, accountability mechanisms, and reward structures. The second dimension examines the extent to which the day-to-day interactions within the organization reflect an equal or unequal distribution of power. For example, who determines the priorities of the organization? How are decisions about its reward structure made? Who receives the most "perks"?

The third dimension (uncertainty avoidance) refers to the extent to which the organizational culture encourages risk-taking activities—for example, in its advocacy efforts, innovation in program development, and methods of dealing with conflict inside and outside the organization. Some organizations provide incentives for such activities; others prefer to follow long-standing approaches to program design and external relationships, and engage in conflict-avoidance behaviors. Finally, although Ting-Toomey and Chung's fourth dimension (femininity-masculinity) reflects in its terminology somewhat outmoded binary gender distinctions, in an organizational context it assesses whether the organization promotes fluid and overlapping or complementary and distinct gender roles in its patterns of leadership and decision making, distribution of organizational functions, and program design.

Leadership/Management Styles

One of the key reflections of an organization's culture is its style of leadership and management. Think about the organizations in which you have worked or are currently working. Is leadership a core value of the organization? What are the qualities of the organization's leaders? How does the organization make decisions and solve short- and long-term problems? Is the process collaborative or individual? How do managers and supervisors treat staff members on a daily basis? Figure 4.1 depicts the varieties of management styles and their relationship to organizational culture.

Figure 4.1 A Matrix of Management Styles

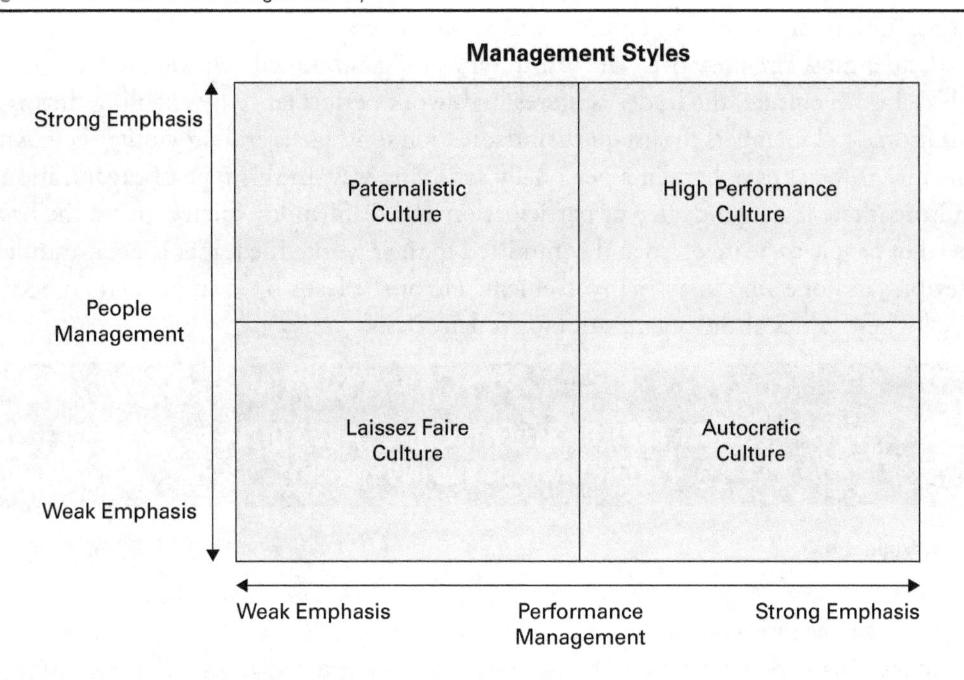

Blake and Mouton (1964) described four types of organizational culture that emerge from different management styles. In one type, which they called an *impoverished* culture, the leader (or manager) exerts (and expects) minimal effort and has little concern for either staff satisfaction or work targets. This person goes through the motions of the job. She or he is indifferent, noncommittal, resigned, apathetic, and is doing just enough to keep their job. This type of manager may appear in the phase of the organizational life cycle in which the organization is in decline. His or her behavior may also exacerbate the conditions that produced the decline.

In the second type of culture, the *country club*, the leader is attentive to his or her staff's needs and has developed satisfying relationships and work culture—but at the expense of achieving effective outcomes for clients or constituents. People inside the organization view the leader as someone who is agreeable, eager to help, nonconfrontational, comforting, and uncontroversial. While staff members may rue the organization's "drift," they may not speak up about it because their jobs are secure and the work environment is "cushy."

At the opposite end of the spectrum is the leader who creates an *authoritarian* culture. She or he is controlling, demanding, and overpowering. This type of leader concentrates almost exclusively on achieving results at the expense of interpersonal relationships and employees' job satisfaction. This leader views the organization's staff members merely as commodities to be used to get the job done and, often, to promote his or her self-image.

In this type of organization, administrators deemphasize communication and use suppression to resolve conflicts, even constructive conflicts.

Under most circumstances, the fourth type of organizational culture, the *team*, is the ideal. In this culture, the leader achieves high work performance by enabling the organization's staff members to sustain their dedication to its goals and providing them with the means to achieve them in a personally satisfying way. In this type of organizational culture, there is a high degree of participation and teamwork, which satisfies the basic need of people to be involved and committed to their work. The leader is open-minded, flexible, and one who inspires involvement. He or she leads by example and embodies the highest values of the organization on a daily basis.

IN-CLASS EXERCISE
WHAT TYPE OF STAFF MEMBER ARE YOU?—A PERSONAL STYLE INVENTORY

Introduction

Each line below lists two contrasting traits. Your task is to spread seven points between the two statements on each line to reflect the balance of how each describes you. You may distribute the points in any manner you wish, but both sides together must total seven points. Give high points to the description that describes you well; give the other side low points. For example, people who see themselves as quick in the way they handle things might fill out the first line in this manner:

__5__ Likes a fast pace OR __2__ Likes a slower, more deliberate pace

	A			B
4	Likes a fast pace	OR	3	Likes a slower, more deliberate pace
3	Energetic involvement in things	OR	4	Relaxed involvement in things
3	Emphasis is on action	OR	4	Emphasis is on planning and thinking
2	Likes to influence people	OR	5	Prefers to "live and let live"
3	Likes competitive activities	OR	4	Prefers casual, cooperative activities
4	Takes control of problems		3	Tries to let things work out
2	Tends to be impatient		5	Shows a good deal of patience
6	Expresses opinions openly	OR	1	Holds opinions to self
27	**TOTAL FOR COLUMN A**		29	**TOTAL FOR COLUMN B**
	1			**2**

	Column 1			Column 2
2	Moderate enjoyment of social events	OR	5	High enjoyment of social events
2	Most concerned about facts	OR	5	Most concerned about feelings
3	Controls emotions	OR	4	Expresses emotions
3	Likes to take independent actions	OR	4	Prefers to be part of team activities
3	Rational decision maker	OR	4	Intuitive decision maker
2	Conversations focus on tasks	OR	5	Conversations have a people focus
1	High concern for accomplishment	OR	6	High concern for emotional satisfaction
4	High expectations of self and others	OR	3	Easy-going with self and others
20	**TOTAL FOR COLUMN 1**		36	**TOTAL FOR COLUMN 2**

*B - 2

The Four Basic Styles

Your "Style" is shown below with the letter and number combination, which is your highest score between Section A or B, plus the highest score between Section 1 or 2.

A and 1—CONTROLLER (control specialist): achievement-oriented. Exerts strong influence in getting things done. Assertive in expression of ideas. Prefers being in charge. Has strong opinions. Bottom-line orientated.

Common strengths: determined, requiring, thorough, decisive, efficient, gets results, direct, takes charge

Potential excesses: dominating, unsympathetic, demanding, critical, superior, loner, harsh, impatient, combative

A and 2—ENTHUSIAST (social specialist): Expresses opinions and emotions easily. Is active and moves at a lively pace. Prefers strong interaction with people. Usually has many interests. Tends to be image conscious.

Common strengths: personable, stimulating, enthusiastic, dramatic, inspiring, innovative, expresses easily

Potential excesses: opinionated, excitable, undependable, phony, flighty, reactionary, exaggerates, show-off

B and 1—ANALYZER (technical specialist): Likes things to be well organized and thought out. Prefers to work on specific projects and activities systematically. Enjoys putting structure to ideas. Thorough and careful about details.

Common strengths: industrious, persistent, serious, vigilant, orderly, rational, methodical, factual, thorough

Potential excesses: indecisive, picky, cold, withdrawn, data-bound, uncommunicative, critical, unsympathetic

B and 2—AFFILIATOR (adaptive specialist): High concern for good relationships. Likes being part of cordial and friendly groups. Seeks stability and predictability. Stays out of the limelight. Wants to be part of a larger picture.

Common strengths: cooperative, supportive, friendly, willing, dependable, personable, sincere, helpful

Potential excesses: conforming, retiring, uncommitted, overly sensitive, dependent, sarcastic, hides true feelings

Organizational Structure and Organizational Culture

Another important facet of an organization that reflects its culture is the organization's structure. As discussed in Chapter 3, this refers to how an organization makes decisions, allocates roles, and coordinates work tasks (Jackson & Morgan, 1982). Look (again) at the different types of organizational models in the figure that follows. What does the organizational chart in your organization look like? Is your organization hierarchical or flat? What does its structure reveal about the organization's culture?

Figure 4.2 Models of Organizational Structure

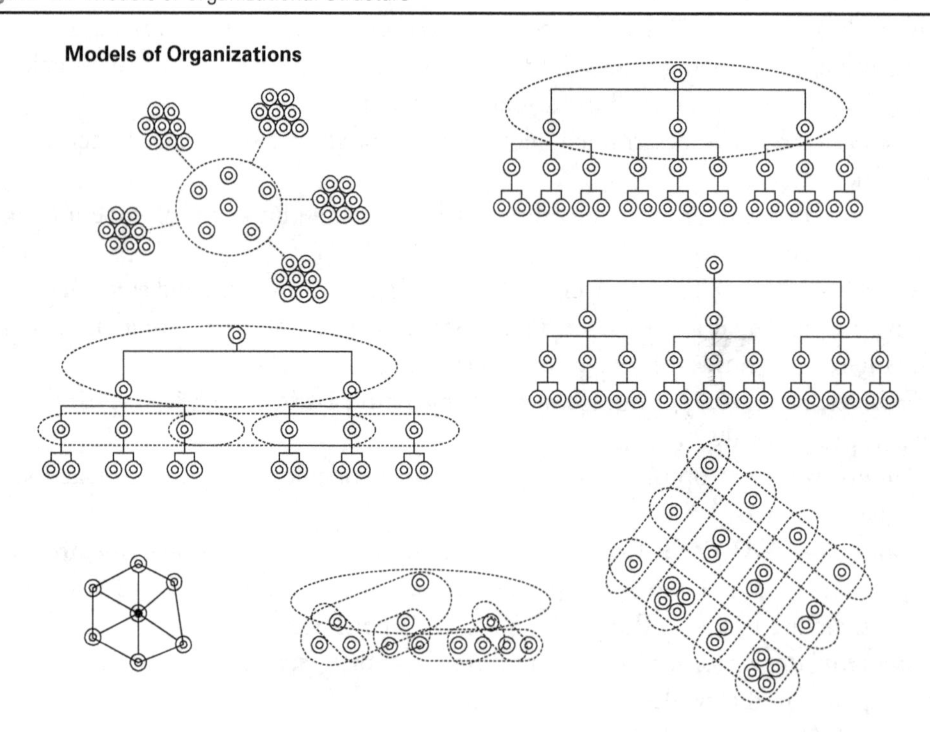

The Interpersonal Components of Organizational Culture

Hasenfeld's (1972) depiction of HSOs as "people processing organizations" underscores the role that interpersonal relationships play in creating and sustaining an organization's culture. A number of organizational features affect the quality of these relationships, which, in turn, influence the character of the organization's work environment and the effectiveness of its programs and services.

For example, the physical environment of an organization reflects its underlying values and has an immediate and lasting effect on both staff members and clients. Weissman, Epstein, and Savage (1983) argued that the most important person on an organization's staff is the receptionist, because in many ways this person sets the "tone" of the entire agency and influences clients' initial impression. The quality of staff performance and morale, and the ways in which staff members interact are different if people work in offices, cubicles, or open work spaces.

Think about an organization in which you work or have worked. Is the organization's physical space in good condition? Do offices have windows, adequate light, and sufficient privacy? Is the equipment up-to-date and in good working order? Are offices conveniently situated near clean restrooms, meeting rooms, elevators, or staircases? Does the organization make reasonable accommodations for staff members with disabilities? Are there common areas that encourage informal staff interaction and communication, such as a reception room, a kitchen, or a lunchroom? Does the physical structure of the organization facilitate or impede interpersonal interactions among staff members?

Another critical dimension of organizational culture, particularly in today's changing demographic environment, is whether the organization's staff and leadership reflect the diversity of backgrounds, experiences, and beliefs of the community it serves. The composition of the organization's staff not only affects its ability to serve its clients and constituents effectively, it also shapes the interpersonal dynamics of the organization itself. Patterns of staff interaction reflect the extent to which an organization has become sufficiently diverse.

In this regard, the organizational culture can have a major effect. Is the environment highly structured, intense, and impersonal, or is it collegial, relaxed, and more informal? Is staff input encouraged in agency decision making? The answers to these questions influence both organizational effectiveness and efficiency. Organizations that neither diversify their staff nor value the ideas of diverse staff members—particularly the ideas of racial minorities and women—often experience resistance to change and high staff turnover. (*See Chapter 15.*)

Although people work in HSOs for a variety of reasons—economic necessity, value congruence, personal satisfaction—they generally appreciate symbolic rewards as much as decent salaries and benefits. Some organizations recognize the importance of these intangible benefits through the distribution of job titles. Other organizations place little stock in how they label staff members' functions. In assessing an organization's culture, it is useful, therefore, to consider: Are staff titles important and meaningful? For example, are there many vice presidents or program directors? Do employees perceive their own roles and those of their colleagues differently depending on their job title? Does this perception affect their performance? What is the overall relationship of the formal and informal reward structures of the organization?

In addition to the distribution of titles, organizations express their cultural values—much as families, communities, and societies—through their traditions and celebrations. Some organizations formally acknowledge (through newsletters or parties) the personal successes (marriages, births, awards) of staff members; they recognize the longevity and loyalty of their employees, and major milestones such as retirements. They institutionalize social rituals—e.g., annual picnics—to strengthen interpersonal bonds and increase staff members' allegiance to the organization. Organizations that treat employees more as family and respect the diverse contributions they make to the organization's goals are less likely to experience high staff turnover and employee "burnout."

One thing that all new employees notice immediately is the work pace of an organization. (The author has worked in organizations where staff members waltzed in at various times in the morning, always took a lunch hour, and invariably left before 5 p.m. In other places, no matter how early the author arrived at the office or how late he stayed, there was always someone else who was working.) In some organizations, everyone seems to be working fast, almost frantically, all the time, while others have a more moderate pace. This could be the result of external pressures on the organization (an atmosphere of perpetual crisis, a growing number of clients, insufficient staffing, budget cuts, poor leadership), or it could be a product of a culture that stresses productivity over all other things. While there is no correlation between the pace of work in an organization and its effectiveness, it affects employees' morale and their ability to achieve a satisfactory work/life balance (Delecta, 2011). It is particularly important to be aware of the effect of this feature of organizational life on individuals who come from cultures with different approaches to work or, as many staff members, have caregiving responsibilities.

Another way in which organizations create and sustain their cultures is through the development of an internal language. While the use of agency-specific terminology can sometimes make communication more efficient, the excessive use of jargon can also serve as a means to separate those who are "in" from others who are unfamiliar with key terms. Awareness of this possibility is particularly important for organizations that are striving to integrate new staff members, particularly those from other cultures, who may not initially understand the organization's idiom. It is also a critical factor in communicating with clients from diverse backgrounds and with the public. The use of language that, intentionally or not, excludes others from the conversation can turn off the people with whom we work and those whose views we are trying to influence.

Differences in Communication

Cultural differences in communication appear in a variety of ways, not all of which are obvious to the casual observer of interpersonal action within an organization. These include (Thomas, 1991):

Conventions for Courtesy. An important difference—which exists even among different regions of the United States—is how people express anger or disagreement. In some places, people are "up front" about their feelings and regard those who withhold them as dishonest. Other cultures interpret passionate disagreement, however respectful, as anger, and regard genuine expressions of anger as a form of bullying. Because of these different cultural norms and expectations, it is important to ask the right questions, listen carefully to what people say and how and when they say it, attempt to understand the underlying cultural values behind communication, and offer colleagues or clients options for expressing their opinions.

Phasing and Sequencing of Ideas. People from some cultures prefer to communicate their ideas in a "logical," "orderly," and linear manner; they build their arguments step-by-step starting with a premise, adding evidence, and reaching a conclusion. In other cultures, it is important to contextualize the conversation—both historically and also in terms of how the topic relates to other issues. People from these cultures present their ideas through a series of "loops" and "spirals" that emphasize the interconnectedness of different parts. Those who argue in a linear fashion may feel that this style is "illogical" and that it introduces tangential issues into the discussion. Conversely, those who speak in this manner may find that a linear style is cold and fails to acknowledge the effect of a variety of factors on the subject at hand. A related issue is phasing—i.e., when it is appropriate to discuss certain topics. In the dominant Western culture, people in work situations prefer to "get down to business" right away. In many other cultures, however, it is rude not to start a conversation by asking about people's family and health.

Objectivity and Specificity. Some cultures value precision and specificity in argumentation; they focus on the substance of the matter at hand. Other cultures, however, emphasize style as much as substance; they prefer ambiguity and state ideas more generally, particularly when discussing sensitive subjects. People from the former culture may interpret the latter style as dishonest, cowardly, or passive-aggressive, when it may reflect a more nuanced approach to the issue, a desire not to give offense, or a preference to maintain group equanimity. Another difference occurs between cultures whose style of argument is impersonal ("just the facts, ma'am"), in contrast with those cultures that recognize the important role played by emotions.

Assertiveness and Candor. In some cultures, people demonstrate interest in another person or that person's ideas by inquisitiveness and assertiveness; in other cultures, silence reflects respect for others' privacy. Cultures also define what constitutes candor differently. Some cultures favor a style that seeks the "truth" (the "whole truth and nothing but the truth") at all costs. Other cultures contextualize the importance of truth and balance truth telling with courtesy and the need to maintain social harmony. The key here is to recognize both forms of behavior as honest; they express real meaning in different ways. One way to overcome this gap in communication styles is to summarize the conversation by stating a specific action that both parties agree to take.

Humor. Although humor can be an effective tool to defuse tension in a conflict-ridden situation—such as in a tense staff meeting, forging a personal bond or "breaking the ice" in social relationships—it is very difficult to translate across cultural lines. A remark that is considered funny or witty in one culture may, at best, fall flat among individuals from another culture or, at worst, be offensive. Above all, one should always avoid jokes of an ethnic or sexual nature or anything that reinforces cultural stereotypes. This is not merely good practice; it is a legal requirement. Title IX of the Civil Rights Act includes inappropriate humor as one means of creating a hostile work environment. In sum, if you are unsure whether something might be offensive, do not say or do it.

Use of Digital or Social Media. This relatively recent issue involves a different type of cultural distinction, one that might cross generational rather than racial or ethnic boundaries. On the one hand, it reflects the difference between personal, face-to-face contact and more distant, virtual, and impersonal contact. The widespread use of digital media has also created the challenge of how to use or interpret gestures and vocal expressions during interpersonal interactions, and how to express or read others' feelings accurately in digital formats. The key here is to use all media strategically and not assume that all media have the same effect or that all people are equally familiar with a particular set of media conventions or "language." As discussed in Chapter 8, it is also critical not to assume that any message sent through digital or social media is confidential.

One way in which communication styles reflect cultural differences is in the physical distance people place between each other when communicating. In Western culture, this follows four distinct patterns. In *intimate distance*, when people are in emotionally close situations, they are 0–18 inches apart. Both parties anticipate physical contact; the other person is visually blurred and vocalization plays a minor role in the communication process. Each person can smell the odor and feel the body heat of the other person. Speech often occurs in whispers. If such situations arise unexpectedly in non-intimate relationships, one of the parties can interpret such behavior as a sign of hostility. Think of the expression "getting in someone's face."

In *personal distance*, 1.5 feet to four feet apart, touch is also possible but there is no longer a visual distortion of the other person's physical or facial features. The other person is kept at arm's length, just within the realm of physical contact. This phase is the limit of physical domination. In these situations, one has to be particularly careful of how the other party might interpret a touch. What one person may consider a supportive, friendly gesture (a pat on the shoulder, a squeeze of the hand or arm), another person may view as aggression or sexual harassment.

In *social distance*, four to 12 feet, the parties have no physical contact, voice levels are normal, and intimate facial details are less visible. This is the distance in which personal business occurs; informal communication is more likely to take place at a closer distance within this range than the formal communication involved in business and social discourse.

In *public distance,* people are well outside the circle of involvement. In the close phase (12–25 feet), people are on guard, evasive, and somewhat defensive in protecting "their space." Speech patterns tend to be formal and people speak in louder voices. The far phase (25-plus feet) is generally used in public presentations, which tend to be more theatrical. Facial expressions and movement, particularly the use of one's hands, are amplified and gestures are an important part of the communication process (Luckman, 1981). Cultural differences influence people's behavior and their reaction to the behavior of others in each pattern of communication.

Awareness of these cultural differences in communication is important for several reasons. First, members of the dominant culture may falsely assume that the rules that govern their speech and communication patterns apply equally to everyone. Second, the nature of organizational life may compel people to communicate in spaces that are not commensurate with their behavioral norms (e.g., cubbyholes, small meeting rooms, and conversations by the coffee pot). Third, because many types of interaction in organizations occurs spontaneously, we often do not have sufficient time to prepare ourselves properly for the cultural rules that may arise.

As the staff members and clients of HSOs become more diverse, there is also the danger that efforts to be sensitive to cultural differences will create an environment that diminishes the quality of organizational performance. The fear of offending people of different cultures through criticism, in supervision or evaluations, for example, is the opposite of judging people harshly if their behavior does not conform to dominant cultural patterns. Yet, "walking on eggs" can lead to the lack of meaningful performance evaluations and attenuated supervisor-supervisee relationships. This, in turn, can produce further employee dysfunction and withdrawal. The key here is to use specific behavioral examples when engaged in constructive criticism and to encourage a dialogue about how to improve performance.

The Perpetuation of Organizational Culture

As in any community or society, an organization's culture is a self-perpetuating phenomenon. Through the maintenance of their cultural norms and values, agencies define and select "desirable" staff members and clients and remove "troublemakers." In an extreme version, to perpetuate its organizational culture, an organization does not keep clients or staff members equally informed; it also treats clients and workers unequally. To use Marx's term, the organization's culture serves as the "superstructure" that rationalizes and maintains the organization's political and economic foundation, goals and objectives, leadership patterns, and decision-making processes.

According to Sathe (1984), an organization perpetuates itself through seven distinct, yet interrelated, processes:

1. Preselection and hiring of new members: This includes the qualities it deems desirable in a new staff member, the wording of a job announcement, and how it advertises a staff opening.
2. Socialization into the organization: Does the organization treat certain staff members differently in the orientation phase of the hiring process due to their race, ethnicity, or gender? Does the organization assign mentors to all new employees through a careful selection process?
3. Removal of "deviants": What does the organization consider "deviant" behavior? How flexible is the organization in respecting new ideas or different work styles?
4. Establishment of patterns of behavior (rituals that define what is "normal"): To what extent does the organization explain its subtle rituals, norms, and unspoken expectations to new staff members, particularly those from different cultural backgrounds?
5. Development of official rationales (justifications) and rewards for desired behavior: Does the organization distribute rewards fairly and make clear the criteria for their distribution? Does the organization have a flexible or rigid definition of desired behavior?
6. Reinforcement of cultural norms and behavior through official and unofficial communication, formal rituals, rewards, and punishments: Does the organization communicate these norms clearly, using a variety of forms of communication?
7. Use of **intimidation rituals** that sustain the existing culture (Kotter, Schlesinger, & Sathe, 1986, p. 385).

The last item is particularly relevant to the challenge of cultural and gender diversity because such rituals often reflect implicit bias. Intimidation rituals can be either direct or indirect. The former includes:

1. Defamation—an attack on an individual's character or motives.
2. Distortion of events or behaviors, which often include fabrication of instances of misconduct, including spreading of rumors through the organization's informal system.
3. Questioning the competence or mental health of someone who challenges long-standing practices in the organization.
4. Efforts to destroy the reputation of a staff member to compel her or him to retreat into silence or resign.
5. Subjective performance evaluations that lay the groundwork for future expulsion.

6. Expulsion, either for "cause" or, as in many "at will" organizations, on the basis of an arbitrary reason for dismissal.
7. Transfer to another branch, department, or program, to separate the "trouble-maker" from any potential following.

These intimidation rituals purposefully serve as a warning to others who challenge the basic tenets of the organization's culture and prevent further opposition to the status quo from emerging. Because of the potential damage to an organization's reputation if there are appearances that it fires "reformers," those who implement intimidation rituals prefer to have such individuals leave the organization voluntarily.

In most organizations, however, intimidation rituals are indirect and sometimes hard to detect. The most common form of an indirect intimidation ritual is "nullification." In such circumstances, a supervisor will assure the "reformer" or potential **whistle-blower** that his or her accusations or suggestions are invalid or the result of a misperception, lack of information, or misunderstanding. A variation on this phenomenon is to indicate that the individual's suggestions are "duly noted" and will be "investigated," and that the individual should allow the "usual channels" to handle the problem. The goal here is stop the questioning of an organizational practice before it gathers momentum or attracts widespread attention and support.

Another frequent example of indirect intimidation is isolation—the separation of organizational "rebels" from their peers and potential allies. This can take numerous forms including physical transfer to a less visible position or location, restrictions on communication or "movement," reduction or elimination of critical resources, and failure to respond to future criticisms and suggestions. The purpose of isolation is to reduce the effect of internal protests on the organization and make it difficult to mobilize support for reform efforts.

Under such circumstances, a staff member has only three viable alternatives to protect her or himself. One is reference to the NASW *Code of Ethics* (2015), particularly the sections that address obligations to clients and colleagues. A second option is to rely on the stated policies and procedures of the organization itself. A third is to utilize legal rules and regulations regarding employment practices in the relevant jurisdiction. It may also be possible to use internal strategies of organizational change such as "functional non-capitulation" (Reisch, Wenocur, & Sherman, 1981–1982). (*See also Chapter 15.*)

Power and Organizational Culture

Our culture often uses the phrase "office politics," but we do not always understand its relationship to power within organizations very well. Power operates everywhere and affects all aspects of practice in an organization. Each person's **positionality** and **standpoint** influence their relationship to power and reflect their personal or group identity in the context of the organization's culture. At its worst, power within organizations can involve the self-serving and manipulative behavior of individuals and groups to promote their self-interests at the expense of others, and sometimes even of the organization's goals.

As energy in physics, power in organizations can be both active and latent. Active power involves the connection between a need and a means to address it. This produces a relationship characterized by influence and dependence and is often associated with the use of force, influence, control, and—at worst— domination. The degree of power an individual or group possesses within an organization can be determined by measuring these two factors. Do employees depend on their supervisor's approval for a raise or promotion? How much discretion do employees have in determining the nature of their work?

The possession or absence of a variety of tangible and intangible resources also influences the power of an organization as a whole or the power of individuals within an organization. Tangible resources include money; staffers and volunteers with appropriate skills; space and time; relevant technology; the presence of strong, competent leaders; and adequate external support, including organizational allies. Intangible resources include a clearly articulated vision, the presence of solidarity among staff members regarding the organization's values and goals reflected in issue consensus, effective decision-making processes and patterns of communication, the ability to mobilize people, and an inclusive organizational culture that creates a sense of belonging and a fair distribution of rewards (Cameron & Quinn, 2005). Factors of race, gender, ethnicity, sexual orientation, class, and religion shape both the distribution and application of these resources. Different types of power can facilitate action for change or block such actions from occurring.

Hasenfeld (2010) lists a number of sources of personal power within organizations. These include formal sources of power such as the authority given to certain positions that grant certain individuals control over resources, organizational goals, work processes, and people's careers; organizational policies that determine the distribution of responsibility and roles; and external policies and laws. They also include informal, occasionally less visible sources of power, such as knowledge and expertise, personal style, or membership in a particular group or clique. Finally, all organizational cultures have certain norms, traditions, and customs that have the power to coerce and compel staff members to conform to certain behavioral patterns through intense social pressure. These range from informal dress codes to how staff members address one another, and from the obligation to attend all staff meetings to whether staff members keep their doors open or not.

Organizational politics, therefore, can reflect many things—a struggle for resources between departments or programs; personal conflicts (over program goals or based on long-standing animus); and competition for power and leadership. In organizations, people use politics—in the broadest sense—to acquire power, build one's personal stature, control access to information, conceal one's real intentions and ambitions, or build coalitions to effect organizational change. Attempts to interpret the power dynamics within an organization, therefore, must be recurrent and should analyze the ways in which the organization's structure, culture, decision-making processes, and interpersonal relationships reflect and shape the organization's politics. This analysis can lead to regular negotiation of boundaries within the organization, create opportunities to work for change, and prevent future contests over power.

A variety of factors hinder workers' personal power and empowerment within their employing organization and the power of the organization to effect change in the community. Staff members' power is affected by administrative and personal standards and expectations; the type of supervisory relationships that exist; the organization's decision-making processes; the context of work tasks, including the nature of the agency's clients; the organization's reward structure; and the community's attitudes toward social work itself. The next section focuses on the meaning of empowerment in an organizational context. It also examines how to create empowering organizational cultures.

REFLECTION EXERCISE

1. Who has power in your organization? Who has formal power? Informal power?
2. How do people use or express this power?
3. What organizational politics have you encountered?

Empowerment in Macro Social Work Practice

For four decades, empowerment has been a major theme in the social work practice literature, although the precise meaning is often ambiguous and suggestions as to how to apply empowerment concepts to practice have varied widely. The following are some examples of these differences. Barbara Bryant Solomon was the first social worker to use the concept of empowerment in her scholarship. She defined it as a way "to manage emotions, skills, knowledge, and/or material resources in a way that effective performance of valued social roles will lead to personal gratification" (Carr, 2003). In her history of empowerment practice, Simon (1990) defined empowerment as "a reflexive activity, a process capable of being initiated and sustained only by the agent or subject who seeks power or self-determination" (Simon, quoted in Finch, Lurie, & Wrase, 1997). Gutierrez (1995) refers to empowerment as "the process of increasing personal, interpersonal, or political power so that individuals, families and communities can take action to improve their situations" (p. 230). In sum, empowerment enables individuals, groups, and the community to consciously take control of the environmental conditions that affect their lives.

Despite these different emphases, each definition expresses certain common themes. First, empowerment occurs on both personal and collective levels and involves a synthesis of political-economic and psychosocial factors. It involves the development of a more positive and potent sense of self and a more critical comprehension of one's environment. The ultimate goal of empowerment is to inspire action by individuals and groups.

Second, empowerment can only occur through respectful dialogue and recognition of the mutuality that exists between workers and clients. This includes the cultivation of functional competence to attain personal and collective goals. It is a process of mutual reinforcement facilitated by respectful dialogue. Third, social workers can neither give people power nor determine who needs to be empowered.

There is some disagreement and several unresolved issues, however, on the practice implications of empowerment. For example, what are the limitations of empowerment in achieving social change goals? What is the relationship between different forms of power and empowerment, and between empowerment and privilege? What is the connection between client or community empowerment and the pursuit of social justice? What if an "empowered" community sought to create a change that violated some conception of social justice?

In this book, "empowerment" is defined as a concept that incorporates three primary dimensions:

1. The development of a more positive and potent sense of self, individually and collectively.
2. The construction of a more critical comprehension of the web of social and political relations that comprise one's experienced environment.
3. The cultivation of resources and strategies, or functional competence, which are required for the efficacious attainment of personal and collective sociopolitical goals.

Empowerment, therefore, is both a state of being and a process of becoming. Individuals, groups, and communities are empowered as they become able to participate in the dynamic social relations that surround them with a personal sense of potency, critical political awareness, and practical strategic skills. In sum, empowerment is the process of developing "participatory competence" and, in Freire's (1971) words, becoming subjects rather than objects in the world.

In organizational and community change efforts, the ability of participants to be empowered often depends on a combination of factors. These include:

- their personal interest or investment in the change effort;

- the extent to which they believe in the possibility of a successful outcome;
- the development, recognition, and effective application of individual and group resources;
- the opportunity to take action and make contributions to a broader cause;
- recognition of common interests and common risk taking; and
- the availability of mentorship and "role modeling" that encourages people to become involved in a change effort.

Classroom Discussion

1. How do you define "empowerment?"
2. What are the implications of this definition for your practice?

As stated in Chapter 2, Rivera (1995) asserts that social workers have rarely examined the phenomenon of citizen empowerment as an issue of human development and learning. He argued that while considerable scholarship exists on citizen participation, community organizing, and the experience of powerlessness and alienation, it often focuses on people's problems, deficiencies, disadvantages, and constraints. The deficit models so prevalent in psychological research are frequently implied—in models of social change. These models—have failed to provide insights into the successful cultivation of abilities, understandings, and awareness that characterize "participatory competence."

In this sense, the concepts of empowerment and disempowerment refer to the relationships among conscious and unconscious experiences, identifiable skills, and people's perceptions of their social and political relationships. As Freire (1971) noted, "powerless" individuals (or groups) are viewed as "objects" in the world—as individuals who are acted upon by dominant and frequently oppressive forces—rather than as "subjects" who are active in and acting upon the environment. Powerlessness or disempowerment, therefore, implies alienation from positive participation in the construction of social reality. Because dominant social and structural relations reinforce this passivity and cultural mystification—in sophisticated and often subtle ways—the powerlessness of individuals, groups, and communities reflects their submersion in and loss of the sense of control over those complex, interwoven relationships.

Similarly, the definition of empowerment derived from Freire emphasizes the role of "critical consciousness" in its development. According to Freire (1971), critical consciousness is a process through which "… people develop their power to perceive critically the way they exist in the world with which and in which they find themselves" (p. 100). The convergence of this notion with theories of personal "competence" is important for social workers engaged in macro practice to comprehend.

In sum, the purpose of empowerment is to enable those who possess little power, or who are in a power-dependent position, to engage in activities that will correct this imbalance (Perlman, 1976). There are three components, therefore, of the empowerment process: behavior (action); perception or awareness, specifically consciousness-raising;

and the linkage of thoughts, emotions, and actions through an iterative reflective process referred to as praxis.

In this regard, consciousness-raising does not refer to sensitivity sessions that solely address private matters. Rather, based on Freire's (1971) concept of **conscientization**, it refers to the process by which people become aware of themselves as social actors. From this perspective, the environment is not a fixed reality to which people must accede or adjust. It is a problem people can address and solve through critical thinking and individual or collective action (Jani & Reisch, 2011). This transaction occurs through political participation in the broadest meaning of politics (Reisch & Jani, 2012). Thus, people initiate the process of empowering themselves by demythologizing their social reality and acting upon their new view of themselves and their environment. The critical element in this process is reflection upon the current context, and development of new ways to "read" or interpret it.

If successful, this process—which occurs between clients/constituents and social workers, between staff members, and, above all, within and between clients/constituents themselves—not only generates greater ability to interpret problems and to assert one's "stamp" on the world, it also helps break down barriers of distrust and engenders greater intragroup and intergroup cooperation. An essential part of this process is removing the artificial and socially constructed obstacles that exist between social workers and the people with whom we work. This requires a different view of the professional role that may produce considerable anxiety among some social workers (Rivera & Erlich, 1997).

An important behavioral component of empowerment is learning how to manage conflict rather than resolve it permanently or ignore it entirely. (*See Chapter 15 for further discussion of this issue.*) When applied this way, empowerment can become a means to link organizational, community, and policy change. This connection is particularly important in today's environment in which societal conditions often marginalize both social workers and clients, and multiple forms of conflict occur on a daily basis.

Social workers can help forge people's connection between awareness and action through several interrelated processes that were developed outside of the United States: **conscientization**, created by Brazilian educator and activist Paulo Freire; **praxis** (created by the so-called Frankfort school in Europe); and ***animation***, originally developed in France and Francophone Quebec (Quirion, 1972). Conscientization emphasizes the transformation of one's role through dialogue and a shift in one's self-perception from object to subject. Praxis refers to the ongoing integration of action and reflection. *Animation* stresses both the existential and political aspects of individual and community agency. It is based on the recognition that people can best control their destiny through participation in social groups that work in a self-directed manner to achieve goals the group itself established (Reisch, Wenocur, & Sherman, 1981–1982).

These concepts have significant implications for contemporary practice. In today's environment, social workers, particularly those engaged in macro social work practice with diverse populations, must develop both a new conceptualization of their relationship with the people with whom we work based upon the establishment of trust in the motivation of others, and also the willingness to use nontraditional forms of cooperative action to effect social change. The persistent micro-macro dichotomy within social work practice reflects false assumptions on the nature of individual and institutional change, and the misguided belief that social workers' ability to control and define their community and organizational environments is separate from similar efforts by clients and constituents (Rothman & Mizrahi, 2014).

There is growing recognition, however, particularly among younger social workers and their allies in various social movements, that changing the focus of our practice must begin with changes in our self-perception vis-à-vis our environments and the development of similar revised perceptions about the colleagues and constituents with whom we work. This recognition emerges from pressures within our work environments that are analogous but not identical to the pressures experienced by the people who rely on the services we provide and the policies for which we advocate. In effect, the causes and consequences of what has long been labeled worker "burnout" is not that different from the battering our clients experience daily. Framing these problems solely as staff "burnout," or focusing primarily on the symptoms of structural problems that affect clients and constituents, transforms what are essentially political issues—requiring political solutions—into personal ones that lead to a focus on "self-care" and "resiliency" rather than resistance (Lewis, 1980; Reisch & Jani, 2012).

Creating an Empowering Organizational Culture

The structure and decision-making processes within an organization reflect its conceptions of power and empowerment. Through the social climate they produce, they determine the extent to which staff members and clients feel empowered. As discussed in Chapter 3, there are four basic patterns within organizations. Hierarchical organizations, such as large bureaucracies, tend to have authoritarian cultures in which formal power resides almost exclusively at the top. At the opposite end of the spectrum are *laissez-faire* organizations in which power is diffused and leadership plays little role. (*See Chapter 2.*) In between these poles are democratic organizations in which power is exercised to some extent through participatory decision making, guided by facilitative leadership and consensus-oriented organizations that diffuse power—at least formally—to all members. Figure 4.3 illustrates this continuum.

Figure 4.3 Organizational Governance Structures & Empowerment

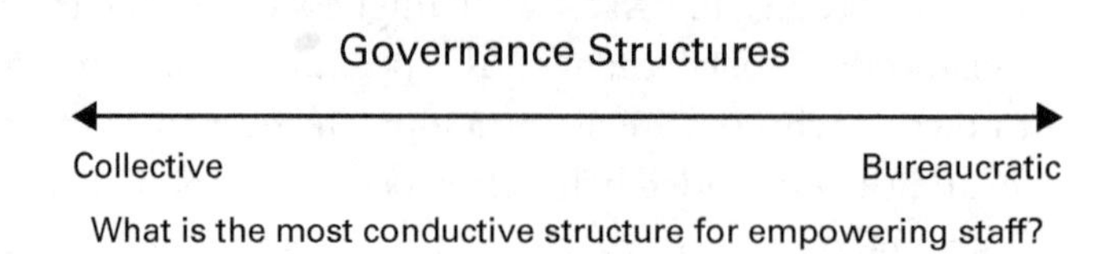

Despite their differences, most descriptions of the empowerment process in organizations agree that it involves developing positive group identification (to the community or organization) and more critical comprehension of one's context, ceasing self-blame, developing self and collective efficacy, and using praxis (Garvin & Ortega, 2016). As in our work with clients, creating an empowering organization requires staff members to develop a personal interest or investment in the organization's goals. It also requires a belief in the possibility of successful outcomes and recognition of one's personal resources and those of the organization as a whole. In addition, an empowering organization creates a sufficient range of viable choices for staff members and clients, and develops opportunities for staffers to contribute to the organization as a whole. In such organizations, the staff becomes aware of its common interests and the potential risks involved in change, and makes use of mentorship and "role modeling" to encourage others to take collective action (Reisch & Garvin, 2016; Cohen & Austin, 1997).

In an organizational context, empowerment occurs on three levels. Between workers and clients or constituents, it requires sharing information, promoting skill development, mutual participation in problem definition, and the planning and evaluation of interventions. This gives clients or constituents more control and investment in the helping process.

Organizations can facilitate the empowerment of the groups or communities with which they work either through the efforts of individual staff members or through the organization as a whole. Examples include promoting greater ownership of the change process by community residents; actively involving them in a problem-posing approach to community issues; using community members to collect and analyze data needed in the assessment process; and giving the community a substantive rather than a symbolic or nominal role in making recommendations for change. If used effectively, community empowerment can be a powerful approach that encourages HSOs to view community members as full partners, participants, stakeholders, collaborators, and **consumers** in the process of community change.

Lastly, empowerment can occur within HSOs themselves in ways that enhance overall organizational effectiveness and improve the working conditions and productivity of staff members. According to Cohen and Austin (1997), empowering staff members requires that workers be involved in organizational improvement efforts in an ongoing and meaningful way and not merely through token roles, such as nonvoting membership on the board of directors. This can only occur if the organization integrates such participation into the organization's structure and decision-making processes. The organization's leaders must give this participation formal sanction and employees' job descriptions must reflect this role.

Organizations can take several concrete steps to empower their staff members. One way is to enhance the quality of the physical environment of the workplace by paying attention to its appearance, giving staff members a role in aesthetic choices, however limited they may be, and making sure that employees have facilitated access to the resources they need to do their jobs and maintain their physical comfort. Another tangible effort that organizations can make is in personnel benefits. While many public and nonprofit HSOs are often strapped for funds, they can still demonstrate a commitment to their workers by the expansion of non-salary benefits such as work-life policies—e.g., time off for caregiving and volunteer work—staff development programs, sabbatical leaves, and the provision of increased educational and promotion opportunities (Delecta, 2011).

Organizations can also empower their staff members in other nonmaterial but equally significant ways. They can provide workers with increased autonomy and responsibility in determining how to do their jobs. This requires active encouragement and support from supervisors, administrative superiors, and even peers. It is advisable for organizations to avoid micromanaging employees and to develop diverse, qualitative ways of evaluating employees' performance.

Finally, organizations can promote greater internal collaboration among staffers by sanctioning decentralized authority in program development, providing grants or other rewards to encourage innovation, creating a "research mentality" that requires greater employee participation, and promoting work support groups.

Creating Effective Multicultural Human Service Organizations

Responding to the demographic and cultural changes in the United States is no longer merely desirable, it is essential to the development of responsive and effective services. A few statistics underscore why the creation of multicultural HSOs is both an ethical and practical imperative. In 2000, the U.S. workforce was more than three-quarters (76%) White. By 2020, people of color will constitute one third of the workforce, and by 2050, they will represent a majority. Already, 85% of new workers are women and people of color; nearly one quarter are immigrants (Mor-Barak, 2005; U.S. Department of Labor, 2016). Yet discrimination in the workplace continues to exist. "Women and members of ethnic minority groups commonly find themselves excluded from networks of information and opportunity [and] are more likely to occupy the lowest-ranking positions" (Mor-Barak, 2005, pp. 341–342). Recent statistics reveal that workplace discrimination based on religion, age, and sexual orientation persists (Equal Employment Opportunity Commission [EEOC], 2016).

An organization's staff composition signifies the effects of discrimination. These effects also appear in how staff members and clients are treated, and what services the agency offers. Agencies that do not respond to the multicultural imperative tend to select "desirable" clients who may be more compliant with the organization's cultural norms. As research by the author and other scholars on welfare reform revealed, they may also fail to keep clients adequately informed about changing eligibility requirements or application procedures (Reisch & Sommerfeld, 2003; Soss, Fording, & Schram, 2011). Agencies may treat clients from racial, ethnic, or sexual minority backgrounds unequally and exclude them from some programs. Administrators may remove from the organization clients and staff members whom they considered "troublemakers." These consequences occur despite the guidelines in the NASW *Code of Ethics* (2017) and the presence of anti-discriminatory rules and regulations at the federal level and in many states.

Racism, sexism, homophobia, and other "isms" in human service organizations are neither accidental nor conspiratorial phenomena, but they frequently serve multiple, interconnected purposes and are manifest in various ways, from institutional inequities to micro aggressions. Often, despite the best intentions of organizational leaders and staff members, these forms of "invidious discrimination" (Wilson, 1976) pervade many features of the organization's culture, often in subtle and unnoticed ways. Above all, their persistence in organizational cultures has multiple consequences for practice. It fosters divisions between people and within groups. It encourages acceptance of the status quo. It prevents us from developing alternative ways of envisioning the world. Above all, it diminishes an organization's ability to respond effectively to increasingly diverse environmental conditions.

In an organizational context, racism and sexism—and all forms of discrimination, for that matter—occur through explicit acts, such as institutional discrimination and individual prejudice, and in unstated assumptions about people's problems, intentions, and abilities, sometimes referred to as **implicit bias**. An organization's staff composition, program design, decision-making and reward structures, communication style, and external relations inevitably reflect these tendencies. Although they have lasting effects on historically marginalized and excluded populations, they also serve to maintain traditional patterns of power and privilege.

Ironically, these "isms" also have a negative effect on their primary beneficiaries—members of the "majority" culture. This majority—largely White, heterosexual men of higher socioeconomic background—generally accepts the world as a "given" and often has difficulty envisioning an alternate reality. For example, one assumption of this dominant cultural perspective is that the distribution of goods, power, roles, and status in a community, organization, or society is a "zero sum game"—that is, any gains for historically marginalized groups must come at the expense of the dominant group. Because of this assumption, the historic "majority" group often feels threatened by social change and views "others" as competition, sometimes even as "enemies." In response to this perceived threat, it shapes the language, customs, invisible "rules," and role expectations of the organization in a manner to sustain the status quo.

Working in this type of environment creates constant challenges for social workers who do not accept its premises, who want to overcome its effects where they exist, and who desire to transform the culture of their organizations. One well-intentioned but flawed approach is to view organizational diversity as a problem administrators must *manage*, rather than a potential asset (Thomas, 1991). Once we acknowledge the existence of this issue, however, it is important neither to dictate solutions nor to think of the "answers" to the "problem" as residing only in oneself. It is far more effective to recognize the mutuality of the situation and the shared and different risks experienced by staff members and clients of diverse characteristics. The goal should be to create an organizational culture in which people from different backgrounds each contribute in his or her own way something valuable to the whole rather than to compel assimilation into a homogeneous or even a hybrid organizational culture.

Creating a multicultural organization, therefore, requires awareness of the visible and invisible rules than exist in the culture—both inside and outside the organization—and how different actors might interpret them. It also requires awareness of the different ways people learn and the importance of developing role models and mentors who understand the background and experience of their new colleagues. Above all, it requires us to separate our assessment of individuals' personal qualities and character (often based on socially constructed preconceptions) and their actions in the organizational context.

Traditional approaches to addressing the challenges of demographic and cultural diversity have largely failed for three reasons. First, as stated previously, they viewed diversity as a "problem" in need of a solution rather than a resource to be employed. Second, from the myth of the American "melting pot" to the promotion of Affirmative Action, they required individuals from minority groups to assimilate—by choice or coercion—into the values, norms, and behaviors of the dominant majority culture rather than recognize the potential contributions that non-majority cultures could make to organizational effectiveness. This is what Gutierrez et al. (1996) referred to as *ethnocentric practice*. Third, even those organizations that were aware of cultural differences (who Gutierrez et al. termed ***ethnic-sensitive organizations***) tended to emphasize individual issues and interpersonal relationships as the key to the successful integration of racial and ethnic minority and female staffers, and ignored the role of organizational culture and systems.

In some instances, organizations go further and become ***ethno-conscious organizations*** that embrace cultural **pluralism** and stress the importance of cultural competence (Lum, 2004). In these organizations, employees with distinct differences work side by side, willing to affirm one another's dignity, benefit from one another's experience, and acknowledge one another's contributions to common goals. Quoting Cross et al.

(1989), Yan and Wong (2005) assert that a culturally competent organization reflects "a set of congruent behaviors, attitudes, and policies that come together in a system, agency, or profession that enables that system, agency, or profession to work effectively in cross-cultural situations" (p. 182). Rather than viewing the creation of such organizations as a fixed target, it is better to view them as a goal to strive for constantly, not to attain for all time. Majority staff members in particular have to disabuse themselves of the idea that they can ever completely understand another culture. Instead, they should adopt the role of a constant learner.

Although it is not possible to achieve complete cultural competence, by adopting a posture of a learner and approaching situations with cultural humility, we can come closer to understanding the context and perspectives of people from other backgrounds. Under some circumstances, to acquire this mind-set it may be useful to draw analogies to one's own life experiences. While there is never true equivalency across lines of cultural difference, recalling what it felt like to be marginalized in a specific situation may give *some* insights into what people who are marginalized in *many* situations experience.

Table 4.1 Four Levels of Diversity Awareness in Organizations

Level 1	Token employment opportunity organization
Level 2	Affirmative Action organization
Level 3	Self-renewing organization
Level 4	Pluralistic organization

Gutierrez, however, suggests there is a further stage beyond a pluralistic, ethno-conscious organization—a *multicultural* organization. These organizations not only embrace differences but also apply a social justice perspective. "Creating multicultural service organizations means changing transitive goals by developing ethno-conscious services for clients but also creating new reflexive goals and organizational ideology" (Gutierrez et al., 1996, p. 206).

Although this seems a formidable task, HSOs can take a number of formal and informal steps to make progress in this direction. One formal step involves redefining the responsibilities of the organization as a whole and the individuals who work within it. It is particularly important to establish clear expectations for staff performance, program objectives, and the organization itself. It is also critical that the organization's energy focus on the collective well-being of its various stakeholders, rather than regarding them as distinct, atomistic entities. This requires the organization to define its "success" in interactive, qualitative terms, and in quantitative outcome measures.

A more informal and challenging process involves paying greater attention to trust issues within the organization. First, organizations have to recognize how a lack of trust—often a response to fear, ignorance, and prejudice—afflicts virtually all organizations, especially those that have not had a great deal of experience addressing issues of diversity or fostering a multicultural environment. It manifests itself in a variety of ways, including negative reactions (formally and informally) to the energy and assertiveness of "newcomers," lack of receptivity to staff members with different communication styles or a different balance of interpersonal and analytical skills, and diverse cultural rules and norms of relationships.

Trust issues emerge initially in the organization's recruitment and retention processes. The creation of a genuine multicultural organization requires its leaders to engage in some difficult, self-effacing behaviors. If the organization's goal is to bring its staff's talent to its fullest potential to advance the organization's mission and vision, it needs to resist the temptation to apply dominant cultural standards in its personnel practices, particularly in its assessment of candidates for staff positions and in the evaluation of their performance once they are hired.

There are several key principles to keep in mind in this regard. First, that skills of equal quality and potential may not appear, at first examination, to be identical. Appreciation of the influence of different personal, educational, and experiential backgrounds—and of different ways of expressing one's skills—can lead to greater fairness in an organization's culture. It can also help previously excluded populations overcome their invisibility in organizations once they join the staff.

The ability of organizations to integrate diverse staff members into the organizational culture requires both modifications of that culture and the identification of mentors who can facilitate the entry of new staff members. This requires organizations to recognize the barriers created by a lack of informal relationships and a sense of belonging. These barriers often mean that historically excluded groups have to work twice as hard (or more) to succeed and receive acknowledgments for their accomplishments. Full inclusion in an organization's culture also requires ongoing coaching and the nurturing of informal relationships, which are often difficult to establish across racial, gender, and cultural lines because of a lack of trust and mutual suspicion or wariness. The latter often leads to a failure even to acknowledge, no less confront, the obstacles that prevent the formation of these relationships. Ideally, new staff members, particularly those from "minority" populations, should have three mentors: their supervisor, someone of the same level as their supervisor but not in the same "decision-making" line, and a peer who has worked in the organization for some time.

Communication is a critical element in the creation and maintenance of effective relationships in all phases of staff development: recruitment, hiring, supervision, training, and evaluation. In creating an effective multicultural environment, organizations need to determine to what extent they are willing and able to adjust or adapt while maintaining individual and collective efficacy. Clarity about organizational rules and performance expectations is particularly important. All staff members should know which rules are inviolable, which standards are inflexible, and which are not.

Supervisors and administrators should be prepared to change at least some of the organization's rules to support its goals of diversity, particularly in recognizing that different cultures value different styles of communication, leadership, and decision making. Especially in the early stages of their relationship, they should ask new supervisees questions about their preferred help-seeking behavior and their attitudes on authority, receiving advice, praise, criticism, and recognition. They should also be careful about acting upon real or perceived assumptions—of themselves and the staff members with whom they work. In this regard, it is also important to note that different outcome expectations do not mean lower standards. The goal is to strive to create the best possible match between the needs of the organization and the people it serves and the unique qualities of the staff.

Administering Multicultural Organizations

The dominant culture has both a direct and indirect effect, and explicit and subtle influences on the administration and management of HSOs. It determines the visible and invisible roles assigned to staff, expectations regarding staff members' potential to grow and learn, and the organization's communication style. To create genuinely multicultural organizations, administrators have to overcome the tendency to equate individuals' demographic characteristics with their behavior, stress the importance of modeling by supervisors, and build trust among staff members with different backgrounds and experience. This takes time, patience, ongoing reflection, flexibility, and self-effacement, which are often in short supply given the pressures many agency administrators face today. Yet, as Gutierrez et al. (1996) point out, "if ethnic-sensitive services do not lead to structural changes in organizations and greater participation of people of color in the governance of the agency, efforts toward change can be mostly symbolic and marginal" (p. 501).

Table 4.2 From a Monocultural to a Multicultural Organization

Differences = Deficits	Differences Tolerated	Differences = Assets
Enforces the status quo through formal and informal practice. Low expectations for disenfranchised groups.	Committed to inclusion and the elimination of discrimination but still retains many features of the dominant culture.	Sees the benefits of a broader cultural perspective in all aspects of its work.

Exclusive-------------Passive--------Symbolic------Attitudinal------Structural------Inclusive

Table 4.2: *L. Gutierrez and B. Nagada; eds. P.R. Raffoul & C.A. McNeece, "The Multicultural Imperative for Human Service Organizations," Future Issues for Social Work Practice, 1996.*

Table 4.2 provides a broad outline of the steps involved in creating a more multicultural organization that has the following features:

1. A work environment that respects and values the contributions of all staff members and taps everyone's potential creativity.
2. The ultimate elimination of culturally inappropriate behaviors, including microaggressions.
3. The recruitment, retention, and promotion of "nontraditional" employees regardless of their race, gender, age, ability status, or sexual orientation.
4. Creating cultural competence among all staff members and, eventually, going beyond cultural competence to achieve cultural humility.

Administrators, managers, and supervisors can implement these broad steps through the following specific actions. They can conduct "cultural audits" to locate the policies and practices in the organization that are discriminatory or dysfunctional. They can use focus groups, confidential surveys, personnel records, and exit interviews to identify areas of needed change. They can review the organization's written and internet materials (e.g., brochures, reports, website) regularly to ensure cultural sensitivity and appropriateness. They can demonstrate in formal and informal ways that the organization's leadership supports and values these goals (i.e., "walk the walk"). They can promote and value teamwork and collaboration across departments. As Table 4.3 demonstrates, this often occurs in three steps.

Table 4.3 Steps in Creating a Multicultural Organization

Step 1: "Talking the talk"	• Organizational leaders embrace diversity. • Leaders are willing to make changes. • Leaders commit necessary resources to initiative.
Step 2: "Thinking the talk"	• Relate diversity to mission, vision, culture, policies, and procedures. • Conduct a "cultural audit." • Prioritize actions for changes. • Include education and training for all staff members.
Step 3: "Walking the talk"	• Changes are made based on cultural audit. • Ongoing dialogue on progress occurs. • Plans for continuous improvement are developed.

Throughout this process, organizational leaders—at all levels—can encourage individual workers to support and facilitate the changes involved. While the contributions of individual staff members largely occur in the attitudinal realm, they can also be manifest in subtle changes in their behavior. Particularly through modeling, supervisory staff can influence employees to respect the opinions and skills of all coworkers regardless of their background; work willingly and cooperatively with people who are different; recognize that everyone is a product of his or her background; and embrace the notion that there is more than way to analyze and resolve issues. Individual staff members can also be involved from the outset in the assessment of the organization's strengths and weaknesses in the area of diversity.

In this regard, it is important to link efforts to promote organizational diversity with the goal of enhancing all aspects of practice in the agency. Research reveals a close relationship between organizational effectiveness and its efforts to be more multicultural. These efforts help develop a closer match between clients or constituents and staff members, and between clients or constituents and the community. In addition, heterogeneous groups are more innovative than homogeneous groups because the presence of multiple perspectives creates more chances for staff members to learn, more ways to appeal to different stakeholders, more innovative programs, and a more productive workforce (Ortega, 2017).

Communication in a Multicultural Organization

To create a genuinely multicultural organization, it is important that all staff members learn how to communicate with and influence people different from themselves in positive ways. This can only occur if they make an effort to get to know colleagues with different backgrounds in ways that go beyond formal contacts, such as meetings, and to include them in informal networks. It is also important to demonstrate real interest in the ideas of people who think differently and to make a conscious effort, without being self-conscious, to refrain from using language that reinforces stereotypes. Sometimes this may involve taking the risk of interrupting others' derogatory comments and correcting colleagues who generalize individual behaviors or attitudes to an entire group. Finally, it is important to learn to respect different communication styles and to avoid the "hot buttons" discussed previously. None of these steps are easy. They involve painful self-assessment and risk taking. Yet, if we are truly committed to "walking the walk" and to making our organizations more responsive to the needs of a changing society, these steps are absolutely necessary.

Gutierrez et al. (1996) summarize the features of a multicultural HSO as follows:

1. The organization is transformative: It focuses on social change and social justice not just the delivery of services to a wide range of clients.
2. The organization's programs and practices emphasize empowerment and praxis.
3. The organization's structure, goals, norms, and values reflect a multicultural ideology.
4. The organization links its programs horizontally to the communities it serves and their organizations and informal networks.
5. The organization actively participates in shaping public policies and public opinion through advocacy and popular education.
6. The organization connects its work to other local, national, and international networks around common themes.

In sum, multicultural organizations seek to combine diversity, innovation, and effectiveness. They aspire to be so-called "creategenic organizations" (Anderson, Potocnik, & Zhou, 2014) that possess the following qualities:

- They encourage staff members to develop and express new ideas and to forge new external contacts;
- They embrace the value of staff heterogeneity;
- They value research and planning in developing programs and strategies;
- They take risks—internally and externally—and experiment with new ideas;
- They decentralize decision making;
- They encourage staff members and volunteers to have fun and are receptive to different work styles;
- They strive to be flexible in their work-related processes and policies and original in their approach to problems; and
- Although they embrace diversity and risk taking, they try to do this in a stable environment and avoid crisis-driven decision making.

Figure 4.4 depicts these features graphically.

Figure 4.4 Features of a Multicultural Organization

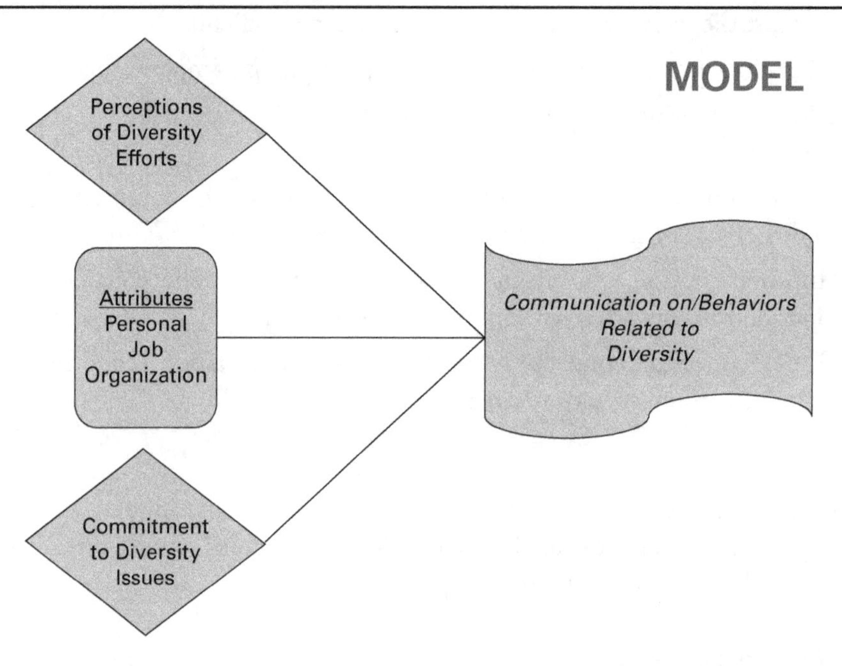

Summary and Conclusion

This chapter focused on the various dimensions of organizational culture. It examined how an organization's culture influences practice and shapes the relationships staff members have with clients and with one another. Chapter 5 looks at how cultural issues affect the critical relationships all HSOs have with key organizational actors in their external environment.

END-OF-CHAPTER EXERCISE
ASSESSING YOUR ORGANIZATION'S CULTURE

1. What values, behaviors, and symbols—both explicit and implicit—are most important in your organization's culture? In what ways does the organization's culture promote or resist acceptance of human diversity?
2. How are racism, sexism, heterosexism, ableism, and other forms of systemic privilege and oppression manifest (e.g., economically, politically, socially) in your organization?

3. How are the manifestations of racism, sexism, heterosexism, ableism, and other forms of systemic privilege and oppression denied, minimized, and justified?
4. What demographic differences do you see among the various stakeholders of your organization (clients, constituents, board members, staff members, and funders)? In what ways are these differences important?
5. Where does your organization fit on the continuum of multicultural practice? Why did you place it there?
6. What challenges in your organization hinder anti-oppression work and progress toward social justice?
7. What assets does your organization possess that can be mobilized to further equity and justice? What steps has your organization taken to oppose and undo systems of privilege and oppression? What steps would you propose?

END-OF-CHAPTER EXERCISE
ASSESSING YOUR CROSS-CULTURAL AWARENESS

Part 1

1. Describe a work situation in which you had or continue to have difficulty with an employee, colleague, or coworker who comes from a different racial/ethnic/cultural background.
2. What are the components of this situation that are particularly troublesome for you (those that create the most emotional or practical difficulties)?
3. Ask yourself:
    a. Is this the type of situation that is difficult for me when it occurs with a person of my own race/ethnicity/culture?
    b. Is there a recurring pattern to these problems? If so, what is it?
    c. How well do my usual means of addressing and resolving similar problems work?
    d. Does the problem have an effect upon my overall job performance?
    e. How does the above situation influence my response to all that involve this person or with individuals from the same racial/ethnic/cultural background?

Part 2

1. List what you believe are the most important personal characteristics of the people with whom you work.

2. For each of these traits, identify the behaviors that you believe provide evidence of the presence or absence of these characteristics. Write the personality trait on the left side of the page and the ways in which an individual demonstrates this trait on the right side.

	Character Traits	Behaviors
Ex:	Honesty	Always tells the truth

1. Look carefully at each of the above traits and their related behaviors and assess how each reflects the values of the culture with which you identify (group discussion).
2. Try to identify other ways in which people from another culture may express characteristics you believe are important in a different way (group discussion).
3. Think about the possibility that other cultures may give higher priority to character traits different from the ones you prefer OR give other interpretations to behaviors that you believe are reflections of particular character traits.
4. What are the implications of these differences on how you work in organizations and communities?
5. As a class, discuss your answers to questions 1–4.

END-OF-CHAPTER EXERCISE
CONDUCTING AN ORGANIZATIONAL DIGNITY AUDIT

[Adapted from Locke, B., Garrison, R., & Winship, J. (1997). *Generalist social work practice.* Belmont, CA: Brooks/Cole. (May be reproduced for classroom instruction.)]

Answer the following questions on the overarching trends in your agency.

I. People seeking services from my agency are more likely to experience:

____ A poorly maintained waiting room	____ A warm and well-furnished waiting room
____ A place to sign in and be told to wait	____ A courteous and personal greeting
____ Having their named called out and being told to "follow me"	____ Being personally met and invited to an office
____ Negative nonverbal cues from staff	____ Positive nonverbal cues from the staff
____ Treating clients as a "case"	____ Treating clients as a person

II. Persons seeking assistance from service providers in my agency are more likely:

____ To be treated as a "problem"	____ To be treated as a "partner"
____ To receive treatment based on the "medical model"	____ To receive treatment based on a "strength/competency model"
	____ To be seen as people with needs and issues
____ To be seen as needing an expert	____ To be seen as an expert on their lives

III. Employees within my agency are more likely to experience:

____ Receiving memos about changes	____ Being asked for input on changes
____ Being on the firing line alone	____ Being supported in their roles
____ Wishing for another job	____ Joy in coming to work
____ Feeling like their consumers are not important to the agency	____ Feeling their consumers are important to the agency
____ Feeling like they are a drain	____ Feeling like they are a resource
____ Feeling unimportant to the agency	____ Feeling important to the agency
____ Lack of respect for other employees	____ Respect for other employees

V. My experience with, and observations of, my agency tells me that:

____ Respect for diversity is ignored	____ Respect for diversity is valued
____ Involvement is blocked to those deemed "different"	____ Involvement is open to all
____ Appropriate social services are at best tolerated	____ Appropriate social services are willingly supported

V. Sources for this audit: ____

CHAPTER 5

The External Environment of Macro Social Work Practice

Human behavior is more influenced by things outside of us than inside. The "situation" is the external environment.

—Philip Zimbardo

A fully integrated culture would be like the dinosaurs, which had to perish because they were no longer able to adapt themselves to changes in the external environment.

—Carroll Quigley

Introduction

In an era of increased fiscal austerity, competition among organizations has become fiercer even as the necessity for inter-organizational cooperation has increased. Drawing upon the literature of organization studies, social change groups, social service agencies, coalitions, inter-organizational collaboration, social networks, social movements, and emerging "hybrid" organizations, this chapter includes a description of the various components of the external environment (the "**environmental set**") of community-based HSOs. It includes the following content:

1. An overview of the complex "environmental set" of organizations and the role that "bridging social capital" plays in organizational success.
2. A discussion of the various types of inter-organizational relationships: their common and differential features and the reasons for their creation.
3. A discussion of inter-organizational collaboration: its key features, the motivations behind collaboration, the problems involved in developing collaborative efforts, and the skills required to develop effective collaborative partnerships, particularly in interdisciplinary or interprofessional settings.
4. The role of coalitions in producing change at the organizational, community, and societal levels; the purposes of coalitions; the steps involved in building effective coalitions, particularly across cultural and social differences; and the skills involved in sustaining coalitions.

The Role of Organizations in Community Building

Organizations help build community in several interrelated ways. Through human capital development, they help reform existing social services by making them stronger and more responsive to people's needs, or by creating new services to fill gaps in service delivery. Through physical and economic capital development, they expand or enhance the economic and physical infrastructure of a community. Through social and political capital development, they help organize and mobilize residents through processes of empowerment and self-determination. Community groups can often link their members to larger bureaucratic organizations and external institutions whose support and resources they require (Austin, 2002).

Assumptions about the Organizational Environment

As with individuals and families, HSOs do not exist in a vacuum. As Figure 5.1 that follows illustrates, the environmental context (or organizational "set") plays a critical role in determining the issues HSOs address and how they attempt to address them. This context consists of broader political-economic forces, such as globalization, the political and ideological climate of the nation and region, the demographic and cultural composition of the population the HSO purports to serve, the history of this population, and the issues it presently confronts.

Figure 5.1 The "Environmental Set" of Organizations

Fig. 5.1: *Elizabeth A. Mulroy, "Theoretical Perspectives on the Social Environment to Guide Management and Community Practice: An Organization-in-Environment Approach," Administration in Social Work, vol. 28, no. 1. Copyright © 2004 by Haworth Press.*

Figure 5.1 illustrates several critical features of the relationship between organizations and their external environments. First, it is impossible for any organization to insulate itself from the effects of outside forces. Their boundaries are porous and subject to the dynamic changes that occur in the wider economy and political and cultural climate. This requires staff members of these organizations to be strategic by engaging in continuous environmental "scanning" in order to understand the effects of the changing context on the organization and the people with whom it works, and to develop effective solutions to the problems generated by these changes.

The chart also suggests that, in response to this strategic assessment, an agency's structure and the resources (tangible and intangible, material and nonmaterial) with which it works are constantly changing. This occurs for three reasons: (1) the aforementioned porous boundaries of the HSO; (2) the organizational life cycle, which is partially a response to environmental influences (*See Chapter 3*); and (3) the need for active collaboration with other organizational entities to survive and thrive in its environment. This means that HSOs must cooperate with other service providers, government agencies, local businesses, community groups, and coalitions to effect change in their environments and to improve the circumstances of their clients and constituents. (*See Chapter 12 for further discussion.*) In sum, to achieve the goal of providing effective and efficient services, organizations must adapt their internal processes to the rapidly changing and often unpredictable environments in which they are situated. Figure 5.2 below illustrates the pattern of these relationships.

Figure 5.2 The Multiple External Relationships of Organizations

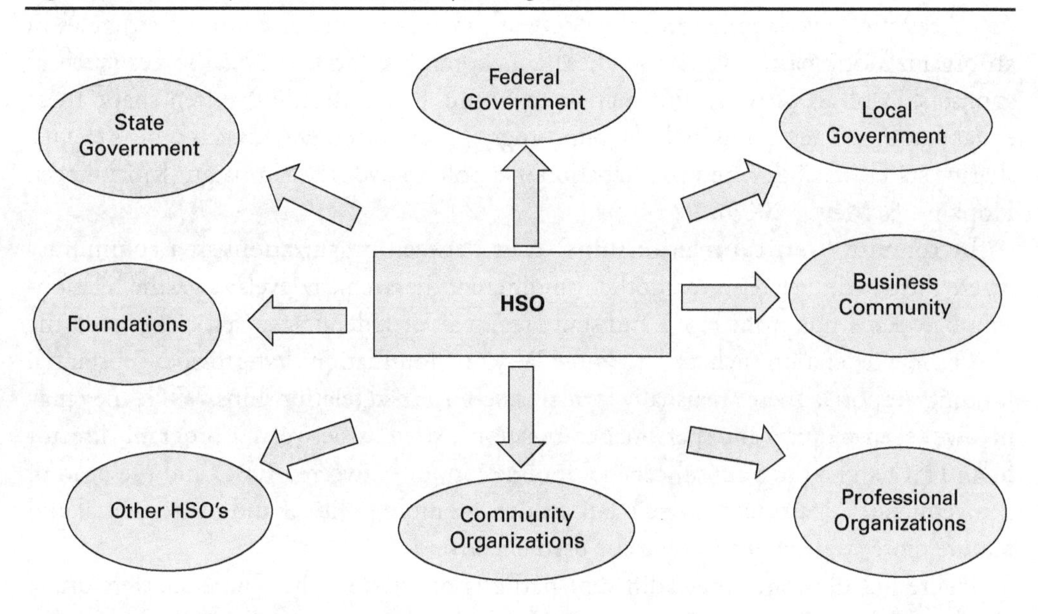

All organizations operate within an environmental set that influences their internal and external activities on a regular basis. The structure, activities, and resources of HSOs are ever changing due to the effects of these external forces. This occurs because as an "open system" the organization has porous boundaries and, consequently, needs to engage in a wide range of collaborative and competitive activities within its environment. These activities vary depending upon the organization's position within its life cycle. (*See Chapter 3.*) Thus, as organizations strive to create effective and efficient services they make decisions based not only on their history, culture, and context, but also on how their internal forces respond to developments in the task environment.

This dynamic relationship with the external environment affects the organization's strategic approach as well. Organizations must engage in continuous assessment of the environment to identify problems as soon as they emerge, analyze their causes, and seek effective solutions. They must also collaborate with a range of community stakeholders and influential actors to effect desired changes (Woodford & Preston, 2011). As discussed below, these collaborative efforts take a variety of forms.

The task environment of an HSO consists of two types of relationships and involves a variety of "players" or stakeholders, including funders, policy makers, clients, constituents, and the public at large. An HSO has **"horizontal relationships"** with groups and organizations in the same community that are on the same hierarchical level. For example, two organizations in a city of similar size that address the needs of low-income children and families would probably have a horizontal relationship.

These relationships have informal linkages and frequently engage in short-term collaborations. Sometimes colleagues with similar backgrounds initiate these relationships. At other times, overlapping group or network memberships, or common struggles in an organization's past, give rise to these collaborative efforts. Political forces (such as sponsorship of an activity) and market/economic forces (funding) often shape these collaborations. They could include joint programs, endorsement of each other's events, sharing staff or facilities, and participation in a policy advocacy campaign (Knickmeyer, Hopkins, & Meyer, 2003).

By contrast, **"vertical relationships"** exist between organizations in a community where the entities relate to each other on different hierarchical levels (e.g., the relationship between a nonprofit HSO and state, regional, or federal agencies, or between the HSO and a federation such as the United Way or a foundation that provides substantial funding support). These are usually formal, rule-governed relationships. While they may involve (even require) interpersonal connections, such as between a program director in an HSO and a program officer in a foundation, or between a CEO and the head of a government department, these relationships are more political and instrumental and require more strategic planning to be used effectively.

Figure 5.2 illustrates these different patterns of relationship. There is, therefore, a clear connection between an organization's internal structure, goals, and environment and its external "set." As the environment of an HSO is constantly changing, its inter-organizational relationships will shift, depending on the relative importance of horizontal and vertical relationships between the agency and institutions in its community at a particular juncture in the organization's development (Mulroy, 2003). These relationships reflect the presence or absence of "bonding" (horizontal) social capital and "bridging" (vertical) social capital within the community and the organizations that operate within it (Dasgupta & Serageldin, 2000).

A wide range of environmental factors can have a significant effect on an organization and the services it provides. These factors fall into five broad categories: physical, sociodemographic, economic, political-cultural, and physical/technological.

Physical changes to a community, such as the construction of a highway through a neighborhood or new residential or commercial development, affect not only its appearance, but can also transform existing social relationships, restrict access to vital services, and alter a community's self-concept. The construction of highways that ran through long-standing neighborhoods in major cities such as Detroit, New York, Philadelphia, and San Francisco are prime examples of this phenomenon, as are so-called "urban renewal" projects. These developments had a particularly deleterious effect on well-established communities of color. They were often the consequence of policy decisions made by majority culture political leaders in response to significant demographic shifts (Massey & Denton, 1993).

Sociodemographic factors include changes in the race, ethnicity, income distribution, religion, age, and educational level of the community's population. These changes produce new needs or new forms of long-standing needs among residents, new types of help-seeking behavior, and new priorities among community groups.

CASE ILLUSTRATION
RESPONDING TO DEMOGRAPHIC CHANGES IN THE NEIGHBORHOOD

Early in his career, the author worked for a multiservice community center in New York City that received much of its funding from the Federation of Jewish Philanthropies. The Federation stipulated that at least 50% of the clients served by the center must be Jewish to receive its financial support. Over several decades, the demographics of the community changed and the organization's original client base moved away. The center faced a crisis: How could it balance the need to preserve its funding with the desire to serve the people who now populated the neighborhood in which it stood?

The executive director came up with a brilliant multipart solution. He purchased several vans that the center employed to transport children and adults from outlying neighborhoods to programs delivered at the center. The center also hired staff members to deliver programs on sites in the neighborhoods where its former clients had relocated. These steps protected the agency's major source of funding—the Federation. At the same time, due to its stabilized funding base, the center could diversify its staff and develop new programs that specifically addressed the needs of the community's new residents.

Economic factors, such as changing rates of poverty and unemployment, or changing patterns of poverty (e.g., more female-headed households or more long-term poverty) and unemployment (e.g., more chronic joblessness among teenagers and young adults) can also influence the problems a community experiences or the expectations community members have regarding the HSO's role. These changes can bring a community's needs into sharp focus, or they can exacerbate existing problems and increase residents' sense of frustration and hopelessness. These changes have significant implications on how HSOs respond. For example, over the past several decades the effects of deindustrialization compelled many HSOs to put greater emphasis on job training and economic development, and to respond to the immediate, concrete needs of community residents such as food, energy, and childcare.

The external environment can also change along political-cultural lines, sometimes in response to changes in a community's demographics or economic situation. A community may resist the construction of new services for a stigmatized population, such as a shelter for people experiencing homelessness, a substance abuse treatment program, or a job-training center for recently incarcerated individuals. This NIMBY ("Not in My Backyard") phenomenon reflects value conflicts between community residents and service providers and calls into question the meaning and boundaries of community "self-determination."

Alternately, new groups may appear, or new leaders with different priorities and personalities may emerge in long-standing groups. Changes in the population of a community, or the effects of external events, such as a natural disaster, can also have dramatic effects on the level and intensity of political participation in a community with major consequences for inter-organizational partnerships. The aftermath of Hurricane Katrina in New Orleans is a prime example of this development (Bates & Swan, 2010).

In addition, significant changes in public policy can alter an organization's environmental set. Examples include the effects of welfare reform, the uneven implementation of the Affordable Care Act, and recent attempts by the Trump administration to place restrictions on immigration. In addition, changes in the roles of nongovernmental funders, such as foundations, federations, or corporations, could have significant effects on how HSOs operate. The emphasis on greater organizational accountability through outcome-based funding is a prime illustration of this development.

Finally, the introduction of new technology, particularly computers and social media, has had a dramatic effect on HSOs' relationships with surrounding communities. It has changed the nature of inter-organizational communication and interprofessional relationships, and the expectations community residents have regarding the content and sources of critical information. The presence of a technology gap, particularly between "mainstream" HSOs and those established in historically excluded and marginalized communities, has exacerbated persistent resource and power divisions among these organizations along racial, class, and generational lines. It also reflects the different ways diverse cultures use technology itself.

The critical question every HSO faces is how can the organization respond internally to these changes in its external environment?

REFLECTION EXERCISE
ASSESSING THE EXTERNAL ENVIRONMENT

Draw a sketch of the external or task environment of your organization.

1. How does the external environment affect your agency's everyday operations and practices, its pattern of organizational development, and its response to change? In particular, how are these features affected by the following:
   - **a.** Funding sources
   - **b.** Public policies
   - **c.** Inter-organizational relationships
2. What opportunities and threats does the external environment present to your agency? How does the agency respond? (Is there a pattern of proactively and strategically planned responses, or are responses reactive and haphazard?)
3. Who are your agency's most important partners in the community? What characterizes these partnerships? In what ways do these partnerships support and/or hinder your agency's efforts to achieve its mission?
4. In what ways does your agency collude with those in the community who oppress, marginalize, and exclude? In what ways do power holders attempt to co-opt the organization?
5. In what ways does your agency challenge existing power structures?

At their best, HSOs can help build and strengthen communities in several complementary ways. Through the reform of existing services or the creation of new programs, they can help community residents develop their individual human capital as part of the process of empowerment. Examples include job-training programs, parenting classes, individual (assets) development accounts (IDAs), and various types of public health education on such issues as proper diet, disease prevention, smoking cessation, and exercise. Alternately, they could enhance the collective capital of the community through the creation of cooperatives and the construction or rehabilitation of community assets, such as recreation or cultural centers, community gardens, and resident-owned housing developments.

By helping a community construct or rehabilitate its physical or social infrastructure, organizations can enhance the community's economic capital development. This can occur on a large scale, such as housing renovation, or on a smaller scale, such as the creation of community gardens, after-school tutoring programs, or neighborhood cleanup projects. Some HSOs combine efforts at physical and social rehabilitation by training community members to do the rehabilitation work rather than contracting with outside groups. In this way, they enhance community members' future employment prospects while improving its current physical surroundings and increasing its property values.

HSOs can also strengthen a community's political and social capital. The latter takes two basic forms. The first, "bonding social capital," refers to the social relationships that exist among the members of a given community. As discussed later in Chapter 9, individuals who are engaged in community organizing and community development often focus on this component of community building. Many low-income communities, particularly those with a strong sense of racial or ethnic identity, already possess or have the potential to develop this type of social capital (Delgado, 1994). What they lack is the second type, "bridging social capital"—connections to powerful and influential social networks outside the community upon which residents depend for economic and political resources. The creation or strengthening of external relationships can help empower and mobilize these communities, increase their ability to become self-determining and participate more fully in the critical decisions that affect their lives and life chances.

Changes in the external environment are not the only environmental shift to which HSOs must adapt. Changes in their internal environments can have an equally powerful effect. In some ways, these internal changes parallel those that often occur in the wider environment. They can include the sudden loss of a director or key staff member, which can be a particularly significant problem for an agency whose leadership has been constant since its foundation. The introduction of new board or staff leaders, who may bring different leadership styles and organizational priorities, can also create challenges for an organization.

Internal economic issues can result from precipitous, unanticipated funding cuts or major shifts in the organization's sources of funding. For example, the author encountered such a problem when serving as president of a national children's advocacy organization. For years, the organization had relied upon foundation or corporate grants to support its work and largely ignored its original base of individual donors. When the dot.com bubble burst, these funding sources were no longer available. In fact, some foundations retracted their original commitments. This created the need to lay off staff members and downsize some departments. Other agencies, faced with similar challenges, have acted similarly. They have sometimes been required to contract out vital agency services, create new staffing arrangements, revise inter-organizational relationships, freeze staff salaries, or make structural changes in the agency itself, such as the closing of satellite programs.

Cultural changes, such as a changing client base or the emergence of new unprecedented needs in a community, can compel an organization to reflect upon its underlying premises and revise some of its basic processes. Organizations that served the LGBTQ community, for example, had to make dramatic shifts when faced with the enormous challenges produced by the HIV/AIDS epidemic. Finally, the physical relocation of an agency—in response to demographic shifts in its client population or increases in the cost of space—often has dramatic effects on its community relationships and with other actors in its inter-organizational environment. It can sever long-standing community relationships. Longtime clients might feel abandoned, and staff members may have to reorganize the practical details of their workdays. Without proper preparation, changes in the physical relocation of any agency can also affect the organization's internal climate and staff members' morale and overall effectiveness.

Perspectives on Inter-Organizational Relations in the Human Services

According to Reitan (1998), a number of critical factors affect the quality of inter-organizational relationships in the external environment of HSOs. These include the degree of formalization in the relationship, the intensity of the relationship, and the extent of reciprocity in the commitments of the participating organizations. As discussed below, other factors include the origins of the relationship (i.e., whether it was mandated by a third party or developed voluntarily); whether its features are standardized or nonroutine; whether the resources exchanged are tangible or intangible; and what disciplines or professions are involved.

Reitan presents a number of theories for assessing inter-organizational relationships. For purposes of simplicity, this chapter will focus on two of them: a client-need perspective and a professional perspective. The advantage of the former is that the focus on clients requires organizations to respond to their needs. The downside, according to Reitan, is that this approach is apolitical and avoids the question of how clients' needs or demands became valid issues to which HSOs must respond. She further argues that this perspective ignores the element of control and coercion HSOs exercise, and the conflicts that may arise between agencies and their clients or constituents.

A professional perspective considers bureaucratic organizations (individually or in collaboration) as the antithesis of professional autonomy. It focuses on the potential tensions between different professional groups (e.g., social workers and physicians) and their effect on inter-organizational cooperation and effective service delivery. It also addresses the issue of how professionals may develop collegial relationships that transcend agency boundaries to overcome or get around rigid bureaucratic requirements, or because they believe that cooperation among professionals is valuable in itself.

The advantages of this perspective are that it focuses attention on the human dimensions of HSOs and on the importance of the different types of expertise, technologies, and values that organizations possess. In addition, it acknowledges the effects (positive and negative) of power and ideological conflict among agencies. A critique of this perspective is that it ignores the role of "semiprofessionals" in inter-organizational relationships and that it assumes professional loyalty supersedes organizational loyalty.

Patterns of Inter-Organizational Collaboration

To respond effectively to the dynamism in their environments, all organizations collaborate with individuals and groups who share a common focus or interest. These collaborations occur in different combinations: between private (nonprofit and for-profit) agencies, between public and private agencies, and between different public agencies. Most partnerships occur at the horizontal level, although major policy shifts, such as welfare and health care reform, can promote and even necessitate partnerships of a vertical nature.

Fellin (2001) described four levels of inter-organizational relationships in which HSOs participate. They range from lay informal service systems involving families, friends, and neighbors to formal, rule-governed collaborative entities. In between lie quasi-formal mutual aid or self-help systems and the occasional contacts that professional service agencies have with one another on a case-by-case basis.

Litwak and Meyer (1974) regarded these relationships as potential vehicles for neighborhood integration. Several factors determine the extent to which this integration occurs:

- the "openness" of membership in the inter-organizational relationship;
- whether the relationship reflects overlapping social and political ties and activities in the community;
- whether the relationship complements, rather than conflicts, with other group activities; and
- whether the inter-organizational relationship retains a focus on local issues—i.e., those issues that matter most to its clients and constituents (as opposed to becoming involved in causes that affect clients and constituents indirectly).

Other important issues affect the nature of inter-organizational relationships at the community level. Is the relationship part of a larger regional or national network? Did it emerge due to developments (or pressures) from outside the community? How might these external inducements affect its character? In addition, HSOs need to consider if the inter-organizational relationship will have a social justice focus. If so, through what specific issues will it express this focus? What roles will people of color and women play in the relationship? How will the participating organization remove barriers to their participation and leadership?

The goals of collaboration vary considerably depending on the underlying motives and the circumstances that produce it. Legislation may require the distribution of resources at the local level and give community residents a greater role in program design and implementation. This is what occurred through the Community Action Programs (CAPs) during the "War on Poverty" in the 1960s (Bailey & Danziger, 2013;

Moynihan, 1970; Rose, 1972). Alternately, foundations or corporate funders may insist on collaboration among community agencies as a prerequisite for the receipt of substantial funds. The author helped evaluate a public health project in Philadelphia funded by the Robert Wood Johnson Foundation that included a major focus on collaboration among its outcome objectives.

HSOs with different foci may collaborate with peer organizations to provide comprehensive "wraparound" services or to create a "continuum of care" in the service delivery system. Finally, organizations may initiate collaborations because they recognize they lack the resources, staffing, space, skills, or standing in the community to develop effective programs and services. In such cases, they seek partners who can help fill these gaps.

For example, an emerging organization that seeks to assist recently incarcerated individuals in a low-income neighborhood could collaborate with a well-established, better-funded organization that has worked on community development projects for years. In this case, the newer organization brings greater knowledge of the community, fresh ideas, and energy to the relationship, while the more established organization can provide tangible resources, fund-raising expertise, and connections to the media and policy makers. Each type of collaborative relationship produces its own set of issues and challenges. Perhaps the most troublesome challenge occurs when inter-organizational relationships develop between organizations whose staff members come from different racial or cultural backgrounds.

These differences can appear along a variety of demographic lines depending on the issues involved, the population affected, and the targets of change. Sometimes the diversity is a result of different sectors of society forming a partnership, or because organizations from different geographic regions (each with its own history and culture) must collaborate due to political circumstances, the requirements of funders, or policy stipulations. Efforts to develop multicounty collaborations in response to the growing problem of homelessness illustrate the dimensions of this challenge. Other forms of organizational diversity include differences in HSOs' size, in their professional cultures, and the amount and type of resources each organization brings to the partnership. These resources include financial capacity, of course, but may also involve an organization's legitimacy, credibility, reputation, ability to mobilize its constituents, knowledge and expertise on the issues to be addressed, physical facilities, access to the media and key decision makers (its political capital), and the extent of its other inter-organizational relationships.

The Purposes of Collaboration

The current emphasis on collaborations and partnership ventures has emerged from several externally driven forces, including congressional legislation such as the 2010 Affordable Care Act (Reisch, 2012). Other forces include the spread of managed care programs beyond the health care arena to fields such as public child welfare. Managed care has placed increased emphasis on cost containment and the coordination of services, outcomes that proponents claim inter-organizational collaboration can better achieve. A related factor is the expansion of case management practice as a core technology in human services. The spread of case management in virtually all areas of social welfare is largely an attempt to adapt to an increasingly complex service system and demands for greater fiscal accountability (Frankel & Gelman, 2004; Rose, 1992).

This push for increased inter-organizational collaboration did not emerge solely from the public sector. Funders in the private sector—particularly foundations and socially responsible corporations—have valued and promoted collaboration for two reasons. One is that there is some evidence that collaboration produces easier, faster, and more coherent access to services and benefits. A second reason is that collaborative efforts, particularly at the community level, can have a greater and more sustained effect on system change (Nowell & Foster-Fishman, 2011).

Beyond satisfying the demands of funders, collaboration can serve multiple purposes. These purposes range from modest steps, such as sharing information on new government regulations or community features, to taking joint action to create a new program or engage in an advocacy campaign to effect policy changes (Reisch & Sommerfeld, 2003). Although difficult to create and sustain, collaborative efforts benefit most HSOs in a variety of ways.

One benefit, which is particularly valuable to small nonprofits with limited budgets and staffing, is access to hard-to-find information. This benefit is especially important during a period of extensive policy changes, such as the implementation of welfare reform in the late 1990s or, more recently, the 2010 Affordable Care Act. During these periods of policy transformation, many smaller agencies lack the ability to stay current with changes in regulations or government procedures (Sommerfeld & Reisch, 2003). This places them at a considerable disadvantage in obtaining resources and restricts their ability to respond effectively and promptly to their clients' needs. Having a connection with a better-resourced organizational partner can partially overcome this disadvantage.

A related benefit that partnerships or participation in a network provides is greater access to key decision makers and power holders through the relationships previously established by other network members. These relationships and the more extensive history partners may have with power brokers, enables newer organizations to learn from others' experiences and build their own relationships for future action. Finally, creating connections to a larger like-minded community can help small and mid-sized HSOs, particularly those that serve excluded or marginalized populations combat the effects of political isolation (Alter, 2009).

The Spectrum of Collaboration

No two collaborations are alike. They range from informal relationships that may be initiated by two staff members to more formal connections that may either be temporary (such as cooperation on a time-limited project) or more permanent (such as a joint operating agreement or membership in a permanent advocacy coalition). Because the names for collaborative ventures vary widely, there is often some linguistic and practical confusion in distinguishing the different types of inter-organizational relationships on the spectrum of collaboration.

The most common form of inter-organizational collaboration is participation in a network of other service providers or advocates, such as a citywide or countywide organization of human service agencies. These networks, which may be permanent or temporary, are primarily for information sharing and social/political support. Although they may elect a titular leader (a chair), they tend to be quite informal—for example, holding monthly breakfast or lunch meetings that sometimes include a guest speaker. They have a limited structure—often with a rotating facilitator—and all of the participating organizations maintain full autonomy. Although networks will occasionally take joint action, such as staking a common position on a piece of legislation or promoting a change in the government's budget, for the most part their activities are loosely coordinated.

Occasionally these networks evolve into formal inter-organizational relationships, although the participants may retain the original name. In such instances, the members need to create a more permanent structure and determine how they will share decision making and acquire and use the limited resources they possess. These more permanent collaborations—which could emerge for purposes of enhanced service provision or more effective advocacy—engage in regular coordination of their activities toward goals that the group usually develops by consensus.

To remain effective, however, these more formal collaborations need to resolve a number of structural issues from the outset. First, they must decide: What criteria determine who can become a member of the collaborative? Who determines these eligibility criteria for membership? What are the obligations of membership? (Nowell & Boyd, 2014).

Second, they must decide what level of participation is acceptable to be a "member in good standing." This is important to prevent organizations from becoming "free riders" that benefit from association with the collaboration but make scant contributions to its efforts and take few of the risks involved in joint action (Hibbert, Huxham, & Ring, 2008).

A third issue is whether the collaboration should have a fixed leadership (e.g., elected officers) or rotating facilitators. There are clear advantages and disadvantages of each approach. On the one hand, having an established leadership can promote greater operational efficiency, particularly if the leaders have strong facilitation skills. It can also create clearer lines of communication with the media and key policy makers and enhance the organization's ability to convey a consistent message to the public (Keast, Mandell, & Agranoff, 2014; Mandell & Keast, 2009).

One downside is that fixed organizational roles often prevent certain members—particularly people of color and women—from emerging as leaders. Another potential downside is that the public could begin to identify a single person or small group as the "face" or "voice" of the entire organization. This could distort the public's perception of the organization's breadth and diversity and stifle the organization's ability to attract new supporters.

A related issue is how the collaborative should make decisions. In general, smaller inter-organizational systems can make decisions by consensus. It is important to note here that consensus does not mean unanimity. Most groups use 70–80% approval as their definition of consensus. It also means that *all* members of the group agree to live with the decision and not to undermine it by attacking the decision outside the group. As they grow, however, achieving consensus can be time-consuming and more difficult. This can limit the ability of a collaborative to respond promptly and effectively to environmental changes.

A less tangible but equally important issue involves group identity. Sometimes this involves something as seemingly simple as determining the name of the collaborative. While this may seem trivial, it can have both symbolic and practical significance. On the symbolic level, it can convey a message to the community and the public as to the purposes of the collaborative, who are its members, and the nature of its activities. On a more practical level, it defines the group's identity and establishes the degree to which its members maintain their individual autonomy. This symbolic issue is particularly important when inter-organizational relationships involve HSOs from diverse racial and cultural communities.

Finally, inter-organizational relationships must establish clear logistical guidelines if they are to function in the best interests of all members and the constituencies they represent. These logistics include clear rules about intraorganizational and extra-organizational communication. A collaborative must determine who speaks for the group. What is the process for handling crisis-related responses? What are the most effective ways to communicate within the group and between the collaborative and the public?

A related set of issues involves the scheduling and site of meetings, who will be the chair or facilitator, and how to develop the agendas. A collaborative must also determine from the outset how it will collect the resources it needs to function (e.g., through dues, in-kind contributions, staff time, or some combination thereof) and how it will distribute its limited assets. In addition, it must decide how the group assigns various task responsibilities and holds its members accountable for satisfying the obligations they have voluntarily incurred. As the following case example (based on the author's experience) demonstrates, these tasks are complicated when a collaborative consists of individuals and organizations from different cultures.

CASE ILLUSTRATION FOR DISCUSSION
DEFUSING TENSIONS IN A MULTICULTURAL COALITION

The author helped organize a coalition of ~15 organizations with a wide range of racial and ethnic backgrounds to advocate for the needs of children and families in a major U.S. city. The group agreed to meet from 4–6 p.m. on the fourth Thursday of each month to develop strategies and plan actions. A coalition member from a well-established organization offered space for the meeting, an offer that everyone appreciated. At the first meeting, the group's members agreed to rotate facilitation and note taking. Everything seemed to go very smoothly and spirits were high.

Over the course of the next several months, however, two internal problems appeared. Some members began coming to the meetings late—not just five to 10 minutes late, but 30–40 minutes late. At first, no one said anything in the interests of group harmony, although all the participants had extremely busy schedules and most had family obligations as well. After a few meetings, the irritation of some members surfaced. The failure of a few group members to follow through on routine tasks to which they had committed (sending out minutes or meeting reminders, obtaining certain key information) exacerbated intragroup tensions. The group was on the brink of breaking up. What steps might you take to prevent this from occurring?

On an individual level, there are certain "ground rules" that help prevent or resolve situations such as the one described in this case. First, it is important to respect others' opinions, styles, individual and organizational needs, skills, and limitations. All people, particularly those from different cultural or class backgrounds, bring different abilities to the table in inter-organizational relationships. Sometimes those abilities take different forms that may not be immediately recognizable because they do not fit dominant cultural patterns.

Second, it is important to avoid questioning others' motives for joining the collaborative or their commitment to the group unless there is incontrovertible evidence that they are placing their personal interests or those of their organization above that of the group. In contentious discussions, while acknowledging the role of emotions, be sure to criticize the ideas or actions of those with whom you disagree, not their persons or styles. Do not interrupt when others are speaking no matter how passionately you feel about an issue. Sometimes others will view the interruption itself as disrespectful even if you are interrupting to support the position of the person who was originally speaking.

Conversely, it is equally valuable to give credit where it's due but avoid superficial or gratuitous compliments. Especially in diverse organizations, such behavior can feel patronizing or condescending, and feed suspicion and mistrust. This requires individuals to check their egos at the door and allow others to claim the spotlight. Remember that the goal of the partnership is to advance the interests of the group as a whole, not the individual members or the organizations they represent. This is often difficult, particularly in our individualistic and highly competitive culture.

Third, in this regard, it is important to stay focused in meetings on the issues at hand, to be transparent in the presentation of positions, to be an "active listener," and to avoid even the appearance of having a "hidden agenda." All individuals should be encouraged to participate equally, even if that participation takes different forms, to contribute to the best of their ability, to use the different strengths they bring to the group, and to be accountable for the tasks to which they have committed. Finally, particularly in multicultural groups, it is critical to use humor appropriately, as discussed in Chapter 4. While humor can be a great way to ease intragroup tensions, it can also inadvertently exacerbate those tensions, especially in groups whose members are just becoming acquainted.

The group as a whole will function more effectively if it strategizes collectively before it takes action on an issue. It should agree in advance to discuss difficult issues that many groups resist, such as the effects of race and gender. Brushing conflicts aside, even those below the surface, only makes them worse. Organizations need to take time to manage conflict, solve internal problems, and strive to identify common ground whenever possible. Whatever disagreements may surface in meetings—and in diverse groups they inevitably will (and perhaps should)—group members should agree to disagree, and make sure the group hears everyone's voice by creating safe spaces through different decision-making formats. Participants should also agree to accept the final decision (whether made by consensus or majority vote) and not undermine it outside the group, and to maintain the confidentiality of group discussions, particularly keeping all criticisms of decisions within the group.

Building and sustaining multicultural partnerships, particularly in politically contentious times when resource scarcity has become more widespread, is an ongoing challenge for HSOs. As the case that follows illustrates, one way to overcome this challenge is to find a common issue that unites diverse groups instead of heightening the divisions that exist among them. It is also important to be clear on the reasons why the issue or issues the group wants to address cannot be resolved without a diverse partnership. For the most part, the creation of a collaborative relationship is not useful to bring an issue (such as homelessness) to the public's attention; it may be an effective strategy, however, to address this issue.

CASE ILLUSTRATION
CHOOSING THE RIGHT ISSUE TO ORGANIZE A FRACTIOUS COMMUNITY

Some years ago, community tensions erupted in a New York City neighborhood that had undergone a dramatic demographic transition during the previous two decades from a largely white, multiethnic community, to a community in which a majority of residents were African American and Puerto Rican. Efforts by HSOs in the community to ease these tensions repeatedly failed, in part because each demographic group focused on different real or perceived grievances. Older residents complained of increasing crime and noise; newer residents of the declining quality of local schools and police treatment of youth.

Finally, a few leaders agreed to ask a multiracial group of community organizers for assistance. After careful assessment of the situation (*see Chapter 9 for a fuller discussion of this issue*), the organizers decided to focus their attempts at building inter-organizational relationships on an issue that *all* community residents understood: the decline in the quality of public transportation. This decision had several important consequences.

First, residents' anger was redirected from other groups in the community to an external enemy—City Hall—and gave them the opportunity to collaborate on a solution to a problem they all agreed existed, rather than compete on defining the problem itself. Second, it enabled community members from different groups to know one another on a more personal basis rather than as the "other." Finally, the community's success in extracting concessions from City Hall empowered participants involved in the collaborative effort. It also enabled them to cooperate in the future on more contentious community issues.

A lesson from this case is that organizations that are considering whether to participate in a collaborative relationship should assess, in advance, what their potential contributions to the group would be and what might be the benefits (and problems) from joining the partnership. Part of this assessment involves the identification of common long-term goals and short-term projects that are consistent with these goals. It is equally valuable to enter the collaboration with "eyes wide open" by identifying historical and contemporary factors that could facilitate or impede future cooperation with potential partners. This enables the organization to build upon existing strengths and diminish the effect of these possible barriers. Finally, it is important to recognize that the partnership is probably not going to be permanent, though your organization may aspire to be.

Several critical factors determine the shape and outcome of efforts to forge inter-organizational relationships. One is the history of past efforts to create relationships of this nature in the community or around similar issues. A second is whether the partnership requires the exchange of tangible (money, staffing, physical space) or intangible resources (connections to funders, political influence). Another is the intensity of the relationship that potential organizational partners desire to create and whether the partners initiate the collaboration voluntarily (through a mutually agreeable "courtship" period) or whether third parties, such as funders, mandate the collaboration by imposing a "shotgun marriage" on unwilling partners.

A fourth issue is the extent of formality in the partnership and the degree to which members will have reciprocal obligations to one another. Other differences among potential partners can also affect the success or failure of the collaboration. For example, are the services or activities they perform as independent organizations similar? Are the organizations composed of staff members from the same or different disciplines, professions, and cultural backgrounds?

Bronstein (2003), for example, explored the effects of diverse professional backgrounds on the ability of organizations to establish effective collaborations. She identified four major influences on interprofessional efforts to collaborate at the organizational level. Many of her observations are equally applicable to the challenges of creating collaborative relationships among organizations with diverse demographic and cultural backgrounds.

One factor is the effect of each profession's view of its role, as reflected in its explicit and implicit values and **ethics**, and its overall view of practice (e.g., holistic or fragmented). A second influence is the history of collaboration among key actors. A third factor is the nature of the interpersonal (as contrasted with the inter-organizational) aspects of the partnership relationships. Does the partners' behavior reflect mutual trust, respect, understanding, and effective means of informal communication?

The structure of the partnership itself is another important influence on the success of the collaboration. This includes how the collaborative distributes workload responsibilities and whether members receive adequate administrative support, time, and space to fulfill their commitments. It also involves whether its members can preserve their professional autonomy—as individuals and organizations—while concurrently building a new, inter-organizational culture.

Bronstein found that successful collaborations met the challenges involved by promoting interdependence among the various partners and creating new, shared activities that each of the partners could "own." This required partners to be flexible about their roles and to recognize their collective ownership of the collaboration's goals. It also required them to reflect on the collaborative process on an ongoing basis and to embrace the benefits of the relationship. The role of leaders or facilitators in this regard is particularly important.

As difficult as it is to create an inter-organizational collaboration, particularly among culturally diverse partners, it is even more difficult to sustain this relationship over time. A wide range of external forces, from budget cuts to unforeseen social crises to shifts in the political climate, buffet individual organizations and the group as a whole. No collaborative effort is immune from such forces. Collaborative partnerships, however, can take several steps to increase the possibility they will survive and thrive even during the most difficult circumstances.

From the outset, they should strive through broad outreach to create diverse memberships based on recognition of the benefits multicultural organizational partnerships produce. This may require seeking allies in unfamiliar sources or revising traditional views of what constitutes an organization's assets. Once the collaboration is established, it should develop a clear structure and decision-making process so that there is no confusion (and potential conflict) over how it makes and implements decisions, where authority lies, or how members bring issues to the attention of the group.

Paying attention to the interpersonal dynamics of multicultural partnerships is equally if not more important. Organizations should take concrete, deliberate steps to build trusting relationships among members, many of whom may be justifiably skeptical of the benefits of collaboration and of the advantages of forging partnerships with colleagues from different backgrounds. These efforts take time and a willingness to experiment and learn from mistakes. Key tools in this regard are effective means of intraorganizational and inter-organizational communication and the development of a conflict management process. (*See Chapter 15.*)

Finally, successful collaborations must have a diverse leadership that brings different skills to the complicated process of inter-organizational work. There are several types of inter-organizational leaders, each of which plays a valuable role in the partnership's work. One type of leader is a "movement builder" who has the energy, vision, and connections to create the initial momentum needed to forge the partnership. This person is not only a skilled strategist, she or he is also an effective communicator, someone who can inspire even a cynical audience to take action.

Other leaders are strategists and problem solvers. They remain conscious of the connection between the long-term goals of a collaborative effort and the short-term steps needed to reach them. They are also important leaders when crises inevitably emerge because they understand how a resolution of the crisis affects the overall prospects of the partnership (Tracy, 2014; Kippenberger, 2002).

Because inter-organizational partnerships often explore new territory (e.g., new issues, new strategies, systems changes), they must also have leaders who are skilled communicators. Some of these leaders play the role of "statesperson" (e.g., when dealing with power brokers or the media), while others play the role of negotiators (when meeting with policy makers, for example), or "sparkplugs" who have the ability to mobilize public support when speaking with community stakeholders or acquiring resources from prospective funding sources. As most multicultural partnerships have few successful precedents in U.S. society, some leaders must play the role of group historians, or serve as role models and mentors to younger group members. Finally, if collaborations are to be sustained over the long haul, their leaders must be carefully chosen, held accountable by the group as a whole, and, above all, representative of the diverse communities that constitute the partnership (Perrault, McClelland, Austin, & Sieppert, 2011). (*See Chapter 6 for more discussion of leadership.*)

Coalitions: A Unique Form of Collaboration

A **coalition** is an "organization of organizations" that shares articulated social or political change goals and is characterized by dynamic tensions. A coalition is time limited (under most circumstances); pools relevant resources to achieve its goals; engages in conscious communication regarding its goals, strategies, and tactics; agrees (ideally in advance) on the distribution of the tangible and intangible benefits of its efforts; and develops—by consensus—its structure and decision-making processes. The purposes of a coalition are to achieve objectives that a single organization cannot by "borrowing" power, building the individual organizations of the coalition partners, and, under some circumstances, preventing a serious division among potential allies from erupting. It is important to note a simple rule: 0 + 0 = 0—that is, combining two or more powerless organizations does not create power or enhance the power of any of the coalition's members. As the old song goes, "nothing from nothing leaves nothing."

There are several types of coalitions: (a) direct membership; (b) coalitions of pre-existing groups; (c) compound organizations; and (d) those usually established and often controlled by large agencies. A long-standing problem is that few of these coalitions are multicultural.

Successful coalitions have a number of similar qualities. They have broad, diverse representation, large memberships, clear roles (especially regarding leadership), a distinct ideology, an attractive, clearly stated set of values, concise framing of key issues, a common vocabulary, ease of mobilization, large amounts of tangible resources, and a dominant group of actors to represent it. Perhaps of greatest importance, they are willing to experiment and learn from their mistakes. This requires time and flexibility (of style, strategy, etc.). Much as effective collaborations for service provision, successful coalitions also possess a cadre of skilled, diverse leaders, a democratic decision-making structure, trusting relationships among members, and effective communication and conflict management.

Group leadership is essential in a diverse coalition. Diverse coalitions also have different types of leaders. Some have personal charisma while others possess specific technical expertise, such as around policy issues or media strategy. Others are generalists in their orientation, who bring wise counsel to a range of situations. Each coalition should assess what type of leaders it possesses and which potential partners possess the qualities the group lacks and needs.

Several key points about leadership in diverse coalitions are worth emphasizing. In every coalition members choose the leadership through no fixed criteria. Leaders must represent—in actual, not merely symbolic ways—the diversity of the coalition. Leaders are also accountable to members and constituents for their decisions. This requires an open flow of communication. (*See more on leadership in Chapter 6.*)

As with collaborations, coalitions must resolve several structural issues in advance: Who can be a member? What type of participation is required or allowed? What type of leadership best serves the interests of the coalition? What pattern of decision making should the coalition adopt and for which types of decisions? Should the coalition make all decisions by consensus? How should it make tactical decisions during an unanticipated crisis? How should coalition partners identify themselves? To what extent should coalition partners retain autonomy? What style of communication is best suited for the coalition?

When do you build a coalition? Under what circumstances is it necessary or advisable to forge a coalition (especially one with multicultural partners)? In general, the following preconditions should exist:

1. Potential coalition partners share genuine common interests.
2. Each organization lacks the resources to produce a desired change alone.

3. Partners are aware of the need for the changes the coalition would seek.
4. Potential partners have desirable resources, which if pooled could benefit the coalition as a whole.
5. Connections between coalition leaders already exist.
6. Environmental conditions favor the formation of new inter-organizational relationships. This could be due to common fear of those who hold power or awareness of a common issue that has the potential to unite previously disparate groups.

Each organization takes steps to form a coalition after it develops its own power base and reputation and before it engages in a critical fight over resources or policy decisions. The steps in building a coalition resemble those used in forming a friendship or engaging in a courtship. You gather intelligence about a potential partner. Through some medium, perhaps a colleague or sympathetic journalist, clergy member, or politician, you meet informally, exchange paper contacts, and/or engage with key staff members on specific projects. You work jointly on a short-term project, and if everything goes well, you enter a formal partnership. In sum, the evolution of a coalition goes through specific stages: endorsement, alliance on a single issue, formation of an ad hoc coalition on a single issue, formation of an ongoing coalition, affiliation or merger (permanent), and dissolution (whether due to victory or defeat).

In addition, to construct a solid foundation for a coalition, organizations need to take the following concrete steps:

- identify potential partners, involving as many diverse groups as possible;
- base discussions with these potential partners on hard information (not wish lists);
- learn the major issues each organization addresses and where there is overlap or potential conflict with the issues of other organizations in order to select the right issues around which to partner;
- analyze the costs and benefits of the relationship;
- define initial goals broadly and create a superordinate goal; and
- identify targets and use outsiders (opponents) to unite the coalition.

Many organizations fear joining coalitions because of real or perceived risks. They worry that differences among coalition members or competition over goals, strategies, and leadership could paralyze the group and impede joint efforts. They are concerned about the possible drain of time and energy from their organization and that the costs of participation will outweigh the benefits. They fear that other members might not pull their weight. Conversely, they worry that their organization will lose control over the coalition's agenda, strategy, tactics, or methods of resource allocation, resulting in their organization's loss of identity and autonomy. Finally, they worry that the coalition may become too large which will inhibit effective action. Sometimes coalition members use this rationale to prevent the coalition from diversifying its composition.

Creating and sustaining multicultural coalitions present specific challenges. It is particularly important, therefore, to find an issue that unites people and to be clear why the partnering organizations need the coalition to ***resolve*** the issue, not merely to create it. Identifying how the coalition will frame common goals and short-term projects also have important implications for the success of the coalition. It is equally important to address forthrightly the historical and/or contextual factors that could facilitate or impede the process of coalition formation and to assess each group's strengths carefully.

In multicultural coalitions, partners need to be aware how race, gender, class, and sexual orientation may influence people's behaviors both negatively (in the form of microaggressions) and positively (in the form of different communication or leadership styles). One way to overcome some of the obstacles that multicultural coalitions confront is to forge a new identity or a multifaceted identity that is not associated with any individual group. In addition, the coalition should strive to level the playing field among partners (e.g., around technology), establish clear decision-making guidelines, and be particularly sensitive to questions of process and leadership.

Sustaining a diverse coalition also involves a number of critical challenges. These include addressing the inevitable tension between inter-organizational cooperation and overt or covert conflict among coalition partners that their mixed or divided loyalties can produce. The following list summarizes other issues that coalitions confront:

KEY CONCEPT SUMMARY
ISSUES COALITIONS CONFRONT

- Autonomy vs. accountability
- Unity vs. diversity
- Survival vs. militancy
- Breadth vs. focus
- Product (goals) vs. process (means)
- Local vs. national emphasis
- Resource dependence vs. survival
- Offensive vs. defensive strategies
- Long-term goals vs. short-term goals
- Moving on vs. stabilizing gains
- Formal structure vs. spontaneity
- Experienced leadership vs. "fresh blood"

Despite these challenges, multicultural coalitions have the potential to provide considerable benefits to their members and to their members' constituents. Obviously, in a competitive and hyper-partisan political environment, there is strength in both numbers and diversity. A diverse coalition can mobilize different segments of the population around a common issue. It can bring a broader array of skills to the processes involved in social change. For example, some organizations have experience with direct action tactics, while others have been successful through more conventional "inside" methods. If organized well, coalition partners share the workload and distribute tasks and resources equitably. On an intangible level, diverse coalitions can create greater intragroup and intergroup cohesion and solidarity. Finally, a successful multicultural coalition can become a symbolic microcosm of a more just, decent, and diverse society.

KEY CONCEPT SUMMARY
FEATURES OF A SUCCESSFUL COALITION

- Clarity about each organization's self-interest, goals, and norms
- Knowledge of the culture and history of potential partners
- Clear decision-making rules
- Being a good partner even in difficult times
- Ongoing personal contact with other members
- Distinguishing between group dialogue and joint action
- Provision of different types of incentives to coalition members
- Regular meetings and communication
- Scheduling periodic joint events to maintain group solidarity
- Engaging in proactive planning and decision making
- Being aware of and capitalizing on partners' strengths and assets
- Establishing and sticking to time lines and tasks
- Keeping the big picture in mind
- Maintaining the organizational independence of each partner

There are some important caveats to keep in mind in building and sustaining coalitions, particularly those that involve diverse organizations. Coalitions are "foreign organizations" to most people and groups. Actions, not words, build strong, lasting connections. Be wary of bringing in "experts" to solve any intragroup problems too early. Rotate leadership and responsibilities. Do not formalize the coalition's structure before establishing its overall goals. Yet, do not neglect formalizing the coalition's structure out of fear it will blunt the coalition's momentum. Finally, make sure you think carefully about where your resources are coming from.

To build a truly diverse yet effective coalition, it is important to think "outside the box" about potential allies and to take the time needed to build trust, which is often particularly fragile at the outset. It is also important to make the issue of diversity a priority ***before*** the coalition's initial meeting while remaining aware of the potential effect of diversity on the coalition's ongoing functioning. Leave space for new coalition partners to create new agenda items or revise the coalition's existing agenda. Build informal social time into meetings to forge new interpersonal and intergroup relationships. Remember that diversity equals difference, but not deviance, and think about how the coalition will respond when inevitable differences (some of which may be conflict-oriented) arise.

As is increasingly apparent, diversity takes different forms in our increasingly complex society. In addition to the obvious factors of race, ethnicity, gender and gender identity, class, sexual orientation, and religion, there are also other sometimes more subtle factors. These include the personal backgrounds of coalition partners, their geographic region, the issue or sector of civil society from which they emerge, the focus of their organizations, and their organizations' relative size and duration. Diverse coalition partners also bring different resources to the table. Some of them are tangible resources—money, facilities, technology, for example. Others are intangible, such as legitimacy or credibility (which varies depending on the community), people power (numbers), knowledge and technical expertise, and relationships (social capital). A key question to consider: What types of diversity best fit the goals and strategy of your organization and the prospective coalition as a whole? Which individual and group partners are essential for your organization and the coalition to succeed?

To build trust, coalition partners should reflect frequently on the following questions:

1. Who are we? Whom do we each represent?
2. Why are we here? Why do we care about the issue? What is our long-term agenda?
3. What do we each bring to the table—e.g., perspectives, resources, abilities?
4. What are our limits and limitations?
5. What constraints—internal and external—exist on our partnership?
6. Do we each have the authority to act on behalf of our respective groups or organizations?
7. Are there issues we cannot discuss—now or ever?

Advocacy or Social Change Coalitions

Advocacy or social change coalitions are a particular type of coalition. They are organizations that collaborate—i.e., work with individuals and groups sharing a common interest and policy goal—for purposes that range from sharing information to taking joint action on a legislative campaign. Some of them are informal and temporary (e.g., for a single legislative session around a single bill); others are formal and permanent (Hoefer, 2016). They go under different names—network, coalition, alliance, campaign—whose meanings vary in U.S. and global efforts.

Generally, however, there are differences in form and purpose between networks and coalitions. Networks are generally informal and temporary. They have a limited structure and maintain the full autonomy of participating organizations. One of their primary objectives is information sharing.

The primary purpose of advocacy coalitions is to facilitate joint action. They are more formal and, in some cases, permanent. They need structure to operate effectively. Coalition members share decision-making responsibilities and resources and organize more tightly coordinated activities.

Particularly today, when marginalized groups have limited access to policy makers or power to influence critical policy decisions, these types of collaboration can provide multiple benefits. They help individual organizations obtain hard-to-find information. They enhance access to decision makers and power holders through partners' connections. They provide opportunities to learn from others' experiences about what works well and what does not. They help forge relationships that could serve as the basis for future action. They also avoid organizational isolation by connecting each coalition partner to a larger, like-minded community.

Given the challenges and risks involved in coalition work, it is natural to ask "When is it worthwhile to join or create a coalition?" Several "leading indicators" point to the desirability of forming or participating in a coalition instead of each organization trying to solve a complex problem on its own. The issue must be a high priority in the community the organization serves and must affect a large (and preferably) diverse segment of the community's population. Ideally, coalition partners should avoid framing the issue in a manner that creates the perception it is something only elites care about, or that it affects only the most disadvantaged members of the community. Focusing on the needs of all children, rather than the needs of a specific group of children, is an example of this type of framing. Although there are always potential pitfalls in universalizing an issue, it provides the opportunity to build broad political support that ultimately may facilitate the distribution of additional resources to the populations that most need them.

Another factor to consider is whether joining the coalition furthers the organization's agenda and whether it has the capacity to commit sufficient resources to the coalition's work. A related consideration is whether participation in the coalition will strengthen relationships with clients and constituents and, conversely, have no adverse effects on them. From a purely pragmatic perspective, organizations should join coalitions when no other strategic options exist. Finally, it is important to assess whether the organization's ideology, values, and goals are sufficiently similar to those of potential partners and, if they diverge, whether the coalition can help work through any differences. In sum, there are always pros and cons to coalition work. Organizations must always determine whether the trade-offs required are acceptable or worth the risk.

Alternatives to Coalitions

If an organization answers the preceding question "no," it does not preclude the development of other possible inter-organizational connections. Organizations can resume their "courtship" on individual and structural levels, for example by continuing to share information through informal channels. Another option is for an organization to begin to work on a particular issue while keeping other organizations, which may be potential partners in the future, informed of its work. A third possibility is for two or more organizations to collaborate in a less intense way (e.g., cosponsoring a single event such as a press conference or codirecting a short-term campaign). Finally, two organizations could develop parallel organizations that work toward the same or similar ends in different ways.

Building and Maintaining Interracial and Multicultural Coalitions

This chapter concludes with some recommendations on what is probably the most daunting challenge in today's environment: building and maintaining interracial or multicultural coalitions (Chesler, 1981). This process requires careful planning, ongoing vigilance, and risk-taking behaviors that may be hard for some members to undertake. For such efforts to succeed, all members of the coalition must be aware that contemporary societal divisions will create objective and subjective conflicts among different racial and cultural groups and that these will occur and reoccur at various stages of the coalition's development. Each potential coalition partner must, therefore, commit itself to a set of vital, mutually established common interests and develop goals that are concrete and situationally specific (Robinson & Robinson, 2006).

Coalition members from dominant groups—Whites, men, heterosexuals—have a particular responsibility in this regard. For example, White members must recognize how they have benefited from a historic pattern of institutional and individual racism, and acknowledge the differences that often exist between their interests and those of people of color. They need to take the time to learn how they carry racism and the effects of "whiteness" within themselves and the ways in which well-socialized attitudes and behaviors sustain their privilege and power (Crowfoot & Chesler, 2003; Mullaly, 2010). They should also be clear about the ways in which their self-interests affect both Whites and persons of color in the coalition (McGary, 1999; Browning, Marshall, & Tabb, 2003).

All parties in the coalition, especially groups representing persons of color, should have an already established base of power. The internal operations of the coalition should reflect these power bases and the interests they represent. One means to achieve this is to provide opportunities for each racial or ethnic group to spend time in a separate caucus (if desired) and for leaders of each coalition partner to meet with their own constituents separately, particularly before the coalition makes critical decisions.

The structure and internal processes of the coalition should also support and reward leadership by persons of color and other historically marginalized groups. Leaders must make a purposeful, concerted, cooperative, and sustained effort to recruit some coalition members and groups with common interests that cut across racial boundaries. Individuals and groups that have experience and skills in working in interracial or cross-cultural settings should be particular targets for recruitment. In recruiting members, however, it is important not to cast the net too widely. It is wasteful and potentially tragic to attempt to build a coalition with groups that do not genuinely have common interests or values, or those who want to question or challenge the coalition's agenda constantly (Bobo, Kendall, & Max, 2001; Shaw, 2013).

Because the formation of the coalition itself, whatever the intentions and good faith of its founders, cannot eradicate the lingering effects of racism, sexism, and homophobia, coalition leaders should confront both the incidents of racism (or sexism and homophobia) and also the exploitation of racial issues by persons of color. This difficult challenge requires the development of an internal educational program that teaches all members the competencies required to create positive multicultural relations and help the coalition discipline or correct destructive behavior (Bystydzienski & Schacht, 2001).

Another way a multicultural coalition can begin to correct the effects of history is to create as many equal status interactions and role relations as possible in its internal workings. This may require organizational restructuring, new ways of making strategic decisions, alternative approaches to task distribution, and revised internal relationships, such as concepts of leadership (Mizrahi & Rosenthal, 2001). The coalition should also develop several mechanisms, such as intragroup dialogue (Hubbard, 1997), to facilitate constant processing of the various intense emotions and issues that are bound to arise in the course of its work.

Circling back to where this chapter began—the importance of the external environment—multicultural coalitions should discuss the change strategies they plan to implement with considerable care. This includes an assessment of how authorities will react to the challenges put forth by the coalition (perhaps even the existence of the coalition itself), and how White members of the coalition might respond. As important as it is to determine a coalition's potential enemies or opponents, it is equally important to look for potential allies—covert and overt—who often exist in powerful and unexpected places. For example, on several occasions the author worked with groups that obtained critical support from powerful corporate executives, conservative politicians, and status quo-oriented business groups. Coalitions could consider the possibility of forming a permanent, multi-issue organization or a short-term alliance with these potential partners after the coalition achieves its initial objectives (Delgado, 1993; Shaw, 2013). Finally, because many multicultural coalitions are short-lived, its members should prepare for its possible demise—whether compelled or voluntary—and discuss well in advance how each of the coalition partners will respond to this eventuality.

Summary and Conclusion

This chapter discussed the multiple features of an organization's external or "task" environment and emphasized the importance of inter-organizational relationships to all HSOs. It examined the various forms of these relationships, with a particular focus on collaborations and coalitions, particularly those among organizations with diverse backgrounds. The chapter provided guidelines for the formation and maintenance of successful multicultural inter-organizational relationships. Two issues that it addressed to some extent are the role of power and leadership. Chapter 6 delves into these critical issues in more detail.

END-OF-CHAPTER EXERCISE
SOCIAL SERVICES AND SOCIAL CHANGE

1. What is your organization's stated and unstated mission? Vision? Goals?
   a. What part of your organization's mission, vision, or goals is unstated? Why?
   b. When did your organization decide upon its mission/vision/goals? How did the organization make this decision? Who was part of this decision-making process?
2. How does your organization engage with individuals, communities, and society to achieve its stated mission/vision/goals? What types of activities (e.g., services, advocacy, organizing) does your agency undertake? What are the objectives of these activities? Who benefits from the organization's activities?
3. What changes in the external environment would be necessary to achieve your organization's stated mission, vision, and goals? What would be required to bring about these changes (e.g., new or revised services, additional funding, advocacy, organizing)?
4. What type of organization is your field placement (e.g., government, nonprofit, for-profit, etc.)? How does this shape the organization's mission/vision/goals, activities, and ability to seek social change?
5. In what ways does your organization promote social change? In what ways does it promote social control?
6. How does your organization's history inform its present activities?

END-OF-CHAPTER EXERCISE
ASSESSING RESOURCES IN THE EXTERNAL ENVIRONMENT

1. What funders and other organizational partnerships does your agency rely upon for resources? Why did it choose them? How would you recommend improving them?
2. What is/are the governing body(ies) of your agency? Are there any you would discontinue, or others you believe should exist to improve service delivery? How does the governing body assist or impede the services you offer?
3. Reflect on the agency's external environment. What inter-organizational relationships exist? How do they operate? What relationships are missing that would improve service delivery?
4. Discuss how the external environment (e.g., funding sources, public policies, inter-organizational relationships) affects its everyday operations/practice, its pattern of organizational development, and its response to change. Reflect on how the external environment influences how your organization delivers services; implements rules, regulations, and procedures; engages in program planning and development; relates to the community it serves; and responds to internal and external opportunities and threats.

CHAPTER 6

Power and Leadership in Multicultural Organizations and Communities

There is nothing more difficult to take in hand or more perilous to conduct ... than to take the lead in the introduction of a new order of things.

—Niccolo Machiavelli

Power is not only what you have but what the enemy thinks you have.

—Saul Alinsky, *Rules for Radicals*

Introduction

There is increasing urgency in the field of social welfare to create a new generation of leaders that reflects the social and cultural diversity of society and whose knowledge and skills are adapted to the enormous environmental and technological changes under way. Yet, nonprofits have neither the size nor the resources to develop large numbers of managers internally, as their for-profit counterparts do. The sector also lacks robust management-education and executive-search capabilities. This has produced the leadership deficit illustrated in Figure 6.1.

Figure 6.1 helps explain why there is a growing leadership deficit in the nonprofit sector, where many social work agencies reside. As the chart reveals, there are two major reasons for the emergence of this deficit. The first is the dramatic increase in the number of nonprofit organizations over the past several decades. Many of these organizations are smaller and less well financed. They face increased challenges for scarce resources and public attention in a highly competitive environment. The second owes to the retirement of a generation of seasoned nonprofit leaders. The loss of their accumulated experience, institutional history, political savvy, and commitment to the historic mission of the nonprofit sector will be difficult to replace without conscious, strategic efforts.

To understand the magnitude of this leadership deficit and the challenges involved in fixing the problem, we need to examine what shapes the supply of, and demand for, nonprofit leaders. The supply side of the story begins with the baby boom generation. Because of the baby boom, the pool of American men and women of prime executive age (34 to 54 years) swelled to 35 million between 1980 and 2000. The first wave of this nearly 80 million-strong generation is now retired, and because the boomers did not have as many offspring as did their parents, the cohort that follows them has considerably fewer people. During the first two decades of the 21st century (that is, by 2020), the number of people in the prime leadership age bracket of 34 to 54 will grow by only three million. Clearly, the United States needs to increase the pool of qualified leaders who reflect the growing diversity of the nation. To do this, HSOs will have to revise the ways they recruit, select, retain, and promote the next generation of leaders. They will also have to rethink what is a leader and the concept of leadership itself.

Figure 6.1 The Leadership Deficit

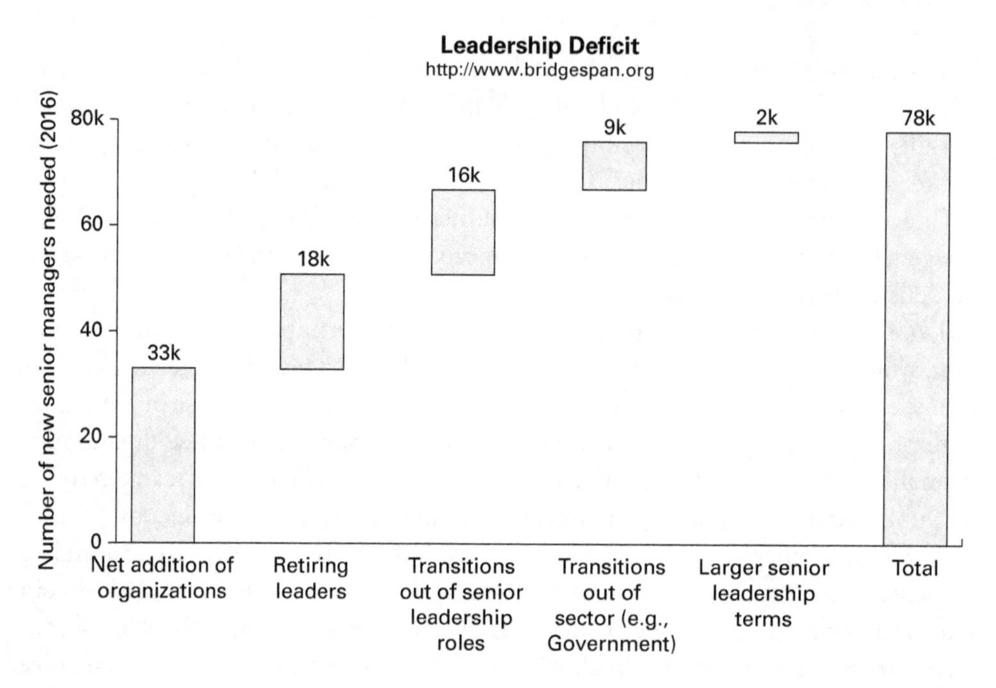

Fig. 6.1: *Source: Thomas J. Tierney, https://www.bridgespan.org/bridgespan/Images/articles/leadership-deficit/leadershipdeficitexecutivesummary.pdf?ext=.pdf.*

This chapter focuses on the role of leadership in both service and change-oriented organizations, and the process of leadership development. It includes content in the following areas:

1. Different conceptions and models of leadership within and across diverse population groups, including the role of leaders in producing organizational and community change.
2. Traditional and alternative views of leadership.
3. The distinction between leaders and the concept of leadership and its practice implications.
4. Gender and cultural differences in leadership styles and their implications.
5. The traits of effective leaders; how to combine effective leadership with respect, inclusiveness, fairness, appreciation of diverse cultures and perspectives.
6. The challenge of balancing external accountability (to sponsors and supporters) with efficiency, effectiveness, and accessibility.
7. Leadership development—how leadership traits can be identified (e.g., in a search process) and cultivated among staff members and community residents.

8. Contemporary problems of leadership and ways to address them.
9. The importance of supervision, including the ways a supervisor can enhance the effectiveness of staffers, particularly in diverse organizations and communities.
10. Practice prescriptions when in leadership situations or when working with leaders.

What is Leadership?

We use the words "leader" and "leadership" so often that we assume they mean the same thing to everyone. Yet, is this really so? In a diverse society, do all people define leadership in the same way? Do we agree on what are the preferred qualities in a leader or what kinds of people make the best leaders? Would we all recognize the potential for leadership in the same individuals?

These are not merely rhetorical questions. How we view leaders, how we define the concept of leadership, and how we distinguish between a leader and leadership has a significant effect on our work in communities and organizations. In our increasingly diverse society, does the dominant portrait of a leader match the types of leaders who emerge in different cultures?

Traditional Views of Leadership

A traditional view of leadership, particularly in Western societies, complements the traits associated with top-down, hierarchical organizations. Leaders exhibit intelligence, masculinity, adjustment, dominance, extraversion, and conservatism (Mann, 1965). This perspective also emphasizes the importance of individual charisma (Weber, 1946) and, therefore, regards membership in the so-called "leadership class" as largely exclusive—i.e., limited to a select few who all exhibit similar qualities and operate in a top-down manner. The application of this conception of leadership to macro practice perpetuates prevailing power dynamics and a dichotomous view of the relationships that exist between administrators and staff members; boards and executives; organizers and community residents; advocates and constituents.

This view of leadership also tends to ascribe change exclusively to individuals (the so-called "great man theory of history"). It ignores the relationship between the context (space and time) and the emergence of leaders (Plekhanov, 1940). The behavioral models it assumes reflect the prevailing individualistic ideology of the socioeconomic system. Hence, we fail to recognize how our culture "socially reproduces" elite views of leadership (Bourdieu, 2003; Gorz, 1968), maintains organizational hierarchies, and excludes many people, particularly women and people of color, from positions of leadership despite their qualifications.

In addition, the traditional hierarchical view of leadership emphasizes the commitment of an organization to a particular mission or belief system and the importance of its leaders' charisma. As Weber pointed out, this charisma is irrational and is counter-poised to the force of bureaucratic rationalization. It transforms the inner lives of people and leads them to transform their environment. It is a top-down, creative force. This elitist concept of leadership has influenced contemporary views of the relationship between leaders and staff members, leadership development, and organizational structure. It focuses on such issues as who becomes a leader and what are appropriate leadership styles and functions?

The 'Iron Law of Oligarchy'

Michels's classic work (1915) provocatively points out several other important consequences of traditional concepts of leadership. According to Michels, in a hierarchical organization relatively few people actually make critical decisions, even if the organization shares authority for these decisions formally with the entire body. Those leaders who have been delegated authority within an organization tend to take on more power than other members. Once in power, they tend to remain for long periods—eventually becoming impervious to influences from "below." To perpetuate the status quo, this leadership cadre generally selects new leaders, who share the same personal qualities and self-interests. As a result, a united, informal group tends to form around these leaders and gradually they develop values at odds with others in the organization. Their different social positions shape their outlooks, as critics ranging from Jefferson to Mao to Milovan Djilas (1957) have noted. Because this leadership is well organized and has nearly exclusive access to vital resources—information, specialized knowledge, communications, and money—those in leadership positions tend to keep power. After time has passed, those in power establish their "legitimacy" as organizational leaders and can claim to represent the organization. Based on your experience, is Michels correct?

Problems Produced by Traditional Views of Leadership

In addition to Michels's critique, other observers have pointed out a number of problems created by the application of traditional views of leadership. First, the goals of an elite leadership cohort often shift from the pursuit of the best interests of the organization (and the people it serves) to the preservation of their power and influence. This reduces their ability to alter their behavior in response to changes and new levels of risk within the **"organizational set"** or to adjust to a news risk/reward calculus. Consequently, this style of leadership may not adapt effectively to the organization's changing needs.

Second, there is a tendency of elite leaders to retreat into isolation. This diminishes their ability not only to respond to internal and external developments, but also reduces their ability to mobilize staff members or constituents on behalf of social change efforts.

Third, traditional leadership models tend to create succession issues. What Weber (1946) termed the "**routinization of charisma**" occurs. That is, an organization tends to try to replicate leadership patterns to sustain the belief system under which it operates. As stated above, these organizations tend to search for a similarly charismatic leader or react to failed ones. Alternately, they may develop a succession process in which the outgoing leader or the "old guard" personally anoints a successor to the departing leader. This succession process often includes the transfer of the previous leader's charisma through organizational symbols, status, and titles. These tendencies create a serious problem for organizations that want to recruit or cultivate future leaders without producing or reproducing elites.

Alternative Views of Leadership

A more contemporary view (Alimo-Metcalfe et al., 2008; Alimo-Metcalfe & Alban-Metcalfe, 2005) distinguishes between leadership qualities and leadership behavior. Desirable leadership qualities include a desire to lead, honesty and integrity, self-confidence, cognitive ability, and knowledge of the field (Kirkpatrick & Locke, 1996, 1991). Leaders also display determination, sociability, humility, and will (Johnson, 2005). Transformational leaders inspire and stimulate the people with whom they work (Mary, 2005).

Most current researchers, however, conclude that personal qualities and values, and leadership competencies are necessary, but not sufficient for effective leadership. Some focus on the attainment of defined outcomes and the ability to influence others to achieve clear goals as a measure of leadership, while others emphasize the importance of behaviors and relationships. There is general agreement that leadership today is situational, not fixed, and is clearly tied to context.

More recently, other ideas about leadership have emerged—for example, that leaders should be representative of the communities they serve. Yet, what exactly does "representative" mean in a heterogeneous society? Does a leader have to be of the same race, gender, social class, age, or geographic origin as the people with whom she or he works? How do factors of multiple identities and intersectionality fit into this picture?

Another model, based partly on feminist concepts, regards a leader as someone who facilitates intragroup and intergroup cooperation and consensus.

In addition to the age-old debate—are leaders born or made?—there are substantial differences among scholars and professionals over what characteristics should be cultivated to develop leaders, the best means to identify and train leaders, what are appropriate leadership roles, and what types of leaders and styles of leadership are best suited to the changing practice environment.

A study by Carol Barner-Barry (1986) of children in playgrounds provides some creative insights on alternative forms of leadership, each of which is suitable for a specific situation. One style, which resembles the traditional model of a leader, she terms "directive–authoritative." These leaders regulate activities, distribute resources, resolve conflicts, determine rules, and decide who is in and who is out of the group. A second style of leadership is similar to that posited by some feminist scholars. These leaders, who adopt a "constituency-stroking" manner, give aid, protection, attention, and affection to others. They control the flow of information and decide how the group will sanction rule-breakers who shatter its unity.

Barner-Barry referred to a third form of behavior as "receiving." These individuals desire proximity to those who have power and influence. They seek permission before initiating action, and attempt to appease, imitate, and defer to those they acknowledge as leaders. Yet, through their seemingly passive behavior, they can sometimes influence the tone and the direction of the group.

Table 6.1 An Alternative View of Leadership (Barner-Barry, 1986)

Directive Behavior	Constituency Behavior	Receiving Behavior
• Regulation of activities	• Aid	• Proximity desired
• Inclusion or exclusion	• Giving information	• Attention solicited
• Conflict resolution	• Protection	• Imitation
• Distribution of resources	• Retaliation for another	• Appeasement
• Rule articulation	• Giving attention	• Permission solicited
• Rule interpretation	• Showing affection	• Deference
• Rule enforcement		
AUTHORITATIVE	STROKING	RECEIVING

There are several potential implications of this interesting study of children at play for the behavior of adults in organizations and communities that could revise our views on leadership. First, circumstances matter; in a given situation, *anyone* can be a leader. Second, in different contexts and cultures, leaders act differently and different styles of leadership are both more acceptable and more effective. Third, that leadership is not an attribute but a behavior—a relationship between a person and a specific situation that can change over time. This implies that even successful leaders may no longer have the "right stuff" if they do not adapt to changes in the environment. Fourth, that a profile of leadership traits among children reflects similar qualities to those we prefer in adults: maturity, intelligence, social competence, creativity, and coordination. Finally, there is no such thing as a "natural leader." Leadership combines interpersonal, political, analytical, and motivational skills. We can develop leaders, therefore, through training, work, and experience if organizations commit the time and resources required, and are willing to shed long-standing myths and prejudices.

IN-CLASS EXERCISE
REFLECTING ON OUR EXPERIENCE WITH LEADERSHIP

Introduction

Our personal and professional experiences and our interpretations of these experiences shape our personal views of leadership. In part, we make decisions on leadership based upon what we have learned from our families, schools, churches, direct encounters with leaders we have known, or from observations of distant "heroes." The following exercise is designed to reveal experiences that shaped your personal view of leadership and influence your current thinking about becoming a leader and/or improving your leadership skills.

Step 1 (5 Minutes)

Think about individuals whom you remember and revere. Think about individuals whom you consider leaders in your current life.

A. List three (3) people who have been important leaders in your past.

1.

2.

3.

B. List three (3) people whom you respect and value as leaders in your current life.

1.

2.

3.

Step 2 (5 Minutes)

A. For each person from your past, jot down the principal results of his or her leadership (successes and failures).

B. For each person whom you currently value as a leader, list the attributes that person reflects that make him or her an effective leader (i.e., the lessons that person taught you).

Step 3 (10 Minutes)

On the following chart, list those qualities and attitudes/behaviors that characterize the leaders you identified previously. Indicate in a few words what you learned from them that has been valuable in your professional and personal lives. After you fill in the chart look for the qualities and attitudes/behaviors that are common to several individuals.

Qualities	Attitudes/Behaviors	Lessons learned
Examples:		
Personal integrity	Constructive/Outspoken	Speak truth to power
1.		
2.		
3.		
4.		
5.		
6.		

Questions: What did you learn from this chart? How do you use what you have learned from these leaders in your daily life? (*Note the patterns in your answers.*)

Step 4 (20 Minutes): For Class Discussion

1. What similar and different insights on leadership did individuals have?
2. How did students interpret leadership qualities in different ways? Which qualities did students interpret differently?
3. What factors may influence these disagreements? What are their implications?

Gender, Culture, and Leadership

In a female-dominated profession such as social work, gender differences in leadership styles have significant implications. During the past century, women have played major leadership roles in virtually every part of the social welfare field, although men have dominated leadership positions in social service agencies, policy organizations, and educational institutions (Stotzer & Tropman, 2006; Rank & Hutchison, 2000; Chambers, 1986). Although it is important to avoid overgeneralizations about women as leaders, studies have found that, in general, women tend to be more transformational and engage in more contingent reward behaviors (Eagly & Johannesen-Schmidt, 2001), team work, and consensus-building (Cheung & Halpern, 2010). They are also more likely to use democratic styles in decision making and apply relationship-oriented skills. The effectiveness of this leadership style depends on the domain. That is why it is important for an organization to select a leader whose qualities and values match its needs at a specific stage of its life cycle and in a specific context.

Too often, organizations respond to leadership changes in one of two unproductive ways. If they have been fortunate to have an effective leader for a long time, they try to "clone" this leader in their search for a replacement when the leader retires or accepts another position. Conversely, if they have endured a leadership crisis, or if major problems emerged during a leader's tenure, they may seek to hire someone with the diametrically opposite qualities of his or her predecessor. Neither approach is effective. Organizations need to assess the current context and future horizon carefully and select a leader whose attributes are best suited to the challenges that exist and may emerge in their internal and external environments. This process takes time but, based on the author's experience, is far more likely to produce successful results (Austin & Gilmore, 1993).

In our increasingly diverse society and interconnected world, cultural differences are another important variable in shaping leadership behaviors. A recent GLOBE study (Waldman et al., 2006) found six types of leadership behaviors around the world: (1) charismatic/value-based leadership; (2) team-oriented leadership; (3) participative leadership; (4) humane-oriented leadership; (5) autonomous leadership; and (6) self-protective leadership. Despite these considerable stylistic differences, the same study determined that across all cultures desirable leadership traits included:

- trustworthiness, fairness, and honesty;
- optimism, dynamism, and confidence;
- foresight, motivation, and dependability;
- intelligence and decisiveness; and
- skills in communication, administration, planning, team building, problem solving, and coordination.

The author's research (Reisch, 2012c), conducted through 20 oral histories of a diverse group of leaders in the human services and in-depth interviews with 100 human service professionals who were self-identified activists, provides some contemporary insights into the nature of leadership in the contemporary social welfare field. The study found particularly striking distinctions between men and women, and persons of color and Whites.

The sample in the oral histories was 45% male and 55% female. One quarter of the sample consisted of persons of color. Subjects ranged in age from their 40s to their 80s. (Two of them are now deceased.) Nearly 90% of the subjects grew up in poor, working class, or lower-middle-class families in diverse geographic regions. Three people were immigrants and two were the children of immigrants. The interview sample (N = 100) was 41% male and 59% female. Approximately one fifth of those interviewed were persons of color and nearly 75% came from poor, working class, or lower middle class backgrounds. They ranged in age from their late 20s to their 80s, and grew up in all regions of the United States.

A near universal response was that exposure to diversity in childhood and young adulthood was a critical influence on the values and behavior of future leaders and activists. Even conservative parents with little formal education provided support and inspiration. One well-established leader remarked, "My dad always let us believe we could do anything we want [although he] didn't graduate from high school until he was in his 40s and took night classes."

Family origins, combined with exposure to diversity in their communities and workplaces, and through their travels, also played a key role in shaping their values and career choices, and in building strength and optimism. Stated one respondent: "As far back as I can remember, I just had a sense that part of what we were on this earth to do was to help other people. Now I don't know if that came from my religious background … or whether … it was just something innate in my family." Classmates, friends, and colleagues from diverse backgrounds also helped respondents develop a clearer understanding of the effects of injustice and oppression and provided insights into the meaning of exclusion in a White-dominated society.

Those respondents who came from unstable nuclear families found support from other family members. This helped some of them rebel against family prejudices, such as anti-Semitism and racism, as this respondent indicated: "My family was very prejudiced in terms of the Jewish population and it just infuriated me. I don't know what it was or why, but I suspect where I got my sustenance and where I heard the other side." Recent research by other scholars supports these findings (Guerin et al., 2011; Li, Arvey, & Song, 2011).

Family background, personal and professional experiences, and the ongoing influence of mentors were particularly important for women and persons of color in shaping their values, goals, and self-confidence. Their mentors included family members, professors, politicians, and radicals such as the Puerto Rican revolutionary Lolita LeBron and social work educator Bertha Capen Reynolds. Some of their family members who played a mentoring role were also active in social and political change efforts. One leader's grandmother "helped Malcolm X set up his first trip to the Middle East [and] led the first demonstration at the U.N." The mother of another respondent "was involved in political organizing in Chicago. … She used to tell me stories about going into the Black community and not being afraid … and going to protests and organizing things."

Changes in the nation's political and cultural environment, such as the social movements of the past several decades and the introduction of Affirmative Action, played a critical role in determining the leadership opportunities that emerged, particularly for women and persons of color. On the other hand, progress has slowed during the past decade due to the conservative political climate, which has implications for future leadership development. These changes underscore the continuing importance of policy advocacy and of the need to adapt our understanding of leadership and our selection of leaders to the evolving cultural context. The expectations of leadership and the skills required have also changed substantially during the past two generations—reflecting changes in the political-economic environment, the nation's communities, and organizational cultures. These changes are particularly apparent in the nonprofit sector. In sum, leadership development correlates with appropriate "matching" of people's abilities to the environmental "set" and the specific issues organizations are addressing.

The leaders interviewed were not, however, passive recipients of changes in their environment, regardless of the era in which they reached personal and professional maturity. Virtually all of them were, in some fashion, involved in social and political action. They participated in anti-war protests, the civil rights movement, local politics, and state-level policy advocacy. They engaged in action research on issues such as prisons, poverty, and juvenile justice. Some of them commented on how international experiences were particularly influential. One mentioned acquiring "a growing realization of global interdependence and awareness of radicalism as a worldwide movement."

Many of those interviewed remarked on the risks involved in taking political positions and in becoming a leader. They stressed the importance of risk taking to create changes in the policies and services that affect vulnerable populations. A number reported that they experienced persecution and professional marginalization for their political beliefs. One remarked, "I think … a lot of people [were] very reluctant to take chances because there was [and is] a price to be paid." Another made the sardonic comment: "My political views have resulted in some difficulties, mostly minor, although one was job loss, and some were very amusing."

Despite their significant accomplishments, those interviewed were modest about their contributions and had collective rather than individualistic conceptions of leadership. They believed in maintaining solidarity with colleagues inside and outside their organizations. They also emphasized the importance of ongoing education of themselves and those they supervised. One expressed this perspective succinctly: "I don't have a need to be the person in charge or in power." On a more personal note, they emphasized the importance of ongoing support from families and friends in maintaining work-life balance and enabling them to engage in long-term struggles. One prominent administrator said she was fortunate to be "married to someone who understands what it's about and who's willing to pick up your slack."

In sum, these interviews emphasize the importance of *history and context* in defining the nature and critical characteristics of leaders. Respondents universally questioned the validity of a "one size fits all" model of leadership. They emphasized the need for diverse methods of education, recruitment, and training in defining and creative "effective" leaders for the future.

They believed that every person can become a leader. In their view, leadership consisted of the ability to create positive changes in the absence of a crisis and without generating other problems. Leaders stimulate dissatisfaction among their constituents and work with them to find better solutions to the issues that affect their lives. They do this by generating excitement around new strategic directions, by speaking truth to power, by using humor effectively, and by emphasizing and building upon the strengths of the people with whom they work.

REFLECTION EXERCISE

1. Do these findings match your experience?
2. What were the major influences in your life and career?
3. What risks have you taken in being a leader?

John Tropman (1997), a distinguished student and practitioner of organizational leadership, proposes several possible antidotes to the nation's leadership crisis that complement the respondents' suggestions just cited. He suggests that leaders instigate conversations on the purposes of social work, the social welfare system, and HSOs in today's environment. We should reinvent ourselves for a changing context by asking such questions as: Why are we here? What do we hope to achieve? This, he asserts, will legitimize our values, and our personal and career goals. It is equally important that we overcome our resistance to discuss the undiscussable and to express uncomfortable truths, particularly to those in positions of power.

In concluding this section, here is a "top 10" list of practice prescriptions for being a leader or working with leaders in a community or organizational setting:

KEY CONCEPT SUMMARY
TOP 10 PRESCRIPTIONS FOR LEADERSHIP

1. Know yourself and know the situation. Be aware of what people say and do *not* say.
2. Distinguish facts and your subjective feelings around them.
3. In meetings, be aware of how and when people expressed their ideas and opinions and also what was said.
4. Know the position of leaders in a particular setting: e.g., how they stand regarding the organization's values.
5. Carefully select the setting in which you engage with others. Make it comfortable or uncomfortable, depending on the circumstances.
6. Be aware of your prejudices—not merely about big issues (e.g., race, gender, sexual orientation) but also about questions of lifestyle, style of dress, and the formality or informality of people's behavior. Confront your prejudices honestly.

7. Set realistic objectives in both your work and relationships and derive satisfaction from limited accomplishments.
8. Raise questions about concrete, specific issues, not abstractions.
9. In groups, notice who listens when someone speaks, who responds to whom (and how), and where people sit.
10. Speak in a language that is natural and understandable. Tailor your message but not your personal style to the group. In other words: always be yourself.

IN-CLASS EXERCISE
ASSESSING YOUR PERSONAL LEADERSHIP STYLE

Introduction

For each item below, please indicate which of two alternative reactions would be most characteristic of you. Some alternatives may be equally characteristic of you or equally uncharacteristic. While this is a possibility, nevertheless choose the alternative that is relatively more characteristic of you. For each item, you will have five points that you may distribute in any of the following combinations.

	A	B
1. If you feel A is completely characteristic of your feelings and B is completely uncharacteristic, write a "5" on your answer sheet under A and a "0" under B, thus:	5	0
2. If A is considerably characteristic of your feelings and B is somewhat characteristic, write a "4" on your answer sheet under A and a "1" under B, thus:	4	1
3. If A is only slightly more characteristic of your feelings than B, write a "3" on your answer sheet under A and a "2" under B, thus:	3	2
4. Each of the above three combinations may be used in a different order; for example, if you feel B is slightly more characteristic of your feelings than A, write a "2" on your answer sheet under A and a "3" under B, thus:	2	3

and so on for A = 1, B = 4, or A = 0, B = 5.

Thus, there are six possible combinations for responding to the pair of alternatives presented to you with each inventory item. ***Use only whole numbers. Be sure the numbers you assign to each pair sum equal 5.*** In general, try to relate each situation in the inventory to your own feelings. Take as much time as you need to make a true and accurate response. Remember, ***there is no right or wrong answer.***

Used with permission.

1. a. ____ As a leader, I focus on raising the level of consciousness on the importance and value of designated outcomes for employees.

b. ____ As a leader, I focus on clarifying goals and roles for employees.

2. a. ____ As a leader, I structure work so that individuals feel a sense of purpose.

b. ____ As a leader, I structure work so that team effort and success are encouraged and rewarded.

3. a. ____ Task clarity is most important in determining effectiveness.

b. ____ Organizational mission is most important in determining effectiveness.

4. a. ____ I enjoy rewarding followers.

b. ____ I enjoy motivating followers.

5. a. ____ I pay attention to being a positive role model on the job.

b. ____ I pay attention to doing fair job-performance evaluations for employees.

6. a. ____ I tend to think long range on what might be.

b. ____ I tend to think short range and accomplish what is realistic.

7. a. ____ I communicate clearly on what employees need to do to get appropriate rewards from the job.

b. ____ I tend to work to change conditions in people's lives.

8. a. ____ I am oriented toward solving problems.

b. ____ I am oriented toward creativity.

9. a. ____ I am more likely to be passionate in presenting my view.

b. ____ I am more likely to be rational in presenting my view.

10. a. ____ A primary value I have is equal justice for all.

b. _____ A primary value I have is honesty in all dealings.

11. a. _____ I focus on how best to keep the system for which I am responsible running.

b. _____ I focus on new ways of doing things in the system for which I am responsible.

12. a. _____ I approach problems in a methodical manner.

b. _____ I approach problems in a speculative manner.

13. a. _____ I cause events to happen.

b. _____ I facilitate events.

14. a. _____ I tend to go with the tried and true.

b. _____ I tend to go with the new and experimental.

15. a. _____ I spend time making sure employees understand their jobs.

b. _____ I spend time making sure employees become excited about their jobs.

16. a. _____ I value the inspirational at work.

b. _____ I value the practical at work.

17. a. _____ I believe in large part that we determine our destiny.

b. _____ I believe in large part that our destiny is determined by factors larger than us.

18. a. _____ My everyday work process encourages and supports people to develop themselves to their fullest potential.

b. _____ My everyday work process is oriented toward giving people a clear sense of their responsibilities.

19. a. _____ I am more likely to have my head in the clouds than to become bogged down in detail.

b. _____ I am more likely to become bogged down in detail than to have my head in the clouds.

20. a. _____ I negotiate clear, attainable objectives with employees.

b. _____ I energize employees, providing them with hopes, dreams, and aspirations.

21. a. _____ I desire my employees to be reliable, detail-oriented workers.

b. _____ I desire my employees to look for new, creative ways of doing things.

Leadership Questionnaire Key

	Transformational Point(s)	Transactional Point(s)
1.	A ______	B ______
2.	B ______	A ______
3.	B ______	A ______
4.	B ______	A ______
5.	A ______	B ______
6.	A ______	B ______
7.	B ______	A ______
8.	B ______	A ______
9.	A ______	B ______
10.	A ______	B ______
11.	B ______	A ______
12.	B ______	A ______
13.	A ______	B ______
14.	B ______	A ______
15.	B ______	A ______
16.	A ______	B ______
17.	A ______	B ______
18.	A ______	B ______
19.	A ______	B ______
20.	B ______	A ______
21.	B ______	A ______
Totals	______	______ **Difference** ______

The Meaning of Power in Macro Social Work Practice

In most macro practice situations power is closely associated with leadership. As discussed in previous chapters, however, there are many definitions of power in the literature. Look at the definitions that follow and note their different emphases. What does each definition reveal about the author's view of power and its implications for practice in the real world?

- "The probability that one actor within a social relationship will be in a position to carry out his own will despite resistance" (Weber quoted in Mills, 1956).
- "The ability to enforce one's moral claims" (Gouldner, 1970).
- "The ability to act, to create change, and to influence others" (May, 1969).
- "A relationship in which one person or group is able to determine the action of another in the direction of the former's own ends" (Easton quoted in Parenti, 1978).
- "The ability to get what you want when you want it, despite the opposition of other people" (Hardcastle et al., 2011).
- "The ability to determine alternatives" (Bottomore, 1991).
- "The capacity to produce a change" (Baker Miller, 1987).
- "The ability to realize one's values in the world" (Homan, 2016).
- "The ability to recognize one's will even against the resistance of others." (Mondros & Wilson, 1994).

These different definitions reflect some common assumptions. First, that power implies the ability to act and to effect a change or, conversely, to prevent a change from occurring or to direct an inevitable change in a particular manner. Second, that in some way power involves control, domination, ascendancy, or influence. Third, that those who have power also possess the capacity to shape the agenda and, therefore, to limit the range of options over which people compete. A key issue that underscores all of these definitions is "what is the purpose of power?" As Martin Luther King Jr. said "Power is the ability to achieve a purpose. Whether or not it is good or bad depends upon the purpose" (quoted in Atlas, 2010).

Classroom Discussion: A Powerful Reflection on Power

> Power concedes nothing without demand. It never did and it never will. Find out just what people will submit to, and you have found the exact amount of injustice and wrong which will be imposed upon them; and these will continue until they are resisted with either words or blows or both. The limits of tyrants are prescribed by the endurance of those whom they oppress (Frederick Douglass, 1849, 2013).

Do you agree with Douglass? What are the implications of his view for practice?

The French scholar Michel Foucault (1995) analyzed how dominant cultural institutions have used power throughout history to control the human body based on gender, sex, and sexuality. Recent authors, such as Michele Alexander (2012), Kimberly Crenshaw (2010), and Ta-Nehisi Coates (2015), have used similar analyses to interpret the oppression of African Americans in the United States. This theme and its corollary, the importance of resistance to power, also resonates through the work of the Black Lives Matter movement.

Patricia Hill Collins expands this concept in her discussion of the various **domains of power** (2009). These include: (1) *Disciplinary* (knowledge of how organizations work). She argues that the inequities produced by organizational dynamics require resistance from within and without. (2) *Hegemonic* (use of culture, ideas, and ideology to absorb and thereby depoliticize oppressed groups' dissent). This can occur at multiple levels as means to rationalize unjust practices and institutions. In this domain, change requires consciousness-raising, the examination of underlying assumptions, the rediscovery of subjugated knowledge and history, and the introduction of new symbols and ways of thinking. (3) *Interpersonal* (everyday lived experiences, microaggressions, and inequities). These manifestations of power are systemic, recurrent, familiar, and usually unnoticed and unchallenged. Changing them requires consistent monitoring of transactions (e.g., microaggressions or instances of implicit bias) and creating relationships with people from different cultures (*see Chapter 4*) who can offer regular feedback and work together to uncover and eradicate discriminatory dynamics. (4) *Structural.* This refers to the interconnections among societal institutions that maintain an unequal and unjust distribution of resources and perpetuate social exclusion. Change in this area requires new laws, policies, and social practices.

From a different perspective, Freire (1971) regards **conscientization**—the process of attaining critical consciousness—as a source of power. This implies the importance of ongoing critical reflection on the relationship between theory and practice. According to Freire, people can acquire power through **praxis**, through understanding and analyzing their environments and circumstances. Engaging in praxis increases their capacity to act effectively and resist the forces that block action for social change.

In this regard, Wilson (1976) distinguishes between active power (its exercise) and power ability (its potential). (Think of the analogy of potential and kinetic energy in physics.) "Active power" defines the relationship between a need and a means to address. This produces a relationship characterized by influence and dependence. The degree of power can be determined by measuring these two factors. This interpretation of power is often associated with the application of force, influence, control, and domination.

Another important issue is whether one defines power as *power over* (coercion), or *power to* (influence). An additional issue is whether one views power as a finite commodity over which people compete, or whether it is a quality based on a relationship that people can expand and transform through cooperation and collective effort. The implications of each perspective on power for leadership in communities and organizations are profound because power dynamics shape most policy, community, and organizational decisions, and power inequities are a primary source of social and personal problems and societal oppression.

REFLECTION EXERCISE
DEFINING POWER AND ASSESSING ITS EFFECT ON PRACTICE

Please reflect upon the following questions:

1. How would you define power? How do your race, class, gender, ethnicity, sexual orientation, and religion shape your definition?
2. Why do you think power is an important concept? What do you regard as its significance for macro social work practice?
3. In what ways do you see the overt use and effect of power in the organizations and communities in which you work and live? In what ways do you see the covert use and effect of power?
4. Who are the constituents (or clients/consumers) of your field agency? In what ways are they economically oppressed, socially marginalized, and/or politically excluded?
5. What systems are working effectively or not working for the people your agency serves? How do these systems oppress, exploit, exclude, and underserve this population, intentionally or unintentionally?
6. Who defines the nature and extent of the problems that your field placement seeks to address? To what extent do the agency's clients or constituents play a role?
7. Based on how the organization defines people's problems, what does the organization regard as the primary sources of the problem(s)?
8. Who determines the ways in which your field placement intervenes to address these problems? To what extent do the agency's clients or constituents play a role?
9. If your agency's clients or constituents thought some program or intervention was ineffective or inappropriate, how would they express their views? To what extent could they influence the agency to change?
10. Who has formal power in your organization? Who has informal power?
11. What is the nature of "politics" in your organization? What are some examples?
12. Based on your initial experiences, do you believe you have any power in your organization? If yes, in what ways? If not, why?

In the realm of politics, power refers to the right to command and control the actions of others through lawful instruments of government. Political power often leads to political influence—i.e., the ability to affect the nature of political decisions. Finally, political process refers to the means by which political influence shapes the distribution of resources (e.g., in a society or community).

Some further questions to consider:

1. Is power purposeful (constructive) or innate?
2. What forms does power take?
3. How do you know when someone exercises power?

French and Raven (1968) identify the various types of power that exist in organizations and communities, and their diverse sources. Each type of power has different implications for the ability of those who possess it to produce community, organizational, or social change.

Table 6.2 French and Raven's Classifications of Power

Type of Power	Source of Power
Reward	Control over resources
Referent	Status, organizational role
Coercive	Ability to punish or sanction
Expert	Ability to control discourse
Legitimate	Authority to make decisions; place in the organizational or community hierarchy
Information	Knowledge, contacts
Personal	Charisma, strength, network connections
Spiritual	Faith, confidence

As the above conceptions of power demonstrate, there is considerable difference between viewing the concept of power as something we *have*, as opposed to something we *do*. There is also a distinction between having power *over* someone (or something) and creating power *with* someone else. Patricia Hill Collins (2009) captures the complexity of power in her discussion of the distinct domains of power that exist. Ironically, in many discussions of power its subjective aspect is often unacknowledged. Because all forms of power—personal, collective, and institutional—involve a relationship between people, the perception of control influences the power dynamics of a particular situation as much as the actual distribution of power.

Homan (2016) applies these perspectives on power specifically to their sources at the personal, community, and organizational levels. Possession and access to information and to critical internal and external communication systems (e.g., media) is a major source of power. This concept of power also includes the extent of bonding social capital (e.g., among community residents or colleagues, neighborhood families, and other key constituencies) and bridging social capital (e.g., professional and political networks) a group, organization, or community possesses. Another key source of power is more tangible—access to vital resources, including money, people and their talents, other critical goods, and necessary services.

Knowledge is another important source of power in organizations and communities. This includes knowledge of the organization or community's history, culture, norms, customs, social relationships, and traditions; knowledge of relevant policies that affect strategic options; and various forms of substantive expertise (e.g., knowledge about particular issues, communication or resource development skills). A final source of knowledge is collective in nature. It includes the energy and commitment of community residents, staff members, clients, and constituents and their ability to mobilize to take legal or illegal action (such as a strike or civil unrest) or apply social pressure.

Because power often reflects the relationship between dominant and oppressed or subordinate groups, it is particularly important to understand the different ways each group relates to the realities of power. In general, dominant groups define the parameters of action in an organization, community, or society and determine what is appropriate or legitimate. They believe that they alone are capable of producing needed changes, reflecting their self-image of superiority, control, confidence, and correctness. They tend to ignore the interests or views of others and do not acknowledge the structural and psychological constraints that affect them. They operate on the assumption that their view of reality is the only view, that this view is clear to everyone, and that those who do not share this view are either misinformed or misguided.

Dominant groups in Western society also tend to define social problems in personal terms and focus on issues primarily as they affect individuals. This creates the tendency to become judgmental of others' failures or missteps. When they consider other groups, they tend to "exoticize" or "essentialize" them (Said, 2003; Young, 2011). They neither recognize their privilege nor trust others' ability, especially as leaders.

Oppressed individuals or groups frequently view things from a collective perspective. They tend to look at their problems through both a historical lens and also in their contemporary context. To survive, they need to be "bicultural" in outlook and behavior.

When oppressed or subordinate groups disagree, however, dominant groups often regard these protests, however mild, as disruptive. This reinforces the former's self-image of inferiority or incompetence. It heightens their sense of insecurity, vulnerability, defensiveness, and low self-esteem. It increases the likelihood that these groups will withhold their opinions and feelings in the future, and be evasive when asked to express them.

To a different extent, social workers possess all these types of power in their relationships with clients and constituents yet often lack this power in relationship to the institutions on which they are dependent for resources and sanction. In addition, the type of power one possesses in a practice setting reveals little about the amount of power or its potential effect. This is particularly significant for social workers who are increasingly themselves in a power-dependent position. The degree of control social workers have over strategic resources and their ability to resolve uncertainties in community, organizational, and societal environments significantly affect the extent to which social workers possess or lack power.

Particularly in today's turbulent and hyper-partisan context, the powerlessness of workers often results from two persistent "deficits." One is that the forces inside and outside the organizations in which we work largely possess a monopoly of the strategic resources we require. The second is that to a considerable extent, these external forces do not share our values or those of the people with whom we work. In addition, powerful external entities decide how to resolve environmental uncertainties in ways social workers often cannot anticipate because the "rules" are ambiguous, unstated, or constantly changing. Recent examples of this phenomenon include the implementation of welfare reform, and current uncertainties regarding immigration policy and the future of the Affordable Care Act.

This situation of powerlessness creates an inevitable paradox for social workers who are engaged in efforts to produce institutional, community, or societal change. To create positive change we must challenge the same power structures upon which we are dependent for critical resources and sanction. Yet, we must make these challenges from a base that lacks both adequate resources and traditional forms of power. The resolution of this dilemma will be a major focus of macro social work practice in the years ahead.

IN-CLASS EXERCISE
THE MEANING OF POWER IN MACRO SOCIAL WORK PRACTICE

Part I

Think about a situation in which you possessed power.

1. How did you become aware of the power you possessed?
2. What did it feel like to have power?
3. What were the sources of your power in that particular situation?
4. What—if anything—was different about that situation from others in which you lacked power?
5. How did you use the power you possessed in that situation?
6. How did it feel to use the power in the way you did?
7. What—if anything—was the lasting effect of your use of power? What did it teach you about power and its use?

Part II

Think about a situation in which you lacked power.

1. How did you become aware of your lack of power (be as specific as possible)?
2. What were the effects (psychological and behavioral) of being powerless?
3. What were the causes of your powerlessness in that particular situation? To what extent were they "situation specific" (i.e., was it an unusual situation)? To what extent were the causes of your powerlessness systemic?
4. In what ways—if any—did the experience of powerlessness have a lasting effect?

Part III

[Divide students into small groups for this portion of the exercise.] You are working —as part of a group of social work students—with one of the following populations on a community effort whose goals include public education, group empowerment, and the enhancement of services:

- individuals experiencing homelessness;
- women who have experienced domestic violence;
- TANF recipients;
- elderly residents of nursing homes;
- incarcerated youth; and
- unemployed industrial workers.

Classroom Discussion

Think about your role in working with this population and in working with the other students in your group—**NOT** about the specific strategies/tactics that you might employ in this particular social/political action effort.

1. In what ways would you anticipate issues of power and privilege might emerge:
   - With members of the particular population with whom you are working?
   - Within your group (of students)?
2. How might these issues affect intragroup and intergroup dynamics?
3. What steps might you take to reduce the negative effects of imbalances of power and privilege?

Power, Leadership, and Macro Social Work Practice

For many social workers and social work students, power often has negative connotations ("power corrupts"), although it is an essential component of all social work practice, particularly macro practice (Brodkin, 2010). Ironically, the concept of "empowerment" has primarily positive connotations. How can we explain this contradiction? As discussed previously, in most traditional definitions power is associated with force, coercion, influence, control, and domination. Many people believe that those who have power use it solely to exploit others. Conversely, those who fear power most also believe they lack power and often deny the existence of their own power. This compounds their concerns that leaders frequently use power in negative and abusive ways.

In contrast, as discussed in Chapter 4, social workers generally regard empowerment as a step toward community liberation, individual self-determination, and human agency. It reflects a combination of personal power—how individuals can achieve their goals—and social power—power exercised collectively to obtain what a group needs or values, often through efforts to influence key decision makers, particularly in the political arena, the private sector, and the media (Solomon, 1976; Simon, 1990; Gutierrez, Parsons, & Cox, 1998).

Overcoming powerlessness through collective action also requires challenging dominant, often taken-for-granted worldviews (Hill Collins, 2009). The power of media and other cultural institutions frequently combines with the social and physical isolation of marginalized and excluded communities (Massey & Denton, 1993) to compound their sense of powerlessness. This isolation contributes to their inability to take action to alter their circumstances or even to believe that such action is possible.

In this context, empowerment, therefore, is the process by which oppressed populations acquire the tools to overcome the multiple dimensions of their powerlessness and its consequences. A major component of this process is the development of critical consciousness, what Freire terms the ability to "name the world" and thereby transform themselves from objects acted upon to subjects who can effect change in their environments. This heightened consciousness includes the ability to identify the sources of injustice that afflict their communities—to recognize that these problems are neither natural nor inevitable and that change is possible. It also requires the creation of group identity and solidarity, the acquisition of new or enhanced skills and knowledge, and the ability to take risks and initiate the process of change. As in practice with individuals, survivors of domestic violence, for example, this is often the most difficult step of all and one in which social workers can play a key role.

In the social welfare field, power issues arise from two primary elements: need (for a service, information, material resources, access) and means (money, authority, knowledge, political access and influence). The relationship between need and means transforms those who lack or possess resources into two opposing forces, defined by their dependence and influence through the dynamic of "active power," the most easily recognized form of power. According to this perspective, it is possible, therefore, to assess the extent of an individual, group, or organization's power by measuring either its influence or dependence.

Pressures on social workers and their clients and constituents emerge from similar sources in the political-economic and cultural environment. As the private sector and elites have increasingly assumed responsibility for the definition and provision of human needs, they have also shaped the values that underlie these efforts and fostered widespread powerlessness, particularly within oppressed and marginalized communities. A peculiar contradiction emerges today, however, between the exaltation of individualism and private initiative and the power-dependent position in which many individuals and communities find themselves. Because of their dependency, individuals can appear to exercise initiative only if they act in accordance with the values and goals of power-dominant institutions. This is the result of what Gramsci (1992) termed "cultural hegemony."

One consequence of this phenomenon is that the relationship between people and the institutions upon which they rely for survival and well-being—for income support, nutritional assistance, housing, and health care, for example—has become increasingly depersonalized. More and more, the connection is not based on human interaction or the capacity to create viable and meaningful relationships or social structures. Rather, it reflects the growing power imbalance in society and the shift of power within the social welfare system away from social workers and the people with whom they work (Schram, Soss, Fording, & Schram, 2011; McDonald & Reisch, 2008).

An overarching goal of macro social work practice is to reverse this process of disempowerment. Macro social workers strive to replace the reality of dependency and the perception of helplessness and powerlessness with a sense of individual and collective competence. They believe it is important to reassert the dignity and worth of all people and the institutions they create, and to affirm people's capacity to respond effectively to complex and dynamic environmental conditions. These goals rest upon two underlying assumptions: (1) that the conditions of social workers and those with whom we work are interdependent. Workers and clients will be able to improve these conditions only if they work together; and (2) that power is a core concept of social work practice that bridges individual behavior, social role performance, and organizational-institutional functioning. Empowerment, therefore, is both a social-psychological and political-economic phenomenon (Solomon, 1976) that only exists either in the context in which vital resources are distributed or the social interactions that occur in deciding how organizations and communities will distribute these resources. It is a concept that connects the situation of workers and clients/constituents and provides the basis for bridging micro and macro practice (Rothman & Mizrahi, 2014; McBeath, 2017).

In this sense, power involves a purposeful act closely linked to values. It is relational, not autonomous. It is not the same thing as dominance. It reflects the distinction between power over and power to. In different circumstances, different individuals or groups possess more or less power. People exercise power using different styles; in part this depends on the type of power they possess, the source of that power, and their self-perception and the perception of others on the power dynamics of a situation (whether it is public or private, what constitutes appropriate use of power, etc.).

Power and Social Action/Social Change Organizations

A major goal of social action organizations is the accumulation and effective use of power (Alinsky, 1971). Two major sources of organizational power are the number of people who support its goals and the nature of its organizational structure. This perspective on power assumes that power inequities are a primary source of personal and social problems and the foundation of oppression and marginalization. It also assumes that power dynamics shape most organizational, community, and public policy decisions. It implies that power involves interpersonal and intergroup relationships and that the possession of power is essential to generate support, mobilize people, and overcome opposition. Finally, it distinguishes between actual power and the feeling of being powerful.

Advocacy is the most significant power inequity intervention by social workers to help members of disadvantaged groups obtain resources and access to decision-making authorities. Locating the power resources of those involved in community or political decision-making processes is generally the first step in identifying the "target" for advocacy and/or other action tactics.

Advocates can use power in numerous ways. They can help individuals and groups obtain critical resources by arguing on behalf of a disadvantaged group or community. They can teach people to advocate for themselves. They can lobby for legislative, judicial, or administrative policy changes or participate in electoral politics to influence social change. (*See chapters 12, 13, and 14 for further discussion of advocacy.*)

Power and Empowerment

Rubin and Rubin (1986) define empowerment in terms of the self-efficacy awareness that people acquire when they recognize their ability to solve their own problems and their right to protest the injustices that affect their lives. In this sense, empowerment is a concept that links the personal and political. In macro social work practice, the key issues in the empowerment process are control over the life of the community or organization, gaining the ability to make larger political decisions, and acquiring increased skills and confidence. Central to this is the willingness to challenge formal authority and escape dependency. These changes, however, can only occur gradually. They require patience and persistence on the part of social workers and the people with whom we work.

Disempowerment frequently occurs because people learn inefficacy through societal structures, cultural institutions and norms, and the socialization processes to which they are exposed. As a result, they tend to shift the blame for their problems to themselves. One role for leaders and organizers in the empowerment process, therefore, is to reduce the shame that keeps people from expressing their needs or working together to fight for their collective interests. A key component is the promotion of capacity building for individuals and groups.

There are three steps in capacity building. The first is in the mind: consciousness-raising through which individuals begin to see the connections between solutions to their personal problems and broader social and political causes. The second is more action-oriented: self-assertion of their individual and group interests. The third, often referred to as "bootstrapping," is the process by which small, collective victories lead to a willingness and ability to challenge larger problems. A major role of leaders, therefore, is to encourage collective action and link it to each participant's needs and personal growth (Austin et al., 2011).

As stated previously, a key issue in the empowerment process is control—both actual control and the perception of control. Factors that influence control include the structural biases within many systems, the obscurity of many power relationships, and the belief that the distribution of power in most situations is a "zero-sum" game. One can assess the extent of control possessed by a group or organization by determining who sets its goals, who takes action to achieve these goals, who benefits from these actions, and who evaluates the success of these actions?

Homan (2016) argues persuasively that we cannot promote change without using power. Following Weber (1946), he views power as "the ability to make decisions and to implement them" (p. 202). In sum, these definitions of power assume that power involves a relationship between people and that the possession and perception of power is essential to arouse support, mobilize constituents, and overcome organized opposition.

Undeveloped Sources of Relational Power

Lappe and DuBois (1994) identify a wide range of nontraditional resources that can increase individual or group power. Many of these resources involve personal qualities that social workers already possess or can cultivate with some effort. They include:

1. Active listening skills.
2. Ability to analyze the self-interest and respective power positions of individuals, groups, and institutions with which you are negotiating.
3. Knowledge of existing policy options and the process by which governments choose among them.

4. Disciplined behavior in critical, conflict-oriented settings.
5. Vision—the ability to articulate alternatives to existing problems and not just complaints.
6. The ability to bring together groups with different experiences and perspectives.
7. The ability to develop innovative ideas to solve long-standing problems.
8. Persistence (The author's research on advocacy organizations [1987, 1990] and his professional experience confirm the importance of consistent and constant effort over time in producing effective advocacy.)
9. Appropriate use of humor to defuse tense situations and to help people overcome fear
10. Courage—the ability to take risks and "speak truth to power" when necessary.
11. The ability to be self-critical and self-effacing, particularly when working with diverse populations. These are important components of cultural humility.
12. Organization—spontaneity is good, but usually cannot sustain organizational momentum.

Power, Leadership, and Human Service Organizations

Within HSOs, power is the means by which individuals, groups, and institutions can exert influence on others to establish organizational priorities, determine the distribution of finite resources, and define appropriate means to achieve organizational goals. A number of factors facilitate the constructive exercise of power in organizations. These include the organization's commitment to its workers. Organizations can demonstrate this commitment concretely through decent salaries and benefits, the introduction of work-life policies, and the expansion of staff development and educational opportunities. Organizations can also express this goal intangibly through greater staff participation in decision making, more staff autonomy and responsibility for defining work tasks, increased encouragement and support from supervisors and peers, and the presence of a supportive workplace environment, such as the physical appearance of the work area and adequate support resources (Cohen & Austin, 1997).

Even in the best-intentioned HSOs, several factors can hinder the effective exercise of power. These include administrative expectations, particularly regarding the efficient use of resources and organizational accountability; the quality of supervisory relationships; and the expectations of agency clients or constituents. Social workers may also be reluctant to acknowledge the role that intraorganizational and inter-organizational politics plays in their agencies (Hasenfeld, 2010). Struggles over scarce resources, personal conflicts, and competition for power, status, and leadership sometimes produce self-serving and manipulative behavior by individuals and groups to promote their self-interests at the expense of others, and even the goals of the organization itself. Politics can also be used to build personal stature, control access to information, conceal real intentions, and build (or destroy) coalitions.

Other factors that influence the exercise of power include the nature of work tasks within an organization, the availability of resources to complete these tasks, and the community context in which the HSO delivers its services. The latter is important because community attitudes toward the HSO and social work in general shape the power dynamics between the organization and residents of the surrounding area. For HSOs, therefore, community empowerment is a powerful approach that encourages social workers to view community residents as full-partnered participants, stakeholders, collaborators, and consumers in a community change effort (McNulty, 1999; Craig & Mayo, 1995; Hanna & Robinson, 1994).

REFLECTION EXERCISE
POWER IN ORGANIZATIONS

1. Who has power in the organization in which you work or have worked?
2. For what purposes do individuals who possess power exercise it?
3. What types of power do they employ most frequently?
4. How do these individuals use their power? In an autocratic manner, democratically, or *laissez-faire*? What are the consequences?
5. What is the relationship between the organization's structure and the exercise of power?
6. What is the relationship between the organization's culture and the exercise of power? (*See Chapter 4.*)

Leadership Development in HSOs

Leadership development is one of the primary objectives of macro practice in both communities and organizations. Social workers closely link leadership development to the values of self-determination, empowerment, and democratic participation. It is part of a broader strategy to enable people to take responsibility for their own problems and to initiate collective efforts on their own behalf. A fundamental question for macro social workers, therefore, is how can the executives of HSOs or community organizers promote leadership development among their staff members, clients, and constituents?

IN-CLASS EXERCISE
THE MEANING OF LEADERSHIP AND LEADERSHIP DEVELOPMENT

Before addressing the specific steps involved in leadership development, it is important to answer some seemingly simple, but fundamental, questions:

1. What do we mean by "leadership"? What are the preferred qualities and functions of leadership?
2. What characteristics are preferred in a leader? What types of people make the best leaders?
3. Is there a difference between leaders and leadership? If so, what causes our problems with particular leaders if we recognize the importance of leadership?
4. What makes people decide to become leaders? Do specific types of people become specific types of leaders? Do certain cultures produce certain types of leaders? What are the implications of these differences for the development of leadership in a multicultural society?
5. What do we mean by leadership *development*?
6. How does the process of leadership development influence the type of leaders and organizations produced?

Alternative Views of Leadership Development

In today's tumultuous environment, the presence of strong, visible leaders represents a critical counterforce to the various forms of opposition organizations confront in attempting to achieve their goals. Given emerging demographic and cultural dynamics, it is critical that organizations learn how to identify and develop a new cadre of leaders who blend a task and process orientation and reflect the demographic and cultural diversity of the people with whom we work. This approach reflects an underlying assumption that different types of leaders are most effective in different circumstances. For example, task-oriented leaders are most effective in the amorphous early stages of organizational development. Process-oriented leaders are most effective in the "middle stage" when most organizations flounder due to uncertainty.

More than ever, today's emerging leaders need to be able to deal with personality conflicts and the hidden agendas of staff members and allies, with disruptive people or factions even without their own organizations, and with funding and political crises that disrupt organizational functioning. This view of leadership regards it not as an attribute but a behavior. Behavior is a relationship between a personality and the situation in which that personality finds itself. This relationship can change over time.

Si Kahn (2010), an experienced organizer, defines a leader as someone who helps people determine the direction they want to go and facilitates their movement in that direction. Another veteran organizer, Shel Trapp (1976), defined a leader as someone who already represents a constituency or possesses the ability to develop a constituency focused on a particular issue. These definitions, however, beg the age-old question: Are leaders born or can organizations develop them? What do we really mean by leadership development?

Steve Burghardt (2013) argues that leadership development is not a hallowed goal, but a political process by which people change themselves and their relationships with the world. Unfortunately, many organizations go about the process in the wrong way. Some attempt to change the situation of the organization (its funding base, goals, auspices) to the exclusion of leadership development. Others strive to develop leaders who possess concrete organizational skills but lack critical consciousness. Burghardt asserts that the cultivation of critical consciousness is essential. It can be accomplished through linking personal and political issues and attributes during the process of leadership development, viewing history as a change process in which people take action (as subjects) and are not acted upon, and engaging in multidirectional dialogue that allows people, in Freire's memorable phrase, to "name the world."

In fact, Freire (1971) regards leadership development as a process of education and humanization, a potentially emancipatory or liberating process. How the process is carried out contributes to whether organizations replicate (socially reproduce) existing patterns of leadership and social structure or replace them with more egalitarian, democratic, and justice-centered alternatives.

Kahn believes that leaders are not born, but that organizations can nurture the emergence of leaders through training, work, and experience. The developmental process needs to start small and includes the following steps:

- broadening individuals' experiences within and outside the organization;
- adding specific skills (e.g., communication, political, management) gradually, starting with what individuals know best;
- expanding responsibilities and varying skills through experiences;
- using self-analysis and exercises to sharpen analytic ability and praxis; and
- allowing potential leaders to learn how to handle the stress of leadership, and the physical, intellectual, and emotional demands of the work.

This approach recognizes that leaders are real people with jobs, families, personal needs, and obligations beyond the organization in which they are working. The key goal is to develop survival skills to sustain effective leadership within the organization. (*See Epilogue for a brief discussion of these issues.*)

Desirable Leadership Skills and Styles in Diverse Organizations and Communities

Leadership skills include "hard skills"—the ability to develop coherent strategies, analyze policies, budgets, and the political situation, and write coherent proposals—and "soft skills"—effectiveness in interpersonal communication, the ability to run meetings, and to motivate staff members. Effective leadership styles vary depending on one's role in the organization. Sometimes, a leader needs to serve as an enabler or catalyst for actions taken by others. At other times, she or he broker compromise solutions among staff members or coalition partners. A leader may alternately be a teacher in a mentoring role, or a learner when engaging in dialogue with staffers, clients, or constituents. In all circumstances, a leader must be a role model to those with whom she or he works, someone who helps people develop critical consciousness through a dialogic process.

By such active work and sharing of oneself, a leader can balance the attainment of group or organizational goals (tasks) with the development of cooperative problem-solving skills (process). By sharing decision making and through active listening, a leader can help people take responsibility for their own futures. Finally, by breaking down the artificial dichotomy between leaders and followers, an effective leader can redefine the situation through reciprocal sharing of analytic and task roles.

Figure 6.2 demonstrates how different types of leadership produce different organizational cultures and management styles in HSOs.

Figure 6.2 Management Styles

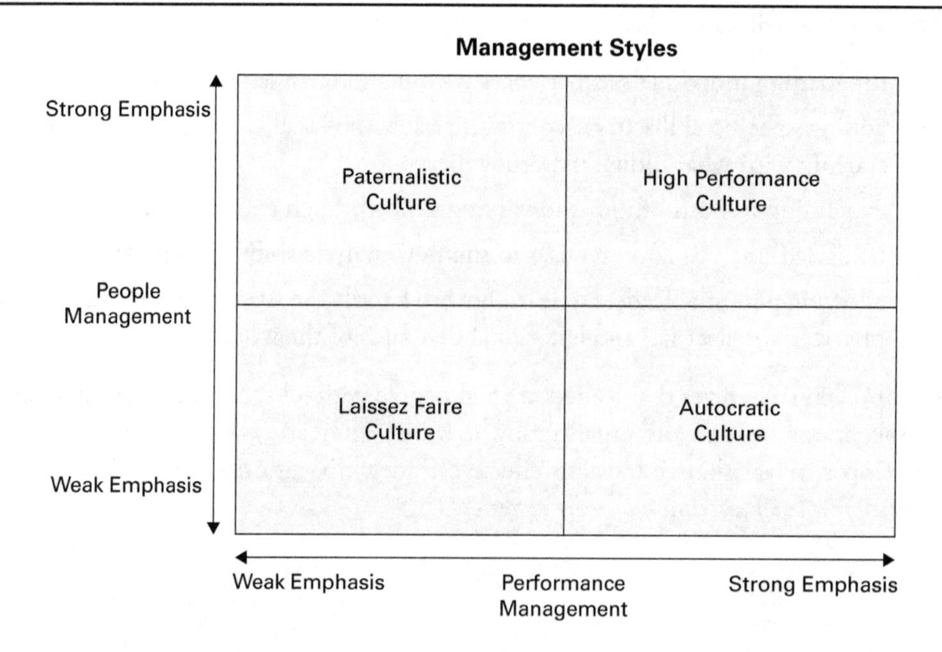

Summary and Conclusion

This chapter discussed the critical issues of power and leadership in human service and social action organizations. It summarized and criticized traditional views of leadership and power and introduced several alternative perspectives on these concepts. It also discussed how to apply different forms of power and leadership in organizations and the important role of leadership development. Subsequent chapters will demonstrate the application of these concepts in both organizational and community practice.

END-OF-CHAPTER EXERCISE
LEADERSHIP AND DEMOCRACY IN HSOS

1. What is the leadership structure of the organization in which you work or have worked?
   - What does the agency's organizational chart reveal about its leadership structure?
   - What is not included in the organizational chart that would help you understand its leadership structure and organizational culture?
2. Who are the leaders in your organization? What is the prevailing leadership style in the organization? How do staff members respond to this leadership style? What qualities do the organization's leaders have in common?
3. What is the prevailing management style in the organization? Reflect on how the agency's leadership and management styles are similar and different.
4. What types of opportunities exist in your organization for staff members and clients to lead and to develop themselves as leaders? How does your organization facilitate and support such opportunities? How could it?
5. Does your agency value the development of critical consciousness among staff members and clients? How do you know?

   a. How does your organization help its staff members and clients to develop critical consciousness? How might it?

   b. How might a more critically conscious constituency help your agency to achieve its mission and vision?

   c. How does your organization promote democracy (e.g., harm reduction, the service/advocacy dialectic, leveling the structure, participatory budgeting)? How might it?

   d. How do administrators manage staff members and volunteers? Is leadership development a core value of the organization? How are decisions made and problems solved? Is the process collaborative or individual?

END-OF-CHAPTER EXERCISE
CONDUCTING AN ORGANIZATIONAL LEADERSHIP AUDIT

To what degree:

1. _____ Do leaders in your organization regularly interact with staff members ("manage by walking around," attend meetings)?

2. _____ Do leaders project a positive attitude (via trust and respect, for example) toward staff members?

3. _____ Does your organization have clearly defined values that are well known, well understood, and well accepted by members?

4. _____ Do leaders help develop and articulate an inspiring and shared vision, purpose, and mission for the agency that drives strategy and programs?

5. _____ Do leaders in your organization use appropriate management styles that motivate you to achieve high performance?

6. _____ Do leaders articulate high ethical standards and ensure that they are maintained?

CHAPTER 7

Working With Diverse Groups in Macro Social Work Practice

If we are to achieve a richer culture, rich in contrasting values, we must recognize the whole gamut of human potentialities, and so weave a less arbitrary social fabric, one in which each diverse human gift will find a fitting place.

—**Margaret Mead**

Diversity—The art of thinking independently together.

—**Malcolm Forbes**

Introduction

For many social workers, meetings are the bane of their existence. A meeting can be an important tool, however, in enhancing practice in an organization and in promoting change efforts. Yet, many meetings are unproductive and, frankly, make poor use of practitioners' scarce and valuable time.

As so much of our professional life is spent in meetings, however, one of the critical skills that *all* social workers need to acquire is how to run a meeting effectively and how to contribute effectively to the work that occurs in meetings. In addition, as social workers progress in their careers, they will be increasingly required to interact with boards of directors, advisory boards, and commissions, either as organizational or community leaders or as key staffers. To help students develop these skills, this chapter includes the following material:

1. The purpose of meetings in organizations and communities
2. Factors that make meetings difficult or unproductive
3. The structure of a good meeting—planning an agenda
4. Tips to enhance the quality of meetings
5. Key roles in task-oriented groups and meetings
6. Developing "ground rules" and guiding principles for effective meetings
7. Ways to ensure effective communication in meetings, particularly in diverse organizations and communities
8. Skills to avoid meeting problems and skills in solving them when they occur
9. Types of agency boards and their functions
10. Responsibility of board members
11. Board/staff relationships: problems, opportunities, skills in negotiating them
12. Skills in developing relationships with external bodies (e.g., commissions, government agencies, legislative committees)

What Makes Meetings So Difficult?

For many people who work in organizations, meetings seem a waste of time, a distraction from more important work, and an arena for unproductive competition and conflict. Many of us have often fervently wished that the hours we spend in meetings would not count toward our allotted time on earth.

Yet, meetings are very important, and successful organizations use them effectively to advance their goals and objectives. Meetings can be a place where vital social interaction occurs; they can strengthen informal relationships and help channel potentially damaging conflicts into healthy directions. At meetings, participants often share or explain vital, complex information in a manner that eases staff members' anxieties about upcoming changes. Meetings can also be a setting in which staff members can air diverse perspectives on controversial subjects and apply insights from multiple viewpoints to solve vexing problems. These possible uses of meetings are particularly valuable in diverse organizations and communities.

Then why are so many meetings boring at best and fruitless or even counterproductive at worst? There are several possible reasons. Schools usually do not teach skills in planning and running meetings to aspiring professionals. Some human service workers hesitate to take charge, even in the relatively nonauthoritarian role of a facilitator. Motivating disinterested staff members and overcoming their resistance to participate in meetings is a considerable challenge, especially in large meetings with distinct status hierarchies and impersonal staff relationships.

There are other reasons meetings can be unsuccessful and frustrating. The absence of a clear agenda, distributed in sufficient time for participants to prepare, can lead attendees to wonder: "*Why* am I here? I put aside my more important work *for this*? How will I meet that critical deadline?" This is why the person responsible for calling and leading (or facilitating) the meeting should send a reminder to participants a week in advance (unless, of course, it is an emergency meeting called to address a crisis) with the date, time, and site of the meeting. The reminder should include the minutes of the last meeting (if it is a meeting of a committee or regularly scheduled group), supplementary materials (of reasonable length), and a clearly stated agenda. If there is a particularly important item on the agenda, the announcement should also state the purpose of the meeting and the decisions participants need to make.

Another reason that people dislike meetings is that they feel nothing of importance is ever accomplished, groups meet too frequently, and meetings are much too long. Staff members at meetings often convey a lot of information—most of which they could share by other, more efficient means—but there is little substantive discussion of difficult issues and the group makes few decisions. If organizational or group leaders want people to commit their time, energy, and talents to the work involved in meetings, it is critical that participants feel that their sacrifice was worthwhile.

For example, the author was once part of a small group of activists who organized a meeting to protest inequities in the state's tax system. We invited an influential leader of the state legislature to the meeting and expected about 40–50 people to attend, at best. Much to our surprise and delight, about 300 people showed up. They were full of enthusiasm and ready to take action. That was the good news.

The bad news was that we convinced ourselves that the issue of tax policy was so complicated that we needed to educate the group about its various intricate components. We planned each subsequent meeting to include a "mini-seminar" on some aspect of taxation. Unfortunately, we neglected to include any action items. As a result, interest in the group waned and attendance badly declined. In sum, because of poorly planned meetings, we lost the opportunity to mobilize a committed constituency on an important issue.

There is the potential for similar problems to emerge in any organizational setting. They can be diminished if meetings are only called when they are needed, not merely to fill "white space" on people's calendars or because a committee has "always met" every week (or month). Except in an emergency or crisis, administrators or managers should never call meetings merely to convey information. Ideally, there should be at least one item on the agenda that requires deliberation and concerted action, and one that requires discussion for future action consideration.

During the late 1990s, a major children's advocacy organization in a large U.S. city recruited the author to be a board member. The issues were important, the organization had an excellent reputation, and the list of board members (on the organization's letterhead) was impressive. I initially attended board meetings with high hopes and considerable enthusiasm.

Unfortunately, I soon discovered that virtually the entire agenda of board meetings consisted of reports by the executive director and major program staffers. There was little discussion and no opportunity for board members to have any input into the organization's activities. Although the board listed more than 30 locally prominent individuals, the average attendance at board meetings never exceeded eight to 10 members. Even I soon lost interest in attending meetings.

Often staff members regard meetings as an inefficient and unnecessary use of time because of a lack of leadership and direction by the person(s) responsible, traits that contribute to a poor use of time. (*See Chapter 6.*) Running a meeting well takes skill; one cannot just "wing it." Particularly when there are difficult issues on the agenda, a group leader or facilitator must know how to balance competing interests, enable different opinions to be expressed, allow controlled, productive conflict to emerge, maintain the overall harmony of the group, and motivate meeting participants to take action and agree to follow up on the decisions they have made. This seems a daunting list of tasks, but anyone can learn how to run a meeting well. It takes planning, keen observation of others' behavior, patience, and confidence.

REFLECTION EXERCISE
MEETINGS IN YOUR ORGANIZATION

1. What characterizes the meetings in your organization? (These might include meetings with the full staff, teams, committees, task forces, case conferences, clients, and the board.)
2. Who leads these meetings? Is the leadership consistent or does it change? Do the leaders represent staff members from across the agency or from one portion/level of the agency?
3. Who participates in the meetings? What is the nature of their participation?

Meeting Agendas

The agenda of a meeting is similar to a script of a play: to be effective it follows a particular pattern or rhythm. Tropman (1996) suggests that the best meetings last between 90 minutes and two hours. The agenda should take the shape of a bell curve and look something like this:

1. Welcome and introductions (5%)
2. Overview of agenda and approval of minutes (if necessary) (5%)
3. Update of vital, current developments (essential information only) (15%)
4. Action item(s) (30%)
5. Discussion item(s) (30%)
6. Follow-up and reminders of action steps (5%)
7. "Good and welfare" (end on a positive note) (5%)
8. Set next meeting date and time (5%)—consistent dates are best; doodle polls also help

IN-CLASS EXERCISE
PLANNING AN AGENDA

Introduction

Think of an organization in which you are currently working or have been involved in the past. Imagine that you are going to facilitate the next meeting of the staff and/or volunteer members of the group.

Step 1: Make a list of the items the meeting needs to cover and what decisions the group needs to make.

Step 2: Identify the order in which you will cover these items.

Step 3: Estimate how much time you will allocate to each item.

Step 4: List the problems you anticipate might emerge in addressing the items on your agenda.

Step 5: Briefly indicate how you might respond to these problems.

In addition to creating a clear structure and purpose for the meeting agenda, it is important to remember that most of a group's work occurs *outside* of meetings—i.e., in the space between meetings. This requires the group, or its subcommittees, to develop ongoing, effective means of communication between meetings. If this occurs, the discussions that occur in meetings are far more likely to be focused and productive.

Finally, meetings can seem like dreary exercises in institutional allegiance if they follow the same predictable pattern week after week, month after month. As in any social encounter, variety is important. It stimulates the senses, inspires creativity, and energizes the group. Keeping a group "on track" (i.e., task-oriented) while avoiding the bog of boredom requires some thought and planning. Occasionally, an outside speaker can "juice up" a conversation that often slides into routine. Short, multimedia presentations are far more effective, particularly among the millennial generation accustomed to digital media, than are wordy reports or PowerPoint slides. A brief simulation or small group exercise can also break the routine.

In sum, here are some tips for conducting successful meetings:

1. *Select a good chair or facilitator.* Either choose someone who is acceptable to all group members or rotate responsibility for facilitation.
2. *Plan and distribute the agenda in advance.* Consult with key staff or group members. Distribute the agenda and supporting documents a week in advance if possible.
3. *Serve refreshments* or encourage people to bring their lunch for lunchtime meetings.
4. Build in a brief "social time" but *start the meeting's business promptly.*
5. Welcome everyone, but keep introductions brief. (*The author has been at meetings where introductions took up to one third of the allotted time.* This is an example of a well-intentioned but inefficient gesture.)
6. *Review the whole agenda at the beginning.* Highlight the key items and major objectives.
7. When a group initially convenes, *explain the rules of discussion and decision making.* Address cultural issues regarding intragroup behavior before they arise and become *the issue.*
8. *Limit discussion on each item and stick to the agenda.* It sometimes helps to put time limits on each agenda item. Refer side or tangential issues for future meetings.
9. *Unless they are the background to a critical decision, do not waste time on lengthy reports.* Distribute them in advance and ask presenters to summarize key points and highlight items that require a decision or further discussion.
10. *Do not get bogged down in small details.* Make a list of issues that require future clarification, corrections, or follow-up.
11. *Make sure you take some action or people will stop coming*—trust me, this is a painful lesson from the author's experience, as described previously.

12. *Encourage broad participation.* Consider setting a ground rule that no one can speak twice until each person who wishes to speak has spoken once. Avoid side conversations or one-on-one "debates."
13. *Be flexible when necessary* (e.g., if a crisis occurs). This may require a last-minute alteration of the agenda. If so, explain the reason, and ask the group's permission to make necessary revisions.
14. Summarize the meeting and get commitments for follow-up actions.
15. *Thank everyone for working together.* Conclude the meeting on an upbeat note even when the group is facing serious issues. The author worked in an organization that ended each meeting with a short "good and welfare" period, during which each person had to report on one good thing that happened—in his or her personal or professional life—since the last meeting. This helps people leave the meeting on a more optimistic note.
16. *End on time.* If the group concludes the business of the meeting early, end the meeting. Do not fill the time allotted by introducing other items. People will really appreciate your consideration.
17. *Follow up promptly* regarding the minutes, next steps, etc.

Ground Rules

In addition to preparing for meetings in advance and creating effective meeting structures, every group, but particularly diverse groups, should establish clear ground rules or group norms. These principles should cover such issues as: (1) how the group leader will run meetings; (2) how group members will interact; and (3) what kind of intragroup behavior is acceptable. Making these ground rules part of the group or organization's culture will avoid many potential conflicts and help keep meetings focused.

There are a few basic ground rules to consider when conducting a meeting. These include: civility (basic conversational courtesies); confidentiality; clear assignment of roles and tasks; clear decision-making processes and procedures; rules about attendance and punctuality; ways of managing conflict; whether the group will have rotating or fixed roles (facilitator, chair, minute taker, etc.); how the group will evaluate its own performance; and how the group will acknowledge and celebrate its accomplishments.

Civility

Although they may seem obvious, in the heat of discussion people often let passion or self-interest override the importance of basic conversational courtesies. These include:

- listening attentively and respectfully to others;
- not interrupting (a particular problem for men);
- holding only one conversation at a time;
- keeping disagreements focused on the issues and not permitting personal attacks; and
- turning off all electronic devices and focusing on the business at hand.

Confidentiality

Confidentiality is a well-established ethical principle in the social work literature (Wilson, 1980; NASW, 2017), but the literature often overlooks its application to group discussions. Yet, maintaining the confidentiality of group discussions is critical to establishing and sustaining intragroup trust, especially in groups that consist of individuals from different backgrounds or different organizations. At the outset (at its first meeting), a group should decide whether certain information should not be discussed outside the meeting and, if so, only under what circumstances and, in the case of advocacy groups, by whom. Ideally, it should also agree that once the group makes a decision, however contentious the issue and heated the discussion, group members will not criticize the decision outside the group. To paraphrase the slogan about Las Vegas: "What happens at the meeting stays at the meeting." This helps build and sustain group solidarity, a particularly important concern for culturally diverse groups.

Accountability

As stated previously, most groups do most of their work between meetings. It is important, therefore, for all group members to complete their assigned responsibilities on time. Groups need to establish clear, mutually agreeable accountability mechanisms in advance of assigning tasks to group members. If possible, they should also agree, by consensus, what sanctions the group should impose on group members who fail to fulfill their agreed-upon responsibilities.

Focus

Even in a well-planned meeting, discussions of complex issues can often stray off course or be inconclusive. It is important, therefore, for group leaders to identify the problem or issue to be addressed at the meeting (e.g., an impending budget cut), define it clearly and carefully, and provide participants with sufficient information in advance (whenever possible) to enable them to contribute to resolution of the problem. Leaders should also diagnose the problem and its causes—assuming they are clear—and present alternative solutions and their foreseeable consequences. The group leader should allot time for group members to offer their own interpretations, although all members should avoid finger-pointing and assignment of responsibility to individuals, rather than systemic or structural causes (Bronstein & Abramson, 2017).

Once the group has analyzed the problem carefully and participants have presented multiple perspectives, the leader should guide the group to make an action decision, particularly if a timely action is required. After the group makes its decision, the group needs to develop an implementation strategy, making sure that everyone in the group commits to the action—either directly through accepting a task assignment, or indirectly by supporting the group's decision outside the group. Finally, the group should arrange for follow-up and then follow through on its decision. The importance of leadership at each stage of this process cannot be understated.

Decision Making

Today, many HSOs, neighborhood organizations, and coalitions prefer, whenever possible, to make decisions by consensus rather than through a "majority rules" vote. This is particularly important in multicultural organizations because it can prevent the emergence or the appearance of factions within the organization or group. As with a number of frequently used terms, however, the meaning of "consensus" is often misconstrued.

Reaching consensus does not require unanimity. Although there is no fixed percentage within a group that marks the achievement of consensus, it usually implies that somewhere between two-thirds and three-quarters of the group agrees with a particular decision. All group members, however, agree to accept the decision of the group as binding and commit to the following:

- I can live with it;
- I can accept it;
- I understand it;
- I will support it;

- I will make it happen;
- I will explain and sell it to those outside the group;
- I will not be neutral about it;
- I will not subvert it;
- I am at least 70% comfortable with it; and
- I am 100% committed to it.

Attendance

Woody Allen's famous line that 90% of success in life is due to showing up applies to the success of groups in communities and organizations as well. For this reason, groups should place a high priority on *all* members attending *all* meetings and establish legitimate reasons for missing a meeting. They should also establish a procedure for bringing absent members up to speed without disrupting or slowing the progress of future meetings. Groups that fail to hold members accountable for chronic absence risk undermining their overall morale and effectiveness.

Punctuality

As stated previously, to maintain everyone's commitment to the group's work and the effectiveness of the group as a whole, meetings should start and end on time. This is not as simple as it seems as people from different cultural backgrounds have a different sense of time. All groups, therefore, should consider these cultural differences and decide by consensus what constitutes being "late." The following exercise, based on the author's experience described in a previous chapter, illustrates the potential dangers of not making this determination in advance.

IN-CLASS EXERCISE
HANDLING A DIFFICULT MEETING PROBLEM

You are a social worker who has organized a multicultural coalition of agency directors and community activists to develop a legislative advocacy agenda on behalf of low-income children and families. The 15-person coalition schedules lunchtime meetings on the last Thursday of the month at rotating sites. You are responsible for facilitating the meetings.

A few members of the coalition have complained to you that some of their colleagues are not arriving to the meetings at the time everyone had mutually agreed. At the last meeting, these concerns led to a personal confrontation between two of the coalition participants that disrupted the flow of the meeting and now threatens to break up or weaken the coalition. The next monthly meeting of the coalition is in a week and you are concerned about what might occur.

Questions to Consider

1. What might you do in advance of the meeting to address this issue?
2. How would you handle a discussion of this issue at the meeting itself?

Participation

Just as everyone's attendance at a meeting is critical to a group's success, it is equally important that the group create an environment that recognizes that everyone's contribution is important (Ortega, 2017). Groups should decide how to ensure that every member has an opportunity to speak. For example, as stated previously a group could establish a rule that no one can speak twice on an issue until everyone who wishes to speak has an opportunity to do so. Groups often control participation in a quasi-formal manner (e.g., raise one's hand for the group leader to call on her or him). A more informal, but equally important, component of a group's culture requires all members to agree that the group will listen respectfully to all points of view. Particularly in groups that bring together individuals who have little or no history of interaction, active listening is critical to understanding diverse perspectives that may analyze a problem or propose solutions in ways not previously considered or experienced. It is both disrespectful and unproductive to dismiss out of hand views that diverge from mainstream patterns of discourse.

Rotation of Roles

In addition to determining guidelines for group participation, each group should decide how to assign its major roles. In some groups, the rotation of roles facilitates greater involvement of members and promotes a broader variety of perspectives (Smith, Buccio, & Turnage, 2017). Other groups favor fixed assignment of roles to ensure continuity and to take advantage of the skills and experience group members acquire by performing certain functions over time. Each approach has its advantages and drawbacks, although rotating roles might be somewhat more likely to promote diverse leadership. Groups that decide to rotate roles need to determine how they will do this. Groups that prefer fix roles need to decide how long members will remain in these roles, how to ensure that the group's leadership reflects its membership, and how to avoid what Michels (1911) referred to as **"the iron law of oligarchy"**—in which a few people (e.g., the executive or steering committee of an organization) dominate all decision making.

Whatever method of role assignment is used, the group should spell out the responsibilities of each role (sometimes by including them in the organization's bylaws) and clearly explain them, particularly to new members. It should also establish clear accountability mechanisms. Mentoring of new members is particularly valuable in this regard.

Key Roles in Task-Oriented Groups

Although the following role distribution will vary somewhat depending on the size and function of the group, most task-oriented groups have the following roles:

1. *Facilitator (or Chair).* The tasks of the facilitator are: (1) review the agenda and the purpose of the meeting; (2) identify others' roles; (3) keep the group focused on the issues at hand; (4) facilitate discussion and encourage participation; (5) help evaluate the meeting; and (6) summarize and close the meeting and remind everyone of follow-ups.
2. *Timekeeper.* This role is generally more useful in large groups when the facilitator has the added challenge of maintaining order. Smaller groups can combine the roles of facilitator and timekeeper. In large groups, the timekeeper: (1) helps keep the group on track, reminding the group if there is a "time certain" on the agenda; (2) identifies the time allotted to each agenda item; and (3) intervenes when necessary to keep the group focused on the established agenda and the time frames it has agreed upon.
3. *Notetaker.* This person takes minutes, which involve: (1) recording key topics taken up by the group and the main points of a discussion (it is important to note that minutes are not the same as a process recording); (2) highlights the group's decisions; (3) collects future agenda items; and (4) maintains and distributes minutes and handouts. While many groups rotate the role of notetaker, it is probably advisable to give one person the responsibility for maintaining the group's records.
4. *Scribe.* This role arises only when a group engages in detailed discussions or a planned problem-solving exercise. In such circumstances, the scribe: (1) posts ideas clearly and legibly on a flip chart, board, or computer screen to maintain

the group's focus and memory; and (2) checks periodically with group members for accuracy. It is helpful to use different colors or symbols where needed to highlight key points.

5. *Reporter.* If a meeting breaks down into small groups, the reporter: (1) summarizes the key points and decisions made by the group process; (2) checks for consensus among group members; and (3) *briefly* reports outcomes to the larger group.

KEY CONCEPT SUMMARY
TIPS FOR COMBATING COMMON MEETING PROBLEMS

1. Bad Attendance
   - Make the meeting a priority for members.
   - Schedule meetings at a consistent time.
   - Begin and end meetings on time.
   - Send members an agenda in advance.
   - Include only items of consequence on the agenda.
   - Get people involved through assigned tasks.
   - Serve food.
2. Starting/Finishing on Time and Handling Latecomers
   - Make punctuality an obligation for everyone.
   - Start on time consistently.
   - Schedule routine or less important items first or begin with some sort of group discussion.
   - Test the starting time with the group to see if it is convenient.
   - Appoint one or two punctual members to help latecomers "catch up."
3. Spending Too Much Time on Reports
   - Time the agenda—script it in writing.
   - Tell the presenter the maximum time in advance. Secure his or her agreement.
   - Put reports in writing. Summarize at meeting.
   - Include reports only when specific actions or results have occurred. (Not every committee needs to report at every meeting.)

4. Some Group Members Dominate the Discussion
    - Do not allow interruptions.
    - Insist that new agenda items brought from the floor be referred to the appropriate committee prior to further consideration or action.
    - Ask everyone in the group for their opinion. Make a special effort to involve quiet members.
    - Do not allow attacks on people's ideas or person.
    - Defuse personal confrontations by focusing on problem solving.
    - Keep track of who has indicated a desire to speak.
5. Cutting off a Long-Winded Speaker
    - Politely interrupt to ask if others have questions or need clarification.
    - Interrupt to summarize what the speaker said.
    - Set up a general rule limiting all comments to a specific time. Enforce the rule.
6. Getting an Apathetic Group to Respond
    - Break into small discussion groups to focus on the issue at hand. Ask for reports back.
    - Use brainstorming about issues to remove pressure and allow group to be imaginative.
    - Send materials to the group in advance.
    - Be sure the agenda contains important items.
    - Ask the group: Do we really need to meet this often?
7. Avoiding Hasty Decisions
    - Do not force a decision—watch for signals you send, *especially nonverbal ones.*
    - Do not use a "majority rules" approach until all members have had an opportunity to speak.
    - Be sure the group fully understands and appreciates the ramifications of its action (Ephross, Vassil, & Rose, 2017).
8. Running Out of Time
    - Start the meeting on time and keep to the script.
    - Send the agenda and other materials in advance.
    - State clearly the expected outcomes for each item.
    - Avoid excessive announcements (write them).
    - Use visual aids.
    - Prioritize the agenda items. Cut nonessentials.
    - Do not include reports unless the group took a specific action or the group needs to issue a response (e.g., to a complaint or report by an external body).

9. Handling Disruptive Behavior

- Keep members' attention on the agenda. Do not allow tangents or interruptions.
- Briefly acknowledge irrelevant comments or expressed feelings before returning to the agenda.
- Respond as nonjudgmentally as possible.
- Solicit everyone's opinions and ideas.
- Summarize, summarize, summarize.
- Request a two or three minute "timeout" to diffuse tension (Schulz, Israel, & Lantz, 2017).

Sustaining Community and Human Service Organizations

Meetings are an important tool to maintain the focus of an organization. Yet, they are not the only tool. In addition to effective meetings, all organizations also require three other key elements to sustain themselves over time: a sound structure and decision-making apparatus that meets all legal requirements and political needs and allocates tasks and roles effectively and efficiently; adequate tangible and intangible resources; and certain cultural qualities. The latter include:

- a sense of unity or solidarity that often comes from a sense of belonging;
- effective means of communication and decision making;
- energy and motivation and the ability to mobilize staff and constituents to take concerted action;
- issue consensus;
- a clear and well-articulated vision and mission;
- well-defined strategies and tactics to achieve its goals;
- good relationships with other organizations; and
- an effective system of distributing rewards.

Each of these features requires an effective organizational leadership structure, usually embodied in some type of board of directors. Without a well-designed and well-functioning board, no organization can sustain itself for very long.

Goal Setting and Decision Making

The most important consideration in organizational decision making is time. Creating sufficient time to make critical decisions gives an organization control over what action(s) it needs to take. It is particularly important, therefore, not to feel compelled to make a premature decision.

What makes a good decision? First, it is important to separate facts and values in your analysis and be clear where values influenced your perception of an issue and your judgment about what strategy to adopt. Second, wherever possible, try not to bias the results by the process used to reach a decision.

As discussed earlier, there are a variety of decision-making styles in HSOs that reflect the nature of its leadership and organizational culture: (1) an autocratic (proprietary) system; (2) bureaucratic management; (3) consultative management; and (4) participatory management. Although the latter may appear the most congruent with social work values, it is not easy to implement. It requires full and free communication among staff members and reliance on a consensus model for decision making.

Particularly in large organizations, the range, complexity, and frequency of decisions require delegation of most decision-making to standing or ad hoc committees and task forces. These groups tend to fall into one of three categories. Some are advisory in nature; that is, they exist to inform the organization's leadership about community issues, or plan innovative solutions to these issues or persistent problems. Others have the charge of decision making. They receive a set of action alternatives and have the authority to select among them. Finally, there are implementation committees, whose responsibility is to determine how a decision made by another group or the organization as a whole will be put into effect. Given these different purposes, it is important to determine who should make up each committee and how to staff them.

Working with Boards

At some time in their careers, virtually all social workers and human service workers will work for an organization that has one or more variety of board. To be effective in communities and organizations in all sectors of society, all social workers need to understand how boards operate, what are their functions and responsibilities, and how their role differs from that of staff members. It is also important to recognize that different types of organizations have different types of boards.

Advisory Boards

Some public (government) organizations have ***advisory boards***, often required by law, that are generally appointed by the executive branch (the governor, mayor, county executive, city manager, or departmental administrator) for the purpose of obtaining citizen input into the organization's policies, procedures, or appointment processes. In most cases, these boards have no legal authority or responsibility for the operation of the organization, although they can be an effective channel for citizen participation and for public accountability. Sometimes a state or city uses advisory boards to help select a new leader of a key government agency (e.g., the Department of Human Services), or to obtain comments on the implementation of a new policy, such as welfare reform.

Some nonprofit organizations create advisory boards to provide guidance to the executive on specific issues, programs, or projects. Sometimes the role of an advisory board is to evaluate the overall quality of an agency's services, and recommend improvements, additions, or consolidation (often for purposes of fiscal efficiency). They can also be used to help determine consumers' needs and to publicize the organization's activities through the media or through their connections in the community. A major exception in the public sector is a board of regents, which has considerable power over the policies, procedures, and budgets of public institutions of secondary or higher education. In many states, the voters elect the board of regents, the governor appoints its members, or the state employs some combination of the two methods.

Governing Boards

In contrast to advisory boards, private nonprofit (and some for-profit) organizations are directed by ***governing boards***, which have legal sanction to manage the organization and are accountable for all aspects of its operation. These entities go by several different names: the board of trustees or directors, the governing council, or the board of governors. In the nonprofit sector, board membership is always voluntary and unpaid (hence the original name of this sector, the "voluntary sector") and the board itself determines its members and bylaws.

Under whatever name, these entities have a similar purpose. Their primary duties are policy making, legal oversight, fund-raising, and political/public relations. Except at the initial stage of organizational development, boards rarely have day-to-day oversight responsibilities. In fact, the blurring of board and staff roles can produce considerable organizational dysfunction, especially during periods of organizational growth or transformation (Reid & Turbide, 2012). Not every board fulfills every function described below except for legitimization.

As the legal and fiscal agent of the organization, the board of directors provides legitimacy and sanction for an agency's work. It ensures that the agency has the necessary resources to carry out its functions, including adequate access to the media and political process. The board also plays an important role in formulating agency policy. For example, it decides whom the organization will serve, under what conditions the organization will provide these services, and what types of benefits or services it will provide via its programs.

Finally, the board has a major accountability function. It establishes and maintains evaluative standards, both fiscal and programmatic. It measures the productivity of staff members and the effectiveness of agency services. In this regard, it is important to distinguish the roles of public and private boards. In addition, new accountability requirements imposed by external entities (e.g., government departments and private sector funding sources) have increasingly technical features that often give the CEO more power than the board because of her or his presumed expertise.

According to Independent Sector, a national organization that advocates for non-profit organizations (2015), the specific responsibilities of a board of directors are to:

1. Establish the legal structure of the organization including its bylaws and its tax exempt [501(c) (3)] status with the Internal Revenue Service and the state in which the organization is incorporated.
2. Recruit new board members and engage in self-assessment of its performance.
3. Formulate the organization's vision, mission, broad goals, policies, and programs.
4. Help the organization obtain the resources it needs to fulfill its mission and goals.
5. Ensure that the organization uses its resources in a responsible and accountable manner through fiscal oversight and approval of the organization's annual budget.
6. Represent the organization to and in the community.
7. Hire, supervise, support, evaluate, and (if necessary) fire the executive director (CEO).
8. Establish and maintain standards for organizational performance through the promotion of education and training, periodic evaluation of the organization's overall effectiveness, and assessment of its attainment of specific outcomes through various means, such as strategic planning or contracting with an outside consultant.
9. Ensure that the organization complies with relevant external policies, professional standards, and accreditation requirements and that it fulfills all reporting obligations.

KEY CONCEPT SUMMARY
THE TOP 10 RESPONSIBILITIES OF NONPROFIT BOARDS

1. Determine the organization's mission and purpose.
2. Select the chief executive.
3. Provide proper financial oversight.
4. Ensure adequate resources.
5. Ensure legal and ethical integrity and maintain accountability.
6. Ensure effective organizational planning.
7. Recruit and orient new board members and assess board performance.
8. Enhance the organization's public standing.
9. Determine, monitor, and strengthen the organization's programs and services.
10. Support the chief executive and assess his or her performance.

(Source: *R. T. Ingram (2003). The ten basic responsibilities of nonprofit boards. Washington, DC: BoardSource)*

Given these responsibilities, desirable characteristics of a board include political capital (to help the organization have access to and influence with key decision makers); community connections (both bonding social capital within the community and also bridging social capital outside the community); fund-raising and development experience; and legal expertise. Small boards (six to 12 members) require members to have multiple skill sets and play multiple roles. Larger boards have the luxury of having several members who are knowledgeable in the same area and of not requiring each board member to be able to perform multiple functions. Of whatever size, good boards are diverse, talented, networked, engaged, and effective fundraisers.

In private agencies, the preferred composition of a board includes:

1. People who can acquire resources (business and political contacts).
2. People who have political influence.
3. People with expertise in law, finance, accounting, services.
4. People familiar with the community.
5. People who give the agency legitimacy within the community.

Holland and Jackson (1998) identify the following six dimensions of board competency:

1. *Contextual*: The board understands the cultural norms and values of the organization.

2. *Educational*: The board understands the mission of the organization and its own roles and responsibilities.
3. *Interpersonal*: The board nurtures the development of its members and maintains a strong sense of cohesion.
4. *Analytical*: The board recognizes organizational and mission complexities and draws on diverse perspectives to find solutions.
5. *Political*: The board accepts that relationship building is paramount to its mission.
6. *Strategic*: The board uses a strategic approach to direct the organization.

IN-CLASS EXERCISE
DEVELOPING ORGANIZATIONAL BYLAWS

Introduction

You are a member of an ad hoc committee charged with the development of bylaws for a new community-based nonprofit organization. The committee will present these bylaws to the agency's advisory board for consideration and action at its next meeting.

Step 1 (10 Minutes)

The chair of the committee has asked each member to bring to the meeting a list of items to be covered in the bylaws. In the space below, write those items that you believe need to be included. Remember to keep in mind the specific issues confronting a community-based nonprofit organization.

Step 2 (15 Minutes)

The committee will compare each member's lists and reach consensus on the articles to be included in the bylaws and the order or their placement.

Step 3 (20 Minutes)

The committee will divide into groups to write the specific content of each article. Identify the issues or concerns that each article is designed to address.

Step 4 (30 Minutes)

Each group will present its recommendations to the entire committee for discussion and action. In its presentation, the group spokesperson should identify those issues (if any) around which the group could not reach agreement.

Questions for Discussion

1. How did the specific purposes and environment of the organization influence the development of its bylaws?
2. How might changing circumstances in the future necessitate revisions to the bylaws?
3. Which articles were most difficult to draft? For what reasons?
4. In reviewing the committee's work, what issues were omitted that should have been included? What issues were included that could have been omitted?

Questions for Discussion

1. How did the specific purposes and environment of the organization influence the development of its bylaws?
2. How might changing circumstances in the future necessitate revisions to the bylaws?
3. Which articles were most difficult to draft? For what reasons?
4. In reviewing the committee's work, what issues were omitted that should have been included? What issues were included that could have been omitted?

To maximize the assets of the board, it is important to assess each board member's personal strengths, technical specialties, areas of interest, and particular expertise. It is also worthwhile to consider what current and prospective board members want from their participation in the organization. What issues do they care about? What outlets do these board members have for speaking out on issues of concern?

Such assessments help determine the role each board member can play with respect to the organization's visibility and reputation in the external environment. Each organization must select the strategies that will bring out each board member's strengths to capitalize on opportunities when they arise. It is equally important to assess the benefits and drawbacks of each strategy and to decide how to motivate board members to engage in these strategies.

One possible strategy is for board members to participate in the activities of other agencies, coalitions, professional groups, neighborhood associations, and civic organizations. Another is to establish a "speakers' bureau" and help board members write speeches and identify opportunities to publicize the work of the organization and the issues or causes in which it is involved. A third strategy is to help board members develop as experts on particular issues and use media contacts to engage in public education. A relatively simple component of this strategy is to have board members write op-ed essays or letters to the editor on potential policy solutions to the problems the organization addresses.

Questions for Discussion

Think about your field placement or agency of employment (or an organization in which you previously worked) and answer the following questions:

1. What is the composition of the agency's board? What is the relationship of the board to the organization's staff?
2. Who participates in the organization's board meetings? What does participation look like?
3. How effectively and efficiently does the board operate?
4. Are there key members (or types of persons) missing from the board?

The Role of the Executive Director

The executive director of an organization, sometimes called the chief executive officer (CEO) or, more recently, the president, is in charge of its day-to-operations and is the instrument of the board of directors. Her role is to implement the policies and strategic direction for the organization as established by the board, to manage the organization's staff, and to develop the organization's programs in cooperation with the board and other staff members, and in a manner consistent with the organization's mission. Although large organizations may also have a chief financial officer (CFO), the executive director has overall responsibility for the financial management and stability of the organization and for the administrative oversight of all its programs and internal operations. In many organizations, she is a nonvoting member of the board of directors, attends all board meetings at which she gives a report of the organization's activities since the previous meeting, and informs the board of any issues that arise. She works closely with the officers of the board, particularly the board president (or chair), the chair of the board's fund-raising (or development) committee, and the treasurer of the board (about fiscal matters). Because the executive director (and indirectly, the staff) report to the board, the composition of the board is critical and should not be the product of accident (Daley, 2002). Maintaining good relationships between the executive director and the board is critical to sustain the organization and to maintain the internal equilibrium of the board and the morale of staff members.

Another important function of the CEO is supervision of staff members, which consists of both administrative and educational tasks whose purposes are to promote staff development and enhance services to clients (Furman & Gibelman, 2012). Although the CEO is responsible for the performance of all the organization's employees and volunteers, the number of staff members she directly supervises (i.e., who are "direct reports") varies depending on the size of the organization and its geographic dispersion. For example, large organizations with multiple programs and branches in various locations will have program and/or branch directors who are responsible for the operations of their programs, departments, or branches. These directors will supervise the employees in their programs and, in turn, they will report to the CEO. Other "direct reports" of the CEO within large HSOs include the director of development, the chief financial officer (CFO), and various associate directors (e.g., for programs, human services, communication, government relations, or administration).

It is important to understand that the supervisory functions of the CEO and many of the aforementioned leadership within an organization differ from clinical supervision. Clinical supervision has a psycho-educational component that enables workers to develop insights into their professional use of self and its effect on clients. The functions of nonclinical supervision include a different sort of education—for example, training on the implications of a new legislative policy or on the use of new software; ongoing support; administrative assistance; and ensuring performance accountability (Kadushin & Harkness, 2002). The distinction between these types of supervision is particularly important in community or advocacy work because of the different challenges staff members face and the primacy of their public role.

Potential Problems

A number of problems may arise that affect the functioning of a board or mar the relationship between the board and staff members, particularly the executive director, and especially in challenging economic times (Marx & Davis, 2012). This occurs most often when both the CEO and the board president have strong egos and want to control the direction of the organization (and the agenda of board meetings). It can also emerge when these two leaders are of different genders, race/ethnicity, or professional backgrounds (Ephross, Vassil, & Rose, 2017; Toseland, 2017).

Another major potential problem involves the mutual accountability of the board and the executive to one another. The CEO must give board members detailed, honest, and timely information regarding what she wants the organization to do and how. The CEO must also tell the board what are her indices of success. At times, it is necessary to develop these indices with the board in small, selective ways. For example, the CEO could give the board some small evaluative function of its own, such as assessing a random sample of clients.

There may be problems, however, with the board's role as an accountability mechanism. Most board members are seldom present in the agency and do not observe the day-to-day work in which staff members engage. They generally lack expertise in social work or knowledge of the issues the agency addresses. On occasion, board members join the board for superficial or self-serving reasons. Finally, some board members attend meetings infrequently and are no help to the organization when a crisis appears and the board needs to make critical decisions. Under such circumstances, the board may become a "rubber stamp" and stop carrying out its policy making, political leadership, and accountability functions.

The board, therefore, must be as committed as the CEO to the agency and its goals and support the CEO when she attempts to implement the policies and directions established by the board. Extended conflict within the board or persistent tensions between the CEO and the board (or any of its members), therefore, is potentially destructive to the organization's mission. If such circumstances should appear at a board meeting, the board should defer making a decision on important matters, even if a clear majority exists, to avoid permanent splits or factions.

A final set of problems may emerge in the overall relationship between staff and board members. This is more likely to occur in new organizations or organizations that have evolved from informal entities, largely staffed by volunteers, to more formal organizations with more clearly defined roles and responsibilities. One issue that often reflects staff/board tensions is whether staff members should attend board meetings.

In the author's experience, there is no universal answer to this question. Factors to consider include the size of the staff and the reasons for staffers to attend board meetings. An additional issue is whether staff members have other opportunities to inform the board of their activities and to receive recognition and validation for their work. Especially for junior staff members, it may be helpful to attend a board meeting to acquire a better understanding of the role of the board and to dissolve the mystique that sometimes surrounds board meetings. Staff members may imagine that these meetings are dramatic events when, in fact, they are usually fairly dull and routine affairs.

Summary and Conclusion

This chapter has discussed the key components of effective meetings, the functions of an organization's board, and the qualities of successful boards. The next chapter will address the variety of ethical dilemmas that confront macro practitioners in all fields of practice.

END-OF-CHAPTER EXERCISE
PLANNING A NEIGHBORHOOD MEETING

You are a social worker working with a group of community residents. You have organized the first meeting of a community association you have helped develop to address the issue of truck traffic on residential streets. The meeting, scheduled for 5:30 p.m. next Wednesday, will be at a local church; its pastor has been supportive of your efforts. The church seats about 100 people; it is situated on a busy street about four blocks from the homes of the community leaders with whom you have built a working relationship.

You have invited the mayor and City Council representatives from the community to address the community's concerns and asked them to arrive at 6 p.m.

You canvassed the community surrounding the church two weeks ago announcing the meeting, and the community leaders had the responsibility of making reminder phone calls to their neighbors. The pastor volunteered use of the sound system but asked that the residents share in cleaning up after the meeting, especially the bathrooms. You plan to distribute a media advisory five days before the meeting.

You need to create an agenda for the meeting and a list of everything you think could possibly go wrong, so that you can prepare for these contingencies.

1. Draft an agenda for the meeting, which includes: (a) the order of agenda items; (b) the objective or purpose of each agenda item; and (c) the amount of time you will allocate to each item.
2. Make a list of everything you think might go wrong with the meeting and briefly indicate what your response would be if this contingency arose.

IN-CLASS EXERCISE
BOARD DEVELOPMENT

You are a social worker who has been asked to consult on the development of a board of directors for a three-year-old organization, Tomorrow's Adolescent Fund, which focuses on increasing the access of low-income and racial minority youth to a college education. The organization's work has expanded since its creation. It has become more formal in its operations and is applying for 501(c)(3) status to increase its opportunities for external funding support.

You have a list of 10 possible candidates for the board. You have to recommend which candidates should be priorities for recruitment and why. Capsule bios follow:

- Richard: The founder and executive director of Tomorrow's Adolescent Fund. He started the organization three years ago based on a family member's need for her child.
- Bill: Richard's close friend and a strong supporter of the organization's mission. He has made substantial contributions to the organization during the past three years.
- Mark: Richard's life partner; he assisted Richard with the organization's technology and website design. His background is in communications and organizational "branding."
- Rachel: She is a parent of one of the children supported by the fund. She believes passionately in the mission of the organization because it "saved her daughter's life."
- Tanya: She is a prominent African American business leader in the community. She travels frequently for her international marketing firm and is ranked in the Top 20 Women in Business in the state.

- Jesse: He is an African American attorney specializing in medical malpractice. He serves on two other community advisory boards for nonprofits and is active in his neighborhood association.
- Victoria: She is a semiretired certified public accountant. She runs a part-time business out of her home and maintains her certification for consulting purposes.
- Joe: He is an all-pro member of the local NFL team. His son attends elementary school with one of the current board members of the organization.
- Anna: She is a practicing physician, specializing in pediatric mental health research. She has never served on a nonprofit board.
- Juan: He recently began a career as a real estate agent. He has chosen to focus his business on supporting first-time homebuyers in multiethnic communities.

Questions for Discussion

1. Which of these board candidates would you recommend (in priority order)?
2. What are your reasons?

CHAPTER 8

Identifying and Resolving Ethical Dilemmas in Macro Social Work Practice

Ethics are more important than laws.

—Wynton Marsalis

Action indeed is the sole medium of expression for ethics.

—Jane Addams

Introduction

As members of a value-based profession, social workers are deeply committed to the fulfillment of critical ethical imperatives and to the maintenance of high ethical standards in their practice. In recent years, a combination of fiscal austerity, political polarization, social/cultural diversity, and the increasing complexity of organizational and community problems has compounded the challenge of achieving these goals.

As our world and our practice become more complex, there is increased concern about the potential for ethical misconduct in all spheres of society, including the organized social work profession. We design ethical codes to guide our behavior in situations that are often morally ambiguous and to help us do the right thing in difficult situations. Yet, what exactly is "doing the right thing"?

A variety of factors influence our sense of what is the right thing. These include the values our families, communities, places of worship, and schools teach us; the laws and customs of our society also play an important role. We are conscious of some of these values, while others influence us more subtly. In today's environment, a growing challenge is to determine what is the "right thing" when there are multiple stakeholders who profess different personal values. Reflect for a moment on the differences that exist in your community on such personal issues as corporal punishment, abortion, the death penalty, and same-sex marriage. An additional challenge is that in our increasingly inter-professional workplaces, professional ethics vary, sometimes in significant ways.

The presence of diverse perspectives on what values should guide societal priorities and conflicts over the meaning of social justice itself underscore the importance of self-awareness in all aspects of macro social work practice: community organizing, administration and management, and policy practice. We need to broaden our conceptualization of macro social work practice beyond the *goals* of these activities to incorporate the social justice components of the processes involved. We also need to recognize that the dimensions of socially just macro social work practice parallel those of socially just practice with individuals.

Although this book stresses the ethical components of macro social work practice in every chapter, this chapter focuses specifically on this topic to ensure that students acquire an in-depth understanding of its dimensions. The chapter includes:

1. A definition of key terms.
2. A discussion of the major approaches to ethics.
3. Material on the relationship of ethical practice to social justice, empowerment, and multiculturalism, including the potential conflicts involved.
4. The relationship between law and ethics.
5. The role and limitations of the NASW *Code of Ethics*.

6. Various examples of ethical dilemmas that arise in macro social work practice.
7. Models of ethical decision making.

Figure 8.1 The Challenges of Ethical Decision Making

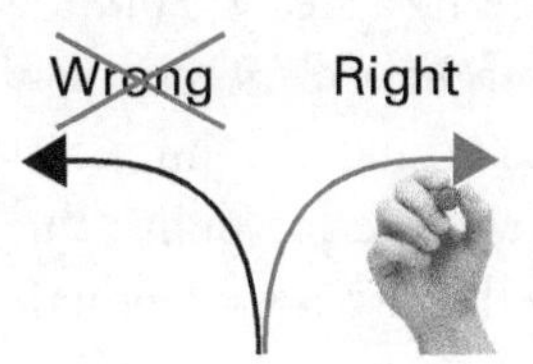

Fig. 8.1: *Copyright © 2013 Depositphotos/ivelin.*

Ethics and Social Work Practice

Since the late 19th century, the social work profession has used principles derived from religious and secular moral philosophy to justify its efforts to improve workplace conditions, promote civil rights and civil liberties for racial/ethnic minorities and the LGBTQ population, advocate for policies and services for women and children, and support peace and economic conversion (Reisch & Andrews, 2002). Social workers have linked these moral principles to their practice based on several underlying assumptions. First, government has the potential to play a relatively benign role in promoting individual well-being and social change. Second, social work's constituents have a common understanding of their needs and of the components of social justice. Third, organized social and community action can respond effectively to economic and cultural changes of considerable magnitude. Finally, that under the proper circumstances, social work values would be widely accepted in U.S. society.

Given the scope of external changes that have occurred over the past several decades, it is worthwhile to ask are these assumptions still valid? What are the implications of these changes for the ethical basis of social work practice, particularly in the sphere of macro practice?

For example, it is widely acknowledged that the consequences of economic globalization have transformed the context and very nature of social work. Globalization has exacerbated long-standing inequalities, both locally and globally. It has dramatically altered the relationship in the social welfare field between the public and nonprofit sectors. It has changed the mission, goals, and cultures of HSOs, especially nonprofit organizations. It has influenced the ideology and vocabulary of the profession. It has depoliticized the focus of the profession's efforts (Reisch & Jani, 2012). This transformation calls into question many long-standing assumptions that have shaped U.S. social welfare and social work practice—on the role of the state in social welfare provision; on relationships between workers and clients or constituents; on the relevance of prevailing practice theories and constructs to new practice realities; and on the goals of social work itself (Reisch, 2013c).

On the positive side, globalization has heightened practitioners' awareness of the linkages between local and global issues and change initiatives. It has stimulated or revived interest among social workers on such issues as climate change, global poverty, civil conflict, and human trafficking (Healy, 2008; Wronka, 2017). This has created the potential—and one could argue the necessity—to forge new multicultural and cross-national coalitions, to understand the implications and possible usages of new technologies, and to define a new role for politics in social work practice. Finally, it makes the examination of the ethical bases of practice even more important than in the past.

Key Ethical Concepts

It may be useful to begin by clarifying the meaning of key concepts often used interchangeably in the popular and professional literature.

Ideology. Although politicians and the media sometimes use the word "ideology" to connote a rigid philosophical or political perspective, in its origins the term actually has a neutral connotation. According to Weber (1946) an ideology is a systematic, coordinated body of ideas about human life and culture; a unified worldview. (The German word, *weltanschauung*, best encapsulates this meaning.) Marx (Marx & Engels, 1959), however, viewed ideology as a by-product of the socioeconomic system that reflects the perspectives of the dominant class and culture of a society, what he referred to as the "superstructure" of society that acquires an identity of its own. Durkheim (1972) also regarded ideology as a belief system of a group or class that systematically distorted reality, sometimes unconsciously, to preserve the status quo.

Definitions in the social work field have somewhat broader applications. Gil (2013) defined ideology as the reflection "of the interests of individuals and classes who supported a status quo from which they benefited objectively and subjectively" (p. 50). Lewis (1982) viewed it as our preferred system of values that we accept for ourselves and apply in our interactions with others—for example, whether freedom or equality should take priority in the distribution of rights and responsibilities.

Values. Values are the enduring beliefs we hold on what is preferred as good and right in our conduct and in our existence as human beings. Our personal and professional values emphasize the "oughts" (what we should do) and not merely what is interesting and desirable. Values are also guides to moral judgments that shape our behavior and ways of thinking.

Ethicists in social work such as Reamer (2013) identify four types of values: instrumental, intrinsic, objective, and potential. Of closer relevance to macro social work practice, Levy (1976) identified three basic value dimensions in professional practice:

(a) preferred conceptions of people; (b) preferred outcomes for people; and (c) preferred instrumentalities for dealing with people. It is important to note, however, that while ideology and values are "in the mind" they are not merely abstract entities. They are, instead, expressions of class, racial, or group self-interest that prevailing economic, social, and political conditions shape and reinforce. These conditions ultimately maintain or transform our values.

Recurrent social work values (as reflected in the preamble to the NASW *Code of Ethics* [2017]) include respect for all people, an emphasis on rights, the imperative of working toward social justice, and the pursuit of the common good. In this chapter and in subsequent chapters we will examine how to apply these values in macro social work practice.

Morals. Morals are those principles or habits with respect to right or wrong conduct that often have their origins in an external source of authority (such as religion). They lead to the development of specific rules and standards of behavior and practice. They also shape the generally accepted customs of a community and define what we consider a proper way to live and to relate to others in a society or community.

The purpose of morals is to help us determine what choices create the greatest good. Moral principles, however, do not always provide the best answer. They are often based on absolute directives on what constitutes right and wrong frequently derived from an external authority. Particularly in a diverse society, what is right for the majority may not be right or just for the minority or for individuals who live in unique circumstances. Because of the ambiguity in many practice situations, we must balance our assessment of the inherent "rightness" of an act by determining whether a particular act in a particular context produces a desired outcome. For example, although it may always be wrong to steal money to provide better services to our clients, under certain conditions it may be morally proper to "bend" the rules to help a person in dire need.

Value Conflicts in Practice

The media make us constantly aware of the value conflicts that exist in our society. But why in a value-based profession do such conflicts exist in social work practice? One reason is that practitioners are human and that our practice occurs in complex, often ambiguous circumstances. We are constantly trying to reconcile the multiple dimensions of values we all must address all the time: our personal values; the values within the *Code of Ethics*; the values of our constituents and clients; the values of the organizations in which we work; the values of our allies; and the values of society. Another reason is that we deal with conflict-ridden issues for which there are no clear ethical solutions—abortion, assisted suicide, transracial adoption, LGBTQ rights, Affirmative Action, the rights of parents and children, the balance between personal and societal responsibility, the respective roles of the market and the state, just to name a few.

This underscores why it is very important to be aware of the personal values that guide our choices and behaviors. For example, recognizing how important financial security is to you is critical in determining what job you will accept and what risks you will take in your practice. It is also important to know that your concept of social justice may differ from that of your clients, constituents, colleagues, and supervisors, and that these differences may create conflicts in practice settings.

Lastly, the very nature of our practice in a multicultural, increasingly contentious environment produces value conflicts over what constitutes a "need" and appropriate forms of assistance (Green, 1998). Demographic and cultural differences, and power imbalances—within agency staffs or between organizations and the communities in which they work—can also produce major trust issues. This sometimes appears in the form of ideological or political polarization, religious and moral differences, or different concepts of social justice. The growing separation of people's work from their private lives, and the increasing isolation and fragmentation of our communities, particularly along racial and class lines, exacerbate these value conflicts. Finally, growing economic and social insecurity and resource scarcity in communities and organizations intensifies conflicts that could be more easily resolved during prosperous times.

Haynes and Mickelson (2010) argue that social workers are often reluctant to address these conflicts, in themselves and in their environments. They identified a number of reasons for this avoidance. One is what they term the reactionary consequences of our focus on professionalism and professional status enhancement (Wenocur & Reisch, 1989; Specht & Courtenay, 1994). We often define professionalism as the maintenance of impartiality or "objectivity," rather than staking out a partisan position, as our ethical imperatives to pursue social justice and to prioritize the client's interest appear to imply. Another factor is that we often base our practice on conservative, system-conserving assumptions about individuals, society, and social change. This is both cause and consequence of our practice in conservative institutions whose missions and goals are incompatible with our social justice principles. As a result, social workers tend to emphasize specialized forms of practice—that is, we address people's problems in "silos"—rather than seek systemic or structural solutions. The recent emphasis on "evidence-based" practice is merely the latest iteration of this morally neutral position. In sum, the orientation of social work practice, even in the macro arena, has become fundamentally apolitical (Reisch, 2008a).

Figure 8.2 Dealing with Value Conflicts

Fig. 8.2: *Copyright © 2013 Depositphotos/jordenmac.*

CASE ILLUSTRATION
RESOLVING A CONFLICT OF VALUES

You are a social worker at the counseling center of a local community college. One of your clients, Janet B., is a student at the college. At your last session, she told you that she is pregnant and wants to get an abortion. She is 23 and, under the Affordable Care Act, she has health insurance coverage through her mother's employment-based plan until the age of 26. The plan her mother selected, however, does not provide coverage for abortions. Although your state's abortion laws are liberal, if Janet sought to obtain individual coverage her only option under the new law would be to purchase an expensive individual policy that would cover abortions. This would be difficult for her to afford since she is only working part time and cannot ask her mother for help (for both economic and personal reasons). Janet cannot obtain a subsidy for the more expensive health insurance plan because the new law bars the use of government subsidies for plans that cover abortions. What do you advise her to do? What are your reasons?

Ethics

Finally, we get to the oft-confused meaning of the term "ethics." Ethics are propositions derived from values and morals that form the basis of actions to achieve their ends. In a sense, they are the behavioral dimension of values and morals. Another way to define ethics is that they constitute rules of conduct that link morals and values to action.

The meaning of ethics is confusing because we sometimes use the word to refer to things that are not quite equivalent. One definition is that ethics are what conduct is customary in a particular group, community, or society (its mores). In some cases, it is equated with formal law—although as we shall see, ethical and legal imperatives can and do conflict. In other cases, we equate ethics with rules of behavior based upon religious prescriptions. This equation can lead to conflicts between one's personal and professional values and obligations.

In the social work literature, ethics are formally codified concepts of etiquette (Reamer, 2013). Social workers have a particular ethical responsibility to the people with whom we work because of the fiduciary (trust) relationship that is an essential component of all practice (Lewis, 1982). Ethics, therefore, implies a duty owed to others by virtue of a specific responsibility. There are two categories of this duty: prescriptive principles or rules—that is, idealized "oughts" or "shoulds" (what we must do); and proscriptive rules or taboos (what we must never do). A profession enforces violations of these rules through sanctions, punishments, or the imposition of specific remedies.

These various definitions all assume, however, that ethics are primarily an end. While this is true to some extent, this book offers another complementary interpretation: Ethics are also a process, or a systematic framework to examine the underlying assumptions of our practice and to establish a consistent basis for resolving the value differences or moral dilemmas that inevitably arise in our work.

It is equally important to clarify what ethics and ethical practice are not. Ethical practice is not merely competent practice. The author knows several colleagues who were extremely competent who behaved unethically and faced sanctions by the profession. One former colleague (and friend, in fact) who was the successful longtime director of a major social service agency that received national attention, including a visit from former President Reagan, was fired for ethical (and legal) misconduct.

Ethical behavior is also not equivalent to one's personal feelings about right and wrong. Ethics connote obligation not "gut instincts," however accurate they may be in some practice situations. Similarly, one can be an ethical practitioner without connecting one's practice principles to a particular set of religious beliefs, which derive their authority from a higher (divine) power. Ethics should apply to all people equally, including those who are atheists.

Being ethical is also not always compatible with obeying formal laws, policies, rules, and regulations. Sometimes deferring to the law is ethical—for example, stealing is both illegal and unethical. Ideally, laws and policies incorporate ethical standards, but they can also be unethical. Examples of laws from the not-too-distant past that are unethical include apartheid, slavery, Jim Crow, and the Nuremberg laws. Rosa Parks broke the law when she refused to give up her seat on a Birmingham bus; so did "righteous Gentiles" who sheltered Jews in Nazi-occupied Europe. More recent examples of the conflict between law and ethics include the military's "don't ask, don't tell" policy; so-called "Religious Freedom Acts" adopted by many states, including Indiana; California's Proposition 187, which prohibited agencies from providing services to undocumented individuals; and municipal "stop and frisk" policing procedures.

In addition, sometimes there is no law to guide our conduct. For example, it may be legal to accept a gift from a grateful client, but it raises certain ethical concerns. To complicate the issue further, what if refusing the gift is offensive to the client whose culture requires her to offer it? Is it offensive to a community resident if you decline a cup of coffee she offers and counterproductive to your efforts to recruit her for a group you are organizing?

Finally, ethical practice is not always doing what is socially acceptable. Behaviors that some societies or communities often condone or tolerate—e.g., the use of racial or homophobic slurs, sexual harassment, making anti-Semitic remarks—are unethical. In sum, ethics are a set of rules to which we hold ourselves accountable. If applied consistently, they are effective guides in our personal lives and for our professional conduct.

There are certain recurring themes in social work ethics throughout its history. One theme is respect for people, often rooted in the concept of equality. This focus is particularly important as our society becomes increasingly diverse.

NASW Code of Ethics

The NASW *Code of Ethics* (2017) establishes principles that all social workers are obligated to follow. These principles reflect six broad values, or ethical imperatives:

1. Service—putting the needs of the people with whom we work above self-interest.
2. Social justice—challenging social injustice and working for social change on behalf of vulnerable and oppressed populations.
3. Dignity and worth of person—being respectful, mindful of differences and cultural and ethnic diversity, and promoting the self-determination of all people.
4. Importance of human relationships—engaging people in the helping relationship; empowering individuals, communities, and organizations.
5. Integrity—being trustworthy and practicing in a manner that is consistent with social work's mission, values, and ethics.
6. Competence—demonstrating a commitment to competent practice and ongoing professional development.

The *Code* further stipulates that all social workers have ethical responsibilities to multiple stakeholders, including clients, colleagues, their practice settings, the profession of social work, and society as a whole. The standards it establishes are prescriptive (e.g., informing people of the risks involved in a particular intervention) and proscriptive (e.g., not disclosing confidential information to a third party without authorization). Unfortunately, the *Code* is often ambiguous in its statement of values (for example, it does not define "social justice") and in its ethical guidelines (e.g., the use of phrases such as "to the extent possible"). This ambiguity places additional responsibility on practitioners to use good judgment in resolving ethical dilemmas.

Another theme in the *Code* is the pursuit of social justice and the emphasis on rights or legal entitlements. These rights are legal and moral, individual and social. They are linked to other major themes such as the pursuit of the common good (Lewis, 2003) and the importance of individual and community self-determination. Although in practice the application of these principles frequently overlaps, the NASW *Code of Ethics* distinguishes the responsibilities of social workers to clients (or constituents), colleagues, the employing organization, the profession as a whole, and the broader society. Each of these categories of responsibility applies equally to clinical and macro social work practitioners.

For example, major ethical principles such as self-determination, informed consent, boundary issues, confidentiality, and truth telling apply equally to all social workers, although the manner in which these ethical issues arise may be different. In addition, ethical practice in community work may be different from practice with individuals and families. It influences the selection of interventions that could put people at risk, value conflicts that may arise between community practitioners and community residents, conflicts of duty that exist around such issues as reporting criminal activity among constituents, and the difficulty of choosing between short-term and long-term gains.

In today's environment, it is particularly difficult to translate social work values into ethical macro social work practice. Hardina (2004) goes as far as to argue that community practitioners confront different ethical issues because of the nature of their work. For example, the goal of community practice is social transformation through community, organizational, or policy change, not individual change. Many macro practitioners regard the people with whom they work as constituents, consumers, partners, or allies rather than clients. This implies that *both* workers and constituents must develop critical consciousness about the sources of the issues they are addressing and about the social and economic conditions that contribute to the marginalization of oppressed groups.

Despite the profession's long-standing emphasis on "person-in-environment," the perspective of many clinical practitioners is that social work occurs primarily in the context of a dyadic relationship between worker and client. In contrast, awareness of the environment in macro social work practice is critical and the ethics of practice are more likely to be situational (Alinsky, 1971). "Clients" are primarily constituency group members, residents of target communities, and members of marginalized populations. In many instances, organizers do not have direct contact with all members of the client group.

Because creation of a partnership is particularly important in macro practice, and macro practitioners frequently belong to the communities with which they work, there is the increased possibility of dual relationships. These conditions underscore the need for understanding the implications of cultural diversity, the different meaning of self-determination and empowerment, the importance of partnership and mutual learning with constituents, and the challenges of translating a commitment to social justice into the distribution of tangible and intangible resources.

In addition, in macro social work practice most interventions take place in partnership with constituency group members. In fact, in some situations the constituency group serves as the organizer's employer. The organizer may also be a member of the target community. As a result, in some situations, the organization may prefer to hire a member of its geographic community or a person who identifies with the community served (for example, a person with a disability or a gay man or lesbian).

Finally, working with people to gain power often requires the use of confrontation tactics, targeting powerful groups in society. What constitutes ethical conduct, therefore, is often situational, requiring practitioners to assess the seriousness of the situation, accessibility of key decision makers, and possible risks to targets before deciding on the appropriate use of tactics.

Other ethical issues that are specific to community practice or advocacy include:

1. How should practitioners deal with involuntary participation in social and community action?
2. Should community residents be free to withdraw from the group at any time if they have freely committed to its goals?
3. What should be the response to "free riders"?
4. Are community practitioners or advocates required to obtain informed consent from their constituents if the strategies and tactics they are contemplating involve individual or group risk?
5. What are the limits of confidentiality in practice that takes place in the public arena?
6. What is the legal liability of community practitioners for malpractice if, as leaders, they make inadvertent strategic mistakes that cause irreparable harm to their constituents?
7. At a broader level, how can macro social work practitioners reconcile cultural differences regarding the meaning of community, leadership, group roles, group styles, group values, and goals? (*See also chapters four through six.*)

In sum, community practice requires macro social workers to examine the implications of the *Code of Ethics* carefully for the following reasons:

- Most practice occurs outside of organizations;
- Practitioners frequently will encounter opposition when helping people fight for power;
- Opponents and targets of change efforts may engage in unethical tactics;
- Colleagues and opponents may not be social workers;
- Limited supervision exists, especially from social workers, in the development of strategies; and
- Strategies that may be good for individuals may not help produce the community or societal change that is often the goal of community practice.

Organizational practice also creates different types of ethical dilemmas, particularly for administrators and managers. As most social work practice occurs in agencies, it is important to reflect on how practitioners can apply ethical standards in these settings. Here are some issues that may arise in the organizational context that are different from those that appear in clinical practice:

1. Is it ever ethical to use resources (e.g., a foundation grant) for purposes other than their original intention, even in emergencies?
2. Given the increased computerization of record keeping, how extensive should security measures be to maintain confidentiality before they impede the intraorganizational and inter-organizational flow of vital information?
3. As many organizations are under severe fiscal constraints, is it ethical to establish waiting lists for services that do not treat all potential service users equally—for example, by giving priority to people who can pay a fee for service or have insurance?
4. If the organization will use certain funds to further the goal of social justice, is it ethical to accept contributions from individuals, groups, or organizations whose core values are in conflict with those of the organization and the social work profession?
5. Is it ethical for an agency not to provide certain benefits or wages to its staff members while it advocates on behalf of related issues for its constituents?
6. Should organizations establish blanket policies on accepting gifts from clients to address boundary issues and the possibility of dual relationships?
7. Should supervisors discuss among themselves confidential issues that reflect the shortcomings of their supervisees?
8. Should an agency accept additional clients when its current caseloads are so high it cannot provide competent services?

Classroom Discussion: Group Membership and Personal Morality

1. Are there universal ethics or are ethics culturally relative?
2. What do you believe should be the role of religious or secular ideologies in defining professionally ethical behavior?

Law and Ethics

Laws, organizational policies, and regulations shape much of social work practice. They establish eligibility requirements, determine benefit levels, and provide organizations with rules, formal processes, and performance standards. They dictate what social workers must, can, and must not do in our practice. For example, if you are a social worker in a public high school that accepts state funds for abstinence education programs, the state prohibits you from discussing contraception or safe sex practices with students. The policies in sex-segregated homeless shelters may determine the placement of transgendered persons. Some may dictate that transgendered persons be housed in a facility that matches their birth gender, and some will allow these persons to be housed according to the gender with which they identify.

In other words, laws provide guidance but they do not insulate us from ethical conflicts. Under most circumstances, however, compliance with the law is a useful guide to ethical behavior. The most important legal guidelines include:

1. The obligation to meet reasonable standards of care and comply with best practices.
2. The requirement to advise people of the costs and risks of a particular intervention.
3. The protection of confidentiality in the communications between social workers and those with whom we work, including digital and electronic communication (*Jaffe v. Redmond*).
4. The duty to warn and protect (*Tarasoff v. Regents of the University of California*).

Figure 8.3 Intersection of Ethics and Law

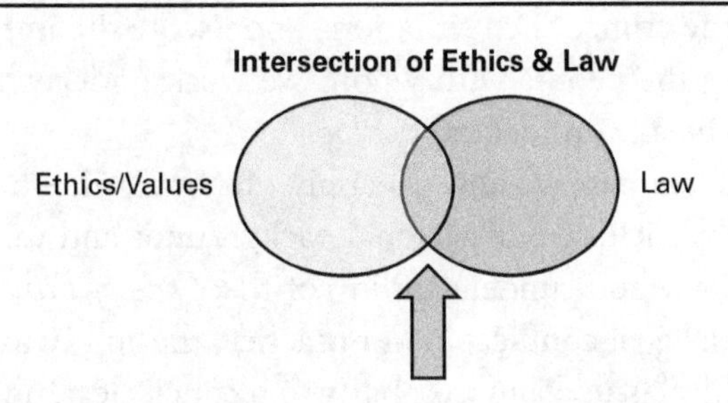

Ethical Dilemmas

Figure 8.4 The Nature of Ethical Dilemmas

Fig. 8.4: *Copyright © 2015 Depositphotos/bakhatiarzein.*

Even when our ethical obligations are clear, we may confront ethical dilemmas in our practice situations where no clear solution exists. Macro practitioners make judgment calls all the time. According to Hardcastle, Wenocur, and Powers (2011), ethical dilemmas occur when "two ethical principles require equal but opposite behavior and the ethical guidelines do not give clear directions or indicate clearly which ethical imperative to follow" (p. 22). These dilemmas usually arise for one of several reasons. Two ethical principles may conflict and we are obligated to choose between two competing "goods" or rights. Sometimes the reasons to act or not act are unclear due to a lack of sufficient or adequate information or there is insufficient time to make a reasoned judgment (e.g., in a crisis). On occasion, ethical principles conflict with legal or organizational obligations. Finally, we are sometimes compelled to choose between equally bad options.

An example of the latter occurs when a client or constituent discloses that he committed a serious crime. If you report him to the authorities, you will break the fragile bond of trust you have worked hard to establish. If you fail to report him, however, you will be complicit in the crime. Such situations underscore the importance of informed consent and of telling the people with whom we work under what circumstances we might be required to break confidentiality.

To resolve these dilemmas, we have to apply our own value hierarchy. Critical elements of this hierarchy include our personal backgrounds and values, our professional education and experience, our understanding of the *Code of Ethics* and its limitations, recognition of potential goal conflicts in our practice, the ability to distinguish between practice issues and ethical issues, and the ability to reconcile legal and ethical obligations.

As suggested earlier, in some situations different stakeholders may have different views on what constitutes an ethical response. For example, how would you respond if you observed a parent in a grocery store spanking a child for wandering off? Would you say something? Or, what would you do in your place of employment if you noticed that one of your colleagues was consistently late and playing video games on his computer during work hours? Is there a difference between stealing something for personal gain and behaving as the legendary Robin Hood? If you had a voice in policy making, how would you respond to a situation in which a critically ill patient declines to undergo a lifesaving medical procedure because of religious beliefs? Should health care professionals, legislators, and the courts attempt to overrule her decision as they did in the case of Terry Schiavo during the G. W. Bush administration?

There are other examples of ethical dilemmas that occur regularly in macro practice, some of which the cases below will illustrate. They include:

- telling the truth versus pursuing the group's (constituents') interest;
- determining how to allocate scarce resources;
- resolving conflicts of duties or loyalties;
- reconciling the use of certain means and the attainment of certain ends;
- deciding whether to comply with laws or regulations you consider unjust; and
- deciding when to blow the whistle on a colleague.

Making Ethical Decisions

Figure 8.5 Actors Involved in Ethical Assessment and Decision Making

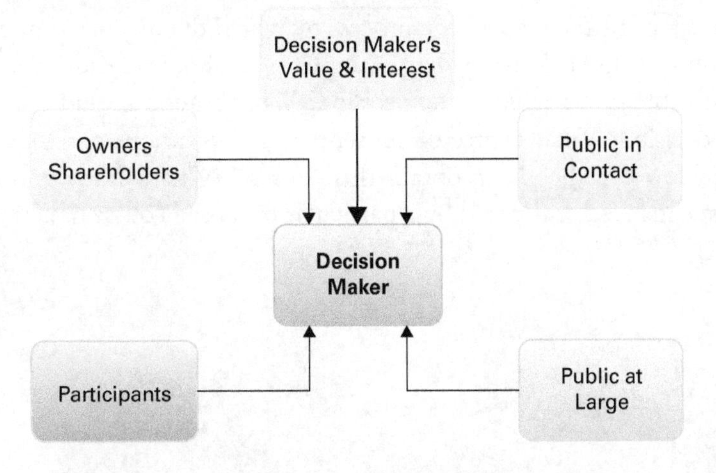

Fig. 8.5: *Michael Reisch and Charles D. Garvin, Social Work and Social Justice: Concepts, Challenges, and Strategies.*

Reamer (1999) asserts that the people with whom we work "... have a right to expect ... that social workers involved in decision making will be thorough, thoughtful, sensitive and fair" (p. 91). Because the *Code of Ethics* is frequently not explicit on what constitutes an ethical response to the dilemmas practitioners confront, and because many situations involve a conflict of duties, we are obligated to use our professional judgment and apply a consistent approach to the resolution of ethical problems. For example, suppose you are a supervisor in an agency and are aware that one of your staff members has a sexually transmitted disease. Although he is under treatment for his ailment, you have observed that he has not been able to carry his fair share of the program's workload. To what extent are you required to maintain confidentiality? Do you also have an obligation to other workers in the organization—to their safety and to the effect on their jobs? What would be the consequences for the organizational culture and climate if you revealed this individual's health condition?

It is important to note that while the *Code of Ethics* does not dictate how to resolve such dilemmas, it provides broad guidelines that help us critically assess and take action in such complex situations. In other words, we do not have the option of electing whether to adhere to a specific ethical standard, but we have to determine how we will uphold it. One criterion to use is whether our decision enhances or impedes good practice in our organizations. Another is to determine what the consequences would be if our decision in a specific situation would be generalized to all circumstances. In today's multicultural environment, a third criterion should involve assessing whether the decision is consistent with the goal of cultural competency.

Lewis (1982) suggests that to conduct an ethical assessment of a practice situation, social workers should address two categories of questions. One set of questions involves the nature of the action itself—the desired end. It requires examining such issues as: Who are the actors? What is the proposed action or actions? What is the context in which the proposed action will occur? What is the intention or purpose of the possible action? What are the probable consequences?

The other set of issues involves the process by which the organization or group will make an action-oriented decision. For example, who should decide what to do? On whose behalf is the group making the decision? What criteria should the group use in making the decision? What degree of consent from the various participants does the group need? How can the group obtain this consent? What, if any, moral or ethical principles are enhanced or negated by a particular proposed course of action?

Figure 8.6 Analyzing an Ethical Dilemma

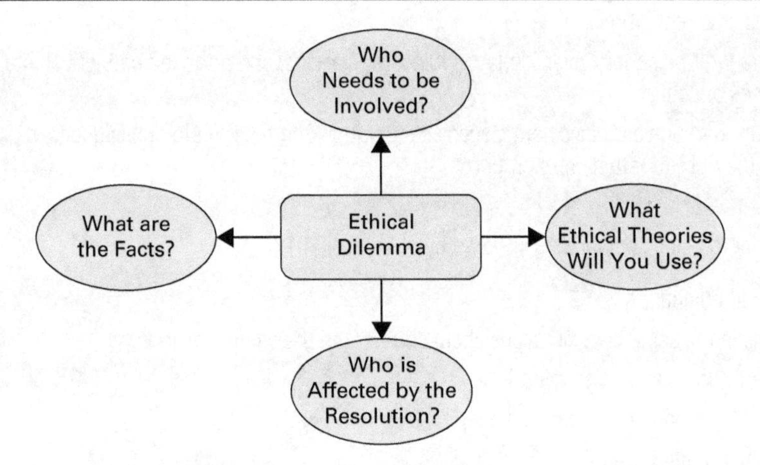

Macro social workers can resolve the ethical dilemmas they will inevitably confront in several ways. Briefly, here are some major approaches to the resolutions of these dilemmas:

- Always put the interests of clients or constituents first;
- Use a "prime directive" (i.e., impose externally imposed values);
- Create a hierarchical ordering of values—what ethicists refer to as a *deontological* approach;
- Assess the potential consequences of various options—what ethicists refer to as a *teleological* or *consequentialist* approach. A prominent example of this approach is utilitarianism, a method of seeking the "greatest good for the greatest number"; and
- Use a *relativist* approach that considers the context of the dilemma. This often leads to means versus ends debates.

The following are some examples of a deontological approach.

Table 8.1 Two Hierarchies of Values

Reamer's Hierarchy of Values (2013)

1. Rules against basic harms to the necessary preconditions of action (e.g., life, health) take precedence over rules against harms such as lying or revealing confidential information.
2. The right to basic well-being takes precedence over another individual's right to freedom.
3. The right to freedom takes precedence over the right to basic well-being.

4. The obligation to obey laws, rules, and regulations to which one has voluntarily and freely consented ordinarily overrides the right to engage voluntarily and freely in a manner that conflicts with these laws, rules, and regulations.
5. The right to well-being may override laws, rules, regulations, and arrangements of voluntary association in cases of conflict.
6. The obligation to prevent basic harms such as starvation and to promote public goods (e.g., housing) overrides the right to retain one's property.

Dolgoff, Harrington, and Loewenberg's Hierarchy of Values (2012)

1. Protection of human life
2. All persons in the same circumstances should be treated the same way (equity)
3. Autonomy/freedom (self-determination)
4. Principle of least harm (such as medicine)
5. Better quality of life for all
6. Privacy and confidentiality
7. Truthfulness and full disclosure

Addressing Means vs. Ends

With which of these statements do you agree:

> "The end may justify the means, as long as there is something that justifies the end." —Leon Trotsky
>
> "The end justifies the means only when the means used are such as actually bring about the desired and desirable end." —John Dewey
>
> "One's concern with the ethics of means and ends varies inversely with one's personal interest in the issue." —Saul Alinsky (1971)

Probably no one in the field of macro social work practice discussed the issue of ends and means more candidly or controversially than Saul Alinsky in his famous book, *Rules for Radicals* (1971). Honestly, some would say cynically, Alinsky framed this classic dilemma in contemporary and highly contextualized terms. The key question in his view was does a particular end justify a particular means? Here is his full list of the "rules" regarding means and ends. What do you think of them? How would you apply them to macro social work practice?

Table 8.2 Alinsky, on Means and Ends (1971)

1. One's concern with the ethics of means and ends varies inversely with one's personal interest in the issue.
2. The judgment of the ethics of means is dependent upon the political position of those sitting in judgment.
3. Judgment (regarding means and ends) must be made in the context of the times in which the action occurred and not from any other vantage point.
4. Concern with ethics increases with the number of means available and vice versa.
5. The less important the end ... the more one can afford to engage in ethical evaluations of means.
6. In war, the end justifies almost any means.
7. Generally, success or failure is a mighty determinant of the ethics of a particular means.
8. The morality of a means depends upon whether the means is being employed at a time of imminent defeat or imminent victory.
9. Any effective means is always judged by the opposition as being unethical.
10. You do what you can with what you have and clothe it in moral garments.
11. Goals must be phrased in general terms of higher purpose (e.g., liberty, equality, fraternity) (pp. 26–45).

Questions for Discussion

1. Are Alinsky's tactics ethical?
2. Are they consistent with social work ethics?

The Process of Ethical Decision Making

The examples cited in this chapter illustrate different hierarchical ordering of the values that could guide the resolution of ethical dilemmas. They do not, however, outline the steps involved in applying these values. Here are a few possible approaches.

The first is the "E.T.H.I.C. Model of Decision Making," developed by Elaine Congress (1999). She proposes the following steps:

- **E**xamine the relevant values (personal, societal, professional, client, agency).
- **T**hink about the ethical principles and laws that apply to the situation.
- **H**ypothesize the consequences of various options.
- **I**dentify who will benefit or be harmed by your decision.
- **C**onsult with supervisor and colleagues before you act.

Reisch and Lowe (2000) proposed the following seven-step framework specifically for macro social workers:

1. Identify the ethical principles that apply to the situation.
2. Collect additional information needed to examine the ethical dilemma in question.
3. Identify the relevant ethical values and/or rules that apply to the ethical problem.
4. Identify any potential conflicts of interest and those likely to benefit from such conflicts.
5. List the appropriate ethical rules in terms of importance in this situation.
6. Determine the consequences of applying different ethical rules or ranking these rules differently.
7. Determine who needs to resolve the dilemma.

Lastly, there is the "Ethics Work-Up," which the author adapted from Thomas (1978), "Training in Medical Ethics: An Ethical Workup." This model assumes that we can apply the discipline of ethics in a rigorous manner to social work practice to help us understand (a) the value questions ethical dilemmas raise; (b) the ethical dimensions of various options confronting the parties to the situation; and (c) the merits of various reasons offered in support of each option.

Table 8.3 Steps of the Ethics Work-Up

1. Identify the facts of the situation and their likely consequences as best as you can.
2. Identify all related value factors (personal, professional, social, and human) present for all actors (individuals, groups, organizations) involved in the situation and the major value conflicts.
3. Set priorities for the values you identified as in conflict in Step 2. State the reasons that would support this priority setting in your view.
4. Identify and present the argument in support of the reasons advanced in Step 4 by answering the following questions:
   a. What underlying ethical norms support your view?
   b. Why should you accept these norms as guides for conduct in this situation?
   c. What do these norms imply for how you should arrange values in a priority order? (Revise the priorities established in Step 4 if required to do so at this point. That is, Step 5 requires one to make an argument showing why we should accept certain value priorities and what their implications are for how one should act in the situation.)
5. What are the policy implications if your decision on this situation was generalized (i.e., via laws, regulations, specific ethical canons, precedents)?
6. How could one challenge the value priorities developed in Step 4 and defended in Step 5?
7. Criticize the arguments given in steps four through six.
   a. How could one challenge your priorities?

b. Do the implications identified in Step 6 follow from the priorities developed in Step 4 and defended in Step 5?

c. How would you defend the position you developed from these critiques?

Table 8.3: *Adapted from David C. Thomasma, "Training in Medical Ethics: An Ethical Workup," Forum in Medicine, vol. 1, no. 9. Copyright © 1978.*

CASE ILLUSTRATION
APPLYING AN ETHICAL FRAMEWORK

You have been working with an ad hoc coalition of health care providers and consumers in a major metropolitan area regarding a range of issues that focus on access to health care, quality of care, and consumer sovereignty in the health care arena. One of the major partners in the coalition is the local Health and Hospital Workers Union. The union, which has successfully organized health care and social workers in nonprofit and private hospitals, managed care companies, and HMOs in the region, is involved in serious and conflict-ridden negotiations over its contract. Among the issues: (a) differential salary levels for new and longtime employees; (b) health and pension benefits; (c) improved working conditions; and (d) enhanced quality of care. In addition, the union has pressed for greater influence for workers and consumers in making health policy, especially on matters of client care and the distribution of institutional resources.

After weeks of negotiations, however, the two sides are at an impasse. It appears the employers' side is not bargaining in good faith because it doubts the union's ability to sustain an effective strike or job action. The employers also contend that the unionization of some hospital staff members, including social workers, nurses, interns, and residents, violates professional codes of ethics and renders the employers under no moral or legal obligation to engage in collective bargaining with the union.

Last night, the union members voted overwhelmingly to strike effective next Monday. The union's representative to the coalition asked you to use your influence to persuade the coalition to endorse the strike. While you are sympathetic to the union's position, you know that a strike will affect the quality of care (at least temporarily) for the constituents you represent. What do you do? What are your reasons for your decision?

Questions to Consider

1. What is the nature of the ethical dilemma?
2. Who created the dilemma?
3. What is the locus of responsibility for its resolution?
4. What is the nature, basis, and extent of your ethical obligation? To whom?
5. What are the short- and long-term consequences of your decision for your constituents?
6. What social work values or ethical frameworks help guide you in your decision making?

If used properly, models of ethical decision making allow us to weigh the relevant factors in a situation and develop a consistent ethical response. One benefit of working in an organization is that we often do not have to resolve ethical dilemmas in isolation. We can talk to colleagues and other professionals to acquire their perspectives, gather information, identify alternatives, and learn about past actions on similar dilemmas. Unlike family members and friends, who may be sympathetic and supportive but not bound by any ethical codes, your colleagues will maintain confidentiality.

If you are the only social worker in an agency—a common situation for macro social workers—it may be advisable to seek external consultation from someone who is knowledgeable of the NASW *Code of Ethics*. These private conversations will help you generate options and enable you to identify the pros and cons of each alternative. In host settings, such as hospitals, which have established ethics committees, it is better to exercise caution before seeking ethical advice, because such committees often focus primarily on risk management for the organization (Reamer, 1987).

It is also useful to consult the literature for guidance and to reflect on how you have dealt with similar dilemmas in the past. Think about what you did in those circumstances. How did your attempt to resolve the dilemma work out? Is the present situation different? If so, in what ways is it different? Finally, you can try to find out whether your agency has specific guidelines about such situations.

Recurrent Ethical Dilemmas in Macro Social Work Practice

The following section looks at some recurrent ethical issues and the dilemmas they create for macro social work practitioners. Case examples, based largely on "real world" experiences, will provide readers with the opportunity to apply one or more of the decision-making models outlined previously.

Confidentiality

The NASW *Code of Ethics* (2017, Standard 1.07 (c)) states: "Social workers should protect the confidentiality of all information obtained in the course of professional service, except for compelling professional reasons ... [This] does not apply when disclosure is necessary to prevent *serious, foreseeable, and imminent harm* to a client or *other identifiable person*" (emphasis added). Confidentiality is a core ethical obligation of social work because it serves a number of central purposes. It maintains clients' and constituents' ability to self-determine (i.e., preserves their agency) and sustains the trust between them and workers that is essential for effective practice. Maintaining confidentiality also protects the people with whom we work, practitioners, and employing agencies against legal risks. Finally, the principle helps preserve our professional integrity by preventing us from engaging in any deceptions (Bok, 1999; Wilson, 1980; Reamer, 2013).

As the *Code* indicates, however, confidentiality is not an absolute. There are certain circumstances in which practitioners can make exceptions. For example, confidentiality can be broken to protect a third party from harm. In fact, courts have determined that in some situations social workers have a "duty to warn" and are *required* to break confidentiality (Kagle & Kopels, 1994; Weil & Sanchez, 1983). Yet, it is not always clear in macro social work practice settings what constitutes a "serious risk of harm," to whom is the duty owed, or how to determine whether a risk is "foreseeable" or "imminent."

Conversely, practitioners can violate confidentiality to benefit their clients or constituents or a third party such as a family member or a minor, for example by providing useful information to colleagues. It is important, however, to assess whether such actions are paternalistic and deprive individuals or groups of their right to self-determine. Under certain conditions, social workers may be obligated to break confidentiality in response to a subpoena or court order. All of these possible exceptions underscore the importance of obtaining informed consent in advance from the people with whom we work. Yet, this is far more difficult in macro social work practice settings because we do not know all the people with whom we are working, nor can we foresee all the possible consequences of actions taken to produce community, organizational, or societal change.

CASE ILLUSTRATION
CONFIDENTIALITY VS. NATIONAL SECURITY

(This case is adapted from actual events.)

Shortly after the terrorist attacks on New York and Washington on September 11, 2001, law enforcement officials arrested several Arab American men in Detroit and one near Chicago on charges of using false information to obtain specialized driver licenses that would have allowed them to transport hazardous materials. Although suspicions were cast that these men might somehow be connected to the individuals responsible for the September 11 attacks, no evidence to this effect has subsequently been presented. In the course of its investigation, the FBI learned that several of these men had participated in a training course for truck drivers operated by ACCESS, the largest social service organization for Arab Americans in the United States, which is in Dearborn, Michigan. Government and private sector dollars fund the course—one of several employment-related programs ACCESS delivered successfully for years.

The FBI approached ACCESS and requested the files of the arrested men. Citing concerns over national security, government agents explained that they were seeking any information in the files that might identify the men's links to terrorist organizations or provide information on other potential terrorists. They argued that as the government funded the training program, the organization's records should be open to government officials. Of greater importance, they asserted that since the national interest was involved, protection of the public's safety took precedence over protection of the men's confidential records.

The director of ACCESS refused to comply with the FBI's request. He argued that the protection of clients' confidentiality was necessary to safeguard their privacy and well-being and to ensure that future clients would trust the organization and its staff. In addition, he asserted the government had not demonstrated a clear connection between its request for information and its national security interests. Finally, given the fear of increased official and unofficial discrimination toward Arab Americans (and other persons of color) in the aftermath of the September 11 attacks, he argued the protection of clients' rights was part of a broader effort to protect their civil liberties.

Questions to Consider

1. Which argument do you find more compelling? What values did you prioritize?
2. How did you arrive at your decision? What decision-making process did you use?
3. What ethical principles can you derive from your decision?
4. What are the implications if you generalized these principles to other similar circumstances?
5. How is this case relevant to recent policy developments regarding immigrants and refugees in the United States?

Paternalism and Self-Determination

Figure 8.7 Paternalism and Self-Determination

Fig. 8.7: *Copyright © 2011 Depositphotos/lightkeeper.*

Figure 8.8 What is Paternalism?

Fig. 8.8: *Copyright © 2014 Depositphotos/samuraitop.*

In *Doing Good: The Limits of Benevolence* (Gaylin et al., 1978) the authors (philosophers, historians, and legal experts) discussed how even the most well-intentioned actions by professionals, institutions, and society can create problems for those whom the actions are designed to help. Margolin (1997), based on ideas derived from Foucault (1995), goes even further to criticize the social work profession for using its alleged benevolence as a means of social control. How can this happen? To understand these arguments and their application to contemporary macro social work practice, it is useful to examine the meaning of the complex phenomenon known as paternalism and to recognize how our attitudes toward paternalism complicate our efforts to help people, particularly those who have different cultural values and norms, and sometimes conflict with our goal of maintaining their self-determination.

John Stuart Mill, in his classic work *On Liberty* (1859, 1910), presented a clear statement outlining the limits of our ability to assist others against their will:

> … The only purpose for which power can be rightfully exercised over any member of a civilized community, against his [sic] will, is to prevent harm to others. His own good, either physical or moral, is not a sufficient warrant. … Over himself, over his own body and mind, the individual is sovereign (pp. 72–73).

More than a century later, a modern philosopher, Gerald Dworkin (1972), defined paternalism as "interference with a person's liberty of action justified by reasons referring exclusively to the welfare, good, happiness, needs, interests, or values of the person being coerced" (quoted in Beauchamp, 1980, p. 122). If Mill and Dworkin are correct, policies as different as restrictions on abortion, laws banning smoking or the use of trans fats in restaurants, the Affordable Care Act's requirement that people purchase health insurance, and mandatory work requirements to obtain social welfare benefits would be proscribed. HSOs could not compel their clients to participate in any programs as a condition for the receipt of other services. Advocates could not insist on constituents testifying at public hearings. Organizers could not hold community residents responsible for failure to attend meetings unless they could demonstrate that nonattendance hurts the community as a whole.

Figure 8.9 illustrates how paternalism influences social policies at all levels.

Figure 8.9 The Spectrum of Paternalism

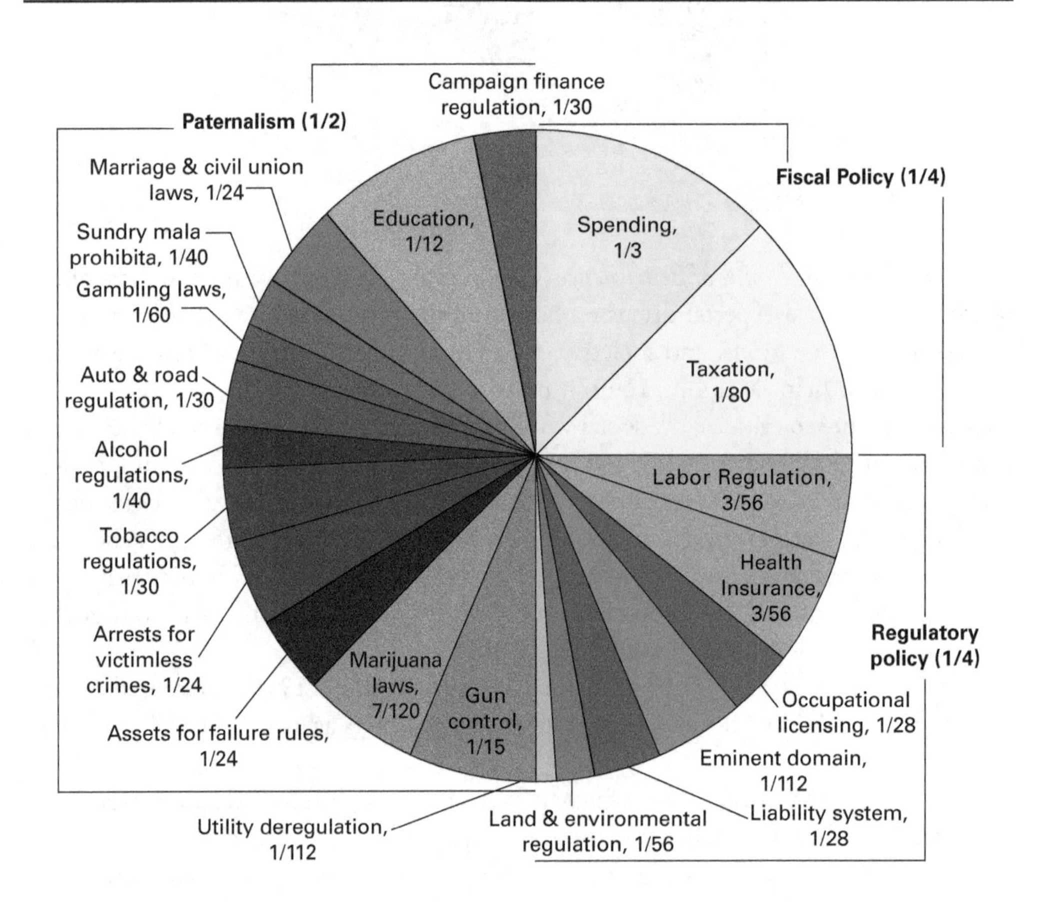

Fig. 8.9: *Copyright © /Jim Riley and Geoff Riley.*

Paternalism takes many forms in social work practice and social policy. In macro social work practice, it could involve the deliberate withholding of information from community residents for their own good (e.g., the likelihood that a favored program will soon be cut). Alternately, it could involve lying to constituents on what a coalition partner said about their organization. HSOs sometimes act against the stated wishes of clients or constituents by allocating resources to programs preferred by the agency instead of those desired by the community. Social policies reflect paternalistic attitudes in their determination of what benefits to provide. For example, health insurance policies may cover prescriptions for Viagra but not female contraceptive devices.

Macro social work practitioners rationalize paternalistic behavior in several ways. They often claim that constituents do not understand the issues, that if "they knew what we knew" they would go along with our decision. This justification smacks of elitism and it possibly reflects unacknowledged racist, sexist, or classist bias. A similar rationale is that our constituents are incapable of comprehending complex policy details, either temporarily (due to their age or condition) or permanently (due to a lack of education, sophistication, experience, etc.). Sometimes practitioners justify paternalistic actions based on the assumption that their constituents (or coalition partners) have implicitly given prior consent to a decision on strategy or tactics. Alternately, they may argue that in the likelihood the decision will produce the results constituents want, they would most likely consent after it has occurred.

While the proscription against paternalism appears to be straightforward, there are persistent issues that complicate this seemingly simple ethical principle. For example, how can we develop helpful community interventions that do not—in some way—interfere, constrain, or restrict the actions of those we intend to assist? In our work with excluded, marginalized, and dependent populations, whose sense of justice do we serve if we act or fail to act paternalistically? In macro social work practice, when we often have to make decisions without the luxury of consulting with constituents, what are acceptable and unacceptable grounds for paternalistic intervention? Is it more acceptable to engage in paternalistic behavior if certain issues—for example, a public health or environmental crisis, or the protection of a particularly vulnerable population—are involved?

Macro social workers, particularly those working with populations different from themselves, and who may be especially sensitive to behavior that appears to be paternalistic, should consider the following criteria in assessing their behavior:

1. If I (or we) engage in this paternalistic action, is it consistent with our constituents' long-term goals and preferences?
2. Can we provide our constituents with the relevant information that would enable them to be full partners in the decision-making process in a sufficiently timely manner?
3. Can our constituents acquire the necessary sophistication to understand the complex issues and optional solutions that exist?
4. Do we have to make an action decision immediately? What other options exist?
5. What is the balance between what we would gain and lose by failing to allow constituents to participate in the decision-making process as full partners?

6. What would be the effects on our group or organization, and on our relationship with our constituents, if we fail to involve them in the decision?

In general, three circumstances may justify paternalistic behavior. First, when the harm done by failing to act paternalistically would be irreversible. Second, paternalism is permissible if we can protect and preserve constituents' current and future well-being, long-term interests, and future self-determination only by restricting their decision-making role *temporarily*. Third, such actions are not ethical violations if there is an immediate and compelling need to act, such as a crisis, or when we cannot defer a vital decision (Reamer, 2013; Dworkin, 1972).

Self-Determination

Figure 8.10 Self-Determination

Fig. 8.10: *Copyright © 2013 Depositphotos/iqoncept.*

There is a close relationship between dilemmas regarding self-determination and those concerning paternalism. Self-determination—for individuals, groups, and communities—is a core social work value. Social workers believe it is a universal right that is particularly significant for vulnerable populations. According to Levy (1976) there is no justification for depriving clients of a benefit or a right merely because they sought or were compelled to participate in a service. Self-determination is considered both an end and a means; it is a precondition (what ethicists call a "side constraint") to the fulfillment of individual or community goals. It assumes people have the ability to make their own decisions and thereby maintain their dignity and sense of self-worth.

As Mill wrote more than a century and a half ago, self-determination is a near absolute right. If we are going to violate people's right to self-determination, there must be a clear justification. Yet, when laws, agency regulations, or community norms are ambiguous, or when constituents' capacity to act is not easy to determine, who decides when it is acceptable to violate people's self-determination and how are such decisions made? A key principle to apply is that any limitation on people's right to self-determination must match the importance of the other interests involved. Another principle is that we must also consider the effect of this violation on third parties.

Although the NASW *Code of Ethics* (2017) comments on this dilemma, its statements reinforce rather than clarify the inherent ambiguities involved:

> Social workers' primary responsibility is to promote the well-being of clients. ... However, social workers' responsibility to the larger society or specific legal obligations *may on limited occasions supersede the loyalty owed clients*, and clients should be so advised (1.01) (emphasis added).
>
> Social workers respect and promote the right of clients to self-determination and assist clients in their efforts to identify and clarify their goals. Social workers may limit clients' right to self-determination when, *in the social worker's professional judgment, clients' actions or potential actions pose a serious, foreseeable, and imminent risk to themselves or others* (1.02) (emphasis added).

The autonomy-paternalism debate involves a series of ethical dilemmas at the heart of contemporary macro social work practice. One is the relationship between the satisfaction of clients' and constituents' interests, rights, and values and our professional role and goals, and between the rights of the people with whom we work and societal priorities and needs. Another issue is how the unequal distribution of resources and power (in communities, organizations, and society as a whole) influences our perspectives on this debate. A third is whether social work practice, however well intended, is actually a form of social control and a means to achieve the dominant culture's goals and objectives, or a liberatory form of practice (Day, 1981; Dominelli, 2010). A fourth involves the conflict between clients' or constituents' right to self-determination and autonomy ("negative freedom") and their right to assistance that will protect their well-being and increase their ability to self-determine in the future ("positive freedom"). In other words, a conflict exists between the interests of clients or constituents, as they define them, and our desire to "do good" and protect them (Gaylin et al. 1978). Finally, this conflict raises the question of whether we should prioritize what is good for an individual, group, or community or balance that good against what is good for society as a whole.

Figure 8.11 Cartoon

"I didn't get my 'Hail, Caesar' from you this morning."

Fig. 8.11: *Copyright © 2014 Depositphotos/andrewgenn.*

CASE ILLUSTRATION
THE LIMITS OF SELF-DETERMINATION

Introduction

Eastville is a community of about 100,000 people within a large Eastern metropolitan center. Its population is "in transition" from predominantly White and middle income to one with a mixed racial, ethnic, and class composition. At present, approximately 40% of the residents are African American, 30% are White, 25% are Latino, and the remaining 5% are Asian American. The overwhelming majority of the families with school-age children is composed of people of color. While the White population has lived in the community for generations, most of the people of color arrived during the past 10 years. The newest arrivals are Asian American and Latino immigrants, who have been in the community less than five years.

Over the past two decades, much of the industrial base of the community has disappeared. There are few large employers and most of the new jobs in Eastville are in the service sector, pay minimum wage, and have few benefits. Consequently, the poverty rate in the community is about 30%, with pockets of severe poverty in certain neighborhoods. Unemployment is about 25%, with higher rates among youth. In some neighborhoods, about 50% of the population is on some form of public assistance (TANF, SSI). Social indicators of distress (e.g., homelessness, alcohol and drug abuse, crime) reflect the economic problems at the core of the community.

While the community elects its own mayor and City Council, it receives most of its services from the surrounding county. This county is more affluent and less demographically diverse than Eastville. Its political leadership resides in the office of the county executive and the Board of Supervisors. Voter turnout in Eastville is lower than that of the surrounding county and its political influence on county elections has diminished in recent years.

Eastville has lost many of the nonprofit organizations that once provided social services and recreational and cultural activities to the community. Several of the major nonprofits have relocated from Eastville to newer areas in the county. The Catholic archdiocese has closed the churches in a few parishes. Community residents have difficulty accessing services or cultural institutions in the surrounding region, in part because of their poverty and in part because of poor public transportation. This contributes to the growing sense of social isolation in Eastville.

On the positive side, churches remain a strong force for social cohesion in certain neighborhoods, most notably in the African American, Polish, and Italian communities. A new church has opened in the Latino community and Asian Americans built a temple to serve Buddhists in the community. Several of the churches have developed social service and/or child care programs. There are a few emerging grassroots multiservice community organizations, including agencies that focus on the needs of immigrants.

The Dilemma

At the request of the local community board and an ad hoc coalition of concerned community residents, Eastville asked a team of community social workers from a metropolitan area-wide community development corporation for assistance. You are part of that team.

After working with the community residents for some time, they have identified a variety of issues of concern and formed an organization Community United for a Revitalized Eastville (CURE). One of the most compelling issues is the declining quality of the public schools. There is incontrovertible evidence of this problem. Following considerable discussion, the leadership of CURE voted to make a campaign for a school voucher initiative its top priority. The proposed initiative would provide cash grants or tax credits to families who send their children to private schools, including religiously based schools. Although community members regarded other issues as equally important, CURE selected this issue because of its broad appeal and its potential for uniting the community. The leaders of CURE asked you to play a major role in developing this campaign.

You are a strong proponent of public schools and believe the voucher initiative, while well intentioned, is a misguided effort that will ultimately further undermine the quality of public education in Eastville and fail to produce the desired results for its residents and their children. You believe strongly that public education is a fundamental prerequisite for the preservation of democracy—another core value of social work. You also believe (based upon research of the experience of other communities) that the issue has been promoted as a distraction from more fundamental concerns of the community and that there are more feasible solutions to the problems of education in Eastville. On the other hand, you believe deeply in the concepts of community self-determination and community empowerment. They are both fundamental values of social work. What do you do?

Whistle-blowing

Figure 8.12 Whistle-blowing

Whistle-blowing involves a choice between silence and full-scale disclosure of collegial misconduct, choices often complicated by the many "shades of gray" that such situations reflect. These shades of gray reflect conflicting moral and ethical obligations. These include the conflict between obligations to colleagues and one's organization (loyalty) vs. obligations to clients, constituents, and society.

The NASW *Code of Ethics* proposes a two-stage process to resolve such dilemmas. In general, the *Code* suggests that social workers should first approach the colleague suspected of misconduct and address the issue through the organization's established channels (Standard 2.11 (c)), particularly for less severe or ethically egregious matters. There may be reasons, however, when this approach is not viable.

If lower-level approaches fail or are not possible, the *Code* stipulates that a social worker is obligated to be more assertive. This may lead to formal whistle-blowing by notifying the individuals inside or outside the organization—such as licensing or regulatory boards—who are in a position to address the salient issues (Standard 2.11(d)). This step is particularly important when failure to stop the alleged behavior has serious potential consequences for clients or constituents, the reputation of colleagues, or the morale or survival of the organization itself.

Before taking on the risks involved in whistle-blowing, a social worker should ask:

1. What are my motives for doing this? Am I acting out of principle or engaging in self-serving behavior?
2. Do the facts warrant this action? How strong is the evidence? Am I confident that my allegations rest on a solid foundation? Consideration must be given to the possibility that, in the long run, conforming may be more beneficial than disloyalty to colleagues and victims.
3. Whom am I accusing? Is it fair to accuse this person or organization? If no one can reasonably be held responsible—as in the case of a natural disaster—then the warning does not constitute whistle-blowing.
4. Have I pursued all feasible and reasonable alternatives to full-scale whistle-blowing, such as mediation, taking corrective actions, strict supervision, or continuing education?
5. Finally, if I am going to engage in a breach of loyalty, will my whistle-blowing make a difference? If I pursue this course of action, how can I minimize the potential harm to the organization and to my colleagues?

Bok (1980) similarly suggests whistle-blowers should exhaust all existing avenues for change within the organization before sounding the alarm. They can, however, reject alternative approaches for three reasons: (1) There is no channel within the organization to address the problem at hand; (2) There is insufficient time to go through existing channels; or (3) The organization is so corrupt there is imminent danger of being silenced. She proposes the following guidelines to determine whether to blow the whistle:

1. The accusation should not be trivial. It should concern a matter of morality or ethics that is basic and serious.
2. The accusation must be specific and refer to a situation that is immediate and current.
3. The whistle-blower should seek, if possible, objective advice regarding his or her decision before going public in order to minimize the risk of personal bias.
4. The whistle-blower should exhaust all channels for internal remedies before sounding the alarm.
5. The whistle-blower must have specific evidence.
6. The accusation should be commensurate with the whistle-blower's responsibility.

7. The accusation should be articulate and must arouse the ethical sense of its audience to be effective. In other words, it should have some chance of success.

Lewis (1985) also spells out clear guidelines for whistle-blowing. First, the individual must decide, whether all things being equal, speaking out is in the public interest. Second, the individual must decide whether his or her responsibility to serve the public interest in the particular situation outweighs his or her responsibility to colleagues and the organization, and to their personal reputation and the livelihood of their families. The individual must also consider "what are the least harmful methods at my disposal?"

CASE ILLUSTRATION
SHOULD YOU BLOW THE WHISTLE?

You are the assistant director of a nonprofit, community development agency in a low-income urban neighborhood. You have worked for the agency since you received your MSW degree five years ago and have been in your current position for 10 months. The director of the agency, Nancy Jones, has headed the organization for 10 years. The agency has prospered under her leadership and she enjoys a good reputation in the community. Jones has been your mentor since you were a graduate student. Your career has thrived under her guidance and you have turned down several lucrative job offers to remain at the agency and work with her.

Two months ago, as part of a routine annual audit of the agency's books, auditors asked you to explain a discrepancy of approximately $10,000 in the agency's accounts. Apparently, the organization charged a steady flow of funds, in relatively small amounts, to program accounts but spent them on other, undetermined purposes. On closer examination of the records of the past five years, you discover that a similar pattern exists. In short, without going further than six years back, you discovered that more than $50,000 in agency funds were used for other than program purposes with no apparent explanation.

You bring this matter to the attention of Jones, who has the ultimate authority to sign off on all agency expenditures. After initially pleading ignorance of the matter, she "takes you into her confidence" and tells you that she used these funds to establish a "Director's Discretionary Account" to cover those out-of-pocket costs she regularly incurred in her work, but which cannot be reimbursed through the grants and contracts that comprise the bulk of the agency's budget. Items paid out of this account included meals, tickets to special events (e.g., fundraisers), and extraordinary travel. Although somewhat troubled by this matter, you accept Jones's explanation. As you investigate the issue further, however, you learn that about half of the reimbursed expenses were for private, not professional, purposes. You are required to sign off on the agency's audit prior to the next board of directors' meeting. The organization files a copy of the signed audit with the state tax bureau and the local United Way, a major funder of the agency. Hence, you will be legally liable for subsequent discrepancies.

Jones has called you this morning to ask what is delaying the processing of the final audit report. The board meeting will take place in only 10 days and the directors must have the report a week in advance to approve it at their meeting. Jones is someone you admire—someone who is clearly a dedicated and talented leader. If you "blow the whistle" on her it could result in serious harm to her career, the reputation of the agency, the well-being of the community the agency serves, and, of no small significance, to your career as well. If you do not blow the whistle, you face both legal liability and the effect of nonaction on the agency and its constituents. What do you do? What are your reasons for doing so? (Reisch & Lowe, 2000)

Truth Telling

What do we mean by "the truth"? What do we do when people believe "multiple truths" may exist, particularly in an era of "alternative facts"? What is the difference between not lying and telling the truth? In brief, is truth telling an absolute?

Figure 8.13a Truth Telling: The Different Meanings of "Truth"

Fig. 8.13a: *Copyright © 2013 Depositphotos/kikkerdirk.*

Figure 8.13b Truth Telling: Magnifying Truth

Fig. 8.13b: *Copyright © 2013 Depositphotos/AndreyPopov.*

Figure 8.13c Truth Telling: Direction Post

Fig. 8.13c: *Copyright © 2011 Depositphotos/iqoncept.*

Figure 8.13d Truth Telling: Pinocchio

Fig. 8.13d: *Copyright © 2015 Depositphotos/memoangeles.*

Why is telling the truth so important? There are several critical reasons that serve as guides to macro social work practice, particularly in an environment in which racial and cultural divisions have intensified long-standing mistrust. A primary reason is that truth is the basis for establishing and maintaining professional relationships and is the foundation of a practitioner's credibility with the individuals, communities, and colleagues with whom we work. In this regard, it is important to distinguish between purposefully conveying false information—for example, misrepresentation of oneself or one's organization—and making misstatements or inadvertent errors. It is also important to distinguish between acts of commission and acts of omission, such as withholding information from clients or constituents.

This raises several important questions: What situations would justify lying? Is there a higher good than telling the truth? Is it permissible to lie under any of the following circumstances?

- to protect yourself or others from physical harm;
- to protect yourself or others from property loss;
- to preserve your personal liberty or that of others;
- to protect your reputation, the reputation of a colleague, or the reputation of your organization; or
- to help a client or constituent circumvent a law or regulation you consider unfair in order to meet her need.

To resolve these dilemmas, macro social work practitioners should consider the following factors:

- the "magnitude" of the deception;
- the degree of falsehood;
- the issue being lied about;
- who is being lied to;
- the actual or potential consequences of the act;
- the unique aspects of the situation (e.g., available options); and
- the purpose(s) of the lie—i.e., is it a case of "benevolent deception" (e.g., to preserve an organization's funding or an individual's reputation)?

To resolve ethical dilemmas in which there may be some uncertainty over the value of truth telling, macro social workers should use the following criteria:

- the extent to which the well-being of clients or community members is protected or enhanced;
- the likelihood that the well-being of the community will be harmed in the absence of using the deception; and
- the lack of legitimate means to protect the community's well-being (Reisch & Lowe, 2000).

Finally, Bok (1999) summarizes an ethical approach to this common dilemma. She argues that under some circumstances a lie may be acceptable or even necessary. She concludes, however, that where a lie is a possible choice, it is imperative first to determine if telling the truth is a viable option.

CASE ILLUSTRATION
TRUTH TELLING AND A CONFLICT OF DUTIES

You are a social worker on the staff of a community-based agency that serves primarily low-income clients, including large numbers of immigrants, some of whom are undocumented. Some of the latter have family members nearby who are citizens or legal immigrants. Although most of your undocumented clients have jobs, they do not receive health insurance from their jobs and cannot purchase individual plans through the new insurance exchanges the state has established. One of your coworkers has suggested that the agency should assist the children of these undocumented clients by adding them to their relatives' health care plans. You are concerned about the consequences of engaging in potentially fraudulent conduct that could have repercussions for your clients, your agency, and yourself. How would you respond? What are your reasons?

Allocating Scarce Resources

Figure 8.14 Allocating Scarce Resources

Fig. 8.14: *Copyright © 2016 Depositphotos/vaeenma.*

There are three common dilemmas regarding the allocation of scarce resources in macro social work practice. One involves the distribution of personal resources—how practitioners should address role conflicts, the risk of burnout, and the amount of time they set aside for self-care. (*See Chapter 15 and Epilogue.*) A second, increasingly frequent dilemma concerns how organizations should distribute finite resources through the design of their programs, the construction of their budgets, and their determination of eligibility requirements and benefit levels. Finally, in an increasingly partisan political environment, there will be constant struggles over the allocation of societal resources—struggles shaped by an ever-changing combination of political, economic, and ideological factors.

Philosophers have proposed a number of possible criteria to resolve these dilemmas of distribution. They include prioritizing the needs of the least advantaged (Rawls, 1999); promoting equality of opportunity or outcome (Ryan, 1981); measuring the value of past or potential future contributions to society; providing compensation for past injustices (Coates, 2016); and basing distribution on merit, "desert" (Dworkin, 1978), ability to pay, or the ability to take advantage of a specific benefit. What do you think are the pros and cons of each approach? Under what circumstances would you apply each approach?

CASE ILLUSTRATION
ALLOCATING SCARCE RESOURCES AT THE ORGANIZATIONAL LEVEL

You are the associate director of a large, nonprofit multipurpose social services organization that employs more than 100 people (professionals, paraprofessionals, and support staff) at various sites. The agency has always provided noncontributory health insurance to its employees, in part to compensate for its relatively modest salaries. In recent years, the organization has experienced increased fiscal challenges due to cutbacks in government grants and contracts, a decrease in full-fee clients, and increased operating costs.

The Board of Directors has mandated a 10% cut in the agency's budget during the next fiscal year and expressed a preference for making cuts in employee benefits rather than cuts in services or staff. A primary target of these cuts would be health insurance. It argues that under the new health care law employees would be able to purchase coverage through the state's insurance exchange and that most employees would be eligible for subsidies for this purpose. Depending on the type of coverage selected (and how much they were willing to pay), the agency's employees could obtain coverage equal to, greater than, or less than the coverage the agency currently provides. Under the new law, the penalty the agency would pay for not providing coverage would be less than its existing costs. The executive director has asked for your views on this matter. What would you recommend? What values would guide your decision?

CASE ILLUSTRATION
ALLOCATING SCARCE RESOURCES AT THE POLICY LEVEL

The Harris County Coal Company operates 10 small mines in West Virginia with an average of 30 miners each. Congress is considering revising the Affordable Care Act to create a single-payer, national health insurance program. It would provide government-financed health care for all with a provision that the insured pay the first $50 in any given year. Within the past year, scientists have developed a number of techniques to minimize the effect of coal dust on miners, who develop black lung disease from prolonged exposure. The problem is that the most effective prevention techniques are expensive. They required both massive ventilation systems and also costly hourly monitoring of the air quality throughout the mine. Analysts estimated the full prevention program would cost $7,500 per miner. The mine workers' union demanded that the company initiate the program, but recognized that small-scale mines, such as those run by Harris, were marginal operations. The added cost, according to management, would close the mines. By coincidence, a government study has just shown that the predicted cost to the government for treatment of black lung disease from the mine under present conditions would also be about $7,500 per person, prorated over all miners.

The government raised several serious policy questions. Should it require the mine to install the black lung disease prevention program to protect the miners and to promote the public interest by lowering the cost of national health insurance? Should the government allow the mining companies to pass the cost along in the form of a pay cut or higher prices?

The mine management proposed another plan, giving the miners a choice between working in the mines with the prevention program installed and taking a pay cut and working in the mines in their present condition without taking the pay cut. Without the prevention program, the national health insurance program would not cover those working in the mines if they developed black lung disease.

Questions to Consider

1. Which option would you recommend?
2. What are your reasons?
3. How would you apply the principles that guided your decision to other policy issues?
4. What would be the implications of applying these principles more broadly?

Summary: Taking Ethical Action in a Frequently Unethical Environment

Recognizing the difference between a practice problem and an ethical dilemma is the first step toward becoming an ethical practitioner. Determining how to analyze the situation is the second. These are necessary but insufficient steps. You also need to take action.

Taking action involves risk. Colleagues may criticize your decisions. It may anger clients or constituents and weaken the relationship you have long struggled to establish with them. It may lead to a power struggle with your supervisor that threatens your job security. You might make a mistake and have to deal with the consequences, including those you did not foresee. A good decision may produce a bad outcome because of faulty implementation.

It is reasonable, therefore, to ask: Why should I take action in this situation when others won't? Conversely, could you live with yourself if you did nothing? Behaving ethically often requires moral courage because we are dealing with serious issues, large and small, in an environment that is often unethical (Reisch, 2014). This courage includes "the capacity to overcome the fear of shame and humiliation in order to admit one's mistakes, to confess a wrong, to reject evil conformity, to renounce injustice, and also to defy immoral or imprudent orders" (Miller, 2000, quoted in Strom-Gottfried, 2007, p. 12). It helps to keep your own moral compass clear and unclouded by repeated adjustments to an unethical environment and to recognize that, in the long run, doing the right thing is of value to the organization in which you work and to the people with whom you are working.

Finally, it is important to ask: Why am I selecting this particular course of action? Make sure your personal beliefs, biases, and interests are not clouding your judgment. Reflect on your motivations for acting. If time permits, go over the process by which you made a decision to ensure you did not omit something important.

Conclusion: Ethical Dilemmas in the Future

Due to a combination of economic, political, and cultural factors, the ethical dilemmas macro social workers face today will probably intensify in the future. Unless the nation makes significant changes in how it allocates resources, it will be increasingly difficult to establish and maintain trust with people and communities from different demographic backgrounds. This lack of trust will compound the ever-present problem of understanding the worldviews and interpretive lenses of diverse communities, particularly as these communities become further isolated from one another. Under conditions of chronic resource scarcity, macro social workers will face persistent challenges regarding their relationships with people and institutions in authority. In their efforts to assist excluded and marginalized communities, they may fear compromising their professional and personal values and widening the gap between their rhetoric and the harsh realities of practice. They may feel constrained between the pressure to acquire cultural humility and the effect of outsiders perceiving them as overly "politically correct."

There are no simple prescriptions to these serious issues. As mentioned in other chapters, adopting the position of a learner, becoming aware of one's ignorance, particularly in complex situations, may help resolve seemingly intractable dilemmas. We will need ongoing courage and patience. Perhaps above all, we will need to forgive the mistakes we make in our attempts to apply high-minded ethical principles to the gritty world of macro social work practice. It will be worthwhile to keep these guidelines in mind as you read the chapters that follow.

END-OF-CHAPTER EXERCISE
VALUES CLARIFICATION

Introduction: Underlying Assumptions

1. Our activities as social workers in community, organizational, and societal settings reflect our personal beliefs and goals and emerge from our personal experience.
2. Social work practice, therefore, can never be value-free (or "objective").
3. All social work practice—and all aspects of our social lives—is political.

Think about your vision of society—the one that shapes your personal, professional, and social goals, and affects the nature of your present and future work. Indicate where you stand in relationship to the following statement:

"My vision of society can best be achieved within existing economic, social, and political institutions."

1	2	3	4
Strongly Agree	Agree	Disagree	Strongly Disagree

Questions to Consider

Think about the ethical and practice implications of your answer.

1. Do you believe you have the right to impose your view of society and change on the people with whom you work in communities and organizations?
2. If so, under what circumstances?
3. If not, why not? And if not, how will your view of society ever be realized?
4. How are issues of politics and power influential in determining both your answer above and also in implementing its implications?

The following are some decision making models that can be used to problem solve and determine actions when assessing an ethical dilemma. Each provides a slightly different series of steps to use, but you will note commonalities. The model that you choose to apply is not as important as is identifying a consistent process to help you critically analyze the ethical dilemmas you may face.

Table 8.4 Models of Ethical Decision Making

Problem-Solving Approach (Reisch & Lowe, 2000)	**Strom-Gottfried (2007)**
1. Identify the ethical principles applying to the situation at hand.	**1.** Who will be helped?
2. Collect additional information necessary to examine the ethical dilemma in question.	**2.** What are my choices?
3. Identify relevant ethical values and/or rules that apply to the ethical problem.	**3.** When have I faced a similar dilemma?
4. Identify potential conflict of interest and people who are likely to benefit from conflicts; how it will affect individuals, groups, organizations?	**4.** Where do ethical and clinical guidelines lead me?
5. Identify appropriate ethical rules and rank them in terms of importance.	**5.** Why am I selecting a particular course of action?
6. Determine the consequences of applying different ethical rules or ranking rules differently.	**6.** How should I enact my decision? What are my next steps?

ETHIC Model (Congress, 1999)	**Reamer (2013)**
1. **E**xamine personal, professional, client, agency, and societal and other relevant values.	**1.** Identify the ethical issues, including the values and duties that may conflict.
2. **T**hink about the ethical standards, laws, and legal precedents that apply.	**2.** Identify the individuals, groups, and organizations most likely to be affected by the ethical decision.
3. **H**ypothesize different decisions, their outcomes and the effect on relevant systems.	**3.** Identify all possible courses of action. Consider the participants who would be involved in each course of action, along with the possible benefits and risks for each.
4. **I**dentify who will benefit or be harmed by these specific decisions, keeping in mind the profession's values and mission.	**4.** Examine the reasons for and against each possible course of action. Consider relevant (a) ethical theories, principles, and guidelines; (b) practice theory and principles; (d) personal values (including religious, cultural, and ethnic values, and political ideology); and (e) NASW *Code of Ethics.*
5. **C**onsult with your supervisor and colleagues and others who are appropriate.	**5.** Consult with appropriate experts.
	6. Make a decision and document the decision-making process.
	7. Monitor, evaluate, and document the decision-making process/implementation.

Dolgoff, Harrington, and Loewenberg (2012)
1. Identify the problem and factors maintaining the problem.
2. Identify all persons, groups, and organizations involved in the situation.
3. Determine who should be involved in the decision making.
4. Identify the values involved in the situation—client, family, worker, professional, group, institutional, societal.
5. Identify the goals and objectives that may resolve or reduce the problem.
6. Identify alternative interventions to reach the goals.
7. Assess the effectiveness of each of these alternative strategies.
8. Select a strategy.
9. Implement the strategy.
10. Monitor the implementation of the strategy.
11. Evaluate the results.

Table 8.4: *Based on information from Michael Reisch and Jane Isaacs Lowe, "'Of Means and Ends' Revisited: Teaching Ethical Community Organization in an Unethical Society" Journal of Community Practice, vol. 7, no.1, 2000; Elaine Piller Congress, Social Work Values and Ethics: Identifying and Resolving Professional Dilemmas, 1999; Frederic G. Reamer, Social Work Values and Ethics, 2013; Frank Dolgoff, Donna Harrington and Frank M. Loewenberg, Ethical Decisions for Social Work Practice, 2000.*

CHAPTER 9

Defining 'Community' and Assessing its Needs and Assets

What is community? Not just where you were born or where you lay your head down to sleep. Community is a mix of history, experience, stories, and imagination: possibility. The man who went away twenty years ago can still be very much a part of a community—as can, I believe, a woman who has not yet been there, who will not cross paths with a given community for another twenty years.

—**Rick Bass, "Round River,"** ***Orion*****, Summer 1997**

We have all known the long loneliness, and we have found that the answer is community.

—**Dorothy Day**

Introduction

I came across the first quote at Parsons Memorial Lodge, Tuolomne Meadows, while hiking in Yosemite National Park a few summers ago. It stuck with me and reinforced the idea that *all* social work practice occurs in a community context. Yet, the meaning of community has changed considerably in recent years, a change that has significant implications for community practice, particularly in an increasingly diverse society. The boundaries, structures, and dynamics of communities have become increasingly fluid. A number of factors have shaped their development, some old, some new. More than ever, communities interact with other internal and external systems through a process of dynamic, mutual influence. This chapter discusses various conceptions of community, including geographically bound communities, communities based on identity, and issue-based communities. After providing different definitions of what is a "community," the chapter includes the following content:

1. Theories of community change and community practice: behavioral, structural-functional, conflict, and social movement.
2. The major functions of a community.
3. Features of a "competent" community.
4. Factors that promote and interfere with the development of competent communities.
5. Different categories of community needs.
6. Purposes of a community needs assessment.
7. Different means of assessing community needs, their challenges, and their implications
8. The distinction between needs and assets assessment: A strengths-based approach to community practice.
9. Steps involved in determining a community's assets.
10. Using assets assessment to build stronger communities.
11. Synthesizing the two approaches: Creating a community profile.

The Meaning of Community

Since the 19th century, the sociological literature has contrasted the concept of community with the idea of society. Community represented tradition and the horizontal relationship of community subsystems to one another to maintain tradition and stability (***gemeinschaft***). In contrast, society represented change and the structures and functions connected to systems outside of or above the community (***gesellschaft***) (Tonnies, 1957). This distinction, which reflects a conservative intellectual response to industrialization and the emergence of alienation and anomie among the population, continues to resonate in popular discourse. The so-called populist response to economic globalization and mass immigration, as exemplified by the "Brexit" vote, the 2016 election results in the United States, and the rise of right-wing nationalist parties in Europe, is the recent manifestation of this conflict.

In contrast to this traditional perspective on community, cultural modernism emphasized limited, partial, segmented, even shallow commitments to a variety of diverse collectivities—no one of which commands an individual's total loyalty. In cultural terms, modernism reduces, not eliminates, the total control that communities have over individuals in favor of the diffusion of constraints among several collectivities in which persons have differing degrees of partial involvement. Viewed favorably – we call this freedom, a relief from the restrictions traditional communities placed on individual autonomy and self-expression. Viewed unfavorably—we call it "alienation" because without strong community ties individuals have no central identity, or we term it "anomie" because people in the modern world receive contradictory or incompatible signals regarding the norms and values of the diverse communities to which they belong.

Yet, most people are only dimly or partially aware of the "taken-for-granted culture" of everyday community life, what Bourdieu (2005) refers to as "habitus." We are only partly conscious of the connections between these taken-for-granted beliefs and their location in social spaces or social structure. What Gramsci (1992) termed "hegemony" refers to the consent and compliance induced by habitual socialization by an authentically felt common culture of implicit, self-evident values and behavioral norms. Without this compliance, routine social interaction and ordinary civil discourse would be just about inconceivable.

Whatever else it means, community always refers to commonly held values and behavioral prescriptions, the honoring of which are ultimately conditions of membership. This requires frequent face-to-face interaction among its members (more frequent than with nonmembers), even in this digital age of virtual relationships. These interactions create the possibility of new memberships and reduce the cost of expulsion from old memberships.

According to Fukuyama (2014) and Durkheim (1972), if the negative side of freedom is alienation, anomie, and egoism, the negative side of community is the eternal power struggle over limited resources, and over the authority to interpret the ultimately ambiguous shared culture in a way that ensures optimal conformity and continuity of members.

Modern society requires a minimalist conception of community. In the postindustrial world, community members share the fewest possible cultural ties necessary for social order. Constant struggles (ideological and political) exist over what we are obliged and constrained to accept and what we are free to choose, dissent from, and rebel against.

The history of liberation from the authority of communities is part of the struggle for personal freedom. Yet, without a sense of community, what will be the bonds that tie us together and prevent social chaos? This ongoing tension persists in the 21st century.

The modernist image of communities often offends conservatives because it contradicts their definition of community as of birth, ascription, fate, or irrevocable "commitment," rather than choice. In their view, the vocabulary of kinship should dominate the discussion of community—e.g., the "family of nations," "sisterhood," or "Black brothers and sisters." At its most extreme, it produces right-wing ethnic nationalism, as recent events in the United States, Europe, and India reveal.

To summarize, it is important to understand all ideas, including the idea of community, in terms of its group origins and potential to reproduce or change the social order. The image of autonomous individuals always choosing their communities of affiliation is a myth. The choice of one's community is to some extent structured, constrained, and habitual. A number of factors, such as race, class, gender, age, and geography, influence our history and place in the social order.

Dimensions of 'Community'

There are several ways to conceive of community. The most common is as a physical space. Yet, the application of even this relatively simple idea becomes more complex in the real world. Think of the neighborhoods in which you have lived. Do natural boundaries, such as a river, or human-made boundaries, such as a highway or railroad tracks, define them? What historic boundaries gave them shape? To complicate matters further, for purposes of service provision we may organize geographic communities today by zip code, area code, census tract, school district, electoral precinct, sanitary district, zoning laws, or catchment area. We sometimes refer to such communities as communities of administration.

Another way to conceive of community is as a group of people with shared identity, networks, culture, history, norms, institutions, and values, as a social system or set of social systems (Fellin, 2001). These communities maintain their boundaries through the horizontal and vertical interaction of community subsystems. These subsystems establish patterns of resource production, distribution, and consumption. They engage in various forms of socialization and social control, although they can also be an arena of conflict. Finally, they promote social participation and mutual support.

To what communities do you belong? That may seem a simple question, but when I ask students, their answers vary widely and include as many as 10–12 different answers per student. For some students, their community is the neighborhood in which they grew up or currently live; for others, it is their churches or places of work; their community of identity (race, ethnicity, sexual orientation, profession); their friends and family; and the people who share the same tastes in music, sports, or leisure activities. At the same time, increasing geographic mobility often creates circumstances in which people look outside of the space where they live to find genuine "community." In addition, with the rise of "virtual communities" through social media, a person's community can now include individuals whom one has never met and may never meet face-to-face.

A quarter century ago, Garvin and Tropman (1992) wrote that a community exists when a group of people form a social unit based on common location, interest, identification, culture, and/or activities. Today, one's community is more likely to be an amalgamation of a geographic place; other people with whom he or she shares common interests, identity, and/or social concerns; a set of common social relations; or even a unit of an organization or people who are seeking a common solution to a social problem. One's "personal community," therefore, is a combination of location, identity, and interests.

The recognition of people's complex, multiple, and intersecting communities is at the heart of two critical concepts for macro social work practice: positionality and standpoint. In this context, positionality refers to the effect of a person's various identities on how she or he perceives the world. Standpoint refers to how an individual's social and political experiences (in the broadest sense) shape her perspectives on the world. Understanding the significance of these concepts is particularly important for practice in racially and culturally diverse communities and organizations.

Concept of Neighborhood

The most common form of a geographic community is a neighborhood—a geographic entity within which certain social relationships exist. The definition of a neighborhood varies depending on a combination of the geographic scale used by its residents and outsiders' perceptions. Shared participation on a daily basis and a common cultural perspective help create and sustain the neighborhood as a reality for inhabitants and for the larger community. Neighbors use the same space, such as single residential real estate market area, as a focal point for personal interactions. They have a common relationship with some nearby institution (e.g., church, school) and a local public service office, such as the police. Sometimes they have a common membership in an ethnic group or a local political organization.

We can divide the concept of a neighborhood further depending upon its geographic scope. A person's "immediate neighborhood" refers to a small cluster of houses or apartment buildings around one's own home. A "homogeneous neighborhood" is the area up to where the market value of housing noticeably changes or where the mix of housing types or values changes. An "institution-oriented neighborhood" is the area where residents share common relationships with a local institution (school, police precinct, political ward). Finally, a "regional neighborhood" may consist of an entire suburb, township, or district within a city.

Neighborhoods can also differ greatly in almost all measurable characteristics from one city to another and within a single city. Local residents rather than external observers must define them. People in many residential areas perceive their neighborhoods only on the immediate geographic scale unless local institutions undertake actions that unify residents. "In the last analysis, each neighborhood is what the inhabitants think it is" (National Commission on Neighborhoods, n.d.).

Questions for Discussion

1. How do you define your current neighborhood or your neighborhood of origin?
2. What were its distinguishing features?

Theories of Community and Community Practice

All theories of community practice have four primary components. They attempt to explain the nature of communities and the key features of community life. They provide a framework for the analysis of community conditions. They interpret the causes, effects, and interrelationship between community and social change. They suggest guidelines for effective practice within communities. These theories fall into four major categories: behavioral theories, structural functionalist theories, conflict theories, and social movement theories.

A distinction also exists between theories that *describe* or explain communities, and those that *prescribe* actions. The former examine community systems, patterns of individual and group behavior, and the role of power and politics in creating or obstructing change. The latter emphasize such concepts as community strengths and assets, capacity building, empowerment, resiliency, and resistance. Figure 9.1 is an example of how ecological theory (Bronfenbrenner, 1979) could be applied to an analysis of how a major policy change, welfare reform (PRWORA), affected people at the community level.

Figure 9.1 Ecological Systems

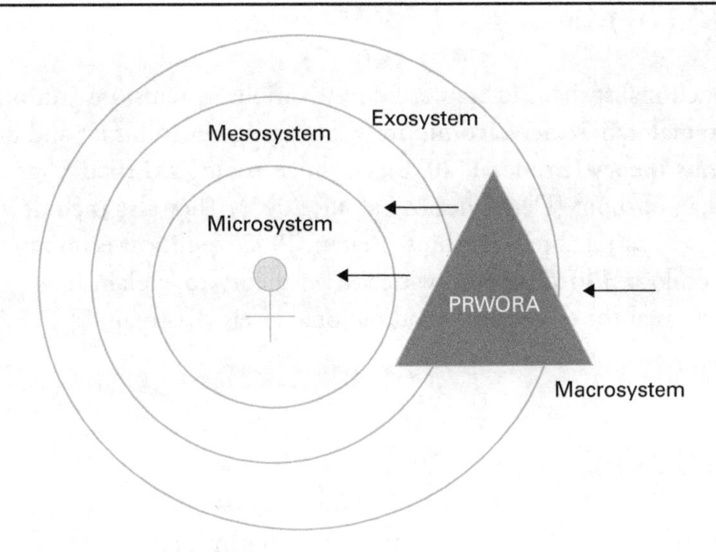

Fig. 9.1: *Based on information from Urie Bronfenbrenner, The Ecology of Human Development: Experiments by Nature and Design, 1981*

Behavioral Theories

Under this category, there are three major types of theory. **Social learning theory** (Bandura, 1977) bridges behaviorist and cognitive learning theories. Its basic premise is that people learn from one another through observation, imitation, and modeling. The socialization process that occurs in all communities provides an example of how this theory helps explain the behavior of community members, who reproduce long-standing roles, customs, and values.

Efficacy theory (Bandura, 1986) focuses on the extent to which people, individually and in groups, believe in their competence to effect personal and political change in their environment. Concepts such as learned helplessness and cognitive liberation emerged from this theory. To some extent, Freire's (1971) emphasis on conscientization applies concepts derived from efficacy theory, as do contemporary theories of empowerment.

Finally, **social exchange theory** attempts to explain the processes of community, organizational, and societal change and stability as the outcome of negotiated exchanges between parties with different self-interests and different amounts of resources, power, and influence (Braithwaite & Schrodt, 2015). These exchanges produce both economic and social outcomes for participants. Ideally, they result in mutual satisfaction, but the imbalance of power and resource in many organizations and communities often leads to unequal costs and benefits.

Structural Functionalist Theories

Structural functionalist theories emphasize how various systems, institutions, or groups fit together to maintain societal, community, or organizational order and balance. They include **systems theory** (Brunczel, 2010), of which **ecological theory** (as illustrated in Figure 9.1) is an offshoot (Deutscher & Lafont, 2017). They also include various theories of inter-organizational relationships (Reitan, 1998), political-economic theory, and institutional ecology. **Pluralism** is a widely used theory to explain how policy makers produce decisions at the community and national levels (Lassman, 2011).

Conflict Theories

While structural-functionalist theories emphasize "dynamic equilibrium," conflict theories focus on disruptive changes. The most influential conflict theory since the mid-19th century has been Marxism and its various corollaries. Marxists made three contributions that continue to inform community practice in the 21st century in valuable ways.

First, they regard change (in all systems) as occurring through a dialectical process rather than a linear or cyclical manner. They posit that each situation contains elements that lead to its contradiction or negation—for example, that even in "stable" communities there are forces of instability—and that the resolution of these contending forces creates a new situation that, in turn, contains contradictory components. In other words, that conflict is inevitable and ubiquitous, even desirable.

A second contribution of Marxism is that it posited the primary driver of this conflict was competition for material resources and the power to control those resources. Third, Marxists assert that societies (and organizations and communities) construct ideological and cultural rationales to justify the prevailing distribution of resources and power. Examples of the latter include widely accepted explanations for persistent poverty and inequality (Hirshleifer, 2001).

Although they do not accept all the premises of Marxism and have added important theoretical dimensions regarding the role of race, gender, and sexual orientation, Marxism has influenced the emergence of critical theory (critical race theory, neo-feminism, queer theory, social constructionism), particularly over the past several decades. Critical race theory is a valuable tool for community practitioners to examine how institutional racism in such areas as criminal justice, education, employment, and housing marginalizes communities of color (Delgado & Stefancic, 2017). Feminist theory, particularly socialist feminist theory, is useful to analyze the differential effects of policies in such areas as welfare, health care, and child care on women (Disch & Hawkesworth, 2016; Holmstrom, 2002).

Social Movement Theories

Although social movement theories address issues on a larger scale than the work of most community practitioners, they have relevance for community practice for several reasons. First, many community change efforts—e.g., to address police violence against African Americans—are closely connected to broader social movements (e.g., Black Lives Matter). Second, social movement theories enable practitioners to examine the relationship between political opportunity and community change. Third, as an important aspect of community work involves community mobilization, social movement theory provides a framework to assess a community's readiness to engage in change efforts and to determine whether it possesses the necessary tangible and intangible resources to do so successfully. Finally, social movement theory focuses on how people frame issues, how ideology influences people's interpretation of social conditions, and how a community's problems are socially constructed (Staggenborg, 2016). These are all important components of change-directed community practice.

What Do Communities Do?

According to Warren (1970), all communities engage in the following five functions:

1. They establish and maintain economic and social systems that regulate the production, distribution, and consumption of goods and services.
2. They socialize community members into the community's culture, its values, norms, customs, traditions, and language—they define what constitutes acceptable and "deviant" behavior.
3. They sustain these systems and enforce behavioral rules by engaging in both formal and informal means of social control, ranging from laws that define and punish criminal activity to extra-legal social processes that can lead to **social inclusion** or **exclusion**, status enhancement or ostracism.
4. They develop mechanisms to encourage social participation for similar reasons of system maintenance, which can include formal processes such as political elections or more informal methods such as providing volunteer opportunities for community members and creating occasions for social interaction, including block parties or street fairs.
5. They provide community members with various forms of mutual aid and mutual support, ranging from financial assistance to advocacy.

What is a Competent Community?

Although all communities strive to fulfill these functions, not all succeed to the same extent, often because of a lack of adequate resources or power. While competent communities take many different forms, they share certain common characteristics. They collaborate effectively in identifying problems and needs. Once they identify these problems and needs, they are able to achieve consensus on their goals and priorities and agree on a strategy to attain them. Competent communities are then able to collaborate effectively on the various actions required to implement the strategy they have developed. Finally, they can work together to evaluate the results of their efforts and use this evaluation to shape future actions (Iscoe, 1974; Cottrell, 1976).

Factors Interfering With Community Competence

What makes certain communities more competent than others? This is a critical question for community practitioners, particularly in our increasingly diverse society. The short answer is that many of the same forces that create community problems also impede a community's ability to take effective action to address them. The presence of these forces creates particular challenges for community members and practitioners with whom they work because they affect both the ends of community work and the available means to achieve those ends. Some of these forces are external to the community and some exist within the community itself.

A principle external obstacle to community competence is the unequal distribution of resources and power in our society. Significant disparities in the level of income, wealth, and political influence exist among communities in the United States primarily on racial, ethnic, and class lines (Rank, 2014; Stone et al., 2015). For example, the average wealth of a White household is 14 times higher than that of the average African American household. Given the widespread prevalence of racial segregation, the aggregate effect of this disparity is significant. The quality of locally funded services, such as schools, reflects this disparity, as does the limited ability of children in low-income racial minority communities to escape poverty (Reisch, 2016). These disparities, which social and physical isolation and marginalization compound, also produce a lack of community control over defining its problems or determining potential means of resolving them.

External barriers both create and exacerbate a community's internal difficulties. One major internal obstacle is that these communities lack essential forms of capital. Increasing socioeconomic inequality, particularly after the Great Recession of 2007–2009, significantly diminished the financial capital of low-income, low-power communities (Edin & Schaefer, 2015; Acs, 2011; Aber & Chaudry, 2010). Studies have shown that these communities also lack political capital—power, influence, and access to key decision makers (Bartels, 2016). In addition, these communities, because of their proximity to toxic waste facilities and industrial polluters, and the indifference of policy makers, have less environmental capital—clear air, water, and arable land (Philip & Reisch, 2015).

What is contested, however, is whether these communities also lack human capital (individual assets), cultural capital (mutual interests and identity based on shared customs, beliefs, and history), and social capital. To some extent, the perception of deficiencies in these areas reflects the views of mainstream society and perpetuates a "victim-blaming" mentality when addressing community issues. The task of community organizers and activists is to help communities correct these misimpressions, overcome these various capital deficiencies, and tap into the alternative sources of capital that exist in every community. By helping residents strengthen the civil society organizations in these excluded communities, social workers can facilitate the development of "organized forms of social autonomy against the dominant economic, political and cultural powers" (Edwards & Foley, 1998, p. 125).

The Importance of Social Capital

Putnam (2001) defines social capital as the features of social organization, such as networks, norms, and bonds of social trust, that facilitate coordination and cooperation for mutual benefit. They include those aspects of social relations that impinge on economic and political life, and that are difficult to incorporate into explanatory models based solely on self-interest (Edwards & Foley, 1998).

Social capital takes two forms. A community's "bonding social capital" refers to its internal social relationships and the degree of mutual trust and cooperation that exists. Communities whose members are struggling to survive, both literally and economically, have greater difficulty in forging and maintaining these bonds, although they do exist even in the most precarious circumstances. The lack of resources produced by social exclusion and fragmentation may lead to frequent conflicts between individuals or groups over scarce resources. The persistence of these conflicts, in turn, results in the community having little or no history of cooperation that could serve as a model to address current or future challenges (Reisch & Guyet, 2007).

Even if a community is able to forge stronger horizontal ties, when residents are marginalized and at a power and resource disadvantage, they lack "bridging social capital"—i.e., vertical relationships with key external individuals, groups, and institutions. This prevents these communities from having a "seat at the table" when policy agendas are being formed and vital resources are being distributed. Working with communities to determine the nature of these problems, identifying these internal and external barriers, and developing strategies to overcome them are the major components of community practice. Figure 9.2 illustrates this process.

The following are some examples of the intangible features of social capital:

1. Relationships between individuals, within groups, and among groups based on a shared commitment to moderating self-interest and collaborating to foster economic and social progress (Fukuyama, 2014).
2. Norms, values, and behaviors of reciprocity that provide resources to individuals in a particular context and facilitate cooperative action.
3. Resources that accompany social integration into solidary groups, networks, or organizations (Fellin, 2001).
4. Social and cultural institutions (Bellah et al., 1991).
5. Social infrastructure (Midgley & Livermore, 1998).
6. Informal and formal networks and associations of ordinary citizens to help them facilitate, coordinate, and cooperate in efforts that benefit the entire community (Kretzman & McKnight, 1993).
7. Focal points of informal affiliation that are capable of massive mobilization and community participation around issues of care and support.

How can we measure social capital in a group or community? What factors facilitate or inhibit its development? Based on the above examples, there are several possible ways to measure a community's social capital:

1. Membership and/or participation in formal associations and organizations.
2. Existence or absence of formal and informal networks.
3. The range and depth of informal support activities.
4. The presence or absence of traits such as tolerance and trust.
5. Linkages to other forms of capital inside and outside the community.

The significance of social capital for community development raises important questions for macro social workers: What is the role of nonprofit organizations in developing social capital, particularly in communities with racial and/or cultural characteristics that differ from that of the organization? What contributions can community organizers or community-based social workers make in this regard? How do we reshape public policies to allow social capital to develop and flourish in low resource, low power communities?

Figure 9.2 Understanding Community Practice

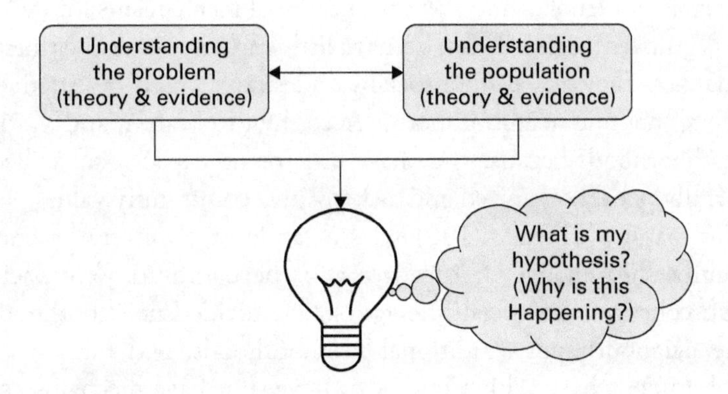

Fig. 9.2: *Based on information from F. Ellen Netting, Peter M. Kettner, Steve L. McMurtry and M. Lori Thomas, Social Work Macro Practice, 2011.*

Models of Community/Neighborhood Types

Warren and Warren (1977) identified different types of communities based on their social identity, degree of internal social interaction, and connections to the wider environment. Although these types are neither rigid nor static, macro social workers can use them to obtain a clearer picture of the character of a community with which they are working.

Warren and Warren refer to one type as "integral neighborhoods." These communities have a high capacity to identify their problems and to take action because they have a strong internal organization and positive links to the outside community. In other words, they possess both bonding and bridging social capital.

A second category, "parochial neighborhoods," have a strong group identity and internal social integration. Residents possess a powerful commitment to the area and a capacity to produce necessary changes for those problems that do not require external assistance. A lack of bridging social capital, however, limits the capacity of these neighborhoods to produce change.

A third type of neighborhood is more diffuse. It has a high degree of collective capacity because of the social capital individual residents possess, but it rarely exercises this capacity because of a lack of bonding social capital, or the absence of a perceived need to use its capital. According to Bellah et al. (2008), it is more of a "lifestyle enclave" than a community in the classic sense.

A "stepping stone" neighborhood is a place whose residents are highly mobile. They have positive but no strong ties to other residents or to the organizations within their community. Some neighborhoods that consist of immigrant populations fall into this category, as do some communities composed of young families in so-called "starter homes."

An extreme version of this type is a "transitory neighborhood." These communities have a high degree of turnover and few organizational mechanisms for dealing with the problems this turnover creates. They also have little capacity to deal with either internal or external changes. They may exhibit socially undesirable or self-destructive tendencies. Finally, there are "anomic neighborhoods." According to Warren and Warren, they are not really neighborhoods because they have little or no capacity for collective action. They are generally poorly organized and lack positive community values.

In a similar manner, Litwak's (1961) classification of communities emphasizes the extent of membership change or turnover and the community's capacity to retain primary group cohesion and social integration. He divided neighborhoods into three types: mobile neighborhoods, traditional neighborhoods, and mass neighborhoods. Mobile neighborhoods have a high rate of turnover but have mechanisms for quickly integrating new residents and for retaining neighborhood cohesion. Some planned communities (such as Columbia, Maryland, and Reston, Virginia) exhibit these qualities, as do long-standing, well-resourced suburbs.

Traditional neighborhoods, such as urban ethnic enclaves (Gans, 1982), reflect stability of membership and are not well suited for integrating new members. Mobile and traditional neighborhoods often have positive values and strong internal organizations. Mass neighborhoods have a high mobility of residents but little capacity for either integration or retention of neighborhood cohesion. They may possess positive values but lack strong organizations. The most disorganized communities, such as some long-neglected public housing projects, may reflect both negative values and poor organization (Fellin, 2001).

Figueira-McDonough's (2001) analysis of community types focuses on a combination of population factors (poverty and mobility) and organizational factors (informal networks, secondary formal networks, and external links). Using these criteria, she developed four distinct categories.

One consists of stepping-stone communities. The residents of these communities are not poor and are highly mobile. They have few primary networks but a large number of secondary networks and external connections. This category is similar to Warren and Warren's stepping-stone neighborhood.

A second category is established communities. These communities are both nonpoor and stable. They have both high primary and secondary networks but few external links. They are similar to the parochial neighborhoods in Warren and Warren's model.

Figueira-McDonough refers to a third neighborhood type as disorganized communities. These communities are poor and mobile. They have low primary and secondary networks, and few external connections. They resemble Warren and Warren's anomic neighborhood.

Parochial communities make up a fourth category. These are poor, but stable. They have high primary networks (bonding social capital), but low secondary networks and external links. They are similar to parochial neighborhoods in Warren and Warren's typology.

Finally, Etzioni (2004) distinguishes communities based on their maintenance of balance between social order and personal autonomy. What he terms "authentic communities" are responsive to the "true needs" of their members, both in the substance of their shared values and in their social formation. These qualities enable such communities to reduce the contradictions between the common good (order) and the needs of individual community members. In contrast, "partial or distorted communities" are either nonresponsive to the true needs of members or fail to balance the need for order with the need for autonomy.

In sum, these authors differentiate among neighborhoods based on their socialization patterns, their ability to cope with internal and external changes, their leadership structures and extent of resident participation, and the manner in which they process information and communicate both inside the community and with the external environment.

Community Assessment

The first step in helping communities is to conduct a community assessment. This is a systematic way to identify the assets, resources, issues, and needs of communities. It includes the following elements: (1) gathering data (from a range of sources) to develop a community profile; (2) soliciting the perspectives of community residents and leaders; (3) surveying current service providers to obtain their views on community conditions; (4) identifying community resources and assets, tangible and intangible; and (5) working with the community to establish priorities for change. A community assessment is a description of a community and its people. The purpose is to identify the needs and assets of a community to provide services appropriate to those needs.

Table 9.1 Features of a Community Profile

Basic Characteristics	• Physical features • Population demographics
Community Functions	• Physical needs • Social and emotional needs • Political needs • Economic needs • Educational and communication needs

Resources to Develop a Community Profile	• Census Bureau data • Publications and directories • State government departments • City and county agencies • Police and fire departments • United Way, other federations, and service agencies

There are several ways to approach a community assessment. According to Netting et al. (2012), these approaches include a problem/need and opportunity perspective, a population perspective, and an arena or community perspective. See Figures 9.3 and 9.4.

Figure 9.3 Understanding Community Practice

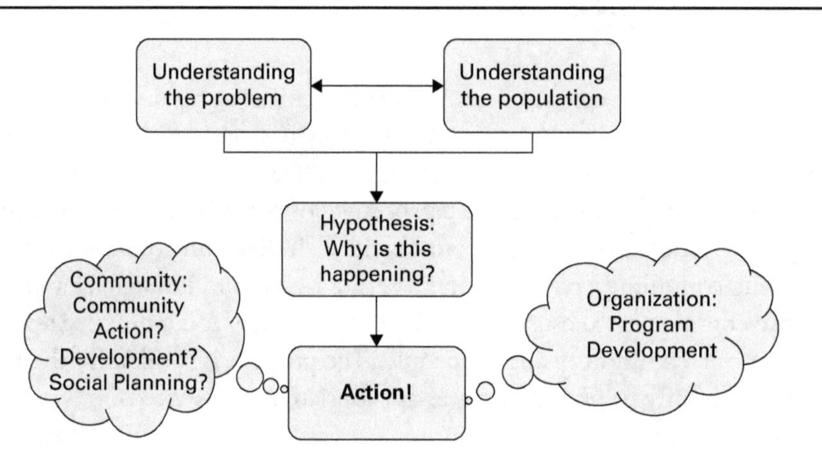

Fig. 9.3: *Based on information from F. Ellen Netting, Peter M. Kettner, Steve L. McMurtry and M. Lori Thomas, Social Work Macro Practice, 2012.*

Figure 9.4 Understanding Problem, Population, and Arena as Focal Points

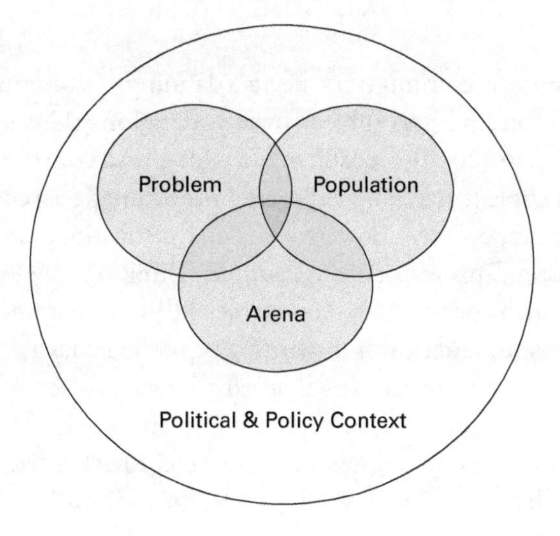

Fig. 9.4: *Based on information from F. Ellen Netting, Peter M. Kettner, Steve L. McMurtry and M. Lori Thomas, Social Work Macro Practice, 2012.*

Needs and Problems

Determining a community's needs is a complex, multiphase process discussed in more detail in subsequent sections of this chapter. It is important from the outset, however, to understand that a community's needs fall into four categories. The "normative" needs of a community reflect those standards established by custom, authority (usually external), or consensus. These could include statutory requirements regarding schools or housing conditions.

Although we can usually measure these needs with relative ease, they do not reveal the whole picture of a community. Another important aspect of community assessment is discovering what do its members perceive, think, and believe their needs are. For example, a community's schools might conform to external standards, but residents may not be pleased with the quality of their children's educational experience.

A third component of needs assessment, therefore, consists of the "expressed" needs of a community. These are needs that the community has already brought to the public's attention and includes those needs that authorities have recently addressed or are currently addressing. Finally, needs assessment, especially in a diverse society, must include a relative or comparative perspective. In metropolitan areas, for example, it is important to analyze the gap between the level of existing services in an inner city neighborhood and those in a nearby suburb.

Defining Community 'Problems'

Similar to determining a community's needs, defining a community's problems or issues involves both objective and subjective considerations (Green, 1998). According to Hardcastle and Powers (2004), a problem is a widespread concern that creates intense worries among the people it affects. To address a problem effectively, several conditions must exist. Of most importance, powerful societal institutions need to recognize the condition as a problem. This is not always simple. Think of how long it has taken our society to recognize such "private troubles" as racial discrimination, sexual harassment, socioeconomic inequality, and health disparities as public issues.

Second, given the power imbalances that exist in society, for better or worse those with power and influence must regard a problem as an undesirable condition, worthy of attention and action. It is not enough, for example, to acknowledge the existence of poverty and chronic homelessness; there must also be a commitment to do something about these problems.

Third, the commitment to act generally occurs only when the problem affects a significant number of people or threatens in some way populations that society generally does not regard as "deviant" or marginal. For example, in the 19th and 20th centuries, the government did not introduce public health measures to combat cholera, tuberculosis, HIV/AIDS, and substance abuse until they affected so-called "mainstream" elements of the population. This often occurs concurrently with a reinterpretation of the problem's causes—from individual responsibility to environmental or social conditions. Finally, those with the power to make change have to believe the problem is capable of solution and that it is necessary to take collective action and spend resources to solve it.

Throughout its history, the social work profession has been involved with communities that are struggling with needs and problems rooted in the macro realm, with often limited control over solutions (Zimbalist, 1977). We engage in community practice to understand—through research—the sources of these problems; to disseminate our findings to the public and key decision makers; and to advocate for resources to address these problems and create planned change. While the problems communities face today are considerably different from those the earliest social workers addressed, certain issues persist: chronic and severe poverty; community violence; inadequate services; and widespread societal indifference to these conditions (Reisch, 2015).

A Problem-Solving Approach

A problem-solving approach consists of three primary tasks. The first is to gather information from key informants in the community. These include formal and informal leaders, longtime community members, and those who are already receiving services. It also involves assessing current conditions and discovering relevant historical antecedents to contemporary problems.

The second task is to explore the professional literature on the community's problems, including existing research and other forms of evidence. We then use suitable theoretical frameworks to interpret the supporting data that are collected. These lead to the third task—the selection of what factors help explain the underlying causes of the presenting problem. By determining the problem's causes, practitioners can work with community members to identify the target for intervention and the form that intervention will take (Netting, Kettner, & McMurtry, 2004).

Think about how you would apply this approach to one of the following community problems:

- opioid abuse;
- community violence;
- unemployment; and
- the reintegration of veterans or formerly incarcerated individuals into their families and communities.

A Population Approach

Alternately, practitioners could use a population approach to develop a strategy for community intervention. For example, they could focus on ex-offenders, people who are chronically homeless, or children in foster care. This approach also contains three basic tasks.

The first task involves the exploration of the professional knowledge base on the target population to understand the basic concepts and issues that affect it. The second task is to seek diverse perspectives on the population. This includes listening to people from this population and those who know them well (e.g., family members) or have worked with them (e.g., service providers). An important component of this task is cultural competence, particularly the ability to avoid making judgments about the population and assuming that the population defines its condition in the same way as you do. The last task is to select those environmental and personal factors that help you understand the target population.

Both the problem and population approaches present a fourth task for community practitioners: Developing a working hypothesis of the etiology of the problem and producing a theory of change. By identifying the underlying causes of a problem or a population's condition, you can identify more solutions. Each potential cause can lead you in a new direction.

This process requires skills in research, data collection, and data analysis. Although data collection does not need to be extensive, it should be adequate to identify needs and priorities in support of planning decisions. It should take into account some of the cultural, economic, and physical conditions that make up the community.

It also requires skills in conceptualization. Think about the social construction of the problem (now and in the past), how that construction reflects, or does not reflect social work values, and how it shapes strategic options for change.

Finally, both approaches require interactional skills and the ability to build trusting relationships, whether you are conducting a one-on-one interview, facilitating a focus group, or running a large meeting. Effective community practitioners also have to be able to assess their own self-interest and the self-interests of those with whom we are working. This involves ongoing reflection, honest self-effacement, and the ability to acknowledge and address even our most deeply hidden biases.

APPROACHES TO NEEDS ASSESSMENT

There are five traditional approaches to conducting a community needs assessment. Under most circumstances, communities can use both formal and informal methods effectively (Austin, 1978). It is generally a good idea to obtain information from at least three sources. The five basic formal approaches are:

- interviewing key informants;
- organizing a community forum or focus group (nominal group);
- analyzing current "rates under treatment";
- examining recent social indicators; and
- conducting a field survey.

Key Informant Interviews

These are interviews or one-on-one consultations with members of the community with whom you have established trust. They might be respected members of the community or a group with which you are planning to work. These could include elected and appointed officials, agency executives and staff members, service providers, and other known community leaders, both formal and informal. These contacts can help you identify the major "players" in the community, perceptions of current community or organizational conditions, and relevant historical incidents that shape contemporary concerns and challenges.

One advantage of this approach is that it is relatively simple to organize and inexpensive to implement (i.e., it takes a considerable amount of time but few other resources). It has the added benefit of face-to-face contact, which can strengthen a practitioner's relationship with the community.

Another advantage is that it generally receives a high response rate and increases the level of community involvement in the change process. Finally, this approach encourages the free exchange of ideas, open communication, and the expression of different perspectives on the community. These can be valuable in formulating a balanced assessment of the community's needs and strategies to address them.

The primary disadvantage of this approach is that the data collected are both subjective, reflecting informants' biases, and also selective, possibly creating significant gaps in the information. It may also be difficult to identify informants and/or to produce a list of key informants that represent the full range of community views, particularly in a diverse and demographically changing community. Lastly, by gathering the opinions of community leaders, residents could perceive the process as elitist and exclusionary. For that reason, it is useful to balance this approach with one or more that involve a wider spectrum of the community.

Community Forums, Meetings, or Focus Groups

A community forum involves a mass meeting or series of large meetings that are open to the public. Forums are generally easy and relatively inexpensive to arrange—provided a community group can supply the space at little or no cost. An advantage of a forum is that helps identify the community members who are most likely to be interested in future involvement in a community change effort. If you advertise the forum well in advance, it also has the potential to obtain ideas from different perspectives.

A disadvantage of a forum is that it is difficult to obtain an audience that is representative of the community as a whole. As a result, the views expressed in the forum may be primarily those of a dominant group or faction in the community. This is a particular problem in racially and ethnically diverse communities. It makes the data collected at a forum hard to analyze. To conduct a community assessment by taking part in community meetings, you must know in advance the role of attendees, including yourself. Finally, holding a forum to discuss specific issues or problems in a community may create unrealistic expectations among community members on the prospects for change.

Focus groups can also be time-consuming and difficult to organize; however, they can reveal information that is not always apparent to project initiators. They can also indicate something about interpersonal or intergroup dynamics in a community.

Rates under Treatment Approach

This method of assessment focuses on existing client populations or service recipients in a clearly defined geographic area or a clearly defined community of identity. It examines existing service programs in the community to identify patterns of resource control and service delivery. If used effectively, this approach can determine the inter-organizational linkages that exist or do not exist in the community, and locate gaps or duplications of services, inconsistencies in service provision, and opportunities for enhanced collaboration.

An advantage of this approach is that the data are usually readily available and inexpensive to obtain. The process itself helps increase awareness of community needs and provides a clearer background of what efforts are already under way to address them.

One disadvantage of this approach concerns the risk of violating clients' confidentiality. This could be a particular problem in smaller or more easily defined communities. Another potential disadvantage involves determining what constitutes a representative sample of the client population to avoid missing service gaps. Two other possible disadvantages are that this approach does not take into consideration services that community members receive from organizations outside the community, and that the approach assumes there is no untapped reservoir of clients—i.e., community members who need existing (or other) services but are not currently receiving them.

Social Indicators Approach

A social indicators approach uses demographic data from the census and other statistical abstracts. It begins with the identification, collection, and measurement of key community data. Types of data to collect could include:

- recent changes and trends in the community's population;
- median household income;
- unemployment rates;
- percentage of children in poverty;
- infant mortality rate and average life expectancy;
- doctors per 1,000 residents;
- number of juvenile arrests;
- housing affordability and the condition of housing stock;
- residential mobility; and
- educational data such as dropout rates, standardized test scores, and college admissions.

One can obtain these data from the U.S. Bureau of the Census, state or local departments, or non-profit organizations. They are accessible to the public and are inexpensive to access on the internet. The use of social indicators enables practitioners to compare conditions in a particular community with other nearby communities, with similar communities in other regions, or with itself in another period. The data can serve as a valuable tool to create a comprehensive index of community needs.

A disadvantage of this approach is that it is an indirect measure of community needs—it relies on data collected by third parties rather than the views expressed by community members. These data may reflect class, racial, and gender biases because of how they were collected and for what purposes. As a result, the data may not accurately reflect a community's views of its pressing needs or service priorities.

Surveys

An effective survey involves the development, implementation, and evaluation of a questionnaire distributed and collected from a representative sample of community residents. The advantage of this approach is that it has the potential to provide scientifically valid and reliable data. A survey is a flexible instrument; it is possible to design a questionnaire to obtain specific data on a particular community need and the current extent of service utilization. It is also possible to tailor a survey to facilitate the specific goals of a community change effort.

Surveys, however, are expensive and time-consuming. Sufficient funding is not always available to conduct a survey; however, on occasion funding might be available to purchase survey results from another source. From experience, I can attest that sometimes surveys get a low (and unhelpful) response rate even after a considerable effort. Especially in communities already distrustful of outsiders, people may be reluctant to share the type of confidential data that are useful. Consequently, the method itself may make the results suspect.

In addition to these formal approaches to community needs assessment, there are a variety of informal methods that could serve as helpful complements. These include:

- *Conduct a "windshield survey."* This involves driving around the community/area you are researching and recording your observations. To do this effectively, it is helpful to get a detailed map of the community, such as those provided by real estate brokers. Optimally, the survey should be conducted at two different times during the week to get different perspectives on the same streets (e.g., midafternoon during the week and on a weekend). It is best to have three or four people in the car—a driver, a navigator, and one or two observers. (*A sample windshield survey is at the end of the chapter.*)

- *Do a walk about around the community/area in which you are planning to work.* Stop in a local restaurant. Talk to various shopkeepers. Look at the posters in storefront windows and the notices on bulletin boards. Visit with people who may be available including people you meet on the street. It is best to conduct this in pairs during the day. Ideally, one of the two observers should either be a member of the community or familiar with its population and culture.
- *Post a suggestion box* in the offices of a community organization or social service agency, or at a site (such as a community school or popular business). This will allow community members to make suggestions or express their needs anonymously. It can help gather information on the extent and intensity of need, how often the need is experienced and for how long, and who actually feels this need.

Summary: The Purposes of a Needs Assessment

Whatever combination of methods you employ, it is important to recognize that all forms of needs assessment have common goals. First, they determine the overall characteristics of a community—its physical boundaries if it is a geographic community, or its ideological or cultural boundaries if it is a community of identity or interest (Kazda et al., 2009). Second, they attempt to identify a community's strengths and the problems and issues it confronts. Third, they try to understand the dominant values of the community that shape its perceptions of these issues and how to address them.

An assessment also strives to recognize the differences that exist within a community and between the community and the external environment, including surrounding communities. This requires considerable skills of cultural competence that go beyond mere sensitivity (Rivera & Erlich, 1997). In addition, practitioners can use the assessment process to identify formal and covert mechanisms of oppression and the forms that actual and potential discrimination take (Lillie-Blanton & Hoffman, 1995).

A critical component of the assessment process is to locate the sources of power within a community and to determine how its tangible and intangible resources are distributed. This includes identifying who are its formal and informal leaders, around what issues they exercise leadership, and over which segments of the community they have influence. Broadly speaking, there are three possible perspectives on community power: (1) *elitist*—a small number of people possess most of the power; (2) *pluralist*—various groups and coalitions of groups arise and acquire influence as issues change; and (3) *amorphous*—there is no consistent pattern of power relationships. Each of these situations requires a different type of response from practitioners.

To design an effective needs assessment, practitioners must answer the following questions:

1. What do we want/need to know about the identified problems or issues and existing programs that address them?
2. What are our reasons for wanting/needing to know this information?
3. What useful data already exist? Where does it exist?
4. What useful data will we have to collect for ourselves? What will be the cost?
5. In what sequence should those engaged in the assessment process utilize each data collection approach to maximize its effectiveness?
6. Which of the available needs assessment approaches will be most efficient (in terms of time and money)?
7. Which approaches to needs assessment will be most effective with the members *of this particular community*?
8. What are the consequences of the approach selected for *future* community-building efforts?

IN-CLASS EXERCISE
NEEDS ASSESSMENT

Introduction

You are part of a team of consultants hired by CURE, Citizens United for a Revitalized Eastville. (See previous chapter for a description of this hypothetical community.) The organization has received $50,000 in funds—in the form of a six-month planning grant—from the state and a local community foundation to initiate a process of community needs assessment and planning for the purpose of **economic and social development**. By the end of this period, CURE is to submit a fuller proposal for a multiyear grant to engage in a community development and revitalization effort. To establish the overall goals of the planning effort, CURE asked your team to conduct a needs assessment of Eastville during the first three months of the planning period. The organization allocated $10,000 for this needs assessment, the results of which CURE will use as the basis of a future proposal for long-term funding. Funds that are unspent on needs assessment will be available for other aspects of the planning process.

The Charge

Your initial task is to determine which methods of community needs assessment you will employ. You have to make your recommendations to the CURE board this evening. The options—along with their costs and time requirements—are:

1. **Conduct a survey of Eastville residents**. Cost: $7,500. Time required: two months
2. **Hold a series of community forums**. Cost: $2,500 each. Time required: one month per forum (for preparation and analysis)
3. **Hold a series of focus groups with key informants in the community**. Cost: $2,000 each. Time required: two to three weeks per group (for preparation and analysis)
4. **Analyze existing data provided by government and nonprofit agencies and business leaders**. Cost: $6,000. Time required: two months.

Questions to Consider

1. Which method(s) of needs assessment would you recommend? What are the reasons for your decision?
2. List the advantages and disadvantages of each method—with particular attention to the context of the situation in Eastville. (See previous scenario for details.)
3. In what ways will your selection of needs assessment methods shape the overall focus of the planning process?

Needs Assessment vs. Assets Assessment

During the past three decades, the traditional approach to identifying a community's needs has come under critical scrutiny by both scholars and practitioners. With considerable justification, they have argued that by focusing on a community's needs, problems, and deficiencies, these approaches view communities through a deficit-oriented lens. This serves to pathologize excluded and marginalized communities and maintain a "victim-blaming" perspective on the causes and cures of the issues that afflict them. It also leaves control over resources and the power to define the change agenda in the hands of those conducting the assessment.

Think about how this occurs. A community's "needs map" is usually drawn by "experts" from outside the community who often have little intimate knowledge of the community's history and culture. These include social scientists, social planners, and social workers. These experts then report their findings to the media, who are often more interested in attracting attention (viewers, readers, and listeners) than getting to the complex heart of the matter. As even the best-intentioned efforts at urban renewal and community revitalization during the past half century have demonstrated, the focus on deficits can produce devastating consequences for the residents of excluded and marginalized communities (Mathie & Cunningham, 2003).

This creates a contradictory situation for community leaders and macro practitioners. They have to draw attention to a community's problems to obtain a response from those who control vital resources. Yet, if outsiders perceive the community solely as a compilation of problems, the community will continue to be viewed as a "tangle of pathologies" that is incapable of taking action on its own behalf. When external entities define communities solely in terms of their needs and problems, they reinforce those aspects of their ineffectiveness.

An alternative approach attempts to correct this dynamic by focusing on the discovery of a community's capacities, strengths, and assets. At best, this approach complements, but does not entirely replace, a needs assessment that involves community members from the outset. This approach assumes that communities that "work" (demonstrate functional competence) are able to bring together people's talents, experience, and expertise, and articulate a community vision based on their strengths rather than their weaknesses.

Before attempting to identify a community's assets, it is useful to consider the following questions:

1. How will you locate all the formal and informal community resources that exist? For example, does a resource directory exist?
2. Can the United Way, another federated agency, or local government provide a list of service agencies?

3. What outreach efforts will you use to engage residents and providers of services in identifying resources?
4. How will you map formal and informal resources?

Kretzman and McKnight (1993) describe the process of assets assessment in terms of five sequential steps:

1. Drawing a map of a community's capacities and assets.
2. Building relationships among local assets.
3. Mobilizing the community's assets.
4. Building a vision and plan.
5. Leveraging outside resources for support.

Asset mapping is the process of locating and making inventories of the gifts, skills, and capacities of individuals, associations, informal groups, and local institutions. Examples that traditional approaches to community assessment do not usually consider include the skills and potential contributions of youth, older people, persons with disabilities, service recipients, artists and other cultural workers, and those involved in the community's informal economy.

Every community, even marginalized and socially excluded communities, possesses local institutions and informal associations (or groups) that are assets or potential assets in a change process. These can include schools and libraries, parks and recreational or cultural facilities, police and fire stations, social service agencies, colleges and universities, health care facilities, religious congregations, and social clubs.

There are a number of ways to find these local associations. You can often find them in community newsletters, neighborhood newspapers, a citywide monthly magazine, the telephone book, or an encyclopedia of associations. The bulletin boards of libraries, parks, recreation facilities, and religious institutions often post their announcements and schedule of events. If practitioners already have contacts in the community, they can conduct a telephone survey of knowledgeable individuals. Finally, social media and the internet are increasingly an excellent source of this information.

Identifying these local associations is an important component of community change because they involve community members in three ways. They determine a community's most pressing problems. They decide the best ways to solve these problems. They also play a key role in organizing association members and others to implement whatever strategies community groups develop. Many well-functioning communities actually consist of informal networks that work together to craft and implement their vision of a good community.

According to Kretzman and McKnight, associations are particularly able to achieve these goals because they possess certain unique capacities. They provide mutual aid that enables people to negotiate the challenges of daily life. They can respond rapidly to problems. Yet because of their limited scope and scale, they can maintain a focus on the individuals affected by these problems. Due to their relatively informal nature, associations provide a context for community members to develop creative solutions to their problems and, in so doing, enable people to exercise collective responsibility for the common good. They become a tool to empower the community, enhance individual and group competence, and foster the development of indigenous leaders and initiatives.

Community practitioners can facilitate this process by helping local groups build or strengthen existing relationships among their assets for mutual gain. This involves connecting individuals' capacities, the participation of marginalized people or groups within the community, the resources of local associations and institutions, the community's physical and economic assets, and the abilities of indigenous leaders. Practitioners also have to determine how to share information on community change efforts to facilitate the mobilization of community members. This involves identifying local communication leaders (formal and informal) where information is currently shared (e.g., beauty salons, barbershops, social clubs, radio stations, taverns, local newspapers, churches, street corners, parks, local websites, social media outlets), and how to strengthen and expand them.

The next step involves convening the community to develop a vision and a plan. Kretzman and McKnight describe this as a three-step process:

1. Begin with the assets currently available to the community.
2. Expand the participants involved in the planning beyond recognized leaders to include people from all areas as "representatives of community assets" such as residents, service providers, and key public and private decision makers who have the power and influence to change existing systems.
3. Combine planning with problem solving so community residents can see small but significant victories and increase their capacity and confidence. This helps ensure that residents recognize and understand the need for systems change.

A major goal of such efforts is to leverage vital external resources in order to support locally driven development efforts and build both bonding and bridging social capital. Participants from outside the community may include foundations, church groups, United Ways and other federations, local government, businesses, and influential individuals. This group engages in a visioning exercise; identifies and prioritizes the community's goals; assigns responsibility for implementing action plans; and reaches consensus on next steps. Ideally, the group bases these decisions on the empowerment of residents that occurred during the initial steps of the community-building process.

These efforts constitute a "claims-making" process by a community whose needs and interests society generally ignores. Communities make a public claim that a problem exists to get policy makers to respond to the claim. If successful, policy makers will offer official recognition of the problem and designate agencies to develop an official response. Over time, this process of problem definition and official response evolves; the problem may take on new forms or influential institutions may perceive the problem differently. If the community acquires sufficient power, it may engage with these powers in an ongoing dialogue about options for intervention. Alternative responses may then emerge, new players may enter the debate, and conflict over models of intervention may arise. Ultimately, these differences may be resolved in some way, although the problem may persist.

CASE ILLUSTRATION
THE COMPLEXITY OF THE NEEDS ASSESSMENT PROCESS

Of the 300,000 veterans of the wars in Iraq and Afghanistan who are already in the Veterans Administration (VA) system, more than one half have been diagnosed with severe mental health conditions and more than 68,000 have been diagnosed with post-traumatic stress disorder (PTSD). The VA currently has a backlog of 600,000 claims. Eighteen vets each day commit suicide.

The problem this community identified is how to organize services to deal with PTSD and other forms of trauma. The population-at-risk is returning soldiers, although similar problems exist among refugees, survivors of natural disasters and terrorist attacks, and victims of sexual abuse. These problems appear in the workplace, in people's homes, in their communities, and in public spaces (e.g., the streets).

Macro practitioners who attempt to address this problem need to acknowledge not only its complexity and its multiple manifestations, but also that virtually no social problem has only one cause or one simple solution. This is particularly true when people suffering from the problem come from diverse demographic and cultural backgrounds. What approach would you take to conduct a needs assessment of this population?

Entering a Community

There are three critical elements to entering a community: (1) educating oneself on the community's culture, history, issues, and institutions; (2) making initial contacts (through one-on-one or group meetings, door knocking); and (3) identifying issues around which organizing and action are possible (Cook, n.d.).

There are two basic sources of initial contacts. The better kind is a reference from a community leader or third person who knows you and the contact, and who can "vouch" for you and/or serve as a liaison. This is particularly valuable when you are an "outsider" and may be unfamiliar with the customs, values, and politics of the community. The more challenging type of contact is similar to a "cold contact" in sales—membership lists of existing organizations and, if all else fails, the telephone directory.

Whether in a one-on-one interview or a group meeting, the initial contact has two key components. First, there is the "tone" of the contact. It is vitally important that you establish your personal presence as someone who is "professional," who is competent, knowledgeable about the community (within limits), and, above all, someone who can be trusted. I cannot emphasize this last point sufficiently in our diverse society. Good intentions are never enough.

The second component is the "what" of the contact—the content of the discussion itself. It is important to recognize that the interview or meeting is the beginning of a process, not an end in itself. This requires that you focus on the substance of the conversation. Think of the interview as a metaphor for dialogue with limited expectations.

To create the most constructive atmosphere for the initial contact, it is helpful to hold it in a place that is familiar to the community members. This could be their home, office, congregation, association headquarters, or a local park or restaurant. During the meeting, it is very important that you are conscious (but not self-conscious) about how race, culture, gender, class, and age differences affect the degree of formality, required courtesies, language used, and pace of the conversation.

Some specific suggestions:

1. Know yourself. Be aware of all the dimensions of the situation, including what tactics you might employ and how others might perceive you.
2. Listen carefully to what people say and do not say (and in what sequence).
3. Distinguish between "objective" facts and people's subjective feelings around them. Note how and when they raise controversial topics during the meeting.
4. Know the critical values of the individual or group with whom you are meeting. What do they consider proper behavior? What are their views on right and wrong? What do they think is fair?
5. Make sure the setting is as comfortable or uncomfortable as possible (depending on how you want to use the initial contact).
6. Be aware of prejudices as they manifest themselves, not just big issues such as racism but also moral issues and questions of lifestyle, dress, and formality/informality. Do not let this get in the way of your work, but recognize it and do not repress it.
7. Set realistic objectives and be satisfied with limited accomplishments. Community change takes time.
8. Raise questions regarding concrete, specific issues, not abstractions. Speak about people or issues one at a time.
9. In assessing body language, look for consistency in response to references on issues or persons.
10. If the initial contact is a group meeting, look to see who listens when an individual speaks and where people sit in relationship to one another.

11. Speak language that is natural and understandable within the context. Do not try to "bond" with the individual or group by using words that make you seem like a phony.

Preparing for the Initial Contact

Before this initial meeting, it is highly recommended that you develop a "script" and practice it in advance. It is important that you use your own style, one that feels comfortable to you, and polish it. Do not imitate others.

Think about the specific aims of the contact. For example, are you just trying to discover what are the community's major issues and plant seeds about the possibility of change? Are you trying to recruit a new member for an existing organization? Are you trying to raise money or get people involved in a specific action? Are you looking to identify a potential leader? Are you seeking simply to familiarize others with you and your organization? Is your objective some combination of the above? Your objectives affect what you will say, the timing of what you say, and how you will say it.

The Contact

Once the contact begins, you should say succinctly and quickly who you are, who you work for, who your sponsors are (or who are the organizational supporters that give you legitimacy), and what you want. If an issue is involved, provide concise information about the issue. In general, try to avoid asking questions expected to elicit a "no" response. As much as possible, your presentation (or "rap") should reflect your knowledge and understanding of the background and culture of the people you are approaching. This means doing your homework regarding the community, its issues, organizations, politics, values, and interests.

In general, you should try to anticipate questions people are most likely to ask. You can answer these questions proactively (before being asked) or be prepared to answer them as they come up. Questions might include what your organization is about, the issues you are addressing, the reasons why it is important to get organized, what organizing around these issues can accomplish, and what you expect of the people with whom you are meeting. Again, rehearsing your answers to these and other possible questions with a colleague is very helpful.

When you are making multiple contacts, start with those offering the most likelihood of success, if you can assess this in advance. You will not succeed in every contact but psychologically you will feel better if you start with easier ones. Whatever sequence you establish, it is useful to put yourself in a good frame of mind before you start. Whatever it takes, try to psych yourself up and get into your task. (This may be particularly difficult for practitioners who are not naturally extroverted.) Meeting new people from different cultures and backgrounds can be very enjoyable and stimulating, but you have to be in a receptive frame of mind to make it work.

Some General Rules

1. *Be yourself.* If you are inauthentic, you will be suspect from the outset, especially if you are from outside the community.
2. *Project confidence.* For example, in most communities (be sure you know when this does not apply) maintaining eye contact is a sign of respect and confidence. Control any distracting mannerisms. Make sure your dress is appropriate—neither too casual nor too formal. Use clear language without vulgarity. Avoid words (e.g., rhetoric or professional jargon) that others may not easily understand. Maintain a tone of voice that is interested and alive, not flat or bored.
3. *Start where the other person is.* Just as in clinical practice, try to have a sense in advance of the interests and values of others—what reflects their context and their definition of reality. If you are out of tune with your contact and push your agenda too hard, whatever its merits, you can be thrown out on your ear or get a polite brush-off.
4. *At the outset.* Explain clearly and simply who you are, what organization you represent. Show your credentials and state your purpose.
5. *When in doubt, be polite and nonthreatening.* You are not there to pick a fight, make a convert, or get involved in things that are not your business. Being polite does not mean being passive. Your style should be assertive. Keep your eye on your objectives and do not let "seductive" opportunities sidetrack you.
6. *Be assertive.* Do not apologize for why you are there, or accept responsibility for what you did not do (e.g., other people's behavior, the community's problems), or for developments over which you have no control. You need to let people know what you want from them. In general, if you do not ask, you will not receive. You may have to be persistent and you can say "no" to requests of you that are more than you can handle or outside your authority.
7. *Try to ask questions and learn from your contact.* Think of the contact, in part, as an educational experience. Find out about the person, the community, the culture, the issues that affect them, the community's history and politics. Communicate your interest in the people and their concerns, your feelings about the situation, your respect for them and their ideas. You can do this by the kinds of questions you ask and how you ask them (e.g., in a challenging way, with carefully chosen humor). When you do not understand something, try to get clarification. On the other hand, you can make people feel either stupid or competent by how

you ask questions. Remember the difference between how good and bad teachers asked and answered questions.

8. *Listen.* Good listening is crucial, especially in a community that is different from yours. This means more than just hearing people's words. Attend to nonverbal cues that may express feelings such as nervousness, impatience, anger, and sadness. Try to understand the meaning of what people are telling you based on their own terms. Above all, good listening means listening to the answers to the questions you have asked and hearing what people do not say as well. It also means giving others a chance to talk and not making speeches.
9. *Keep your eyes on the prize.* One of your objectives is to engage with the people with whom you are meeting and to establish rapport. Try to find some common ground, personal experience, or situation that you share. Get the information you came to get—this includes feelings and opinions on issues, grievances, concerns, skills, and motivations. Do your best not to allow tangential issues to distract you.
10. *Get a commitment of some kind.* Unless this is explicitly *not* one of your objectives, you will want to get some degree of commitment from your contact(s). Are they willing to donate their time, money, resources, or use of a facility they control? Are they willing to participate in a meeting, do preparatory work prior to a meeting, play a role at a meeting, sign a petition, or provide a list of potential contacts or endorsements for a particular change effort? Try not to get a flat "no," but do not waste too much time doing it.
11. *When to end the contact.* If you are convinced you are not getting anywhere, it is better to pass over people whom you cannot clearly persuade or with whom you cannot establish rapport. Do not be tempted to try to make a convert when it is unlikely you will succeed and it takes time away from more positive contacts who offer more opportunity for success. This also means it is important not to spend too much time with each contact. Unless it is culturally congruent, or prearranged, try to limit an initial individual contact to 10–30 minutes. If you need more time, make another appointment.

Finally, it is important to distinguish between your contact with community leaders and "typical" residents (or members of a community group). A community leader has a following in the community. She has some kind of organization, formal or informal. This means she has organizational self-interests (resources, goals, membership, and recognition). She will want to know in what ways organizing will promote the interests of her constituents. She may ask how a particular intervention will help "her people," especially those who face the problems her organization attempts to address.

Leaders also have legitimate personal self-interests different from mere selfishness. These might involve concerns about the organization that will make key decisions, whether the organization will consider their ideas and values, what role they will play, and whether the organizing process will help the leader establish new connections and key relationships. In your contact with leaders, therefore, your main goals are obtaining vital information, acquiring additional contacts, or getting a commitment (e.g., use of her name; introductions to other key players; and agreement to make a presentation, provide space or other resources, attend a meeting, or help plan a meeting).

Residents you might recruit to a change effort, including those who have the potential to become future leaders, do not typically have the same self-interests as leaders; however, they have basic problems they want to solve and personal self-interests analogous to those of leaders. They may be concerned about such matters as whether the group will listen to their views. Will the group provide opportunities to meet new people and make new friends? Will they be able to learn new skills from the organizing process? It is important to note that in both situations a social worker does not offer to solve the community's problems nor decide who the leaders are or will be. The democratic process of the organization is the vehicle for doing this.

KEY CONCEPT SUMMARY
STEPS IN THE INITIAL CONTACT

While these steps will vary depending on the context, there is a general pattern. The pattern can change, however, as circumstances dictate.

1. Establish yourself—why you are there and what you are doing.
2. Learn what the contact thinks and feels about the issue(s).
3. Relate what the contact thinks and feels about the organization you are working for or want to build.
4. Find out how the person with whom you are speaking would like to see things change.
5. Find out what the person is willing to do to bring about the changes she would like.
6. Inform the contact that your job is offering assistance in bringing about the changes the contact would like by helping her become more active in the organization that is going to bring about those changes.
7. Get a definite commitment on what the next step will be on the part of the person with whom you are speaking.
8. Inform the contact what you are going to do next and when.
9. Get a commitment for further contacts.

IN-CLASS EXERCISE
MAKING INITIAL CONTACTS

1. Individual Contacts
   - **A.** You work for a community behavioral health center that is attempting to expand its programs into low-income neighborhoods in nearby suburbs and want to establish an advisory committee to assist in their development. You learned that several community groups could make a valuable contribution to the advisory committee. You have arranged to stop by the home of the president of a neighborhood-based anti-drug group, Wanda Blank, to invite her participation. Blank is a widow, in her mid-50s, who has partial responsibility for raising her grandchildren. She works as a secretary in the local high school and is very active in her church. She greets you at the door politely but suspiciously and invites you in.
   - **B.** You work for a local tenants' action group with the responsibility of contacting residents of low-income housing developments. The organization is interested in establishing tenants' councils in these housing developments. Your assigned task is to determine whether the tenants have problems or grievances around which they would be ready to organize on their own behalf. If you learn that this is what the tenants want to do, you are to help them organize a tenants' council. Since you do not know any of the residents personally, you decide to knock on doors and explore tenants' awareness of problems and readiness to act. You park your car, knock, and a tenant opens the door. She is a young, single parent and a TANF recipient currently involved in a job-training program.
2. Group Contacts
   - **A.** You are on the staff of a local Community Development Corporation (CDC) and work with parents who are concerned about the operation of the local elementary school. During the past two weeks you have contacted a number of parents and, based upon these discussions, you have arranged for a meeting of eight to 10 parents to begin to address their problems. The meeting is in the basement of a local church. Tonight is the meeting night.
   - **B.** You work for a federated agency that raises funds for social service and community education projects. Your supervisor asked you to convene a meeting of individuals who have been major donors to the agency in the past. The purpose of the meeting is to enlist the support of these individuals in a major new campaign to address the needs of women and girls in the community. The agency expects the individuals invited not merely to be donors but to attract other potential donors to the project.

Next Steps

1. Assign roles to the various scenarios.
2. Individuals who will be the social worker should jot down a few notes for their script.

3. Each role play should last no more than five minutes.
4. Students should provide both positive and critical feedback on their peers' participation.
5. If time permits, other students could engage in subsequent iterations of one or more of the above scenarios to integrate the comments and suggestions of classmates.

Some Barriers in the Way of Organizing Communities

To be realistic, a community organization should be alert to obstacles blocking or slowing its efforts to solve its problems. (In this context, "community" refers to a geographic place or a particular population that defines itself as a "community," even it does not live contiguously, or is a large organization that has many of the characteristics of a community.) Listed below are some barriers that may arise in efforts to organize a community to take action on its own behalf.

1. *The "let George do it" attitude*: This amounts to leaning on the other person—a willingness to submit to someone else's brain, decisions, or influence. Every community has its "free riders." Sometimes, of course, there is no "George" and the community suffers.
2. *Apathy:* People often express their frustrations by asking, "Why should I bother? I don't count, anyway." They may be resigned to their situation and see no outlet for their opinions or their energy. They think they do not really belong to the community and/or that nobody cares about them. In many socially excluded and marginalized communities, this response is understandable and it is important not to judge people who express it.
3. *Prestige seekers:* Some individuals and organizations want credit every time they do something for the community. Self-glorification, to them, is more important than community change. They adopt a "I'll do it only if I get my name in the paper" point of view.
4. *The "I'm better than you are" feeling:* This leads to splits and tensions among religious, racial, and income groups, and creates disunity and hard feelings that prevent cooperation around community problem solving. People express this attitude in such forms as "You can't depend on those (fill in the blank), so let's not get them mixed up in this."
5. *Vested interests:* Some groups profit from the "way things are." They resist change for fear they will lose something—control over scarce resources, status, reputation, or influence. Sometimes, however, they are not always sure what they fear losing.

6. *Intense specialization:* The tendency in most communities is to divide work and responsibilities very finely. This leads to fragmented community efforts and to breakdowns in communication among various specialists and specialized groups, organizations, and neighborhoods. They do not talk to one another, or understand one another well when they do. They are often unaware of one another's activities, even when they are on common issues. Such a situation is grist for the gossip or rumor mill, or lends itself to a lack of coordination or duplication of effort.
7. *Lack of time:* Nearly everyone suffers from this. There are just not enough hours in the day for residents to take on more responsibilities, particularly in communities that experience economic stress. Sometimes people lack time because they spread themselves too thin, have poor time management, do not focus on their priorities, or do not care about the issues.
8. *The autocratic approach:* Sometimes people are really committed to democratic values but act as if "only the best people will get the job done, so let's go ahead." They talk democracy but sidestep democratic procedures and actions due either to mistrust of others or impatience.
9. *Inferiority complexes:* A whole community and the individuals within it can lack self-confidence due to historic disempowerment. While a community may have suffered setbacks, usually there are untapped strengths within the community. The community, as a whole, may have internalized the view that outsiders hold about it. One of the purposes of conducting an assets assessment is to help the community overcome this internalized negative conception (Freire, 1971).
10. *Lack of "know-how":* Many communities frequently lack or believe they lack the knowledge and skills needed to change existing conditions or overcome the various obstacles they confront. Here is where an organizer can play a key role.
11. *The "dreamless peace":* This is the obstacle of no vision, the inability to dream big dreams about the "good community," or to imagine alternative realities. This is the result of self-satisfaction, being contented with too little, false consciousness, a lack of hope, or a long history of dashed hopes (Gray, n.d.).

Think about—What other roadblocks have you experienced in your work with communities? How did you attempt to overcome them? What worked? What did not work?

IN-CLASS EXERCISE
IDENTIFYING ISSUES AROUND WHICH TO ORGANIZE

Introduction

Divide the class into small groups, each of which will focus on one of the following cases. Each group has 20 minutes to answer the following questions and prepare a brief report to the class.

Scenarios

1. You are a social worker in a community-based behavioral health agency. The county has announced a proposed cut in funding due to budget shortfalls. The director of your agency reports to the head of the city's Health Department. She, in turn, reports to the city's Health Commission that recommends a budget to the City Council. The director asked you to organize an emergency meeting of the agency's staff, board, clients, and community advisory committee to discuss the proposed cuts.
2. You work in a medium-sized family services agency in a suburban county adjacent to a large city. The new executive director of the agency—with the support of the new chairperson of the Board of Directors—has recently imposed salary freezes, workload increases, and changes in agency procedures that have greatly upset all staff members. Your colleagues asked you to organize a meeting of staffers, contract professionals, and concerned community allies to develop a response to these changes.
3. You work at a large senior services center in a medium-sized, politically conservative county. The county executive has recently ruled that the center may not conduct nonpartisan voter registration on its grounds. The center's senior action committee has called an all-center meeting and asked your advice in framing the issues for impending action.
4. You are a social worker in a large urban Head Start program. Parents of children in the program are concerned because of recent conflicts between parents and staff members regarding children who have tested positive for the HIV virus. Parents want to do something to demonstrate their concerns. They have asked your advice on how to frame the issues before a citywide parents' meeting called to address this problem.
5. You are on the staff of the Human Resources Administration of the state. Some staff members have recently attended meetings of a local welfare rights organization to advise them on how to advocate on behalf of TANF recipients. The director of the agency has recently distributed a memorandum that forbids staff members to meet with representatives of this organization during working hours and strongly discouraging staff from assisting this organization in any way. You are part of an ad hoc committee charged with preparing a response to the director's memorandum.

Questions for Discussion

1. How would you recommend framing the issue(s) around which you would organize?
2. What are your goals in framing the issue in this way?
3. How will framing the issues this way help you attain your short- and long-term goals?
4. In what ways would you frame the issues differently based on the community or group that you might attempt to organize?
5. What questions/problems/issues arose with your group in discussing this situation?

Summary and Conclusion

This chapter focused on various concepts of community and community assessment. It addressed the implications of different definitions of community for contemporary practice, and discussed some of the obstacles involved in making connections in a community and organizing community residents to take collective action on their own behalf. Chapter 10 focuses on various models of community engagement and their implications for the development of strategy and tactics in diverse communities.

END-OF-CHAPTER EXERCISE
EXPLORING YOUR CONCEPT OF COMMUNITY

1. List the communities (of geography, identity, interest) to which you belong.
2. How do you know or demonstrate that you are a member of these communities?
3. How did you become part of these communities?
4. What are the notable features of these communities?
5. What are the requirements of membership?
6. In what ways do your various community memberships complement or conflict with one another?
7. How do different perspectives on community inform your understanding of these communities?
8. What does the concept of community competence mean to you?
9. How would you apply it to the various communities of which you are a member?
10. To what extent would you describe these communities as "ecologies of games"? What games do people play in the community? Who are the players?

END-OF-CHAPTER EXERCISE OR ASSIGNMENT
DEVELOPING A COMMUNITY PROFILE

This is a group activity or assignment in which three to five students identify a community and develop a profile of that community using one or more of several models used for this purpose. The community profiled can be a geographic community (e.g., a neighborhood or a catchment area); a community of identity (e.g., African American youth, the elderly and their caretakers, the hearing impaired, gays and lesbians, victims of domestic violence); or some combination of the two. The assignment focuses on the collection, analysis, and presentation of data and the skills involved in working with task-oriented groups. Students should complete the assignment in the following stages (assuming a 15-week semester):

Week 2: Students will select their topics and form groups. Within each group, students will assign themselves key roles (facilitator, timekeeper, notetaker, scribe, and reporter).

Weeks 2–4: Students will: (1) develop ground rules for their group; (2) select the profile model(s) they will use; (3) identify and assign work tasks; and (4) develop a work plan.

Weeks 4–8: Students will conduct the research needed to profile their community. This includes resolving such issues as: (1) What data will you collect? (2) How will you collect the data? (e.g., analysis of written documents, interviews, focus groups, windshield surveys); (3) How will you allocate responsibilities within the group? (4) When will you collect the data?

Weeks 8–10: Students will integrate the data collected. This will involve: (1) identifying major themes; (2) synthesizing quantitative and qualitative materials; (3) determining what findings should be included/excluded; and (4) resolving conflicts in the data.

Weeks 10–12: Students determine in what format(s) they will present their profiles and begin to develop their presentations. Possible formats include: (1) written report; (2) photo-voice project; (3) geographic information system (GIS) presentation; (4) videotape or DVD; and (5) PowerPoint.

Weeks 12–14: Students turn in a two- to three-page executive summary of their profile and make brief presentations in class.

Week 14: Students turn in their final profile and an evaluation in which they critique their group experience.

Optional addition: Beginning with week four, students will turn in minutes of their meetings and biweekly progress reports every two weeks. Class time will be set aside for brief group meetings, for updates, and for group problem solving.

SAMPLE WINDSHIELD SURVEY (for Community Needs/Assets Assessment)

Block: ____________________ **between** ______________ **&** _____________

Residential Property	**Condition**	**Comments**
Single Family Homes		
Multiple Family Dwellings		
Apartment Buildings		

Commercial Property	Condition	Comments

Restaurants

Food Stores

Bars/Clubs

Liquor Stores

Clothing Stores

Service Establishments

Theatres/Recreation

Parking Lots

Office Space

Non-Commercial Property	**Condition**	**Comments**
Churches		
Health Care Providers		
Social Service Agencies		
Schools/Educational Orgs.		

General Conditions of Block

Litter

Graffiti

Street Traffic (cars)

Pedestrian Traffic (volume)

Demographics of Pedestrians

Hangouts

Street Lighting

Street Conditions

CHAPTER 10

Engaging With and Intervening in Multicultural Communities

The likelihood that your acts of resistance cannot stop the injustice does not exempt you from acting in what you sincerely and reflectively hold to be the best interests of your community.

—Susan Sontag, *At the Same Time: Essays and Speeches*

Without community service we would not have a strong quality of life. It's important to the person who serves as well as the recipient. It's the way in which we ourselves grow and develop.

—Dorothy Height, social worker and civil rights activist

Introduction

Recent newspaper articles about the aftermath of remarkably similar events—the 1992 disturbances in Los Angeles that followed the videotaped beating of Rodney King, and the Baltimore uprising of 2015 after the death of Freddie Gray while in police custody—drew pessimistic conclusions about the underlying conditions that sparked these powerful examples of urban unrest. According to community residents quoted in the articles, little has changed in their communities. A majority of residents believe that a recurrence of civic insurrection is likely within the next five years. Given the indifference of the current presidential administration to the issues afflicting racial and ethnic minorities and the problems facing U.S. cities as a whole, the pessimism of these residents acquires even more credibility.

In this climate, what could social workers who engage in community practice do to promote social change in a socially just manner? What models of community practice would be most effective in producing meaningful change in socially excluded and economically disadvantaged communities? How could efforts to produce social change integrate both socially just ends and means? Building on an analysis of current practice models, this chapter articulates key principles of working with communities in ways that promote social justice, while recognizing the effect of the differences that exist in people's social location and the power within and across communities and between communities and practitioners.

Over the past several decades, there has been a proliferation of literature on the theories and practice models for community work in a multicultural society and in multicultural community organizing. The literature tends to depict multicultural community work as involving a worker of a particular racial or cultural background working with a community whose characteristics differ from those of the worker (i.e., the worker is an outsider). Sometimes the literature focuses on different identity groups working together, e.g., multicultural coalitions and alliances. There is relatively less discussion, however, about how to work with a community with which one shares or does not share a common dimension of identity. This chapter examines the ways in which workers' multiple and intersecting identities influence their work with a community, whose members also have multiple and intersecting identities. The ability to work within or across sociocultural boundaries, whether at the one-to-group or group-to-group level, is necessary for promoting socially just ends through socially just means in an increasingly diverse and globalized world.

This chapter bases its analysis and discussion of working with communities on a strengths perspective and takes into account power differences and structural inequities. Although many communities are affected by a multitude of social problems, no community is void of resources or assets, no matter how depleted it appears. Thus, across various phases and approaches of community practice—e.g., entry to community, assessment, planning, engagement, mobilization, evaluation—it is critical to build on a community's strength. Yet, it is equally critical to address structural inequities that reinforce the marginalization of certain communities, while privileging others. This chapter presents the principles and skills necessary to challenge such structural forces in various aspects of community practice.

Specific topics in this chapter include:

1. Models of community practice and their implications in contemporary society.
2. Global/international influences on community organizing practice.
3. The role of social capital (bridging and bonding) and the means to increase a community's social capital.
4. Fostering increased civic participation within and across diverse population groups: The effect of community participation at various levels and in multiple arenas (e.g., within a neighborhood or the political arena).
5. Designing effective strategies and tactics: The role of evidence, context, and consciousness.
6. How to use social services to build communities and community organizations.
7. The intersectional and transactional nature of the relationship between worker and community and across multiple communities.
8. Monitoring and assessing community change processes and goals.
9. Ways of sustaining effective community organizations.

A (Very) Brief History of Community Organizing

We can trace the roots of community organizing in the United States back to the tradition of civic participation and voluntarism that existed prior to independence. Both Anglo settlers and new immigrants organized at the local level to provide mutual aid, promote various social causes, and resist the intrusion of centralized political power (Stern & Axinn, 2012). Even enslaved African Americans organized at the plantation level and through various underground networks to secure their freedom (Foner, 2015).

During the Progressive Era (~1890–1917), organizers played a critical role in strengthening new immigrant communities, creating labor unions, advocating for a wide range of social reforms, and promoting participatory forms of democracy. These activities continued throughout the conservative 1920s and intensified during the Great Depression of the 1930s in both urban and rural areas. At the end of the 1930s, Saul Alinsky (Horwitt, 1992) introduced a new model of issue-oriented organizing in Chicago whose influence continues today.

The new social movements of the 1960s and 1970s (a resurgent civil rights movement, so-called "second wave" feminism, the lesbian and gay rights movement) had a significant influence on community practice, by shifting the field away from an exclusive focus on geographic communities to one that emphasized communities of identity and interest (Walls, 2012). Throughout history, international influences, such as socialism and anarchism, have shaped both the ends and means of community organizing. These international influences continue today, in such areas as environmental justice and the rights of indigenous peoples.

Fisher and Kling (1993) emphasize the effect of new social movements on community practice today. They argue that most organizing occurs around communities of interest or geography, not the workplace, and that struggles over culture and social identity play a greater role than in the past. Today organizing strategies focus on self-help and empowerment rather than attempts to obtain assistance from external sources. This reflects both the changing character of work in a postindustrial, globalized economy and the decline of labor unions. They also point out the significance of the development of trans-class organizations of constituencies and cultural identities. A neo-populist vision of democracy that defies traditional left-right ideological definitions often provides the conceptual "glue" to keep these diverse groups together.

Delgado (1994) argues that the major accomplishments of community organizing during the past century include upping the political ante, developing local leaders, and achieving local victories by redressing power imbalances and holding local political leaders accountable. More recently, organizing efforts have provided a fertile ground for training youth in civic participation and developing new models of organizing that other communities can replicate. Community fragmentation, particularly along racial and gender lines, lack of clarity over who should be organized, frequent inability to articulate a comprehensive, alternative vision that goes beyond protesting against injustices, and the perpetual problem of insufficient resources have limited the effectiveness of these efforts.

Nevertheless, there are some hopeful signs. Urban communities of color have developed organizations based on racial/ethnic solidarity and focused their concerns on specific issues that primarily affect this population, such as police violence and racial profiling. Community practitioners have incorporated new methods of analysis in their work, bolstered by increased collaboration between community organizations and universities. New training programs offer the promise of developing a new generation of leaders, particularly among youth. New identity-based communities of interest, such as Black Lives Matter, have forged new networks, and have recently begun to connect with organizations that advocate around different forms of social exclusion, such as immigrant rights groups (Butterfield, 2012).

According to Wenocur and Soifer (1997), these trends exist because many social movements that began a half century ago are still alive, albeit in somewhat different form. For example, many community organizations professionalized in recent decades, particularly involving fund-raising and the use of social media. This resulted in many organizing efforts shifting away from confrontational to more collaborative or consensus-oriented approaches (Ohmer & DeMasi, 2009; Eichler, 2007).

We can extract a number of contemporary lessons from this brief historical overview. As recent developments in the United States attest, community organizing cuts across the political spectrum and occurs in a historical context that includes yet transcends local community borders. There is, therefore, a critical relationship among organizing efforts, local and national politics, and national and international social movements. This implies that in many instances the problems that affect both geographic communities and also communities of identity require the expansion of organizing efforts beyond the local level, and demand political organization beyond the neighborhood level. It also stresses the importance of blending political education into all organizing efforts and of organizers articulating their ideological assumptions more clearly (Fisher & Kling, 1993). Finally, community practitioners today must pay particular attention to the effect of persistent racial inequality and its implications for effective practice, and to the expanding meaning of "minority" status in U.S. society (Rivera & Erlich, 1997; Gutierrez & Reisch, 2017).

Why Organize?

Given all these challenges, why should people organize? A longtime organizer, Tim Sampson, defines organizing simply as the process of bringing people together to act collectively on their common interests. (As we will discuss later in this chapter, this is not as simple as it sounds.) He argues that the goals of organizing include:

1. The development of power, a sense of community, and heightened political consciousness.
2. The ability to analyze the root causes of inequality and injustice.
3. The creation of structural and institutional change rather than mere participation within existing systems.
4. The development of alternative institutions.

Heather Booth (1977), the founder of the Midwest Academy, identifies three reasons why people organize: (1) Win concrete reforms (such as anti-discrimination legislation); (2) Change the relations of power (that will shape future social change efforts); and (3) Give people a sense of their own power. Marilyn Adamson summarizes these goals succinctly: to win on an issue while building the capacity to win on other issues.

Community practice, therefore, has a diverse set of goals. Some of them are short term and pragmatic: to solve a specific community problem through the application of various types of expertise or the acquisition of concrete resources, to provide self-help and mutual aid where needed, or to influence the electoral process to produce a specific benefit to the community. More often, the goals are long term and broader in scope.

They include increasing the effectiveness of existing programs and services, and creating new ones to fill gaps in service delivery or access to essential benefits. At times, they strive to achieve major, permanent change in the structure, policies, and practices of institutions to effect a significant alteration in the distribution of power, rights, and resources.

Other goals of community organizing involve less tangible objectives. These include efforts to enhance individual and group identity, to provide social and psychological benefits to community members, and to strengthen their capacity for collective action. They could also involve building alternative centers of power to promote group empowerment and respond more effectively to changing community conditions. At times, the purpose of community organizing is educational. It attempts to heighten people's awareness of the tensions between individually and structurally oriented responses to their issues and problems, to teach them about the processes of social and political change, and to change the value orientation of community members. At the same time, community organizing tries to strengthen the social relationships that exist within a community (its bonding social capital) and between the community and external sources of power, resources, and influence (bridging social capital).

Coser (1966) distinguishes between changes *of* systems and changes *within* systems based on two criteria: the speed of change and the extent of a system affected. Specific examples of these changes might include:

- expanding rights to social or economic benefits, such as nutritional assistance or health care;
- enhancing access to existing services by opening new sites for service delivery or increasing the number of bilingual, bicultural staff members at existing sites;
- educating the public about the nature of a particular issue or about the processes of promoting change through the legislative, administrative, or judicial arenas;
- developing new recreational resources for youth at the community or organizational level;
- providing technical assistance to community groups on fund-raising or board development; and
- constructing coalitions to mediate existing intra-community conflict and engage in collective problem solving with community members.

The organizational forms created to achieve these purposes vary widely. They may refer to themselves as social equity, social justice, self-help, or community identity organizations (Rubin & Rubin, 2008). They may assume diverse titles such as association, congress, advisory committee, neighborhood council, or community development corporation (Homan, 2016).

There are also a wide range of organizing models that community groups use to achieve their goals and objectives. These include grassroots organizing, neighborhood economic or social development, organizing within or in cooperation with existing agencies to create new or revised services, community or social planning, popular education, policy advocacy, participating in broader social movements, and electoral work.

Whatever their name, the demographics of their communities, the organizing model they employ, or the ideologies of their members, most community organizations share certain common assumptions. First, they assume that the major injustices of the world exist because it is not in the self-interest of those in power to end them. Second, that one of the greatest injustices is the denial of people's right to participate in making the basic decisions that affect their lives. Third, that the alienation, loss of dignity, feelings of incompetence, and lack of self-worth that are common among powerless people can only be overcome by those people entering the arena of struggle and action. Fourth, that people will typically enter the arena of struggle when there is a prospect of winning something. Therefore, proposals to people aimed at encouraging them to participate must be believable, immediate, and specific. Finally, that the experience of winning is an essential ingredient for people to develop the self-confidence and civic competence necessary to participate in making bigger decisions on more fundamental problems and issues.

All forms of organizing must also resolve certain persistent issues. These include:

1. What are the goals?
2. Who determines these goals?
3. What means of change will they use?
4. Who will initiate and control the change effort?
5. When does the change effort end? Who decides?
6. How will community members be involved?
7. What strategies and tactics will produce the desired goals?
8. How will the organization determine if it has been successful?

Components of Community Practice

All models of community practice contain similar components. The first set consists of "big picture" factors. These include the overall goals of the intervention and its guiding vision and mission; the definition of "success"; the short- and long-term agendas driving the action; the definition of community underlying the effort; the nature of the analysis of the situation; and the roles that ideology, values, and consciousness play.

A second set of components is structural. They include the role of organization (as opposed to spontaneity) in the success of the action; the range of strategies and tactics employed; the locus of the action (its targets); the importance given to the action's underlying auspices; and the role played by concepts of space and place.

A third set of components addresses the roles played by participants in the action, whether the process is inclusionary or exclusionary. It also includes a perspective on the preferred characteristics of activists (whether they should be similar to or different from that of constituents), what is their preferred function (leader, consultant, or technical advisor), and whether they should be value neutral or value-driven. In addition, this component focuses on the preferred forms of leadership (top-down, bottom-up, or egalitarian, individual or collective).

Lastly, models address the types of process that occurs within social change efforts. For example, should they stress outcomes or the means by which an organized effort achieves these outcomes? They also focus on preferred forms of intragroup and intergroup relationships and decision making (e.g., consensus or conflict); and the group's approach to power. Finally, they include the "nonrational" components of organizing, such as the role of emotions, rituals, and spirituality.

All models of community practice share the following common elements.

KEY CONCEPT SUMMARY
COMMON ELEMENTS OF COMMUNITY PRACTICE

1. *People*: Whom to recruit, where and how to contact them. This also involves identifying their common bonds and interests and their different characteristics.
2. *Structure*: Determining the nature of the organizational vehicle that will implement change efforts. Options include a membership organization, a coalition or collaborative of existing organizations, and an ad hoc committee. It is critical to determine under what auspices (legal, fiscal, and political) the organization will operate.
3. *Process*: How will the organization communicate with its members, community residents, and other groups in the environment? How will its patterns of communication accurately reflect the culture and traditions of the community?
4. *Strategy and Tactics*: What approaches to change and specific actions will the organization adopt? How will it involve community members and other affected parties in making these decisions?
5. *Roles*: Who will do the work of the organization and how will the organization assign key roles?
6. *Resources*: What type of resources will the organization need (e.g., allies, experts, money, facilities, media contacts, political support)? How will the organization obtain these resources?
7. *Action on Issues*: How will the organization identify target(s), and develop specific, immediate, winnable, and unifying issues? (Hardcastle, 2011).

The Importance of Identifying Issues

Through the processes of needs and assets assessment described in Chapter 9, community practitioners can identify the issues around which to organize a community. Although this seems a straightforward task, there are complicating factors that an organizer needs to consider. First, you must recognize that community residents may have different perceptions of the same phenomenon from one another, from outsiders, and from the organizer herself. Second, the identification of significant issues must occur against the backdrop of the organizer's knowledge of the community's history and culture, awareness of contemporary developments about the issue (i.e., its currency), and the ability to project current conditions into the future (e.g., to determine whether the issue is temporary or permanent).

To identify the most salient issues affecting a community, an organizer must cultivate communication skills to acquire the most relevant information. She must possess a non-romantic, realistic view of the community. Above all, she must look at issues in the context of the overall goals of organizing—as tools to engage the community and build a community organization.

As discussed earlier in the book, there is an important difference between a problem and an issue. A problem is a personal, rather than a public or political situation. A problem could also be a socially defined condition that some segments of the public consider worthy of attention but is not personally engaging.

In contrast, from an organizing perspective, an issue is a problem about which an individual (or group) feels strongly and is willing to take action. It is engaging. In sum, an issue is a problem that others also share and about which they have strong feelings.

From the point of view of organizing, a good issue has all or most of the following characteristics:

1. *It is realistic or winnable.* This does not mean the issue is simple, but that some form of collective action can resolve it.
2. *It is immediate.* People affected by the issue must feel strongly about it.
3. Spokespersons can state the issue clearly and simply when they communicate it to others. While the problem might be complex, the issue has to be easy to understand.
4. *It is specific and not stated as a vague generality*, such as "substandard housing." Community members must be able to translate the issue into a clear demand.
5. *The issue unites rather than divides people.* It should not demonize another group, particularly another vulnerable population that could be a potential ally.
6. *The issue affects a large number of people.* It is a "public" or community-wide issue and not merely the concern of a few individuals.
7. Finally, the issue involves the affected population in its identification and resolution through collective action.

Certain factors determine how winnable an issue is. One factor is how motivated the community is to take collective action on the issue. Another factor is whether the issue has the possibility of initial easy victories (so-called "low-hanging fruit") that can build the community's confidence in its self-efficacy. A third factor is how clearly we have defined the issue and whether the process of issue definition validates community residents' perceptions of their daily reality (Alinsky, 1971; Bobo, Kendall, & Max, 2001).

Classroom Discussion

1. If we focus only on simple issues, how can we organize for the long haul and really create meaningful social or community change?
2. How do the above guidelines compare with the way we raise most current issues?
3. If an issue reflects a complex set of conditions, what is the best way to frame it?
4. What are the costs/losses of adhering to the above criteria?
5. How do community demographics (e.g., heterogeneity vs. homogeneity) affect the way we select and frame issues?

Issues, by definition, involve controversy. In fact, in the absence of controversy there is no issue. A problem may be widely shared but the specific solutions proposed for a problem shape the public's perception of the issue. The availability and accessibility of required resources and contemporary political realities also determine the feasibility of proposed solutions. As stated previously, issues must have broad appeal to build a powerful constituency. It is impossible to involve all members of a community but broader issues are "bigger" issues in the sense that they have the potential to involve a larger constituency. This quality affects the ability to mobilize the community to take action. It also influences the range of strategic and tactical options available and the structure of the organization you are trying to create.

The process of learning what issues people care about most is similar to the process of identifying the needs and goals of an individual client. You engage in active listening and encourage people to talk about their hopes, anger, and fears. You visit people in their homes, workplaces, and other familiar community sites—and, in these comfortable surroundings, you get them to talk about what they think, as specifically as possible. You explore around what issues they would take action, and who are their friends and enemies.

Sometimes the issue identification process is more formal. You (individually or with a team) engage in door-to-door canvassing or surveying. In such instances, it is important to distinguish between learning about people's attitudes and their willingness to take action. Alternately, you could organize small group meetings that help to reinforce and validate people's views on the problems that affect their community.

Once you identify an issue or set of issues, it is important to determine how to articulate the issue to the community you want to organize and mobilize. In this phase of the organizing process, it is helpful to explore with community residents and leaders the different ways the issue can be resolved, what they regard as an acceptable resolution of the issue, and how they think the community should state its demands. It is also important to develop fallback positions for those circumstances when others take away the issue to define alternative solutions.

There are a number of ways opponents can "steal" an issue. One way is through pre-emption—that is, making certain concessions that weaken the motivation to act among some community residents. A classic illustration of pre-emption occurred in late 19th-century Germany when Chancellor Otto von Bismarck "stole the thunder of the Socialists" by passing the first modern social welfare legislation.

A second method of undermining an issue is through co-optation. This often involves inducing key community leaders to accept certain benefits that do not accrue to the community as a whole. A related method is tokenism, such as appointing a few community members to a powerful board on which they will have little influence but where they will provide "cover" for the issue's opponents.

Other ways opponents can steal issues include "tid-bitting" (focusing on the more insignificant components of the issue), redefining the issue to conform to the perceptions and interests of the community's opponents, and proposing certain procedural delays, such as forming a committee to "study" the issue in more depth. Finally, opponents frequently use divide and conquer tactics to undermine the power of an organization to press a particular issue. On occasion, this tactic involves the use of personal or ethnic slurs and even spreading lies about other members of the community group.

In sum, to establish the legitimacy of an issue, a community organization needs to define the issue clearly, frame the issue in terms of its breadth, vision, and long-term and short-term goals and objectives, and connect the issue to widely accepted community or societal values, ethics, and sense of morality. A difficult question for a social change organization is how can it acquire legitimacy from external sources without adopting the value system of the structures it is trying to change? Often an issue is the logical extension of the dominant ideology. A possible solution to this dilemma is to exploit the internal contradictions in the ideology. (*Chapter 12 on advocacy will discuss this tactic further.*)

Issue-based organizing also requires a model of organization that allows you to take action soon, not just talk about the problem (which leads only to researching the issue). This requires developing an organizational structure through which people can work together to achieve a mutually agreed-upon purpose (Applied Research Center & Center for Third World Organizing, 1998). Shel Trapp (1976) outlines 10 steps to build such an organization:

1. Identify the issue.
2. Test the issue.
3. Find community leaders.
4. Hold a leadership meeting.

5. Focus the agenda by determining
   a. What is the issue?
   b. What are the things we can do about the issue?
   c. Of these, prioritize what we want to do first.
   d. Decide when and where to hold a larger meeting to get support for this action.
   e. Determine who is going to chair the meeting, what is the specific agenda, and who will publicize the meeting throughout the community—to other groups and to the media—and how.
6. Holding a larger meeting to determine:
   a. What action to
   b. Needed follow-up; and
   c. The next meeting date.
7. After this meeting, build the structure for a community-based organization. Possible ways to do this include:
   a. Work with small community subgroups (e.g., block groups) to develop a more coordinated effort on the issue and create a new more permanent coalition-type organization.
   b. Develop an issue coalition.
   c. Create a more formal structure (e.g., a community council) that will define the issues. As new issue-oriented groups form in the community, bring them into the council.
8. Follow through with subsequent meetings.
9. Alternative conclusions are: (a) victory; (b) partial victory; and (c) defeat.
10. Next steps: Move on to new issues.

Social Justice and Community Practice

As Reisch and Garvin (2016) point out, to be true to the mission and values of the social work profession, social justice should be a central component of all of our practice. This means that we have to infuse social justice principles into our preferred outcomes and the processes we use to achieve them. In the community practice field, this requires us to view social justice as a dynamic, not static, concept and to recognize the critical importance of history, context, power, and people's positionalities and standpoints. We also need to recognize that powerful resistance makes social and political change difficult to achieve and that even small victories are not necessarily permanent.

Community practice with a social justice focus, therefore, emphasizes the educational function of community work, the importance of praxis and the development of critical consciousness, and efforts to integrate excluded and marginalized groups as full partners in the change process, if possible through the creation of multicultural coalitions. It also stresses the role of organizing within and across existing boundaries, mixing issue and identity-based approaches, struggling with the consequences of power and conflict, and infusing global perspectives and ideas derived from other societies into our practice (Iglehart, 2012).

Models of Community Practice

In the 1960s, Rothman (1968) developed a tripartite division of the major community practice models: **locality development**, social planning, and social action. He pointed out that these basic models could be "mixed and matched" depending on the context and goals of a community-based intervention. For over half a century, the field expanded Rothman's original formulation in response to criticisms from feminists, organizers of color, and changes in the practice environment itself.

A comprehensive list of today's models would also include neighborhood and grassroots organizing, organizing in functional communities and existing service agencies, political and social action, advocacy, social reform, community-based social and economic development, program development, coalition work, and social movement work (Rothman & Tropman, 1987; Hyde, 1996; Weil, Gamble, & Ohmer, 2013). Each model represents a particular emphasis within community practice.

For example, the function of grassroots organizing is to enable individuals and groups to grow to the point where they are able to work with others around common goals and build mutual trust while struggling to achieve institutional and systems change. The goal of organizing within existing agencies or groups is to help clients and staff members become more competent and better able to negotiate the systems in which they live and work, and to use external systems/networks to help produce internal change. This could include creating a new service or program, or expanding or modifying existing services.

The purposes of educational work, such as that involved in advocacy, are to increase access, resources, and opportunities for populations-at-risk; inform service providers, policy makers, and the public about unmet or underserved needs; and educate the public and critical decision makers about a particular problem. An overarching goal of educational work is to develop people's ability to understand and act upon their social environment. From this perspective, the ability to engage in power analyses is critical, including the ability to identify the sources of one's individual or group power. It also involves developing specific skills to address power deficits and increasing power resources. The role of the organizer is as a consultant or, through dialogue, facilitator, to avoid replication of traditional power relationships.

A related activity, social reform, strives to link the expansion of rights, resources, and opportunities to changes in the political-economic structure. In this regard, there is a key distinction between "reformist reforms" that leave the basic structure of a system or institution intact (such as the Affordable Care Act) and "non-reformist reforms" that fundamentally alter this system (such as a single payer health care model) (Gorz, 1968).

An emerging model, multicultural community organizing (MCO), builds upon an ethno-conscious approach to practice. It combines an ethnic-sensitive orientation and an empowerment perspective (Gutierrez, 1997; Kirk & Okazawa-Rey, 1998). This model reflects an appreciation of the strengths within communities of color (Rivera & Erlich, 1997; Delgado, 1994). Its core concerns are the acquisition of power and confronting social inequality, especially structural inequality in all of its forms. MCO assumes that building strong organizations within communities of color is a prerequisite for the construction of effective and viable multiracial coalitions.

As Rothman asserted earlier, however, these models are not mutually exclusive. Practitioners often "interweave" them depending upon the needs of a particular situation or the particular phase or goals of a change process. Using a model allows for interventions to be proactive, planned, and strategic, rather than reactive.

In selecting a model, a social worker needs to determine the type of community in which she is working. What is the central problem or issue? What are the community's strengths? Which theory will guide our work together? Theories are useful guides to the big picture. They inform our work, but they do not tell us how to be a **change agent** or organize effectively in diverse communities. Practice models or intervention approaches (which are based on theory), however, can help guide our work. They reflect efforts to use an informed, consistent approach to identify goals and processes that are part of a planned change effort. This includes engaging in critical thinking based on available quantitative and qualitative data, and valuing the participation of clients, constituents, and colleagues in other organizations. As a new social worker, you must find the intersection of where your personal values meet professional values. By integrating these value systems, we can create a lens to think critically about the necessary elements of the process of planned change.

So, how do you choose which model of community practice to use? You need to consider a number of factors. They include:

- the process by which you will identify salient issues;
- goals and targets of the change effort;
- the type of change strategy you will use. This requires an assessment of how cooperative or adversarial the target of change will be;
- the resources required to produce the desired change;
- the respective roles of the organizer, staff, volunteers, community members, and community leaders in the change effort;
- the specific roles of staff, leaders, and organizational members;
- the values, needs, and cultural frame of constituents;

- the local and national political context; and
- your personal framework. This includes how comfortable you are with various change strategies and tactics, whether you are more task-oriented (outcome) or process-oriented, and your perspectives on power. For example, community development is a model if you want to create power. Social planning is an approach that uses available power. Social action is a model that seeks to gain power.

Locality or Community Development

This model of practice emphasizes neighborhood work aimed at improving community life through the participation of a broad spectrum of people at the local level, although its scope can be from local to global. One of its goals is to assist residents organize into block clubs and neighborhood associations to build power and improve the quality of their lives. This model often reflects **communitarian** values; it emphasizes process goals and stresses such concepts as community competency, self-help, and mutual aid. Examples of this model include settlement houses, community development corporations, VISTA, and the Peace Corps.

Sometimes community development focuses on organizing functional communities to change a specific area of concern that affects community members. When the focus is on community economic and social development, a primary goal is the creation of stronger and more sustainable institutions and resources in low-income, oppressed, or isolated communities. On a more modest scale, a goal could be "community transformation" (e.g., the creation of affordable housing, employment opportunities, or the refurbishment of abandoned or deteriorated properties).

The community practitioner plays a variety of roles in locality development. These include:

1. Catalyst (stimulating action in others)
2. Teacher (especially capacity building and leadership development)
3. Facilitator/coordinator (e.g., of meetings)
4. Communicator (within the community and to the media)
5. Motivator (stimulating others to act)
6. Educator (developing potential leaders)
7. Strategist (identifying targets of change)
8. Technical Assistant (e.g., fund-raising)
9. Broker (linking organizations and groups)
10. Negotiator/Mediator (resolving disputes, forging inter-organizational agreements) (Rothman, 1968; Rubin & Rubin, 2008).

Figure 10.1 graphically reflects the approach of community development

Figure 10.1 Resident Participation Model

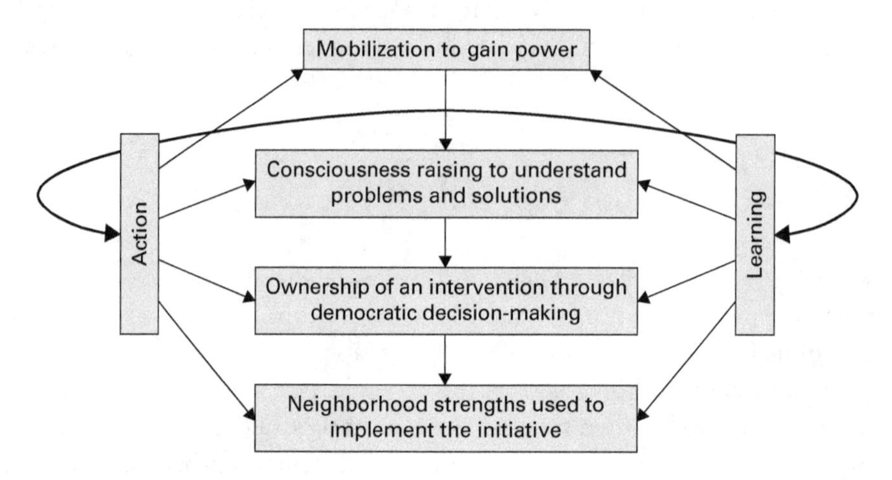

Fig. 10.1: *Daniel Brisson and Susan Roll, "An Adult Education Model of Resident Participation: Building Community Capacity and Strengthening Neighborhood-Based Activities in a Comprehensive Community Initiative (CCI)," Advances in Social Work, vol. 9, no. 2, pp. 164. Copyright © 2008 by Indiana University School of Social Work.*

According to Warren (1970), the community development model seeks to create or recreate the components of the "good community." It takes into account the following factors:

1. *Primary group relationships*: The functions, depth, breadth, and history of these relationships.
2. *Autonomy*: The ability of the community to make decisions on its own behalf and the feasibility of community autonomy in today's complex political-economic environment.
3. *Viability*: The capacity of people to confront their problems effectively through some type of concerted action.
4. *Power distribution*: An assessment of whether the current distribution of power in the community is democratic or hierarchical, and what are the community's values about power.
5. *Participation*: How extensively do community members currently participate in community activities? This has implications for how the community will make decisions.

6. *Degree of commitment*: How important is the community to its members? Do community members have divided loyalties and commitments (e.g., to other communities)? How much commitment is desirable to achieve the goals of the change effort?
7. *Degree of heterogeneity or homogeneity*: By class, race, ethnicity, religion, culture. What mix is desirable? What are the implications for building community power?
8. *Extent of neighborhood control*: Whether present authority in the community is centralized (e.g., in one organization) or decentralized.
9. *Extent of conflict*: How much conflict exists in the community? To what extent should this conflict be encouraged or suppressed? What might be appropriate settings to resolve existing conflicts?
10. *Overall*: How much of the "good community" is actually possible? How much of what seems desirable do we actually want even if the change efforts threaten other values?

The focus on community building underscores the need for organizers to be aware of people's problems, their level of readiness for change and their capacity to change; and the influence of broader social and economic forces on the community. A major component of community building, therefore, involves identifying common ground (solidarity) to break down the community's isolation and achieve power (Etzioni, 1968). Another component is the creation of organizational structures that build collective capacity, a sense of community, and a belief in the possibility of change (Delgado, 1986). A key question in this regard is what types of organizations are most suitable for a particular community at a particular time?

An underlying assumption of community organizing is the importance of starting with people's needs, concerns, issues, and strengths. A challenge for practitioners using a community development model is how to determine what they are. This is particularly difficult in communities that have internalized externally imposed oppression and often lack critical consciousness, the ability to articulate their long-standing concerns, and the belief that positive change is possible. This is why Freire (1971) emphasized the need to create value consensus and people's belief in the possibility of change through transforming their self-perception from objects to subjects capable of acting upon their world.

Another major emphasis in this model is the importance of broad and sustained community participation and leadership development. This requires extensive, ongoing collaboration with community members. It involves recognizing and sharing power in order to develop others' power. In addition, it requires us to decide what form of leadership is best suited for the community at this particular time.

The underlying assumption is that through collaboration, community members will develop the necessary knowledge and skills to make critical decisions on their own behalf. This is why the nature of the organizer's relationship to the community is so critical. Is the organizer a member of the community, an outsider with a similar racial/ethnic/class background, or an outsider of a different background (Rivera & Erlich, 1997)? This influences what roles the organizer can play most effectively.

Another major focus of community development is capacity building. It emphasizes building on a community's strengths and assets, instead of trying to "fix" its problems or deficits. This involves recognizing and validating the skills of community members, which many community change efforts often overlook. This requires the organizer to become familiar with the history of change efforts in the community, particularly its previous successes.

Although this model appears to reflect many long-standing social work values, the use of this model is not without challenges. Organizers require supportive supervision, education, and leadership, and skills in working with community members from different backgrounds. Organizers must understand how critical it is for them to adopt the role of constant learner, and not just teacher, and to distinguish their leadership tasks from those of a facilitator. The latter particularly requires organizers from majority cultures to understand the significance of social location (class, gender, culture) in shaping human experience and making a conscious effort to know the history of others.

Rubin and Rubin (2008) list the major elements of community development as empowerment, collective action to build social capital, expanding community control, strengthening community bonds, and building strong organizations as vehicles through which community members focus power and social solidarity to bring about desired changes. Through this model, community practitioners work with members to achieve the following goals:

1. Build community assets.
2. Increase members' competencies.
3. Develop new leadership.
4. Strengthen interpersonal and intergroup relationships.
5. Create linkages to available resources inside and outside the community.
6. Develop new resources, if possible.
7. Foster a sense of community responsibility, community ownership, control, self-reliance, and confidence.
8. Build self-sustaining organizations to enhance the quality of community life.

Community organizers facilitate the change process by promoting improved intragroup and intergroup community, gathering and disseminating critical information, helping community members frame issues and take initial action, bringing people together to discuss their common concerns, expanding their power, celebrating accomplishments, recruiting new members, and developing new leaders (Homan, 2016).

Although community development efforts emphasize cooperation and democratic participation, they can ultimately lead to concerted social action. Often the process of community participation heightens people's awareness of the connections between their current problems and their structural roots. Small-scale successes at the local level can enhance community members' belief in the possibility of broader changes and the viability of alternative approaches to their problems. Other factors that can promote social action at the community level include the credibility of organizers, the validity of the issues identified by the community, the sustainability of the organization that community members create, and development of a sufficient degree of passion about the issues that is necessary for community mobilization.

Homan (2016) lists the following elements of successful neighborhood organizations:

1. Full-time, paid professional staff
2. Well-developed fund-raising capacity and the acquisition of external financial and political support.
3. Sophisticated mode of operation.
4. Variety of skills among community members.
5. Ability to expand the issue from a local to a regional or national focus.
6. Participation of the organization in effective coalitions and networks.

He proposes the following general guidelines for local organizations:

1. Choose issues within your existing capability.
2. Distinguish between desirable and feasible goals.
3. Move from reactive to proactive strategies.
4. Develop ways to resolve internal disputes and avoid the emergence of factions.
5. Identify and develop leaders. Get children and youth involved early by creating mentor relationships.
6. Find allies in other organizations (including government). Do not hesitate to ask for help when needed.

IN-CLASS EXERCISE
COMMUNITY POWER

Introduction

Please read the following scenario ***carefully***—most of which may be familiar to you from previous exercises. You may assume any information that the background description does not provide as long as it does not contradict any information presented in the case and you make your assumptions explicit.

Background: The Current Situation

Two years ago, an ad hoc coalition of concerned community residents (Citizens United for a Revitalized Eastville, or CURE), composed largely of individuals from the African American and Latino communities, was created. The coalition has focused its efforts on such issues as crime and drugs, the deteriorating conditions of the public schools, and police-community relations.

The Problem

At the request of CURE, you are part of a small team of community organizers sent to Eastville from a metropolitan area-wide community development corporation. Your supervisor has asked you to write an analysis of the situation in Eastville that concisely addresses the following questions:

1. How you will determine the principle sources of power and empowerment in Eastville? What conceptual model(s) of "community," "power," and "empowerment" will you use and why?
2. What do you consider the most significant barriers to organizing the community? What factors influenced this assessment?
3. What role(s) should you—as an organizer—play in working with the people of Eastville? What frameworks or models of community organizing and development will serve as your guide(s) and why?
4. How might factors of race, gender, social class, and/or religion influence your work—in terms of the roles you play, the strategies you adopt, and your overall relationship with the community?
5. You will convene and facilitate your first meeting with the coalition next week. Develop an agenda for the meeting. Explain your overall goals for the meeting, why you selected each agenda item, how you hope to achieve your goals, and how they fit into your long-term strategy.

Economic and Social Development

A subset of locality development focuses on economic and social development at the neighborhood level. One of its goals is the generation of economic production through microenterprises, the creation of so-called "enterprise zones," strengthening existing local businesses, and forming cooperatives. Another goal is the creation of more economic capital in the community. This occurs by changing the lending practices of financial institutions, attracting external sources of investment (e.g., foundations, government, philanthropists), and developing internal sources of capital (through peer lending, community loan funds, and individual assets accounts or IDAs). A third goal is to expand local employment opportunities by creating job training and skill development programs, and enhancing the quality of education in the community. To increase local standards of living, community developers also attempt to help the community produce local goods and services for internal use and export, identify potential consumers of these goods, and enhance the local infrastructure and direct it toward economic activities that benefit the community as a whole.

There are numerous examples of neighborhood economic and social development. The most widely recognized involve enterprise zones that require extensive cooperation between government and the private sector. They often involve relaxation of tax policies and environmental rules, and produce inconsistent benefits for community residents.

"Buy Black" initiatives, such as Recycling Black Dollars in Los Angeles, represent another approach. They include encouragement of banks and corporations to invest more in the communities that consume their products. They also emphasize the need to end the practice among financial institutions of redlining (failing to loan money to) low-income, racial minority neighborhoods, and to support local educational and recreational projects.

In other nations, this linkage of economic development with the creation of supportive social services is common. A major example is the Brotherhood of St. Laurent Project in Australia (Johnson, Brotherhood of St. Laurence, & Taylor, 2000). Some leading international efforts, such as the Grameen Bank in Bangladesh, focus primarily on microenterprise development through small loans to individual entrepreneurs (Holcombe, 1995; Karim, 2008). The extent to which such programs have an effect on community development is unclear.

More generally, the emphasis of community development on viewing the neighborhood as a center of coproduction has several important implications for the future of community practice. First, in this "back to the future" approach, the citizen role in a neighborhood replaces that of a paid professional. Examples include using "natural helpers" or developing helping networks, which work to diminish crime and violence or provide mutual aid in such areas as child care and after-school tutoring.

Second, in this model neighborhood associations replace some of the functions of local government through cooperatives, community development corporations, citizens' planning boards, and neighborhood groups that focus on specific issues such as housing. The development of participatory budgeting in diverse communities from Brooklyn, New York, to Sao Paulo, Brazil, are examples of this phenomenon (Lelieveldt et al., 2009).

A hybrid form of this model occurs when a neighborhood citizen entity and a professional, governmental entity outside the neighborhood share responsibility for the delivery of an essential service. Examples include private-sector initiatives aimed at redevelopment or rehabilitation of a particular area and federal projects such as Hope VI. This approach differs from community outreach or citizen participation in two ways: (1) Neighborhoods can initiate actions without awaiting formal approval for government or private programs, and (2) It includes an element of spontaneous development in which the objective is not merely to replace existing actors but to change systems.

Another type of community development involves a synthesis with approaches more commonly associated with social action models of community organizing. One example is the living wage campaigns organized by the now-defunct ACORN organization in such cities as Baltimore, Portland, Oregon, and Milwaukee (Figart, 2004; Freeman, 2005). Another example involves attempts at political restructuring—that is, to expand the boundaries of "inelastic cities" to include their suburbs through annexation and city-county consolidation to create metropolitan governments. The goal of this approach is to compel affluent suburbs to accept their fair share of responsibility for poverty in the region through metro-wide affordable housing requirements, public housing programs, and revenue sharing. To some extent, this has occurred in the development of regional solutions to transportation issues or problems such as homelessness (Rusk, 2013). A third example are programs such as the Neighborhood Jobs Initiative that focus on urban areas of high poverty and unemployment, high welfare utilization, and other indicators of social problems. These programs tailor work incentives to local financial and nonfinancial conditions; provide job-training, job-placement, and job-retention services using a best practices approach; and expand access to capital for residents and local entrepreneurs (Molina & Nelson, 2001).

There are numerous challenges involved in initiating and expanding these economic development efforts. The technical challenges involved constitute an obvious problem. Low-income, low-power, excluded communities frequently lack the requisite skills, organizational networks, technology, resources, and internal and external linkages to develop successful projects. There is also the risk, particularly within "top-down," externally controlled economic development efforts, that they will exclude those most in need from both the process itself and from its benefits. This risk is particularly strong among people of color, women, the elderly, youth, and immigrants. The mixed results of enterprise zones are a prime illustration of this phenomenon.

Another potential danger is that the search for local solutions may further isolate the community, and that the emphasis on local development may provide a rationalization for further abandonment by external sources of power (e.g., government). Historically, this was one reason the African American community had ambivalent feelings about self-help, mutual aid approaches. The failure of major public and private institutions to pay sufficient attention to marginalized communities (e.g., Asian American and Latino immigrants) that had attempted to develop their own services justified African Americans' reluctance to adopt a similar strategy (Iglehart & Becerra, 2010; Carlton-LaNey, 1999).

Conceptually the tension between organizing and development is, perhaps, inevitable. Development focuses on pragmatic, transactional, time-limited, immediate projects, while community organizing is often messy, quirky, and more time-consuming. In addition, as racial and class divisions widen and harden, it becomes increasingly difficult to persuade community members to act in a manner that appears to go against their short-term self-interests.

Community and Social Planning

This model of community practice generally occurs at the neighborhood, city, or regional level. (For historical and ideological reasons, there has always been considerable resistance in the United States to centralized social and economic planning.) Community and social planning, whether for purposes of physical renovation, economic development, or service planning, emphasizes careful study of a community's political, social, economic, and demographic characteristics (Mayer, 1972). The goal is to create the basis for identifying agreed-upon problems and determining a range of solutions. City and county planners and funding federations, such as the United Way, Associated Jewish Charities, and Catholic Social Services, often use this process (Lauffer, 1978). Practitioners could use this model to create a new service (e.g., a citywide universal pre-k program), expand or revise existing programs to improve their responsiveness to long-standing community needs (such as youth unemployment), or develop programs to meet the emerging needs of a specific population, such as unaccompanied immigrant youth.

The practitioner's roles in this aspect of community work are quite distinct. They include:

1. Conducting research and analyzing community needs (*See Chapter 9*);
2. Translating identified problems into needs that programs can address;
3. Establishing new ways of providing services through innovative program development and by serving as a community liaison;
4. Technical problem solving around a specific issue, such as housing, education, or substance abuse; and
5. Evaluating the effectiveness of existing services (Rothman & Tropman, 1987).

The roots of planning emerged from Weber's (1946) emphasis on organizations as rational entities. The planning process, therefore, is research-driven and strives to be "objective" by relying on expert opinion and rationality. It emphasizes task goals, rather than process, such as the delivery of more effective services. It generally follows a prescribed pattern of problem identification, assessment, goal development, implementation, and evaluation. Social planning is the "problem-solving model" of social work, although it is a practice shared with other disciplines such as public health, urban planning, public administration, and public policy.

Critics of this approach point out that its "top-down" orientation tends to exclude low-power groups from the process of identifying and assessing community problems, and participating in the development of alternative solutions. The emphasis on expertise also implies a devaluation of the acquired, experiential wisdom of community members. Finally, the reliance on objective data obscures the issue of whether research is used to help understand problems as experts define them and to solve them without making fundamental changes in the social or political structure that created them in the first place (Yiftachel, 1998).

Social Action

The primary goals of social action are to correct societal inequities by changing existing policies or procedures, patterns of resource distribution, or power arrangements within societal institutions and systems that particularly disadvantage oppressed and marginalized groups of people. The targets are usually those community institutions that control and allocate resources and power, such as financial institutions, corporations, or local government. Prominent examples of the use of the social action model include landlord/tenant conflicts, welfare rights organizing, union or workplace organizing, and political organizing, both inside and outside the electoral arena. Practitioners employ a wide range of tactics that are often confrontational, such as strikes, protests, boycotts, and demonstrations. People exercise power through their numbers, particularly through their participation in coalitions or social movements.

The roles of the community practitioner in social action are considerably different from those emphasized by other models. They include:

- Initiator
- Agitator
- Catalyst
- Spokesperson
- Leadership identifier and developer
- Strategist/tactician
- Risk taker (Alinsky, 1971; Weil, Gamble, & Ohmer, 2013).

Homan (2016) suggests there are a number of elements of successful social action. Some of them are similar to the components of effective community development, such as knowledge of the affected community; framing a compelling issue based on sufficient information; acquiring sufficient numbers, tangible resources, and expertise; developing new leadership, a strong organization, and culturally compatible patterns of communication; and matching strategies and tactics to the context. It is also critical to forge a power base larger than the issue and to make sure the environment is sufficiently receptive to the goals of the social action effort. Domhoff (2003) adds that effective social action must include the following three components: (1) an in-depth analysis of the issues; (2) a clear vision of an alternative future; and (3) a clear road map on how to achieve this vision.

Because of the political risks and controversial nature of the issues involved, social action efforts often emerge in different places from efforts that focus on community development. They often arise in "free spaces." During the civil rights movement, these included beauty parlors, social clubs, and churches (Morris, 1986). The feminist movement emerged through small-scale activities in major organizations such as the YWCA and in less visible consciousness-raising groups in women's homes (Rhode, 2014). Similarly, LGBTQ activism began in safe spaces such as gay bars and bathhouses (Adam, 1995). The freedom these spaces provided allowed oppressed groups to acquire a heightened sense of self away from external threats, and enhanced their ability to create individual and group change.

This growing confidence or empowerment enables people to expand their ability to fight for their rights, and to promote fundamental institutional change. In the process, they change the ways they acquire and interpret critical knowledge and learn how to form and maintain new types of social relationships. Above all, they develop a deeper sense of self-definition and heightened social and political consciousness.

The creation of safe spaces enables oppressed populations to develop organizational autonomy. It also allows these populations to expand their cultural freedom from dominant ideologies and, potentially, become more open to working with diverse groups. In effect, social action can help overcome the conflict between traditional and new modes of behavior, particularly regarding such challenging issues as racism, sexism, xenophobia, and homophobia (Seif, 2010; Nasir & Al-Amin, 2006; Peters, 2003).

Organizing in Communities of Color

Delgado (1994) described a wide range of organizational configurations within communities of color that overlap with but do not conform to traditional models of community organizing. These include the following:

- single-issue mobilizations such as Black Lives Matter and the Dreamers;
- multiracial community organizations such as those that emphasize the unequal treatment of racially minority children in public schools;
- mono-racial community organizations;
- immigrant rights organizations such as CASA de Maryland;
- community-based workplace initiatives such as organizing among janitors in Los Angeles;
- economic development efforts such as "Buy Black" initiatives; and
- professional advocacy organizations such as the NAACP, Urban League, and MALDEF.

These organizations share a common perspective: that racism is the primary mode of oppression in the United States. Based on critical race theory, they define most issues primarily in racial terms. They emphasize the importance of capacity building, particularly among youth, and the revitalization of indigenous cultures and values. In recent years, these organizations have acquired more of an international perspective and, with some exceptions such as the Obama campaigns, increased skepticism toward electoral-based reform. There is still the possibility of collaboration with progressive White organizations if there is adequate representation of people of color "in the mix" and if organizations of people of color can maintain their ability to act independently.

Marable (2009) regards these developments as critical steps in the promotion of a multicultural democracy. He makes a strong connection between the ideals of democracy and the complementary goals of social justice and diversity. This connection has significant implications for our sense of history, language, religion, economic philosophy, and leadership patterns. In the area of community organizing, it influences how we view power sharing and resource allocation and the meaning of self-determination. It promotes the goal of creating an economic system centered on human need rather than profit. Finally, it infuses contemporary politics with a common sense of ethics and spirituality that challenges the structures of oppression, power, and privilege within the dominant social order.

Social Reform and Advocacy

This model is a mixture of social action and social planning that involves collaborating with other organizations to promote system or policy change. It addresses such issues as increasing child care options for working parents, raising the minimum wage, addressing inequities in the funding of public school districts, and creating more affordable housing opportunities (Weil, Gamble, & Ohmer, 2013).

The roles of a practitioner in this area include:

1. *Building Coalitions*: Groups of diverse organizations that pursue common goals, coordinate resources, and adopt a common strategy (e.g., a domestic violence coalition).
2. *Working with Social Movements*: Individuals and groups inside and outside social work join in efforts toward social justice goals (e.g., the civil rights movement).
3. *Policy Advocacy*: Developing and/or revising institutional policies or legislation.
4. *Public or Popular Education*: Through media, cultural activities, and other vehicles.

(See chapters five and six for further material on coalitions and chapters 12–14 for a fuller discussion of advocacy.)

Implementing a Model: Developing Effective Strategies

A strategy is the overall plan that determines how we are going to get where we want to go. Put simply, it is also the answer to the question, "How are we going to reach our goal?" To answer this question, good organizing requires that you propose a solution when making a demand. Two important factors in this regard are choosing the right target and choosing the right tactics. (*See section below for more on tactics.*) This requires good research and good press and media coverage (*The Gray Panthers Organizing Manual,* Vol. 1, n.d.).

A good strategy must also be rooted in politics, either explicitly or implicitly. This includes ideas about: (1) how society and its institutions function (i.e., who rules and why); (2) the nature and cause of social, economic, and political problems; (3) the nature and scope of political participation; and (4) appropriate means to produce or induce change.

Strategies are distinct from tactics in that they involve the overall plan of a group or organization. A strategy frames the organization's desired goals in means/ends terms. The central question in developing strategies is how are events and actions used to identify people's self-interests and to help people learn how to engage in a long-term struggle?

In sum, strategies are the vehicles we use to produce or induce change. They reflect a plan that in some way challenges, debates, and acts to resolve differences in a group's favor. A group's ideology and goals shape its strategies. In turn, strategies determine a group's selection of tactics.

The veteran organizer Si Kahn (1991) identified eight qualities of a good strategy. It should be thought out well in advance (i.e., not the result of impulsive, spontaneous action). It should build on the experiences of the people with whom we are working and should involve them in both planning and implementation. A good strategy is also flexible and suited to its specific context. It has depth. It is feasible. It is consistent with the culture of the population with whom we are working. Finally, it is educational.

If a strategy is well developed, it will produce several desirable outcomes (Coover et al., 1985). It will provide a long-range lens through which to assess short-term actions. It will enable the organization to assess the consequences of proposed tactics and outline the critical features of the tactics selected. A good strategy will assist in choosing tactics that are consistent with the organization's basic goals. It will help the organization analyze future successes and setbacks to its advantage.

In addition, a good strategy helps an organization determine how to use people's abilities and energies most effectively, and to measure whether offers of "help" from local groups, foundations, or government bodies would restrict or impede the program for change. It provides a framework for action that the organization can continually evaluate and modify by experience when necessary. It helps the organization connect local change efforts to larger national and transnational movements for change. On a personal level, it suggests creative ways for people to live, work, and relate to one another in a manner that is supportive of collective goals. Finally, it can help resolve tensions between people's personal lifestyle and their protracted involvement in political and economic change by enabling them to prepare for long-term struggles.

Common strategic approaches generally fall into the following broad categories:

1. *Legislative*: This strategy focuses on passing or defeating a proposed law, or influencing the allocation of government's fiscal resources through the budgeting process.
2. *Political*: In this strategy, an organization uses its influence to inject an issue into the political process and force political leaders to take a stand on it.
3. *Economic*: This approach emphasizes an organization's ability to hurt the image, profits, or reputation of a business enterprise to win concessions. Sometimes this strategic approach tries to embarrass the targets of change.
4. *Disruptive*: This broad category covers those activities designed to create so many problems for the power structure that some elements therein will do something about the organization's key issue(s).

Within each of these approaches, organizers also have to decide which of the follow six methods to utilize:

1. *Mass Mobilization:* This is best suited for organizing individuals at the grassroots level around issues that affect them such as substandard housing (Fisher & Kling, 1993).
2. *Citizen Participation*: This strategy attempts to involve community members in policy planning and program implementation conducted by nonprofit organizations and government agencies (DeSario & Langton, 1987).
3. *Policy Advocacy*: In this strategy, the organization represents group interests in established institutional arenas, such as the legislature, to effect policy change around economic or social issues that affect the community. (*See chapters 12–14 for more on this topic.*)
4. *Service Development*: This strategy strives to empower people to create more responsive, community-based services, such as in health care.
5. *Social Action*: The main goal of this strategy is to build powerful community organizations that identify an effective issue, focus on that issue, and then move on to other issues identified by the community.
6. *Popular Education*: This strategy's objective is to raise community members' critical consciousness as a step toward empowerment and ultimate mobilization to take action (Kane, 2001).

Another way to conceptualize community intervention strategies is in their relationship to their opponents. In this regard, there are three general approaches:

Collaboration or Consensus: This type of strategy, usually associated with the locality development or social planning model, is best suited for situations in which the target and action systems agree on a common goal and a working relationship already exists between groups or organizations. It focuses on capacity building, and involving members of the community in the change effort. A consensus model works best when the groups involved share power so that they are dealing with one another as equals. Another precondition for the success of this approach is that the goals of the change effort are distributable. In other words, there is common ground and the potential exists for a win/win outcome. A final precondition is that the groups involved share certain values and interests, or it is at least possible to forge a value consensus (Ohmer & DeMasi, 2009; Eichler, 2007).

Campaign: This type of strategy involves a group effort to convince a target system that a problem exists or that some significant change needs to occur to solve an acknowledged community problem. The approach is usually associated with the social planning and social reform models, although it sometimes fits with the community development and social action models. It focuses on public education and persuasion to change the opinions of key decision makers. It assumes that communication between opposing groups is possible despite their differences. Depending on the outcome of its attempts to persuade, it could lead to the use of another strategic approach (Narro, 2005).

Both the consensus and campaign approaches require skills in bargaining and negotiation.

Contest: This strategic approach, commonly associated with the social action model, occurs when organized change efforts become an open, public conflict. It focuses on changing the balance of power, the use of confrontation and pressure tactics, and working both inside and outside existing systems. The conflict model is best suited for circumstances in which power disparities exist and one group dominates the other. In such situations, the potential outcomes of the change process reflect a "zero sum game" (Alinsky, 1971) and there are sharp differences in the values and interests of the respective parties.

Sample (1979) further distinguishes these strategies in terms of such characteristics as:

1. Their general orientation to the change process and their assumptions as to why people seek change.
2. The role of organizing in the change of process.
3. The significance of ideology.
4. The functions of communication and the use of information.
5. Their attitude toward opponents (dialogue with or defeat them; understand or attack them).

6. How they deal with conflict.
7. Their perspective on alliances (broad or narrow).
8. Whether they take an "inside" or "outside" approach to systems change.

A major challenge for community practitioners involves deciding which strategic approach best matches the situation and needs of the community. Community practitioners also need to determine whether those in power want to create change, whether they have the resources to do so, and whether they can achieve the change goal within the structure of existing institutions.

Factors to consider in selecting the best strategy include:

1. The group's clarity about its goals.
2. The nature and power of the forces to be defeated or neutralized.
3. The range of potential allies.
4. The most effective approach to offset the strengths of the opposition.
5. The risks involved for people and the organization.
6. The potential consequences of victory or defeat (including unintended consequences).
7. The timing and context of a change effort.

Strategies and Group Mobilization

Most analyses of mobilization for social change and group contention for power take group interest for granted. Yet, many organized groups fail to mobilize. Some mobilized groups fail to act collectively. Some collective actors fail to contend for power and many actors on the stage of social change come and go with little lasting effect (Tilly, 1978).

These painful realities raise two key questions for organizers:

1. How do we identify a group's interests to help formulate strategies?
2. What are the implications of this process of identification for our practice?

There are two basic answers to the first question. We could infer a group's interest from its words and actions. But, to which part of a diverse group or community do we pay closest attention? Which of its actions are most significant? Another option is to infer a group's interests by conducting an analysis of the connections between its interests and its social position.

There are problems, however, with either approach. Groups are often unaware of their interests. Evidence that reveals these interests is frequently difficult to identify, challenging to synthesize, in conflict, or simply scarce. Another problem stems from the arrogance of outsiders attempting to organize a community. A conflict exists between the short- and long-term interests of the organizer and the community, and even within the community itself. This makes it hard to determine the real interests of a group. One could resolve this problem by applying a preconceived analytical framework, such as Marxism, or critical race theory, to predict the group's long-term interests, while relying on the group's articulation of its interests in the short term.

Another problem is how to distinguish and act upon differences between individual and group interests? A possible resolution is to recognize differences as a factor in the ability to identify and achieve collective interests. The greater the conflict, the costlier collective action is to individuals and groups.

Another major consideration is whether the organization has the capacity to mount and maintain the effort to implement the strategy selected. A small neighborhood organization should think about a campaign that does not go beyond two months. A large, older organization can think about a campaign that may extend as long as two years. The ability of an organization to sustain a change effort also has implications for the issue it chooses to address.

Richan (2006) proposes four basic rules for strategy formulation:

1. Know your agenda.
2. Decide between incremental and fundamental change goals.
3. Be clear about your priorities.
4. Develop fallback positions.

An expanded "top 10" list of other potential guidelines might include:

1. Let the people with whom you are working know what you are all about and keep them informed of activities.
2. Keep planning as much within your interest group as possible. The less opposing forces know, the longer it will take them to counterattack.
3. Know the groups(s) with which you are allied and those in opposition. Use research to plan and prevent the organization for moving too fast without adequate information.
4. Make sure the group with whom you are working sees progress (tangible gains) even if they are initially small.
5. Know what resources are available to your group—keep them on file and accessible.
6. In your meetings focus on short-term goals. Allow time occasionally for group members to vent their feelings, particularly about highly charged issues, and encourage the free flow of ideas.

7. In utilizing resources, it is sometimes good to pick people who know one another and share common ideologies. "New blood" is often helpful, however, in generating new ideas and creative directions. Constantly expand your network of resources and influence.
8. Plan activities in stages. This enables less experienced group members to follow the strategic process.
9. Keep progress reports or document activities or actions taken and the responses they elicited.
10. When the timing is right, try to get as much positive coverage of your activities as possible.

Classroom Discussion

1. What are the implications of these different strategies and concepts for your practice?
2. What different conceptions of power and empowerment do they reflect?
3. Which approaches would be most effective in the community in which you are working? For what reasons?

Developing Effective Tactics

> "Tactics means doing what you can with what you have." —Saul Alinsky, *Rules for Radicals*

> "Tactics relate to the manner in which a strategy is enacted and the tools that will be employed." —*The Gray Panthers Organizing Manual*, Vol. 1.

> "Tactics are designed to create the pressures necessary to win on particular issues. They also help to build the organization through the participation of members ..." —Si Kahn, *Organizing: A Guide for Grassroots Leaders*

As these quotes indicate, tactics are the *specific things* that we do to help us reach our goals and objectives. They are activities carried out by an organization as part of its selected strategy. To accomplish these purposes, tactics focus on three pivotal issues:

1. The context of a group or an organization's overall functioning.
2. The actual resources at hand that the group can mobilize for a strategic goal.
3. A clear understanding of the potential risks and benefits.

Good tactics have the following qualities. They are winnable, imaginative, simple, fun, and exciting. Ideally, they involve and affect large numbers of people and unite the members of your organization or community in order to strengthen them. Conversely, they divide the opposition and take advantage of rivalries and competition among your opponents.

Good tactics also contain an educational component. They help the organization learn as much about the opposition while revealing as little as possible. They are flexible and, under most circumstances, are either legal or designed to call attention to existing legal inequities. Finally, although the purpose of many tactics is to precipitate a reaction that polarizes or clarifies a conflict, they are at an acceptable level of risk for the people involved.

Types of Tactics

Kahn (1991, 2010) organized tactics into five broad categories. The first he termed "social tactics." These include marches, sit-ins, rallies, mass meetings, picket lines, shop-ins, pray-ins, and demonstrations. They serve two useful purposes. They can mobilize people prior to taking other more extensive actions, and they can be a way of calling attention to the potential power of your organization's mobilization efforts. The women's marches on January 21, 2017, were a good example of this type of tactic.

Kahn refers to a second category as "real power tactics." These can be either economic or political. Economic power tactics include boycotts (such as the 1955 Montgomery bus boycott), strikes, and proxy solicitations to influence a vote at a corporate board meeting. Political tactics can include civil disobedience, disruption, or harassment (such as those used by ACT/UP in its efforts to change government policies toward people with HIV/AIDS). They can be either peaceful or violent. Sometimes participants direct the violence against property (such as in many anti-globalization protests); at other times, they direct it at people, such as the police, in response to police shootings of African Americans.

Kahn calls a third category "political/normative" tactics. These tactics are clearly within the mainstream. They include endorsement of a candidate or **ballot initiative**, voter registration and get-out-the-vote drives, testimony at public hearings, and mass lobbying efforts. Sometimes called "inside actions," they involve confrontations or negotiations with a particular party or parties who control vital resources.

A fourth category consists of "terminal tactics." Kahn uses the metaphor of a wave to describe such tactics. They do not arouse the reaction that is essential for development of a conflict or for building an organization. Organizations only use these types of tactics to finish a conflict.

Lastly, Kahn calls certain tactics "self-help" tactics. These often consist of programs run by and for the organization's membership, independent of the power structure.

The primary purpose of such tactics is to establish separate (parallel) institutions that enable the group to become more independent and self-sufficient. Groups such as the Kensington Welfare Rights Organization in Philadelphia have employed such tactics as part of a multi-faceted strategy.

Organizations have to be strategic in the selection of any of these tactics. For example, "outside tactics" that involve confrontations usually focus on secondary targets (e.g., financial institutions). They can be particularly useful for grassroots organizations to build their reputations and demonstrate their power or potential power. The more newsworthy the target and the issue, the more effective the tactic will be.

While mass demonstrations are a good way to demonstrate widespread support, they require a lot of work. If this is a primary tactic of your organization, then to maintain momentum each demonstration must be larger than the preceding one or the opposition, the media, and the public will argue that you are losing support. Another major problem with mass demonstrations is that, with rare exceptions, they do not lend themselves to specific demands on specific institutions (Mahaffey, 1987). Think about the wide range of topics addressed by speakers at many such events. In sum, this tactic is most useful when combined with inside actions in which a delegation negotiates a specific commitment from a target during the demonstration.

Other outside tactics present similar challenges. An exposé involves releasing damaging information about targets by your organization or through an ally in the media. It is important to decide which approach will generate maximum coverage and make the news most credible. It is best to combine this tactic with a proposal to correct the exposed problem and with other tactics such as a protest. The major concern is whether the public will really care about *this particular scandal*. You can sometimes use a related tactic, embarrassment, to break down the morale of the opposition, attract attention, and build the morale of your members, especially in the early stages of organizing or when facing a serious obstacle.

The use of other outside tactics, such as civil disobedience (which might lead to arrest) and other disruptive activities, such as a strike, often frightens many people and is generally not effective in recruiting people to your cause. For these tactics to be effective, the issue must be deeply felt (e.g., the civil rights movement, HIV/AIDS, or the Black Lives Matter movement) and well understood to engender sufficient participation and support.

Even with legal disruptive tactics, the power lies in the effects of the tactic itself, not in its symbolic meaning. Boycotts, for example, only work if they have a real economic effect on the businesses targeted (King, 2011; Chasin, 2000). As with the use of civil disobedience, it is very important to assess whether an action would increase support for your cause among those *outside your organization* or isolate you.

"Inside tactics," such as public hearings, take two basic forms. In organizing a self-sponsored hearing—such as a hearing on police violence—the key issue is maintaining control of the event and using testimony to define the issue(s) in the ways you want the public to perceive them. It helps to provide a visual setting to make media coverage more interesting and to ensure the space selected is small enough to give the impression of a crowded room. A successful self-sponsored event can:

- establish your organization as a force on a particular issue through a show of numbers;
- help educate your organization's members and the general public;
- obtain valuable media attention;
- demonstrate who are your important supporters and allies; and
- provide a range of activities in which members can participate and acquire new skills.

In contrast, hearings sponsored by others, such as legislative committees, are generally less effective in achieving an organization's goals. They are usually long and boring, especially if they are about technical issues, such as tax policy, which may make it difficult for members to participate. In such hearings, only expert witnesses should testify. Witnesses have a limited time to testify (usually three to five minutes) and, unless they are invited, do not get the opportunity to answer follow-up questions.

To maximize the effectiveness of this tactic, it is important to sign up for a specific time to testify. Otherwise, you may wait for hours and still never get a chance to speak. It is helpful to combine testimony with a picket line or rally, either before or after the hearing. To give an impression of strength, pack the hearing room with your supporters when your group's witnesses are about to testify. It is also important to bring copies of your written testimony, which might be more extensive than your oral remarks, to distribute to committee members and the media. Finally, unless you want to create the impression of a confrontation, it is better to avoid appearing at a hearing at the same time as an opposition group (Reisch, 2015a).

Other inside tactics include accountability sessions—meetings with responsible public officials, *not* members of their staff. If these meetings are to be effective, numbers are critical—either through petitions, letters, or large attendance at a community forum.

On the other hand, petition drives or letter-writing campaigns, while an easy form of community participation, are ineffective unless you combine them with a hearing or accountability session. Letters, phone calls, or emails are particularly useful when you combine them with personal visits during the negotiation phase of an advocacy campaign. They can demonstrate a base of support in a specific geographic area or among a specific constituency, because legislative staff multiply each letter by a factor of 10 or more in terms of what it reveals about popular support for an issue. Letters, phone messages, and emails should be brief and are more effective when not mass-produced (i.e., original) (Rusk, 1999).

Educational or cultural activities, such as a teach-in or benefit concert, can generate publicity and demonstrate the strength of your organization. The major challenge is to make them interesting events and to use them to promote further actions by assigning follow-up tasks to those who attend.

IN-CLASS EXERCISE
DEVELOPING A 12-STEP COMMUNITY CHANGE OUTLINE

Introduction

You have been working as a member of the organizing team consulting with Citizens United for a Revitalized Eastville (CURE) for nearly a year. You are aware that many members of the community have become increasingly frustrated with the slow pace of change and the lack of responsiveness of government officials to persistent concerns. While community development and community planning efforts are under way, they have not yet made any progress in ameliorating any of the social and economic problems the community members confront on a daily basis. You worry that the coalition will lose community support and, perhaps, dissolve if it does not take some concrete actions soon.

After considerable discussion with key leaders of CURE, the group's Steering Committee decides it needs to take some form of social action to reinvigorate the community and produce some tangible results. By its next meeting, it has formed five subgroups around the issues that could become the inspiration for social action efforts. These issues are:

1. Quality of schools, particularly the underfunding of the Eastville School District by the county Board of Education.
2. Racial profiling of youth and young men of color by local police.
3. Lack of adequate services for women and girls who are victims of domestic violence and rape.
4. Redlining of certain Eastville neighborhoods by local banks.
5. Absence of jobs at a living wage.

Each group of three to five students will develop a proposal based on the 12-step outline below and present it to the class (which will act as Eastville's Steering Committee) for discussion.

1. How would you frame the specific issue around which you would organize? (For example, an issue that affects the entire community or a specific population? And what implicit values would you express in how you framed the issue?)

   Issue: ____

2. What is the overall goal of the change effort?

   Goal: ____

3. What would be the target of the change effort?

   Target: ____

4. What are the possible obstacles (people, organizations, resources, history, etc.) that could impede attainment of this goal?

Obstacles: ______________________________

____

____

5. What groups might have the power to facilitate the desired change(s)?

Sources of Power: ______________________________

____

____

6. Who might be your potential allies in a change effort toward this goal? What assets might they contribute to your change effort?

Allies: ______________________________

Assets: ______________________________

7. What overall strategic approach would you recommend—consensus, campaign, or conflict? What are your reasons for selecting this approach?

Approach: ______________________________

Reasons: ______________________________

8. What tactic(s) would you recommend be adopted as part of this strategy?

Tactics: ______________________________

____

9. Indicate the relationship of the tactic(s) you selected to your overall strategy

	Tactic	Relationship to Strategy
a.		
b.		
c.		
d.		
e.		
f.		

10. Identify the criteria you believe should be used to assess the merit of the tactics you chose. What made you choose these criteria?

	Criteria	Reasons for Selection
a.		
b.		
c.		
d.		
e.		
f.		

(You may add others)

11. Apply the criteria you selected above to the tactic(s) you chose. Which tactics do/do not meet the criteria you identified?

	Criteria	Meets the Criteria (Y/N)
a.		
b.		
c.		
d.		
e.		

f. What ethical issues might arise in the implementation of the strategy and tactics you selected above?

Questions for Discussion

1. How did the manner in which you framed the issue influence the choice of strategies and tactics?

2. To what extent did personal experiences and values influence your choice of strategies and tactics?

3. In what ways did the definition of community shape the choice of strategy and tactics? What differences—if any—existed between those efforts that focused on the geographic community of Eastville and those that focused on one or more communities of identity?

Selecting Tactics and Targets

Social and political action requires focusing an organization's demands on specific institutions and individuals (often called targets). A "handle" is the term used to describe the combination of a specific demand and the power to back it up. A major strategic consideration in organizing involves determining what kind of power you can apply against a particular target.

Successful organizing campaigns often require many issues, targets, and handles, not just the use of a single issue or slogan. A major consideration in tactical selection, therefore, is avoiding the pitfalls that can sidetrack community organizations, such as using the same tactic repeatedly until it becomes predictable. It is important to keep the opposition off guard by combining demands in creative ways and employing tactics that are outside their experience. It also helps to play targets off against each other whenever possible. The enemy of your enemy may become your ally.

Many established organizers argue that one organizing objective is to personalize the issue—to identify an enemy as your target (*The Gray Panther Organizing Manual*, Vol. 1; Alinsky, 1971). Each tactic selected should also try to involve as many individuals as possible, strengthen the cause by generating favorable publicity, and be consistent with the overall goals and strategy of the organizing effort. Another important criterion is determining the extent of organizational readiness to implement a particular tactic. Figure 10.2 illustrates the relationship between tactical selection and organizational readiness.

Figure 10.2 Tactical Selection and Organizational Readiness

Very unready　　　　　　　　　　　　　　　Ready

1　2　3　4　5　6　7　8　9　10

Petition Delegation Boycott　Legal Protest Strike Civil Disobedience　Violence

Characteristics of the Organizations

Very Unready	**Ready**
1. Formality	1. Informality
2. Distance between members	2. Intimacy
3. Real feelings hidden	3. Real feelings open
4. No ability to solve internal conflicts	4. High ability
5. Immature attitudes toward leaders	5. Mature
6. Vague understanding of issues	6. In-depth

Fig. 10.2: *Eugene Nadler, Militant Action and Organizational Development. Copyright © 1971.*

Note:

1. There are degrees of cohesiveness between the two extremes.
2. Deciding where a group stands is a complex judgment.
3. The actions listed above are only illustrative, not exhaustive.

KEY CONCEPT SUMMARY
TOP 10 CONSIDERATIONS IN TACTICAL SELECTION

1. Your power resides in the ability to hurt the target(s) or withhold something the target(s) want(s). The "pain" you inflict can be immediate (a strike or boycott) or potential (bad publicity). Be aware of exactly what kind of power you are using and how it will work.
2. Always assume that your organization is strategically weaker than the target in terms of money, influence, access to the media, and (at least initially) credibility. Therefore, the organization must concentrate all its efforts on the target's weakest point.
3. You can enhance an organization's strength by playing off one target against another. This enables you to use others' self-interests to support your cause.
4. Your organization's power does not derive from the tactics you select. Your tactics reflect the strength and influence of your organization and its supporters. Avoid the tendency to view an action as a symbolic act in which a few people express their moral outrage.
5. The threat of any tactic depends on how little experience your target has had in dealing with similar tactics. (The threat is always greater than its actuality.) Once you announce a target, a period of negotiations with the target should follow. Be open to accepting a concession and backing off, then pressing on a few weeks later.
6. Numbers count more than any other factor because they carry the threat of still larger numbers. Tactical selection, therefore, must take into account (a) reality; (b) the subjective perceptions of the opposition, and (c) expectations.
7. Your target does not have to defeat you directly. It can go around you and defuse your issue(s) through a variety of means. As stated previously in the section on issues, these include redefining the issue, dividing your supporters, outflanking you with other supporters, co-optation, and preemption. You must consider these possibilities in planning a campaign and selecting which tactics to use.
8. Try to use the principle of encirclement. The more tactics you can use at once, the better. This can create a situation in which the target is overloaded or create a good guy/bad guy arrangement. The civil rights movement was particularly effective in this regard.

9. One of your advantages is that your primary resource is people, while the opposition's response to your tactics inevitably involves financial costs. Thus, every tactic you employ can drain the opposition's resources and become a factor in the opposition's calculations; however, only a large and well-developed organization can take advantage of this reality. Smaller organizations must avoid overextending themselves with too many tactics.
10. Time is not on your side. Because the opposition is usually larger and always more powerful, it can wear you down. It is much harder to maintain active interest in a community or workplace on an issue than it is to hire someone to oppose the community. Whenever possible, design short campaigns over long ones and do not become caught up in lengthy legal or administrative procedures, unless you can sustain the momentum on other fronts.

Planning and Implementing an Action

An action is a tactic that is a specific event designed to carry out a strategy and to help one's organization win on an issue. A series of activities, in combination, constitutes a campaign. Actions are the lifeblood of activist organizations. You can have the best theory, analysis, structure, people, and leaders, but if you do not put all those resources into action, they will soon atrophy and die (and so will your organization). An action is also a means of communicating to our constituents, potential constituents, supporters, and opponents. This means that you must be clear about the message you want to communicate through the action, about what you want to win due to the action, and about the reaction you want the action to produce.

Briefly, the purposes of an action are to win something and to advance your overall goals and objectives. In this context, winning means extracting a concession from a target or decision maker to do something; acquiring exposure in the media; or evoking an expected and desired negative reaction from the opposition to widen the arena for future action.

Actions also seek to build your organization. Building enables people to acquire a sense of their power; it helps them learn how to lead, speak, negotiate, deal with the media, and evaluate their efforts critically. It is also a means to help people overcome their fears and raise their political consciousness, excite them about taking action on their own behalf, and, ideally, enjoy themselves.

An action might combine both "inside" and "outside" tactics. The best action combines an encounter with a decision maker with the participation of a large number of people. For example, you might support a confrontation in a small room between a spokesperson for your group and a decision maker with hundreds of people rallying outside and receiving reports on what is occurring inside. Combined actions are more difficult to implement. It is also important to recognize that every action generates a reaction. Planning an action, therefore, also requires that you prepare for the reaction of the opposition, of your group's members and potential members, of your constituents, the media, and the authorities.

Steps in Planning and Implementing an Action

The first step in planning an action is determining its purpose. To implement an action, you must create an action team that consists of the person(s) responsible for planning and orchestrating the event. It is important to involve as many people as possible, and develop a plan with clear responsibilities, expectations, and lines of authority. In planning a protest or demonstration, for example, tasks could include making signs, dealing with the media, organizing transportation or child care, working out details with the police, courts, and attorneys, serving as a monitor or troubleshooter, and maintaining communication among people at a large action such as a march.

Planning an action also involves making a number of specific decisions. These include the details of the scenario, such as where to meet, the timetable of the action, and contingency plans (for example, in the event of bad weather). The organization needs to work out various logistics—supplies, signs, leaflets, media coverage, police permits, legal assistance, transportation, monitors, first aid, and food.

A critical component of an action is getting people to participate. This cannot occur through random, spontaneous activities. You need to create squad sheets with quotas and sign-up lists. You need to determine who is responsible for bringing people to the event. Finally, you need to mobilize people to participate in the event. You can do this through social media, email, sound trucks, widespread use of flyers and posters, and telephone/email "trees."

At the action itself, it is important to keep people informed, and keep the event moving, lively, and enjoyable. Use the experience to educate people. Be sure to connect the action to the issue(s) at the heart of your campaign. Twitter, Instagram, and other social media apps are useful tools in this regard.

Just as in a clinical intervention, it is useful to conceive of an action as occurring in stages. The beginning stage (at a rally, for instance) includes meeting and greeting the crowd, warm-up remarks, introducing leaders, using music and songs to entertain and keep people engaged, and providing people with logistical information, such as how to identify monitors (e.g., by their armbands), and what is the overall plan for the event. In this stage, the individuals who are serving as press or police liaisons perform their duties, including the distribution of media kits.

In the middle stage, it is important to keep people's spirits up, adjust to any contingencies that arise, use the action to educate the people about the issue(s) and the opposition, and employ monitors to keep things moving (through chants, cheers, singing). It is important to have established a clear decision-making structure for the action in case of unexpected situations in order to maintain a short span of control to deal with contingencies.

Finally, in the ending stage, when the action is over, it is critical that the organization critically interprets what occurred. Did we win? How did we build? Where are we going from here? Ideally, have a flyer and squad sheets ready for people to begin mobilizing for the next action. It often helps to end the event with something uplifting (a song, cheer, prayer). Media liaisons should be prepared for post-action interviews (the "spin") (Bobo, Kendall, & Max, 2001; Sampson, 1973).

Shortly after the action is over, the organization should evaluate the event as soon as possible. This includes following up with the media representatives who were present at the event and reaching out to media representatives who were not present as soon as possible to give them your side of the story. Claim victory. At the next formal organizational meeting, update those in attendance on the aftermath of the action. Give people credit for their work but engage in honest, self-critical evaluation. Use media clips to post on the internet, make new flyers, or distribute through Facebook, Twitter, or mass emails.

It is important to recognize that action, especially militant action, is a means to an end, not an end in itself. If it does not move your organization closer to its goals and objectives, it is a failure. Militant action puts a strain on both the opposition and your organization. It can also exacerbate confusion, unresolved conflicts, weaknesses, and latent factions within your group (Nadler, 1971).

Organizations use militant action not only against opponents. It is critically important, therefore, to distinguish among the following: allies, potential allies, neutrals, potential enemies, and enemies. It is never true, for example, that those who are not your friends are automatically your enemies. It is important, therefore, to match your strategies and tactics to the target (Cress & Snow, 1996).

No organization ever uses a single tactic in isolation. It is always part of a carefully planned campaign linked to a broader strategy. Militant action is only one aspect of a many-sided effort to achieve your organization's objectives. Other components include organization building, cultivating allies, developing and refining strategy, and acquiring resources. Militant action can also be educational—especially to the group using it. It gives people practice and experience in social struggle and organization as its lessons sink it.

An action that is appropriately militant can shift people in the right (supportive) direction (see Table 10.1 below). Organizations should be prepared to respond to an unanticipated concession. This sometimes surprises groups for whom militant action is an end in itself. The desire to engage in conflict is insufficient justification for using militant tactics. If an unexpected, acceptable concession appears, capitalize on it by publicizing it and use it to build your organization.

As Table 10.1 demonstrates, another important consideration in tactical selection is the nature of the target. This involves an assessment similar to that discussed previously regarding the use of consensus, campaign, or confrontation strategies.

Table 10.1 Tactical Selection and the Nature of the Target

Target	Tactic
1. Friends	**1.** Support ("consensus")
2. Potential Friends	**2.** Persuasion, favors, "bandwagon" (consensus and campaign)
3. Neutrals	**3.** Create respect and a little fear (not hatred). (campaign and contest)
4. Potential Enemies	**4.** Great deal of fear/"escape hatch" (mostly contest)
5. Enemies (small number)	**5.** Win/lose situation. Defeat them. (total contest)

Friends	Potential Friends	Neutrals	Potential Enemies	Enemies
Consensus		Campaign		Contest

Use the continuum above to determine which type of strategic approach to select. For example, a consensus strategy is most suited when working with friends, while a contest approach is most appropriate when confronting enemies or opponents.

IN-CLASS EXERCISE
THE ETHICS OF TACTICAL SELECTION IN SOCIAL AND POLITICAL ACTION

Introduction

Activists and the groups or organizations with which they are working often have to make difficult decisions about the use of tactics in a social or political action campaign. Issues of power, resources, level of risk, and suitability to goals are all critical dimensions in the process of tactical selection. Issues of values and ethics are also critical. The following questions ask about the "fit" of particular types of tactics with your personal values and ethics. Please indicate your responses to the following questions by checking the appropriate box. Write your comments in the spaces provided.

1. The use of confrontation is an acceptable tactic. Always __Sometimes __ Never__
2. Embarrassing opponents is an acceptable tactic. Always __ Sometimes __ Never__
3. Whistle-blowing is an acceptable tactic. Always __ Sometimes __ Never__
4. Leaking information is an acceptable tactic. Always __ Sometimes __ Never__
5. The use of exposes is an acceptable tactic. Always __ Sometimes __ Never__
6. Lying is an acceptable tactic. Always __ Sometimes __ Never__
7. Legal disruptive actions are acceptable tactics. Always __ Sometimes __ Never__
8. Civil disobedience is an acceptable tactic. Always __ Sometimes __ Never__
9. Violence against property is an acceptable tactic. Always __ Sometimes __ Never__
10. Violence against persons is an acceptable tactic. Always __ Sometimes __ Never__

What is Effective Community Organizing?

Unlike many forms of clinical practice, it is difficult to define the effectiveness of community organizing efforts. This occurs for several reasons. There is a lack of empirical evidence on effective community organizing (with the exception of data on civic participation and self-esteem). The foundation of many organizing models, therefore, is ideology, rather than evidence. Organizers, however, are frequently unable to think outside of their "ideological box." We often equate community organizing solely with certain types of ideologically compatible activities. As a result, organizers rarely learn from the experiences (and successes) of their opponents (Reisch, 2012a).

Often, groups that organize are unclear on their overall goals. This produces ambiguous or conflicting definitions of what constitutes "success." In addition, the breadth of community organizing requires us to distinguish what constitutes effective practice in different settings (e.g., community development, social planning, and social action). We also need to differentiate between effective outcomes and processes and to clarify the meaning of such oft-used terms as empowerment, oppression, and multiculturalism and how to apply these terms to our practice.

In addition, community organizing often focuses on preventing problems from occurring or getting worse. This is particularly hard to measure, particularly when organizations conflate long- and short-term goals and objectives. The use of different organizing models in the same change effort (e.g., from community development to social action) make the measurement of the effectiveness of each approach difficult.

Different theoretical approaches to organizing, however, have attempted to define effectiveness in different ways. Proponents of direct action organizing, such as Alinsky (1971), emphasize building powerful issue-oriented organizations, producing shifts in the distribution of resources and power, creating democratic decision-making structures, and attaining tangible "victories" to inspire people to take further action. In contrast, advocates of so-called "insurrectionary theory" (Piven & Cloward, 1977) regard success as taking advantage of environmental opportunities when they arise. They emphasize spontaneous action, not organization building (which they regard as a drain of energy and resources). Social movement theorists (Gamson, 1990; Staggenborg, 2016; Tilly, 1978) measure the extent to which organizing efforts attain greater resources, power, rights, and access.

Feminist organizers regard enhanced participation, the creation of democratic (horizontal) decision-making processes that emphasize consensus and consciousness-raising as the key components of success (Weil, Gamble, & Ohmer, 2013; Hyde, 1996). Advocates of multicultural organizing (Dobbie & Richards-Schuster, 2008; Gutierrez, 1997; Delgado, 1994; Rivera & Erlich, 1997) stress increased cultural awareness and matching the selection of organizing methods to people's needs.

Table 10.2 Top 10 Sources of Success and Failure in Community Organizations

Success	Failure
1. Clear goals	1. Unclear or contradictory goals
2. The will to succeed	2. Lack of will to succeed
3. Focus on a limited number of goals	3. Conflict of interest
4. Plan and timetable to reach goals	4. Boring programs
5. Tangible victories	5. No plan or timetable for goals
6. Exciting programs	6. Out-of-date or bad bookkeeping
7. Building fun into organizing process	7. Too little money
8. Strong board of directors	8. Too many goals
9. Dependable sources of income	9. Lack of dedicated leaders
10. Up-to-date bookkeeping	10. Lack of paid staff

Community Participation and Mobilization

In today's environment, in which virtual communities and virtual communication appear to replace face-to-face relationships, particularly among young people, the challenge of enhancing community participation and mobilizing people to take collective action is more important than ever. People join community organizations or engage in social protest for different reasons. Sometimes, the motivation is anger, a sense of injustice, or a desire to redress real or perceived grievances (Klandermans, 2004). Another reason, especially in an increasingly fragmented society, is to satisfy a need to belong and to become a member of a supportive community (Polletta & Jasper, 2001). People also join as part of their search for understanding in an increasingly uncertain world, to obtain information, and to increase their sense of control over lives. Finally, people join organizations to restore their dignity and self-respect or self-esteem, and to feel useful to themselves and others (Perlman, 1976).

Given these various reasons, organizations can provide different incentives to attract and sustain members. Sometimes they can provide tangible or intangible material benefits. At other times, they can offer social solidarity in the form of group prestige, respect, or friendship. Finally, some organizations can appeal to higher purposes and attract members based on value fulfillment and a desire to acquire power to achieve long-term goals (Tarrow, 2011).

Nevertheless, people often resist joining or participating in social action or social change organizations. Mullaly (2010) points out that the experience of oppression is a major source of this resistance. He argues that we must understand oppression in terms of the social processes that lead to an unequal distribution of resources, power, and status. Even in the absence of violence, oppression takes various forms, including economic exploitation, social marginalization, and political powerlessness. Oppressed people often respond in a variety of ways that have direct implications on their ability to participate in social change efforts. Often, they withdraw psychologically or socially, or engage in self-destructive behavior. Sometimes they adopt magical ideologies that abet their attempt to escape from their daily reality. They sometimes misdirect their anger toward their oppressors and toward themselves or their peers through in-group hostility, even violence (Fanon, 2004).

When asked to participate in change-oriented activities, they sometimes express their responses to oppression in one of the following ways:

1. Fear of change or the risk of involvement.
2. Claiming a lack of time, energy, resources, skills, information, or experience.
3. Expressing a negative valuation of politics, community participation, and community organizing in general.
4. Focusing exclusively on their individual needs and problems.
5. Hopelessness—the absence of belief in their ability to create change.
6. Emphasizing intragroup and intergroup conflicts (e.g., class, racial, ethnic, cultural, gender, or religious divisions in their community).
7. Absence of belief in their ability to create change (hopelessness).
8. Focusing on intragroup and intergroup conflicts (class, racial, ethnic, cultural, gender divisions).

Table 10.3 Top 10 Excuses for Not Joining a Community/Social Change Effort and How You Might Respond

1. I am too busy/cannot do too much to help out/going to school at night/already a member of another organization.	Are you in support of what we are doing? We encourage everyone who supports us to show it by joining in some way. We encourage people to contribute whatever they can in terms of time, but the first step is to join. That way, we will keep you better informed and you can become more active at any point in the future. OR—Our organization/effort can only show our strength through our numbers. The more members we have, the better our chances of winning changes.
2. I am too old and getting ready to retire.	Not everything we are working on is going to be accomplished in our lifetimes, but we have to look at the future for our children, grandchildren, other working people, etc.
3. I can't afford to pay the membership dues (where applicable).	Dues can be paid in monthly installments. OR—When would you be able to pay the dues? OR—The dues only amount to $__ per month. That is not much for what we do.
4. I am thinking about changing jobs/just lost my job/afraid of losing my job.	The work we are doing will affect all working people in the community.

5. I am afraid my boss/company/neighbors/family will find out.	They do not need to know. We do not identify the organization if we call you at work. (And we don't need to call you at work at all.) What you choose to tell others is entirely your business.
6. I have children/dependent care problems.	Our organization can make some arrangements to furnish you with care, or schedule meetings well in advance, or could work on the issue of providing such care to all families.
7. My spouse/partner/parent doesn't like me to join organizations. I need to talk to him/her.	Wouldn't _______ like you to solve the problem we are working on?
8. How will this organization help me?	The organization will help you in the following ways (be as specific as possible).
9. I already have a friend who keeps me informed about your issues.	Then you must know enough about us to show your support by joining.
10. I am not a _______ (radical, socialist, feminist, activist, etc.).	Not all of our members are _________. (Unless your organization claims to be.)

Competing Values in Community Practice

Throughout the history of community practice, tension existed between three competing values: maximum participation, the application of expertise, and the role of leadership. To a considerable extent, this tension remains unresolved. Different models of community practice focus to a greater or lesser extent on one of these values. Community development (or similar models) and social action emphasize to different degrees participation and leadership, while planning stresses expertise (Hardcastle, 2011).

Other value-driven questions challenge community practitioners on a daily basis. For example, is our practice morally neutral or should we make our values explicit to those with whom we work? If so, what should those values be? (Reamer, 2013).

In today's diverse environment, a number of value dilemmas may confront practitioners. *(Chapter 8 discussed some of these dilemmas.)* How should we respond if differences exist between our values and the values of the people and communities with whom we work? Should we work inside or outside established institutions, or both? To what extent are we obligated to obey laws, rules, and regulations, even those we consider unjust? How can we balance outcome goals ("success") with enhanced participation (empowerment)?

Classroom Discussion

1. What values shape your perspectives on community practice?
2. What are the sources of these values?
3. What are their implications for your practice in communities and organizations?

Skills of the Community Organizer

As all good social workers, organizers listen to people to learn what their problems are and what they are willing to do to solve them. Organizers also inspire and agitate people to take action. They help people think through what organizing methods, values, strategies, and tactics enable them to act on their own behalf with confidence and success. In sum, a good organizer is a creative educator, involved in the development of the whole person (Miller, 2009).

Effective organizers must have a wide variety of interpersonal, intellectual, and technical skills. They must convey empathy and be able to serve as role models. They must be "organic intellectuals" who are capable of both understanding and working to change society through the application of praxis. They must possess analytic skills and also skills in organizational and group management. They must be strategic and "political" in the broadest sense of the word, and sensitive to power dynamics, large and small, in all situations.

There is disagreement in the field on the demographic and cultural characteristics organizers need to possess to be effective in today's environment. Some writers argue that an organizer needs to have a cultural and/or racial identification similar to the community with whom she is working (Rivera & Erlich, 1997). At a minimum, an organizer needs to be familiar with the community's customs, history, traditions, social networks, and values, and have an intimate knowledge of its language and subgroup slang, leadership and decision-making styles, and the conceptual framework it applies to political and economic analysis. In addition, the organization should be aware of past organizing strategies, their strengths and limitations. It is unclear whether a person from outside the community can possess these qualities in sufficient depth. It is clear, however, that a good organizer must be self-aware and reflect constantly on her personal strengths and limitations.

Feminist organizers (Gutierrez & Lewis, 1998; Weil, 1986) add that effective organizers must embrace feminist values, such as valuing process, recognizing the importance of consciousness-raising, and emphasizing the goals of wholeness and unity. They must also be able to think differently about the meaning of power and empowerment, develop organizations that are more democratic, and never forget that personal problems are also political issues.

Summary and Conclusion

Community organizers in the years ahead will face many of the same issues that confronted their predecessors. They have to find a way to balance enhanced participation with increased outcome effectiveness. They have to develop strategies and organizational structures that are compatible with recent technological changes and the changing nature of the political landscape. They will need to find new ways to translate the profession's social justice rhetoric into practice.

Of course, they will have to do this against the backdrop of new issues that require creative responses. These include the effects of economic globalization and climate change, growing social and economic inequality, and the response to unprecedented demographic and cultural changes. Organizers will have to connect local, national, and international issues in their strategies and develop innovative ways to work with communities of identity in diverse coalitions.

An organizing agenda for the 21st century may include the following features:

- forging new types of multicultural and cross-national coalitions;
- identifying appropriate roles for European American (White) organizers (Burghardt, 2012);
- involving more young people and disaffected community residents in politics and legislative advocacy;
- using social media more effectively as a tool for social change; and
- above all, developing ways to combat persistent racism, xenophobia, anti-Semitism, and other forms of invidious discrimination and bigotry, currently masked by the deceptive labels "ethnic nationalism" or "populism" (Reisch, 2016a; Reisch, 2013b).

The next chapter will focus on how macro social work practitioners can promote change through their work designing and implementing innovative programs and services.

END-OF-CHAPTER EXERCISE
PLANNING A COMMUNITY INTERVENTION—PART I

Introduction

Eastville is a community of about 100,000 people within a large metropolitan center in a mid-Atlantic state. Its population is "in transition" from predominantly White and middle income to one with a mixed racial, ethnic, and class composition. At present, approximately 40% of the residents are African American, 30% are White, 25% are Latino (largely Chicano and Puerto Rican), and the remaining 5% are Asian American (largely Vietnamese and Laotian). The overwhelming majority of the families with school-age children is composed of people of color. While the White population, largely of elderly, ethnically Polish and Italian residents, has been in the community for generations, most of the people of color have arrived during the past 10 years. The newest arrivals are Asian American immigrants, who have been in the community less than five years.

Over the past two decades, much of the industrial base of the community has disappeared. There are few large employers and most of the new jobs are in the service sector, pay minimum wage, and have few benefits. Consequently, the poverty rate in the community is about 30%, with pockets of severe poverty in certain neighborhoods. Unemployment is about 25%, with higher rates among youth. In some neighborhoods, about 50% of the population is on some form of public assistance (TANF, SSI). Social indicators of distress (e.g., homelessness, alcohol and drug abuse, crime) reflect the economic problems at the core of the community.

While the community elects its own mayor and City Council, it receives most of its services from the surrounding county. This county is more affluent and less demographically diverse than Eastville. Its political leadership resides in the office of the county executive and the Board of Supervisors. Voter turnout in Eastville is lower than that of the surrounding county and its political influence on county elections has diminished in recent years.

Eastville has lost many of the nonprofit organizations that once provided social services, recreational, and cultural activities to the community. Several of the major nonprofits have relocated to newer areas of the county. The Catholic archdiocese has closed churches in a few parishes. Community residents have difficulty accessing services or cultural institutions in the surrounding region, in part because of their poverty and, in part, because of poor public transportation. This contributes to a growing sense of social isolation.

On the positive side, churches remain a strong force for social cohesion in certain neighborhoods, most notably in the African American, Polish, and Italian communities. A new church has opened in the Latino community and Buddhists constructed a temple to serve some members of the Asian American community. Several of the churches have developed social service and/or child care programs. There are a few emerging grassroots multiservice community organizations, including agencies that focus on the needs of immigrants. These organizations, however, have scant resources.

Part I: Analyzing the Situation

At the request of the local community board and an ad hoc coalition of concerned community residents, you are part of a team of community organizers sent to Eastville from a metropolitan area-wide community development corporation.

1. Based upon the above information and using one or more of the organizing models discussed in chapters nine and 10, how would you characterize the situation in Eastville? Explain your reasons for using this particular characterization and the potential implications for practice.
2. What additional data would you seek to collect about Eastville to undertake an in-depth analysis of its situation? How would your perspective (problem-focused, systems-focused, strengths-focused) shape the nature and outcomes of your data collection process?
3. What common and differential elements might you find within the different groups in Eastville? What are the implications of these similarities and differences for economic and social development efforts?

Part II: Finding Solutions

Your team has completed the data collection process. (You may assume any information that is consistent with the previous description of Eastville.)

1. What do you see as the three (3) major issues confronting Eastville that a coordinated social and economic development effort would need to address?
2. What goals (short term and long term) would you propose to the community board and ad hoc coalition? Be sure to relate these goals to the issues you identified in Part II, No. 1 and to the model you have used to describe Eastville in Part I, No. 1.
3. What model(s) of economic and social development would you propose to achieve the goals identified? What are your reasons for selecting the model(s) you did?
4. What problems would you and your team need to overcome to implement the model(s) you chose? What steps would you recommend to begin to address these problems?

Classroom Discussion

1. What were the major similarities and differences developed by each team?
2. In what ways did the selection of a theoretical model(s) influence the planning process of economic and social development?
3. In what ways was a model at various stages of the exercise useful or not useful?

END-OF-CHAPTER EXERCISE
PLANNING A COMMUNITY INTERVENTION—PART II

Introduction

Your team's analysis of the problems of Eastville identified a growing pattern of neighborhood segregation and isolation. One consequence of this development is the dramatic increase in negative social indicators such as unemployment, family breakdown, drug abuse, out-of-wedlock births, and criminal behavior in the poorer and more isolated portions of the community. The community board and ad hoc coalition agree that two major problems facing Eastville are neighborhood stabilization and chronic poverty in certain sections of the community. They wish to consult with your team again on how to address these two issues.

Theoretical Perspective

1. Identify the theoretical perspective(s) you would use to analyze the problem of neighborhood stabilization in Eastville. (Use the information provided in the case study in the first part of the exercise.) Outline your reasons for selecting this perspective and for not selecting others.

2. Based on the perspective(s) you selected, on what causative factors would you focus?
3. What are the implications of your choices for the development of strategic approaches to the issue?
4. What obstacles or problems might arise in the implementation of these strategies? What new issues might they generate?

END-OF-CHAPTER ASSIGNMENT OR TAKE-HOME FINAL EXAM

Introduction

Answer the following questions **as specifically as possible**. You may answer the questions in the order below or integrate your answers into a less structured essay. In support of your answers, you may use any of the course materials (readings, handouts, and lecture/discussion notes) or materials from outside the course. You are not required to use any materials beyond the course syllabus. Please cite all references you make in your answers using APA format. Please limit answers to eight to 10 pages, typed double-spaced, using a 12-point font and 1" margins.

Questions to Consider

1. Identify a social or economic issue that motivated you to become interested in social work, in general, and community organization in particular. Frame the issue in a manner that facilitates the development of alternative community interventions that might address it. (*The more focused your definition of the issue, the easier it will be to answer the questions.*)
2. If you were to engage in community organizing around this issue, what particular community would be the focus of your work? How might the definition of community that you selected and the particular characteristics of that community influence your work?
3. In what ways do the concepts of power, social justice, and cultural diversity shape the nature of the issue you selected *as it manifests itself within the community you selected*? How would you incorporate these concepts into the development of goals and strategies to guide a community intervention? Be as specific as possible.
4. Which of the major models of community organization or which combination of these models would be, in your judgment, most appropriate for addressing the issue you identified? As specifically as possible, indicate the reasons you would choose this model. Identify the ways in which this model might facilitate and/or impede the process of community empowerment around the particular issue you selected.
5. Within the framework of the model you selected, identify the goals and objectives of a potential organizing effort within a particular time frame. Be as specific as possible. Discuss how these goals and objectives reflect your underlying values and assumptions about the issue and

your views on the nature of the community change process itself. Justify the time frame you developed.

6. **Outline** the steps you would take **during the first six (6) months** of an organizing effort around the issue you chose. Explain briefly the purposes of each step, how it fits into an overall organizing strategy, and the reasons you sequenced the steps the way you did. Link your "plan of action" to the theoretical constructs that inform it as specifically as possible.
7. In the course of implementing your action plan, how would you incorporate sensitivity to issues of race, gender, religion, and other manifestations of diversity?
8. Identify the potential barriers—personal and professional—you might encounter in the development and implementation of this organizing effort. What might you do to overcome them or prevent them from emerging?
9. What ethical or value conflicts might arise in the course of this organizing effort? How would you address them?
10. Indicate what progress you hope to have achieved at the end of six months of organizing in terms of the key features of the model you selected. What would be the criteria by which you would measure the success or failure of your effort? **Briefly state** what your objectives would be during the next stage of this organizing effort.

CHAPTER 11

Planning and Program Development in Diverse Communities and Organizations

A goal without a plan is just a wish.

—**Antoine de Saint-Exupery**

Two types of choices seem to me to have been crucial in tipping the outcomes [of the various societies' histories] towards success or failure: long-term planning and willingness to reconsider core values.

—**Jared Diamond, Collapse:** ***How Societies Choose to Fail or Succeed***

Introduction

Community and organizational practice requires the development, implementation, and evaluation of purposeful interventions. Consequently, planning is an integral component of macro practice in several ways. It is critical to the creation of more effective services and to the mobilization of community members. It can help transform institutions, structures, and meso-mezzo systems to be more inclusive, democratic, redistributive, and decentered. Successful program planning balances strategic effectiveness and ethical consistency in the establishment of both ends (outcomes) and means.

This chapter provides an overview of several varieties of planning. It addresses their similarities and differences and the ways organizations use them in community organizing, administration, policy practice, and policy advocacy. Specific topics include:

1. Varieties of planning at the community level: Skills involved in social planning, community planning, and service planning.
2. Steps in program development in organizations: Linking program development to community and organizational assessment.
3. Identifying, acquiring, and managing essential resources.
4. Enhancing staff and community participation in the planning process.
5. Ethical issues in the planning process.

Why Do We Plan?

The development of new services or the revision of existing programs and services to make them more responsive to community needs and goals cannot occur haphazardly. As are all social work interventions, it is a form of purposive change. Service innovation, the introduction of new ideas on long-standing problems, the revision of an organization's structure or policies to make it more responsive, changes in organizational culture, and the introduction of new technology to an existing service all require careful research, analysis, and the participation of all stakeholders.

Similar to the models of community organizing discussed in Chapter 10, program planning and development is another way to strengthen communities. Similar to community organizing, it requires collective action and it must overcome such challenges as the translation of personal crises into public concerns, insufficient resources, and a lack of influence with powerful forces in the external environment (Checkoway, 2013). Despite these obstacles, successful community or program planning can enhance solidarity within a community or organization, strengthen existing structure, develop new leadership, improve strategic decision making, and increase people's belief in the possibility of positive change.

A number of contextual factors shape the planning process. The overall political-economic environment—how supportive and receptive it is to potential changes—is a major factor. Other factors include the history of the community or organization in engaging in planning and strategic development, the values of community residents or staff members, and the presence of other concurrent demands on the community or organization. Given these diverse variables, successful planning efforts must have clear goals, a consensus on the values underlying these goals, and adequate resources to engage in the planning process and to implement the plan that is developed.

According to Kahn (1991), democratic, community-based planning rests on the following values:

1. Maximum decentralization of authority and decision making.
2. The distribution of the maximum available information to all participants and stakeholders at all stages of the process.
3. Conscious efforts by the leaders of the planning process to make its underlying values, strategic alternatives, and consequences visible throughout the planning experience.
4. The opportunity for various stakeholders to express their views in all phases of the process.
5. Democratization of decision making, whether by consensus or another previously agreed-upon method.
6. The use of a variety of planning devices that make clear the political nature of the decision-making process.
7. Readiness to take risks, to delegate authority to act, and to trust in people.
8. Assigning resources and policy control experimentally to community groups to give community residents control and power over the process.
9. An emphasis on community self-definition and empowerment.
10. Participation of the community in the evaluation of both process and outcomes at all stages.

These values lead to the application of practice principles that stress community autonomy, distributive justice, and the importance of sustaining the process over time (Woodford & Preston, 2011).

The author had the opportunity to work with the Northern California Community Services Council, an offshoot of the United Way of the Bay Area (Buckmaster, 1999), in its effort to develop practice principles for service development and planning. After much effort, the council's stakeholders agreed upon the following principles:

1. Planning efforts should focus on the development of integrated and comprehensive community services (rather than isolated programs).

2. The creation of collaborative partnerships with stakeholders should occur throughout the planning process.
3. The planning process should focus on prevention, rather than remediation, of community problems wherever possible.
4. The planning process should build on the strengths of individuals and communities, rather than respond to deficits (*see Chapter 9*).
5. Planning efforts should emphasize support for families in all their forms.
6. All phases of the planning process should integrate cultural responsiveness.
7. The planning process should use community participation to promote community building.
8. The planning process should focus on progress toward community goals as the community defined them.

Classroom Discussion

1. What do you think of the principles outlined by Kahn and the NCCSC?
2. How would you revise or add to them?

Planning efforts reflect a number of assumptions about the underlying causes of community needs. First, community needs often stem from a lack of resources, tangible and intangible, both in terms of the quantity of resources and also in their quality (i.e., nature or appropriateness). Second, that they frequently reflect ineffective or culturally unresponsive services or programs. Third, that they may be the result of inappropriate structuring of current services or ineffective means of distributing available resources. Finally, that they are the consequence of an overall lack of institutional responsiveness to the needs of a particular community or population (Maybach, 1996). Note that while each of these assumptions, individually and in combination, leads to the development of a different approach to the planning process, all of them reject the tendency to blame the community for its problems.

Given these assumptions, a macro social worker has to play multiple roles in the planning process. First, she has to facilitate the maximum possible involvement of the community in assessing its needs, defining outcome goals and objectives, determining how to measure their attainment, and establishing criteria for program or service effectiveness. Second, she has to work with the community, ideally through community-based participatory research, to acquire new data that further illuminates the issues confronting the community. Third, she has to play the role of educator, teaching participants in the planning process about the nature of the process itself. Finally, she has to provide the planning group with technical assistance where necessary (Weil, 2013).

In addition to these practical challenges, there are a number of ongoing issues with the planning process itself that social workers must address. As in all social work practice, planners must consider if neutrality is possible. That is, how explicit should they make their values and those of community stakeholders?

Although democratic planning is the ideal process, one that best reflects social work values, how extensively should the planning process be decentralized? At what point does the goal of democratic participation produce undesirable inefficiencies? A related issue is how to balance the role of professional expertise with the acquired wisdom of community stakeholders (Chaskin, 2005).

Another concern is the extent to which the planning process should emphasize long-term or short-term goals (Laverack & Lebonte, 2000). From the perspective of community members, failure to address short-term goals in a timely fashion may appear as indifference. From the perspective of the community social worker, however, failure to address the structural sources of community problems (a long-term goal, to be sure) would lead to the frequent recurrence of these problems. At times, the auspice of the planning process determines the outcome of this choice between short-term vs. long-term goals. For example, is the process community controlled and community-driven? What happens if an external entity, such as a foundation, government agency, or funding federation, largely determines the nature of community participation?

Finally, how can the planning process reflect and promote social work values such as social justice, the desirability of social change, and community self-determination and empowerment? This issue is particularly important in our work with members of diverse populations who are justifiably skeptical of outside interventions (Todd, 2016).

Models of the Planning Process

There are multiple models of the planning process in the literature (Carmon & Fainstein, 2013). One distinction is between **policy planning**, which focuses on identifying the goals of organizational activities, and **implementation planning**, which considers the alternative strategies or program approaches that are available to achieve predetermined goals and objectives (Jansson et al., 2013). The former emphasizes problem definition and the establishment of broad desirable outcomes. It ensures that the organization unifies its resources and activities in a single direction. The latter pays closer attention to more specific organizational objectives. These include the determination of operational objectives for selected program approaches and the identification of activities that should result through the implementation of established operational objectives.

For purposes of simplicity, a few common processes are summarized below. One is a **four-step approach** consisting of the following stages:

1. Using one of the methods described in an earlier chapter, identify the needs and assets of the community or organization. Based on this assessment, review the purposes and goals of the planning process from the perspective of the

community-based organization or service agency. Reconcile the findings of the needs and assets assessment process with these goals. The final product of this step should be a clear statement of project (planning) goals and objectives that reflects the views of all stakeholders.

2. In Step 2, stakeholders develop alternative program ideas designed to address the goals and objectives they determined at the conclusion of Step 1. Through discussions and analysis, they assess the relative desirability and feasibility of these ideas and select what they believe to be the best possible program design. The product here is a detailed description of proposed program activities or services.
3. Step 3 involves the development of a detailed plan to create, implement, and evaluate the programs or services selected at the end of Step 2. It also includes the formulation of contingency plans (to implement when something goes wrong, the project is delayed, or the planning process produces unintended consequences, as often occurs), staffing patterns, a project time line, and budget. The result of this stage is the creation of formal implementation procedures for the project.
4. A final step involves the determination of criteria to evaluate the effectiveness, efficiency, and overall effect of the planned intervention. Ideally, this process should begin in Step 1. The planning group selects a data-gathering process and develops evaluation questions. The product is an evaluation plan for measuring the attainment of outcome objectives. Stakeholders must be involved in this step of the process to ensure the integration of their perspectives.

A second model—**a 10-step program planning approach**—divides the above four steps into 10 stages:

1. Determine the project idea.
2. Assess the need for the project and define the problem.
3. Determine the capacity for effecting a solution to the problem and identify the factors that limit this capacity.
4. Identify the underlying assumptions and values of the planning group.
5. Develop the goals and objectives for the program.
6. Choose methods and outline the work plan.
7. Identify the resources necessary to perform the activities.
8. Design an evaluation system to monitor the program's effectiveness.
9. Implement the work plan and monitor the program's effect.
10. Review the program plan and repeat the planning process.

A similar, **problem-solving model** (Cohen, 2001) focuses on the following nine steps:

1. State the problem situation in broad terms.
2. Analyze the nature and causes of the problem situation.
3. Describe the ideal situation and compare it with the present situation.
4. State alternative versions of the problem.
5. Choose one version of the problem (or a combination) to pursue.
6. Inventory existing solutions.
7. Generate new solutions (probably a synthesis of existing solutions).
8. State guidelines for choosing ("decision criteria") and select the best solution.
9. Implement and document the solution selected.

Those readers with an interest in automobiles might prefer this **four-stroke internal combustion engine approach**. The first "stroke" involves the intake of vital information regarding the community or organization's problems, needs, goals, objectives, and resources. It also involves an assessment of which planning or change strategies the community or organization employed in the past, and how effective they were. The second stroke requires the compression or condensation of all this information into usable form through narrowing the amount of information collected into useful summaries and eliminating extraneous data. In the ignition phase, the third stroke, the planning group uses the synthesized ingredients to generate new program ideas. Finally, in the exhaust stage, the group narrows the options available and repeats the four-step cycle in the implementation process. In this approach, the process of inventing and choosing program options is one of alternately expanding and narrowing the thinking of the organization or group.

Lastly, there is the **continuum model of feminist planning**. This alternative model based on feminist theory involves different modes of analysis, reflects different perspectives on life and politics, and integrates different ways of asking questions, searching for answers, and formulating choices. One of its primary purposes is to demystify the planning process by making values and goals explicit and to reject frameworks that reflect the biases of dominant systems of thought and behavior (Hyde, 1989).

This model is designed to address such persistent problems as the low level of women's involvement as planners, the undemocratic dichotomy between experts and community stakeholders in the planning process, false assumptions about women as analysts and planners, and issues of power differentials that arise throughout the planning process. The model's value base incorporates such social work principles as egalitarianism; a reduction of status and power differentials; the importance of cooperation, collaboration, nurturance, and support; sharing of resources; an embrace of divergent ways of knowing and thinking; and recognition of one's responsibility to oneself and others (Gamble, 2013).

In sum, a feminist model of planning involves a reconceptualization of the process from a dichotomous toward a holistic synergistic approach. It also involves a redefinition of power from zero sum to infinite (the basis of the social work concept of empowerment) and a redefinition of planning from an "expert"-driven to a cooperative process. Proponents of this model reject the typical competitive ethos that often drives the planning process. They stress the need to collaborate with community stakeholders and other service providers (Whitzman, 2007).

To implement this model, planners need to switch their focus in the following ways:

> place an equal emphasis on a process orientation to planning—as opposed to a primary focus on outcomes. This requires a shift from a dichotomous to a holistic, synergistic approach to planning;
>
> encourage divergent methods of thinking and the integration of all forms of knowledge into the planning process;
>
> maximize consumer input throughout the process, from the identification of the initial issues to the selection of intervention strategies to evaluation. This is part of a shift from "expert-centered" to cooperative forms of planning;
>
> make all values and assumption statements open and explicit;
>
> use both quantitative and qualitative data;
>
> establish service delivery criteria that address the elimination of bias;
>
> place a major focus on stakeholder empowerment and shift from "zero sum" to infinite views of power and empowerment;
>
> use both process and outcome evaluations; and
>
> commit yourself to the self-determination of all women and human dignity.

Implementing any of these ideas will not be easy. It would require several changes even in the most democratically oriented planning processes. One change involves a reconceptualization of leadership and the qualities that make a good leader. (*See Chapter 6.*) Our culture's view of leadership is deeply ingrained. Think about how this change might occur. Would it ever work? If so, under what circumstances?

There is also no easy way to determine which of the above models to use. Macro social workers have to consider such factors as the political-economic environment, the history of the community or organization, the community's demographics, and the nature of intragroup and intergroup relationships.

Program Development

One of the most common ways in which social workers, even clinical social workers, become involved in macro social work practice is through participation in the development of new programs or services, usually at the organizational or local level. To be successful, a program development process should closely align with the organization's mission, vision, and strategic goals. Otherwise, the organization will be subject to organizational "drift," in which it loses sight of its original purposes. The author once consulted with a nonprofit organization whose programs had changed so dramatically that it had lost both its original mission (serving victims of domestic violence) and also the public's confidence and support.

Successful program development should involve board members, staff members, and community stakeholders (clients, community residents, funders) throughout the process. It is also useful to keep in mind that there is no such thing as a "perfect" program plan. Participants in the program development process, therefore, should be prepared to be flexible and adaptive to unexpected twists and turns.

A theory of change is useful, especially in the design of new programs. It helps participants develop clear goals and provides a coherent framework that matches the program's design to its intended purposes (Funnell & Rogers, 2011). A systems approach to program planning is one example.

A systems approach conceptualizes the program development process in three stages: inputs, throughputs, and outputs (Gross, 1965). Program **inputs** include the various resources needed to run the program, such as money, facilities, clients, program staff, and volunteers. **Throughputs** consist of the processes by which the organization delivers the program's services—for example, family counseling, child care, job training, or education on home ownership.

Outputs are the units of service the program generates, such as the number of clients who receive counseling, the number of children cared for, the number of community members who participate in job-training programs, or the number of households that attend sessions on the process of home ownership. In contrast, **outcomes** are the program or service effects on the clients who receive the services. Did the program improve their mental health, reduce the rate of substance abuse, help children boost their academic performance and youth find employment, or give families assistance in purchasing or retaining a home? Outcomes are the "compass" for the program and help it keep its direction. Today, because of a growing emphasis on accountability, funders increasingly request outcomes-based evaluations from nonprofit organizations that seek financial support. (*These issues will be discussed further in subsequent sections of this chapter.*)

A term frequently used for a program's underlying theory of change is a "**logic model**." It provides a "road map" and action plan to guide the program development process (Funnell & Rogers, 2011). A logic model depicts the various components of a program showing what the program will do and what it is intended to accomplish. It also includes a series of "if-then" relationships that, if implemented as intended, lead to the desired outcomes (Kaplan & Garrett, 2005). Finally, it includes the various steps of the program planning, implementation, and evaluation process. (http://www.uwex.edu/ces/pdande/evaluation/evallogicmodel.html).

In its simplest form, a logic model is a graphic representation that shows the logical relationships between: (1) inputs—the resources that go into the program; (2) outputs—the activities the program undertakes; and (3) outcome—the changes or benefits that result from the program or service. Figure 11.1 reflects this relationship in its simplest form.

Figure 11.1 A Basic Model of a Systems Approach

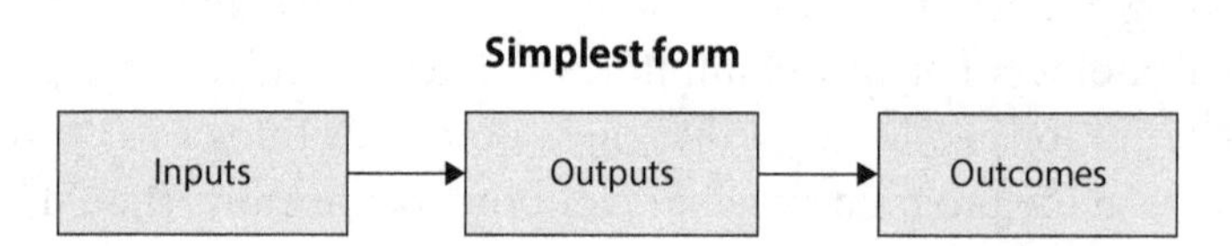

Fig. 11.1: *Ellen Taylor-Powell and Ellen Henert, Developing a Logic Model: Teaching and Training Guide, pp. 55. Copyright © 2008 by Board of Regents of the University of Wisconsin System.*

There are several reasons for an organization to use a logic model. First, it enables those involved in the program development process to focus on and be accountable for what really matters—the outcomes the program or service produces. Second, it provides participants with a common language and makes the underlying assumptions of the process explicit. Third, it encourages planners to refine the program development process continuously. Finally, it promotes enhanced communication among stakeholders. Figure 11.2 demonstrates how we could apply a logic model to an everyday personal challenge. In this simple analogy, it illustrates the utility of a logic model to organizations engaged in program development.

Figure 11.2 Applying a Logic Model to a Personal Problem

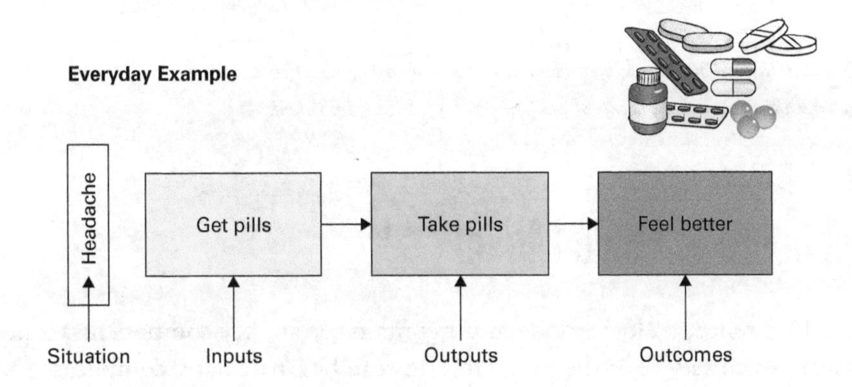

Fig. 11.2a: *Copyright © 2014 Depositphotos/sangoiri.*
Fig. 11.2b: *Based on information from Ellen Taylor-Powell and Ellen Henert, Developing a Logic model: Teaching and Training Guide, pp. 43, 2008.*
Fig. 11.2c: *Copyright © 2011 Depositphotos/baldyrgan.*

Figure 11.3 demonstrates how an organization could apply a sophisticated logic model to the process of program planning and development.

Figure 11.3 Using a Logic Model to Design a Program

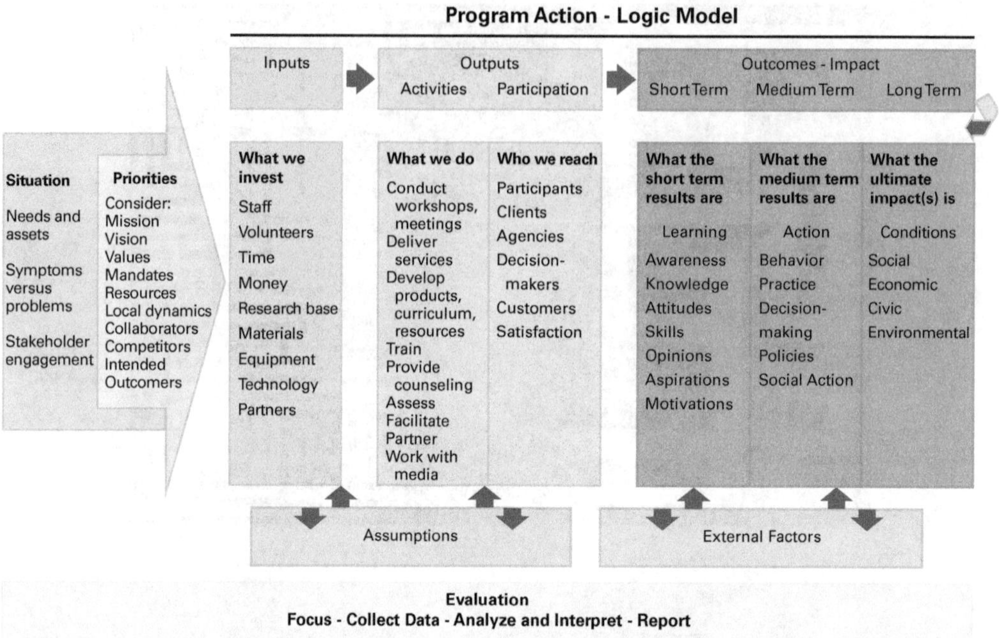

Program Action - Logic Model

Situation: Needs and assets; Symptoms versus problems; Stakeholder engagement

Priorities: Consider: Mission, Vision, Values, Mandates, Resources, Local dynamics, Collaborators, Competitors, Intended Outcomers

Inputs — What we invest: Staff, Volunteers, Time, Money, Research base, Materials, Equipment, Technology, Partners

Outputs — Activities — What we do: Conduct workshops, meetings; Deliver services; Develop products, curriculum, resources; Train; Provide counseling; Assess; Facilitate; Partner; Work with media

Outputs — Participation — Who we reach: Participants, Clients, Agencies, Decision-makers, Customers, Satisfaction

Outcomes - Impact — Short Term — What the short term results are: Learning: Awareness, Knowledge, Attitudes, Skills, Opinions, Aspirations, Motivations

Outcomes - Impact — Medium Term — What the medium term results are: Action: Behavior, Practice, Decision-making, Policies, Social Action

Outcomes - Impact — Long Term — What the ultimate impact(s) is: Conditions: Social, Economic, Civic, Environmental

Assumptions

External Factors

Evaluation
Focus - Collect Data - Analyze and Interpret - Report

Fig. 11.3: *Ellen Taylor-Powell and Ellen Henert, Developing a Logic model: Teaching and Training Guide, pp. 56. Copyright © 2008 by Board of Regents of the University of Wisconsin System.*

Components of Logic Model

As Figure 11.3 reflects, a logic model must contain certain key components. It needs to define clearly each service in the program. This can be particularly complicated when a program has multiple features, such as wraparound services for families. A logic model must also clearly state how a program will deliver its services. For example, will a program aimed at reducing opioid abuse focus on individual counseling, group sessions, community education, or some combination of these activities? A logic model must also indicate what measures of success the organization will adopt for the program. It also needs to provide details on the program's staffing patterns, budget, and non-personnel costs. Finally, it should indicate how the organization plans to advertise the service to potential consumers.

Goals. A program's goals should follow directly from, or be the same as, the strategic service goals participants in the planning process developed to meet the specific needs of specific populations. (Note that there may also be strategic goals other than meeting clients' needs—for example, acquiring a facility to deliver the program.) Goals should specify the desired results of the program services. It is useful to frame them in "***SMARTER***" terms—that is, **S**pecific, **M**easurable, **A**cceptable to those with the responsibility to achieve the goals; **R**ealistic, **T**imely, **E**xtending the capabilities of those working to achieve the goals; and (ideally) **R**ewarding for them, as well. For example, one way to state a program goal could be: Reduce the high school dropout rate in the community by 50% over the next three years and increase the number of high school students who attend a two- or four-year college by 25%.

Components of a Credible Program

In addition to goals that are clearly stated, a credible program must also have a well-defined and unambiguous program plan to achieve these goals. Ideally, the idea behind the program must be both compelling (to stakeholders, funders, and program staff) and feasible. Factors that contribute to the program's feasibility include the organization's possession of relevant expertise; the relevance of the program to the underlying problem or issue facing the community; and the existence of strong, capable leadership in the organization and community to obtain the requisite resources and public support and to keep the program development process focused. The latter more likely exists in stable organizations that have remained consistent in their mission and overall goals and that have a good "track record" with the surrounding community.

Identify Collaborators. In today's complex environment, a single organization often cannot develop an effective program or service on its own. As discussed in a previous chapter, nonprofit social service agencies now engage more frequently, by choice or compulsion, in collaborative arrangements with other providers. At best, a successful collaboration brings two or more organizations together to work in synergy, in an effort that produces "more than the sum of its parts." That is, if both organizations worked separately, they would provide their clients with some benefits, but the services would not produce as many benefits and, possibly, benefits of the same quality as would occur if both organizations had worked together. A major advantage of collaboration, particularly in today's environment of fiscal scarcity, is the economy of scale it creates by two or more organizations sharing resources. By lowering administrative costs, for example, collaborators can focus more resources on clients (Healey, 2003).

In addition, an increasing number of funders are requiring evidence of inter-organization collaborative planning as a prerequisite for a funding application. Many nonprofit leaders naturally struggle with the notion of collaboration, because it involves sharing resources with other organizations and relinquishing a certain degree of organizational autonomy and control. New organizations, especially those in racial or ethnic minority communities, may be particularly upset when funders compel them to collaborate with larger and better-established "majority" organizations (Healey, 2006).

The leaders of many nonprofit organizations, therefore, view collaboration as a frustrating process, a "shotgun marriage" that they accept with great reluctance and some trepidation. The dilemmas created by collaboration require organizational leaders to consider carefully which populations they really want to serve, which issues they want to address, and what compromises they are willing to make to achieve these goals. Ultimately, if collaboration with another agency will produce better services for one's clients or constituents, it may be the right decision, despite the challenges involved.

Classroom Discussion

1. If the organization in which you are working or where you are interning wanted to establish a new program or expand an existing service, with whom might it collaborate?
2. What resources might this potential collaborator bring "to the table" and what could your organization bring?
3. What problems might arise? How would you address them?

Funding the Program or Service

Although most social workers do not enter the field with much interest in discussing money matters, it is critical for organizations engaged in program development to determine how they will fund a new or expanded service (Ciconte & Jacob, 2009). For example, how much of the cost should clients or service users be expected to bear?

Most nonprofits typically do not place the same high priority on charging fees for their services as do for-profits. It is important to note, however, that the funding provided by both foundations and government agencies will not support a program indefinitely. In fact, most foundations require funding applicants to include a plan for program sustainability in their proposals. Consequently, it is always wise for a nonprofit organization to explore how it can generate revenue from a service to offset its operating costs. Nonprofits that rely on federal funding would also be wise to plan programs that recover costs through user fees because federal and state governments are substantially reducing their fiscal contributions.

Several major factors influence how an organization might determine the price of a service. The organization's strategic goals greatly influence pricing. For example, if the nonprofit really wants to get into a new market (such as behavioral health), it might charge lower than usual prices to generate more clients for the service. In addition, the organization might consider changing pricing if the demand for its services is either very high or very low. The fees competitors charge also is an important factor. If competitors are charging much less for a service of comparable quality and accessibility, then it might be strategic to lower prices. Conversely, if competitors are charging much more, then the organization might consider increasing its fees (Andreasen & Kotler, 2008).

Under whatever circumstances, an organization always has to consider the following issues: Can it use fees to recoup the costs it takes to provide the service? If it charged a fee for the program, would clients still be able to participate? Would it be better to implement a sliding-fee scale or volume discounts? How would it design these alternatives?

Finally, it is critical for the organization to identify all laws and regulations it must follow that might affect the implementation of a particular service or program. For example, if an organization decides to open a childcare or after-school program, what requirements exist about the ratio of staff to children, or the type of staffing that the program must have? It is important, therefore, to contact local or state agencies to determine which laws and regulations might apply. Organizations can obtain this necessary information from the offices of their state's attorney general, secretary of state, department of human services, or department of health.

Promoting a Service

To promote a service effectively, an organization must develop a concise—yet meaningful—description of its goals and potential benefits. This can be much more complicated than merely picking a catchy name. Some organizations use consultants to help in naming or branding their products and services, an example of the growing trend toward "marketization" (Gronbjerg & Salamon, 2002). It is not merely a matter of being trendy. An organization must be sure not to use a name that another agency has already trademarked or service marked. It is also important not to adopt a name that closely resembles the name of an established program in your community or service area. If you do, clients may confuse your services with those of a potential competitor. In a worst-case scenario, the other organization may sue for copyright infringement.

In sum, an organization developing a new or substantially revised program or service needs a name that makes sense in the local context, but could also be understood if the program expanded to new communities in the future. In most cases, the name chosen for a particular service will be around for a long time and can have a substantial effect on how the public perceives the service itself and the organization as a whole. It might be a good idea, therefore, if sufficient resources are available, to consider conducting some basic market research to learn how the public reacts to different names. An organization can do this through focus groups of community residents or survey cards.

Marketing a Program or Service

As much as the application of for-profit values and norms may seem unseemly to many social workers, even contrary to the profession's values and ethics, it is an unfortunate feature of today's environment that organizations must market their services to reach potential service users and sustain their programs. Marketing a service includes clarifying which client groups the organization desires to serve (these are target markets). It also involves verifying the needs of this population (a basic form of market research), analyzing the competition and potential collaborators, determining the best fee for services, deciding how to produce and distribute the services, and choosing the best ways to promote the services through advertising, public relations, or recruitment of clients. Finally, the organization must learn what laws and regulations it is required to follow to deliver the proposed service and what name it will use for the service.

A first step is to draft a basic description of each service. Typically, a service is a closely related set of activities that accomplishes a specific benefit for clients. Exactly what determines a service in an organization is unique to the organization itself. A program can have several services. A nonprofit might sell services separately and/or in a package of related services.

As you can see, developing program services is not unlike developing products or services in the for-profit market, particularly as nonprofits look to more innovative methods to earn revenue from products and services. It includes a clear description of each service offered. Each organization possesses the unique capacity to determine what constitutes a service. A marketing plan is a helpful tool in this regard. It includes the type of individuals or groups most likely to become service users, the specific connection between the service and an identified community need, and the cost of a service to potential clients.

Identifying the potential target markets for an organization's program makes it much easier for the organization to ensure that its program remains highly effective. In addition to helping focus the measurement of service outcomes, understanding the target market helps an organization determine where to promote its services (such as through publications, social media, or online advertising), conduct public relations campaigns, and recruit potential clients.

It is very useful to select several possible target markets to ensure an adequate client base. For example, an organization interested in developing an after-school tutoring and dropout prevention program might promote its services among several populations: high school students, parents of high school students, teachers and administrators, the local school board and state department of education, and other community agencies that provide supportive services to this population-at-risk.

In addition, the more an HSO knows about its clients or potential clients, the greater likelihood it will develop a more effective service. Staff members in charge of promoting the service should draft a customer profile or a description of the groups of clients who will use it. This profile should include demographic information on members of this population, their major needs (as they define them), what methods of helping they prefer to address these needs, their physical location, and where they prefer to have their needs met. Demographic information should include their age ranges, family arrangement, educational and income levels, typical occupations, and major cultural interests (McNamara, 2017).

These marketing requirements have several implications for program development at the community level. First, it is important to use diverse approaches to obtain and retain community support. Second, organizations should try to ensure that their standards match the standards of external bodies, particularly in relationship to program effectiveness. Third, organizations should try to co-opt external decision-making bodies that control critical resources by educating them on organizational goals and how the organization's program addresses community needs. Finally, it is valuable to nurture a constituency that understands and supports the goals and effectiveness criteria you have developed for the organization's programs.

Resource Development

Most experienced macro social workers realize that the future survival of human service agencies in an environment of fixed or declining resources and political hostility is dependent upon their ability to secure adequate funding for their organizations. Agency survival means more than just whether an agency exists; it also includes how well the organization is fulfilling its mission and goals, and what percentage of the at-risk population it is reaching (Bray, 2016). HSOs do not struggle for survival in a vacuum; they usually operate in a network of services. This pattern of inter-organizational relationships (e.g., referral resources, funders, political allies and opponents, the media) plays an important role. Sometimes these relationships facilitate organizational survival; at other times, competition among HSOs or political opposition can threaten organizational survival (Kaplan, 2001). Small organizations, particularly those that serve predominantly racial and ethnic minority or low-income communities, are particularly vulnerable in this environment. It is especially important, therefore, that these organizations develop skills in resource development.

An organization's ability to acquire and sustain adequate resource support depends on the following factors: (1) a clear statement of its mission and goals, and the ability to translate this statement into concrete programs and services; (2) official nonprofit—501 (C) (3)—status; and (3) a credible "track record" of delivering on the promises of its services. In addition, when submitting a specific proposal for funding, an application needs to provide evidence of a clear program design, feasible (even exciting) goals and objectives, demonstration that the organization possesses the relevant expertise to implement the proposal, and the presence of strong, capable, stable leadership to guide its implementation (Warwick, 2000). The plan should also reflect recognition of the importance of its underlying ideas and be consistent with the overall direction of the organization.

Setting Funding Priorities

In determining the funding priorities of an organization, it is critical to start with the needs of the community and/or the organization, rather than tailoring funding proposals to funders' priorities. This may seem obvious, but in today's highly competitive environment, many organizations do precisely the opposite. A number of potential problems can arise if an organization decides to "follow the money" instead of responding to its constituents' needs and aspirations. Programs may receive partial or incomplete funding and this strategy may affect the resources available for other programs and distort their implementation. Of greatest importance, this approach may conflict with the organization's mission, create role confusion among staff members, and undermine relationships with the community (Lauffer, 2013).

It is useful to involve as many constituencies in the community as possible in planning a resource develop strategy to help identify expected sources of funding. These can include grants (from government, foundations, or corporations), contributions from wealthy individuals, government contracts, and general solicitation. The next step is to target the organization's resource development strategy by segmenting the market and connecting its interests and needs with those of potential funders. This enables the organization to tailor its fund-raising appeal to each particular audience. For example, in seeking funding for a program designed to help reintegrate former inmates into the community, appeals could emphasize the humanitarian, family strengthening dimensions of the program, its economic benefits to the community, or the cost-savings it can produce by reducing recidivism.

Although the use of market terminology may be uncomfortable in the social work field, it can be helpful in clarifying the essential components of an effective resource development strategy (Cravens & Piercy, 2009). Think of these components as the "5 Ps":

1. **Product:** A statement of what your organization or program is attempting to do and what issue the program intends to address.
2. **Price:** The actual cost of the program.
3. **Promotion:** A clear description of how the program meets a legitimate need.
4. **Place:** Indication of where you will implement the program and who would benefit.
5. **Plan:** A detailed description of how you will implement the program.

Comparison of Fund-Raising Approaches

Each year, nonprofits must raise revenue to meet their needs. To raise revenue, nonprofits develop fund-raising plans, which define the steps a nonprofit will take to gain support. These plans involve a number of important stages.

First, in consultation with the executive staff, the board of directors establishes a fund-raising plan with clear revenue goals. It includes the specific steps required to reach these goals. This overall plan issubject to the board's approval.

Second, in cooperation with the staff and community members, the board creates fund-raising committees to raise the necessary funds. Depending on the size of the organization, it may need to create different committees to address different components of the overall fund-raising program (e.g., donor solicitation, a major fund-raising event). An outreach committee often identifies the most likely donors. A membership committee often makes requests from individual donors.

Third, board members may make requests from major donors. In fact, in some organizations this is an expectation of all or most board members.

Fourth, in some cases, the organization may create a grant-writing committee to assist the executive director in applying for grants to foundations, corporations, or the government.

Finally, special events committees help coordinate fund-raising events. A nonprofit HSO may hold an annual dinner, dance, carnival, celebrity auction, or other event. By charging admission for these events and receiving in-kind sponsorship to cover some or all of the event's expenses, the nonprofit raises much needed income.

Potential Revenue Sources

As stated previously, potential sources of support for nonprofits include grants and contracts, donations, earned income, endowments, in-kind support, and volunteer service (Foster, Kim, & Christiansen, 2009). Here are brief descriptions of some of these various forms of financial support:

Grants and Contracts. Grants often come from foundations—philanthropic organizations that support charitable activities. It is important to conduct research to match the goals of the organization's programs to the stated priorities of potential foundation funders. Grants also may come from federal, state, and local governments, who may issue requests for proposals (RFPs) to address a particular community or societal issue. There is often a requirement for an organization that applies for a particular grant to collaborate with other agencies in its area and demonstrate the ability to sustain a program after the grant period expires. A contract is a legal agreement between a government entity and an HSO to provide a particular service in return for a certain amount of financial support. It is usually time-limited and contains specific programmatic requirements, such as the nature of the program's population and the components of a particular service.

Donations. Many donations come from individuals. Sometimes these individuals join the nonprofit as members. Other individuals may donate to the organization even if they are not members. Some donations come through major donors—individuals, families, or businesses—who may contribute a large sum through a single gift, an annual contribution, or a bequest. In addition, corporations often support nonprofit organizations through an arrangement known as a sponsorship.

Some organizations depend on either an annual fund-raising campaign or a single, major fund-raising event to raise a significant portion of their operating budgets. Both approaches have potential but are fraught with challenges. It often takes considerable time to develop a donor base that is sufficiently large (and affluent) to reap measurable returns through a fund-raising campaign. Campaigns also require an initial investment in "branding" the organization, compiling donor lists, training staff members or volunteers, and creating comprehensive record-keeping systems. Often, fund-raising campaigns do not bring in large amounts of contributions for several years.

Similarly, fund-raising events—luncheons, dinners, celebrity auctions—require extensive planning and investment of staff time and organizational resources, which small organizations are less likely to possess. The author has worked with several organizations that obtained about half of their annual budgets from such activities. Yet, this success only occurred after several years of trial and error. No organization should base its resource development strategy on a single event. If successful, however, such events can provide favorable publicity for the organization, an opportunity to reward staff members and volunteers, and an occasion that donors and the community at large anticipate each year.

Earned Income. Nonprofits also receive revenue by earning it in one of several ways. A common form of earned income is through charging clients a fee in exchange for a product or service, such as counseling. In addition, some organizations earn income through investments. These could include rental properties, interest from organizational reserves, or for-profit activities (e.g., a hospital gift shop). As nonprofit HSOs are tax exempt, the latter form of income raises certain ethical and legal questions. For example, do nonprofits that engage in for-profit activities have an advantage over for-profit competitors? Does participation in for-profit activities change the fundamental character of a nonprofit HSO?

Earned income represents the main source of income for many nonprofits. A nonprofit becomes independent when it earns its own income because it does not need to rely on other sources for funding. Nonprofits often run "sustainable programs" that earn income on a regular basis and keep it running independently. The sustainability of these programs can also provide nonprofits with the flexibility to innovate in other service areas.

This source of income, however, places smaller HSOs at a disadvantage for at least three reasons. First, organizations need sufficient resources to initiate a for-profit endeavor. Most new HSOs, especially those in low-income communities, lack these resources. Second, organizations that serve predominantly low-income clients may be reluctant to charge a fee for their services because their clients may be unable to pay. Even if they charge a token fee—which some analysts recommend—it has minimal effect on the organization's resource base. Finally, to develop a substantial fee-paying clientele, an organization needs to publicize its services and acquire a strong reputation in the community. Many low-budget HSOs, particularly those in racial and ethnic minority communities, do not have the means to advertise their programs, nor have they existed long enough to acquire a well-established reputation in their service areas. This is why such organizations need to be creative in developing resource development plans.

Endowments. Some nonprofits, especially older, more established organizations, also earn income through endowments. Endowments are very large donations (usually millions of dollars in cash or stock) that can generate interest or dividends for a nonprofit. Each year, the organization uses the interest on these investments to augment its general operating funds. Sometimes, the terms of an endowment place limits on how the organization can use its income.

Endowments are very important to nonprofits because they represent continued support. Organizations that have endowments never spend the principal (original gift). They only spend the interest from the investments. Ideally, if invested wisely, the original investment continues to grow and earn interest. If invested wisely, large endowments can support a nonprofit for a long period. Unlike grants and contracts, there is no limit to the time of support, because the endowment keeps earning interest. Unfortunately, small HSOs, particularly those in low-income, racial minority communities, rarely are the beneficiaries of endowments. This form of revenue is a classic example of the old cliché about the rich getting richer. It is one reason why the resource gap between mainstream organizations and newer, community-based HSOs continues to widen.

In-Kind Support. In addition to monetary contributions, nonprofits also receive other types of support. Cash donations are critical because they enable HSOs to buy the products and services they need. Sometimes, however, nonprofits receive these products and services directly. For instance, instead of cash contributions, a shelter for the homeless might receive blankets or toiletries for the people it serves directly from a department store or pharmacy. Organizations refer to this type of assistance as in-kind support.

Another example of in-kind support is free office space, such as in a government building or the headquarters of a larger HSO. In these circumstances, the "host" agency might not charge rent or utilities to the smaller nonprofit. Often, small "start-up" organizations, including those that may have "spun off" from a larger organization, use such in-kind contributions, particularly in the early stages of their development.

Volunteers. For many nonprofit HSOs, large and small, volunteers represent a crucial source of support. Volunteers work without pay to serve nonprofit goals. They fill roles ranging from board members to office help to program aides. The Washington-based organization Independent Sector conducts annual research on the value of volunteer time to the nonprofit sector. According to Independent Sector (2016), the value of voluntarism is in the millions of dollars each year.

Using volunteers, however, is not cost-free. An organization must spend considerable time and resources recruiting, training, and supervising volunteers if their contributions are to help promote the organization's mission (Cnaan & Cascio, 1998). The extensive use of volunteers also raises certain legal questions (e.g., on the organization's liability for the actions of volunteers) and ethical questions, such as the consequences if volunteers take over staff roles (Reamer, 2013).

It is important for organizations to weigh the advantages and disadvantages of each type of funding source in creating a resource development strategy. Given the various pros and cons of each approach to fund-raising, an ideal resource develop plan would reflect a variety of strategies to increase the likelihood of success.

Another important consideration in creating a resource development strategy is an assessment of the stability of potential funding sources. Not all funding sources are equally stable. This factor is particularly important if the program or project has long-term goals and objectives than can only be achieved with steady funding. The table below indicates the relative stability of different funding sources from most stable to least stable.

Table 11.1 Stability of Potential Funding Sources

Most Stable
Government grants or contracts
Federations (e.g., the United Way)
Large foundations (e.g., Robert Wood Johnson, Ford)
Small foundations (family or local community foundations)
Membership fees
Contributions from big donors or corporations
Fund-Raising campaigns
Fund-Raising events
Least Stable

Because resource development will remain a critical part of all social work practice in the future, learning how to write a concept paper, letter of intent, or case statement is a skill every social worker should acquire early in her career. Unlike research proposals to the National Institutes of Health, in general these documents are not very long, usually three to five pages plus a short cover letter. The goal is to frame the program or project proposal in a manner that appeals to the priorities and interests of the potential funding source (Coley & Scheinberg, 2000).

This does not mean, however, that the proposal should pander to the potential funder or distort the purposes of the program or the underlying issues that lead to its development. It does mean that the proposal should emphasize those program components that most closely reflect the stated goals of the funders. For example, if your organization wants to develop a dropout prevention program in local high schools, and one of a foundation's current emphases is the empowerment of women, it is critical to demonstrate how the proposed project would contribute to this result.

These documents have different names: a proposal, a concept paper, a letter of intent, or a letter of inquiry. Under whatever name, each document contain similar elements. It begins with a brief (short paragraph) introductory description of the program's goals, followed by a concise (one or two paragraphs) background discussion of the underlying issue(s) the program intends to address (often called a needs statement). The next component is a more detailed description (one or two pages) of the proposed project, including the target population, program goals, output and outcome objectives, and methods of evaluation. Finally, it concludes with a proposed short-form budget (you can attach this in an appendix) and a time frame for implementing the project. A sample letter of inquiry/intent is in the box below.

KEY CONCEPT SUMMARY
ELEMENTS OF A SAMPLE LETTER OF INQUIRY

Program Description

Our organization's mission is to expand opportunities for children and youth in our community. For many years, we have done this through a variety of well-established programs and services. These include before- and after-school care programs, tutoring and mentoring programs, college counseling, and job-placement services. These programs have transformed the lives of hundreds of children and families in the community. Agencies throughout the state have emulated the service model we have developed and the state legislature and various media sources have favorably cited the beneficial effects of our work.

Background/Needs Statement

As recent research demonstrates, a growing issue in our community and throughout the nation is the urgent and compelling need to target the 6.7 million youth (ages 16–24)—one in every six young people—who do not complete school and are unable to join the workforce. The cost to these youth, their families, and the community as a whole is staggering. Last year alone, taxpayers paid approximately $100 billion in direct and indirect costs to support these young people and to pay for the social services and juvenile justice programs they required. Yet, if these youths receive the right opportunities, they have the potential to infuse our economy with skills, new knowledge, and innovative leadership. Young people who are out of school and work do not see themselves as "failures" or "losers." They have energy and ambition, and are eager to work with established civic and business leaders to develop solutions that improve their lives, benefit their community, and help youth nationwide.

Program Description

Target Population

Our organization, ABC Services for Children and Youth, would like to develop a new program for youth of color, aged 16–25, who have experienced poverty and other barriers to entering the primary labor market. Some of these young people have graduated from high school or obtained their GED certificate. Some have dropped out of school. Others have been involved with gangs or the juvenile justice system. Nevertheless, they are all motivated to advance their knowledge, secure meaningful employment, and contribute to their communities as future leaders and heads of households.

Goal 1: To increase the number of youth who return to school to receive their high school diplomas or GED.

Goal 2: To reduce the recidivism rate among the portion of this population who have been involved in the juvenile justice system.

Goal 3: To increase the number of youth who go on to higher education.

Goal 4: To increase the number of youth gainfully employed in the primary labor market.

Output Objectives

1. In the first year of the program, 100 youth will participate in either educational or job-training programs.
2. Youth participating in the educational program will also receive a minimum of 10 hours per week of job-related skills.
3. Youth participating exclusively in the job-training program will receive, on average, 30 hours per week of services during the program's first year.

Outcome Objectives

1. 50% of participating youth will graduate from high school, complete their GED, or be placed in a full-time job after one year.
2. By the end of the program year, 90% of the youth will still be involved in the program.
3. By the end of the program year, less than 10% of program participants will have a repeat incident with the juvenile justice system.
4. By the end of the program year, 80% of participants who complete the job-training program will enter the full-time workforce or higher education (a community college or four-year college).

Evaluation

Our ongoing approach to evaluation reflects our commitment to measurable results and our organization's record of producing quantifiable results through our programs. We will collect data on a monthly basis through web-based evaluation tools and continuous dialogue with program participants and trainers. We will use evidence-based tools to gather output, outcome, and satisfaction data from program participants and community partners, and additional methods such as individual development plans, 360-degree reviews with feedback discussion circles, and regular participant presentations of their work.

Budget

Our organization is requesting $50,000 to support the operating costs of the job-training program. These costs include instructional materials, trainers' salaries, and stipends for program participants.

Time Frame for Implementation

1. July 2017–September 2017: Recruitment and selection of youth participants, hiring of trainers
2. October 2017–December 2017: Training programs begin. Creation of individual development plans and personal goals for program participants.
3. January 2018–June 2018: Programs continue and participants receive assistance with college applications or job placement.
4. July 2018: First cycle of program ends. Participants graduate.

As stated previously, it is essential to include a cover letter along with a concept paper or letter of inquiry. This serves the same purpose as a cover letter when you are applying for a job: it highlights the importance of the proposal and draws attention to the strengths of your organization. When applying for a foundation grant, address the cover letter to either the director of the foundation or the program officer responsible for a particular funding area. It should identify your organization, provide a little background on its accomplishments, indicate the exact amount of funding support you are seeking, and state the specific purpose(s) of the requested funding. A sample cover letter to accompany the sample letter of intent (above) follows.

KEY CONCEPT SUMMARY
SAMPLE COVER LETTER

Date

Mary Jones

Program Officer

XYZ Foundation

ADDRESS

Dear Ms. Jones:

ABC Services for Children and Youth requests funding in the amount of $50,000 to support the delivery of an innovative new educational and job-training program, which will be targeted at talented young adults from diverse, under-represented backgrounds in our community.

Since the founding of our organization in 1975, we have developed a wide range of innovative, cost-effective programs and services through partnerships with local nonprofit organizations and the business community. To date, more than 10,000 children, youth, and parents have benefited from our programs and services. The program described in the enclosed concept paper continues our tradition of responding to emerging community needs as they evolve. The support of the XYZ Foundation will provide critical assistance to our efforts to change the lives of young people in our community.

As your request, we have enclosed our Letter of Inquiry. Thank you in advance for considering our request for support. If you have questions or require additional information, please do not hesitate to contact me at 555-555-5555 or YourName@ABCServices.org.

Sincerely,

Your Name

Job Title

Another important component of resource development is the ability to persuade people in one-on-one conversations on the value and potential effect of a program or service you want to create. This could occur in conversations with major donors, program officers of a foundation, heads of government departments, or directors of corporate giving. The skills social workers possess in interpersonal communication, including active listening and effective framing of issues, are valuable tools in this regard. The following class exercise helps both to underscore the importance of these tools and also to highlight the areas where students may need further practice.

IN-CLASS EXERCISE
THE PERSONAL SIDE OF FUND-RAISING

1. Step 1: Divide the class randomly into pairs. Identify one student in each pair as the fund-raiser, the other as a potential donor.
2. Step 2: The fund-raiser in each pair has 10 minutes to try to raise as much (real) money from the donor for whatever cause she determines. The student who is acting as the fund-raiser writes down the money pledged on an index card (as a receipt) and turns it in to the course instructor.
3. Step 3: The instructor collects all the pledges and tallies the results.
4. Step 4: Each donor writes on a second card the maximum amount she was *willing to give* to the cause for which the fund-raiser was soliciting a donation.
5. Step 5: The instructor collects these cards and tallies the maximum amounts. The class will then compare the two totals (Step 3 and Step 5).
6. Step 6: The donors then present to the class: (a) what words, actions, or approaches by the fund-raiser would have led them to make the maximum donation they were prepared to make; (b) what approaches the fund-raiser took that were effective; and (c) what approaches the fund-raiser took that were less effective.
7. Step 7: The class then discusses the implications of the comments in Step 6 for resource development in community-based nonprofit organizations.

Budgeting

In addition to securing adequate funding to implement desired programs and services, organizations must also plan carefully how they will distribute these funds internally and monitor their use. There are two key elements in the budgeting process, cost shifting and cost sharing. Together they serve three functions: (1) maintaining records on how the financial plan of the organization reflects realistic program goals and objectives; (2) serving as a device to monitor the organization's financial activities and remain accountable to the government, other funding sources, and the community; and (3) maximizing the efficient use of resources.

The overall purpose of budget planning is to match the organization's available resources to the resources it needs to implement its programs and services (Maddox, 1999). Budget planners must factor in such expenses as personnel (salaries, fringe benefits, and consultants), training costs, space, equipment purchase or rental, travel, photocopying, telephone and utilities, publications, general office supplies, maintenance, insurance, and technical assistance. This process occurs on an annual basis because circumstances change; without an adequate supply of sustainable resources, an organization's programs (and sometimes even the organization itself) will fail. Nonprofits must not only allocate resources efficiently, they must also manage these resources well. In this sense, budgets serve the same purpose for organizations as they do for households.

Much as household budgets, nonprofit budgets have two main sections. The first section lists income, also known as *revenue*. In this section, the nonprofit includes all its sources of income. The second budget section contains expenses, such as those listed previously. These expenses fall into three broad categories: personnel costs, administrative costs, and other program costs (Dropkin, Halpin, & La Touche, 2011).

Annual budget planning helps a nonprofit determine the resources it will need for the next fiscal year. Nonprofits are legally required to have a balanced budget. If projected expenses exceed their projected income (a deficit), the organization either has to locate other revenue sources, make staffing or program cuts, find administrative savings, borrow funds, or dip into reserves (if it has any).

If projected income exceeds projected expenses (a surplus), the nonprofit may do one of two things. It may reinvest the surplus in the organization—for example, by buying new equipment—or it may put the surplus into an invested "rainy day" fund. In general, the IRS permits a nonprofit to have a rainy day fund equal to approximately 10% of its average annual budget. If an organization's rainy day fund becomes too large, it may trigger an IRS audit. (This restriction refers solely to the organization's operating budget. If the organization is raising funds for a long-term capital campaign—for example, to construct a new building—no such restrictions apply.) Under no circumstances, however, may the organization distribute a surplus to the board of directors or as a bonus to its executive director. This is one of the major distinctions between nonprofit and for-profit organizations.

In a nonprofit organization, the board of directors, in cooperation with the executive director and, in large agencies, the chief financial officer, has responsibility for developing and monitoring the budget. A "good" budget is one that is well conceived, clear, timely (especially for comparison purposes), and analyzed periodically, either by the entire board or its finance committee. An effective budget process also prepares the board and the organization's constituents to take action, when necessary, in support of the agency's programs and services.

The budget cycle of most nonprofits is on a July 1–June 30 basis, although a few HSOs construct budgets that follow the calendar year (January–December). For the most part, this is the best way to construct a budget process as it matches the budget cycles of local and state governments, foundations, and most corporations. It does not, however, match the budget cycle of the federal government (October 1–September 30). This can create potential fiscal problems for nonprofits that rely heavily on federal grants and contracts, or funding from local and state governments that essentially involve "pass throughs" from the federal government. In such cases, nonprofits often have to make their best guess as to the level of funding they will receive and develop contingency plans if they receive less than anticipated.

Steps in the Budgeting Process

The budget process begins with listing the organization's program goals and objectives for the coming fiscal year and their estimated costs. These include both operating and capital expenditures, such as staff salaries and benefits, space (rent), utilities, program supplies, support services, training costs, insurance, and the cost of publications. It is important to estimate how much these input costs might increase in the year ahead—for example, due to inflation (Dropkin, Halpin, & La Touche, 2011).

The next step is to project the organization's revenues or income. Most organizations base these projections on their recent experience. They assess whether current grants and contracts will continue; they measure the likelihood of increasing the "take" from current methods of resource development, such as an annual fund-raiser, a fund-raising drive, fees from clients, or income from activities not service-related. They may also factor in the possibility of receiving revenues from previously untapped sources, such as new foundation grants. It is best to be cautious about the latter, however, as excessive optimism can lead to disastrous consequences.

In estimating revenues, it is important to note that the choice of which revenue sources to pursue is not simply a means of solving the organization's fiscal problems. It is also a political and philosophical decision with long-term implications for the organization and its constituents. As the old saying goes, "he that pays the piper calls the tune."

It is equally important to recognize that, in most cases, the sources of an organization's revenue must also get their resources from somewhere else. The more you know about how potential funding sources obtain their money, the easier it is to get it and to understand the implications (i.e., strings attached) to receiving it. For example, during the dot-com bubble of the late 1990s and early 2000s, many corporate foundations made generous grants to nonprofit organizations based on the upward valuation of their stock shares. When the bubble burst, however, many donors not only failed to renew grants they often terminated existing grants and rescinded their previous funding obligations. This created huge fiscal crises for many community-based nonprofits that depended on these funding sources. They laid off staff members and drastically reduced services, in some cases terminating entire programs.

The next step is to compare projected costs and revenues. This analysis may lead to the need for service cuts, reordering of the organization's priorities, further resource development, modifications or additions to existing programs, or the creation of new programs. Once this analysis is complete, the organization develops its final annual budget and submits it to the board for approval review. Note that throughout this process the budget is both a policy document and a political document—a fiscal statement of the organization's priorities—and a mechanism for channeling its resources and monitoring their use.

A largely unacknowledged "dirty" secret of nonprofit organizations is that in tight fiscal times, there is unspoken competition for scarce budget resources between clients and staff members. When faced with finite resources, organizations often have to choose between hiring new staffers and increasing staff salaries, or maintaining or expanding services to clients. In addition to the obvious ethical and practical dilemmas this creates, this unspoken competition can heighten tensions within an organization.

Most organizations present their budgets in classic "line item" fashion. The budget lists each category of expenditure, usually in comparison with that of the previous fiscal years. This form of "operating budget" allows the organization to review its direct (e.g., staff) and indirect (e.g., space) costs, facilitates accountability, and enables it to monitor expenditures closely.

A second type of budget is a program performance budget. This budget model focuses on program products or outcomes. Organizations use this model to estimate and compare the cost of each service unit the organization produces or provides. If an organization employs this model, it is important to distinguish between outcomes and outputs. Outcomes include side effects, including unintended ones. Outputs are the program's products plus waste. (See below for further discussion of this distinction.)

Establishing and Measuring Program Outcomes

Establishing clear outcome objectives and developing ways to measure them are important to achieve and sustain positive effects on the community and the populations HSOs serve (Ott & Dicke, 2012). Organizations also need to develop them to satisfy the accountability demands of funding sources. In sum, they are beneficial to all the organization's key stakeholders: clients and constituents, staff members, funders, and the organization as a whole (Nocon & Qureshi, 1996).

Effective outcome statements must reflect the following criteria. They should be specific, measurable, and time-limited, not vague generalities. For example, the objectives of a dropout prevention program should state that it will produce a 20% increase in high school completion rates during a five-year period, rather than a "substantial reduction" in dropout rates. Outcomes should also be realistic and described in terms that are meaningful to funders, staff members, and prospective service users. Finally, they should be clearly connected to identified program goals and feasible—that is, matched to the organization's available resources and staffing capacity (Mullen & Magnabosco, 1997).

A number of major elements determine the quality of projected outcomes. Using a systems approach, they include:

Inputs: The ingredients necessary for the delivery of a service or a program. These include staffing, facilities, equipment, organizational structure, and potential clients. At the community level, inputs can also be political support, and the availability of the organizational and neighborhood resources required for larger scale efforts.

Process: The interaction of the inputs—i.e., what occurs when the ingredients come together to address the needs of clients or the community in a service or program.

Outputs: The work produced measured in work units (e.g., the number of individuals or families served by a particular program). At the community level, outputs are the products of organizing, developing, and collaborating with other groups and organizations. They can also include documents (e.g., memoranda of understanding), meetings, and the number of people who participate in program planning, implementation, and evaluation. They are distinct from outcomes and should not be confused with them.

Outcomes: The effect of the service or program on individuals, families, or the community as a whole. For example, outcomes describe what benefits clients receive from participation in the program. Organizational documents usually express them in terms of enhanced learning (knowledge, perceptions/attitudes, or skills) or improved conditions—for example, increased literacy, greater self-reliance, etc. They generally include a reduction in a problem or need, accomplishment of specific goals and objectives, or improvement in a previous condition. They can also include changes at the community level such as the reduction or elimination of a community-wide problem.

To assure that outcomes are of high quality, an organization needs to take the following steps before implementing a particular program or service:

Establish Clear Standards: This is a promise the organization makes to the community, the people it serves, and to funders. It establishes the expected performance level (the "bar") by which others can assess the organization. These standards must be measurable, timely, accurate, and meaningful.

Measure Performance: This involves an ongoing assessment on how well the organization is meeting the standards it established. To do this effectively, the organization must develop some form of data collection to document regularly the actual level of performance in the delivery of services or the creation of a community-based program. These include quantitative measures such as surveys, agency records, and the analysis of existing data; and qualitative techniques such as focus groups, in-depth interviews, participant observation, and ethnographic studies.

Maintain Standards: This requires the organization to address the differences between the promises made (goals) in Step 1 and actual performance, and to take concrete steps to close the gap between them. To accomplish this task, the organization needs to develop administrative tools that encourage good performance in its programs (a reward structure) or prevent the continuation of poor performance in the future (e.g., through supervision, staff evaluation, and training).

Major Components of Program Monitoring

To maintain high standards an organization must engage in constant program monitoring (Epstein & Tripodi, 1977). This involves infusing the organization's mission and values throughout the design and implementation of a program or service, and making values the centerpiece of the organization's culture to demonstrate its ongoing commitment to its constituents. This includes making value-based decisions regarding the day-to-day allocation of resources, portraying the organization and its goals in terms of explicit and symbolic value statements, interacting regularly with key individuals and groups inside and outside the organization, and maintaining core values even when they encounter opposition or disfavor from political opponents or some elements of the media.

In program monitoring, it is also important to distinguish among the effectiveness, efficiency, and effect of a service. **Effectiveness** refers to whether the program is meeting its intended goals and objectives. **Efficiency** is a measure of how well the organization is using resources to meet these goals and objectives. An organization can maintain high efficiency (e.g., cost per service unit) but not provide an effective program. Conversely, a program might be highly effective, but cost-inefficient. Finally, a program's **effect** requires an assessment of its overall consequences for the population served by the program, the community as a whole, and the organization itself, including the emergence of secondary and unintended consequences (Lewis, 2003).

Successful program monitoring requires a combination of steps. These include evaluation research, experimentation and risk taking, participatory decision making, worker discretion and autonomy, and organizational flexibility (McDavid & Hawthorn, 2006). To develop appropriate indicators of service effectiveness, organizations must match goals and resources clearly to each other and to the particular context of the program. They must be careful to avoid the danger of identifying goals and objectives based on political pressure, funding fads, or professional trends (Fitzpatrick, Sanders, & Worthen, 2011).

The process of applying standards and the expectations of staff members, service users, and funders in the evaluation of program indicators is not simple. Organizations must provide ongoing feedback to staffers and community members on the program's progress. This requires organizations to determine which organizational arrangements, administrative structures and processes, and methods of communication best facilitate the attainment of effective outcomes. This is complicated because HSOs must balance the attainment of long-term goals and the need to address contemporary political realities, both inside and outside the community, and within the organization itself. These include differences between the goals and values of external political systems, the organization, and the community it desires to serve.

A major reason for these political complications is that resource scarcity often creates conflicts between the internal and external goals of the organization, such as the desire to maintain a stable, high quality staff and the need to implement effective programs and services. The more an organization is successful in mobilizing its constituencies in support of the organization's program goals, the more it can maintain its autonomy, even in a hostile and resource scarce environment.

IN-CLASS EXERCISE
DETERMINING PROGRAM OUTCOMES

Your work with Citizens United for a Revitalized Eastville (CURE) has achieved some measure of success. The initial planning grant has identified several major issues confronting the community: the quality of public education, lack of jobs at living wages, deterioration of the community's housing stock, and neighborhood safety/security. The board of CURE has decided to submit a major community development grant to acquire long-term funding that would begin to address these issues. To develop the proposal, the board divided itself into four task groups, one for each of the previously cited issue areas. The task groups are to meet separately and develop possible program goals and outcomes; the groups will then come together for discussion, consultation, and consensus building.

Part I

Each group will focus on one of the above four areas. Although it is possible to develop many programs in each area, **for purposes of this exercise each group will identify one program only**. (Assume that this program might be part of a more comprehensive program design.) Each group should take the following steps:

1. Identify as specifically as possible the program component in the assigned issue area.
2. List the possible outputs of this program and indicate how you will measure them.
3. As specifically as possible, identify the intended outcomes of this program, with a particular emphasis on their outcomes for the community as a whole.
4. Identify at least two ways in which CURE could ultimately achieve these outcomes.

In addition, each group should reflect on the following questions:

1. What resources and skills would CURE need to measure outcomes in these ways?
2. What obstacles might make it difficult for CURE to identify and/or measure the above outcomes in the ways you indicated?
3. What are the potential consequences for CURE's goals and for Eastville of defining and measuring program outcomes as you have?

Part II

Each group will then report to the class on its responses to the above questions. Other groups will comment on each group's recommendations as follows:

1. What factors influenced your choice of outcomes and outcome measures?
2. What alternative outcomes and outcome measures might you have used?
3. What might be the different short-term and long-term implications of selecting alternative outcomes or choosing alternative means of measuring them?

Part III

As a whole, the class will address the following questions:

1. What were the commonalties and differences in the types of outcomes selected?
2. In what ways could you categorize these outcomes and integrate them into a common proposal?
3. What were the principal means chosen for measuring outcomes?
4. What are the implications for community development and planning of these choices?
5. What major problems did each group identify?
6. What are possible solutions for these problems?
7. What are the implications for community development and planning of such problems and their potential solutions?

Evaluating Progress Toward Program Goals and Objectives

One of the most effective ways to ensure the success of a program is by evaluating the implementation of the program plan. The plans are not laws—they are a set of guidelines and controls (Newcomer, Hatry, & Wholey, 2015). Sometimes plans need to be changed. That is not a problem in itself. It is important, however, to know why the plan needs to be changed and to determine the best way to make the necessary changes (Fitzpatrick, Sanders, & Worthen, 2011).

In assessing the progress of a program plan, an organization needs to reflect periodically on the following question: Is the organization achieving the program goals and objectives as originally defined? (McDavid & Hawthorn, 2006). If it is, the organization should acknowledge this progress, reward those responsible, and communicate the progress to all stakeholders. If there has been no progress or limited progress to date, the organization should consider the following questions:

1. Will the organization still be able to achieve its goals and objectives according to the time lines specified in the plan? If not, what are the main reasons?
2. Should the organization change the deadlines for completing the overall project or for meeting specific goals and objectives? If "yes," it is important to be careful about making such changes. Before making this change, it is particularly important to know why efforts are currently behind schedule.
3. Do staff members have adequate resources to achieve the goals? If the answer is "no," be sure to identify in what specific areas the staff lacks sufficient resources

and assess whether the organization can obtain the additional resources it needs in a timely manner.

4. Are the overall program goals and objectives still realistic?
5. Should the organization shift its current priorities to focus more on achieving these goals?
6. Should the organization modify the initial goals and objectives of the program? Organizations should proceed with special caution before making such major changes. Staff members should know the reasons why the organization is not achieving established goals before making such permanent and significant changes.
7. What can the organization learn from this monitoring and evaluation process to improve future planning activities and monitoring and evaluation efforts?

In addition to involving as many staff members as possible in this assessment process, it is also important to integrate feedback from clients and constituents (Ing, 2001). For example, the organization should consider:

1. How well did potential service users respond to advertising and promotion efforts?
2. To what extent do stakeholders maintain a positive impression of the organization?
3. Was the response of service users stronger (or less strong) to certain program aspects than to others?
4. What type of media seemed to generate the most responses to the programs?
5. What other information does the organization need to learn more about how clients and constituents are responding to the program?

Creating a Nonprofit Organization

Many students and practitioners express interest in creating their own nonprofit HSO. Often this interest arises from a perception of service gaps in their communities that traditional agencies have not been able to fill or are reluctant to fill. Sometimes this interest is an expression of an entrepreneurial spirit and the desire to develop an organization in which the founder can be her own boss. Whatever the motivation, the process of creating a nonprofit organization is relatively simple—on paper—but more complex in practice (Orslene, 2010).

A first step is to draft a statement of purpose. This should be short, clear, and simple. It should identify the issues or problems the organization intends to address and indicate why there is a need for a new organization to address these issues.

The next step is to write a more detailed organizational plan. This includes the organization's goals, proposed leadership, specific activities, physical location, and prospective resources. The plan should clearly link the projected activities both to the needs the organization intends to address and also to the organization's overall goals. Once the plan is completed, it is critical to recruit the people needed to run the organization, including potential members of the board of directors and/or a community advisory board.

The organization then needs to elect a board of directors and draft bylaws. State governments and the IRS require the submission of both an organizational plan and organizational bylaws in considering applications for nonprofit status.

Under most circumstances, it is desirable for a new organization to file with the state for legal incorporation and with the IRS for tax exempt—501 (C) (3)—status. These steps are critical because they limit the legal liability of the organization, including its staff and board members, provide it with a tax exemption (e.g., for the sales tax on purchases and property taxes if it owns property), and enable donors to claim a tax deduction for contributions they make to the organization. For wealthy donors, in particular, this last feature is often an incentive to make a philanthropic gift. It also helps the fledgling organization expand its potential donor base (Hopkins, 2012).

Before completing documents such as articles of incorporation, it is useful to consult with an attorney who specializes in nonprofit law and with an accountant. Sometimes these professionals can become members of the new organization's board. New nonprofits should also be aware that acquiring tax-exempt status also subjects them to certain restrictions regarding the use of funds and lobbying for policy changes.

In applying for tax-exempt status, new organizations must determine into which of 25 possible categories they fit. They must also decide whether they want to be a 501 (C) (3) organization, which focuses on service provision, or a 501 (C) (4) organization, which can engage more actively in policy advocacy efforts. If the organization decides to apply for the former, it must file IRS form 1023 and include a certificate of incorporation, articles of incorporation, signed bylaws, a current balance sheet, and a statement of proposed activities.

In some cases, the founders of a new organization may decide that the costs or sacrifices involved in creating a nonprofit are not worth the time and effort. If this is their decision, several alternatives exist. One is not to organize at all. The organizers can remain an informal group and continue to provide services as long as the organization does not solicit funds.

A second option is to become part of an organization that is already tax exempt. Sometimes an established HSO will integrate into its existing structure a new program or service on a temporary basis. This enables the creators of this new program to wait to establish a separate organization. They will have to weigh the pros and cons of this decision. While it may be beneficial to take advantage of the resources provided by its host, if a new program becomes part of another organization, even temporarily, it might become more difficult to establish an independent identity in the future.

In addition, the organization could decide to become a different type of nonprofit, such as a cooperative, an association, or a mutual aid organization. If it selects this option, state laws generally determine what are the qualifications and legal requirements.

Lastly, the organization could choose to become a for-profit entity. In this case, it would be subject to state and federal laws on limited liability corporations or partnerships, along with the standards of state and national accrediting bodies. Whatever the organization's decision, it is important to identify potential competitors in the surrounding environments. All nonprofits purportedly exist to serve their communities. Yet, it would be naïve to assume that this spirit of service leads all nonprofits to collaborate for "the common good." For better or worse, however, nonprofits frequently compete for resources, clients, media publicity, and community attention. In many cases, they compete for the same grants from funders.

Before developing a new organization, therefore, it is wise to consider the following questions: Who are your competitors? What client needs are you competing to meet? What similarities and differences exist between their programs and services and those you wish to develop? What are the strengths and weaknesses of each of their programs and services? How do their prices compare with yours? To what extent are competitors' programs effective or perceived by the public to be successful?

If you decide to enter the market, how do you plan to compete with other organizations? Would you try to compete by offering better quality services? Lower prices? Would you emphasize that your agency has a supportive, culturally conscious environment? Easier access to services? You must consider all of these complex issues before taking such a big personal and professional risk.

Summary and Conclusion

This chapter presented several models of program planning at the community level. It discussed various components of program design, resource development, and budgeting. Each of these processes are regular features of the work of macro social workers, and increasingly of all social workers who work in organizational settings. Chapters 12–14 will discuss various methods by which macro social workers can effect changes at the policy level, including policy advocacy and participation in the electoral process.

END-OF-CHAPTER EXERCISE
DESCRIBING A NEW PROGRAM OR SERVICE

Think about a service or program that your organization could develop to meet the needs of the people in its community. Write a brief description of this potential service that includes:

1. Current auspices of your organization, whether it is public, nonprofit, or private
2. Type of service (counseling, education, advocacy, etc.)
3. Target market
4. How you would disseminate information about the service
5. How you would fund the service, including what fee (if any) you would charge and to whom.

END-OF-CHAPTER EXERCISE
DRAFTING A LETTER OF INTENT/CONCEPT PAPER

This exercise involves the development of a letter of intent or concept paper for a small grant you will submit to a potential funding source (e.g., a foundation or corporation) to support the development of an innovative program in your organization. The proposal **may not exceed three (3) pages** (single-spaced, double-spaced between paragraphs), not including attachments, and must contain the following components:

1. **Background/Needs Statement:** This includes a brief description of the issue the project will address and why this issue is important. It also includes the identification of a target population or community for the project. *(Include relevant literature, research, and data to document the need for the proposed intervention/project.)*
2. **Goals and Objectives:** State the proposed project's goals and major objectives *(Be sure to link the goals and objectives to your description of the project.)*
3. **Project Description:** Describe the principal components of the proposed project and identify its anticipated measurable outcomes. Discuss its main features and their contribution to these outcomes. *(Include enough information for potential funders to understand how your organization will use their money to address the identified need and achieve the intended goals of the project.)*
4. **Budget:** Estimate the cost of the proposed project. *(Indicate how much money your organization will need to carry out the project based upon its objectives. Include what proportion of the overall project's budget you are requesting from this funder or what specific components of the project you are asking this funder to support.)*

5. **me Line:** Provide a specific timeline for the proposed project. *(This should give the funding source an overall view of the project steps and activities.)*
6. **Conclusion:** End with a final, persuasive, summary paragraph that "sells" the proposed project.
7. **Cover Letter:** Include a cover letter (transmittal letter) with the proposal. The cover letter should highlight the main points of the proposal and indicate to the potential funding source why this project is important to fund. Research community foundations, philanthropic corporations, and social enterprise organizations on the web to determine to which potential funder you might send this cover letter and proposal.

CHAPTER 12

Advocating for Policy Change in the Legislative Arena

We must always take sides. Neutrality helps the oppressor, never the victim. Silence encourages the tormentor, never the tormented.

—Elie Wiesel

The weapon of the advocate is the sword of the soldier, not the dagger of the assassin.

—Alexander Cockburn

Introduction

The current fast-changing, hyper-partisan political and economic environment compels social workers to engage in advocacy efforts on behalf of vulnerable populations more than ever. Advocacy has also become more complex because of the multiple consequences of globalization, major demographic changes, technological innovations, and unprecedented sociocultural transformation. In addition, the locus of policy making and implementation has also shifted. On the one hand, it has moved on some issues from the national to the state and local levels—a phenomenon known as devolution—and on others from the nation-state to supra-national institutions, and on still others from the public to the nonprofit and for-profit sectors, often referred to as privatization. Ironically, advocates must now pay simultaneous attention to transnational issues and the distinctive character of local needs and concerns. Finally, while the creation of socially just policies requires greater democratization, many critical policy decisions are the products of nondemocratic factors, such as the growing influence of wealth on the electoral process.

This chapter explores how advocacy in the legislative policy arena can help create more socially just policies through traditional methods and new forms of community-based participation. It presents the challenges involved in increasing the participation of marginalized populations from low-power communities in the policy-making process and some potential responses to these challenges. These include the use of participatory action research, **community-based policy advocacy**, popular education, and training community members in public speaking, lobbying, and the use of media. In sum, it discusses how advocates can promote progressive social change through a combination of "inside/outside" approaches.

Specific issues that the chapter will discuss include:

1. Definitions of various types of advocacy and their purposes
2. Framing and targeting advocacy efforts
3. Developing advocacy strategies and tactics
4. Guidelines for effective organizational and policy advocacy
5. Legal and practical constraints on advocacy
6. Advocacy etiquette
7. Community participation in advocacy efforts
8. Roles of advocacy coalitions
9. Ethical dilemmas in advocacy

Purposes of Social Justice Advocacy

Policy advocacy involves organizing the strategic use of information to democratize unequal power relations. It is the *most significant intervention* social workers employ to help members of disadvantaged groups obtain resources and access to key decision-making processes. At its best, advocacy empowers weaker sectors of society through the provision of information, resources, and tools, while enhancing people's self-respect, improving their self-confidence, and promoting greater intragroup and intergroup trust. In general, it includes work in the following areas:

1. Assessing the political and policy-making context.
2. Deciding the political arena in which an advocacy effort should occur.
3. Determining what people think about the issue.
4. Agenda setting and strategy development—deciding what result you want.
5. Acquiring and allocating sufficient financial resources.
6. Managing the flow, frequency, and format of information in useful ways.
7. Creating, strengthening, and formalizing interpersonal, intergroup, and inter-organizational relationships.

Given the power imbalance that exists between established institutions and the people with whom social workers work, the specific goals of advocacy to correct this power-inequity include:

- providing direct assistance to individuals and communities to help them obtain resources;
- teaching individuals to advocate for themselves;
- arguing on behalf of disadvantaged groups or communities in the policy-making arena;
- shaping public opinion through popular education and media efforts;
- lobbying for legislative, regulatory, or judicial change; and
- influencing social change through electoral politics

From a social justice perspective, therefore, advocacy has two core purposes:

1. To influence political, economic, and social ***outcomes*** that directly affect people's lives.
2. To change the ***processes*** by which authorities make decisions and create openings for new actors to be involved in making them.

The four core themes of advocacy—participation, representation, accountability, and transparency—reflect these purposes throughout all phases of the advocacy process.

The Three Cycles of Change

Just as in the fields of community organizing, administration, and management, policy advocates need to be aware of the various cycles of change that affect their work. Three cycles of change are particularly relevant in the advocacy arena. One cycle is the "problem-solving cycle." In this cycle, what people experience as a "private trouble" becomes a public issue worthy of attention and action by key decision makers. Advocates propose alternative solutions and, if they are successful, policy makers adopt and implement a solution that, ideally, produces the necessary change.

A second cycle is the "issue life cycle," whose passage resembles the human life cycle. The six stages of this cycle are:

1. *Birth*: A new demand, issue, idea, or proposal emerges.
2. *Childhood*: Advocates nurture the idea and attempt to obtain support.
3. *Adolescence*: Policy makers and the public make preliminary decisions concerning the issue.
4. *Adulthood*: Policy makers construct a voluntary resolution of the issue.
5. *Maturity*: The policy is implemented, monitored, and evaluated in the short term.
6. *Renewal*: The policy's implementation is re-evaluated to make long-term decisions.

The third life cycle—the "organizational life cycle"—concerns the transformation of the advocacy organization itself (Mahon & Waddock, 1992). This follows a similar pattern to the issue life cycle:

1. *Birth*: The organization emerges.
2. *Childhood*: The organization learns new skills and builds an infrastructure.
3. *Adolescence*: The organization experiments with various ways to frame issues and with different messaging and targeting strategies.
4. *Adulthood*: The organization becomes a leader in the advocacy effort, mentors constituents, collaborates with other organizations, and educates the public.
5. *Maturity*: The organization shares the wisdom it acquired through experience.
6. *Renewal*: Depending on the outcome of its advocacy efforts, the organization develops a new strategic focus or new leadership (Lester, Parnell, & Carraher, 2003).

These three life cycles underscore the reality that changes produced by advocacy are largely incremental and that change is a multidimensional process. Organizations produce them by careful planning, reflection, and visioning. They also point out that to be effective an organization needs to match the stage of its life cycle to the issue life cycle, and to use a combination of "inside" and "outside" strategies.

The Goals of Advocacy

The roots of the concept of advocacy are in the legal system. Advocacy refers to the representation or defense of individuals or a community, to speaking on their behalf. As an advocate, a social worker "speaks, argues, manipulates, bargains, negotiates, and confronts" on behalf of a client system. The application of a social justice perspective—a core obligation of NASW's *Code of Ethics*—modifies this traditional, top-down version of advocacy by incorporating the importance of client and community empowerment. This distinguishes the role of social work advocates from those in other helping professions. Social work advocates focus their efforts, therefore, on behalf of individuals, groups, and families through the provision of direct services, but also on the fair administration of programs, the creation of socially just public policies, participatory community organizing and development, and various forms of action-oriented research.

A primary goal of advocacy is to influence another individual or group to make a decision (that the individual or group would not have otherwise made) that concerns the welfare or interests of a third party. Another possible goal is to secure existing services to which clients or constituents are entitled but unable to obtain on their own. A third goal is to engage in social action to secure rights and entitlements for marginalized and excluded populations. This may require major structural, systemic, or institutional changes in society (Hoefer, 2016; Wilks, 2012).

In addition to passing (or blocking) legislation or a budget initiative, policy advocacy can serve other important purposes that advance the long-term goals of an organization, its clients, and its constituents. It can deepen the commitment of legislators to an issue and educate legislators and their staff members on its intricacies. It can help advocacy groups identify points of resistance, disagreement, and support that will assist them in developing bargaining points in the future. The acquisition of expanded media coverage can increase public awareness of an issue and alter public perception of its underlying causes. (Advocacy for legislation such as the Violence Against Women Act, VAWA, is a good example.) Finally, advocacy can strengthen the advocacy organization itself, heighten the skills of staff members, and empower constituents to engage in other advocacy efforts in the future (Reisch, 2015a).

Types of Advocacy

Social workers engage in several types of advocacy. **Case advocacy** refers to an intervention—inside or outside an existing system—on behalf of an individual, family, or group in conflict with an organization to secure a needed service or resource. A goal of this form of advocacy may be obtaining resources (e.g., nutritional assistance) to which a household is entitled but has been unable to receive due to administrative neglect.

By contrast, **cause or class advocacy** involves an intervention on behalf of multiple groups of clients, potential clients, or constituents that seeks to address issues that affect the entire population through generating some form of social change or creating social policies that are more responsive and just. Examples of class advocacy include efforts to increase the minimum wage, create more affordable housing, and pass comprehensive immigration reform.

One form of class advocacy is **legislative or policy advocacy**. This type of advocacy focuses on the creation or modification of legislation (or government budgets) to benefit some category of clients or constituents (Jansson, 2014). **Administrative or regulatory advocacy** has a similar goal but reflects a different process and target. By targeting boards, commissions, government departments, and the leaders of major organizations, it tries to change the interpretation of policy. Its main role is to monitor the implementation of existing policies (Nicholson-Crotty, 2011).

The focus of **judicial or legal advocacy** is on the court system and the decisions of judges. Although social workers do not argue cases in court, they can still play a key role in this form of advocacy (Lens, 2017). **Media advocacy**, discussed in Chapter 13, refers to efforts to use media to influence public opinion and the actions of key policy makers. Finally, **electoral advocacy** involves the use of political campaigns to educate the public, affect policy decisions, and engage the community in efforts on its own behalf (Lott & Fremont-Smith, 2017; Shaw, 2013). This chapter will focus primarily on the various components of policy advocacy in the legislative arena. Chapters 13 and 14 will cover other types of advocacy.

All forms of advocacy require advocates to engage in holistic, qualitative, participatory action research with clients and constituents. This includes conducting research on the "secondary effects" of a policy on organizations and communities. The author's research on the effect of welfare reform on nonprofit organizations is an example of this type of research) (Reisch & Sommerfeld, 2003a; Abramovitz, 2005). On occasion, advocacy-oriented research produces "whistle-blowing" effects—sometimes unintended—such as the author's research on public housing in San Francisco that lead to the federal government placing the Public Housing Authority of the city of San Francisco in receivership (Reisch & Rivera, 1999). These forms of research can help advocates redefine the goals of policies and reinterpret the policy context.

KEY CONCEPT SUMMARY
A PRACTICE FRAMEWORK FOR ADVOCACY

All forms of advocacy use a similar practice framework that includes the following steps:

1. Identifying the issues and framing them clearly.
2. Getting the facts.
3. Developing a strategy.
4. Establishing ongoing connections with key decision makers.
5. Broadening the base of support for advocacy efforts—for example, through coalitions.
6. Implementing advocacy strategies and tactics.
7. Evaluating advocacy efforts.
8. Preparing for the next steps, including monitoring the implementation of policies.

Similarly, all forms of effective advocacy contain certain essential ingredients. Advocates must know their clients or constituents' rights, the avenues of appeal to produce policy changes, and the resources available to support their efforts. They must also be able to devise appropriate intervention strategies and tactics, and conduct research in government documents and other data sources. In addition, advocates need to know how the political process works and how to build coalitions, including those established with groups from different racial, cultural, and ideological backgrounds.

Policy Advocacy

Policy advocacy, sometimes referred to as legislative advocacy or lobbying, is a major form of advocacy in which social workers engage. In fact, social workers have engaged in this form of advocacy for more than a century. Their advocacy efforts have produced such major policy achievements as the Social Security Act, Medicare, Medicaid, and less well known but equally valuable policy changes, such as the development of the juvenile court, kindergartens, and a wide array of public health, housing, and occupational safety measures (Reisch, 2017). All of the skills social workers use with individuals, families, and groups are directly transferable to policy advocacy. These include the interpersonal skills required when making individual contact with policy makers; skills in interviewing, listening, observing, being empathic, supportive, and willing to confront when necessary; the ability to speak effectively before legislative committees, commissions, boards, and community meetings; being comfortable with group process when working with diverse coalitions; and understanding the dimensions and dynamics of power.

Legal Limits on Lobbying

Lobbying refers to deliberate efforts to influence the decisions of legislators and other government officials. A lobbyist is a person paid to influence legislation on behalf of a particular group or organization. As discussed in the following paragraphs, the government establishes rules to define and regulate lobbying. These rules have important implications for nonprofit HSOs. In general, lobbying—as a persuasive activity—is most effective when targeted at those who are undecided or less well informed about the issue(s). Lobbying directed at staunch opponents is least effective. In fact, it might engender stronger opposition (Hoefer, 2017).

According to IRS policies, 501 (c) (3) and 501 (c) (4), organizations are exempt from paying federal income tax or state sales or property taxes. A 501 (c) (3) organization is either a public charity, private foundation, or private operating foundation with open membership. Catholic Social Services and the Ford Foundation are examples of this type of organization. A 501 (c) (4) organization can be a civil league or association operated exclusively for the promotion of social welfare or local associations of employees with limited membership. The Council on Social Work Education is an example.

Unfortunately, some organizations disguise themselves as social welfare organizations to circumvent federal campaign finance law. They use this IRS designation to funnel so-called "dark money" contributions to political campaigns. Since the Supreme Court's decision in the *Citizens United* case this deception has become more common further skewing the nation's electoral process (Mayer, 2016; Smith & Powell, 2013).

According to the IRS, there are important distinctions among various forms of lobbying. For example, there is a difference between direct lobbying and grassroots lobbying. The former involves direct contact with a legislator or member of her staff. It occurs when a representative of an organization communicates the organization's view on a specific piece of legislation to an official (such as a city council member, state legislator, senator, or a staff person of such an official). The latter includes efforts to educate the public and shape public opinion through communication ultimately intended to influence specific legislation. This can take the form of a "call to action," paid mass media advertisements, and lobbying among an organization's members—for example, around a ballot measure. IRS regulations do not restrict nonpartisan analysis, study, or research.

According to IRS regulations, nonprofits must complete a simple, one-time form (IRS Form 5786) to engage in lobbying. A 501 (c) (3) organization with an annual budget under $500,000 can spend as much as 20% of its budget on lobbying. As the size of an organization's annual budget increases, the proportion it may use to cover lobbying expenditures decreases (Alliance for Justice et al., 2011; Smucker, 2005).

In contrast, 501(c) (4) organizations (such as the Sierra Club or the League of Women Voters) may engage in unrestricted lobbying if it relates to the organization's stated purpose. Some of these organizations, such as the National Association of Social Workers, also establish **political action committees** or PACs. (NASW's PAC, PACE, stands for Political Action for Candidate Election.) These arrangements are legal but usually taxable. Violating IRS provisions, such as the prohibition on the use of government funds for lobbying, can produce serious consequences.

Policy Advocacy in Legislatures

As all forms of macro practice, such as community organizing and program development, effective legislative advocacy requires social workers to take a series of sequential steps. Once an organization identifies an issue that will be the focus of its advocacy, it is important to get involved in developing or revising a draft bill through an established unit of government or a nongovernmental organization. The next step is to identify the bill's supporters or potential sponsors and those responsible for managing the bill through the legislature. It is essential to try to arrange a meeting with these individuals or their key staff members as soon as possible.

Through these meetings, advocates attempt to persuade key legislators to sponsor the bill and work on its passage through the often lengthy and convoluted legislative process. A key part of the process is to use legislative staff members as much as possible. Legislative staffers are often more knowledgeable on the issue and more accessible than elected representatives. They are frequently of the same generation as social work advocates, making them easier to relate to in some ways.

After persuading lawmakers to introduce a bill, advocates then work with other outside interest groups to broaden support for the policy change. They attempt to educate the public in a variety of ways—through newspaper articles, op-ed essays, newsletters, public meetings, symposia, and press conferences. Inside the legislative body, they focus on the legislative committees that have initial responsibility to consider the bill. This includes speaking directly to key committee members and asking committee chairs for an invitation to testify at hearings on the bill.

Throughout the process and, eventually, to influence the final vote, it is important for advocates to keep track of their supporters and opponents, contact uncommitted legislators to try to influence their vote by communicating your views in a manner that resonates with their interests, and to seek favorable media coverage of the legislation (Hoefer, 2016; Jansson, 2014; Shaw, 2013).

Direct and Indirect Advocacy

Not all social workers are comfortable engaging in the above activities. It is important, therefore, to note that successful legislative advocacy involves the use of both direct and indirect methods (Kimberlin, 2010). Direct forms of advocacy, such as the methods described previously, include:

- providing expert written or oral testimony to a legislative committee;
- participating in a task force that is developing policy options about a specific issue;
- coalition building;
- drafting interagency memoranda of understanding (MOUs);
- analyzing or drafting bills and budget measures;
- circulating petitions; and
- initiating legal action or assisting in a legal action initiated by other groups.

Indirect advocacy takes different forms. It could involve developing or staffing an issue-oriented hotline or network, training clients or constituents to engage in advocacy, writing or editing publications on critical issues, engaging in action research, using the media to promote a particular issue, and providing legislators with technical assistance in writing bills or regulations. Most social workers have the skills to engage in this form of advocacy, even if they do not consider themselves political activists (Reisch, 2015a).

Preparing for an Advocacy Campaign

Before initiating any form of advocacy, a macro social worker needs to engage in various types of assessment, just as a clinical social worker does. First, she must conduct some self-assessment by asking the following questions: Is it *my role* to take the lead in this advocacy process? Am I the right person to advocate? Do I have the ability and the time to devote myself to the change effort? In this particular situation, what resources and power dynamics might affect my ability to be an effective advocate?

Potential advocates also need to assess the overall context to be certain that the effect of an issue (or issues) on clients or constituents justifies advocacy of any form. In addition, advocates need to assess the motivation of clients or constituents and their ability to participate in a sustained advocacy process. Based on the principle of self-determination, it is important to ascertain whether clients or constituents opt to pursue action. This requires advocates to discuss possible risks and the chances of success if clients or constituents participate in advocacy. It is important in this regard to keep in mind that while participation is a component of the process of empowerment, the enhancement of self-efficacy, and the construction of a sustainable support network for clients and constituents, it can, under certain conditions, produce negative consequences for clients and constituents.

Finally, an advocate must assess the opposition. How open are opponents to change? How have they responded to challenges in the past? What are their values and goals? What are the "keys of influence" that could alter their perspective on the issues (Richan, 2013)?

Whatever form of advocacy a social worker undertakes and in whatever arena it occurs, certain components are critical to the success of the effort. These include:

- conferring with other organizations to learn from their experience and expertise;
- using tactics of persuasion rather than coercion;
- appealing to the values or self-interest of targeted individuals or groups;
- gathering critical data through various formal and informal methods;
- educating relevant segments of the community;
- forming and sustaining coalitions and alliances; and
- organizing client or constituent groups to maximize their participation in the advocacy process.

Finally, before an organization decides to participate in an advocacy campaign, it needs to engage in several preliminary steps. First, it must identify the issue or problem clearly and frame it in a manner that is comprehensible to the public and policy makers and that lends itself to a feasible solution. Second, the organization must decide whether involvement in this particular advocacy effort is feasible and appropriate for the organization at this time. This includes assessing the connection of the issue to the established goals of the organization, calculating the costs and resource implications, and determining the probability of public support (and the potential long-term effects of advocacy on the organization).

The next step is to devise a specific remedy and to decide what venue (the legislature, the executive branch, or the judiciary) would be most suitable to pursue this desired outcome. Once the organization makes this decision, it must create a well-defined strategy to achieve its advocacy goals. This includes conducting background research on the issue, on potential supporters and opponents, and on the advocacy process selected. It also involves broadening the organization's base of support by working with others directly affected by the issue and/or the advocacy process. Finally, an effective strategy balances broad and specific appeals in a unifying, multi-issue vision, presents alternatives of different costs, and matches the advocacy arguments to the local political culture and current fiscal realities (Shaw, 2013).

KEY CONCEPT SUMMARY
DEVELOPING AN ADVOCACY STRATEGY

In developing an advocacy strategy, an organization has to consider the following specific questions:

1. What do we want? What is the "real" issue? What are our goals?
2. Who can give it to us? Who are the key decision makers?
3. What do they need to hear? For whom are we advocating?
4. From whom do they need to hear it?
5. How can you get them to hear it?
6. What resources do we have? How much will our advocacy effort cost?
7. What do we need to develop? How will we raise the necessary resources? What staff and volunteers do we need?
8. Where do we begin? What strategies should we use? What is the timetable for action?
9. With whom should we collaborate? Should we do it alone? If not, whom else should be involved? How will constituents be involved?
10. How do we determine whether our strategy is working? What are our indicators of success? (Hoefer, 2016).

Issue Framing and Messaging

One of the most critical aspects of advocacy is proper framing of the issue and creating a message that presents the framing clearly to the public and policy makers. The message is the central organizing idea of an advocacy strategy. It is important to keep it simple, focused, and consistent. The language, images, tone, and content of the message are all crucial in shaping public opinion on the causes and solutions of the problem(s) that your advocacy addresses. The goal of framing and messaging is to make the issue resonate most effectively with probable supporters by appealing to their values and objective needs (Dorfman, Wallack, & Woodruff, 2005).

To select the most effective framing of an issue, advocates need to decide whether their demands will focus on a single issue or multiple demands; whether their advocacy goal is expansive (system changing) or small (incremental); and whether their demands will be perceived as radical or non-radical (Shaw, 2013). Advocates also need to determine whether they want to influence current policy actors or change the composition of these actors. Another question is how explicitly to present the ideological or value dimensions of the issue. Finally, advocates must assess whether the issue (as framed) is winnable in the current climate. Is the issue immediate, specific, and sustainable (Lens, 2005)?

KEY CONCEPT SUMMARY
GUIDELINES FOR ISSUE FRAMING

1. Develop a clear distinct message for *every issue.*
2. Target the audience you need to persuade—not the audience that already supports you.
3. Focus on the needs of clients or constituents.
4. After stating the issue, reframe it if necessary.
5. Put a *face* on the issue (people love stories)—but connect the issue to a specific policy solution.
6. Base messages on the data collected through research.
7. Use diverse presentation styles before different audiences but maintain a consistent theme.
8. Use unlikely allies to help reframe the message to undecided or resistant audiences.

IN-CLASS EXERCISE
INITIATING AN ADVOCACY CAMPAIGN

Introduction

After considerable discussion with key leaders of CURE, the group's Steering Committee decides that an advocacy approach is best suited to produce some tangible results in the community. CURE has created five issue-oriented groups around the issues that could become the inspiration for advocacy efforts. These issues are:

1. The quality of schools, particularly underfunding of the Eastville School District.
2. The racial profiling of youth and young men of color by local police.
3. A lack of adequate services for victims of domestic violence and sexual assault.
4. The redlining of certain Eastville neighborhoods by local banks.
5. Absence of jobs at a living wage.

Group Exercise

Each small group will address the following questions:

1. How would you propose to frame your issue to the public and to political decision makers?
2. What avenues for advocacy and policy change might social workers pursue to address this issue? At what levels of government should the group direct these efforts? For what reasons?
3. Who might be potential allies or opponents in such advocacy efforts?
4. What skills and knowledge would community members need to participate in this process? How would you enable them to acquire the knowledge and skills?
5. What specific obstacles might your group face? How would you attempt to overcome them?

Group Discussion

1. In what ways were each group's answers similar or different?
2. In what ways did the issues selected shape the approach for advocacy and policy change?

Two Dilemmas of Policy Advocacy

All policy advocates most try to resolve two persistent dilemmas. The first is the "dilemma of perception." According to this dilemma, the most "realistic" framing of an issue has the most inhibiting effect on the public's conceptions of who or what is responsible for the problem. In today's climate, framing the solution to a problem in terms of how it will benefit particular groups will weaken rather than strengthen public support. A powerful contemporary example is the issue of chronic poverty and higher levels of unemployment in communities of color.

The second dilemma is the "dilemma of power." Effective advocacy requires persuading those with power, authority, and resources that the changes you propose are in their self-interest. Yet, the institutional settings in which policy issues are decided largely exclude or ignore many of the clients and constituents of advocacy organizations (Bartels, 2016).

How do you overcome these dilemmas? How do you balance "winning" with the maintenance of personal and organizational integrity around the issue? As will be discussed in the following section, how do you balance effectiveness with enhanced community participation in the policy-making process? If faced with a choice, should advocates compromise on the solution or the process? Advocates face these tough issues on a regular basis. That is why values play a central role in the advocacy process.

Value-Based Approaches to Advocacy

Whether their origins are in religious beliefs or secular ideologies, values play a critical role in the advocacy process (Prilleltensky, 2001). They influence people's attitudes and behaviors about issues, their support for the status quo, their desire for change, and their views on the change process itself. The success of an advocacy campaign often depends on the extent to which it reflects or contradicts prevailing cultural norms and values.

Think about the major values that shape the community in which you work. How do these values influence how the community views the issues that might form the basis of advocacy efforts? How does the public perceive the issues that affect this community?

There are several ways to use a value-based approach to promote the advocacy goals of an organization and its constituents. One way is to challenge the current hierarchy of values by contrasting them with the organization's values. This approach is part of an overall conflict perspective on social change—it is a form of ideological contest. A second approach is to demonstrate how an organization's position maximizes the opposition's values, even if it originates from a different set of assumptions. This approach fits best with a "campaign-style" strategy. A third approach is to argue that the opposition's solution is not consistent with its own values. This educational approach tries to point out the contradictions between the opposition's stated values and their actions.

Just as in all forms of social work practice, it is essential to assess the value context (ideological or cultural environment) in which an advocacy intervention will occur. Part of this assessment is determining whether the desired change is controversial or highly politicized. Is the magnitude of the desired change incremental or fundamental? Does the policy solution involve the infusion of new resources, the reallocation of existing resources, or a reconceptualization of the issue and its potential solutions? The overarching question is how to use an advocacy campaign to convert a private trouble into a public issue (Mills, 1963).

Classroom Discussion

Think about the values and symbols that might appeal to you in framing an argument on an issue. How do they reflect or conflict with prevailing cultural values?

Targeting

Targeting refers to focusing advocacy efforts on specific individuals, groups, or organizations to achieve desired results. It includes deciding who has to hear your message (the primary and secondary targets), how to make decision makers listen to your appeal, how to influence the public's knowledge and perception of the issue, what are the most compelling parts of your message, and who are the best messengers. Developing a targeting strategy involves analyzing the salience of an issue to those who shape public policy by examining their past records and recent pronouncements on the issue. It also involves determining who are the probable supporters and opponents and estimating the extent of their support or opposition (Olson & Green, 2009). Finally, it helps to identify the media outlets that are potentially friendly or hostile. Ideally, an organization should closely align its media strategy and its overall strategy (Minkler, 2012). (*See Chapter 13.*)

There are several ways to find out what you need to know. Obviously, it is important from the outset to be clear on what you want and need to know about targeted groups. Traditional methods include polling, public opinion surveys, and focus groups of representative sections of the public (Lake, 1987). Methods that are more sophisticated (and expensive) include media trend analyses and the statistical evaluation of data on the issue. In developing a targeting strategy, it is most effective to use different methods of analysis for each targeted group, different ways of conveying the message to each group (without abandoning the overall theme of your advocacy), and different messages at different stages of the advocacy process (Shaw, 2013).

Richan (2013) suggests that to maximize the effectiveness of advocacy efforts, it is useful to divide potential targets into the following four categories. The first category he terms "active allies." The goal with members of this population is to keep them engaged in the advocacy process and to provide them with supportive information in a timely manner.

The second group are "committed opponents." It is very difficult to change the perspective of this group. Richan recommends that the best approach is to ignore this group and redirect one's advocacy efforts to targets who might help advance your agenda.

A third group consists of uninvolved individuals or organizations. The goal here would be to obtain small, incremental commitments of support that might provide the foundation for more substantial commitments in the future. An example might be to call a legislator to express concern about a particular issue or to invite the lawmaker to attend a community meeting. The final category is "the ambivalent." The goal with this group is to get its members to acknowledge the existence of the problem as the starting point of an advocacy effort.

Based on this analysis, the next step is to determine which type of argument is best suited for each target and how it reflects the underlying premises of the overall advocacy message. Richan notes that there are three basic categories of arguments. One reflects the need to define an issue more clearly or redefine the problem. An example is to reframe substance abuse as a physical or psychological condition rather than the result of moral failing.

A second type of argument is a cause/effect argument. This form of argument reassesses the reason a problem or issue exists. For example, advocates might assert that a primary reason for homelessness is the lack of a sufficient supply of affordable housing, instead of the mental health conditions of the people at risk of homelessness.

The final type of argument is an argument that justifies taking action on the identified issue. This argument addresses four basic questions:

1. Why there is a need for policy change.
2. Whether the proposed policy change will meet that need.
3. Whether the policy change is fiscally, politically, and culturally feasible.
4. Whether the benefits of the policy change would outweigh any potential harmful consequences, including those that might affect third parties or society as a whole.

IN-CLASS EXERCISE
TARGETING ADVOCACY EFFORTS EFFECTIVELY

Introduction

Divide the class into groups of three or four students. Each group will have 30 minutes to answer the following questions and prepare a brief report to the class.

Scenarios

1. You are on the staff of the state chapter of a national organization, the Coalition for a Fair America. Its goal is to overturn the effects of recent federal policies that restrict the entry of immigrants and refugees to the United States. You have to decide how to frame the coalition's issues in the following communities:
   - **A.** A low-income African American neighborhood
   - **B.** A predominantly White, working-class community in an inner-ring suburb
   - **C.** A community with large numbers of Latino/a immigrants and Arab Americans
   - **D.** A relatively affluent, liberal, mid-size city
   - **E.** A mid-size, politically conservative city
2. You are on the staff of a community-based behavioral health agency that is working in cooperation with the county to implement a 10-year plan to eliminate homelessness. You have to identify how you might frame the initiative in various communities.
   - **A.** An organization of homeless people and providers of services to this population
   - **B.** A coalition of faith-based organizations
   - **C.** The business community in the county
   - **D.** A more rural community, where issues of housing and homelessness look different
   - **E.** A group of health and behavioral health professionals

Discussion Questions

1. What are the target's presumptions of reality and how might you modify them?
2. What are the presumed value preferences of the target? How can you integrate them into your argument?
3. Which of the following categories best characterizes your target(s)?
   - **A.** The active ally
   - **B.** The committed opponent
   - **C.** The uninvolved
   - **D.** The ambivalent
4. How would you recommend framing the issue around the category picked to advocate?
5. What are your goals in framing the issue in this way?
6. How will framing the issue as you recommended facilitate advocacy efforts?
7. How will you link framing the issue this way to your long-term strategy?
8. What questions/problems arose in your small group in discussing this situation?

Questions on the Nature of Your Advocacy Argument

1. Under which category does your argument best fit?
   - **A.** A (re)definition of the issue
   - **B.** A reinterpretation of cause/effect regarding the issue
   - **C.** An incitement to take action on an issue already recognized
2. Assess whether your argument addresses the following basic concerns:
   - **A.** Is there a need for change?
   - **B.** Does your proposed solution address this need?
   - **C.** Is your proposed solution feasible?
   - **D.** Would the benefits of your solution outweigh any harmful consequences?

Final Question for Discussion

How did the issues themselves shape the ways in which you framed them?

Developing Effective Advocacy Strategies

In general, effective advocacy involves making three separate appeals to your audience —to their heads (through information and ideas), to the hearts (through values and emotions), and to their pocketbooks (i.e., to their economic self-interest). No single approach works equally well with all audiences.

The best way to appeal to people's objective needs is through the clever use of data—always keeping in mind Mark Twain's aphorism: "There are lies, damn lies, and there are statistics." It is best to present statistics in a manner to which people can easily relate, using what advocates call "social math." When discussing the effect of a particular problem, large aggregate statistics can cause people's eyes to glaze over. (The Soviet dictator, Josef Stalin, once famously stated, "The death of one person is a tragedy; the death of millions is a statistic.")

In contrast, a statistic that makes the issue immediate can be quite effective. For example, in discussing the spread of homelessness, it is more powerful to state, "On a given night, x number of people in our community are at risk of homelessness," than to state, "Last year, x number of people experienced some form of homelessness." Similarly, when discussing the cost of a piece of legislation, such as a request for additional funding for individuals on general assistance, it is better to frame the request as "we are asking for 50 cents per person per day" than to request $x million.

A second approach that works is to manipulate the symbols of dominant actors. If lawmakers emphasize the importance of strengthening families, frame a request for universal pre-k programs as a means to achieve this goal. As stated previously, an alternative approach is to demonstrate how the policy position presented by key lawmakers contradicts their espoused values. For example, proposals to cut programs for job training contradict the stated value of encouraging work over welfare and promoting economic self-sufficiency (Chambers & Bonk, 2013).

A third approach consistent with social work values is to design policy solutions that maximize the effect on the most vulnerable intended beneficiaries (Rawls, 1999). Too often, in the interest of achieving a partial "victory," advocates accept a compromise that leaves their constituents little better off. While compromise is often necessary, when deciding what type of compromise is acceptable, advocates should never abandon their original purpose.

Effective advocacy also requires the creation of organizations that support policy goals. Sometimes this takes the form of an organization separate from the original HSO, one that can engage in advocacy-oriented activities that IRS rules prevent the HSO from participating in. At other times, the advocacy organization may use an existing or newly formed coalition to promote its goals (Shaw, 2013; Smucker, 2005).

In addition, advocacy strategies need to be flexible and adaptive to rapidly changing circumstances. These changes can be the result of unexpected economic developments, such as a recession, or the emergence of another issue that becomes a legislative priority, such as the effect of a natural disaster or political scandal. Finally, advocates need to overcompensate by appealing to the strongest component of their argument—for example, the proposal's long-term economic benefits, the humanitarian need it will address, or the rights the proposal will acknowledge.

Another element of an effective advocacy strategy is clarity on its overall goals. Is the primary purpose popular education, community mobilization, or a specific policy change? A goal might also be the development of increasing public receptivity to the issue to prepare for future advocacy efforts, or the creation of sustainable inter-organizational alliances.

IN-CLASS EXERCISE
ASSESSING AND SELECTING ADVOCACY TACTICS ON A CONTROVERSIAL POLICY

1. Identify the overall strategy and goals of proponents and opponents of comprehensive immigration reform. Assess whether their tactics match their overall strategies and goals.

	Strategy/Goals	Tactics	Examples
Pro			
Anti			

2. What have been the most/least effective tactics used by both sides in the debate?

	Most Effective	Least Effective	Reasons
Pro			
Anti			

3. Imagine the following scenario in the not-too-distant future: Congress passed and the president signed highly restrictive immigration legislation, comparable to legislation passed in the 1880s and 1920s.
   - What tactic(s) would you recommend be adopted in response to this situation?
   - How do these tactics fit together into a comprehensive strategy (campaign)? What goals would you propose?

Tactic	Relationship to Strategy

4. Identify those criteria you would use to assess the merit of the tactics you chose. What made you choose these criteria?

Criteria	Reasons for Selection
1.	
2.	
3.	
4.	
5.	
6.	
7.	
8.	
9.	
10.	

(You may add others)

Discussion Question

Apply the criteria you selected above to the tactic(s) you chose. Which tactics do or do not meet the criteria you identified?

Sources of Legislation

In most legislative bodies, there are four possible sources of legislation. One is a member of the legislature, often a legislative leader or chair of a major committee. Another is a legislative caucus, such as the Congressional Black Caucus or the House Freedom Caucus. A third is the executive branch of government, although this varies considerably among the states because different states give a different constitutional role to the governor that affects his or her power to influence policy decisions. Finally, external pressure groups, particularly those that are well established and well financed, can often propose legislation, usually in cooperation with legislative allies (Staller, 2017; Healy & Sofer, 2017).

There are important differences, however, between policy advocacy in Congress and advocacy in state or local legislatures because of the rules that govern the legislative process. Here are a few of the many differences:

1. State legislatures have more casual committee consideration than Congress, making it easier for advocates to become involved.
2. Party leaders (e.g., the speaker, majority leader, majority whip) play key roles in both settings but have a different array of powers depending on established procedures. Thus, it is important for advocates to learn the rules and the informal customs (Reisch, 2015a).
3. The influence of legislative caucuses is particularly important in one-party states. This means that the center of actual power may not reside in formal structures and advocates may need to do more of their work "behind closed doors" (Hoefer, 2017).
4. State legislatures override executive vetoes less often and reconvening state legislatures, which do not meet as frequently as Congress, is difficult. This implies that advocates need to try to get what they want in regular, not special, legislative sessions (Shaw, 2013).

Budget or Fiscal Advocacy in Legislatures

Budgets are the best indicators of a government's priorities. They are not value neutral. The process of budget development in state or local legislatures presents advocates with the opportunity to obtain additional resources for their constituents. It involves an assessment of both the revenue and expenditure sides of government policy making. It requires a sophisticated understanding of the components of the budgetary process, which varies from state to state. The budget process in Congress is also substantially different from that of state governments (Staller, 2017).

Despite these differences, there are common key points in the process:

- establishment of fiscal targets (usually by the leadership);
- committee budget and tax hearings;
- development of committee bills and tax estimates for those bills; and
- decisions in conference committees.

Advocates have an opportunity to influence the process at each of these stages. As the process advances, however, it becomes more difficult for advocates to have an effect (Healy & Sofer, 2017).

Budget or fiscal analysis focuses on:

1. The nature and adequacy of proposed revenues. What taxes exist? What potential sources of revenues does the government currently ignore? Which revenue sources have increased in recent years and which have declined? What laws, constitutional measures, or state propositions (ballot initiatives) govern the budget process, especially regarding taxation and resource allocation?
2. The economic and social effect of tax policies, especially on one's constituents.
3. The degree to which proposed expenditures are adequate—over time—to address evolving social needs. What are the long-term budget trends? How can advocates put a face on cold budget figures?
4. The role of key actors, such as the executive branch, prominent legislators, government agencies, and external interest groups, in the budgetary process (Rosenthal, 2006).

Budget Advocacy in the Executive Branch

As in budget advocacy in legislatures, it is important for advocates who want to influence the budget process in the executive branch to know the key points in the process. In most states, these include:

- determining the baseline budget for the coming fiscal year (for the entire state and each government department);
- forecasting revenues and expenditures based on projections on the economy and service utilization;
- developing agency maximum and minimum proposals; and
- creating a final budget for submission to the legislature.

In some states, the legislature cannot make substantive changes to the budget once the governor submits it. In other states, the legislature has considerable authority to add new taxes and reallocate projected revenues.

Specific tactics that advocates find helpful include:

- persuading the legislature to create a line item for a new program with a modest first-year investment;
- inserting specific language in the proposed budget regarding program requirements that provide some benefit to constituents rather than trying to pass a separate bill that has less political support; and
- intervening in as many points in the budget process as possible, particularly during the early stages of budget development. The key points in the process are:

(1) development of fiscal targets; (2) hearings of the committees responsible for the budget and taxes; (3) development of committee bills and revenue estimates for those bills; and (4) budget decisions made by conference committees to reconcile differences between the two houses of the legislature (Hoefer, 2016).

Advocacy groups in a number of states have used the budget process to enhance the well-being of their constituents. Examples include a tax check-off campaign for quality child care in Colorado; passage of a minimum family budget in the state of Washington; and New York's "counter-budget project," through which a diverse statewide coalition proposed an alternate budget to the one under consideration by the state legislature.

The 'Keys of Influence'

Advocates use several tools to enhance their ability to influence the outcome of the legislative process. They conduct extensive, ongoing research on the political orientations, voting records, and interests of legislators and their staffs. They provide technical and political information to legislators on a regular, proactive basis, not merely when they are asking for support. They maintain frequent, consistent, and constant contact with legislators and their staff members. Finally, they use informal, issue-specific groups to educate legislators on the substance of issues and the needs of their constituents (Reisch, 2015a). As discussed in a later section of this section, the personal qualities of advocates are critical in making these keys as influential as possible.

Legislative advocates who are promoting a specific piece of legislation increase their likelihood of success if they use the following tactics:

- introduce the bill early in the session before it gets lost in a flood of other legislation or the frantic conclusion of the legislative session when legislators are rushing to pass the state budget;
- get multiple sponsors ideally from both houses of the legislature and from both parties (and from factions within each party where they exist). Choose sponsors carefully. You want workhorses not show horses;
- get the support of both legislative leaders and the executive branch;
- in cooperation with constituents and allied organizations, orchestrate the hearing process as much as possible and coordinate contact with the media;
- use the amendment process when necessary to keep a piece of legislation alive; and
- above all—be patient! Policy making in legislatures usually takes years. For example, a bill introduced in the first year of a four-year legislative session may

not pass until the third year. (If a bill requires the additional outlay of funds or new taxes, it is less likely to pass in the fourth year of a legislative session when legislators are up for re-election.) (Hoefer, 2016; Shaw, 2013).

Advocates will inspire confidence if the information they provide is timely and balanced; they present viable, fiscally sound and political feasible alternatives; respond to other requests from legislators; and, above all in these times of fiscal austerity, they provide cost estimates and the programmatic consequences of different levels of funding (and do not just make demands for "more").

KEY CONCEPT SUMMARY
20 GUIDELINES FOR EFFECTIVE ADVOCACY

1. Know the rules (Alliance for Justice, Harmon, Ladd, & Evans, 2011).
2. Know the legislative calendar and legislative process.
3. Work year-round, not just during the legislative session.
4. Get to know the players in all areas that affect the policies in which you are interested.
5. Educate legislators about the issues on an ongoing basis by providing data in accessible formats.
6. Build relationships with key players inside and outside the legislature.
7. Target your advocacy efforts.
8. Support your constituents, not political parties or candidates.
9. Do the heavy lifting. Do not depend on legislative staff members.
10. Track and analyze relevant legislation.
11. Define your goals clearly.
12. Develop a well-thought-out legislative strategy that includes several contingency plans.
13. Provide data and research to support your position.
14. Provide information in accessible formats.
15. Target information to specific legislators.
16. Use multiple strategies to reach out, such as personal visits, drafting legislation, offering testimony, and working with the media.
17. Use coalitions and networks through phone calls, letters, email, hearings, rallies, and events.
18. Reach out to heads of executive departments.
19. Say "thank you!" in public to your supporters.
20. Follow up—monitor the implementation of the policy.

KEY CONCEPT SUMMARY
ADVOCACY ETIQUETTE—DO'S AND DON'TS

Always

- Return phone calls.
- Let them posture.
- Be self-critical—blow the whistle on yourself.
- Educate enemies.
- Find funding ideas.
- Rely on leadership and legislative "champions."
- Be honest.
- Frame the issue clearly and tailor it differently for each target.
- Keep the message as simple as possible.
- Admit ignorance and follow up quickly if needed.
- Be polite and positive.
- Use political capital frugally.
- Practice! Practice! Practice!

Never

- Embarrass public officials in public
- Threaten anyone
- Lie or "fake it"
- Write anyone off—ask questions instead
- Rely on numbers alone in counting votes
- Forget your long-term overall goals
- Be long-winded, self-righteous, rude, threatening, or demand anything
- Mention more than one bill at a time
- Remind legislators you are a taxpayer
- Be apologetic, vague, or deceptive
- Write only to those who agree with you
- Assume the legislator is an expert
- Give up—persistence matters!

Policy Advocacy in Conservative Times

Even in today's conservative political environment in which neoliberal or fiscally austere ideas are ascendant, it is still possible for advocates to find policy solutions (Feldman, Strier, & Koreh, 2016). As Nancy Amidei (1982) wrote 35 years ago, advocates can be effective in this climate, "but it means setting out deliberately to change public attitudes toward public programs and the people who benefit from them. That will require a conscious effort to set the record straight whenever misinformation about social programs or those who depend on them appears; it means joining with others to form 'truth squads' of people who view willing a better understanding of social programs as part of their civic or professional responsibility" (p. 38).

In times of fiscal austerity, it is also important to remember the cost of legislation and to locate new potential sources of revenue from both traditional funding streams and untapped areas. The days when advocates can simply "bang on the castle door" demanding "more!" are long over. It also helps to reduce the cost of proposed legislation, demonstrate its economic benefits, or show how it ultimately saves the government money.

It is also important for advocates to keep the big picture in mind and take the long view, by using policy advocacy as a means of building future efforts. This requires advocates to focus on winnable battles, instead of engaging in righteous but hopeless policy pursuits, and to identify minimum and optimum desirable outcomes in the short term. From the author's research (Reisch, 1987) and experience, consistency and constancy in advocacy work are critical factors that determine an organization's effectiveness, as is the importance of building a reputation as a realistic, informed, principled, and credible advocate.

KEY CONCEPT SUMMARY
TWO BASIC RULES OF POLICY ADVOCACY

1. Nothing happens overnight.
2. You can't change rule No. 1.

IN-CLASS EXERCISE
DELIVERING AN 'ELEVATOR SPEECH'

Introduction

You are seeking a change in a policy based on an issue that affects the community in which you live or work. This could involve the enactment of a new law, the revision of an existing law, new funding for a program or an increase in government funding, the addition or modification of an administrative regulation, etc. Assume that you have been working with a group (or coalition) to bring this issue to the attention of the public and key policy makers. This has involved meeting with legislators, department heads and their staffs, and testifying at legislative hearings and/or "town hall" events.

One day while you are in Washington (or your state capital, city hall, or the offices of the county government), you find yourself riding alone in an elevator with a key legislator or administrator whose influence is critical in getting the policy change you are seeking. He or she is someone you have previously attempted to meet without success. You have 60 seconds to introduce yourself and present a brief summary of your group's advocacy message. Your goal is to learn the policy maker's position on your proposal and/or to get her or him to agree to schedule an appointment with you.

Part I

1. Divide the class into groups of three or four students.
2. Each group should identify an issue for its advocacy and the key components of its message and draft a "script" for the elevator speech.
3. Each group should identify two members to deliver the message.
4. Each group should rehearse its message.

Part II

1. Each group will take turns role-playing its elevator speech. (Either the instructor or a member of another group will play the role of the legislator or administrator.) The instructor will time the speeches and cut off the students at exactly 60 seconds.
2. After each presentation, students will comment upon their classmates' speeches and have the opportunity to redo their speeches based on these critiques if they desire.

Part III

After each group has practiced its elevator speech, the class will process the exercise as a whole to extract general points on advocacy from students' experiences.

Community-Based Policy Advocacy

Community-based policy advocacy combines approaches used in community organizing, popular education, and participatory development. From community organizing, it borrows a focus on mobilizing geographic communities or communities of identity (Formicola & Hernandez-Cordero, 2011). From popular education, it emphasizes the importance of experience, dialogue, and consciousness-raising (Kane, 2001; Freire, 2013). Similar to participatory development, it assumes that people in the community should "drive" the change process (Schneider & Libercier, 1995; Nelson & Wright, 1995). The overall goal of community-based advocacy is to create an alternative structure through which people articulate and meet their own needs over the long haul, and work with marginalized groups to gain collective power to shape existing systems for the better (Minkler, 2012).

The core values of community-based advocacy include maximum participation, social justice, capacity building, prioritizing the interests of the most vulnerable populations, community control, sharing power, sustainability, and taking the long view. Advocates who engage in this type of advocacy share certain core attitudes and beliefs. They regard community members as constituents or allies, not clients. They have confidence in the wisdom of the people. They adopt a role of learner and listener who asks questions. Finally, they use a variety of participatory tools and techniques to build community members' confidence, strengthen relationships, and engage in a process of mutual education (Israel et al., 2010).

Unlike traditional, top-down advocacy methods, community-based policy advocacy reflects objectives that go beyond the passage of a particular piece of legislation. Besides being more consistent with democratic values and social work's emphasis on empowerment, one goal of this form of advocacy is to create a constituency for change by framing issues in a manner that increases public support and accountability among policy makers. Another goal is to expand the participation of those affected by problems and policies in the policy-making process. A third goal is to monitor the media's portrayal of issues that affect one's constituents (Shaw, 2013).

A number of factors affect the degree and intensity of a community's participation. One factor is the community's values and behavioral norms, particularly whether there is conflict or consensus within the community on the issue, and whether the community has previously been active around this issue and with what result (Martinson & Minkler, 2006). Another is the structure of the participation process—for example, whether existing policies facilitate or constrain public participation—and the nature of community participation required to produce meaningful outcomes (Bowes & Sims, 2006).

Internal factors within the community are also critical. These include the presence or absence of internal boundaries and the strength or weakness of intra-community and intercommunity relationships (i.e., the level of bonding and bridging social capital).

The degree of demographic and cultural homogeneity or heterogeneity within a community is also critical because it determines the leadership structure of the community, the extent and intensity of organization within the community, the manner in which the community makes key decisions, and the location of power and influence in the community (Theiss-Morris & Hibbing, 2005). Think about how you would assess these factors in a community in which you live or work.

KEY CONCEPT SUMMARY
10 STEPS IN PARTICIPATORY ADVOCACY

1. Research the issue(s)
2. Engage in outreach to current and potential constituents
3. Jointly forge an overall idea
4. Jointly craft a vision for change
5. Define and plan the advocacy project
6. Create the organizational structure
7. Increase the capacity of the organization
8. Develop adequate resources and support
9. Build a grassroots network
10. Implement the project vision

The promotion of heightened community engagement recognizes certain constraints that may limit the potential of civic participation (Hindsworth & Lang, 2009). One constraint is the existence of racially, economically, and culturally homogeneous communities whose members have little experience working with populations or organizations from different backgrounds. This raises a fundamental question: Under what conditions can diverse populations learn to work together in an advocacy effort (Manzo & Perkins, 2006)? Another is the distrust many people justifiably share about politics in the broadest sense—a distrust that frequently produces cynicism or apathy (Rosenvallon & Goldhammer, 2008). Ironically, particularly in the initial stages of an advocacy campaign, the more people participate in policy advocacy, the more they come to possess negative views of government. In addition, the goals of a group or community may on occasion be incompatible with the use of democratic decision-making processes. Community members also often have limited time to become involved effectively in advocacy campaigns. This reality compounds the risk of widespread "free rider syndrome" emerging within the community (Skocpol & Fiorina, 2004).

Despite these obstacles and challenges, proponents of community engagement assume that heightened civic participation builds interpersonal trust, increases people's self-awareness, expands their skill set, and increases a community's level of both bonding and bridging social capital. To overcome the inertia of nonparticipation, advocates can help community members identify the beliefs, attitudes, misinformation, and imagery that underlie the status quo. Once this occurs, they can help neutralize and counter status quo ideas by replacing them with new alternative perspectives.

To be successful in mobilizing previously disengaged communities, advocates must overcome a number of personal challenges as well. They have to learn to listen and recognize how their ignorance of other cultures can be an obstacle to their work. They have to examine their underlying assumptions about their targets for mobilization. They need to avoid the naïve view that insists people should always not only do the right thing, but that they should also do it for the right reasons. Finally, in their practice repertoire they need to integrate a strategy of community participation with other change strategies, such as the use of social media (Ekman & Amna, 2012; Brulle, 2010). Mobilizing a community's civic capacity almost always involves a major dislocation of the status quo. The overall challenge is how to encourage community participation in a large enough sphere of activities to make a difference but not so large as to constitute an impossible task for community members.

Why is this so difficult? One reason is that political participation is foreign to the experience of most community members (Portney & Berry, 1997). Another is that few individuals have experience working cooperatively with people from different racial, class, and cultural backgrounds (Costa & Kahn, 2003). A third reason is the hyper-specialization of employment, including in the social work field.

Different groups use a variety of models to overcome these problems. The Industrial Areas Foundation (IAF)—the descendant of the organizations Saul Alinsky created from the late 1930s to the early 1970s—relies on the common values of faith communities to serve as a binding element when attempting to organize and mobilize diverse populations (Coles, 2004; Robinson & Hanna, 1994). IAF organizers believe this facilitates the formation of linkages between leaders across racial and class lines by fusing religious traditions and power politics (Warren, 2016). In their model, lay leaders play a central role in the advocacy process; it is not restricted solely to leaders of established organizations. This approach reflects a conception of power as "power to" rather than "power over."

Other models place greater emphasis on the use of technology to enhance civic participation in policy change efforts. Although social media have been effective in disseminating information and mobilizing people to take collective action more rapidly, advocates who rely on technology need to recognize the importance of equity and equality in the distribution of this technology and its effects. The key issues here are the importance of humanizing the application of technology, ensuring equitable participation in decisions made by technological means, stressing interactivity among diverse participants, and focusing on the need to build a supportive community among alternative networks and virtual communities (Uldam & Vestergaard, 2015). A fundamental question, however, is whether people can "do" politics solely in a virtual setting, or if some synthesis of in-person human contact and digital relationships is more effective in the contemporary political environment.

Why People Participate

Community members participate in community-based advocacy both as a response to "negatives" in their environment and also for proactive purposes. Among the former are a sense of violation (e.g., the Black Lives Matter movement), loss or a fear of loss of economic security, social status, or physical well-being (e.g., the Tea Party), the existence of a threat or perceived threat, and the effect of a catastrophic event such as a hurricane. Examples of a proactive purpose include a desire for individual or group economic gain, the creation or strengthening of community identity, the need to express deeply held values (e.g., the evangelical movement), and a desire to prevent a problem from occurring or becoming worse.

The goals of community-based advocacy, therefore, can include concrete gains such as a redistribution of resources and power, a specific policy change, or greater accountability of elected officials. They can also include more intangible successes, such as heightened community, media, and public awareness of issues; changes in people's attitudes, behaviors, or relationships; and the development of a strong constituency for lasting policy change.

The transformation of how people conceptualize power is one of the most important aspects of community-based advocacy. Traditional ways of viewing power focus on control over resources, access to hierarchies, the ability to punish, reward, or sanction, the status of organizational affiliation, and personal charisma or connections. Successful community-based advocacy, however, can revise people's previous conceptions of power. Rather than regarding power as a finite commodity, community members can learn to view power as infinite and relationship-based; rather than defining power as "power over," define it as "power with" and "power within." In community-based advocacy, the construction of relational power has a number of sources: knowledge, numbers, discipline, vision, diversity, creativity, persistence, humor, courage, organization, and collective responsibility. (*See Chapter 2 for further discussion of power.*)

In sum, in policy advocacy, community-based power can mean several things:

- ability to effect a policy change;
- ability to determine alternatives or set the agenda;
- ability to influence the terms of policy discourse; and
- ability to prevent change.

Classroom Discussion

1. What should be the limits of a community's power around an advocacy issue?
2. What should you do if the community or its leaders are bigoted or corrupt or if they express values that conflict with social work values?

Essential Ingredients of Community-Based Advocacy

To make the transition from traditional models of advocacy to one that prioritizes community participation, advocates must take several steps. First, they must recognize that the definition of community or societal problems and issues must begin with those groups most affected. This requires extensive dialogue, collective research, and in-depth analysis to enable the community to "own" the process and influence the vision driving the advocacy effort. By analyzing the problem in this manner, community members have the opportunity to increase their understanding of issues and to clarify their self-interest in resolving them. Peer communication to achieve this objective also contributes to building social capital and raising critical consciousness.

Second, the community needs to create the organizational mechanisms and structures that will facilitate a systematic, collective approach to problem solving and decision making. Through this structure, the community can establish its own goals and objectives for the advocacy campaign. Third, the community must take action to test the viability of its goals and objectives in the crucible of reality. Finally, the community needs to be involved in the evaluation of the advocacy effort in an ongoing manner, not merely at the conclusion.

Taking these steps, however, is not without challenges. Advocates need to address two fundamental questions when they attempt to promote greater community participation. One question concerns how to balance competing interests within diverse communities and between the affected community and stakeholders outside the community. A related question that is particularly pertinent today is how to manage the growing complexity of interests in a geographically dispersed, politically divided, and economically and culturally diverse nation.

Some means of creating a sense of common purpose include encouraging more intragroup and intergroup dialogue, developing new and more egalitarian collaborative networks, and revising the focus of existing inter-organizational entities. The objective is to create a climate of discovery to build a strong case of the need for policy change. This involves multiple steps:

1. Careful assessment of the competing and complementary interests and goals of participating organizations.
2. In-depth analysis of the complex factors that shape the current policy environment.

3. Use of a variety of methods to diagnose the situation and to frame an advocacy message in a manner that enhances the possibility of positive change.
4. Construction of a database of allies, supporters, and potential bridge builders.
5. Willingness to break from traditional advocacy patterns and be more inclusive in decision making, goal setting, strategy development, and leadership selection.

KEY CONCEPT SUMMARY
STEPS TO PROMOTE COMMUNITY PARTICIPATION IN ADVOCACY

1. Establish Overarching Values and Norms
    - Reorientation of values (prioritizing human needs, not profit)
    - Inclusivity
    - Equal opportunity; removal of barriers
    - Emphasis on constituents' beliefs
    - Stating issues in a clear and comprehensible manner
    - Creating incentives for community building
    - Reciprocity of exchange (principles of equality, mutuality, and commitment)
2. Restructure the Process of Participation
    - Focus on fairness and inclusivity
    - Emphasize partnership, not competition
    - Promote community cohesion (regarding vision, identity, goals)
    - Stress an egalitarian view of leadership, power, and control
3. Clarify the Nature of Participation
    - Focus on genuine participation not the "efficiency" of task completion
    - Emphasize breadth, depth, and frequency of community participation
    - Prioritize the strengthening of intra-community relationships
    - Promote individual responsibility, mutual accountability, and reciprocity
    - Place community interests and goals above individual choice and freedom
    - Develop a shared conception of the knowledge needed to participate
    - Understand the role of internal and external policies
    - Be clear on the level of government to be targeted
    - Understand the limited effect of policies and services
    - Identify the source, type, and extent of resources needed
    - Be clear on the role of professionals in the advocacy process and the nature of their formal and informal helping roles

4. Identify Community Boundaries and Relationships
    - Establish a clear identification of "we" and "they"
    - Distinguish between deep and broad relationships
    - Clarify local and global issues and goals
5. Define the Overall Purpose of Community Participation
    - Big vs. small decisions
    - Narrow vs. broad role

Enhancing Community Participation

Fabricant and Burghardt (1992) outline five stages in the promotion of greater community participation in advocacy. First, it is essential to explain to constituents how major changes in the political economy and the sociocultural environment shape the issues about which they are concerned. Second, advocates must help constituents assess how current policies and programs affect their daily lives. Third, they have to be realistic and evaluate conditions as they are rather than as they ought to be. Fourth, they need to devise a new form of political action suitable to the history, culture, and strengths of constituents. Finally, they have to recognize and learn from past successes and failures in efforts to influence policy around similar issues. Advocates must apply critical analysis of these issues throughout the advocacy process, particularly when working with increasingly isolated communities.

Mondros and Wilson (1994) add that constituents must play a significant role in four aspects of an advocacy campaign: (1) its overall orientation to the change process; (2) the development of outcome and process goals; (3) the selection of targets; and (4) the identification and assessment of available resources. Wallack et al. (1999) point out the importance of clarity regarding goals before an advocacy group can develop effective overall media strategies.

In sum, advocates must answer five critical questions in cooperation with their constituents:

1. What is the problem or issue?
2. What is the solution?
3. Who (e.g., an individual, an institution) has the power to make the necessary change (i.e., solve the problem)?
4. Who must we mobilize to apply pressure for change?
5. What message would persuade those with power to act for change?

Answering these questions helps advocates initially focus their target selection.

Next, advocates and community members must break down the target identification process in more detail. They need to determine whom they should approach first to obtain access to those with decision-making power (i.e., the gatekeepers). They need to assess the strengths and weaknesses of each potential target and determine what is in their self-interest. Based on this assessment, advocates then have to figure out how to acquire power or influence over key decision makers. Alternately, they need to decide whether redefining the issue would change their targets and their overall strategy of persuasion (Shaw, 2013).

In working with diverse community groups, it is equally important to pay attention to the internal processes involved in making critical strategic choices. After advocacy groups clearly define the scope of their decision-making process, they should articulate a few breakthrough choices in order to map a narrative of change. This helps create a road map for future decision making and define simple rules or principles that can transform the complexity of community members' interests into a common purpose (Olson, 2009). This may involve the development and mobilization of new networking vehicles of people rather than a coalition of organizational representatives.

Based on his extensive study of social movements, Tilly (1978) found that the likelihood of a group's collective action is a function of the following six factors:

1. The extent of its shared interests.
2. The intensity of its organization.
3. The degree the organization is mobilized.
4. The degree of repression that exists in the environment.
5. The amount of power it possesses.
6. The existence of an opportunity and/or a threat.

A variety of structural and environmental conditions influences these factors. These include the community's long-standing values and behavioral norms, the structure of the participation process, the presence or absence of strong internal community boundaries and intergroup relationships, the extent of bonding and bridging social capital, and the historical role of advocacy organizations and other nonprofit agencies in the community (Ostrom, 2014).

Despite this complexity, macro social workers can intervene in a number of ways to promote enhanced community participation in advocacy efforts. They can be what the French and Quebecois refer to as an *animateur*, who inspires greater community activism (Quirion, 1972) by stimulating people's critical awareness. Social workers can also help organize community groups or facilitate greater participation by existing groups. Lastly, they can serve as a liaison between the community and outside advocacy groups (Reisch, Wenocur, & Sherman, 1981–1982).

In the latter scenario, advocates can enhance a community's level of participation through several means. They can initiate dialogue between community members and allies outside the community to develop "outside the box," policy-oriented solutions to community problems and create a sense of common purpose. Through dialogue, they can create a process of inquiry and construct counter-narratives to connect people's conditions to their systemic roots and to the actions required to address them. In addition, social workers can help the community build a database of allied and potential "bridge builders." This helps establish new networking vehicles that can be mobilized for future efforts, articulate a few breakthrough choices, and produce a road map for advocacy strategies (Isaacs, 1996).

It is also important for social workers to determine what type of community participation an advocacy organization desires or needs in a particular social action campaign (Speer et al., 2003). For example, should the primary role of community members be to help frame community problems and issues and identify those who are most affected? Alternately, should their role be to identify the underlying causes of the problems and to contribute to the development of policy solutions and strategies to achieve them? Should communities contribute to the development of a policy solution or advocacy strategy based upon predetermined options? How should the community contribute to the implementation of that strategy? Finally, in what ways should the community help evaluate the outcome of the advocacy effort? Overall, advocates need to decide which participatory roles are most suitable for a *particular community* within a *specific advocacy campaign*, and how the advocacy process facilitates or impedes the community's participation (McNutt & Boland, 2007). This is particularly important when developing advocacy strategies in communities that have traditionally been excluded from the policy-making process.

In this regard, advocates face three recurrent challenges: (1) how to mobilize and sustain a community's interest in taking organized political action; (2) how to link a community's sense of civic obligation to political participation; and (3) how to use the community's strengths and available tools, such as technology, effectively to promote greater community participation. The following chart lists 10 ways advocates can increase the likelihood of a community's sustained involvement in the advocacy process.

KEY CONCEPT SUMMARY
10 INGREDIENTS TO PROMOTE SUSTAINED COMMUNITY PARTICIPATION

1. Knowledge of the issue
2. Sound organizational structure
3. Effective intragroup communication
4. Clear distribution of responsibilities

5. Established accountability for performing assigned tasks
6. Skills in the resolution of the conflicts that inevitably arise
7. Conscious efforts to redress long-standing inequalities in the community
8. Creation of a sense of common community, particularly among diverse groups
9. Development of trust among community members and between external advocacy groups and the community
10. The use of praxis—the ongoing integration of action and reflection—by all participants in the advocacy process

Social workers can also help promote internal organizational cohesion and intragroup solidarity through the means by which community members express these values. As facilitators and educators, they can assist people undertake specific actions, such as strategy development or the drafting of policy documents. In their broker role, social workers can serve as intermediaries with other organizations, enable residents to establish external contacts, and introduce people with limited advocacy experience to unfamiliar processes. This helps community members develop alliances and participate more effectively in established networks and coalitions.

Ethical Issues in Community-Based Advocacy

As in all forms of macro social work practice, ethical issues arise even in the best-intentioned efforts to promote community participation in advocacy campaigns (Hynes, 2017). One ethical issue emerges from the unequal relationship between advocates and constituents. Advocates generally possess more power, greater familiarity with the issues and the advocacy process, and higher levels of technical skill. Above all, they assume less risk by their involvement in policy advocacy (Reamer, 2013).

There is also the issue of distinguishing between the "mobilization" and the "manipulation" of constituents. Advocates must consider at what point do their efforts to mobilize a community cross the line into paternalistic behavior (Ezell, 2001). This relates to the ethical and practical question of who determines the priorities of an advocacy campaign (McCarthy, 1998). How much of a role should community self-determination play? This is a particularly important issue because advocates may take the "long view" while community members may assume that their participation will produce more immediate benefits. Finally, the inevitable compromises that accompany the policy advocacy process raise the issue of when compromise (for whatever reasons) betrays a community's interests, or when the community perceives any compromise as a form of betrayal.

Advocates must also constantly address a number of other persistent practical issues to increase the possibility of success for community-based efforts. Above all, they have to figure out how to balance the value-driven goals of community mobilization with political feasibility—that is, how to achieve both process and outcome objectives. In other words, how can advocates balance doing the right thing and doing it for the right reasons?

In addition, advocates must determine under what conditions members of a diverse community can collaborate in a coordinated effort. This is particularly challenging in today's diverse and divisive climate. Particularly in communities with a scant history of political participation and in communities whose residents deal with a variety of daily stress factors, advocates must be creative in their attempt to involve community members in the policy advocacy process and to sustain their involvement in the face of repeated setbacks and disappointments. An issue with particular relevance today is how to enable virtual communities (i.e., those based primarily in social media) to do "politics" or engage in common efforts to promote social change (Uldam & Vestergaard, 2015; Hick & McNutt, 2002; Blanchard & Horan, 1998).

Advocacy Coalitions

As discussed in Chapter 5, a coalition is an organization that reflects an agreement among individuals or groups to cooperate in joint action for a common cause while preserving its own self-interest. The alliance may be temporary or semi-permanent. It may be a matter of shared principle, convenience, or necessity (*See chapters five and 10 for further discussion of coalitions.*)

Coalitions represent a form of collaboration in which individuals and groups who share a common interest work together in pursuit of that interest. Under various names—coalition, alliance, campaign, or network—their activities could include anything from sharing information to taking joint action on a legislative advocacy project.

In today's environment, it is particularly important for social workers to be aware of the importance of building and sustaining multicultural coalitions. "Broad-based coalitions allow groups of disparate interests to consolidate their resources for greater impact" (Amidei, 1982, p. 41). They have other benefits as well. Coalitions can enable advocacy groups, particularly those with limited resources, to access hard-to-find information and use partners' connections to establish relationships with key decision makers. Through collaborative endeavors, low-power advocacy groups can learn from the experience of their more established partners and build relationships for future action. Especially in today's partisan environment, participating in a coalition can help marginalized groups avoid political and social isolation by strengthening their connections with a larger, like-minded community (Shaw, 2013).

From an internal, organizational perspective, coalition work allows advocates to "borrow power" and use diverse sources of support to achieve policy goals. When coalitions function well, they share workload and resources, provide important efficiencies for cash-poor groups, and help to build newly established organizations. On a less tangible note, coalitions promote inter-organizational cohesion and social solidarity, creating a small-scale model of a just, multicultural society (Bobo, Kendall, & Max, 2001).

Nevertheless, many organizations, especially those in minority communities, fear participation in coalitions with majority-dominated organizations (Delgado, 1993). They are concerned that differences around goals, strategies, or tactics could result in paralysis and reluctance to work together toward common ends. They worry that coalition work could drain time and energy from constituents and diminish the overall value of the investment. With some justification, they fear loss of control over the policy agenda and over the methods used to achieve it. Lastly, they dread losing their autonomy in the competition to determine the coalition's direction.

To attain the potential benefits of coalition work and diminish these realistic fears, it is essential for advocates to find an issue that unites diverse populations, even if the issue affects these constituencies in different ways, or if the constituencies initially frame the issue differently (Barvosa-Carter, 2001). Advocates should also be clear on why it is essential to create the coalition to resolve the issue. In general, coalitions are not useful vehicles to create an issue. They are, however, potentially effective mechanisms to heighten public awareness of an issue and build support for a policy solution.

When working with an existing organization, it is also important to be clear about what contribution one's group would bring to the coalition and how participation in the coalition would advance the interests of the organization and its constituents. Advocates need to keep in mind that "working in a coalition makes it possible to track several issues at the same time, while still maintaining specialized expertise" (Amidei, 1982, p. 41).

Dialogue helps potential partners identify common goals and develop short-term projects that help the coalition frame the issue(s) in a more consistent message. It also helps identify the historical and contemporary factors that might facilitate the coalition's formation or impede the progress of its work. This requires critical analysis of how each group within the coalition could apply its strengths and diminish the negative effect of potential barriers to cooperation (Alexander et al., 2004). Finally, advocates need to be conscious that while a coalition may not be a permanent entity, one's organization and the needs and interests of one's constituents may be.

So, when should a group join an advocacy coalition? Here are some general guidelines:

- when joining the coalition will further the organization's agenda on an issue that is a high priority for the organization;
- when the organization has the capacity to commit resources and time to the coalition;
- when joining the coalition will not have any adverse effects on constituents; and
- when no other strategic options exist. In other words, the trade-offs are worth it.

If an advocacy organization decides not to participate in a coalition—for whatever reasons—it has several options. It can continue to build and strengthen its relationships with key individuals and groups working on similar issues and continue to share critical information through existing networks. It can work independently on the issue and keep potential future partners informed on its progress. It can collaborate with other groups in less intensive and costly ways, such as organizing a single event (e.g., a press conference) or a short-term activity (e.g., a petition drive). Lastly, it could work on a "parallel track" toward the same goal.

There are a few caveats particularly relevant to forming multicultural alliances. Coalitions are foreign to most people. It is important, therefore, to overcome distrust through acts, not words (Crowfoot & Chesler, 2003). To equalize inter-organizational relationships, it is useful to rotate or share leadership roles and responsibilities and to ensure that the funding sources for the coalition do not create or recreate imbalances among the participants. Keep in mind that a successful coalition needs leaders who are socially diverse, exhibit different leadership styles, and possess different skill sets. (*See Chapter 6 for further discussion of leadership.*)

In a multicultural coalition, it is essential that all partners be aware of the effects of race, gender, class, sexual orientation, and immigration status on members' behavior (Bystydzienski & Schacht, 2001). It often helps to develop a multiple identity for the coalition or create a new identity (Barvosa-Carter, 2001). It is equally important to level the skill and knowledge playing field (e.g., regarding technology), to take risks in the development of strategies and tactics, and to be sensitive to decision-making processes and leadership selection (Steinstra, Waztke, & Birch, 2007).

Finally, to build an effective diverse coalition, partners need to think "outside the box" in choosing potential allies (Ungar, 2001). This requires the coalition to leave space for the creation of a shared agenda and to have sufficient flexibility to revise the group's goals as other organizations join the coalition. Internally, coalition partners should create informal time and space to build interpersonal relationships and trust. The coalition also needs to establish the central importance of diversity before its initial meeting (Luihbeid & Khokha, 2001). Diversity means differences and the organization should prepare how it will respond before any conflict-laden differences arise.

Reflection and Classroom Discussion

1. What types of diversity best fit the strategy you would adopt to pursue a particular policy goal?
2. Which groups are essential for your coalition to succeed?

KEY CONCEPT SUMMARY
GROUND RULES FOR SUSTAINING EFFECTIVE DIVERSE COALITIONS

- Mutual respect: Do not question the motives or commitment of others.
- Criticize partners' ideas, not their persons. Keep all criticisms within the group.
- Give credit to others and hold each other accountable.
- Do not permit hidden agendas.
- Strategize collectively—make sure all voices are heard when making decisions.
- Discuss the "undiscussables" (race, gender, etc.).
- Agree to disagree while contributing to the best of your ability. Take time to manage conflict and solve internal problems.
- Get to know partners well and be a good partner.
- Do not confuse words with actions.

Evaluating Advocacy Efforts

As in all forms of practice, evaluating one's advocacy efforts is critical for a number of reasons and involves several components. First, an **outcome evaluation** measures, as objectively as possible, what an advocacy campaign actually achieved. For example, did it pass a particular piece of legislation or obtain certain budget concessions?

Second, a **process evaluation** determines what strategies and tactics worked or did not work in the advocacy campaign. Was testimony effective? Did media outreach influence public opinion? Were efforts to forge alliances successful? An evaluation also demonstrates the relative efficacy of the advocacy organization to funders, potential political supporters, constituents, and the public. Finally, it helps the organization find ways to improve future efforts (Starling, 2010).

Evaluating the advocacy process also requires an assessment of short-term, medium-term, and long-term results. This is particularly important for community-based advocacy. This assessment addresses such questions as how did the organization make decisions? Who made the decisions? Was the decision-making process effective? Was it genuinely participatory? What actually happened when the organization engaged in strategy development? For example, how did it select targets and decide on its framing message? Finally, which parts of the community actively engaged in the advocacy effort and to what extent? An effective process evaluation requires both direct and indirect observations (Teles & Schmitt, 2011).

A third component of evaluating advocacy involves monitoring the overall policy context. This includes assessing the effect of an advocacy effort on the internal functioning of the advocacy group, organization, or coalition. It also involves assessing the effects of the campaign on the organization's reputation, public opinion, the targets of advocacy, and relationships with allies, affiliated groups, political supporters, funders, and the media.

In addition, assessing the outcome effect of an advocacy effort requires a clear definition of what constitutes "success." This needs to occur at the outset of the advocacy campaign, not at its conclusion. It also requires the use of a combination of objective and subjective measures. Advocates must analyze what the campaign produced and what were the consequences of each substantive outcome. The challenges here are to analyze cause and effect with validity and reliability. For example, how can you determine what would have happened if the organization had not launched an advocacy campaign? What social or political indicators could the organization use in the evaluation? Finally, and perhaps of greatest importance, the organization has to determine whether the achievements of the advocacy campaign were worth the effort (Shaw, 2013).

Other challenges in conducting a comprehensive evaluation include the lack of time, resources, and expertise. Evaluating an advocacy campaign is both similar to and different from evaluating a program or policy change (Coffman, 2007). In addition, some organizations may resist conducting an evaluation because they perceive it as a distraction from other purposes. Finally, there may be internal disagreements about definitions (for example, of effective "participation"), or over how to measure the accomplishments of the advocacy campaign (i.e., whether it was "successful").

Organizations can use a number of mechanisms to assist them in their advocacy efforts. Polling is a common tool that organizations employ. If this is the primary means the organization uses to evaluate its advocacy it needs to answer two questions before it initiates the polling: What information does it really need to know and why does it want this information? Answering these questions contributes to the preparation of a meaningful sample and an effective questionnaire. Once the polling is completed, the organization needs to analyze the results thoroughly and draw only limited implications from the data.

Throughout the evaluation process, the organization also needs to be careful to avoid a number of potential pitfalls. In preparing participatory polls, these failings include insufficient training of volunteer coders and interviewers, inadequate construction of the poll questions, poor selection of the survey sample, sloppy record keeping, and overreliance on the wrong outside experts. Once data are collected, possible problems include overanalyzing the results, focusing on meaningless relationships, overstating the connections between cause and effects, and confusing changes in the attitudes and behaviors of the public and key decision makers. Overall, evaluators need to be sure not to ignore the effect of the context in which the advocacy campaign occurred.

Hoefer (2016) developed an "advocacy map" to assess a group's advocacy efforts. Elements of the map include clarity on the specific issues addressed; desired short-term and long-term outcomes; assessment of available resources, and those the organization acquired or created; and an analysis of how well the organization fulfilled required tasks—in other words, who did what, when, how, and how effectively. In addition, the map evaluates the short-term, intermediate, and long-term outcomes of an advocacy campaign, particularly regarding its effect on the ultimate social justice outcomes for affected communities and society as a whole.

Another component of the mapping process involves monitoring the different components of the context in which an advocacy effort occurs. These include the effect of the context on the dynamics of the organization and its reputation, relationships within the organization's community and with outside groups, and the response of the media and the public at large to the organization's work. To put it simply, evaluating an advocacy effort requires an organization to determine what would have happened had it done nothing, and to identify exactly what occurred due to its efforts. This requires a comparison of "baseline" data with the results of its advocacy campaign through the use of direct and indirect observations (surveys, focus groups, open-ended interviews with key informants, analyzing media coverage) in order to obtain critical assessments from multiple sources. The ultimate objective of this mapping is to revise the organization's advocacy strategy based on this assessment.

Table 12.1 presents a five-part framework for assessing the effects of community participation in an advocacy effort.

Table 12.1 A 5-Part Framework for Evaluating Community Participation

Axis 1: Principles to Measure Community Power and Participation in Decision Making	• All stakeholders will have equal access to information. • Decision-making principles will be based on human rights. • The organization will ensure that everyone has the right to contribute to the advocacy agenda, so it ultimately reflects the entire community's will. No one will be voiceless. • All final decisions will be transparent. • The organization will reach critical decisions by consensus. Decision-making power is shared, autonomous, and nonhierarchical. The organization will rotate leadership.
Axis 2: Identification of the Community's Boundaries	• The community's boundaries will be clear, but permeable. • The organization will strive to develop a positive, self-determined identity that external forces will accept. The process will reflect an attempt to give every member a sense of belonging, history, and continuity. • The organization will reflect respect and appreciation of diversity in all its forms. • The organization will seek to empower members to find their unique place in the community's advocacy process. • The organization will foster positive relationships between individuals, systems, and institutions both inside and outside the community. • The organization's processes will reflect a common standard of behavioral norms.

Axis 3: Utilizing the Community's Needs, Strengths, and Assets	• Community residents will participate fully in defining their own needs, strengths, weaknesses, assets, and goals in order to emphasize its strength and address its weaknesses. • The community will contribute to the creation of well-defined goals in its advocacy efforts. • The organization will allow outsiders to be involved if they operate from an empowerment framework (as opposed to a deficiency model) in assessing the community's interests and goals in an advocacy campaign. The organization would use outsiders to provide consultation and recommendations based upon community input.
Axis 4: Community Relationships and Problem Solving	• The organization will strive to be a safe place for community members. It would be characterized by inclusivity and reciprocity, and the existence of dynamic relationships between individuals and groups. It would ensure that it treats different subgroups within the community with mutual respect. • The organization will develop mechanisms to handle internal and external conflicts effectively and to ensure that the solutions it produces are responsive to stakeholders. • The organization will share knowledge, resources, assets, and power with all community members to the extent possible.
Axis 5: External Structures and Community Well-Being	• The organization will attempt to ensure that external institutions take into consideration the wants, needs, and cultural diversity of the community. • The organization will strive to create open communication with external structures. • In developing policy solutions and advocacy strategies, the organization will make every effort to make decisions on behalf of the community rather than having decisions imposed from outside. The goal is for the community to have the ability to advocate for itself and possess sufficient power to be self-determining. • The organization will prioritize a healthy sharing of knowledge, assets, resources, and power.

IN-CLASS SIMULATION EXERCISE
POWER BROKER

Objectives and Timing

The purpose of this simulation is for participants to gain experience in bargaining and negotiation, wielding power and influence, understanding what it is like to possess or lack power, and engaging in coalition building as they try to obtain political support to establish one or more social welfare-related programs in the community. The challenge is that there are many more proposed programs than there are resources to support them.

The simulation takes about 90 minutes, with 16–25 an ideal number of players; 12 players is a minimum for a viable simulation. It is possible to conduct the simulation with more than 25 players but it will take longer and the facilitator will need to adjust the number of roles and points.

Setting up the Simulation

Each player needs a role (a list of potential roles follows). The instructor can modify these roles to fit the community context. The instructor can add more roles if necessary—e.g., some players could be given roles as agency clients or constituents.

Each role has a certain number of power points. No player has sufficient points to create a program alone—i.e., without forming an alliance with one or more other players. Colored paper "coupons" can represent the power points. The instructor distributes these coupons along with the brief role description at the start of the simulation.

Note: There should be a sufficient number of total points to create about two viable programs and one marginal (shaky) program. Adjust the number of points needed to create these programs based upon the total number of power points in the simulation. For example:

1. With 15 players, about 100 points constitute a viable program and 75 points a shaky program. Total points would be about 275.
2. For a 25-player simulation, use about 350 total points with ~10 players having few power points (e.g., as clients or ordinary community residents). A viable program would need 125 points; a shaky program needs 100 points.
3. For a 40-player simulation, use about 550 total points. A viable program needs 200 points, a shaky one 150 points.

Give each player a name tag identifying his or her role and provide each player with a brief description of his or her character. Players can reveal as much or as little about themselves as they choose. They can add anything to their role description as long as it does not contradict the information they are given.

Orientation to the Simulation

This is a simulation of bargaining, influence wielding, and coalition building. Each player's role is representative of a community constituency.

Write the name of each potential program or project on the board or newsprint (for easy visibility) and on an envelope. The class will use these envelopes to collect participants' "power points" at the end of the simulation. Either the participants can develop the list of potential programs before the start of the simulation, or the facilitator can construct the list in advance. Suggested program ideas include:

- a child care program;
- a job-training program for veterans and former prison inmates;

- a reproductive health center;
- a youth cultural center or LGBTQ community service center;
- legal services for low-income residents;
- subsidized housing for low-income elderly;
- a community behavioral health program;
- a citizen/police anti-crime program;
- a convention center;
- a foster home development project; and
- a transitional shelter for the homeless.

After the roles and power points are distributed, there is a 30-minute period of negotiation and coalition building. During this period, agreements can be reached, points can be exchanged, coalitions formed, etc. Participants may do anything they feel is needed to wield or acquire influence and power.

At the end of this period, each player distributes power points to the programs he or she supports or opposes by placing power points in the appropriate envelopes. (Players may cast "negative" power point by marking a ballot with an "x.") Subtract negative power points from the total positive points received by each program.

At the conclusion of the balloting, the instructor posts the vote tallies and the group discusses the experience.

Questions for Discussion

1. In what ways did the simulation reflect the realities of practice?
2. Through what process did participants identify and interpret the social problems or issues?
3. How did participants who were successful obtain the resources they needed?
4. Which aspect of the simulation did not reflect participants' experiences of reality? Which were oversimplifications? What aspects of reality that more accurately capture the experience of power or powerlessness could have been included?
5. How did you approach other players? What factors affected your choice and the manner in which you approached others?
6. What assumptions did you make about your own power and the power of other actors? Did you reveal your power points to anyone? If so, for what reason(s)?
7. How did the number of power points you possessed make you feel or behave?
8. What did you do to obtain power and influence?

9. How did the distribution of power actually affect the outcome of the simulation? In what ways did this outcome reflect the real world? In what ways did it mirror (or not) elitist and pluralist perspectives on power?

Some Suggestions

1. Relate the simulation to concepts of empowerment, power-dependency, privilege, and personal and collective self-efficacy (i.e., a participant's self-appraisal of the power and position she or he possesses, and the explanations of the causes of any inadequacies or advantages the participant perceives or experiences in the course of the simulation).
2. Discuss the multiple forms of power the simulation reflected. These could include social power, charisma, knowledge, technical expertise, and other personal qualities. Connect these forms of power to the participants' previous knowledge and experiences.

Sample Simulation Roles

Role	Power Points

Recent Graduate — 2

Characteristics

You are a recent college graduate who cannot find a job. Your undergraduate major was in psychology. You are living with your parents, but cannot stay with them for much longer.

Coffee Shop Owner — 5

Characteristics

You recently opened a coffee shop in a downtown neighborhood. You are interested in economic development in the neighborhood and managing the increasing drug trade and crime.

Primary School Teacher — 5

Characteristics

You are a second-grade teacher in a low-income neighborhood. You are interested in improving the facilities of your school, which has crumbling ceiling tiles, broken fountains, and poor lighting.

Parent — 5

Characteristics

You are a parent of three kids who is interested in improving the school in your community. You work as a secretary at the local university and are angry about how the city has spent millions of dollars building new stadiums but not on improving local schools.

Unemployed Steel Worker 2

Characteristics

You are a 55-year-old married male with two grown children and have been out of work for five years, after the steel plant where you worked closed. You have been seeking other employment but have not been successful. You are involved with your local neighborhood association and take pride in being an active citizen. You are getting close to using up your savings and are at risk of not being able to continue paying your mortgage.

Elderly Woman 2

Characteristics

You are 75 years old and are about to be evicted from your apartment because neighborhood rents have increased due to gentrification and you are on a fixed income from Social Security.

Iraqi War Veteran 2

Characteristics

You are 25 and a returned Iraq War veteran. You have been experiencing PTSD symptoms and are currently receiving mental health services but have not been able to find employment or stable housing.

Local Rap Artist 10

Characteristics

You are an up-and-coming local rap musician who has developed a local following.

Your music focuses on the tough economy, the poor public education system, the prison industrial complex, and struggling youth in the inner city.

Poet 4

Characteristics

You are a poet who writes on the plight of the poor in urban America.

You regularly attend open mic nights to read your poetry and have published a small compilation of your work. Your mother is a secretary in City Hall and your father passed away five years ago.

Assistant to the Mayor 20

Characteristics

You are an attorney well connected to the local Democratic Party. You have known the mayor for more than a decade and have considerable influence in City Hall. You will be the campaign manager of the mayor's reelection bid next year. You have close ties to real estate developers.

Police Officer—Head of Community Relations 8

Characteristics

You have lived in the same neighborhood since you were a child and watched it change over the past several decades. You are actively involved in one of the parish churches. Your wife is a teacher in one of the city's Catholic high schools.

Radio Talk-Show Host and Journalist 15

Characteristics

You host a daily talk show on the local NPR affiliate. You write two op-ed columns each week for the local newspaper. Your spouse is a social worker who works in the field of substance abuse.

Physician and Head of a Community Clinic 10

Characteristics

You are married and the mother of two children who attend local public schools. You grew up in the city, moved away for college and medical school, and returned after your residency. Your husband is the owner of a large local car dealership.

NASW State Chapter President 10

Characteristics

You are a former child welfare worker with more than 20 years' experience in the field. You have been divorced, have a child from your marriage, and have been involved in a lesbian relationship for the past 10 years. You married your partner after your state established marriage equality.

Professor in a University MSW Program 8

Characteristics

You are married to a college administrator and the mother of a young son in kindergarten.

For a number of years, you have been actively involved in housing issues in one of the poorest sections of the city. You are also interested in local cultural activities, such as music and theater.

Owner of Local Football team 25

Characteristics

You made your fortune as developer of shopping malls in various U.S. cities and suburbs.

You have considerable influence with the mayor, particularly around economic development issues. You are culturally conservative and a strong opponent of abortion, gay marriage, and Affirmative Action.

Senior Professor in a University MSW Program 8

Characteristics

You recently returned to the city after working in other institutions for more than two decades.

You have been extensively involved with welfare and civil rights organizations.

You have two grown daughters and have care-giving responsibilities for your elderly mother.

You are friendly with the talk-show host.

Junior Professor in a University MSW program 5

Characteristics

You are an unmarried 40-year-old woman who recently lost her mother. You are concerned about the increase in neighborhood violence and the consequences it has wrought, particularly among youth and their families. You have close ties to the Baptist church whose pastor is politically influential.

Person without Housing 1

Characteristics

You are a single male who recently became homeless when the temporary construction jobs you were working on dried up. You have been actively seeking work and affordable housing but have not been able to find either. Your health is beginning to suffer from living on the streets.

Bar Owner 5

Characteristics

You recently opened a bar in a downtown neighborhood. You are interested in economic development in the neighborhood and stopping the increasing drug trade and crime.

Elderly Man 2

Characteristics

You are 72 years old and at risk of losing your home. You are on a fixed income from Social Security and have had difficulty paying your property and city taxes for years. Your house is about to be foreclosed upon and you need affordable housing.

Clergyman/woman 15

Characteristics

You are chairperson of a citywide interfaith council of churches. Your church operates community programs that work with substance abusers and formerly incarcerated neighborhood residents. You have considerable political influence in the African American community. The mayor often calls on you for advice regarding issues facing your congregants.

Community Association President 8

Characteristics

You are a retired firefighter who has lived in the city all your life. You are married, the father of three children, and the grandfather of six. You are close friends of the head of Community Relations in the Police Department.

TANF Recipient 2

Characteristics

You are a mother of two young children. You have some work experience as a cashier, but had to quit your job when your youngest child got sick and needed health insurance that your job did not provide.

Summary and Conclusion

This chapter discussed the concept of advocacy in macro social work practice and various ways of using advocacy in the legislative policy-making arena to promote social justice, particularly for excluded and marginalized communities. It also discussed the challenges and potential of revising current practice models to include greater participation by community members and constituents in the advocacy process. Chapters 13 and 14 will address different aspects of advocacy in more detail to provide a fuller picture of the role of advocacy in social work practice and its increasing importance in the current political environment.

END-OF-CHAPTER EXERCISE
ADVOCACY, ORGANIZING, AND SOCIAL WORK PRACTICE

Introduction

1. Identify a social or economic issue that motivated you to become interested in social work, in general, and community organization in particular. Frame the issue in a manner that facilitates the development of alternative community interventions that might address it. Be as specific as possible. (*The more focused your definition of the issue, the easier it will be for you to answer the questions that follow.*)
2. If you were to engage in community organizing around this issue, what particular community would be the focus of your work? How might the definition of community that you selected and the particular characteristics of that community influence your work? (*Again, being as specific as possible will be helpful to you.*)

3. In what ways do the concepts of power, social justice, and cultural diversity shape the nature of the issue you selected as it manifests itself within the community you selected? How would you incorporate these concepts into the development of goals and strategies to guide a community intervention? Be as specific as possible.
4. Which of the three major models of community organization (community development, community planning, or social action) or combination of these models would be, in your judgment, most appropriate for addressing the issue you identified? As specifically as possible, indicate the reasons you would choose this model. Identify the ways in which this model might facilitate and/or impede the process of community empowerment around the particular issue you selected.
5. Within the framework of the model you selected, identify the goals and objectives of a potential organizing effort within a particular time frame. Be as specific as possible. Discuss how these goals and objectives reflect your underlying values and assumptions on the issue addressed and your views on the nature of the community change process itself. Justify the time frame you developed.
6. Outline the steps you would take during the first six (6) months of an organizing effort around the issue you chose. Explain briefly the purposes of each step, how it fits into an overall organizing strategy, and the reasons you sequenced the steps the way you did. Link your "plan of action" to the theoretical constructs that inform it as specifically as possible.
7. In the course of implementing your action plan, how would you incorporate sensitivity to issues of race, gender, religion, and other manifestations of diversity?
8. Identify the potential barriers—personal and professional—you might encounter in the development and implementation of this organizing effort. What might you do to overcome them or prevent them from emerging?
9. What ethical or value conflicts might arise in the course of this organizing effort? How would you address them?
10. Indicate what progress you hope to have achieved at the end of six months of organizing in terms of the key features of the model you selected. What would be the criteria by which you would measure the success or failure of your effort? **Briefly state** what your objectives would be during the next stage of this organizing effort.

Optional Assignment: Advocating for Social Change

Introduction

By the third class session, students should select an issue, cause, or group of constituents about which they are concerned. Each student will then engage individually in the following tasks:

- **Research the evolution of this issue from its emergence to the present.** This will require an assessment of the current situation and a review of relevant literature (social work and other). Note evidence in the literature supportive of your position.

- **Select the proper venue for your presentation.** This may be a public hearing, legislative committee session, community forum, or a meeting of a special commission authorized to deal with your issue (such as a county board of commissioners, the regents of a university or community college, school board trustees, the planning commission of a unit of government, or the board of directors of a human service organization). Do some background research on the nature of this venue and what are the expectations regarding presentations in this setting.
- Outline the key points of your presentation and the goals you hope to achieve through your advocacy.

Choose one (1) of the following options to complete the rest of the assignment:

1. Write three (3) pages of testimony in support of your constituents or cause and schedule a time on the agenda of the venue you selected to present it. Distribute copies of your testimony to those hearing your presentation.
2. Draft a three-page (3) written plan to mobilize and/or train constituents in this advocacy effort. This could include popular education on the effect of an issue affecting these constituents, training in advocacy, or a leadership development for community members.
3. Write a 750-word op-ed essay on the topic and submit it to a newspaper or reputable website for publication. (*See Chapter 13 for information about op-ed essays.*)
4. Write a three-page (3) letter of intent or concept paper for a small grant to support some program innovation that reflects this advocacy agenda and submit it to a foundation or other funding organization (e.g., a corporate funder). (*See Chapter 11 for a sample letter.*)

Optional Assignment: Drafting an Intra-Agency Memo Regarding Advocacy

This exercise asks students to draft a two- or three-page intraorganizational memorandum designed to encourage the organization to take an advocacy position on a specific issue.

Memorandum

Date

To: Board of Directors OR Executive Director OR Executive Team of Your Organization

From: Your Name and Role

Subj: Proposed Advocacy Campaign Regarding __________ (Be specific)

1. **Purpose**: Explain briefly the purpose of the memo (i.e., the goals and objectives of the memo, not the proposed advocacy campaign) and summarize what the memo contains.
2. **Background of the Organization's Previous Involvement With This Issue**: Explain briefly the history of the organization's involvement on the issue and the status of the issue.

3. **Goals and Objectives of Proposed Advocacy Campaign—Outline**: The intended goals and objectives of the proposed advocacy campaign (e.g., pass or defeat a specific piece of legislation or ballot initiative, increase or cut spending on a particular policy or program, heighten the public's awareness of a particular issue). ***Be as specific as possible***.
4. **Suggested Budget**: Indicate what will be the organization's commitment of resources, staffing, time, etc. to the proposed campaign. List the other organizations or groups with whom the organization will be working and how the various tasks of the campaign will be distributed and coordinated. ***Be as specific as possible***.
5. **Time Line**: Develop a proposed time line for the campaign including the benchmarks or objectives achieved at various points in the process. Indicate how you will determine whether the campaign is successful at various stages. ***Be as specific and as realistic as possible***.
6. **Organizational Benefits and Risks**: Briefly assess what you believe to be the potential benefits and risks for your organization on its involvement in this campaign.
7. **Concluding Paragraph**: Indicate how the recipients of the memo can provide you with comments, feedback, etc., and what will be the next steps in the planning process.

Note: You should assume that the recipients of the memorandum are knowledgeable about the issues (of substance and strategy) to which you refer. You may also assume that this memorandum is confidential and, therefore, you can be particularly candid.

Attachments: Attach any materials that you believe are essential to assist the readers of the memorandum understand it better. This is not required.

CHAPTER 13

Using Media as a Tool of Community, Organizational, and Social Change

Education is the most powerful weapon which you can use to change the world.

—**Nelson Mandela**

When widely followed public figures feel free to say anything, without any fact-checking, it becomes impossible for a democracy to think intelligently about big issues.

—**Thomas L. Friedman, *New York Times* columnist**

Introduction

In today's environment, the use of various forms of media is critical to the survival and success of community organizations, social service agencies, and policy advocacy campaigns. Yet, there has been insufficient attention to how social workers can employ media to promote progressive change and further the profession's social justice goals (McNutt & Menon, 2008). This chapter presents several aspects of this arena of practice. It emphasizes the importance of an informed population as a prerequisite for community, policy, and social change.

The chapter discusses how the use of media can heighten public awareness of an issue and help advocates translate broad policy goals into specific social programs. It also discusses ways that community organizations, coalitions, and advocacy groups can use media to influence the change process, safeguard any achievements they may have obtained, and evaluate their effect. Finally, it discusses how organizations can use technology in socially just ways to increase client participation, staff involvement, and community engagement with their programs.

Other topics included are:

1. How media influences community and social change efforts and social movements
2. Goals of media advocacy
3. Pros and cons of using media to promote change
4. Vehicles of media advocacy: Challenges and opportunities
5. Developing a media strategy
6. Identifying targets and framing an issue
7. Using social media and other digital technology
8. Organizing a media campaign and media events—e.g., press conferences, media blasts
9. Being interviewed in print, electronic, and digital media
10. Raising funds through media
11. Ethical issues in using media

Media Advocacy

Media advocacy involves "the strategic use of mass media to advance public policy by applying pressure to policy makers and opinion leaders" (Wallack, 1999). It helps fill the information gap that often impedes development of public awareness about an issue and the formulation of effective policy responses to social problems (Jernigan & Wright,

1996). The goal of media advocacy, therefore, is neither media coverage nor individual change, but policy change (Tan & Weaver, 2009).

Social workers can also use media advocacy to achieve other goals. It can help position an HSO or advocacy organization as a credible source of important information. It can help an organization or group maintain positive relationships with its contacts in the media. Perhaps of greatest importance, it can help an organization communicate its message on salient issues to a variety of audiences clearly and consistently—a critical feature of effective advocacy groups (Reisch, 2015a).

Media strategy needs to be part of the overall strategy of an advocacy campaign. It can play a critical role in assessing the fundamental questions that all advocacy efforts must address:

1. What is the problem or issue?
2. What is the policy solution to this problem?
3. Who has the power to make the necessary change?
4. Which individuals or groups must advocates mobilize to apply the necessary pressure?

Types of Media

Advocates use three types of media to promote their causes. One is paid media. This includes ads in newspapers, radio, television, the internet, and paid public service announcements. This use of media can be effective if advocates employ it strategically, coordinate the timing of media ads with other activities, and repeat the content and message with considerable frequency. It is expensive, however, and its cost is often beyond the reach of small organizations that operate on a shoestring budget. Particularly during legislative sessions or political campaigns, it is also difficult to make an organization's message stand out among the cacophonous media din.

Two other types of media are more accessible to low power, low budget groups. One type consists of earned media. This includes stories, editorials, or op-ed essays in national or local newspapers, radio or television coverage, and reporting on websites or blogs. As discussed elsewhere in this chapter, advocates can employ a range of tactics to enhance the profile of their organization and its core issues through this form of media. Although earned media also have indirect costs, these costs are generally associated with other, ongoing activities and may not create an unbearable fiscal burden for an advocacy organization.

Another type of media, which is even less expensive, is social media, including Facebook, Twitter, Instagram, YouTube, and other apps. Like all forms of media, social media have both advantages and disadvantages. They are particularly effective in communicating a message rapidly, motivating certain populations—such as younger people, especially those from communities of color—to take immediate, coordinated action, and, as recent electoral campaigns demonstrated, raising large amount of funds quickly and at minimal cost (Guo & Saxton, 2012). There is some question, however, on whether the use of social media is sufficient to sustain a long-term advocacy effort and whether it enables people to soothe their consciences without taking any meaningful risks (Edwards & Hoefer, 2010). As events of recent years demonstrate, the increased misuse of social media to spread false information also raises both ethical and practical questions about its ultimate utility (Gunitsky, 2015; Kwon, et al., 2013).

Vehicles of Media Advocacy

Advocates have many tools at their disposal in their efforts to use media to promote the interests of constituents (Anderson, Miller, & McGuire, 2012). These include:

1. A press release, press advisory, news brief, fact sheet, photo, or profile of a local person
2. A press conference or other staged media event
3. An op-ed essay, guest editorial, letter to the editor, or letter-writing campaign
4. An appearance on a radio or television talk show or podcast
5. Internet blogs by a representative of the organization or coalition, or a sympathetic supporter
6. An article on the organization's website
7. Press coverage or an interview by web reporters or bloggers
8. A TED talk
9. Various forms of social media, such as a Twitter account (Guo & Saxton, 2014; Lovejoy, Waters, & Saxton, 2012; Dorfman, 2003)

Guidelines for a Press Release

A press release is the most basic, but often the most effective vehicle to obtain more in-depth media coverage of an issue. A press advisory is a more concise way of informing the media about the organization's upcoming use of another media tactic, such as a press conference.

To heighten its effect, a press release contains certain key features. As with all good journalism, an effective press release always includes the "5 Ws" of the narrative being conveyed: who, what, where, when, and why. Although there are a number of ways to introduce the story, "leads" (the first one or two sentences) that begin by emphasizing "what" are strongest; "why" or "how" leads are more difficult to write, but can also be effective. "Where" and "when" leads are the worst choice because they detract focus from the substantive issue (Wallack, 1999). Just as in a newspaper story or radio broadcast, the lead must give essential information to generate interest in the story and provide the basic facts (Wallack, 1999). As illustrated in Table 13.1, the overall format is to use an inverted pyramid.

It is useful to include an illustrative quote from a leader of the organization or coalition, and/or a supportive quote from a well-known and respected source, either an expert on the subject or a politically influential figure. Although they are generally short, a press release should concisely state both the nature of the problem and the solution advocates propose. It should also include all contact information about the organization at the top to facilitate follow-up.

Ideally, a newspaper or website will quote or paraphrase the press release and make it the heart of a story on the issue advocates want to disseminate. In writing the copy for a standard press release, therefore, it is useful to note that six or seven lines of copy are the maximum for the average newspaper paragraph. (Web-based stories are generally briefer and have shorter paragraphs.) To ease transmission and avoid errors in communication, it is desirable to end each page of the press release with a complete paragraph and never divide a word at the end of a line. At the bottom of each page of a multiple page story, write the word "more" so that the editor is aware that the narrative continues. On succeeding pages, put the headline and page number at the top of each page (e.g., "Advocacy Campaign—2") and place an end mark (#) at the conclusion of the story. These details may seem petty and technical, but they matter.

Writers of press releases also need to follow certain style rules. When referring to a person, use his or her full name (e.g., President Donald Trump) when mentioning the individual the first time. After this, use only the person's last name or title (e.g., Trump or the president). Try to avoid the use of lengthy titles before a person's name, but if used, they need to be capitalized (e.g., Governor), except for occupational titles (e.g., social worker or school principal). When you include the title, do not separate it from the name with a comma. Finally, do not capitalize titles following names; set them off with a comma (e.g., John Smith, president of the XYZ Community Association).

Abbreviate months when accompanied by a date (e.g., Sept. 1, 2017), otherwise spell them out (e.g., the hearing will be held in September). Capitalize the titles of books (e.g., *The New Jim Crow*), songs, and speech titles, and place them within quotation marks or in italics (e.g., "The New Jim Crow" or *The New Jim Crow*). When using numbers, such as in citing important statistics, spell out figures of nine or less and use numerals for 10 or more. Finally, use two dashes (–) or a computer-generated em dash (a long dash) to indicate parenthetical explanations (e.g., John Smith—who had previously testified before the Senate committee on this issue—will testify again next week). Newspapers will be less likely to use press releases that do not follow these style rules. Failure to use them may also diminish an organization's reputation among media representatives.

What type of event attracts media attention and interest? There are several ways to generate increased media access. Journalists refer to these methods as "news pegs." One effective news peg is to link the organization's story to the anniversary of an important event, such as a civil disturbance or natural disaster, or a local historic milestone, such as the founding of a city. Another device is to highlight the release of a groundbreaking research report.

In addition, media generally respond to stories that involve a celebrity, reflect an emerging or ongoing controversy or a serious injustice, or contain certain humorous or ironic elements. If a story has a local, personal, or seasonal angle, media are also more likely to run it. An example of the latter is to connect an advocacy campaign that focuses on school funding cuts with the "back to school" time of the year.

Table 13.1 A Model Press Release for an Advocacy Campaign

Note: This is an outline for a press release announcing the kickoff of an advocacy campaign or some other type of social/political action effort. It should be ~two pages (500–750 words), single-spaced, and double-spaced between paragraphs.

I. **Basic Guidelines:** Make sure your press release covers the "5 Ws and H"—i.e., who, what, where, when, why, and how.

II. **Leads:** The first sentence or two must either provide essential information to catch the reader's interest and provide the most important facts, or whet the reader's appetite if you wish to sell him or her on your idea.

III. **Format:** Use an inverted pyramid form for organizing and writing information. Start with the most important fact (the lead), followed by the second most important fact, etc. Then follow with details.

Here is a model of how to structure the press release:

Opening Paragraph:

LEAD FACT

[e.g., announcement of start of a campaign, event, release of a report, etc.]

SECONDARY FACT OR INFORMATION

[e.g., purposes of the social action effort]

DETAIL No. 1

[e.g., summary of activities of the social action effort]

DETAIL No. 2

[e.g., summary of participants in the social action effort]

DETAIL No. 3, ETC.

Subsequent Paragraphs:
SUMMARY LEAD (concise)
[e.g., reasons for the social action effort]

DETAILS OF FIRST POINT IN SUMMARY
[e.g., more details on the issue]

DETAILS OF SECOND POINT IN SUMMARY
[e.g., specific goals of the social action effort]

DETAILS OF THIRD POINT IN SUMMARY

ETC.
[e.g., more details on participating organizations]

Table 13.1: *Lawrence Wallack, Katie Woodruff, Lori Dorfman and Iris Diaz, News for a Change: An Advocate's Guide to Working with the Media. Copyright © 1999 by SAGE Publications.*

Figure 13.1 Examples of a Press Advisory and a Press Release

FOR IMMEDIATE RELEASE:
August 19, 2013

CONTACT:
Steve Burdo – (415) 261-4784
Stephen@kathleenrussells.com

San Francisco Village
OUR GENERATION. OUR CHOICE.

New Castro Senior Group to Host September 28th Open House
Network of Older San Franciscans Expands to the Castro

~ OPEN HOUSE (Open to the public) ~
Saturday, September 28th at 1:00-3:00 p.m.
San Francisco LGBT Center
1800 Market Street
Refreshments served

San Francisco, CA - San Francisco Village – citywide network empowering older San Franciscans – is organizing a local chapter in the Castro neighborhood. The group will kick off their organizing efforts with a **free informational open house on September 28th at the San Francisco LGBT** Center. All residents of the Castro community are welcome to attend.

Fig. 13.1: *San Francisco Village, "Example of a Press Advisory." Copyright © 2013.*

Figure 13.2 Examples of a Press Advisory and a Press Release

Max Litter
Catbrella Inc.
1-800-MeowNoMore
max@catbrella.com

FOR IMMEDIATE RELEASE: 10/30/16

Catbrella Inc. Celebrates Their Tenth Twitter Follower

Customized Cat Umbrella Company Experiences Rapid Growth on Twitter

Boston, MA: Today, Catbrella Inc., a custom umbrella company specializing in umbrellas for cats and kittens, announced that they have reached 10 followers on the social media platform Twitter. After creating a Twitter account two years ago using the handle @catumbrella, Catbrella is seeing a return on its Promoted Tweets with their follower base reaching an all-time high this morning. Catbrella's tenth follower is @kittenhatz, who tweets frequently about cat couture.

Of the company's recent Twitter success, Catbrella CEO Max Litter said, "Reaching 10 Twitter followers this morning has been one of my proudest moments in my 20 years at Catbrella. We have a pretty niche offering and adapting to the digital age has really helped us increase our reach; ten years ago, @kittenhatz never would have heard of us. I couldn't be more elated. Who knows, this time next year we could have 30 followers."

To gain this momentous following, Catbrella planned and executed the following tactics:

- After deciding, based on gut instinct, that Promoted Tweets were far easier to leverage than organic content, Catbrella allotted $500.00 to Twitter in their social media budget.
- By using phrases like 'The purr-fect way to stay dry' and 'Next time it rains, paws and think' in their tweets, Catbrella was able to optimize the 140-character limit.

About Catbrella Inc.: Catbrella Inc. is a cat umbrella company based in Boston, MA. Founded in 1982, Catbrella has designed, produced, and distributed over 2 million custom umbrellas for various types of cats and kittens. Catbrella was voted Most Innovative Company of the Year in 2007 by the Feline Business Awards.

###

Fig. 13.2: *Hannah Fleishman, "Example of a Press Release," https://blog.hubspot.com/marketing/press-release-template-ht. Copyright © 2013 by HubSpot.*

Another skill that helps promote an advocacy cause is the ability to write powerful headlines—whether as part of a print media story or on a website page. At best, a headline should express the heart of the story concisely and convincingly, often based on how the "lead" framed it. It needs to be specific and focus on the key point of the story. Most good headlines are short; they can omit articles (a, an, the) and use few punctuation marks. They can imply a subject (i.e., assume readers will "fill in the blanks"). Capitalize all words with few exceptions.

Press Conferences or News Conferences

Many advocacy campaigns use this vehicle effectively for one of several purposes. A press conference is particularly valuable when introducing a new program, policy idea, or initiative. It is also helpful to promote the release of a final report (e.g., of a commission studying a particular issue), newly discovered statistics (e.g., about poverty in a specific community), or conveying a community's protest over a recent event (e.g., the police slaying of an unarmed person). Advocates should only call a press conference, however, when there is a specific reason to do so and when its intention is to provoke additional action. It is counterproductive for advocates to acquire a "boy who cried wolf" reputation.

Several tips can enhance the effect of press conferences. From a practical perspective, it is wise to fax or email press advisories five business days in advance and follow up with phone calls the day before the event. (Obviously, emergencies constitute an exception to this rule.) It is better to schedule a press conference in the morning to avoid competition with other breaking stories and to facilitate media coverage in the noon hour and on late-afternoon programs. Ideally, the location should be accessible and, if possible, connected to the theme of the press conference (e.g., a public housing project if the focus is on housing issues). Serving food is always a good way to attract journalists, particularly in the morning.

Effective press conferences provide those who attend with press packets that include "fast facts" and relevant background information. In today's digital age, they also use vivid visuals (graphs, photos, charts). If possible, organizers should involve people most affected by the issue, such as local residents who suffered from budget cuts or families of shooting victims, and include a local celebrity as one of the speakers if the person is not controversial. Although the press conference may cover a lot of territory, especially if the issue is complex or new, it is important to leave time for journalists to conduct individual interviews with organizational spokespersons.

Media Events

Media events are other types of staged activities or actions designed to produce a particular effect on the public and to influence decision makers. To capture favorable and widespread coverage and attention, media events must contain some extraordinary features. Three powerful examples come to mind from the author's experience. One were protests by the Kensington Welfare Rights Organization in Philadelphia against welfare cuts held at the Liberty Bell to emphasize how these cuts violated the nation's founding values. Another consisted of actions organized by members of the AIDS Coalition to Unleash Power (ACT-UP) to protest against the failure of the federal government to process antiviral vaccines more rapidly. ACT-UP members chained themselves to the fence surrounding the federal building in San Francisco (Duberman, 2014; Powers & Voegele, 1997). More recently, in several cities, the Black Lives Matter movement staged "die-ins" to illustrate the number of African Americans who had been victims of police violence (Rickford, 2016). As these examples demonstrate, advocates and activists need to be creative in their tactical selection and to provide journalists and the public with visual images. These are especially effective in generating extensive television coverage and enabling the issue to "go viral" over the internet (Stienstra, Watzke, & Birch, 2007).

Op-Ed Essays

Publication of an op-ed essay or guest editorial is another effective tool for advocates. It is more powerful than a letter to the editor because it illustrates the paper's interest in the issue and establishes the author as an expert. It may also stimulate further dialogue, such as an editorial, an op-ed piece responding to the original essay, a feature story, or letters to the editor. Although an op-ed piece can be influential, it is important for advocates to weigh the time and resources expended in writing the essay against the size of its potential readership. This "cost/benefit" analysis is similar to the process advocates use in assessing the utility of any tactic (Lens, 2005).

The structure of a guest op-ed (which differs from essays written by a regular columnist) follows a straightforward pattern. It is better to write the essay in an active voice, including facts and analysis, problem descriptions, and proposed solutions. Most op-eds range from 600–1,000 words divided into three roughly equal parts: problem statement, problem explanation, and problem solution (Wallack, 1999).

An op-ed will attract more attention if the author links its theme to a major study produced recently by a reputable organization or expert, or if it illustrates the issue through a powerful personal narrative. If relevant, it may be helpful to connect the essay to contemporary events or ongoing controversies. Sometimes, meeting with editorial boards (in the case of a guest editorial) or station managers (in the case of a radio or television spot) to ascertain their interpretation of issues helps advocates determine how to frame an essay (Shaw, 2013).

Finally, an advocacy organization should carefully consider who should be the stated author of the essay. Although the organization's leader may often be the best choice, under certain circumstances it may be strategic to "ghost write" the essay and have it published under the name of someone who is less controversial, better known, or representative of a group not usually associated with a particular cause. On more than one occasion, the author drafted an op-ed essay as a "ghost" for a powerful and unexpected spokesperson on an unpopular issue. For example, in his role as president of a statewide welfare rights organization, the author wrote an op-ed supporting an increase in welfare benefits. The essay appeared under the name of the former *U.S. News and World Report* CEO, a highly respected corporate executive, who also happened to be the chair of the governor's Advisory Council for the state's Department of Human Resources. The appearance of the essay seemingly from an unexpected source gave the op-ed more credibility among the business community and certain key policy makers. As the old adage goes, "there is no limit to what you can accomplish, if you don't care who gets the credit."

Letters to the Editor

Letter-writing campaigns are another vehicle to attract attention to an issue and inform policy makers of widespread support for an advocacy cause. They are an effective means of involving members of the community affected by the issue, particularly those members who have limited time or who may be less willing to engage in more risky activities. They are also a relatively easy way to engage other professionals and allies in an advocacy campaign, particularly around a local matter.

The best way to initiate a letter-writing campaign is to use existing networks or coalitions. The more letters that address the same issue, the better. The same applies for comments in response to an online news article or opinion essay. It is important, however, for writers to include their names with these posts. Anonymous comments carry little weight. To facilitate the process, advocates can draft a template of a letter that leaves room for writers to include content drawn from their personal experiences or written from their personal perspectives. (Sending identical "form" letters is less effective.) If all of the signers have a common identification—e.g., students or faculty members in the same school or staff members in the same agency—a single letter signed by many people can be just as influential (Galer-Unti, Tappe, & Lachenmayr, 2004). The same strategy applies to posting comments on media blogs or Facebook pages (Galer-Unti, 2010).

Media Interviews

As in the use of all tactics, it is important for advocates to be clear in advance on their reasons for participating in an interview—whether it is with a print, electronic, or digital media journalist. It is critical to know the standpoint of the reporter (his or her frame) and the likely perspective of the audience. Advocates must be wary of falling into traps and allowing themselves to be used by journalists—e.g., those more interested in generating ratings or upping readership than analyzing complex issues—as foils or targets of derision. (In this regard, the author's experiences as a guest on a few right-wing radio talk shows are too painful to recall.)

Advocates need to convey three clear messages when participating in interviews:

1. What is the problem that the public needs to recognize and address?
2. What is the solution to this problem?
3. Why does this matter, particularly to people who are not directly affected?

For the most part, it is better to emphasize point No. 2, not point No. 1.

Certain stylistic tips also help create a successful interview. Advocates should avoid using the "I" word and speak in terms of "we," particularly when referring to an issue campaign organized by an alliance or coalition. This also enables the audience to perceive the advocate as one of them rather than as an outsider. It helps to use one or two vivid examples to express the realities of a complex issue. These can be stories, visuals, or colorful metaphors. The audience often responds better when the writer expresses an issue through a personal narrative.

As stated in Chapter 12, it is better to describe the quantitative components of an issue by using "social math" rather than academically oriented statistics. It is also helpful to use shorter words in responding to interviewers' questions, such as verbs that convey passion, action, and ownership of the issue. As with the best debaters, savvy advocates reframe questions to their advantage. They pose "imagine if" questions (e.g., "imagine what it would be like if every child could afford to attend college?") rather than rhetorical questions (e.g., "what would it take to enable every child to afford to attend college?").

The manner in which you speak also affects the quality of the interview. With print reporters, it is wise to slow down and pause to collect your thoughts. Silence between answers demonstrates thoughtful reflection, not hesitation or ignorance. Remember, whatever you might say, nothing is really off the record.

On television, radio, or in a live podcast, use a relaxed style. Vary the cadence and pitch of your voice so the audience will not fall asleep because of your monotone. Radio is a "hot" medium. Passionate responses, if clearly formed and not overly emotional, are effective. In contrast, television is a "cool" medium; an understated approach generally works better.

To the extent possible, use complete sentences to tell a comprehensive narrative. (This is why experienced advocacy organizations rehearse for scheduled interviews at least a day in advance.) Particularly in radio or television interviews or podcasts, do not respond to questions by stating, "I have several points to make about this issue." Jump in with one or two of your best points. You do not need to tell everything at once. Those one or two points are what the audience remembers.

Finally, try not to make overly broad statements or grandiose pronouncements or predictions. Focus instead on specific goals. The objective is to balance the journalist's desire to inform the public with your objective of educating the public (from a particular perspective) and pressuring policy makers. Avoid interjections (such as "um"), especially on radio. In addition, resist including too much technical detail and do not use any jargon if you can avoid it. It is not necessary to flaunt your expertise or credentials; the audience will assume you are qualified unless you prove otherwise (Wallack, 1999; Dorfman, 2003).

KEY CONCEPT SUMMARY
TIPS FOR MEDIA INTERVIEWS

1. ***Control the Agenda***: It is critical to link a media strategy to an overall advocacy strategy and the specific policy outcomes it hopes to achieve. Remember: *An interview is not a conversation. It is an opportunity (or series of opportunities) to make a point.*

   Example: A children's advocacy organization should consistently articulate the following points in media interviews (Children Now, 2003):

   a. Policies should "put children first."

   b. Policies should reflect a comprehensive view of children.

   c. Policies should create a safe, healthy environment for children.

   d. Policies should create/expand opportunity.

   e. Policies should enable children to contribute to society.

   f. Policies should "collectivize" our shared values.

   g. Policies should reflect the diversity/reality of a multicultural society.

   h. Policies should reflect and reinforce social solidarity and interconnectedness.

   Note: These are the reasons why advocates should constantly use "we" language in media releases.

2. Divide your message into three parts:

   a. What is the problem?

   b. What is the solution?

   c. Why does it matter? (The "so what" factor)

3. Stylistic Tips

   a. Keep your sentences short. Use shorter words to convey complex ideas.

   b. Vary your cadence. ***Slow Down*** (especially with print media). Wait for the next question. Restate the question for emphasis. Try to keep your style relaxed, especially on television; this "cool medium" encourages reflection.

   c. Restate powerful images/messages (e.g., "children are exposed to . . .").

   d. Use colorful language and imagery.

   e. Focus your interview on a specific goal. Do not tell everything at once.

   f. Focus on one component of a problem at a time.

   g. Do not list categories of issues or problems. Try to speak in research/action "bullets" (e.g., "We've learned that . . .").

   h. Do not be afraid to express passion in your use of words (e.g., "We are ***concerned*** that . . .") even when you maintain a measured tone.

i. Use verbs that show ownership of the issues.
j. Do not use jargon, acronyms, or the names of specific programs (only policy wonks will get it). Keep the specific audience in mind.
k. Pose hypothetical statements (e.g., "Imagine if ...").
l. Personalize your response—use good examples to illustrate some of the absurd possibilities of the issue you are addressing. Tell a good story
m. Focus on positives. Do not use terms that frame the issue in negative ways.
n. Avoid excessively broad statements or predictions.
o. Use powerful metaphors and "social math" (quantify the problem) to drive issues home and employ specific examples around emotion-laden issues.

Sound Bites

Most media interviews are not scheduled. They occur on short notice, sometimes at a planned event, sometimes in response to an event that occurred elsewhere. It is difficult if not impossible to prepare for an unexpected phone call, email message, or text from a journalist who wants a quick answer to a question, particularly if it concerns a development you are hearing about for the first time.

Even in these challenging situations, it is possible to produce results that benefit an advocacy campaign. First, keep your answers brief, stick to the known facts, and do not speculate. For better or worse, the media prefer to use short, pithy (and witty) remarks (sound bites) rather than lengthy, more erudite explanations of complex issues (Chapman, 2004). Whether this reflects a "dumbing down" of U.S. culture or the diminished attention span of the audience is a matter of debate. Effective advocates have to respond to the world as it is, not as they would like it to be.

With this in mind, try to match your responses to the message and frame that best reflect your organization's overall goals. (It is unlikely you will receive a spontaneous call or text to discuss an issue about which you have little or no familiarity. Journalists are under considerable time pressure and will always try to go to a reliable source for a pithy quote.) Think about a short, catchy statement you can extract from your overall frame and message. Try to use alliteration, a thoughtful metaphor, or a clever analogy to make your remarks more vivid (Quiroz et al., 2014).

IN-CLASS EXERCISE
THINKING OF AN EFFECTIVE SOUND BITE

Introduction

The purpose of this exercise is to develop skills in expressing an advocacy message concisely and powerfully in a few words. The message should be one you would share with a larger audience. It should employ frames that will persuade the audience and advance the policy goals of your organization.

Step 1

In small groups, identify a cause about which each group member feels strongly. Brainstorm different sound bites (messages of 7–15 words) that express one or more of the following:

- why people should care about this issue;
- how your group's solution to the issue is different from those that have been ineffective in the past; and
- how you would respond to people who believe that the responsibility for addressing this issue lies exclusively with the individuals it affects.

Try to make each message memorable, witty, and/or touching.

Step 2

Each group should introduce their issue to the class and select one or two best sound bites for each question to share with the class.

Step 3

The class should identify what features made sound bites more or less effective.

(Source: D. H. Jernigan (n.d.). Applying media advocacy to the reduction of college alcohol problems. Baltimore, MD: Johns Hopkins University, Bloomberg School of Public Health.)

Debates

Sometimes advocates have the opportunity to participate in a debate, such as an issues forum organized by the League of Women Voters or a neighborhood group or church, or to be part of a panel discussion of an issue on radio or TV that includes spokespersons from groups with widely different perspectives. If handled properly, these events can help advocacy organizations advance their cause. Remember, however, that they are competitive situations; media often pronounce the "winners" and "losers" of a debate or debate-like program (Wallack & Dorfman, 1996).

With this in mind, when participating in debates advocates should focus on taking up as much airtime as possible, even if this requires repeating the same message or restating the same pithy facts more than once. Conversely, try not to provide opportunities for opponents to shape the conversation—for example, by posing open-ended rhetorical questions. As in all advocacy, it is critical to stay on message, employ pivot phrases, and reframe questions to steer the debate in the direction that best serves your purposes. It also helps to be familiar with the opposition's arguments and style. This requires both research and practice.

Especially when debating before a large live audience or on television, it is preferable to use a low-key style and try not to let opponents' accusations or tactics rattle you, no matter how personal or wild they are. (This is one reason rehearsals are critical.) Finally, the audience is as likely to recall how you appeared as what you said. Be aware of body language and facial expressions at all times, even when you are not speaking. They can detract from your intended message. Keep your emotions in control no matter how disturbed you are by what opponents say. This means no headshaking, eye-rolling, finger-wagging, or other derogatory gestures. Let the power of your arguments, not some incidental or spontaneous behavior or gesture, convey your advocacy message (Berkeley Media Studies Group, 2003).

Developing a Media Strategy

As stated elsewhere in this book, a media strategy must reflect the overall strategy of an organization or advocacy group. Its tactics and message must be consistent and avoid counteracting the effects of other activities in which advocates engage. It should augment, not distract or detract, from other aspects of an overall advocacy effort (Kanter & Fine, 2010).

Advocates also need to be careful not to overuse the media. To avoid this problem, it is best to set three priority objectives in developing a media strategy. Advocates also need to be realistic and consider the staff time and resources available to pursue media advocacy effectively. This awareness is particularly important for newer and smaller advocacy groups, especially those that represent excluded constituencies.

In addition, it is important for advocates to target both the content of their advocacy message and also the vehicle through which they convey it to a specific audience. For example, a media strategy that works well in a racially diverse urban setting may fail in a homogeneous rural community (Shields et al, 2004). This requires advocates to be creative to provide the media and their audiences with a new angle on an old issue or a new lens through which to view it. Whenever feasible, it often helps to involve constituents in designing an advocacy message and thinking of how to access media targets. Constituents are often more aware of how to "reach" certain audiences than advocates (Minkler, 2012).

There are both pros and cons to using the media to advance an advocacy campaign. News media shape the environment rather than just reflect it. If media perceive an advocacy campaign as a threat to the institutional or cultural status quo, they could withdraw coverage of the issue. An invisible campaign may as well not exist.

Because of this delicate relationship, advocates must balance the interests of their constituents and their organizations with those of the media. This is an increasingly difficult challenge in a globalized economy in which corporate ownership of the media is more common and corporate influence in the media and the legislative process more pervasive. Nevertheless, the media have cleavages—along political, regional, ideological, and ethnic lines—that advocates can exploit to promote their cause. Media also have an economic interest in promoting interesting stories. The bottom line, therefore, is that attracting media attention and integrating media advocacy into an overall advocacy strategy is a calculated risk. It requires thoughtful judgment by advocates, preferably in consultation with their constituents and allies (Shaw, 2013).

There are five basic elements of a media strategy:

1. Creating news (e.g., through a press release)
2. Piggybacking on an existing news story (e.g., through a press conference)
3. Using the hook of an unexpected event to promote an issue
4. Writing editorials, blogs, or op-ed pieces
5. Employing paid media (e.g., ads or public service announcements)

Advocates must decide when and why to use each element, and which ones are best to promote their particular issue (Wallack, 1999).

Whatever vehicles advocates employ, they also have to consider two distinct targets for their advocacy: policy makers and the public. Each target responds differently to different ways of conveying an advocacy message through the media. The following chart demonstrates these differences.

Table 13.2 Targets of Media Advocacy—What Works (Wallack, 1999; Dorfman, 2003)

Policy Makers	The Public
Op-ed essays	TV stories
Editorials	Newspaper articles
Letters to the editor	Radio coverage/talk shows
Targeted press releases	Cable TV segments
Media events	Special publications for specific groups
Blogs (sometimes)	Blogs (if good)
Social Media (e.g., Twitter)	Social media (Facebook, Instagram, YouTube, etc.)

Table 13.2: *Adapted From Lawrence Wallack, Katie Woodruff, Lori Dorfman and Iris Diaz, News for a Change: An Advocate's Guide to Working with the Media. Copyright © 1999 by SAGE Publications and Lori Dorfman; eds. R. J. Bensley and J. Brookins-Fisher "Using Media Advocacy to Influence Policy," Community Health Education Methods: A Practitioner's Guide. Copyright © 2003 by Jones & Bartlett Publishers.*

Two other components of a media strategy are crisis communication planning and developing strong media relations. The former involves preparing a mechanism within the advocacy organization capable of generating a rapid response to emerging issues and training regular spokespersons for the group. The organization also has to be careful to present each response with the proper tone. For example, it should not appear to exploit a situation, particularly a tragic event, even if the story is accurate and could advance the organization's policy goals. It is better to address the issue carefully.

Particularly if the story involves specific individuals, it is important to avoid focusing excessive attention on these persons or to engage in victim blaming. It is preferable to broaden personalized stories and shift the focus to the larger issue(s) they reflect. If media contacts request interviews on such subjects, and the organization opts to decline interviews, it helps to clarify to journalists that a spokesperson for the organization will be available to discuss how the story relates to its broader concerns.

Building ongoing personal and reciprocal relationships with media representatives is another critical aspect of a media strategy (Reber & Kim, 2006). As with legislators (*see Chapter 12*), advocates can strengthen media relationships by offering journalists and editors a service and not merely seeking them out for desired coverage. This service can include helping reporters and editors meet their deadlines or providing proactive briefings on an issue to help them keep abreast of rapid developments.

As different communities rely on different types of media for information, advocates should do research to determine how best to communicate with each part of their target audience. They should also try to find creative ways to reach journalists who work for these media outlets. Although it is necessary to employ different approaches to establish contact with journalists in different communities, it is still important to maintain a consistent advocacy message, even when exploiting a local angle to convey the message.

Framing

In media advocacy, framing is the process of selecting "some aspects of a perceived reality [to] make them more salient in a communication text" (Entman, 1993). Frames are broad descriptors that reflect unstated underlying principles and assumptions. Within frames, "cues" are words or categories (labels) that have rhetorical effect because they trigger certain emotional responses. Note how using different frames casts the following issues in entirely different lights:

- urban sprawl vs. suburban development;
- reproductive rights proponents vs. advocates for abortion;
- insurgents vs. terrorists;
- estate tax vs. death tax;

- social rights vs. entitlements; and
- activists vs. militants.

According to Wallack (1999), there are three basic elements to framing an issue in the media. The first is a statement of concern or diagnosis. Advocates need to express this statement in specific rather than broad terms. For example, the statement "we need to stop the unnecessary deaths of African Americans at the hands of the police" is more effective than "we need to eradicate institutional racism in our nation's criminal justice system."

Second, a framing statement needs to provide a clear rationale as to why the issue is a serious concern. What makes the issue a problem now and for whom? What are the current effects of the issue and what are the consequences if society fails to respond?

Third, advocates need to impart in their issue framing a clear proposal for what they seek to achieve and a prognosis on the effect of "success." This includes information on the specific policy change they are seeking and the identification of who has responsibility to effect the change.

Here is an example of this tripartite media framing:

Issue: High Rates of Alcoholism in a Particular Neighborhood and the Social Consequences

1. Statement of Concern
   - "There are too many liquor stores in X community."
2. Why is this a concern?
   - "Liquor stores create safety hazards and are hurting community cohesion."
3. What do we want?
   - "We want the City Council to pass a moratorium on all new liquor licenses and create a $600 annual fee on all liquor stores in X community."

Conversely, incorrect framing of an issue can lead to confusion or misunderstanding of the issue by the public and misguided public policy responses. The media ads provided by the Partnership for a Drug Free America illustrate this pitfall. Although well intentioned, the ads focused on educating people on the dangers of substance abuse. They assumed the problem of substance abuse stems from a lack of knowledge and bad personal behavior rather than federal and state drug policies. The ads also failed to consider contextual factors—e.g., economic conditions, health problems, and the physical environments of communities with high rates of substance abuse—in their assessment of the issue and promotion of potential solutions.

When working with the media, advocates need to be aware that no story, however well documented by evidence, starts on a "clean slate." History, contemporary events, and the political and cultural context also contribute to the frame through which people and the media interpret a story. To be compelling, stories first need a character. The

Black Lives Matter movement would have less power if it did not attach its narrative to the tragic loss of specific individuals. Although the use of personal portraits is a powerful tool, advocates have to use portraits—of both victims and villain—carefully to avoid blaming victims for their plight, creating unjustified sympathy (for villains) or distancing the audience from the narrative (because its details or implications are too painful to confront).

The two photos and their accompanying text that follow illustrate how alternative framing of virtually the same behavior reflects unstated underlying assumptions and preconceived perceptions of people based on their race. Note the different effect of these two different framings.

Figures 13.3a and 13.3b

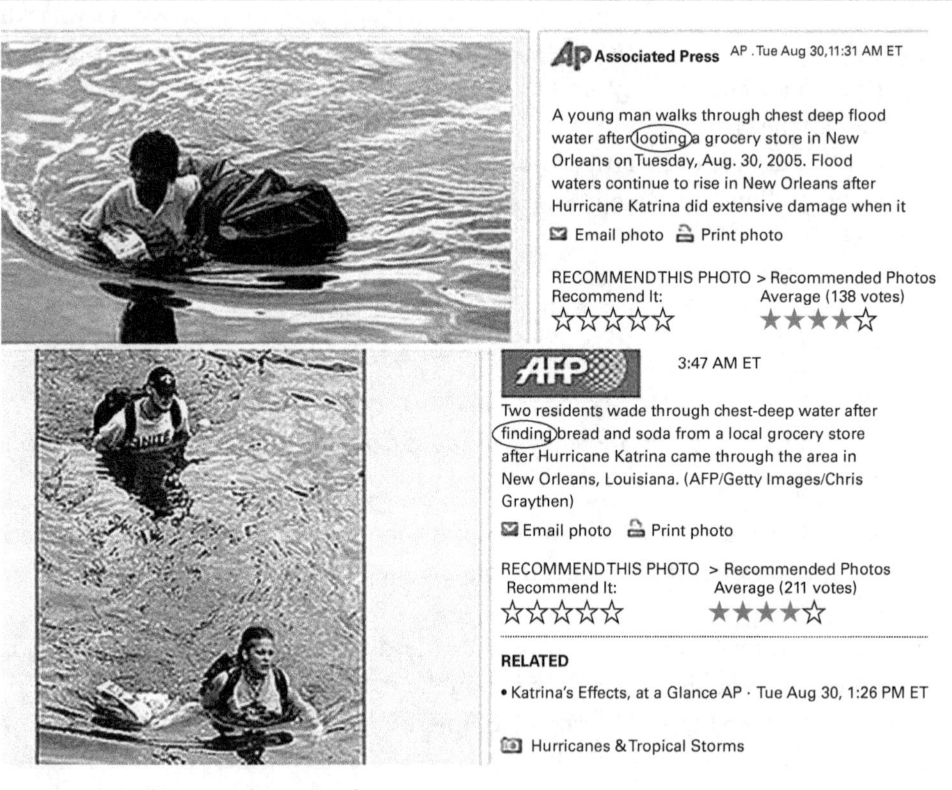

Fig. 13.3a: *Copyright © 2005 by Associated Press.*

Fig. 13.3b: *Copyright © 2005 by Agence France-Presse.*

Classroom Discussion

1. What message does each image and its accompanying text convey?
2. What are the underlying assumptions (about the persons in the image and the attitudes of the media audience) reflected by these two different framings?

Types of Message Framing

The contrast between how the media and advocates tend to frame issues creates significant challenges for groups promoting social justice causes. For example, the media tend to present social issues in episodic terms. They emphasize their short-term effect on individuals (or families) rather than thematically (in collective, long-term, and structural language). This is because media reflect the dominant culture that views issues through the lens of individuals, rather than society as a whole (D'Angelo & Kuypers, 2010; Chong & Druckman, 2007). The financial interests of media (what "sells") also contribute to the adoption of this perspective.

News coverage, particularly on television, also focuses on the competitive aspect of politics and policy development, which side "won" on a given day, which players are "ahead" in the game, instead of the substantive components of a policy debate. This emphasis treats the issues that advocates care about as a "sport," divorcing the process and outcomes from their real-world consequences for people and communities. In addition, media tend to construct issues in terms of opposing rights, principles, or values, instead of addressing their economic context or the pragmatic challenges involved in solving complex social problems (Dorfman, 2003).

The message frames through which media operate interact with the predisposition of their audience and the level of knowledge (or ignorance) audience members possess about particular issues. The effects of framing, therefore, are not uniform. They are filtered through the cognitive structures of the people who see or hear the framing (their "schemas"), and the constellations of knowledge and pre-existing worldviews (ideologies) people use to help them process new information.

The manner in which media framed the issue of welfare reform provides an excellent example. Although when Bill Clinton pledged to "end welfare as we know it" during the 1992 presidential campaign, the majority of welfare recipients were White and 70% were children, the media promoted the impression that most recipients were young African American women having multiple children out of wedlock and relying on the government for financial support. This framing of the issue significantly affected the substance of the 1996 welfare reform legislation, as reflected in its official title: "The *Personal Responsibility and Work Opportunity* Reconciliation Act" (Emphasis added; Avery & Peffley, 2003).

In constructing a message for an issue-oriented campaign, therefore, advocates need to consider the following questions:

1. What preconceptions or stereotypes are associated with the issue or with people affected by the issue?
2. What institution, system, or powerful decision maker is responsible for the problem?
3. What is the organization's vision and solution?

4. What action(s) do you want your target audience(s) to take?
5. What will happen if these targets do not take the action you desire? What is at stake?

IN-CLASS EXERCISE
BIG IDEA FRAMING

Identify an issue that affects the clients or constituents with whom you are working.

1. What question are people currently asking regarding the issue?
2. What new question (or restatement of an existing question) do you want to ask about this issue?
3. What makes this issue important? What is really going on and why should people whom the issue does not directly affect care about it?
4. What values are at the heart of the issue?

(Source: J. Quiroz et al., Center for Media Justice, 2014)

Social Media

Social media provide powerful tools to educate the public and mobilize supporters to take collective action. As with all strategies and tactics, the effectiveness of advocacy through social media depends to a considerable degree on how it complements an organization's overall strategy and to what extent it involves constituents and allies (Kanter & Fine, 2010). In addition, the use of social media presents certain unique challenges and features. First, the presence of digital literacy gaps among the population limits the utility of social media as an instrument of both education and organizing. If a process goal of advocates is to democratize advocacy campaigns, they need to take conscious steps to narrow this gap or find ways to compensate for its existence.

Second, for individuals who possess a modicum of digital literacy, social media are accessible, easy to use, and capable of widespread effect. Advocates can use social media to mobilize people rapidly for an action and create the potential to globalize social justice issues. Yet, the lack of individual accountability, the attraction of anonymity, the blurred boundary between personal and professional use, and the potential to disseminate false information in a plausible format through social media complicate the need for advocacy organizations or coalitions to speak with a single voice, stay on message, and maintain their credibility.

In addition, although social media foster immediacy and breadth of contact, they tend to produce weak ties with their audience. For example, recipients of social media messages can "click" on a link to demonstrate their support for a cause and contribute funds online. This is often helpful, but research demonstrates that virtual contact is considerably different from the bonds formed by face-to-face relationships (Gladwell, 2010). The lack of ongoing personal contact contributed to the difficulty that recent social change efforts—from the Occupy Wall Street movement to the "Arab Spring"—had in sustaining popular interest and participation (Cook, 2017; Gitlin, 2012).

Media, Social Movements, and Social Change

As Todd Gitlin (2003, 1980) pointed out in his classic *The Whole World is Watching*, media coverage is essential to sustain social movements. If employed strategically, it can be an effective mechanism for using an established institution for nonestablishment or antiestablishment goals. Media coverage can confer legitimacy on change efforts (such as occurred during the modern civil rights movement) or stifle them through selective reporting, a blackout of coverage, misrepresentation of the organizations involved or their leaders, and a distortion of a group's overall message. The response of the media to an advocacy campaign or social change effort also influences an organization's selection of strategies and tactics, the types of actions planned and executed, and sometimes even its goals. In some instances, distorted media coverage can produce an escalation of conflict between the establishment and a social change organization, especially when the lack of a public response frustrates the organization's leaders or members.

Evaluating Media Efforts

The evaluation of media advocacy serves a similar purpose to the evaluation of a legislative advocacy campaign or a new program or service. The basic purpose is to make judgments on what worked (or did not work), and generate knowledge to facilitate improvements in future media efforts. To conduct an effective evaluation, it is important first to determine:

1. What exactly do you want and need to know?
2. Is this information available?
3. How will you get this information?
4. How will you use this information if you obtain it?

This type of evaluation requires the assessment of the different components of a media advocacy campaign. Advocates need to examine whether their efforts were sufficiently strong, intense, and sustained. They need to analyze how well their media tactics matched the targeted audiences. They need to explore in what ways the nature and saliency of the issue they championed affected both their media advocacy efforts and the response they received from various audiences (Wallack, 1999).

Advocates can do this in several ways. By consulting with allies and somewhat detached third parties, they can analyze the effect of specific media events (e.g., an interview, press conference). They can engage in self-criticism as to whether their actions at these events matched their original intentions. They can measure how media frame their issues and the extent of media coverage. They can examine the effect of their tactics on relationships with key media players. Finally, advocates can assess how their media activities affected the level and intensity of support among their constituents and allies (Kegler, Twiss, & Look, 2000; Kegler et al., 2009).

Summary and Conclusion

This chapter examined some media strategies that advocates can use to promote their issues and the interests of their constituents. Although relationships with the media can often become frustrating or adversarial, it is important for advocates to remember that, under most circumstances, the press is not the enemy. It is fruitless to blame the press for bad coverage; complaints about poor coverage can even generate additional bad publicity about the advocacy campaign and its goals. It is better to maintain a sense of humor and a focus on the long-term purposes of the advocacy effort. Because personal relationships play such an important role in shaping media coverage, it is similarly foolish to hold a grudge against a reporter, radio personality, or television announcer. It is better to be polite or simply limit contact with such individuals.

As stated above, advocates benefit from making the media's job easier. They can do this in several ways. They can provide media contacts and media outlets with consistent messages and information tailored to their respective audiences in formats the media representatives find most useful and timely. Advocates can also employ a variety of media vehicles to expand coverage of their issue(s). This requires advocates to understand how different vehicles affect different audiences in different ways and how to use these vehicles for maximum effect.

Although using multiple media vehicles is generally a wise approach, advocates need to ensure that they stay on message throughout a campaign. For this reason, it is better to limit the number of campaign spokespersons and make sure to brief them regularly. It is also important for advocates to be careful on what they commit to paper and to remember that, particularly in today's multimedia environment, nothing is ever truly "off the record."

Chapter 14 will explore other means for advocates to initiate policy change: the court system, the monitoring of policy implementation, and the electoral process.

END-OF-CHAPTER EXERCISE
ASSESSING MEDIA COVERAGE OF AN ISSUE

Over the course of one week, follow the media coverage of a specific issue. Track how this coverage evolves, how different media (TV, radio, newspapers, and the internet) frame the issue and how different outlets within the same medium interpret it (e.g., the difference in coverage between Fox News and MSNBC).

1. What were the different ways media framed the issue?
2. How did media convey these framings?
3. What underlying assumptions did these framings reflect?
4. What facts did various media emphasize or exclude in framing the issue?

END-OF-CHAPTER EXERCISE
STORY FRAMING

Identify an issue that affects the clients or constituents with whom you are working.

1. What specific place, trend, or scene best illustrates the frame in which you would prefer to present this issue?
2. What is the conflict expressed or implied in this framing?
3. What is the historical, social, and/or political context that influences the framing?
4. Who are the "good guys" and the "bad guys" in this story?
5. What is the morale of the story?

(Source: J. Quiroz et al., Center for Media Justice, 2014)

Optional Assignment on Media Advocacy

1. Select an issue that affects the clients or constituents of the agency where you work or are doing your internship. Develop a three-page plan for a media advocacy campaign. This could include the creation of an overall media strategy, the development of campaign materials, organizing and holding press conferences or press events, or writing op-ed pieces.
2. Write an op-ed piece on this issue and submit it to a local newspaper.

CHAPTER 14

Advocacy in the Judicial, Executive, and Electoral Arenas

Politics is social work with power.

—**Former Senator Barbara A. Mikulski**

There is hardly a political question in the United States which does not sooner or later turn into a judicial one.

—**Alexis de Tocqueville, *Democracy in America***

Introduction

Despite their best efforts, advocates in the legislative arena often do not achieve their policy objectives. Entrenched political and ideological opposition to the expansion of social welfare policies, the stigma attached to beneficiaries of anti-poverty programs, a climate of fiscal austerity, and the growing influence of wealthy donors create a hostile environment for proponents of social reform. As a result, advocates often have to adopt alternative strategies to advance the interests of their clients and constituents, sometimes concurrently with their ongoing legislative advocacy. This chapter discusses three of these alternative approaches to advocacy: through the courts (judicial advocacy), through the electoral process, and through monitoring the implementation of policies after adoption. Although social workers may regard these advocacy strategies as outside their role or beyond their skill set, social workers have engaged in each activity for decades. As the various sections in this chapter demonstrate, they possess many of the skills required to contribute effectively in each of these arenas.

Advocacy in the Legal System

The concept of advocacy emerged from the legal system. To advocate means to argue on behalf of another party to help that party redress a grievance or obtain a benefit to which she or he is entitled. Given these legal origins, it is not surprising that attorneys dominate this approach to social and policy change. Nevertheless, social workers can and do play an important role in this type of advocacy. In fact, social workers have participated in legal advocacy for more than a century, beginning with the landmark 1908 Supreme Court case *Muller v. Oregon* (1908).

In this case, the court permitted the plaintiff's attorney (the future Supreme Court Justice Louis Brandeis) to integrate social scientific research into his brief (the famous "Brandeis brief"), which defended an Oregon law regulating the maximum number of hours women could labor in a week. Settlement house workers supplied Brandeis with research they had collected on the physical effects of long work hours on women's health to help support his arguments (Woloch, 1996). The introduction of such evidence marked the first foray by social workers into the realm of judicial advocacy (Reisch & Andrews, 2002). It was part of a broader "maternalist" approach to social reform, which ultimately lead to federal and state policy changes in such areas as health care and income support (Stern & Axinn, 2012).

This critical incident in the history of U.S. social work and American jurisprudence illustrates that legal advocacy is usually part of a broader strategy of social and political change. For example, the cases that ultimately lead to the 1954 *Brown* decision banning segregation in public schools were part of the multifaceted modern civil rights movement. For a number of reasons, using the courts is usually not advocates' first option for producing change. Instead, advocates generally coordinate legal advocacy with other forms of advocacy as part of a comprehensive long-term campaign.

Legal or judicial advocacy is complicated because of the unique features of the U.S. system of jurisprudence. In the United States, courts must act on a specific case, not on abstract issues as they may do, for instance, in European courts. Courts also have the authority to rule on both legislative acts and administrative policy decisions, such as a regulation or executive order. Despite their occasional influence on the outcome of judicial proceedings, such as those cited previously, empirically based arguments founded on social or behavioral science data have only a limited effect on courts' decision making (McAfee & Mcguire, 2007). More often, judges rely on precedent (the principle of ***stare decisis***) in deciding cases; at least they claim to use precedent as the basis of their rulings. In fact, courts are not immune from politics (see the decisions in *Bush v. Gore* [2000] and *Citizens United* [2005]) and public pressure (Neubauer & Meinhold, 2016).

U.S. courts also have a number of features that affect the strategies advocates might employ. As stated earlier, they decide cases, based on their interpretation of common law, rather than merely determining how to apply existing statutes on a large scale. In the United States, there are also two distinct court systems—state courts and federal courts—each with three levels (generally, district courts, appellate courts, and supreme courts). These systems operate on parallel tracks and intersect only at the level of the U.S. Supreme Court (Carp, Stidham, & Manning, 2010).

In discerning the meaning, intent, and constitutionality of both legislative and administrative laws, judges apply different interpretations of the U.S. Constitution. Some look specifically to language in the text (textualists), taking the words literally much as religious fundamentalists read scripture. Others purport to infer the intention of the men who wrote the Constitution (originalists), although the authors of the Constitution wrote it in a very different political and social context. Some justices and legal scholars, referred to as developmentalists, take a much different approach. They regard the Constitution as a living document; this position rationalizes a more expansive reading and the recognition of rights, such as the right to privacy, not explicitly stated in the Constitution (Lens, 2017).

Courts can also be reactive or proactive in their decisions. They can support or reject plaintiffs' claims on the discriminatory application of a statute (reactive) or issue an injunction against an executive order or federal regulation that the government has not yet implemented (proactive). They can rule on the substance of a policy or the processes used to develop or implement it (Howard & Steigerwalt, 2011).

Goals of Judicial Advocacy

Because of this complexity, advocates can use the judicial system to achieve diverse goals. Advocates can prevent government or private entities from engaging in certain conduct, such as discriminating against a specific population in the provision of a benefit or service, or polluting the nation's waterways. Judicial advocates can hold organizations (including government departments) and individuals, inside and outside the government, accountable for their actions or inaction. Court decisions can also modify or block legislation, or compel the government to implement a law in a particular manner. In the broadest sense, therefore, advocates use the courts for three purposes (Lens, 2017):

1. Protect established rights (e.g., voting rights).
2. Create new rights (such as the right for gay and lesbian couples to marry or the right to privacy, the basis for the *Roe v. Wade* (1973) decision).
3. Reinterpret long-standing rights (e.g., the expansion of the right of those arrested for an alleged crime, as in the 1966 *Miranda* case, or the Constitutional provision against "cruel and unusual punishment," used in cases involving the death penalty or life sentences for juveniles).

In addition, judicial advocacy can establish, expand, or restrict the right to a particular societal benefit, such as health care or education. For example, the Supreme Court ruled that state governments could not withhold access to public education from undocumented immigrant children. Courts have often dictated or defined the appropriate remedy in response to the violation of a person or group's rights, or as compensation for physical or economic harm inflicted by others. Through issuing an injunction, courts can force or delay legislative or executive policy decisions, or shift the burden of proof (the rationale for a new policy) to the legislative branch. Finally, of particular interest to social workers, court decisions can halt, reduce, or increase spending on a specific social program (Chambers & Bonk, 2013).

Certain recurring legal and constitutional issues influence the ability of advocates to use the judiciary to effect social or policy change. One long-standing issue is the extent to which the Constitution gives power to the states or the federal government. This is a particularly salient issue today because of the wide disparities among the states in their implementation of policies affecting issues ranging from reproductive rights to health care to environmental regulations.

Another important issue is whether the courts will interpret a law narrowly (based on its specific language) or broadly (based on an assessment of its sponsors' intent). This could determine how government defines and applies the "entitlement" (right) to a particular benefit, such as mental health care or special education. It could also influence the scope of proposed government regulations on issues such as environmental protection, the treatment of immigrants and refugees, and use of the internet.

The ambiguous language of certain constitutional amendments makes them subject to different judicial interpretations that have enormous implications for social policies that affect people's rights and well-being. For example, the 10th amendment states: "The powers not delegated to the U.S. [the Federal government] by the Constitution, nor prohibited by it to the States, are reserved to the States respectively, or to the people." What exactly does "nor prohibited by it to the States" mean? What body represents "the people?" How is the will of the people distinguished from the decisions of the people's elected representatives? (Epstein & Walker, 2009).

Similarly, the critical 14th amendment, adopted just after the Civil War, includes the significant phrase "... No State ... shall deprive any person of life, liberty, or property, without due process of law, nor deny to any person ... the equal protection of the laws." What is the meaning of due process? Does this principle apply to the federal government or only to the states? How can we assess what constitutes "equal protection of the laws"? These questions continue to vex constitutional scholars, policy makers, and advocates alike to this day.

In recent years, both Democrats and Republicans have condemned "judicial activism" when court rulings produced results contrary to their party's agenda. In the current highly politicized environment, advocates must be both careful in their use of the judicial system and also choose carefully which policy issues to promote through this means. As stated previously, whatever the issue, judicial advocacy works best when combined with other strategies.

If legal advocacy is so complicated and time-consuming, why should advocates use the courts at all to promote reform agendas? As the history of the past century demonstrates, one reason is that successful legal advocacy can win victories for unpopular causes ranging from ending racial segregation to establishing women's right to an abortion and the right of gay and lesbian couples to marry. Particularly in local cases, it can sometimes produce faster results for marginalized clients who find themselves in legal or economic jeopardy or physical danger.

Advocacy in the courts can also provide socially excluded groups with access to important information through disclosure rules (e.g., regarding the environmental effects of hydraulic fracking or the dumping of toxic materials in low-income communities). High profile cases often draw public attention to a problem that media outlets would otherwise ignore. On occasion, a lawsuit will compel a legislative body to increase funding for a particular social issue. In a recent example, a decision by the Supreme Court of Kansas compelled the state to change its method of funding public schools because the court found its current method violated the state's constitutional guarantee of a decent education for all children.

Sometimes even the threat of litigation can force policy makers to respond to an issue. As the president of a statewide advocacy coalition, the author was indirectly involved in one such effort that lead to major revisions in a state's foster care system. This use of legal advocacy also demonstrates how it can increase the credibility of an organization as a potential threat to the status quo (Lens, 2003).

Based on an assessment of how legal advocacy fits with their overall change strategy, advocates must decide whether the benefits of filing a lawsuit outweigh the costs and risks. Key factors to consider include:

1. *The nature of the remedy sought.* (For example, could advocates obtain a better and more sustainable remedy through another strategic approach such as legislative advocacy?)
2. *The likelihood that the government will implement a remedy in a timely manner.* (Note the typical gap between a court decision and its effect. The slow pace at which states and localities implemented the *Brown* decision is an important and painful reminder of this component of policy development.)
3. The possibility that the executive branch or the legislature will reverse, delay, or obstruct a favorable court ruling.
4. *The time, cost, and difficulty of filing a lawsuit.* This is particularly important to consider when advocates file a suit against a major corporation. Powerful business interests can stretch out the legal proceedings until plaintiffs can no longer afford to continue.
5. *The effect of filing a lawsuit on supporters and potential supporters in government.* For example, will they slow or abandon their efforts to promote an advocacy cause if they believe the courts will decide its outcome? Will winning the lawsuit inadvertently lead to a shift of funds away from other programs advocates support? (This is a classic example of an unintended consequence.)
6. *The prospects of winning and the risks involved*—financial, political, and psychological—if advocates lose.
7. The extent to which the suit will help advance solutions in other advocacy venues (Stoner, 1995).

Table 14.1 Pros and Cons of Judicial Advocacy

Pros	Cons
Process is open to all	Cost often precludes participation
Right of appeal exists	Complexity of appeals process
Egalitarian in principle	Time commitment involved; slow pace
Rules apply to all	Unpredictability of outcomes
Less political than legislative advocacy	Controversial and often unpopular
Principles matter in shaping outcomes	Expertise required may deter participation
Courts are less concerned with costs	

If after assessing all these factors, advocates decide to pursue a lawsuit, they must then determine which type of litigation to use. One option is to file a suit to change an existing law—for example, on the grounds it violates some provision of the state or U.S. Constitution, as advocates did recently in Kansas. A plaintiff in such cases could be an individual; alternately, a group of similarly affected individuals could file a class-action suit. Recent Supreme Court decisions, however, have made it more difficult for judges to certify similarly affected individuals as a "class."

Advocates could also file for an injunction. If approved, an injunction places a hold on the implementation of a policy developed by the executive branch. Examples include recent court decisions that enjoined presidential executive orders regarding the entry of refugees and immigrants from certain Muslim-majority nations.

Advocates could also support a lawsuit filed by another group by submitting an ***amicus curiae*** (literally, "friend of the court") **brief**. Although the parties that file such briefs have no technical legal standing in a case, often the arguments they present can supplement those of the plaintiff and influence the court's decision. For example, social workers can provide evidence of the social repercussions of certain policies that attorneys can integrate into plaintiffs' briefs (Galowitz, 1999).

Two other legal options exist that are particularly well suited for social work advocates. One is a request filed under the Freedom of Information Act (FOIA) to obtain government records that advocates could potentially use as ammunition in a future lawsuit or media advocacy campaign. Anyone can file such a request, although it often takes considerable time to obtain the requested information. Another option is a form of quasi-litigation—a complaint filed with an investigative agency, such as concerning violations in local housing regulations. Through research conducted with a colleague and several graduate students in San Francisco, the author uncovered information that became part of a complaint against the San Francisco Housing Authority (SFHA) filed with the federal Department of Housing and Urban Development (HUD). Ultimately, this complaint lead to a decision by HUD to place the SFHA temporarily under federal receivership until the city corrected the problems identified (Reisch & Rivera, 1999).

Ezell (2001) proposes that advocates use the following criteria to determine whether to pursue their constituents' interests through the judicial system:

- the seriousness and immediacy of the issue;
- the effectiveness of past strategies on the issue;
- the extent of public and legal support for constituents' cause;
- the possibility of getting a "day in court";
- the presence or absence of relevant legal precedents on the issue;
- the availability of effective legal counsel (possible legal resources include legal aid bureaus, law school clinics, public interest litigators [plaintiffs' law firms], public

interest clearinghouse, local bar associations, and legal advocacy organizations such as the American Civil Liberties Union); and

- the range of possible outcomes and their direct and indirect consequences.

Regarding the last criterion, Canon and Johnson (1999) suggest that advocates should ask four basic questions before making a strategic decision to use judicial advocacy:

1. Would the court's decision negate earlier legislation or an executive policy?
2. To what extent would the decision alter past precedents (and possibly establish a precedent that could be used in future advocacy efforts)?
3. What are the specific consequences of the range of possible court decisions and for whom?
4. How would the decision affect future administrative actions and the range of policy options available to the legislative branch?

To these four questions, I would add a fifth: How will participation in judicial advocacy affect the ability of an organization to pursue its constituents' interests in other ways in the future?

Electoral Advocacy

Many Americans, particularly younger people and communities of color, often regard electoral politics with a combination of apathy, cynicism, and disgust. They consider it an unattractive and ineffective form of activism, one tainted beyond redemption by corruption, dishonesty, and failure to recognize the issues that affect excluded and marginalized communities. Voter participation rates among these groups during recent election years reflect these emotions (Leighley & Nagler, 2014; Felchner, 2008). Social workers and social work students may also feel that the explicitly partisan nature of electoral politics contradicts the profession's value of objectivity and that the policy outcomes of elections rarely produce results consistent with the ethical imperative to pursue social justice (Rocha, Poe, & Thomas, 2010; Clark, 2000). Despite justifiable skepticism bordering on cynicism, and the frequently disappointing outcomes of recent elections, involvement in electoral politics can and often has produced policy changes that have real world consequences for clients and constituents (Shaw, 2013).

Promoting social or policy change through electoral politics, however, is considerably different from other forms of advocacy or the social action component of community organizing for a number of reasons. First, the overall purposes, particularly the short-term purposes, of electoral politics are different, as discussed in a subsequent section. Second, electoral politics—similar tofootball and basketball games—takes place within a time-limited frame. Advocates cannot reschedule or postpone the preset date of an election for any reason.

Third, before engaging in electoral politics, advocates must decide whether they will use a campaign to promote a specific issue or set of issues or to elect (or re-elect) a particular candidate. This decision affects the essential character of an electoral campaign, its overall strategy and tactics, staffing patterns, required resources, targeting, and definition of success (Shaw, 2013).

Finally, if the focus is on a candidate, much depends on whether the person seeking advocates' support is a challenger or an incumbent. If advocates back an incumbent, they must assess the value of people perceiving the candidate as an incumbent, particularly in an era where widespread dissatisfaction with the "establishment" exists at both ends of the political spectrum. Some incumbents overcome this problem by adopting the mantle of a political "outsider" even when they are a consummate "insider." This tactic is essential in districts in which incumbents face primary election challenges from opponents in their party who are considerably more to the right or left ideologically (Ansolabehere et al., 2010).

On the other hand, to be successful a challenger must address an entirely different set of problems. She or he must quickly acquire substantial voter recognition and obtain sufficient resources to mount a viable campaign. Media often keep "score" on early fund-raising totals as leading indicators of a candidate's popularity. A challenger must also decide if he or she wants to run a negative (personality-driven) or positive (issue-oriented) campaign. This decision is important because of voters' attitudes about the electoral process. Studies have shown that voters may vote for negative reasons, but want to believe they are voting for positive ones. They may bemoan the negativity of political campaigns, particularly campaign ads, but they respond to them viscerally (Ansolabehere & Iyengar, 1995; Kamber, 2003).

Whether an electoral campaign focuses on a candidate or a ballot initiative, *its overall purpose is get people to do one thing on one day in one place*. How can advocates produce this result? One way to conceive of the problem is to view elections much as promoting a movie: Advocates must figure out how people decide to go (i.e., vote) and use this knowledge to induce them to vote—and to vote in the way they want. This is not altogether different from determining how people decide to search for or use a particular program or service.

As in other forms of advocacy (*see chapters 12 and 13*), there are numerous potential goals of an electoral campaign. The most obvious one is winning—electing (or defeating) a candidate or passing (or defeating) a ballot initiative. Campaigns, however, are also useful vehicles to increase the public's awareness of an issue, strengthen an existing advocacy organization, obtain greater name recognition for an individual planning to run for elected office in the future, test the effectiveness of various tactics, and support allies engaged in a related struggle.

Advocates engaged in electoral politics could define "success," therefore, in different ways. It could mean winning an election, forcing a runoff, or even acquiring a much larger share of the vote than predicted. Success could also mean recruiting a certain number of donors or volunteers whom advocates might call upon for financial or practical assistance in future campaigns. (The author once directed a congressional campaign in which the candidate's district had changed substantially after the federal census. This change required the candidate to establish a "presence" in the new parts of the district and to attract a new cohort of backers who could support her in future campaigns. These goals determined much of the focus of the author's work.)

Other possible objectives of an electoral campaign are increasing a candidate's name recognition, gaining a favorable reception in a new district, and paying one's "respects" to powerful institutions or individuals, such as politicians, media representatives, churches, unions, or business leaders, to line up their support for future efforts, inside or outside of election campaigns. Finally, a campaign might seek to empower staff members and constituents by building their competence (skill set) and confidence.

To overcome resistance to participation or concerns that their skill set does not match the needs of politics, it might be useful for social workers to think of an electoral campaign in social work terms. In such terms, one can conceive of a political campaign as consisting of the following goals and components, as previous chapters discussed:

KEY CONCEPT SUMMARY
GOALS OF A POLITICAL CAMPAIGN

1. Organization building and sustenance—especially regarding the organization's infrastructure, staff ability, and methods of decision making.
2. Acquisition of adequate resources and creation of the means to allocate these resources effectively and efficiently.
3. Building and maintaining diverse coalitions and alliances.
4. Popular education and successful use of media
5. Community mobilization
6. Leadership development (Gerdes, 2010).

Similarly, the strategies proven most effective in political campaigns resemble those employed in other forms of advocacy, program development, or community organizing efforts. First, it is useful to begin a campaign by building on natural constituencies. This is analogous to identifying a community's strengths and assets.

Second, advocates in the electoral arena need to neutralize potential opponents and build communication bridges and interpersonal relationships with established collaborators and new groups and organizations as community organizers or individuals who initiate intraorganizational do. Third, as previously discussed, organizations are stronger when they combine geographic and affinity groups (i.e., those based on a common identity or issue). Finally, successful electoral campaigns, similar to those focused on legislative advocacy, need to frame the issues carefully, create and disseminate a clear, consistent message, and target their finite resources effectively (Hollihan, 2009).

KEY CONCEPT SUMMARY
TOP 10 BASIC COMPONENTS OF AN ELECTORAL CAMPAIGN

1. Clearly defined objectives
2. Focused research (on issues, opponents, voters) compiled in a technologically current database and management information system
3. Creation and testing of a campaign message
4. Mechanism to raise funds throughout the campaign
5. Adequate resources (money, paid staff, volunteers, space, technology)
6. Viable organization with a well-established infrastructure and clear lines of accountability
7. Targeting analysis (*see section on targeting*)
8. Overall strategy that matches specific tactics to the campaign's goals and objectives
9. Ability to respond to opponents' attacks and unexpected developments in a timely manner
10. A get-out-the-vote (GOTV) strategy

Effective campaigns also need three critical types of resources: money, people, and time. A brief comment on each type of resource may be helpful here. *People* are especially important in local campaigns; they have less significance in statewide campaigns (especially in large states) or national campaigns. Particularly in local campaigns, marginalized communities can often compensate, to a certain extent, for their lack of resources through "people power."

As discussed elsewhere in this and other chapters, social workers also have to overcome their repulsion about money. Although the consequences of the *Citizens United* decision reflect the sinister relationship between money and politics (Levitt, 2010; Kennedy, 2015; Mayer, 2016), *money* is not always "dirty." It is, in fact, an essential ingredient of virtually all electoral campaigns, as the Bernie Sanders campaign demonstrated in 2016. Finally, it is best to think of the third resource, *time*, not merely as a linear phenomenon, but in different ways during different phases of an electoral campaign.

A few additional observations are in order here. First, campaign *organizations* are both more effective and more critical in local races, where the physical connection between the campaign and voters is much closer (Woo, 1980). Second, as recent events illustrate, primary and general election campaigns are very different—in terms of their goals, strategies, and tactics. In some districts, where one party is clearly dominant, the primary election is the critical election. The general election merely confirms the results of the primary. Voters in primary elections are also different from those in general elections. They tend to be more political active, committed to specific issues, and to come from the ends of the ideological spectrum.

Third, especially in campaigns focused on a ballot initiative, the campaign organization is more important than visible symbols, whether these symbols appear over social media or in more traditional campaign venues (signs, buttons, T-shirts, stickers). Fourth, whatever the type of campaign it is critical to assess the district (voters) well and use these data to target efforts at persuasion, fund-raising, and voter turnout. Finally, advocates and organizers must recognize that all organizations have "outside limits" of their effectiveness. The best organization cannot compensate for a weak candidate, poorly conceived tactics, a hostile political climate, or an opponent with vastly superior resources.

Campaign Resources: People and Money

Volunteers. The two most critical resources in an electoral campaign are the people involved in the campaign and the funds raised to support it. The media sometimes portray the recruitment of large numbers of volunteers as a sign of a campaign's popularity and an early indicator of "success." This is somewhat misleading. As in HSOs, the effective use of volunteers requires careful screening, training, and supervision. It also requires strategic use of volunteers to maximize their effect.

One way to do this is by developing a "volunteer budget." This involves calculating the number of volunteer hours required to perform certain essential campaign tasks, such as entering data, preparing a mailing, arranging a campaign event, distributing literature, or making phone calls. It is important to be realistic in creating this plan, particularly to give volunteers realistic tasks (this is where proper screening and training are critical), and to pace the use of volunteers reasonably and compassionately. (Some campaigns burn out their volunteers before the critical last phases begin.) It is also useful to do the groundwork for volunteers to make their jobs easier, by providing them with adequate space, time, and equipment.

Campaign events, such as rallies, are a good place to recruit volunteers, and social media postings are increasingly effective in attracting people to work on a campaign—if staffers follow up with in-person contacts. Whatever their age or demographic characteristics, volunteers need lots of "tender loving care" throughout the campaign, not merely in a "volunteer appreciation celebration" at the end of the campaign. Remember—volunteers are giving up their time, energy, and skills because they care about the issues and/or the candidate. They may also see volunteering as an opportunity to expand their social networks and learn new skills.

Even in the most well-run campaign organizations, tensions between paid staff members and volunteers will inevitably arise, particularly during crises and the frantic last days of a campaign (Nielsen, 2011; Cogburn & Espinoza-Vasquez, 2011). There are several ways to minimize these tensions. First, just as one would in an HSO or neighborhood organization, it is important to define the roles of paid and volunteer staff clearly and early. Second, campaigns should establish clear lines of supervision and accountability.

Third, make sure all volunteers receive sufficient training before assigning tasks, particularly complex tasks that require critical judgment. Fourth, keep the campaign's spokespersons separate from volunteers. Authorize only paid staff or carefully selected surrogates to speak for the campaign. Fifth, do not hesitate to ask volunteers to leave the campaign organization if they do not fulfill their responsibilities effectively or in a timely manner, or do anything to sabotage the internal climate of the campaign organization or its external image. Just as firing an employee for incompetence or ethical violations, such actions are most effective if done promptly and efficiently.

Money: The Mother's Milk of Politics. Although volunteers can provide enormous assistance to a campaign, particularly one that is relatively strapped for cash, no number of volunteers can entirely replace money. The cost of advertising alone makes it prohibitive for a campaign to rely primarily on "people power" (McCarthy, Poole, & Rosenthal, 2016). Although in recent years online fund-raising has replaced traditional fund-raising methods, some of the old rules on fund-raising still apply (West, 2013). First, unless a campaign possesses a large donor base of "fat cats," it should not rely on fund-raisers to reach its resource goals. Second, from a strategic perspective, it is important not to confuse fund-raising (which has a clear instrumental purpose) with other campaign objectives, such as educating the public.

Third, advocates should never apologize for asking for money, particularly when approaching someone who has expressed interest in the campaign and has sufficient means to contribute. The author recalls the first time he had to make such a request to the representative of a **political action committee** (PAC) or a potential major donor. The words initially seemed to stick somewhere in my throat. Once I was able to get the words out for the first time, and received an affirmative response, it was much easier to ask for money in the future. The same process applies, of course, to fund-raising for programs in HSOs, as discussed in Chapter 11.

All campaign contributions, however, are not of equal value. As the name of the feminist PAC EMILY's List reflects, early money is best (the acronym EMILY's List stands for **E**arly **M**oney **I**s **L**ike **Y**east) (Pimlott, 2010). Finally, in allocating campaign resources, it is best to use multiple budgets for different aspects of the campaign (e.g., media, campaign events, get-out-the vote [GOTV] efforts). This is similar to developing program budgets in an HSO.

Phases of an Electoral Campaign. Just as in a legislative advocacy campaign, community organizing drive, or program planning process, it is important to distinguish among the various phases of a campaign to focus strategic thinking and action (Burton, Miller,

& Shea, 2015). Most campaigns consist of five distinct phases. The first phase, which can last anywhere from a few months to one or two years, is the preliminary phase. In this phase, the campaign organization gathers data to test the waters to determine the feasibility of its goals.

In phase two, the early phase (several months after the official campaign kickoff), staff members lay the groundwork for the remainder of the effort. Fund-raising begins in earnest, more staffers are hired, and staff functions clearly defined. The campaign organization installs data collection and management systems. Volunteer recruitment and outreach to potential allies begins. During the middle phase of the campaign, the focus is primarily on organization building (staff, volunteers, endorsers, allies) and fund-raising.

The focus shifts during the last three months of a campaign. At this time, the emphasis is on sharpening the campaign's message on issues and communicating it to persuadable voters. This includes more extensive use of media (although some well-financed campaigns saturate the media with ads earlier to drive out competition) and the development of sophisticated targeting strategies. Finally, during the final month, the campaign applies the data collected from its targeting analysis to two fundamental tasks: persuading undecided voters and motivating supporters to vote on Election Day.

Except for the final phase of a campaign, these stages do not have a fixed number of days or months. In this respect, planning an electoral campaign resembles the steps involved in developing a new program or service, or strategizing on legislative advocacy efforts. Advocates need to determine how much time they need to:

- reach the people the campaign requires (donors, supporters, volunteers, voters);
- complete the major priorities of the campaign (as outlined previously);
- develop and implement an effective media strategy;
- raise sufficient funds;
- prepare the candidate adequately or—in the case of a ballot initiative campaign—prepare the campaign's spokespersons; and
- plan and implement the campaign's targeting and get-out-the-vote strategies.

Targeting Analysis: Using Campaign Resources Wisely

Just as in legislative advocacy, targeting a campaign's efforts is critical to its success. In an electoral campaign, the primary goal of a targeting strategy is to identify probableand potential supporters and, in different ways, reach out to persuade or motivate them to behave a specific way on Election Day. A targeting analysis, therefore, needs to reflect the overall goals of the campaign.

Although cities, counties, and states divide the electoral map into districts (or precincts), this division is not a useful way to formulate a targeting strategy. Most people identify with a particular demographic group, issue, or neighborhood; they do not know their specific electoral district. In addition, campaigns today develop their targeting strategies through sophisticated computer-generated statistical analyses and implement these strategies via telephone, mail, or the internet (Karpf, 2012). They use door-to-door outreach only in small geographic areas, such as urban neighborhoods, because it is more efficient to use other means (Nielsen, 2012).

Most campaigns employ the following resource allocation when applying campaign resources to targeting efforts.

Table 14.2 Allocating Resources for Targeting

Population Characteristics	Proportion of Resources	Purpose
Highly favorable/High average turnout	~1/3	GOTV
Highly favorable/Unknown potential turnout	~1/4	GOTV
Undecided/High potential turnout	~1/4	PERSUADE
Undecided/Low potential turnout	~1/6	PERSUADE
Highly unfavorable/Any potential turnout	0	IGNORE

On the surface, this approach may seem undemocratic, but in a competitive campaign in which resources are finite and the outcome is critical, it is the most effective and efficient way to allocate time, personnel, and money.

Targeting and Polling. Many well-financed campaigns make frequent and extensive use of polls to shape their targeting strategies. As the 2016 election cycle revealed, however, polls can distort the sentiments and inclinations of the electorate and fail to reveal the issues animating voters. Campaigns, therefore, can both use and abuse polls, particularly if they rely on polls as the sole means to discern the public's mood (Lake, 1987).

The primary purpose of polls is not to measure the relative popularity of candidates, but to determine which issues voters consider sufficiently important to act (vote). Campaigns can also use polls to assess how to deliver their message in a manner that is consistent with voters' views and values, and to determine how the electorate perceives a candidate (or a ballot issue) and for what reasons. In addition, polls are particularly helpful if campaigns use them to identify the "holes" in their strategies and tactics, where opponents are vulnerable, and how to allocate resources effectively in their targeting strategies.

KEY CONCEPT SUMMARY
10 STEPS IN VOTER REGISTRATION AND GET-OUT-THE-VOTE (GOTV) DRIVES

1. Learn the laws
2. Form a coalition
3. Identify the unregistered
4. Plan the drive
5. Recruit volunteers
6. Conduct the registration drive
7. Disseminate publicity on the candidate and the issues
8. Educate new voters
9. GOTV
10. Evaluate the efforts after the election

Ballot Initiatives

Ballot initiatives or referenda have become an increasingly popular way among activists of all political and ideological persuasions to promote their policy agendas. Advocacy groups have used ballot initiatives to pass conservative policies, such as freezing property taxes (California's Proposition 13), banning Affirmative Action (Michigan's Proposition 2), or defining marriage in traditional heterosexual terms (HoSang 2010; Bowler & Glazer, 2008). Other advocacy organizations have employed referenda to pass progressive reforms, such as laws increasing the minimum wage, permitting same-sex marriage, and expanding educational opportunities for "Dreamers" (Frank, 2017; Nichols, 2013)

There are two primary reasons for the increased use of ballot initiatives. Due to hyper-partisanship, policy deadlock in some state governments and in Congress has become so severe that there is no other way for advocates to advance policy reforms. Conversely, in other jurisdictions, one-party rule frustrates the ambitions of groups at the other end of the political spectrum. Both situations encourage advocates to try to go around existing policy-making mechanisms and make their appeals directly to the people (Shaw, 2013).

These were the precise reasons states originally adopted the referendum process more than a century ago during the Progressive Era. At that time, domination of state legislatures by the "trusts" (corporate interests) had become so pervasive that no alternatives to promote social reforms appeared to be available (Piott, 2003). Although proponents of the referendum process in the early 20th century regarded it as a means to restore American democracy, the ballot initiative process today cannot escape the same influence that shaped legislative policy making during the Progressive Era and continues to shape it today: the dominance of big money. This often results in competing initiatives, sometimes with deliberately confusing wording, appearing on the same ballot, or produces a dizzying array of referenda requiring voters' approval (Bowler & Glazer, 2008).

Despite these problems with the initiative process, it remains an effective tool to expand the rights of marginalized populations, enhance environmental protections, reform criminal justice policy, and allocate more resources to public schools and universities, pre-k programs, and health and behavioral health services. Advocates have also used ballot initiative campaigns to educate the public on issues ranging from domestic violence to wage theft and to block corporate-sponsored efforts designed to thwart anti-pollution measures (Philip & Reisch, 2015).

Randy Shaw (2013), the director of numerous successful initiative campaigns, argues that advocates should follow five rules in using this approach to promote policy change:

1. Determine that there is no other way to produce the desired change.
2. Appeal to voters' self-interests (which are generally economic or value-based).
3. Keep the message of the initiative campaign clear and simple.
4. Involve those most affected by the issue in the campaign process.
5. Evaluate the overall political context.

A further caveat is to remember that ballot initiatives are quite different from candidate elections.

Advocates must also answer a host of fundamental questions in four distinct areas before engaging in this type of activity. First, how permeable is the environment? Is the timing right to mount this campaign? How will you determine this? Advocates can attempt to assess to what extent people are concerned about the issue at the heart of the ballot initiative campaign. Through surveys, door-to-door research, focus groups, conversations with key informants, and an analysis of local media outlets they can measure the degree of discomfort or discontent people have expressed on this issue (Tolbert & Smith, 2005).

Second, advocates need to determine what potential exists to mobilize enough people to mount a successful campaign? (LeRoux, 2007). Is there a large number of disaffected voters who care enough about this issue to contribute to the campaign, volunteer for the campaign, and vote for (or against) the ballot initiative? Can advocates frame the message of the initiative in a manner that increases the likelihood of voter mobilization? Can the campaign target different groups differently?

Third, how popular or unpopular is the issue? How does the public feel about the populations most affected by the issue (e.g., the LGBTQ population, immigrants, or low-wage workers)? Are voters willing to pay the direct or indirect costs of the initiative's passage or failure, particularly if others will be the more likely beneficiaries?

Fourth, advocates need to assess the ability of their organizations to sustain a complex and lengthy advocacy campaign. Does the organization have adequate financial resources, paid staff, volunteers, organizational infrastructure, and technical expertise? Does it have a sufficiently large electoral "base" to win?

In addition, advocates must consider the following issues that parallel the challenges encountered by groups engaged in legislative advocacy. First, they need to identify the connection of the ballot initiative to their organization's long-term strategy. Second, because ballot initiatives invariably require alliances to succeed, advocates have to assess the pros and cons of working with political parties, unions, coalitions, or other advocacy organizations. Third, as with all social change efforts, to ensure that referenda campaigns do not exclude the populations they are intended to benefit, advocates must decide what roles constituents can play and at what points in the process (Bowes & Sims, 2006). Finally, advocates have to determine whether they can frame an issue to reflect a local emphasis and the self-interest and values of prospective voters.

Passing an Initiative. Given the inclination of voters to reject a ballot initiative—particularly if it involves additional expenditures (Shaw, 2013)—it is critical that advocates select, in advance, which strategies and tactics would be most effective in persuading different sections of the electorate. To avoid engaging in top-down advocacy, they also need to determine which campaign methods would most likely enhance community participation. This includes emphasizing the values that are most culturally relevant to their constituents and selecting symbols (e.g., images and slogans) that resonate most powerfully with targeted populations. These choices are especially important if advocates want to encourage new groups or excluded communities to become involved in the campaign, particularly those usually marginalized in the policy-making or electoral process (LeRoux, 2007). Finally, advocates must often choose if their primary goal is to "win" (pass or defeat an initiative) or to use the campaign to build their organization, educate the public, and mobilize their constituents.

Defeating an Initiative. Although campaigns to pass a ballot initiative resemble campaigns to elect a particular candidate in numerous ways, campaigns to defeat an initiative are quite different. (While the purpose of some candidate elections is often to defeat an unpopular incumbent or prevent a challenger from winning, virtually all candidate elections must also have the goal of helping someone *win.*) Shaw (2013) suggests that campaigns use four approaches to defeat a ballot initiative:

1. Educate the public on its potential ramifications, particularly its economic effect or its effects on something about which the public cares deeply (e.g., the environment).
2. Exaggerate the worst parts of the initiative. This is analogous to "playing to your strong suit" in legislative advocacy.

3. Eliminate all extraneous issues in your messaging. Frame the issue narrowly and clearly. The opposition will often try to confuse voters by obfuscating the central issue.
4. Evaluate the public's perception regularly through multiple means (i.e., not just polls).

Shaw also points out that voters are more inclined to oppose an initiative if its wording is unclear, if they perceive it as costly, if they regard it as contrary to their core values, or if it appears to be blatantly unfair.

Media and Ballot Initiatives. As in legislative advocacy, initiative campaigns need to coordinate their media strategy with their overall strategy. This includes researching the media habits of various target audiences, particularly where they receive most of their information, which programs they watch or listen to, which internet sites they visit, and which media personalities they trust. Next, advocates must test the campaign's message, preferably on a small scale to allow them to correct bad choices and limit damage to the campaign (Dorfman, 2003). Once the campaign settles on a certain message, it must convey it consistently and honestly, even if it stresses diverse components of the message in different settings (Iyengar & McGrady, 2007). In addition to testing the substantive theme(s) of the campaign, the organization also needs to test the style and tone of its campaign spots. Pretesting ads with focus groups is an effective and relatively inexpensive way to do this (Leighley, 2004).

Given perpetual resource scarcity, one cost-effective way to test ads is to take advantage of free media as much as possible, albeit with caution regarding the potential pitfalls (*See Chapter 13.*) Free media vehicles suitable for "product testing" include public interest programs, podcasts, and talk shows. Because the complexity of the initiative process further complicates the existing challenges of media advocacy, it is advisable for advocacy groups, especially those with limited experience, to hire a consultant to help develop their media strategy.

This sounds expensive, but some media organizations provide pro bono work for advocacy campaigns, particularly campaigns that have the potential to generate favorable publicity for the consultants. The author worked on an advocacy campaign in San Francisco to pass a "children's budget" measure that would require the city government to spend a certain proportion of property tax revenues on children's programs. The campaign benefited enormously from the visual ads developed pro bono by a well-known consulting firm. Beautiful posters of children from all the city's diverse communities appeared at virtually every bus stop and Metro station. It was impossible for city residents to avoid them. In combination with widespread support in print media and by key surrogates, these powerful images played a critical role in passage of the ballot initiative (Brodkin, 1994).

Administrative and Regulatory Advocacy

All too often after achieving a hard-fought and infrequent victory in the courts, the executive branch, or the legislative arena, advocates celebrate, evaluate their efforts, and move on to the next issue. This is a critical mistake. As a former colleague, the late Jules Berman, who helped develop the regulations that shaped the implementation of the original Social Security Act, once opined, "You can write the law, let me write the rules." In other words, the passage of a statute, however sweeping and precedent shattering, means little if the regulations (or rules) governing its implementation do not reflect the original intentions of whomever drafted the law. It is vitally important, therefore, for advocates to sustain their efforts through the often tedious and highly detailed process of monitoring the implementation of legislation, fiscal decisions made by the executive branch, or court rulings for which they have struggled for months, perhaps years (Staller, 2017; Chambers & Bonk, 2013).

Administrative regulations serve multiple purposes in the policy-making process. They define legislative terms that are often deliberately vague (to gain passage of a law). They respond to the need for flexibility in the administration of legislation because of wide demographic, cultural, and political differences among states and regions. In addition to reflecting the various political considerations and compromises involved in passing a law, regulations fill in critical gaps in the legislation itself (Hoefer & Ferguson, 2007).

For example, suppose Congress passed a law allocating billions of dollars to establish universal pre-k programs throughout the nation and gave the Department of Education (DOE) the responsibility for administering the legislation. How would the DOE determine how much money to give each state (i.e., what funding formula would it apply)? Would the programs established in different states and localities be free to participating families or would the government base fees on the ability to pay? If the latter, what income level would be the cutoff to receive a subsidy? Finally, what features would pre-k programs be required to have to qualify for federal funds? This could affect such areas as teacher-to-student ratios, the number of children permitted in each program, the availability of health personnel, the treatment of children with physical disabilities, and even the requisite square footage per child. This brief example illustrates why advocates must not abandon their responsibilities to their constituents after the initial phase of policy making is over (Nicholson-Crotty, 2011).

The Rule-Making Process

The primary bases of administrative lawmaking are the Delegation Doctrine in the Constitution and the Administrative Procedures Act. The latter established a 10-step process to create the regulations governing the implementation of legislative and executive decisions. The government publishes these rules in the *Federal Register* and the national *Code of Federal Regulations.*

Government regulations serve multiple purposes under the broad function of determining and implementing the intent of legislatures. They clarify vague wording and fill in gaps in the knowledge underlying the provisions of a law. The rule-making process also fulfills the need to inform the public and government departments on the implementation of legislative actions. In addition, rules provide a practical design for policy implementation and define the stages (and pace) of implementing a new law. As described previously, they also help clarify a policy's program components and requirements (Coglianese, Kilmartin, & Mendelsohn, 2008). Of particular interest to social workers, rules may shape eligibility requirements for programs such as nutritional assistance or housing supports by establishing means and assets tests, create noneconomic criteria to determine eligibility for a benefit, and ensure or weaken due process requirements (Brown, 2001).

To influence the rule-making process, advocates need to be aware of its structure and timing, and the venues through which they can apply pressure. Through the development of good relationships with individuals who make the rules and with those who have access to them, advocates can *sometimes* help overcome the gap between legislative intent and implementation (Fox, 2001). Because this process is painstaking and time-consuming, advocates are usually more effective in monitoring regulations if they form an ad hoc coalition with other like-minded groups. As president of a national children's advocacy group, the author participated in such a coalition. The coalition spent more than a year trying to persuade the five members of the Federal Communications Commission to revise *less than one line* in its regulations regarding children's television programming. Although the coalition ultimately succeeded, the effort consumed a great deal of time, resources, and political capital.

KEY CONCEPT SUMMARY
THE 10-STEP RULE-MAKING PROCESS

1. Origin
2. Authorization
3. Planning
4. Development of rules
5. Internal review
6. External review
7. Revision and publication of draft rules

8. Public participation and comment
9. Implementation
10. Post-adoption activities

The last step includes ongoing monitoring by advocates (see below) and potential congressional changes to existing rules. The latter can occur through amendments, rescission of the original rules, or modifications in the rules through the allocation or withholding of funds in the congressional budgeting process (Jansson, 2014).

The Importance of Monitoring

There are several reasons why it is important for advocates to monitor the process of policy implementation. One reason is to assess whether there is a "fit" between the original social problem and the intended and actual goals of legislation designed to solve it (Bell & Bell, 1982). Another is to determine whether the policy inadvertently lead to the stigmatization of beneficiaries. A third reason is to analyze whether the policy's implementation was poorly targeted leading to underutilization or overutilization, or if it distributed benefits to groups other than the original "population-at-risk" (Brown, 2001). Finally, it is critical to monitor policies that include new guidelines for government agencies or private corporations to ensure that enforcement is sufficiently stringent and that regulators hold these organizations accountable (Schneider & Lester, 2001).

In each of these situations, advocates monitor what policy makers refer to as the "implementation gap." Sometimes this gap appears because the policy interferes with a government agency's self-interest. Sometimes it emerges because there are differences among administrators in their interpretation of legislative language. At times, individuals or departments charged with enforcing policies deliberately circumvent their intent, particularly if there is insufficient public pressure or oversight. It does not require an excess of cynicism to recognize that legislators may mask the purposes of a law and administrators may occasionally lack benign intent in its implementation. This is why advocates must continue to be vigilant even after they have achieved legislative success (Jansson, 2014).

Monitoring Unforeseen or Unintended Consequences. A final reason why monitoring policy implementation is a critical component of advocacy is to minimize the effect of unforeseen and unintended consequences. Examples include the effects of welfare policy on the traditional family structure in low-income communities, the effect of deinstitutionalization on the number of homeless people in the United States, the maintenance of a fee-for-service model in Medicare on the cost of health care, and the contribution of welfare reform to the increase in chronic and deep poverty.

Sometimes such consequences occur because of flaws or gaps in the policy development and policy implementation processes. Even the most astute policy advocates may overlook these flaws. Often, however, unintended consequences arise because there are inevitable "unknowns" in the policy-making process (Bloomrosen et al., 2011; Massey & Pren, 2010). These include unforeseen major changes in the economy, such as the Great Recession of 2007–2009; demographic shifts, such as surges or declines in the birth or marriage rate; technological innovations, such as the effect of the internet; and unexpected crises, such as a war or natural disaster. These are part of what analysts refer to as the "Black Box" of policy making (Birkland, 2014).

Policy makers and advocates may be aware of other, known factors in the contemporary environment, including economic globalization, policy devolution, state fiscal crises, heightened resource competition within the nonprofit sector, and the presence of an increasingly multicultural society. They may not understand, however, the full implications of these developments, how they interact with one another, or the nature of their long-term effects. Participants in the policy process may also not be able to assess the effect of vested government or private interests on a policy's implementation, honest differences in interpreting legislators' intent, and genuine confusion and misunderstanding of a policy's purposes. Finally, they may not take into account the absence of benign intent toward the intended beneficiaries of a policy among those charged with its implementation, including the presence of unstated purposes within a policy that reflect racism, sexism, or homophobia (Neubeck & Cazenave, 2002).

How to Monitor Policy Implementation

Advocates have at their disposal a number of means to monitor the implementation of a policy. They can conduct surveys or use surveys conducted by other organizations, such as the Kaiser Family Foundation or the Pew Charitable Trust. They can analyze census data and gain additional insights into the meaning of these data by applying innovative technology, such as geographic information systems (GIS) (Nyerges, Couclelis, & McMaster, 2011). If they possess sufficient resources and staff, advocacy organizations can interview clients and department employees affected by the policy change, evaluate program outcomes at the agency level, and track the assessment of oversight agencies.

Creative advocates also "massage" existing data in new ways by using advanced statistical methods, such as time series analysis, or framing the issue and policy goals in new ways. After they complete their analysis, advocates can disseminate "report cards" detailing how effectively different states or different agencies implemented the policy. In extreme cases of malfeasance or misfeasance, they can "blow the whistle" in the media on incompetent or corrupt administrators who were charged with implementing a policy (Johnson, 2003; Johnson & Kraft, 1990).

Even the most capable advocacy groups, however, cannot monitor all aspects of the policy implementation process or predict all of its intended and unintended consequences. One reason for this limitation is that it is impossible to track clients who drop out of the system or are off the "radar screen." Each time Congress passed "welfare reform," advocates could not determine what happened to individuals and families who were no longer in the welfare system or on the rolls of any other public or private HSOs (Abramovitz, 2005). In other circumstances, clients or constituents are off the radar screen because existing systems fail to account for people's relocation across regional county or state lines. This often causes monitoring problems for advocates concerned about the plight of individuals at risk of homelessness (Fertig & Reingold, 2008).

Another obstacle to effective monitoring is the difficulty of identifying unforeseen or underestimated barriers to clients' utilization of a new policy initiative. For example, were the personnel who staffed a program culturally competent? Was the program physically accessible to clients (in terms of its hours, proximity to transportation)? What was the effect of specific components of the policy on distinct populations? For example, if Congress implements severe cuts in the Medicaid program—which, as of this writing, may be possible—how would various states implement these cuts? How would they affect diverse groups in each state—older adults, childless adults, young families, and individuals with disabilities?

A related problem could arise if a policy change had a significant effect on other systems or programs in similar programmatic areas. Did the receipt of a new benefit affect some clients' eligibility for an existing benefit? Does the process of applying for a new program create an undue burden? What is the policy's effect on the secondary aspects of clients' lives?

In addition, whatever its short-term benefits, advocates can experience difficulty assessing a policy's long-term risks to clients or measuring its potential effects on third parties. Especially in diverse communities, it is particularly important to monitor a policy's effect on population subsets whose members, due to their age, race, gender, income, sexual orientation, or ability status, the policy may affect differently. Finally, it is often almost impossible to determine the overall consequences of a new policy for entire communities, even if a policy affects a large proportion of its members.

Given these limitations and constraints, what can social workers do as advocates? One approach to monitoring would be to engage in holistic, qualitative participatory action research (PAR) that involves clients and constituents to the maximum possible extent (McIntyre, 2007). This is similar to enhancing clients' participation in program development and evaluation (*See Chapter 11*) and expanding constituents' involvement in legislative advocacy campaigns (*See Chapter 12*). An alternative might be to focus monitoring efforts exclusively on the secondary effects of a new policy on organizations or specific features of a community. The author's research (Reisch & Bischoff, 2002;

Reisch & Sommerfeld, 2002) on the effect of welfare reform on nonprofit organizations in Philadelphia and southeast Michigan is an example of this type of monitoring.

Another option is to conduct advocacy-oriented research that investigates the flaws in the implementation process and engages in whistle-blowing if research uncovers serious problems. A final possibility is to use the monitoring process to redefine the policy's stated goals and reframe the context in which government or nonprofit agencies implement the policy. Advocates would only employ this strategy if the policy's initial consequences appear to be quite distinct from its purported original intentions, and if they believe this strategy represents the only way to get their advocacy efforts back on track (Johnson, 2003).

Summary and Conclusion

This chapter discussed three types of advocacy in which social workers are less frequently involved but are just as important to achieve the profession's social justice goals. Advocacy in a less partisan judicial system can sometimes achieve policy changes when various political obstacles thwart legislative advocacy efforts. Legal advocacy can also broaden the scope of policy discourse, draw public attention to issues previously ignored by policy makers and the media, and provide a new policy with greater permanence through the application of a constitutional "seal of approval."

Much as judicial advocacy, regulatory advocacy is critical to ensure that administrative misfeasance or malfeasance does not undermine hard-fought policy victories. This type of advocacy can also promote greater equity in the process of policy implementation, and identify gaps or unexpected problems that emerged in the translation of policy makers' intentions into action.

Finally, advocacy in the electoral arena can serve multiple purposes. It can help elect candidates whose views more closely align with social work values and who will support advocates' policy initiatives in their legislative or executive roles. It can also cast a spotlight on critical issues that advocates have struggled to insert into the public's consciousness or the agendas of policy makers. In addition, despite its costs and risks, advocates can work for or against ballot initiatives to bypass intransigent legislatures or resistant executives through application of the techniques of direct democracy.

The final chapter (Chapter 15) will focus on advocacy within HSOs—to promote intraorganizational change and address the conflicts that inevitably arise in agency settings.

END-OF-CHAPTER EXERCISE
SELECTING AN ADVOCACY APPROACH

1. Think about a policy issue that affects the clients or constituents with whom you work or have worked. What judicial decisions shaped the substance of the policy or its manner of implementation? What role could social workers play in judicial advocacy in expanding the scope or effect of this policy?
2. Identify a ballot initiative whose passage (or defeat) affected the lives of the clients of your agency or the members of a community in which you live or work. How did the framing of the initiative influence the outcome of the campaign?
3. Do you believe social workers should become involved in electoral campaigns in support of or against particular candidates? Is such activity consistent with or in violation of the profession's code of ethics? How would you justify your response?
4. If you believe social workers should be involved in electoral politics, under what circumstances should they be involved? What roles should or could they play? Would you consider running for office?
5. If you believe social workers should not be involved in electoral politics, what other means would you suggest for social workers to influence the outcome of future legislative or executive policy making?
6. Identify a law or executive decision whose implementation is critical for the well-being of your clients or constituents. In what ways could you or your agency monitor the implementation of the law? What obstacles might make this process difficult? How might you overcome these obstacles?

CHAPTER 15

Promoting Change and Dealing With Conflict in Multicultural Organizations

A culture of experimentation is critical to the nonprofit mission.

—John Salls, cofounder, SAS

If you want to bring an end to long-standing conflict, you have to be prepared to compromise.

—Aung San Suu Kyi

Introduction

In our rapidly changing society, organizations must adapt quickly to survive, provide continuously effective services, or promote lasting community and societal change. The forces of resistance to change are ever-present, both internally and externally, and initiating and implementing change efforts often involves dealing with individual and group conflict within the organization. This chapter will focus on several critical components of intraorganizational change and provide students with the specific skills to initiate and manage the change process and to deal with conflict when it arises. It will also discuss how to make effective use of internal conflict. Specific topics covered are:

- the nature of planned change in organizations, including matching a change strategy to an organization's context and culture and sustaining organizational change efforts;
- strategies for dealing with intraorganizational and inter-organizational conflict, including skills for the constructive use of such conflict; and
- ethical issues in promoting change and conflict.

Promoting Intraorganizational Change

As discussed in Chapter 3, all organizations evolve as they go through their life cycle. Many of the changes that occur are "natural" and inevitable. Others appear because of unexpected financial or personnel crises, the unintended consequences of programs or services, demographic shifts in the stakeholder population, and leadership transitions (Lester, Parnell, & Carraher, 2003; Hasenfeld & Schmidt, 1989; Quinn & Cameron, 1983). This chapter, however, focuses specifically on purposive or planned organizational change.

Organizations initiate planned change for a variety of reasons. They recognize the need to respond more effectively to existing or emerging needs among their clients and constituents. Dramatic changes in the external environment are often a prime motivator. Examples of external sources of change include a changing client base, greater emphasis among funders on accountability (outcome-based funding), emergence of new or revised community needs, major policy shifts such as welfare reform and managed care, and annual differences in local, state, and federal budgets. Examples of internal sources of change include leadership turnover (of major staff or board members), significant resource cuts or the acquisition of new funding, downsizing or expansion of staff or new staffing arrangements, physical relocation, or the introduction of new technology (Brager & Holloway, 1978; Austin, 2002; Patti, 2008).

Whatever the source, organizational change follows a similar pattern. It is inevitably disruptive of the organization's culture and climate. (*See Chapter 4.*) It increases the stress experienced by staffers, board members, and clients. Often, this stress leads to individual or group resistance to the proposed changes. Planned organizational change, therefore, requires considerable preparation, adequate resources, and committed and energetic leadership to be successful and sustainable.

Varieties of Purposive Organizational Change

Organizational change also takes a number of distinct forms. Often, the purpose (goal) of the desired change influences its pattern. For example, the creation of a new program or service requires a different approach from the revision or relocation of an existing service or the introduction of a new conceptual or practice model. (*See Chapter 11.*) Similarly, a major restructuring of an organization's policies, staffing patterns, and decision-making processes differs substantially from efforts to change the underlying values, attitudes, and behaviors of the organization's culture or the integration of new technology. The exercises in this chapter provide students with the opportunity to analyze different patterns of organizational change.

IN-CLASS EXERCISE
ANALYZING CASES OF ORGANIZATIONAL CHANGE

Each of the following cases reflects an actual example of organizational change and a different motivation for organizations to engage in a purposive change process. In groups, students should read one case and discuss the following questions:

1. What type of organizational change or innovation does each case involve?
2. What or who initiated the change or innovation?
3. Which theories of organizational change best explain the situation?
4. What would you anticipate as the sources and reasons for resistance?
5. How might the resistance be overcome and the change implemented effectively?

CASE ILLUSTRATION
THE X PROJECT

The X Project emerged in a large West Coast city in response to the HIV/AIDS epidemic that devastated the city's LGBTQ community. It provided an innovative array of services including in-home care and client advocacy. Initially, nearly all of its clients were gay, White men, although its board and staff members were demographically diverse. Over time, however, the nature of the AIDS/HIV population changed; the epidemic now primarily struck intravenous drug users and their partners, many of whom were African American and Latino. The X Project struggled to adjust to the changes. Soon, some members of the board and staff attacked the organization for its institutional racism and demanded fundamental shifts in its character. The issue threatened to destroy the organization, as funders hesitated to renew grants and the publicity undermined the X Project's reputation. Long-standing supporters recognized that some essential change was required.

CASE ILLUSTRATION
THE RENEWAL PROGRAM

The Southeast Asian community in a major U.S. city established the Renewal Program (not its real name) in the aftermath of the war in Vietnam to provide a wide range of services to immigrants and refugees from Vietnam, Cambodia, and Laos. It had a small, diverse, and active board and a dynamic executive director. It obtained numerous large grants from public and private sources to serve its clients and constituents and, for a time, it thrived. Nearly all of its resources, however, came from grants and contracts. Eventually, the flow of immigrants and refugees slowed dramatically, and the needs of the population the agency served changed as a new generation assimilated into U.S. society. As its grants and contracts dried up, the agency faced both a resource crisis and a crisis of purpose. The board began to question the ability of the executive director to address this dual crisis. The community echoed this call for organizational change.

CASE ILLUSTRATION
CHILDREN'S VOICES

Children's Voices (not its real name) is an innovative national research and advocacy organization that focuses on the needs of low-income and working class children and families. When established nearly 30 years ago, it was the only such organization in the state, and quickly developed both a statewide and national reputation for the quality of its work and its innovative approaches to advocacy. After two decades, its highly regarded executive director resigned to accept another position and, for the first time, the organization hired someone from outside. Shortly after accepting the position, the incoming executive director soon learned that the organization faced a number of formidable challenges. First, the organization's finances, which had become highly dependent on foundation grants, was in serious difficulty. The organization had given little attention in recent years to the cultivation of new donors because of its success in attracting foundation grants, but these grants had begun to dry up due to increased competition in the field and the decline in the stock market. Second, the organization had become increasingly less visible in the media and the public eye. Its "products" remained highly regarded but the organization did not always receiving credit for them. Third, the board had become less active, particularly in the area of fund-raising, and had become much less demographically diverse even though the organization's constituents were increasingly diverse. Lastly, many more advocacy organizations had emerged during the past 30 years. The new executive director realized that something major needed to be done to shake up the organization.

CASE ILLUSTRATION
ROOTS & BRANCHES

Roots & Branches (not its real name) began as an innovative, largely volunteer organization in the early 1970s to serve the needs of runaways and other troubled youth in a large Eastern metropolitan area. It acquired a reputation for the dedication of its staff members and the effectiveness of its programs. Even after a decade, its budget had increased to only ~$65,000 annually and it continued to rely primarily on volunteers. Within the next five years, however, the agency received an enormous amount of money from public and private sources to create and administer a variety of crisis intervention and emergency services programs. The agency budget increased more than 500% and the board and staff expanded significantly. At its annual retreat, some members of the board argued that the agency's nonhierarchical structure needed to take on more of the features of a professional agency. Other members of the board and staff countered that such changes would transform the organization's original character.

The Nature of Organizational Change

As these cases illustrate, both internal and external factors can precipitate the need for intraorganizational change. Systems theory reminds us that all organizations have permeable (open) boundaries that produce a dynamic, interactive relationship with their environment. Stakeholders as diverse as funders, policy makers, clients, constituents, public opinion, and the media all influence the stability, vitality, and effectiveness of organizations, and their reputation in the community (Woodford & Preston, 2011).

Although each of these situations has a unique origin, there are similar elements in how organizations can respond effectively to these different circumstances. Gibelman (2003) lists the following common 10 steps to the successful management of organizational change:

1. Define the problem and the reason for the change.
2. Define the desired future state—how should things look when the change process is complete.
3. Identify the level and degree of change required to move from the current state to the desired state.
4. Identify the supporters of change and their influence and those who have a stake in maintaining the status quo.
5. Assess the organization's culture and determine how it supports or inhibits change.
6. Identify the people and the financial, programmatic, and procedural resources of the organization that are required to achieve change.
7. Evaluate the choices involved for bringing about change.
8. Plan and implement the action steps necessary to achieve change.
9. Manage the transition.
10. Monitor, evaluate, and stabilize the change (p. 209).

For Reflection and Classroom Discussion

Identify one change you would like to see occur at your field placement or work site during the next six to 12 months.

1. How will your colleagues receive that change?
2. What will be reactions of other staff members in the organization?
3. What will be the important factors to consider in implementing that change?

Stages of Change or Innovation

Obviously, not all purposive changes must occur. Some develop for "natural reasons" as an organization matures and the environment evolves. As stated above, external or internal crises may precipitate other types of change. In addition, the voluntary introduction of programmatic innovations may spur a third pattern of change.

Because any major change may produce anxiety among staffers, board members, clients, and constituents, it may be useful to consider which aspects of the change process are optional and which are not. Unless external authorities mandate a specific change, or the organization needs to change to survive an internal crisis, the invention or creation of change is optional. As the cliché goes, "If it ain't broke, don't fix it."

Once introduced, for whatever reason, the organization must proceed strategically with its implementation, diffusion, institutionalization, and evaluation. These steps are compulsory. The intentional change process, however, is by definition discontinuous. It is rarely smooth because of the need to balance the rational, political, cultural, and psychological components of change (Glisson, 2007).

Before initiating a change, an organization needs to consider the following issues:

1. What is the origin of the pressure for change?
2. Is the proposed change incremental or a "quantum leap"?
3. How much new learning is required of staff members? What type of learning—a technical skill, a new conceptual approach, a revised attitude or behavior?
4. Does the change affect the entire organization or only part of the organization? Might its effects be "sealed off"?
5. Is the change going to occur immediately or long term?
6. Who are the targets of change?
7. Who will be the initiators, leaders, and supporters of the change? What specific roles will they play?
8. What are the costs of change—financial, emotional, and political?
9. What is the organization's history regarding previous efforts to implement change?
10. What changes are already under way within the organization? How are they going?
11. Should an existing change process be stimulated, accelerated, or slowed?
12. What values should guide the change process?
13. What are the risks and rewards of change or the use of particular change strategies?
14. For whom are the changes beneficial? For whom are the changes detrimental?

Initiating Organizational Change. It is important to engage in a thorough assessment of the organizational environment (an "environmental scan") prior to initiating a planned organizational change. There are clear parallels here to the processes involved in community change (*Chapter 10*), program development (*Chapter 11*), and various types of advocacy (*chapters 12–14*). A first step is determining whether the organization needs to take any action now—at all. If the answer is "yes," the next step is an analysis of what action is feasible in the present context.

The following issues involve an examination of the behavior of people in organizations:

1. Does the staff possess the sense of competency required to implement the proposed change successfully (Busch & Hostetter, 2009)?
2. Do they feel sufficiently "safe" and empowered to take the risks involved? (Cohen & Austin 1997).
3. Is the organization's leadership capable of providing them with enough support and tangible and intangible rewards to sustain the effort (Shier & Handy, 2016; Mary, 2005)?

Assessing these issues carefully can provide guidance on how to promote change within your organization.

IN-CLASS EXERCISE
ORGANIZATIONAL CHANGE IN RESPONSE TO A CHANGING ENVIRONMENT

Introduction

Divide the class into groups of four or five students. Each group should imagine it consists of the staff members of a sexual assault crisis center in a neighboring community. The organization has multiple stated goals: (1) to provide support, advocacy, and other crisis services to survivors of sexual assault; (2) to reduce or eliminate sexualized violence in the community; and (3) to improve the ways that the criminal justice and health care systems interact with people who have experienced sexual assault.

Problem Statement

During the past year, the number of women who have contacted the organization increased 25%. A higher percentage of the agency's clients are now experiencing behavioral health problems and other disabilities. A large proportion have no insurance and cannot afford to pay for assistance from private providers. Consequently, staff members are regularly working overtime without additional compensation and are exhausted.

During the past several months, a higher than usual percentage of those seeking assistance have been unwilling to make police reports about their assaults. They feel emotionally unable to tell their stories to multiple persons or in public. Many clients also do not believe the government will prosecute the alleged perpetrators even if they report the crime.

In addition, some women have complained about their treatment by the police—officers have asked them about their previous sexual history and expressed skepticism that a sexual assault actually occurred. There have also been delays in the collection of evidence via the rape kits in the local hospital's emergency room. These problems have increased the time demands on the staff members, who advocate assertively with hospital staffers and police, whose behaviors may be adding to the stress and trauma of already traumatized people.

The agency has a full-time staff of five well-trained crisis workers, several of whom are also quite skilled in community work, although they are having less and less time to do the latter. Several experienced volunteers are available to spell the regular staff on some telephone shifts and others help with educational speaking engagements to community organizations and groups.

The agency works closely with the county's mental health center, which provides the organization with critical funds and offers longer-term services to those who need more than the center can provide. The city's assistant district attorney and the director of the social work department at the main community hospital are members of the center's advisory council. The center also has good relationships with a detective on the local police force who seems especially concerned about victim rights and services. Finally, in a recent newspaper article, the president of the City Council expressed outrage about persistent threats to safety, noting a recent brutal assault as an example.

Questions to Consider

1. What internal and external issues have produced the need for organizational change?
2. What additional information would you need to assess the situation before you develop a plan of action?
3. Who are the key players you would need to involve?
4. What theories and concepts might help you understand this situation, develop change goals, and create a strategy for organizational change?
5. How might the demographic and cultural backgrounds of the staff members, clients, and community influence your assessment of the change process?

Ethical Dimensions of Organizational Change

No matter how compelling the reasons, individuals who initiate any type of organizational change must also be conscious about the risks of violating critical ethical norms. For this reason, it is advisable to adhere to the following guidelines in planning and implementing any change of significant magnitude or scope.

First, use non-obtrusive means whenever possible, particularly if the proposed change may compromise the needs and rights of clients or potential clients. Second, employ these means only when you have exhausted formal organizational mechanisms that might produce similar results or when, based upon previous experience, you are reasonably certain these approaches to change will not succeed. Third, ensure that all steps in the change process comply with social work values. Finally, take responsibility for the consequences of the actions required to implement the planned change. Make certain not to put staff members, clients, or constituents at unnecessary risk and be sure to obtain their permission before subjecting them to any risk at all. (*See Chapter 8 for further discussion.*)

Barriers to Organizational Change

No change, however necessary or desirable, is ever easy. Much as physical objects, people who work in organizations are susceptible to inertia even in circumstances they consider unacceptable. Similar to the response of oppressed communities, they could redefine the situation as acceptable, a symptom of false consciousness. They could abandon the situation by quitting, burning out, or dropping out (withdrawing from ongoing engagement). Alternately, they could identify the situation as unacceptable but then rationalize their acceptance of it. This rarely solves the initial problem and often leads to demoralization. Ideally, they could recognize that the situation is unacceptable and try to change it.

In addition to normal "inertia," there are a number of recurrent barriers to change, particularly those initiated from outside the organization or in a top-down manner. One obstacle is an excessive focus on the costs of change. While resource scarcity is a chronic problem for many HSOs, an emphasis on the costs of change often overlooks the fiscal, political, and social costs of *not* changing. This frequently results from the presence of a second barrier—the failure to perceive the potential long-term benefits of change.

Another obstacle to change is psychological. Many staff members and organizational leaders avoid uncertainty even when circumstances dictate the need for change. They prefer the "devil they know" to something new and untested. Sometimes this resistance stems from a fear of loss—of power, status, comfortable routine, or even one's position. At other times, it reflects suspicion of any change imposed in a top-down manner. Finally, staff members may resist change because the manner in which administrators introduce or implement the change demonstrates a lack of coordination, planning, and collaboration. With forethought, however, some (not all) of these obstacles can be overcome.

For Reflection and Classroom Discussion

Think about a purposive change that occurred in your professional or personal life and the various emotions it produced.

1. How did you respond?

2. How did these feelings affect the rational development of the change, even one you may have initiated?

Now imagine that change occurring on a larger scale, one that affects many people, some of whom you know and others who are complete strangers. This illustrates the scope and potential effect of a major organizational change.

Because of people's complex responses to planned change efforts, among the most difficult things to master in promoting change are the subtleties involved in empowering others to take the necessary risks, develop effective strategy and tactics, and negotiate and maintain the agreements (and compromises) required to sustain the change effort. The key is to cultivate and unlock your own creativity and the creativity of staff members, and to discover and fill the gaps in the organization's knowledge and skills (Shier & Handy, 2014).

Because leadership skills are critical components of successful organizational change, it is important that organizational leaders be aware of some common pitfalls of change efforts that could find them vulnerable. One potential "trap" reflects overconfidence in one's abilities, especially one's ability to convince others of the value of the change goal and to sustain what may be a long-term process. A second, related pitfall is taking others' support for granted. Often staff members with little formal authority may seem to acquiesce to a proposed top-down change but do not "buy in" to its ultimate purpose or necessity. As a result, they may resist the change passively. A third possible problem emerges from the frequently complex, slow, and incremental nature of the change process itself. In her zeal to succeed, the person who initiates the change may spread herself too thin, become impatient with the routines involved in implementing the change, and lose track of the multiple components of the process (Evans, Hanlin, & Prilleltensky, 2007).

Overcoming Resistance to Organizational Change

Organizational leaders can take several proactive steps to overcome resistance to internal change. First, they can communicate to all stakeholders the need for change clearly and in a nonthreatening manner, using a method of communication most suited to the particular subset of the organization's population. Involving the entire organization is critical from the outset to avoid misunderstandings during the implementation phase of change.

The identification of a proposed change, especially if it includes a major innovation, needs to match an identified need. Innovation for its own sake will inevitably generate greater resistance and make staff members more reluctant to support required changes in the future. It helps to implement the change in small increments with a clear sequential pattern; the concept of "partialization," widely used in clinical practice, is applicable here. It is also useful to base the change, at least to some extent, on concepts, programs, or values that are familiar. Stakeholders are more likely to accept changes that do not represent a radical break from long-standing norms or practices.

In addition, it is critical to get genuine support from the organization's leadership, particularly senior staff and board members. Sometimes, overenthusiasm for a suggested innovation or a heightened sense of urgency can lead the initiator of a change effort to move too fast before explaining the importance of the change to major organizational decision makers. As the author learned from painful experience, this can create a backlash even in situations in which the leadership agrees with the substance and purpose of the proposed change.

To prevent such developments, the initiator of a change needs to analyze how the agency's culture affects its everyday operations and practices, its development, and its traditional response to change (Jaskyte & Dressler, 2005). This includes reflection on how the organization delivers its services and administers its rules, regulations, and procedures. In addition, it helps to assess the organization's former approach to program planning and development, its relationship to the community, and its response to internal and external opportunities and threats.

Preparation for planned organizational change also involves assessment of the agency's assets, strengths, weaknesses, and recurrent challenges. What features of the organization appear to facilitate or impede organizational effectiveness? What components of the organization need change or improvement before the change effort can proceed? What barriers to organizational change exist that you must remove or diminish prior to initiating the change process?

Finally, as with all change efforts, it is important to anticipate the type of resistance that may arise (and from what sources) in order to develop a plan to address this resistance in whatever form—and at whatever stage—of the change process it appears (Cohen & Hyde, 2014).

IN-CLASS EXERCISE
HUGS AND KISSES

Introduction

Put a pile of chocolate Kisses on the table in front of the classroom. Ask the students to form pairs in which the partners are of roughly equal size. Tell the students to arm-wrestle (or thumb-wrestle) several times. Each time the winner receives a chocolate. Keep track of how many times each person wins. After 10 minutes, stop the exercise and engage in the following discussion:

Questions for Discussion

1. How did the rules established at the beginning of the exercise influence how you behaved?
2. Did you assume fixed rules or that you could modify the rules?

3. How hard did you compete for a chocolate?
4. What did the exercise reveal about our approach to organizational or societal conditions? About our approach to competition, conflict, and change?

Using Force Field Analysis to Promote Organizational Change

Kurt Lewin, one of the pioneers of social and organizational psychology, developed the concept of force field analysis after World War II, based on his study of intragroup behavior. Lewin based this concept on the assumption that resistance to change is natural and that it appears in the conflict between what he termed "driving" and "resisting" forces. One way to visualize this conflict is through the metaphor of a "tug-of-war." The driving forces are pulling the group or organization in the direction of a desired change, while the oppositional forces resist it. The goal of the change agent is to strengthen one or more of the driving forces and/or weaken one or more of the resisting forces to increase the likelihood of creating the desired change (Lewin, 1997, 1948). The following exercise illustrates how to apply these concepts.

IN-CLASS EXERCISE
APPLYING FORCE FIELD ANALYSIS TO ORGANIZATIONAL CHANGE

Step 1: Identify a problem in your internship or workplace that you would like to change.

Step 2: List five forces driving toward the desired change in the spaces below.

Driving Force 1 ______________________________ Strength __________

Driving Force 2 ______________________________ Strength __________

Driving Force 3 ______________________________ Strength __________

Driving Force 4 ______________________________ Strength __________

Driving Force 5 ______________________________ Strength __________

Step 3: List five forces resisting the desired change in the spaces below.

Resisting Force 1 ______________________ Strength __________

Resisting Force 2 ______________________ Strength __________

Resisting Force 3 ______________________ Strength __________

Resisting Force 4 ______________________ Strength __________

Resisting Force 5 ______________________ Strength __________

Step 4: In the spaces above marked "Strength," rank each of the driving and resisting forces on a scale from one through five, with one (1) being a weak force and five (5) being a very strong force. (Note: Each force can have a different level of strength. It is not necessary to prioritize them in order of strength.)

Step 5: Chart the strengths of the driving and resisting forces in the space below as if you were drawing a graph.

Step 6: Examine the chart you created. If you wanted to influence the change process in a particular direction, which two or three driving forces would you try to strengthen and which two or three resisting forces would you try to weaken? List your reasons for making these choices.

Step 7: Identify the initial steps you would take to strengthen or weaken the driving and resisting forces you selected. Indicate your reasons for deciding to take these steps. How might they affect your overall change strategy?

	0 (Forces are Equal)	
DF-1	+	RF-1
	+	
DF-2	+	RF-2
	+	
DF-3	+	RF-3
	+	
DF-4	+	RF-4
	+	
DF-5	+	RF-5
	0	

Strength 5 4 3 2 1 1 2 3 4 5

Transforming a Monocultural to a Multicultural Organization

Because of the dramatic demographic and cultural shifts in the United States already under way, one of the most important types of organizational change today involves transforming an organization that reflects dominant cultural values and staffing patterns into one that reflects emerging social realities and incorporates heightened ethno-consciousness (Gutierrez et al., 1996). One framework that provides guidance for this process is the multicultural organization development (MCOD) model (Jackson & Holvino, 1988). This model outlines a multistage process for organizations to: (1) assess the organization's current location on this continuum; (2) select a desired end state; and (3) identify a strategy to achieve this goal. The model consists of the following phases (Holvino, 2008):

1. *The Exclusionary Stage*: Organizations explicitly seek to maintain current patterns of privilege and domination. (This rarely occurs today—at least openly.)
2. *The Passive Club*: Organizations do not expressly advocate the dominance of a particular group but perpetuate this dominance through informal rules and status quo-oriented systems.
3. *The Compliance Stage*: Organizations indicate a passive commitment to greater inclusion but make no substantive changes to their internal policies and practices. The commitment to change is more symbolic and rhetorical than real. It produces tokenism.
4. *The Positive Action Stage*: The organization engages in targeted efforts to be more inclusive and tolerant of different work styles. Yet, in subtle ways, its organizational culture retains many of the previous features that favored the dominant cultural group.
5. *The Redefining Stage*: At this point, the patterns of a fully multicultural organization begin to emerge due to changes in both formal and informal, and explicit and subtle practices. The organization is "testing the waters" here and has not yet institutionalized the changes under way.
6. *The Multicultural Stage*: If an organization reaches this stage, it has become diverse, inclusive, and equitable. It integrates all types of difference (knowledge, values, work styles), treats all of its stakeholders fairly, and engages in genuine democratic decision making (Holvino, 2008, pp. 2–3).

In making an initial assessment, those charged with leading the change process need to examine the following organizational features at every one of the above stages:

- vision, mission, and goals;
- decision-making structure and role division;
- formal policies and procedures (e.g., personnel policies);
- informal systems, culture, norms of behavior;
- individual and group interpersonal relationships;
- formal and informal leadership;
- relationship to its external environment (clients, constituents, etc.);
- type of technology employed; and
- language used by staff members (Holvino, 2008, p. 6).

As described in other types of change efforts throughout the book, organizational change requires clarity on its overall purpose and goals, the strategies to be employed, the level and intensity of stakeholders' interest in the change process, and the composition of the various constituencies (organizational subgroups) in favor of and resisting the change process (Hyde, 2012; Chesler & Crowfoot, 1992).

IN-CLASS EXERCISE
ORGANIZATIONAL CHANGE IN A MULTICULTURAL COMMUNITY

Introduction

Last spring, an ad hoc group of parents in Eastville invited you to assist them in organizing the community in response to recurrent concerns on the quality of public schools in the district. (*See background information on Eastville in previous chapters.*) During the past six months, your collective efforts have created a parent-run organization, Parents Alliance for School Survival (PASS), whose stated goals are to improve the quality of education in the community's elementary and middle schools and increase the level of parents' involvement in educational policy making. To date, the local school board and school principals have made significant concessions in response to demands from PASS. They have expanded after-school programs, hired new teachers, and increased the role of parents in the schools' decision-making processes. Yet, there is still much work to do.

During these six months, the original core group of 15–20 parents expanded to nearly 150. Each member contributes $5 per month to the organization. There are weekly meetings of the entire organization and subcommittees that meet several times each month. All of the members are volunteers, with the exception of a part-time secretary, who is paid through membership dues. The group publishes a monthly newsletter that volunteers write and distribute. Lately, however, you have noticed signs of several emerging problems within the organization that are cause for concern:

- attendance at meetings has declined about 25%;
- those who attend meetings participate less frequently and with less enthusiasm;
- Several of the subcommittees have cancelled their scheduled meetings;
- you have heard talk "on the street" that the organization is dominated by a small number of parents and that the views of new members are largely ignored; and
- perhaps of most serious concern, there has been growing discontent among the White parents (who comprise about one third of the members) that the organization is ignoring the needs of their children. They have threatened to leave PASS and start a separate organization.

Assessing the Problems

1. What do you believe are the problems—both immediate and underlying—that the organization is facing at this time?
2. What steps might you take to address these problems before they become more serious?

Taking Action to Sustain the Organization

After conducting this assessment, you have called a special meeting of PASS's steering committee to discuss the organization's problems. The members of the committee are:

- Roberta Jones: A 26-year-old mother of two school-age children and one of the original founders of PASS. She cochairs the organization.
- Reverend Charlie Woods: Pastor of the largest neighborhood church, parent of three children in local schools, and a longtime community activist. The other cochair of PASS.
- Alberta Johnson: A lieutenant in the city's police department who has worked as a volunteer for many years with local youth. She is one of the original founders of PASS.
- Mary Lyons: A 40-year-old teacher in the district whose children went to local schools. She is one of the newest members of PASS.
- Juanita Lopez: A 29-year-old social worker; her daughter attends the local elementary school.
- Pat Chambers: A 33-year-old accountant who returned to Eastville last year with her spouse and two school-age children. Her parents are retired and still live in the community.

You have discussed your concerns with the two cochairs in advance of the meeting. Jones is chairing this meeting but has asked you to facilitate the discussion of these issues.

Questions to Consider

1. What are your objectives in bringing these issues to the steering committee?
2. What potential problems might arise in your discussion of these issues?
3. How will you deal with these problems should they arise?

Role Play of the Committee Discussion (optional)

Evaluating the Meeting

1. What was the outcome of the discussion? What results had you anticipated? What results were unexpected?
2. What are the next steps you and the committee might take to follow up on the results of the meeting?
3. What problems would you have to address to take these actions? What fallback strategies might you adopt?

Evaluating the Exercise

1. What did the exercise teach you about the process of organizational change?
2. What skills would you need to learn or enhance to be able to address such issues in the future?

Creating a Learning Organization to Encourage Social Innovation

Another compelling reason for organizations to change is the need to innovate to survive in an increasingly competitive environment and to provide effective services as clients' needs evolve within a rapidly changing context. The development of a culture that embraces ongoing learning is a prerequisite for promoting continuous social innovation within an organization.

A learning organization has two major components. Overall, it refers to the extent to which an organization supports the ongoing learning and development of its staff from within the organization (Busch & Hostetter, 2009). Its policies and practices facilitate staff members' acquisition of new knowledge and skills through training, the encouragement of new ways of thinking, and the promotion of innovation throughout the organization. A learning organization also transforms itself through a continuous process of self-examination, reflection, and renewal—similar to the concept of praxis discussed in previous chapters (Kernan et al., 2012). Organizations that develop the capacity to engage in transformation are generally more effective in pursuing change efforts on behalf of the communities they serve.

Garrow and Hasenfeld (2014) suggest that organizations advocate for change to benefit their clients and constituents directly (e.g., establish or expand a right) or to benefit themselves directly and their clients or constituents indirectly (e.g., acquire additional resources to produce better outcomes for service users) (Mosley, 2012). In response to problems generated by government policies, decisions made by the private sector, and events in the communities themselves, organizations also promote social change through efforts that affect their external environments economically and politically (Shier, McDougle, & Handy, 2014; Green & Goetting, 2010). Often, this involves revising existing programs to meet emerging or shifting needs (Fairbanks, 2009; Shier & Graham, 2013) or developing a more expansive social innovation project aimed at producing progressive outcomes (Cnaan & Vinokur-Kaplan, 2015).

Shier and Handy (2014) identify three types of social innovation that organizations undertake. One consists of "socially transformative innovations." These involve such activities as public or popular education to alter public perceptions about an issue, promote greater civic engagement, influence policy development, and engage stakeholders more actively in decision making. These activities are similar to those involved in advocacy efforts. (*See chapters 12–14.*)

A second type of innovation is "product-based." This category includes the creation of new or more inclusive programs, the adaptation of existing services to improve outcomes, restructuring or changing the focus of existing programs to attain different outcomes, and—on occasion—establishing satellite programs or even a new organization. Finally, there are "process-based" innovations. These may involve greater engagement with key stakeholders, rearrangement of intraorganizational or inter-organizational relationships to enhance decision making, revision of organizational procedures, refocusing staff development efforts, and the creation of new staff roles (Shier & Handy, 2016, p. 117).

The literature identifies a number of factors that contribute to an organization's ability to develop successful socially innovative initiatives. They include internal cultural cohesion (Jaskyte & Dressler, 2005) and a transformational leadership style (Jaskyte, 2010; Ruvio, Rosenblatt, & Hertz-Lazarowitz, 2010; Shier, Graham, Deane, & Jones, 2013). Based on their research, Shier and Handy (2016) identified four major components of effective innovation projects: staff engagement, staff development and hiring, board involvement, and the nature of executive leadership (p. 119).

Staff engagement includes a number of key features. First, staff members need to be intimately familiar with the issues experienced by the agency's clients and constituents. Second, the organization needs to consult staff on a regular—not nominal—basis in core decision-making activities and at all levels of the organization's initiatives. In addition, the organization needs to make conscious efforts to empower organizational staff members to participate in these processes (Cohen & Hyde, 2014).

Staff development and hiring can also contribute to social innovation, provided the organization takes several interrelated steps. First, administrators must make it clear to staff members that they need to think about enhancing client outcomes from the outset. Second, the organization should recruit and hire staff members not merely based on their skills, but on their commitment to the organization's mission and goals. Similarly, organizations should design staff training to emphasize social change, not merely the acquisition of new knowledge or capabilities.

As discussed in Chapter 7, the structure and active involvement of the board (in the case of nonprofit organizations) is also critical to the organization's ability to engage in social innovation of any type. Finally, the executive leadership of the organization needs to possess a social change orientation and a "belief that *they were responsible for providing overall direction* for the organization's social change efforts" (Shier & Handy, 2016, p. 125. Italics in original). They demonstrate this commitment "by providing direction and facilitating action" at all levels of the organization (p. 126).

Conflict and Organizational Change

Take a few minutes to think about a conflict you are now experiencing or a recent conflict, personal or professional, in which you were involved. With whom did you conflict? What was the conflict about? What were the consequences? How did the conflict make you feel at the time? How does it make you feel now? Write a few words that describe your thoughts and feelings about the conflict.

Now, examine the words you wrote. What emotions do they express? Who were the winners and losers in the conflict? Did you describe the conflict in negative or positive terms? Ask yourself, what did you like or dislike about conflict at the time? In hindsight, do you see any positive functions of conflict?

Most likely, most or all of your words and emotions about conflict were negative. This raises a number of issues that are critical for macro social work practice, particularly those aspects of practice that involve promoting change. Why does conflict make us uncomfortable? Why do we avoid it so often? How do we avoid it? What consequences occur when we avoid conflict? How do these consequences affect us personally and as practitioners? What effect do they have on our organizations and our clients?

IN-CLASS EXERCISE
THREE CONFLICT SCENARIOS—HOW WOULD YOU RESPOND?

Scenario 1

You are making a presentation to your organization's board of directors for the first time. You worked very hard on the presentation. You are nervous and excited. After making the presentation, which you felt went pretty well, a colleague approaches you and says, "Your presentation put the board to sleep. I think you wasted their time." How would you respond?

Compete	Avoid	Accommodate	Compromise	Collaborate
Challenge your colleague and tell her, "Well, I thought it went really well."	Ignore your colleague's remark and excuse yourself, saying you have to get back to your office for an appointment.	Do not respond to your colleague, but go back to your office and think for hours about how to "recover" from your presentation.	Agree with your colleague that the presentation did not go as well as you hoped, thank her for the criticism, but say you tried your best.	Tell your colleague that her remark hurt your feelings. Then suggest that maybe you could work together on the next presentation.

Scenario 2

You are about to go to a second interview for a job you want very much. You have chosen a new outfit, gotten a new hairdo, feel great, and are looking forward to the interview. Before you leave your apartment, your roommate says, "I can't believe you are wearing that to the interview!" How would you respond?

Compete	Avoid	Accommodate	Compromise	Collaborate
Fight back. Tell her, "You look like '*&%$' too when you go to an interview."	Walk away. You do not want to be late.	Say to your roommate: "Do you really think I look bad? I will go change. What should I wear?"	Tell her that you do not have time to change now, but ask her to help you pick out an outfit if you have another interview.	Tell her that she hurt your feelings. Acknowledge her good taste and suggest you shop together soon so she can teach you.

Scenario 3

You come into work and you inadvertently overhear your supervisor say, "I wish [YOUR NAME] would follow up on her commitments more promptly. I am getting tired of reminding her of deadlines." How would you respond?

Compete	Avoid	Accommodate	Compromise	Collaborate
March into your supervisor's office and tell her, "If you have something to say about my work, say it to my face!"	Pretend you did not hear the remark. Carry on with business as usual, but do not change your behavior.	Make an appointment with your supervisor. Tell her you overheard her remark and apologize. Promise to improve in the future.	At your next regular supervision session, bring up the topic without indicating you heard your supervisor's remark. Ask her how to improve this aspect of your job performance.	At your next regular supervision session, tell your supervisor you overheard her remark, ask her to be more forthright if she has future criticisms of your work, and for tips on how to manage your time better.

Common Responses to Conflict

There are considerable differences among cultures in their response to conflict. Some cultures view conflict—within certain boundaries—as a constructive phenomenon, a normal part of social interaction. Other cultures prioritize the maintenance of social cohesion and eschew open conflict in any form. Individuals from the latter culture may regard those from the former culture as arrogant, angry, or insensitive. Those from the former culture may view those from the latter as passive-aggressive or deceitful.

Similar differences also exist among people of seemingly identical cultural backgrounds (e.g., European Americans) who live in different parts of the United States. What strikes a native New Yorker, including the author, as ordinary conversation may appear rude to someone from the Midwest, South, or Northwest. (I learned this painful truth in my professional travels.) There are also substantial differences in how men and women participate in groups, particularly if there is a disagreement (Gilligan, 1983). Now imagine facilitating a contentious meeting of staff members from diverse cultural backgrounds! What problems might arise? How would you handle them?

Although different cultures respond to conflict differently, some scholars maintain that there are five common approaches to addressing interpersonal conflict (Lewicki, Tomlinson, & Gillespie, 2006; Ting-Toomey et al., 1991). A prominent response is avoidance, particularly among social workers, who often prefer consensus and regard conflict as unprofessional. Individuals who avoid conflictual interaction frequently avoid potentially conflict-ridden ideas or situations and people they perceive as more likely to spur conflict. They do not want to make waves and behave much as a turtle in a shell. Consequently, they do not get their needs met and frequently end up feeling resentful. If an organization (or community) has too many members with this approach, conflicts may fester for some time before they blow up.

A second, somewhat similar response to conflict is suppression—to deny that a problem that might lead to conflict exists. People may do this by changing the topic or keeping silent on issues or processes that upset them, even those they believe are wrong. They may also ignore their feelings about the issue, or keep these feelings to themselves. To some extent, this response is similar to avoidance, although its emotional consequences may be more severe.

A third approach, most common among men, is to force a resolution of the conflict by overpowering the opposition, attempting to control the situation, and trying to impose a solution. This approach sets up a competitive situation, regardless of whether a resolution of the issue requires it. It usually produces an escalation of the conflict and a "hard" method of negotiation. It often involves an attack on others' ideas or personal qualities. Above all, this approach is about winning, about being "right," and about getting what you want at others' expense. It is not always about finding a real solution. People who attempt to do this may use their formal position or purported expertise to dominate the conversation and try to intimidate those with different views. Others may compete through passive-aggressive behavior.

A fourth type of response, similar to suppression, is to accommodate oneself to the conflict—to acknowledge the existence of the conflict but attempt to minimize its significance or smooth over the situation. People may reflect these feelings by saying, "It's not really that bad," "I can handle it," or "Don't worry; it's not really a problem." The condition, however, is usually much more serious than they admit and, by minimizing its importance, they preclude efforts to address the issue. People who adopt this approach regard conflict as a win/lose situation. Yet, because they tend to be "soft negotiators" and shape shifters, they usually give in and end up feeling resentful.

A final way to respond to conflict is through compromise or collaboration. Contrary to some beliefs, compromise does not mean capitulation; nor does it involve a betrayal of values or principles. There are important distinctions between compromising one's values or principles and compromising on one's goals or change strategies. Genuine compromise occurs when you try to get others to give up *some* of what they want in exchange for *some* of what you want.

Collaboration requires creation of a win/win outcome that includes solutions that are mutually acceptable to all parties and satisfies their interests to a considerable extent. Participants in the conflict view the result as fair. Successful collaboration has other benefits as well. It sets standards for future decision making regarding contentious issues. It helps build better trust and stronger interpersonal relationships. It leads to coworkers making feasible commitments to one another and to themselves.

Getting to a win/win result is not simple. It requires persistent effort and effective, multifaceted communication. Participants must trust one another to listen respectfully to their different views and, after they reach an agreement, hold up their end of the bargain. In sum, how you view conflict from the outset influences the range of possible outcomes. Those who view conflict and the emotions associated with conflict through a negative lens may avoid it. Those who view such emotions as a normal part of conflict may have more compassion for others and be better able to engage in a "learning conversation." The ultimate goal is to manage conflict in a productive manner (Fisher, Ury, & Patton, 2011).

For Reflection and Classroom Discussion

1. How does your culture, gender, age, or geographic origins influence your attitude toward conflict and your approach to conflict resolution?
2. What are the implications for your practice in diverse organizations and communities?

Theoretical Perspectives on Conflict

Different theoretical perspectives frame and explain the phenomenon of conflict in different ways. Social systems theory, for example, regards society as a network of interrelated parts: e.g., individuals, families, organizations, communities, the economic and political systems. In this network, no one exists in isolation. Therefore, all parties in the system seek balance (homeostasis) to survive and thrive.

From this perspective, conflict, especially sustained conflict, is not healthy. It is a threat to the social order. Through its existing institutions, societies need to stop and control conflict as quickly as possible. Although periods of imbalance may appear, a return to quiescence soon follows. Systems theorists refer to this process as "dynamic homeostasis." Scholars of organizational change refer to this process through the image of freezing–unfreezing–refreezing (Brager & Holloway, 1978).

From a pluralist perspective, conflict is inevitable but capable of relatively simple and balanced resolution. Pluralists assert that resolving a conflict begins by bringing a critical problem or issue to both the attention of those affected by the issue and also those who have the authority and power to resolve it. Pluralists assume that all stakeholders contribute equally to the dialogue and that participants hear everyone's voice. They also assume that in attempting to resolve the conflict, participants debate different solutions and eventually choose the fairest and most comprehensive outcome (Novak, 2016; Lassman, 2011).

Yet, anyone who has ever worked in an organization or advocated for social change knows that some individuals or groups have more power and influence. They define the agenda, the terms of debate, and the range of possible outcomes. The process literally excludes the views of marginalized population members unless they force the powerful to pay attention. This is precisely what occurred during the civil rights movement, the HIV/AIDS crisis, and the current struggle for environmental justice (Dierenfield, 2013; Shilts, 2007; Sandler & Pezzullo, 2007).

Because these theories do not pay sufficient attention to the importance of conflict and the relationship of conflict to issues of power and inequality, it is useful to examine the phenomenon from the perspective of ecological theory or other conflict-oriented theories, such as Marxism or critical race theory (Delgado & Stefancic, 2017; Crenshaw, 2010; D'Amato, 2014). These theories regard conflict as a naturally occurring phenomenon, an ongoing part of life, and the foundation of social relations. Although these theories may differ on the sources of that conflict, they agree that conflict determines the allocation of tangible and intangible resources in a community, organization, or society and leads to the formation of dominant and subdominant units (classes, races, genders, castes). It is a condition to be accepted, not eliminated. The notion that we can eliminate conflict is a symptom of false or naïve consciousness (Jost, 1995; Freire, 1971).

Because of conflict, inequality in a given system is inevitable; intergroup competition for scarce resources generates and perpetuates this inequality and the opposing interests that defend and attack it. Power is a critical component of this conflict. Many macro social work practitioners operate from one of these perspectives. They reflect the idea that no social or political change can occur without conflict and the pressure it creates that compels the powerful to cede some of what they possess (Alinsky, 1971). They also emphasize how social roles and the distribution of power contribute to the recognition of issues and to the significance attached to their resolution. (*See Chapter 2.*)

Types of Conflict

In general, there are two types of conflict. The first type, which people often do not recognize as "conflict," is normative or institutional conflict. These conflicts are conventional and occur frequently. For the most part, they follow established rules and procedures, and are a natural part of the social landscape. This controlled form of conflict is actually a means to maintain the structural status quo. Two common examples are politics and professional sports. These conflicts rarely disrupt or challenge institutional norms or their underlying values. In fact, they reinforce the dominant culture by channeling conflict into rule-bound competition and restricting change to the incremental variety.

A second form of conflict occurs outside of traditional norms. This rancorous or extra-institutional conflict may include violence (economic, political, and/or cultural) or hostility. It is invariably disruptive of the status quo. At times, this type of conflict may be necessary—as Jefferson wrote on the need for revolution—although societies typically channel it into institutional (i.e., normal) patterns of conflict (Medina et al., 2005; Afzalur Rahim, 2002).

Causes and Consequences of Intraorganizational Conflict

Conflicts are inevitable in any complex organization, particularly those that are demographically and culturally diverse, confront chronic resource shortages, work with challenging clients who have complex needs, and need to navigate turbulent external environments. Each of these conditions can generate internal conflicts—among staff members, between staff members and the administration, between workers and volunteers (including the board of directors), and between the organization as a whole and its stakeholders. The initiation of planned or imposed changes often precipitates conflict within an organization, particularly if imposed by external authorities or internally in a top-down manner. In effect, any attempt to protest or alter the status quo has the potential to provoke conflict, especially if it involves a redistribution of resources, roles, rules, or routines.

When conflicts erupt, they produce several serious consequences that organizations need to address as quickly and thoroughly as possible (Guerra et al., 2005). As in families, they polarize existing social relations, both within and between departments and programs. They could lead to the formation of opposing groups or factions as positions become more entrenched. On the positive side, conflict could facilitate the emergence of new leaders, an increase in energy and commitment to the organization's mission, and more intense interpersonal communication. (*See below*.)

Process of Conflict

The process by which conflicts unfold in organizations is similar to the way they evolve in our personal lives. Initially, one or more of the parties in conflict identifies the issue to be resolved. As awareness of the issue spreads and intensifies, it disrupts the equilibrium of the environment and other issues appear, including those previously suppressed. The expression of these issues often reflects unspoken beliefs about "opponents." Unless the conflict is resolved, the issue is soon personalized and each side begins to regard the other as 100% bad (or wrong); all nuances of perspective are lost. If this occurs, the dispute becomes independent of the initial issue that precipitated it. (Watch the video "Duel at the Mall" on YouTube for a humorous depiction of this process.)

Positive Functions of Conflict

Conflict within organizations, even intense conflict, can also have a positive effect. It may even be necessary at times during an organization's life cycle. It helps to establish and maintain people's personal and professional identities and boundaries. If managed well, it can create an opportunity to relieve stress and frustration, vent long-simmering hostility, and express dissent in a constructive manner, ultimately maintaining and, perhaps, strengthening interpersonal relationships and intragroup and intergroup cohesion.

Conflict can also provide the opportunity for an organization to assess its power and influence in relationship to an external entity (the "enemy"). This might lead to coalition building, within the organization and with potential allies. Internally, it could increase the energy level of a group and add depth to staff discussions by allowing challenges to emerge concerning long-held ideas. This, in turn, promotes clarification of fixed positions, more in-depth understanding of the connection between an organization's day-to-day activities and its mission and goals, and more creative solutions to ongoing problems. Finally, managing conflict when it appears could also prevent the eruption of more serious conflicts in the future (Rahim, 2010).

Difficult Conversations vs. 'Learning Conversations'

Resolving conflicts within an organization usually requires engaging in contentious conversations, either one-on-one or in small groups. These conversations fall into several categories (Ford, Ford, & McNamara, 2002; Ford, 1999; Ford & Ford, 1995). One type is a conversation of discovery; participants are interested in understanding others' perspective. They are comfortable dealing with the emotions connected to these perspectives.

A related form is a conversation of interpretation. It focuses on determining what occurred during a recent interaction that may have precipitated the current conflict. Such conversations, however, are not only about what happened; they involve dissecting the participants' perceptions and the underlying values these perceptions reflect. Sometimes they also involve clarification of participants' identities and self-image. To resolve the conflict, all of the participants need to "take a step back," acknowledge that there may be one than one "truth," and look at the various sides of the argument. This helps overcome the natural tendency in conflict-ridden situations to make assumptions about people's intentions and read more into their behavior than may actually be there.

A third type of conversation emphasizes the feelings people have about the circumstances surrounding a conflict. These are often the most difficult conversations because they often involve sharing deeply held emotions that reflect our core selves. Although it is a mistake to avoid such conversations because they influence our ability to resolve conflicts, colleagues should handle them with the greatest sensitivity. For example, it is better to initiate such conversations after the intensity of a conflictual situation subsides, to hold it in a neutral space, and to engage in the conversation only by mutual consent (Earl & Timperley, 2009).

Using Dialogue to Resolve Conflict

By encouraging constructive dialogue, staff members in organizations can use conflict to facilitate problem solving and produce more "win/win" solutions (Fisher, Ury, & Patton, 2011). Whether in one-on-one or group settings, whomever is facilitating the conversation should encourage participants to state their views clearly using non-judgmental language and to listen carefully to one another's views. Next, they should distinguish their areas of agreement (e.g., goals and underlying values) from areas of nonagreement (e.g., underlying assumptions and strategies). It is useful in such situations to pause periodically to make sure the participants do not misunderstand their areas of disagreement or misinterpret the motives of the other "side." When emotions run high, a "time-out" may help to cool things off and prevent participants from adopting fixed positions (Schein, 1993; Zuniga & Nagda, 1993). By following these steps, organizations can resolve most conflicts without creating permanent internal divisions or precipitating the hasty departure of key staff members.

Summary and Conclusion

As discussed in this chapter, organizational change and conflict can magnify the normal pressures on staff members in HSOs and intensify the strains they experience daily. Increasing pressures from the external environment can further exacerbate their stress. This combination of internal strain and external stress creates what Lewis (1980) referred to as "the battered worker." Whereas the image of "burnout" could lead to victim blaming and a focus solely on workers' self-care (Bride, 2007), the alternative framing Lewis provides acknowledges the multiple sources of staff members' frustration, dissatisfaction, and conflict.

As I often tell my students, preparing for a career in social work, particularly one focused on social and political change, is similar to training for a marathon, not a sprint. How can we, as individuals, avoid or diminish the likelihood we will abandon our careers when circumstances become "too much to bear"?

First, I think it is important to remind ourselves periodically why we chose this field in the first place. What underlying values guide all our work? Remember why you are doing what you are doing. This self-reflection renews our sense of meaning and importance even in the midst of seemingly intractable challenges and petty disputes. It also helps to distinguish between possessing a hard-headed, clear-eyed recognition of "real world" conditions, and accepting the inevitability of these conditions. This enables us to follow through on our commitment to ourselves and to our clients, constituents, colleagues, employers, and profession.

Second, make a conscious effort to develop the skills you draw upon regularly—not just the "technical" skills but such skills as the ability to broaden your perspective on the environment and others' viewpoints. Focus on learning what you need to get your work done well. As much as possible, be prepared for the dynamic environment of future practice. Your success produces successful outcomes for your clients and constituents.

Third, take risks. Especially in macro social work practice, you cannot be effective without taking risks and enabling others to take risks as well. Do not be afraid to make mistakes and do not become bogged down in criticizing or correcting the mistakes of others. Engage in reflexive practice to assess whether your actions (and their underlying assumptions) are working for you. Neither set arbitrary limits on what you can accomplish nor make excuses when you fall short of your aspirations. Do not worry about always "being right." That can lead to off-putting self-righteousness. Allow others to share the credit and acknowledge their contributions.

Fourth, never hesitate to call upon colleagues and friends for support. Create different types of support groups for different aspects of your work life. These may change throughout your career.

Finally, as discussed in the book's epilogue, take care of things that are important to you personally by attending to your life apart from your job. Have fun—at work and away from work. Sometimes it is better (and necessary) to "eat dessert first." Try to find humor even in the midst of a crisis. As the Cretan partisans reportedly said during the Nazi occupation when they engaged in activities to humiliate their oppressors: "Those who laugh are not afraid" (Demopoulos, 2012).

CASE ILLUSTRATION AND IN-CLASS EXERCISE
HOMELAND MEDICAL CENTER

Homeland Medical Center is a large urban medical center consisting of several buildings at several locations. The Medical Center provides all general services, including cancer, renal, and burn centers and has a large major trauma/emergency unit. Increasingly there have been charges that patients who are poor, of color, or experiencing homelessness receive substandard services throughout the hospitals and outpatient units. There have been rumors about unnecessary delays and deaths, rude treatment of patients, and the denial of services to some people. The Medical Center initially attributed these problems to inadequate reimbursement of expenses from Medicare, Medicaid, and increasingly from private insurance plans. The consequences included insufficient personnel and outdated equipment in some areas. Community members, however, consider the emergency unit the most efficient and fair in terms of how its staff members interact with city residents, particularly those experiencing homelessness.

Recently, an investigative reporter has been doing a series of articles for the city newspaper about conditions at the hospital. He has been conducting interviews at various levels and locations of the Medical Center with anyone willing to talk with him. He has also filed a number of freedom of information requests for patient care statistics and mortality figures throughout the system, critical incident reports, and medical review board minutes and records. Hospital attorneys are fighting release of these reports and minutes, saying it will jeopardize the Medical Center's ability to monitor itself honestly, and arguing that legally it is not required to release these records as the center is a private institution. The newspaper is arguing that the Medical Center is at least, in part, a public institution since it receives federal and local government funds and that the center's CEO and medical director report to a board that the mayor partly appoints. The newspaper further argues that the work and performance of medical institutions should be open for public scrutiny, and that the center should be willing to release the requested documents to reassure the public. The one article the reporter filed so far indicates that nurses throughout the hospital report extreme stress, feel that many doctors treat them disrespectfully, and believe that a lack of communication across race and gender lines compromises the quality of patient care.

The hospital CEO states that he is interested in learning how the hospital could be more responsive to community concerns and work better internally. He became CEO six months ago; the hospital board recruited him from another state, and he arrived with a reputation as a reformer. He has begun to reorganize the administrative infrastructure of the center, but has mostly been trying to learn as much as he can about the staff's perceptions of the system's strengths and problems. He has been having informal breakfast meetings with cross-sections of hospital personnel, during which he asks multiple questions and encourages freewheeling discussions of the issues he is raising, including soliciting ideas for change. As the Medical Center's personnel learn about these meetings, they are beginning to have some hope that the hospital administration may finally be able to hear their opinions and ideas.

Recently, the CEO and medical director appointed a nine-person internal committee to advise them about necessary changes and make some suggestions on how to initiate a change process. The initial step is a fact-finding one—to "audit" the current situation, emphasize social justice and quality issues throughout the system, and identify the system's strengths and problems. They are willing to provide a budget for this committee, including money to hire a consultant if the panel believes this would be useful. The administration provided committee members some release time for their participation on the committee, which some supervisors are grumbling about since it leaves them further short-staffed. One of the system vice presidents, who is the highest-ranking African American at the Medical Center, heads the committee. He is not a physician, but holds a doctorate in public health. His job entails overseeing finances and records. Other participants include the director of nursing, the associate director of social work, the director of the emergency services unit, the former medical director, and representatives from housekeeping, clerical units, laboratories, and intake units. Women represent about half of the committee, which is also racially mixed.

Questions for Discussion

If the hospital hired you as an external consultant, how would you address the following issues?

1. What types of data should this audit include? (Use the various theories on change to consider what types of assessment you would want to make, what sort of "data" you would want to gather, and how you would go about gathering that data.)

2. How would you use this audit to help people prepare for a change process, and to consider the types of change processes you would like to recommend?
3. How would you want this committee to operate? Internally? With people and systems external to it? What resources will the committee need or desire for its work?

END-OF-CHAPTER EXERCISE
RESTRUCTURING A WELL-ESTABLISHED HUMAN SERVICE ORGANIZATION

Introduction

The ABC Project to Combat Drug Abuse and Violence is a private, nonprofit agency established in the mid-1980s. It provides a variety of programs for individuals who abuse drugs and for the victims of drug-related violence. Soon after the founding of the agency, it developed separate branches in five city neighborhoods. Each branch coordinator established an advisory committee drawn from the surrounding area to encourage local participation in planning and service utilization. These committees included health care and social service professionals, community activists, clergy, educators, and business owners. All of the branch coordinators report directly to the organization's executive director.

Problem

In recent years, two branches of the agency have experienced enormous growth. Those in other parts of the city have grown more slowly. Some advisory committees are functioning well, while others are barely operating. The visibility and effectiveness of the agency's programs, therefore, vary widely.

The agency's board of directors met recently and decided that the branch programs are too scattered, disparate, and loosely controlled, particularly in the current unstable political and economic environment. The board approved additional funding for the next fiscal year to create a new position of associate director for programs who would supervise each of the branch coordinators. The board also asked the executive director to restructure the agency, tighten the coordination and control of central administration over branch programs, and clarify the roles and responsibilities of the staff members at each of the branches. The executive director has several options. Each choice, however, requires the executive director to "unfreeze" the system, make the changes, and "refreeze" it in a more productive pattern.

Option 1: You are the executive director. You have decided to inject "new blood" into the agency by hiring an outside person to be the associate director for programs. How would you go about unfreezing the agency's structure to accommodate the change and assure a more effective structure? Draw the new plan.

Option 2: You are the executive director. You have decided to promote the coordinator of one of the two successful branches to be the new associate director for programs. How would you go about restructuring to assure an effective "refreeze"? Draw the new plan.

Option 3: You are the executive director. You have decided to throw the problem to the branch coordinators. How would you help them participate in the restructuring process?

Questions to Consider (in all three options)

1. What steps would you take to initiate the process?
2. What information should you provide to staff members?
3. How would you motivate staff to support the change? (What rewards would you offer?)
4. How would you go about "refreezing" the agency at the conclusion of the restructuring?
5. What role should the board of directors play in this process?

END-OF-CHAPTER EXERCISE
DEALING WITH CONFLICT IN MACRO PRACTICE

Introduction

Macro social work practice involves working with groups and individuals who often express their frustrations in the form of heated confrontation. At times, individuals who have remained silent most of their lives may vent their pent-up frustrations in the form of anger. In the community, people may direct their anger at the first person from outside the community who has taken the time to listen. In organizations, staff members may direct these emotions at the person who initiates or implements a change process. Individuals from different cultures may express and respond to anger and conflict differently. Learning how you respond to anger and conflict in different types of situations, and understanding the influence of your background and culture on your attitudes about anger and conflict, are important components of your professional development.

Ask yourself, "How do I respond to conflict?" Try to answer as honestly as possible.

I keep quiet in such situations.	Always	Sometimes	Never
I withdraw to avoid conflict.	Always	Sometimes	Never
I simmer for days and then vent my anger in a big blowup.	Always	Sometimes	Never
I appear to be hurt when actually angry.	Always	Sometimes	Never

I express anger and deal with conflict directly, but I do not label the other person or group.	Always	Sometimes	Never
I direct my anger at someone other than the person at whom I am angry.	Always	Sometimes	Never
When confronted by someone who is angry with me, I respond directly and effectively, with composure and try to understand the grievance's source.	Always	Sometimes	Never
I feel hurt and withdraw when someone is angry with me.	Always	Sometimes	Never
I sometimes mistake assertiveness or passion for anger.	Always	Sometimes	Never
I carry the scars of a confrontation with me for a long time.	Always	Sometimes	Never

EPILOGUE

The Personal Side of Macro Social Work Practice

Never doubt that a small group of thoughtful committed citizens can change the world. Indeed, it is the only thing that ever has.

—**Margaret Mead**

In the long run, we shape our lives, and we shape ourselves. The process never ends until we die. And the choices we make are ultimately our own responsibility.

—**Eleanor Roosevelt**

Although social work and other professional programs address the ethical components of practice, they rarely provide students with the opportunity to discuss the personal dimensions of their work beyond the recent concern about the importance of "self-care." Yet, from the author's experience, these issues have become increasingly salient in the lives of students and most practitioners. They influence the direction of our careers and the level of satisfaction we derive from our work. I have found that giving students the opportunity to raise and discuss these issues not only provides an emotional outlet, it also helps them plan their careers and their postgraduation lives more effectively. It is often helpful to discuss these issues at the end of the academic semester, when students have become more comfortable with one another, and the instructor has created a "safe" classroom environment. I have placed this short epilogue, therefore, at the end of the book to discuss briefly such topics as:

- balancing personal and professional values;
- financial considerations in pursuing a career in social work;
- balancing work, family, and friendships;
- being strategic about your career; and
- avoiding burnout through self-care.

To the extent possible, I addressed these issues from the perspective of my professional experience and the reflections of colleagues with whom I have worked or interviewed. Instructors, of course, may insert their own views to revise or augment this discussion.

Balancing Personal and Professional Values

One of the main benefits of being a social worker is the daily satisfaction and sense of integrity we feel in living a life consistent with our fundamental values. Yet, all social workers inevitably confront conflicts between their personal values and their obligations to the profession's code of ethics. Sometimes we have to counsel a client who has committed a reprehensible act of violence against his children. On other occasions, we must work with community residents who resist the construction in their neighborhood of a shelter for people who are homeless. In both situations, our commitment to the underlying values of social work, such as respect for human dignity and self-determination, are sorely tested (Levy, 1976; Frankel, 1969).

At other times, implicit biases influence our judgment and behavior in a wide range of practice settings. In our society, these biases are part of our psychological DNA from birth. We may not be consciously aware of them, but we cannot escape them and we cannot ignore them. This is why ongoing, honest self-reflection is a critical component of all social work practice. Participation in trainings that enable us to recognize and confront our own prejudices is also very helpful throughout our careers.

How can we deal with these challenges to our personal values and professional ethical commitments? First, we have to recognize that these problems are not easy to resolve and to cut ourselves some slack if we struggle with them repeatedly. Many of them cannot be resolved for all time. We also need to separate our personal feelings, however genuine and justified, from our freely entered professional obligations, which make the interests of our clients and constituents a priority. This does not mean abandoning our commitment to the principle of social justice and to assisting the most vulnerable populations in society. It does require us, however, to be strategic in circumstances when the path of remaining true to these values is not clear. Let me present an example from my personal experience.

Some years ago, leaders of the regional AFL-CIO invited me to meet with hundreds of union members who had lost their jobs due to deindustrialization and a particularly harsh recession. My purpose was to advise them on how to obtain available social welfare benefits, including job training and counseling. While I was speaking, some members of the audience, who were understandably anxious, angry, and uncertain about their future and their families' well-being, made racist remarks about who benefitted from the current social welfare system.

This presented me with a dilemma that required an immediate response: I could have challenged them directly and probably lost their attention, confidence, and trust, as I was clearly an "outsider" and this was the first time nearly all of those present had met me. Alternately, I could have ignored the comments, kept the focus of the meeting on its original objective, fulfilled my responsibility and walked away. If I followed the former path, I would have been "true" to my personal values, but I would have failed in my commitment to those who asked me for assistance. If I took the latter course, I would have betrayed my values. What would you have done?

I chose a third path. I did not immediately respond to the racially charged expressions of anger, but met after the meeting with union officials whom I knew to convey my concerns on what had occurred. I urged them to address their members' responses (and the underlying attitudes that produced them) not merely because of their racist foundation but because they were inaccurate and ultimately would undermine their members' attempts to receive the benefits and services to which they were entitled. The union leaders with whom I spoke appeared to understand and share my concerns, though frankly I do not know how they dealt with their members after I left. I do know, however, that most of the people with whom I met successfully accessed at least some of the programs for which they were eligible.

Another problem stems from value differences within the social work profession itself. Recently, some social workers have expressed concerns about the profession's ideological bias. They contend the professional mainstream marginalizes students, faculty, and practitioners with conservative beliefs. Although research demonstrates that a large proportion of social workers hold liberal or progressive views, there are a considerable number of social workers and social work students with more conservative perspectives on particular issues, often emerging from their religious beliefs (Canda & Furman, 2010; Sheridan & Hemert, 1999).

Here, I would draw a crucial distinction. Reasonable persons can disagree on the most effective ways to address difficult social issues such as poverty, substance abuse, and homelessness. Social workers may also differ on the extent of individual or societal responsibility to address these issues and the respective roles of the government and private sector. These differences do not diverge from the profession's core values as long as they do not represent an abandonment of social work's commitment to help excluded and vulnerable populations. They are differences in strategy, not goals.

There are, however, instances in which personal values—particularly those based on religious precepts—may conflict with the core values of the profession. Two examples that come to mind are positions on abortion and LGBTQ rights. I have heard students who said hurtful things to their classmates that they rationalized by their genuine religious beliefs. There is no obvious consensual resolution of such issues. They rest on views that have a "nonrational" (*not irrational*) foundation. Nevertheless, they can lead to the denial of the basic humanity of some people with whom we work—a clear violation of the NASW Code.

After much reflection, there are, in my opinion, only two options in this circumstance. One option is for a prospective social worker to choose another career that will not involve this conflict between her or his personal and professional values. An alternative is to recognize this conflict, treat all clients and colleagues with respect, and seek other ways to meet their needs that would not involve a rejection of one's religious beliefs. For example, two of my former students, both highly skilled advocates who held diametrical positions on abortion, agreed that to work effectively together and to maintain their friendship they would never discuss this issue. This might sound extreme or an instance of ignoring the elephant in the room, but it worked. In an increasingly diverse society, I think we have to find solutions to this dilemma that neither compromise our core values nor exclude individuals who share a commitment to these values but express them in different ways. To do otherwise would be to mirror the bigoted behavior of others we justifiably oppose.

Financial Considerations

Many social work students today encounter financial obligations during and after their education that are considerably greater than previous generations. In addition to incurring considerable debt as undergraduates, the increasing cost of graduate school tuition and the failure of most schools to make commensurate expansions in financial aid place students and new MSW or BSW graduates in a financial hole at the start of their careers. Some observers have commented that unless they have a wealthy partner or a trust fund, or prefer to live a life of penury, choosing a social work career is irrational solely from an economic perspective (Stoesz, Karger, & Carrilio, 2011).

Despite this hyperbole, the problem is real. Some solutions are, however, beyond the reach of individuals. They include government policies that establish free or subsidized undergraduate tuition at public colleges and universities; fund increased financial aid packages, Pell grants, and work-study programs; and provide loan forgiveness for social work graduates who enter public service careers. Schools of social work could also expand their part-time programs and provide both applicants and students with financial counseling.

These ideas are not new. Some of them may be adopted if the political climate changes. Others require more advocacy by leaders of the social work profession. I believe, however, that even in the absence of immediate policy changes, it is still possible to pursue a social work career and not face decades of financial deprivation. Doing so requires careful forethought and a certain amount of self-advocacy.

Prospective students need to think carefully on whether they can afford to undertake graduate study *before* they apply for admission. Some students do not think through the time and resource commitments involved in graduate professional education. They assume they can work part time (even full time) as they may have done as undergraduates without sacrificing the quality of their learning experience or diminishing their performance in their courses or internships. Based on years of professional education and my personal experience, I believe few students can balance all these tasks, particularly if they also have family obligations or health challenges. When reality sets in, usually during the first semester, they often find themselves in academic jeopardy and under enormous personal stress.

Schools can help somewhat to alleviate these problems. They can schedule more classes in the evenings, on weekends, and during the summer. As stated previously, they can provide more financial aid and financial counseling. They can create more flexible curriculum structures (e.g., part-time programs, online or hybrid courses, block placements) that respond to the different demands that students face today. They can rethink the traditional model of offering most courses in 15-week, three-hour blocks. If necessary, they can advise students to wait before entering graduate school or to take a leave of absence when financial pressures become too great.

After graduation and throughout their careers social workers can do a better job advocating for themselves individually and collectively through our professional organizations. While there is widespread admiration for the work we do, this admiration does not translate into adequate salaries, particularly in the private sector. In contrast, MBA graduates, who also attend two-year, full-time programs and are usually the same age as new MSW students, make on average two or three times as much immediately after graduation and within five years earned five to eight times as much as social workers (U.S. Department of Labor, 2016). It is hard to argue that the contributions of MBAs to our society are that much more valuable than the contributions of social workers.

While the market-oriented nature of U.S. society contributes to this discrepancy, other factors influence the gap between the salaries social workers command in large organizations and those of competing professions, such as nursing, public health, public policy, and administration. Particularly in the case of macro social work practitioners, the problem stems as much from the nature of their educational preparation as from their reluctance to engage in self-advocacy. Based on several conversations I have had with directors of major organizations, they would like to hire social workers for top positions—based on their values and ability to work effectively with diverse populations—but hesitate to do so because most MSW graduates lack some of the advanced skills required to do these jobs effectively. Schools of social work could address this problem, but it would require a major restructuring of curricula and greater flexibility in the type of internships available to students. After years of promoting such changes, I am not optimistic most schools will implement them any time soon (Reisch, 2016a).

Being Strategic About Your Career

Just as it is important to plan your graduate school education, an intervention with a client or community, and a new program or advocacy campaign, it helps to take a strategic approach to one's career. This does not require you to write a script for the rest of your life before you graduate. That would not only be impossible, it would be foolish given the rapid and unpredictable changes in our environment and the likelihood that unexpected personal developments will disrupt even the most carefully crafted life plans.

I never anticipated doing most of the things I have done in my career. Fortunately, I was open to the possibilities that emerged and benefitted from the support of family, friends, and colleagues in making the choices I did, no matter how ad hoc or risky. Not all of them worked out, but I think it far better to have taken these risks than to wonder "what if . . .?"

There are ways, however, that foresight can help maximize the opportunities before us and optimize our work experience. For starters, it is useful to think of the first job we obtain immediately after graduation as a springboard for future positions, rather than as setting us on an irreversible career path. This perspective alters what we might seek in this job. I think it is more important, for example, to accept a position that offers new challenges and the chance to learn new skills, instead of taking a job that may be familiar and comfortable but does not push us or compel us to grow. These challenges might involve working with a different population or working with the same population in different ways. It might involve acquiring new talents or using our existing skills in different combinations.

In sum, it is critical not to choose the path of least resistance. This does not mean abandoning the cause that motivated you to become a social worker. Think of it as enhancing your ability to advance this cause over the long term.

Another valuable component of one's first postgraduate job is good supervision. Unless no other options exist or economic pressures are unavoidable, I would opt for a position that provides excellent mentoring and ongoing staff training over one that offers a slightly better salary or benefits. I would also prefer a job that provides opportunities to collaborate with individuals and organizations outside of the agency, including those in other professions and disciplines. These collaborations not only contribute to one's continuing professional education, they often lead to future employment opportunities.

We face similar choices throughout our careers as we change jobs out of desire or necessity. It is better sometimes to make a horizontal move (take a position at a similar level with a different organization) than to "move up" either within one's place of employment or another agency—not because it offers a higher salary, but because it provides more opportunity to cultivate new skills, meet new people, take new risks, and overcome new challenges.

Finally, as discussed below, we need to take the long view about our career choices and the overall context of our personal lives. This means that we may have to forgo some attractive offers if they might produce undesirable consequences for our families, such as our partner's career or our children's education and emotional well-being. It is important, therefore, to discuss any major career decisions openly, honestly, and—where possible—proactively with affected family members.

Balancing Work, Family, and Friendships

At every stage of our career, it is impossible to separate our professional work from the broader context of our lives. Not only do we carry the stress of our work around with us all the time—whether it is a form of "secondary trauma" or the pressure of meeting a proposal deadline—we also cannot escape the effects of planned or unanticipated developments in our personal lives. Many of us want to sustain long-term intimate relationships; some of us want to have (or already have) children. We have to relocate out of choice or necessity. We often have caretaking responsibilities for relatives, sometimes while we are taking care of our own children. Unanticipated health challenges create unexpected physical, financial, and emotional burdens. Throughout our lives, we acquire new friends and colleagues and, sadly, lose others.

For all of these reasons, we need to find ways to balance these diverse aspects of our lives. The old adage about "all work and no play" applies even to social workers with unshakable commitments to social justice and human betterment. Our commitment to our families, friends, and to ourselves needs to be just as strong. It does not contradict or conflict with our commitment to society and to vulnerable populations. In fact, if we do not nurture these personal commitments we will be unable to fulfill our professional obligations over the long haul.

I am fortunate to have two wonderful daughters whom I helped raise when I acquired my social work education and during a critical phase of my subsequent career. Even when my professional obligations were particularly intense, I tried my best to make time for my family. As a campaign manager or head of a statewide advocacy coalition, I often came home to have dinner with my children before racing out to an evening meeting or event. With a few painful exceptions, I made my children a priority on weekends and during vacations. Of course, this added to my stress, but I never regretted these decisions. It saddens me today to see parents (particularly fathers) pay more attention to iPads and iPhones than to the pleas of their children to play with them.

The same applies to maintaining friendships, especially if you move as often as I have during your career. The bad news is that geographic distance, career paths, and the phases of our family life produce some obstacles to friendship that no effort can overcome. Your postgraduate friendships may not be identical or as numerous as those you made in school, but they are just as valuable. The good news is that digital technology makes it easier to stay in contact even if "virtual" communication cannot compare with face-to-face, spontaneous conversations. Some students solve this problem by making conscious efforts to form support groups or intentional communities after graduation.

It is impossible to deny that creating this balance affects one's professional "output." If you measure your work life primarily by the amount you produce, spending time with family or friends will seem a distraction from the pursuit of career goals. I have seldom heard anyone, however, wish they had spent more time at work when they think back on their lives. You have to reflect seriously on what really matters before making these everyday choices.

Avoiding Burnout Through Self-Care

Nurturing personal relationships also requires that we take care of ourselves. A number of books and articles have appeared recently on the importance of self-care (Carter, 2012). I will not summarize their suggestions here. It would be redundant and somewhat hypocritical to do so, as I have not always followed their advice.

I will profess, however, that when I have built into my daily routine regular exercise and relaxation, made sure to eat properly, and tried to get decent sleep (a perpetual problem since childhood), I have not only felt better, I have been more effective in my work and more accessible to family, friends, and colleagues. Whatever means of self-care you choose, make a sustained commitment and do not succumb to any feelings of guilt that you are taking time away from other, "more important" priorities. Think of it as making an investment in yourself so that you can invest more of yourself in the people and work that matter most to you. Think of it as training for a marathon not a sprint, or as contributing to the construction of a soaring and lasting edifice, not a temporary lean-to. After all, the struggles in which social workers, particularly macro social workers, engage in today have been going on for centuries and will continue in different forms well into the future.

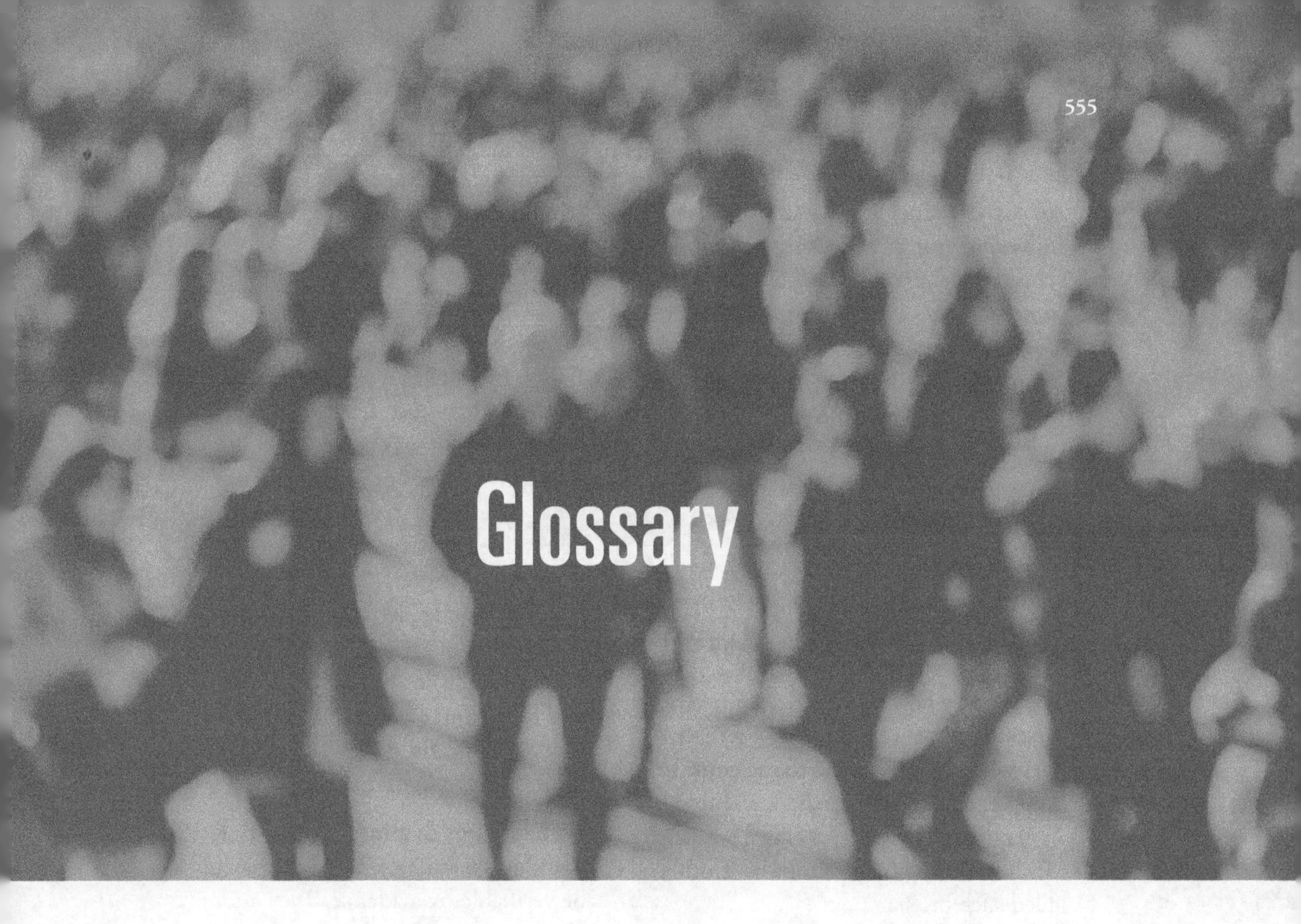

Glossary

A

Action In the literature of community organizing, an action is a specific event designed to implement tactics and carry out a strategy to help one's organization win on an issue. In most cases, it is a component of a broader campaign. An action is also a means of communicating an organization's goals to its constituents, potential constituents, supporters, and opponents.

Action System In systems theory, as it is applied to social work, an action system consists of the people who work together to create a purposive change in a community, organization, or society.

Advisory Board A group of volunteers, often consisting of professional experts and influential community members, who provide information, consultation, and political support to the executive staff of a nonprofit or public sector organization. Unlike the board of directors (or **governing board**), members of an advisory board do not have any legal or fiscal responsibility for the organization's activities.

Advocacy To speak up, to plead the case for another, or to champion a cause, often for individuals or groups unable to speak out on their own behalf. Types of advocacy include self-advocacy, **case advocacy** (for an individual client), and **class advocacy** (advocacy on behalf of a group or category of individuals). Other forms of advocacy focus on the arena in which advocacy occurs. They include **legislative** or **policy advocacy**, **media advocacy**, **judicial advocacy**, **electoral** or **political advocacy**, and **administrative** or **regulatory advocacy**.

***Amicus Curiae* (Legal Brief)** Literally, a "friend of the court" brief filed by individuals or organizations to demonstrate their support for the position of a party to a lawsuit. They often present research evidence and/or an alternative perspective on the issue to the court to supplement the arguments presented by a plaintiff or defendant. Social workers and advocacy organizations have often filed such briefs.

Animation A concept developed in Francophone Canada and France that refers to community organization and mobilization of a population to take action on its own behalf. It combines elements of the confrontational approach to community organizing developed by Alinsky (1971) with more consensual styles (Eichler, 2007; Ohmer & DeMasi, 2009). The French use the phrase *animation sociale* to refer to what English speakers call community organizing.

Assets Assessment The enumeration and evaluation of a community's strengths (individual, organizational, and collective) in the initial stage of community development. It represents an alternative approach to a "deficit model" of assessment that focuses on a community's problems, issues, and needs (Kretzmann & McKnight, 1993).

B

Ballot Initiative A proposition placed on the ballot—also referred to as a referendum—that enables voters to shape the policies of a city, county, or state. Ballot initiatives can be used to determine tax policy, pass a bond issue for a capital project, commit the government to spend a certain proportion of its revenues on a particular population (e.g., children) or need (e.g., education), and to expand or restrict the rights of a specific community (e.g., immigrants or the LGBTQ population).

Beliefs Ideas that individuals or group members assume are true but may not be verifiable by evidence. They attempt to explain how people think the universe and its component parts operate.

Bureaucracy/Bureaucratic Organization An organization characterized by a highly structured, formal division of authority, roles, responsibilities, rule-governed behavior, and limited professional discretion. A state's Department of Social Services is an example of a bureaucratic organization.

C

Campaign/Campaign Strategy A planned effort to effect change in a community, organization, or specific policy area. In electoral politics, it refers to the combination of strategies and tactics designed to elect a candidate, or pass or defeat a ballot initiative.

Capabilities/Capabilities Perspective A concept developed by the economist Amartya Sen and the political philosopher Martha Nussbaum that expands on the theory of social justice developed by the philosopher John Rawls. They posit that social justice involves more than the redistribution of material resources; it also includes enabling people to fulfill their capabilities as humans and social actors through the distribution of nonmaterial, intangible resources. They also argue that the attainment of social justice requires the genuine participation of marginalized individuals and excluded groups in the policy development process.

Change Agent/Change Agent System The individual worker, group, or organization of which she or he is a part that engages in the process of producing a change in people's life circumstances, the policies that affect them, or other significant institutional arrangements.

Civic Participation/Engagement The involvement of a community or subset of the population (e.g., youth) in political and/or social activities that affects their well-being and addresses problems or issues of concern. It is often associated with the concepts of community empowerment and community mobilization.

Coalition A group of organizations and individuals formed to advocate for changes in a public policy or to support a particular cause. It may be a temporary or semipermanent.

Collective Action A joint effort of individuals and groups in a community or organization to achieve a specific purpose. Community development, policy advocacy, and organizational change are examples of collective action.

Collaboration/Collaborative A form of collective action often used to describe a joint effort to create and/or implement a particular service that a single organization cannot deliver as effectively. A collaborative can emerge voluntarily among like-minded organizations; alternately, a funding source may require the formation of a collaborative as a prerequisite for the receipt of financial assistance to support a specific project.

Communitarian/Communitarianism A philosophy that emphasizes the mutually supportive connections between individuals and the community. It stresses the importance of community relationships in shaping a person's social identity and the value of developing collective solutions to individual and social problems.

Community Action Programs (CAPs) Neighborhood programs created by the 1964 Economic Opportunity Act to develop local social services. The legislation required these programs to provide "maximum feasible participation" to community residents.

Community-Based Policy Advocacy An effort that combines approaches used in community organizing, popular education, and participatory development. From community organizing, it borrows a focus on mobilizing geographic communities or communities of identity (Formicola & Hernandez-Cordero, 2011). From popular education, it emphasizes the importance of experience, dialogue, and consciousness-raising (Kane, 2001; Freire, 2013). Similar to participatory development, it assumes that people in the community should "drive" the change process (Schneider & Libercier, 1995; Nelson & Wright, 1995). The overall goal of community-based advocacy is to create an alternative structure through which people articulate and meet their own needs over the long haul and work with marginalized groups to gain collective power to shape existing systems for the better (Minkler, 2012).

Community Competence The ability of a community to assess its problems, identify salient issues, and take action to promote its overall well-being. Social workers can facilitate the attainment of community competence through the provision of technical assistance, leadership development, and other efforts that empower community members.

Community/Locality Development A model of community practice that emphasizes neighborhood work aimed at improving community life through the participation of a broad spectrum of people at the local level, although its scope can be from local to global. One of its goals is to assist residents in organizing block clubs and neighborhood associations to build power and improve the quality of their lives. This model often reflects communitarian values; it emphasizes process goals and stresses such concepts as community competence, self-help, and mutual aid. Examples of this model include settlement houses, community development corporations, VISTA, Americorps, and the Peace Corps.

Community/Social Planning A model of community practice that generally occurs at the neighborhood, city, or regional level. Community and social planning, whether for purposes of physical renovation, economic development, or service planning, emphasizes careful study of a community's political, social, economic, and demographic characteristics (Mayer, 1972). The goal is to create the basis for identifying agreed-upon problems and determining a range of solutions. City and county planners and funding federations, such as the United Way, Associated Jewish Charities, and Catholic Social Services, often use this process (Lauffer, 1978).

Conflict/Conflict Strategy Open confrontation between individuals or groups with competing interests or values. According to Durkheim (1972), there are three basic types of conflict in communities, organizations, or societies (1) *routine conflicts* (such as elections) that—ideally—renew shared beliefs on a regular basis; (2) *anomic forms of conflict* (such as radical cultural or social movements) that shake up shared beliefs; and (3) *restorative conflict* (e.g., reforms passed in response to protest), which recreates social integration after periods of disruption.

Conflict Theory Conflict theories focus on the role of disruptive changes in communities, organizations, and society. They regard conflict as inevitable and posit that it can have both positive and negative consequences.

Conscientization A concept of popular education and social development created by the Brazilian educator and theorist Paulo Freire (1971). Grounded in critical theory, it focuses on developing people's **critical consciousness** and learning how to become subjects rather than objects in the world.

Consensus/Consensus Strategy An approach to conflict resolution or decision making that emphasizes reaching general agreement—not necessarily unanimity—among the various individuals and groups involved.

Consumers/Constituents Individuals, groups, families, organizations, or communities that benefit from a service, program, or policy intervention.

Contingency Theory (of Organizations) A theory of administration that posits there is no optimal way to administer an organization or make key decisions. Instead, the best course of action depends on an analysis of specific internal and external circumstances.

Cooperative An organization or business jointly owned and operated by its members for their mutual benefit. Cooperatives range in size and scope from the multifaceted Mondragon cooperatives in the Basque region to neighborhood food co-ops.

Critical Consciousness A process through which "… people develop their power to perceive critically the way they exist in the world with which and in which they find themselves" (Freire, 2013).

Critical Theory/Critical Race Theory A theory originally developed by legal scholars such as Derrick Bell (1992) and later applied to sociology and other branches of the social sciences. It focuses on analyzing the underlying assumptions (regarding race, gender, etc.) that often prevent people from understanding the realities beneath the surface.

Cultural Imperialism/Hegemony The imposition of the values, norms, attitudes, beliefs, and behaviors of a dominant group or class on subordinate populations. This often occurs in subtle ways, for example, through the **social construction** of certain problems or the social reproduction of these values and norms through societal institutions, such as schools and the media.

D

Dialogue A method of intragroup and intergroup interaction that stresses the importance of active and reflective listening to others, particularly individuals who have different perspectives and different cultural backgrounds.

Domains of Power According to Patricia Hill Collins (2010), the various arenas of society in which dominant groups exercise control over oppressed populations. They include societal structures, cultural norms and values, and individual interpersonal interactions.

E

Economic/Social Development A subset of locality development that focuses on economic and social development at the neighborhood level. One of its goals is the generation of economic production through microenterprises, the creation of so-called "enterprise zones," strengthening existing local businesses, and forming worker and consumer cooperatives. Another goal is the creation of more economic capital in the community. This occurs by changing the lending practices of financial institutions, attracting external sources of investment (e.g., foundations, government, philanthropists), and developing internal sources of capital (through peer lending, community loan funds, and individual assets accounts or IDAs). A third goal is to expand local employment opportunities by creating job-training and skill-development programs, and enhancing the quality of education in the community.

Effectiveness/Efficiency/Effect/ **Effectiveness** refers to whether a particular service or program is meeting its intended goals and objectives. **Efficiency** is a measure of how well an organization is using its resources to meet established goals and objectives. An organization can maintain high efficiency (e.g., cost per service unit) but not provide an effective program. Conversely, a program might be highly effective, but cost-inefficient. Finally, a program's **effect** requires an assessment of its overall effect on the population served by the program, the community as a whole, and the organization itself, including the effect of secondary and unintended consequences

Efficacy Theory A theory that focuses on the extent to which people, individually and in groups, believe in their competence to effect personal and political change in their environment. Concepts such as learned helplessness and cognitive liberation emerged from this theory.

Empowerment The process of increasing personal, interpersonal, and political power so that individuals, families, communities, and organization members can take action to improve their life circumstances or achieve an established goal. Empowerment incorporates three primary dimensions: (1) the development of a more positive and potent sense of self; (2) the construction of a more critical comprehension of the web of social and political relations that make up one's experienced environment; and (3) the cultivation of the resources and "functional competence" that people require for the efficacious attainment of their personal and collective sociopolitical goals.

Environmental/Organizational Set The overall community and societal context in which HSOs are situated. This includes economic conditions, the political climate, the demographic configuration of a community, and the prevalence of certain cultural norms and values.

Ethics The behavioral dimension of values; rules of conduct that guide individual and professional behavior both prescriptively and proscriptively. Ethics also refers to the development of a consistent framework for resolving value dilemmas when they emerge in practice.

Ethnic-Sensitive Organizations Organizations that are aware of differences based on race, ethnicity, and gender but that have responded to these differences largely through superficial actions.

Ethno-Conscious Organizations According to Gutierrez et al. (1996), an organization that has moved beyond ethnic sensitivity to take more deliberate and strategic efforts to integrate cultural awareness into its daily operations and staffing patterns.

Evaluation (Outcome and Process) An **outcome evaluation** measures, as objectively as possible, what an advocacy campaign, service, or program actually achieved. In the former example, did it help pass a particular piece of legislation or obtain certain budget concessions? A **process evaluation** determines what components of a program, service, strategies, and tactics were more or less effective. An evaluation also demonstrates the relative efficacy of an organization to funders and various stakeholders. Finally, it helps an organization find ways to improve future efforts

Evidence-Based Management An approach to the administration and management of organizations that relies upon the latest research—for example, in program planning, resource development, human resource management, and community relations.

F

Framing The presentation of a specific cause or issue in a manner that is both easily understood and capable of evoking the most support for its proponents among the public, the media, and policy makers.

G

Gemeinschaft Often defined as "community," this concept, developed by Ferdinand Tonnies (1957), refers to spontaneously arising social relationships characterized by strong reciprocal ties and common traditions.

Gesellschaft Often defined as "society," this concept (Tonnies, 1957) refers to a group or society characterized primarily by formal organization, impersonal social relationships, the lack of common cultural norms, and a detachment from tradition, often including religious beliefs.

Goal Displacement A process by which a HSO or community group focuses on other ends, such as resource acquisition or organizational survival, instead of its original mission and goals.

Governing Boards The volunteers who are legally and fiscally responsible for the operations of a nonprofit organization. Also called the board of directors.

Grassroots Organization/Grassroots Organizing An aspect of community practice that focuses on work at the neighborhood level or among a particular population directly affected by a specific issue or problem. Also called direct action organizing.

H

Hegemony The consent and compliance induced among subordinate populations by habitual socialization to an authentically felt dominant (common) culture of implicit, self-evident values and behavioral norms (Gramsci, 1992).

Horizontal Relationships The interpersonal and inter-organizational connections that exist among individuals, groups, and organizations engaged in similar activities and that, in general, are on the same "plane" of power, resources, and interests. The relationship between two behavioral health organizations in the same community is an example.

Human Rights/Human Rights Perspective Rights inherent to all human beings, regardless of their nationality, gender, race, ethnicity, religion, or other status. The principle of respect for the individual forms the basis of human rights, as does the assumption that each person is a moral and rational being who deserves to be treated with dignity. The 1948 *U.N. Declaration of Human Rights* establishes these political, social, and cultural rights as universal, interrelated, interdependent, and indivisible.

Human Service Organizations (HSOs) A formal entity that provides one or more of a wide range of services to populations in need. It can be a government or private-sector entity (both nonprofit and for-profit).

I

Ideology A unified, generally coherent collection of beliefs or worldview, of religious or secular origin, that explains a multitude of phenomena and provides the framework for an individual or group's interpretation of its environment.

Implementation Planning A type of planning that considers alternative strategies or program approaches that are available to achieve predetermined goals and objectives (Jansson et al., 2013). It pays close attention to more specific organizational objectives. These include the determination of operational objectives for selected program approaches and the identification of activities that should result through the implementation of established operational objectives.

Implicit Bias A concept that refers to the attitudes, stereotypes, and prejudices that affect people's understanding, actions, and decisions toward others in an unconscious manner. Recently, it refers to the unacknowledged behavior of members of dominant groups toward individuals from "minority" populations, particularly racial or ethnic minorities.

Intersectionality A concept that one's relationship to power and oppression are not solely determined by a single social, cultural, or demographic factor, such as race or gender, but result from a combination of these characteristics. The concept emphasizes the multiple identities all individuals possess that influence their perspective on the environment.

Intimidation Rituals A range of explicit and subtle activities in which some organizations engage to suppress dissent or isolate staff members who engage in "deviant" behavior or challenge prevailing norms and beliefs.

Iron Law of Oligarchy A concept developed by the political philosopher Robert Michels (1915) that power in an organization or society inevitably ends up in the hands of a few individuals, based upon their personal relationships, formal roles, and/or ideological compatibility. These individuals devote much of their time, energy, and resources to the preservation of their dominance and exclude others from critical decision-making processes.

L

Learning Organization An organization that encourages ongoing staff development, innovation, and constant renewal of its goals, processes, knowledge, and skills.

Legislative Advocacy The activities in the political arena that focus on the promotion of the common good or on obtaining, expanding, or protecting the rights and benefits of a specific population. It can serve as a means to mobilize people, raise political consciousness, and accentuate the contradictions within a society's policies. Sometimes called **lobbying.**

Libertarian/Libertarianism A political philosophy that establishes liberty or freedom as its core principle. A libertarian promotes the maximization of political freedom and personal autonomy, and emphasizes freedom of choice, self-ownership, and voluntary association. A libertarian opposes government involvement in the market economy except to enforce the sanctity of contracts and to protect people's physical security. A libertarian also opposes all paternalistic activities, such as restrictions on drug use, abortion, or the consumption of certain foods.

Logic Model A term frequently used to describe a program's underlying theory of change. In its simplest form, a logic model is a graphic representation that shows the relationships between: (1) inputs—the resources that go into the program; (2) outputs—the activities the program undertakes; and (3) outcomes—the changes or benefits that result from the program or service. It provides a "road map" and action plan to guide the program development process (Funnell & Rogers, 2011). It also includes a series of "if-then" relationships that, if implemented as intended, lead to the desired outcomes of a planner (Kaplan & Garrett, 2005). Finally, it includes the various steps of the program planning, implementation, and evaluation process.

M

Management by Objectives A model of management, designed by Peter Drucker (2008), whose purpose is to improve organizational effectiveness by establishing clearly defined performance objectives developed in combination by management and staff.

Marginalization The process of relegating an individual, group, or population to a secondary position in a community, organization, or society. It is associated with social disadvantage and **social exclusion**.

Marxism The most influential conflict theory since the mid-19th century. Marxists made three contributions that continue to inform macro social work practice in the 21st century in valuable ways. First, they regard change (in all systems) as occurring through a dialectical process rather than a linear or cyclical manner. That is, they posit that each situation contains elements that lead to its contradiction or negation—for example, that even in "stable" communities or organizations there are forces of instability—and that the resolution of these contending forces creates a new situation that, in turn, contains contradictory components. A second contribution of Marxism is its assertion that the primary driver of conflict is competition for material resources and the power to control them. Third, Marxists assert that communities, organizations, and societies construct ideological and cultural rationales to justify the prevailing distribution of resources and power.

Mechanistic Organization An organization in which there is a formal structure, rule-governed behavior, and a strict division of authority and decision making. Bureaucracies are mechanistic organizations. A mechanistic organization usually demonstrates little flexibility and provides limited opportunity for staff members to exercise professional discretion and judgment.

Mobilization The organization and application of constituents' resources toward a particular community or policy goal. In this context, mobilization is the process of increasing the ability of constituents to act collectively by building their loyalty to a common set of objectives and increasing their ability to influence the course of events. Mobilization can take multiple forms: defensive, offensive, and preparatory, depending upon the availability of resources, the relative power of advocates, and the particular issues at hand.

Morals Behavioral principles or rules of conduct often derived from a higher authority, such as religious beliefs.

Multicultural Organizations/ Multicultural Organizing A multicultural organization (Holvino, 2008) represents the highest stage of organizational awareness regarding the importance of cultural diversity and cultural humility. It is an organization whose leaders and staff members not only "talk the talk," but also "walk the walk." In community practice, multicultural community organizing (MCO) is an emerging model that builds upon an ethno-conscious and empowerment approach to practice (Gutierrez, 1997; Kirk & Okazawa-Rey, 1998). It also reflects an appreciation of the strengths within communities of color (Rivera & Erlich, 1997; Delgado, 1994). Its core concerns are the acquisition of power and confronting social inequality, especially structural inequality in all its forms. MCO assumes that building strong organizations within communities of color is a prerequisite for the construction of effective and viable multiracial coalitions.

Mutual Aid Organization/Society A collective entity through which people help one another to accomplish their individual and social goals, and address common issues through the provision of social support, tangible and intangible resources, information, the promotion of emotional expression, and advocacy. Mutual aid organizations developed in the United States in every racial, ethnic, and religious minority community to fill gaps in services and policies that mainstream organizations neglected to provide or failed to provide in a culturally sensitive manner.

N

Neoliberal/Neoliberalism A political philosophy that emerged during the 1960s and 1970s that emphasizes deregulation of the economy, reduction in government involvement in social welfare, privatization of services, and substitution of the concept of the "public good" with a focus on "individual responsibility" and "human capital" development. Neoliberals generally prefer market-based and individualistic solutions to social problems.

Nongovernmental Organizations (NGOs) Private, nonprofit organizations whose primary purpose is to provide a public good—e.g., through educational, cultural, social service, or health-related programs. Also called voluntary sector or third-sector organizations. Many HSOs in the United States are nongovernmental organizations and, as such, have special tax status as 501 (c) (3) organizations.

Norms Expectations of group behaviors. They can be formal (expressed through laws or policies) or informal (expressed through customs, mores, and traditions). They provide guidance as to what is proper or necessary behavior within particular roles or settings. They define what is acceptable and what is deviant. They also define the boundaries between and within social structures.

O

Oppression The sustained cruel and unjust treatment of an individual or group by an established authority. Oppression takes diverse forms in different circumstances and affects various populations in different ways. It can be physical, economic, political, social, cultural, and psychological, or a combination of these conditions.

Organic Organization In contrast to a **mechanistic organization**, an organic organization is flexible, adaptive, and open to new information, diverse ideas, and external influences. It is often better suited for a turbulent and rapidly changing external environment.

Organizational Culture/Organizational Climate An organization's culture is the system of shared assumptions, values, and beliefs that governs how people in the organization behave. In turn, organizational culture influences the organizational climate, which reflects the immediate experiences of staff members and clients and the effect of internal forces (such as a leadership transition) and external forces (such as changes in the political environment).

Organizational Life Cycle The various stages through which an organization passes, from its creation to its demise, that are somewhat analogous to the human life cycle. Organizations have different needs and must meet different challenges at each stage of their life cycle.

Organizational Mission The overall purpose of an organization, such as a HSO, usually expressed in a formal statement. For example, an organization's mission could be "to promote the successful re-integration of formerly incarcerated individuals into their families, communities, and society." An organization develops goals and programs based on its mission.

Organizational Vision The ultimate outcome desired by an organization, such as a HSO, that inspired its creation and shapes its mission. Organizations often undergo a "visioning process" in their early stages or during a restructuring process. An organization's vision could be "the creation of a society in which all individuals are given the maximum opportunity to achieve their full human potential."

Outcomes/Outputs **Outputs** are the units of service a program generates, such as the number of clients who receive counseling, the number of children receiving care, the number of community members who participate in job-training programs, or the number of households that attend sessions on the process of home ownership. **Outcomes** measure the effect of a program or service on the clients who participate.

P

Participatory Action Research (PAR) An approach to the design, implementation, and evaluation of research that integrates stakeholders into all aspects of the research process and emphasizes the role of research in producing social and political change.

Pluralism The belief that diverse groups can coexist in a community, organization, or society and resolve social and political disagreements through a process whose outcome all competing groups accept as legitimate.

Policy Planning A type of planning that focuses on identifying the goals of organizational activities. It emphasizes problem definition and the establishment of broad, desirable outcomes. It ensures that an organization unifies its resources and activities in a single direction.

Political Action Committee (PAC) A formal entity created to raise funds in support of (or opposition to) a political candidate or issue. Federal and state laws restrict the fund-raising and spending activities of a political action committee, although the Supreme Court's decision in the *Citizens United* case removed or relaxed many of these restrictions.

Positionality The various social statuses a person occupies (e.g., race, class, gender) that influence her or his view of the world and how others perceive him or her.

Praxis The dynamic and iterative process by which a practitioner acts based on principles derived from ongoing reflection on personal experience filtered through a coherent theoretical framework.

Privilege Unearned advantages of an individual or group usually associated with social categories—such as class, race, and gender—that have higher social status.

Problem-Solving Systems in Communities The systems that—ideally—work together to promote community change and solve community problems as the community defines them. They include the **initiator system** (the individual or group that begins the change process); the **support system** (the group that provides the resources needed to carry out the change process); the **controlling system** (the institutions or structures that define the boundaries in which change can occur); and the **host/implementing system** (the entity that maintains the change process).

Program Inputs/Throughputs/Outputs Three concepts in a systems approach to program planning and development. Program **inputs** include the various resources needed to run a program, such as money, facilities, clients, program staff, and volunteers. **Throughputs** consist of the processes by which an organization delivers the program's services—for example, family counseling, childcare, job training, or education on home ownership. **Outputs** are the units of service the program generates, such as the number of clients who receive counseling, the number of children cared for, the number of community members who participate in job-training programs, or the number of households that attend sessions on the process of home ownership. Similar to organic systems, all organizations also produce "waste," often in the form of paperwork.

Program Planning/Program Development The process of designing, implementing, and evaluating a program or service within a HSO.

Q

Quality-Oriented Management or Total Quality Management (TQM) A comprehensive approach to management that involves all departments, staff, and clients in an organization with the goal of maximizing the effectiveness of its programs.

R

Rational Choice Theory A theory derived from economics that states individuals and organizations always make decisions based on their greatest benefit and on what is in their highest self-interest.

Routinization of Charisma A concept developed by the German sociologist Max Weber (1946), which postulates that personal charisma becomes stabilized through its integration into existing structures of authority.

S

Scientific Management A theory of management, developed by Frederick W. Taylor, that analyzed how individuals did their work in an effort to improve corporate efficiency and productivity. It was one of the earliest attempts to apply science to management processes.

Self-Help Organization An organization established and run by individuals or groups sharing a common problem or possessing a common need. Examples of self-help organizations range from Alcoholics Anonymous to babysitting cooperatives.

Social Action An approach to community organization whose primary goals are to correct societal inequities by changing existing policies or procedures, patterns of resource distribution, or power arrangements within societal institutions and systems that particularly disadvantage oppressed and marginalized groups of people. The targets of social action are usually those community institutions that control and allocate resources and power, such as financial institutions, corporations, or local government. Prominent examples of the use of the social action model include landlord/tenant conflicts, welfare rights organizing, union or workplace organizing, and political organizing both inside and outside the electoral arena.

Social Capital A concept that analyzes the features of social organization, such as networks, norms, and bonds of social trust, that facilitate coordination and cooperation for mutual benefit. They include those aspects of social relations that impinge on economic and political life and that are difficult to incorporate into explanatory models based solely on self-interest (Edwards & Foley, 1998). Social capital takes two forms. A community's "bonding social capital" refers to its internal social relationships and the degree of mutual trust and cooperation that exists (Reisch & Guyet, 2007). Even if a community forges stronger horizontal ties, when residents are marginalized and lack power and resources they lack "bridging social capital"—i.e., vertical relationships with key external individuals, groups, and institutions. This prevents these communities from having a "seat at the table" when policy agendas are being formed and vital resources are being distributed.

Social Construction A concept developed by postmodernists that posits that what people define as "reality" is actually a subjective reflection of the values and beliefs of the dominant group. The use of this conceptual lens helps social work practitioners acquire a different perspective on the origins and meaning of social problems and issues.

Social Enterprise Organization A hybrid form of organization that combines features of a for-profit corporation and a nonprofit agency. Social enterprise organizations sell a product or service and distribute all or some of the profits to support a specific cause or set of causes.

Social Exchange Theory A theory that explains the processes of community, organizational, and societal change and stability as the outcome of negotiated exchanges between parties with different self-interests and different amounts of resources, power, and influence (Braithwaite & Schrodt, 2015). These exchanges produce both economic and social outcomes to participants. Ideally, they result in mutual satisfaction, but the imbalance of power and resource in many organizations and communities often leads to unequal costs and benefits.

Social Inclusion/Social Exclusion The World Bank defines social inclusion as the process of improving the ability, opportunity, and dignity of disadvantaged people to take part in society. Social exclusion is the process that systematically denies certain individuals or groups full access to the rights, opportunities, and resources normally available to members of a different group.

Social Justice A philosophical concept, based originally on social contract theory that emphasizes fairness or equity as a primary principle of social and political organization.

Social Learning Theory A theory that bridges behaviorist and cognitive learning theories. Its basic premise is that people learn from one another through observation, imitation, and modeling. The socialization process that occurs in all communities and organizations provides an example of how this theory helps explain the behavior of community members and agency staffers, who reproduce long-standing roles, customs, and values.

Social Movement A social movement is an organizational structure that attempts to empower an oppressed or disadvantaged population to challenge dominant structures and institutions. In general, it focuses on a specific set of political or social issues. Examples include the civil rights, feminist, and LGBTQ movements.

Social Reform This model of community practice is a mixture of social action and social planning that involves collaborating with other organizations to promote system or policy change. It addresses such issues as increasing childcare options for working parents, raising the minimum wage, addressing inequities in the criminal justice system or the funding of public school districts, and creating more affordable housing opportunities (Weil, Gamble, & Ohmer, 2013).

Social Sustainability The ability of a community or organization to develop processes and structures that meet the needs of its current members and support future efforts to meet these needs.

Standpoint/Standpoint Theory Refers to how a person's social and political location and historical experiences (in the broadest sense) shape her or his perspectives on the world.

Stare Decisis The principle in Anglo-American law that legal precedents should be the primary determinants of a court's decision.

Strategy The science and art of orchestrating community or organizational resources toward clearly defined goals and objectives.

Structural Functionalism A set of sociological theories that emphasize how various systems, institutions, or groups fit together to maintain societal, community, or organizational order and balance. They include **systems theory** (Brunczel, 2010), of which **ecological theory** is an offshoot (Deutscher & Lafont, 2017). They also include various theories of inter-organizational relationships (Reitan, 1998), political-economic theory, and institutional ecology. **Pluralism** is a widely used theory to explain how policy makers produce decisions at the community and national levels (Lassman, 2011).

Symbolic Interactionism An approach to human behavior based on the premise that people respond to social reality through their different perspectives and the interpretations they apply to different objects (such as cultural artifacts) or interpersonal experiences.

Systems Theory The interdisciplinary study of entities with interrelated and interdependent parts defined by their boundaries. In social work practice, systems theory helps explain the process of individual, group, community, or organizational change.

T

Tactics Tactics are the *specific activities* in which communities and organizations engage to help them reach their goals and objectives. They are the specific activities carried out by an organization as part of its strategy.

Target System The individual, group, community, or organization that practitioners attempt to change or influence.

Targeting/Targeting Analysis Targeting refers to the focus of advocacy efforts on specific individuals, groups, or organizations to achieve desired results. It includes deciding who has to hear a particular message (the primary and secondary targets), how to make decision makers listen to an appeal, how to influence the public's knowledge and perception of an issue, what are the most compelling parts of a campaign's message, and who are the best messengers.

Targets of Benefits Usually this refers to the specific clients or constituents on whose behalf advocacy efforts are undertaken. Sometimes, however, the public may be the intended beneficiary of legislative or policy advocacy.

Targets of Influence The individuals and groups that are the focus of community organizing or legislative advocacy efforts. They could include government officials, corporate executives, legislators (and their staffs), other political stakeholders, department heads (and key staff), the media, and other influential opinion makers and advocates.

Targets of Mobilization Those individuals and groups whose resources and energy advocates and organizers need to promote a particular agenda and achieve their goals and objectives.

Theory of Change A component of the planning process that helps organizational participants develop clear goals and provides a coherent framework that matches a program's design to its intended purposes.

Total Quality Management (TQM) A system of management based on the principle that every staff member must be committed to maintaining high standards of work in every aspect of an organization's operations.

V

Values The enduring beliefs an individual, group, or community considers important in that entity's life and practice. Values define a system of preferences regarding desirable goals and outcomes. From an ethical perspective, values indicate what people consider as good and right in their actions and those of others.

Vertical Relationships The interpersonal and inter-organizational connections that exist among individuals, groups, and organizations that are on different "planes" of power, resources, and interests. For example, a nonprofit HSO has a vertical relationship with a funding source, such as the state government or a major foundation.

Voluntary Organization The former name for a nonprofit or nongovernmental organization. Its name stemmed from the fact that originally volunteers staffed these organizations. Many social work organizations, such as the Charity Organization Societies and social settlements, began as voluntary organizations, a unique feature of U.S. social welfare history.

W

Whistle-Blowing The exposure of information or an activity regarded as illegal or unethical within a public or private-sector organization. Examples include violation of company policy/rules, fraud, and corruption. Whistle-blowers can bring information or allegations to surface, either internally or externally, or by contacting a third party such as the media, a government official, a law enforcement agency, or those affected by the violation.

References

Aber, L., & Chaudry, A. (2010, April). *Low-income children, their families, and the Great Recession: What next in policy?* Paper prepared for the Georgetown University and Urban Institute Conference on Reducing Poverty and Economic Distress after ARRA, Washington, DC.

Abramovitz, M. (2005). The largely untold story of welfare reform and the human services. *Social Work, 50*(2), 175–186.

Abramovitz, M. (2012). Theorizing the neoliberal welfare state for social work. In M. Gray, J. Midgley, & S. A. Webb (Eds.) *The Sage handbook of social work* (pp. 33–50). Thousand Oaks, CA: Sage Publications.

Acs, G. (2011). *Downward mobility from the middle class: Waking up from the American dream.* Washington, DC: Pew Charitable Trust.

Adam, B. D. (1995). *The rise of a gay and lesbian movement.* New York, NY: Twayne Publishers.

Akimoto, T. (2014). Social justice in an era of globalization: Must and can it be the focus of social welfare policies? Japan as a case study. In M. Reisch (Ed.), *The Routledge international handbook of social justice* (pp. 48–60). London, UK: Routledge.

Alexander, M. (2012). *The new Jim Crow: Mass incarceration in the age of colorblindness*, revised ed. New York, NY: New Press.

Alexander, R., Lord, M., Novick, T., Nielsen, S., & Ross, D. (2004). *Strategies for building statewide progressive power: An examination of seven state coalitions.* Amherst, MA: State Strategies Fund.

Alimo-Metcalfe, B., & Alban-Metcalfe, J. (2005). Leadership: Time for a new direction? *Leadership, 1*(1), 51–71.

Alimo-Metcalfe, B., Alban-Metcalfe, J., Bradley, M., Mariathasan, J., & Samele, C. (2008). The impact of engaging leadership on performance, attitudes to work and wellbeing at work: A longitudinal study. *Journal of health organization and management, 22*(6), 586–598.

Alinsky, D. S. (1971). *Rules for radicals: A practical primer for realistic radicals.* New York, NY: Random House.

Alliance for Justice, Harmon, G. M., Ladd, J. A., & Evans, E. A. (2011). *Being a player: A guide to the IRS lobbying regulations for advocacy charities.* Washington, DC: Alliance for Justice.

Alter, C. (2009). Building community partnerships and networks. In R. Patti (Ed.), *The handbook of human services management*, 2nd ed. (pp. 435–454). Thousand Oaks, CA: Sage Publications.

Amidei, N. (1982, Summer). How to be an advocate in bad times. *Public Welfare*, 37–42.

Anderson, J., Miller, M., & McGuire, A. (2012). Media advocacy: A strategy for helping communities change policy. In M. Minkler, (Ed.), *Community organizing and community building for health and welfare*, 3rd ed. New Brunswick, NJ: Rutgers University Press.

Anderson, N., Potocnik, K., & Zhou, J. (2014). Innovation and creativity in organizations: A state-of-the-science review, prospective commentary, and guiding framework. *Journal of Management, 40*(5), 1297–1333.

Andreasen, A. R., & Kotler, P. (2008). *Strategic marketing for nonprofit organizations*, 7th ed. Upper Saddle River, NJ: Prentice Hall.

Ansolabehere, S. D., Hirano, S., Hansen, J. M., & Snyder Jr., J. M. (2010). Primary elections and partisan polarization in the US Congress. *Quarterly Journal of Political Science 5*(2), 169–191.

Ansolabehere, S. D., & Iyengar, S. (1995). *Going negative: How attack ads shrink and polarize the electorate.* New York, NY: Free Press.

Applied Research Center & Center for Third World Organizing (1998). *Colorlines: Race, culture, action.* Oakland, CA: Author.

Atkinson, A. B., & Marlier, E. (2010). *Analyzing and measuring social inclusion in a global context.* New York, NY: United Nations.

Atlas, J. (2010). *Seeds of change: The story of ACORN, America's most controversial antipoverty community organizing group.* Nashville, TN: Vanderbilt University Press.

Austin, M. J. (1978). *Management simulations for mental health and human services administration.* New York, NY: Haworth Press.

Austin, M. J. (2002). Managing out: The community practice dimensions of effective agency management. *Journal of Community Practice, 10*(4), 33–48.

Austin, M. J., Anthony, E. K., Knee, R. T., & Mathias, J. (2015). Revisiting the relationship between micro and macro social work practice: A springboard for discussion in our academic and practice communities. Unpublished paper presented at the 2015 Annual Program Meeting of the Council on Social Work Education, Denver, CO.

Austin, M. J., & Betten, N. (1977). The intellectual origins of community organizing, 1920–1939. *Social Service Review, 51*(1), 155–170.

Austin, M. J., & Gilmore, T. N. (1993). Executive exit: Multiple perspectives on managing the leadership transition. *Administration in Social Work, 17*(1), 47–60.

Austin, M. J., & Lowe, J. I. (Eds.) (1994). *Controversial issues in communities and organizations.* Boston, MA: Allyn & Bacon.

Austin, M. J., Regan, K., Samples, M. W., Schwartz, S. I., & Carnochan, S. (2011). Building managerial and organizational capacity in nonprofit human service organizations through a leadership development program. *Administration in Social Work, 35*, 258–281.

Avery, J. M., & Peffley, M. (2003). Race matters: The impact of news coverage of welfare reform on public opinion. In S. F. Schram, J. Soss, & R. C. Fording (Eds.), *Race and the politics of welfare reform* (pp. 131–150). Ann Arbor, MI: University of Michigan Press.

Bailey, M. J., & Danziger, S. (Eds.) (2013). *Legacies of the war on poverty.* New York, NY: Russell Sage Foundation.

Baker Miller, J. (1987). Women and power. *Women & Therapy, 6*(1–2), 1–10.

Bandura, A. (1977). *Social learning theory.* Englewood Cliffs, NJ: Prentice Hall.

Bandura, A. (1986). The explanatory and predictive scope of self-efficacy theory. *Journal of social and clinical psychology, 4*(3), 359–373.

Barner-Barry, C. (1986). Rob: Children's tacit use of peer ostracism to control aggressive behavior. *Ethology and Sociobiology, 7*(3–4), 281–293.

Bartels, L. M. (2016). *Unequal democracy*. Princeton, NJ: Princeton University Press.

Barvosa-Carter, E. (2001). Multiple identity and coalition building: How identity differences within us enable radical alliances among us. In J. Bystydzienski and S. Schacht (Eds.), *Forging radical alliances across difference: Coalition politics for the new millennium* (pp. 21–34), Lanham, MD: Rowman and Littlefield.

Bass, R. (1997, Summer). Round River. *Orion*.

Bates, K. A., & Swan, R. S. (2010). *Through the eye of Katrina: Social justice in the United States*, 2nd ed. Durham, NC: Carolina Academic Press.

Beauchamp, D. E. (1980). Public health and individual liberty. *Annual Review of Public Health, 1*(1), 121–136.

Bell, D. (1992). *Faces at the bottom of the well: The permanence of racism*. New York, NY: Basic Books.

Bell, W., & Bell, B. (1982). Monitoring the bureaucracy: An extension of legislative lobbying. In M. Mahaffey & J. W. Hanks (Eds.), *Practical politics: Social work and political responsibility*. Silver Spring, MD: National Association of Social Workers.

Bellah, R. N., et al. (2008). *Habits of the heart: Individualism and commitment in American life*. Berkeley, CA: University of California Press.

Bellah, R. N., et al. (1991). *The good society*. New York, NY: Vintage Books.

Berger, A. E. (2014). *The queer turn in feminism: Identities, sexuality, and the theater of gender* (Trans. by C. Porter). New York, NY: Fordham University Press.

Berger, P. L., & Neuhaus, R. J. (1977). *To empower people: The role of mediating structures in public policy*. Washington, DC: American Enterprise Institute for Public Policy Research.

Bergh, A., & Nilsson, T. (2010). Good for living? On the relationship between globalization and life expectancy. *World Development, 38*(9), 1191–1203.

Berkeley Media Studies Group (2003). Training guide. Berkeley, CA: Author.

Betten, N., & Austin, M. J. (1990). *The roots of community organizing, 1917–1939*. Philadelphia, PA: Temple University Press.

Birkland, T. A. (2014). *An introduction to the policy process: Theories, concepts and models of public policy making*. New York, NY: Routledge.

Blake, R. R., & Mouton, J. S. (1964). *The managerial grid: Key orientations for achieving production through people*. Houston, TX: Gulf Publishing Co.

Blanchard, A., & Horan, T. (1998). Virtual communities and social capital. *Social Science Computer Review, 16*(3), 293–307.

Bloomrosen, M., Starren, J., Lorenzi, N. M., Ash, J. S., Patel, V. L., & Shortliffe, E. H. (2011). Anticipating and addressing the unintended consequences of health IT and policy: A report from the AMIA 2009 Health Policy Meeting. *Journal of the American Medical Informatics Association, 18*(1), 82–90.

Bobo, K., Kendall, J., & Max, S. (2001). *Organize! Organizing for social change*, 3rd ed., Washington, DC: Seven Locks Press.

Bobo, K. A., Kendall, J., & Max, S. (2001). *Organizing for social change: Midwest Academy manual for activists*. Santa Ana, CA: Seven Locks Press.

Bok, S. (1999). *Lying: Moral choice in public and private life* (Rev. ed.). New York, NY: Vintage Books.

Bok, S. (1980). Whistleblowing and professional responsibilities. In D. Callahan & S. Bok (Eds.), *Ethics teaching in higher education* (pp. 277–295). New York, NY: Plenum Press.

Booth, H. (1977). *Direct action organizing*. Chicago, IL: The Midwest Academy.

Bottomore, T. (1991). *A dictionary of Marxist thought*, 2nd ed. Cambridge, MA: Blackwell Reference.

Bourdieu, P. (2003). *Firing back: Against the tyranny of the market 2* (Trans. by L. Wacquant). New York, NY: Verso.

Bourdieu, P. (2005). Habitus. *Habitus: A sense of place, 2*, 43–52.

Bourdieu, P. (2003). Social reproduction. *Culture: Critical Concepts in Sociology, 3*, 63.

Bowes, A., & Sims, D. (2006). Advocacy for Black and minority ethnic communities: Understandings and expectations, *British Journal of Social Work, 36*(7), 1209–1225.

Bowler, S., & Glazer, A. (2008). *Direct democracy's impact on American political institutions*. New York, NY: Palgrave MacMillan.

Brace, C. L. (1872, 1973). *The dangerous classes of New York and twenty years work among them*. Washington, DC: NASW Press.

Brager, G., & Holloway, S. (1978). *Changing human service organizations: Politics and practice.* New York, NY: Free Press.

Braithwaite, D. O., & Schrodt, P. (Eds.) (2015). *Engaging theories in interpersonal communication: Multiple perspectives*, 2nd ed. Thousand Oaks, CA: Sage Publications.

Bray, I. (2016). *Effective fundraising for nonprofits: Real-world strategies that work*, 5th ed. Berkeley, CA: Nolo.

Bride, B. E. (2007). Prevalence of secondary traumatic stress among social workers. *Social Work, 52*(1), 63–70.

Brisson, D., & Roll, S. (2008). An adult education model of resident participation: Building community capacity and strengthening neighborhood-based activities in a comprehensive community initiative (CCI). *Advances in Social Work, 9*(2), 157–175.

Brodkin, E. Z. (2010). Human service organizations and the politics of practice. In Y. Hasenfeld (Ed.), *Human services as complex organizations*, 2nd ed. (pp. 61–78). Thousand Oaks, CA: Sage Publications.

Brodkin, M. (1994). *From sandboxes to ballot boxes: San Francisco's landmark campaign to fund children's services.* San Francisco, CA: Coleman Advocates for Children and Youth.

Bronfenbrenner, U. (1979). *The ecology of human development: Experiments by nature and design.* Cambridge, MA: Harvard University Press.

Bronstein, L. R. (2003). A model for interdisciplinary collaboration. *Social Work, 48*(3), 297–306.

Bronstein, L. R., & Abramson, J. S. (2017). Group process dynamics and skills in inter-disciplinary teamwork. In C. D. Garvin, L. M. Gutierrez, & M. J. Galinsky (Eds.), *Handbook of social work with groups* (pp. 491–509). New York, NY: The Guilford Press.

Brown, B. (September 2001). *Tracking the well-being of children and youth at the state and local levels using the federal statistical system.* Washington, DC: Urban Institute.

Browning, R., Marshall, D. R., & Tabb, D. H. (Eds.) (2003). *Racial politics in American cities*, 3rd ed. New York, NY: Longman.

Brulle, R. J. (2010). From environmental campaigns to advancing the public dialog: Environmental communication for civic engagement. *Environmental Communication, 4*(1), 82–98.

Brunczel, B. (2010). *Disillusioning modernity: Niklas Luhmann's social and political theory.* New York, NY: Peter Lang.

Buckmaster, N. (1999). Associations between outcome measurement, accountability and learning for non-profit organisations. *International Journal of Public Sector Management, 12*(2), 186–197.

Burghardt, S. (2012). Blues-influenced reflections on the negative impact of racism on white identity. Unpublished paper presented at Symposium on "Interdisciplinary Scholarship for Community Practice in the 21st Century," University of Michigan, Ann Arbor, MI.

Burghardt, S. (2013). *Macro practice in social work for the 21st century*, 2nd ed. Thousand Oaks, CA: Sage Publications.

Burghardt, S. (1982). *The other side of organizing.* Cambridge, MA: Schenkman.

Burton, M. J., Miller, W. J., & Shea, D. M. (2015). *Campaign craft: The strategies, tactics, and art of political campaign management*, 5th ed. Santa Barbara, CA: Praeger, ABC-CLIO.

Busch, M., & Hostetter, C. (2009). Examining organizational learning for application in human service organizations. *Administration in Social Work, 33*(3), 297–318.

Butterfield, A. (2012). Reflections on identity based organizing. Unpublished paper presented at Symposium on "Interdisciplinary Scholarship for Community Practice in the 21st Century," University of Michigan, Ann Arbor, MI.

Bystydzienski, J., & Schacht, S. (Eds.) (2001). *Forging radical alliances across difference: Coalition politics for the new millennium.* Lanham, MD: Rowman and Littlefield.

Cameron, K. S., & Quinn, R. E. (2005). *Diagnosing and changing organizational culture: Based on the competing values framework.* New York, NY: John Wiley & Sons.

Canon, B. C., & Johnson, C. A. (1999). *Judicial policies: Implementation and impact*, 2nd ed. Washington, DC: CQ Press.

Carlton-LaNey, I. (Ed.) (2001). *African American leadership: An empowerment tradition in social welfare history.* Washington, DC: NASW Press.

Carlton-LaNey, I. (1999). African American social work pioneers' response to need. *Social Work, 44*(4), 311–321.

Carmon, N., & Fainstein, S. (Eds.) (2013). *Policy, planning, and people*. Philadelphia, PA: University of Pennsylvania Press.

Carp, R., Stidham, R., & Manning, K. (2010). *Judicial process in America*, 8th ed. Washington, DC: CQ Press.

Carr, E. S. (2003). Rethinking empowerment theory using a feminist lens: The importance of process. *Affilia*, *18*(1), 8–20.

Chambers, C. A. (1986). Women in the creation of the profession of social work. *Social Service Review 60*(1), 1–33.

Chambers, D. C., & Bonk, J. F. (2013). *Social policy and social programs: A method for the practical public policy analyst*, 6th ed. Boston, MA: Pearson.

Chandler, S. K., & Jones, J. (2003). 'You have to do it for the people coming': Union organizing and the transformation of immigrant women workers. *Affilia: Journal of Women and Social Work*, *18*(3), 254–271.

Chapman, S. (2004). Advocacy for public health: A primer. *Journal of Epidemiology and Community Health*, *58*(5), 361.

Chasin, A. (2000). *Selling out: The gay and lesbian movement goes to market*. New York, NY: St. Martin's Press.

Chaskin, R. J. (2005). Democracy and bureaucracy in a community planning process. *Journal of Planning Education and Research*, *24*(4), 408–419.

Checkoway, B. (Ed.). (2013). *Citizens and health care: Participation and planning for social change*. New York, NY: Elsevier.

Chesler, M. A. (1981). Creating and maintaining interracial coalitions. In B. P. Bowser & R. G. Hunt (Eds.) *Impacts of racism on white Americans* (pp. 217–244). Beverly Hills, CA: Sage Publications.

Chesler, M. A. (1995). Racetalk: Thinking and talking about racism. *The Diversity Factor*, *3*(3), 37–45.

Cheung, F. M., & Halpern, D. F. (2010). Women at the top: Powerful leaders define success as work + family in a culture of gender. *American Psychologist*, *65*(3), 182.

Children Now (2003). Media style guide. Oakland, CA: Author.

Chong, D., & Druckman, J. N. (2007). Framing public opinion in competitive democracies. *American Political Science Review*, *101*(4), 637–655.

Chow, J. C. C., & Austin, M. J. (2008). The culturally responsive social service agency: The application of an evolving definition to a case study. *Administration in Social Work*, *32*(4), 39–64.

Ciconte, B. L., & Jacob, J. G. (2009). *Fundraising basics: A complete guide*, 3rd ed. Sudbury, MA: Jones & Bartlett Publishers.

Clark, C. L. (2000). *Social work ethics: Politics, principles and practice*. New York, NY: MacMillan Press.

Cnaan, R. A., with Boddie, S. (2002). *The invisible caring hand: American congregations and the provision of welfare*. New York, NY: New York University Press.

Cnaan, R. A., & Cascio, T. A. (1998). Performance and commitment: Issues in management of volunteers in human service organizations. *Journal of Social Service Research*, *24*(3-4), 1–37.

Cnaan, R. A., & Vinokur-Kaplan, D. (2015). Social innovation: Definitions, clarifications, and a new model. In R. A. Cnaan & D. Vinokur-Kaplan (Eds.), *Cases in innovative nonprofits: Organizations that make a difference* (pp. 1–16). Thousand Oaks, CA: Sage Publications.

Coates, T. (2015). *Between the world and me*. New York, NY: Spiegel & Grau.

Coates, T. (2016). The case for considering reparations. *The Atlantic*, *27*.

Coffman, J. (2007). What's different about evaluating advocacy and policy change? *The Evaluation Exchange*, *13*(1), 2–4.

Cogburn, D. L., & Espinoza-Vasquez, F. K. (2011). From networked nominee to networked nation: Examining the impact of Web 2.0 and social media on political participation and civic engagement in the 2008 Obama campaign. *Journal of Political Marketing*, *10*(1–2), 189–213.

Coglianese, C., Kilmartin, H., & Mendelson, E. (2008). Transparency and public participation in the federal rulemaking process: Recommendations for the new administration. *George Washington Law Review*, *77*, 924.

Cohen, B. J., & Austin, M. J. (1997). Transforming human services organizations through empowerment of staff. *Journal of Community Practice*, *4*(2), 35–49.

Cohen, D. (2001). *Problem-solving partnerships: Including the community for a change*. Washington,

DC: U.S. Department of Justice, Office of Community Policing Services.

Cohen, M. B., & Hyde, C. A. (2014). *Empowering workers & clients for organizational change.* Chicago, IL: Lyceum Books.

Coleman, J. S., & Fararo, T. J. (1992). *Rational choice theory: Advocacy and critique.* Thousand Oaks, CA: Sage Publications.

Coles, R. (2004). Moving democracy: Industrial areas foundation social movements and the political arts of listening, traveling, and tabling. *Political Theory, 32*(5), 678–705.

Coley, S. M., & Scheinberg, C.A. (2000). *Proposal writing,* 2nd ed. Thousand Oaks, CA: Sage Publications.

Collins, P. C. (2010). The new politics of community. *American Sociological Review, 75*(1), 7–30.

Congress, E. P. (1999). *Social work values and ethics: Identifying and resolving professional dilemmas.* Chicago, IL: Nelson-Hall.

Cook, R. (n.d.). Entering a community: Handout. Baltimore, MD: University of Maryland, School of Social Work.

Cook, S. A. (2017). *False dawn: Protest, democracy, and violence in the new Middle East.* New York, NY: Oxford University Press.

Coover, V., Deacon, E., Esser, C., & Moor, C. (1985). *Resource manual for a living revolution.* Philadelphia, PA: New Society Publishers.

Coser, L. (1966). *The functions of social conflict.* New York, NY: Free Press.

Costa, D. L., & Kahn, M. E. (2003). Civic engagement and community heterogeneity: An economist's perspective. *Perspectives on politics, 1*(1), 103–111.

Cottrell, L. S. (1976). The competent community. *Further explorations in social psychiatry,* 195–209.

Council on Social Work Education (2015). *Educational policy and accreditation standards* (EPAS). Alexandria, VA: Author.

Council on Social Work Education (2012). *Statistics on social work education in the United States.* Alexandria, VA: Author.

Council on Social Work Education (2014). *Statistics on social work education in the United States.* Alexandria, VA: Author.

Craig, G., & Mayo, M. (Eds.) (1995). *Community empowerment: A reader in participation and development.* Atlantic Highlands, NJ: Zed Books.

Cravens, D. W., & Piercy, N. F. (2009). *Strategic marketing,* 9th ed. Boston, MA: McGraw-Hill Irwin.

Crenshaw, K. W. (2010). Twenty years of critical race theory: Looking back to move forward. *Connecticut Law Review, 43,* 1253.

Cress, D. M., & Snow, D. A. (1996). Mobilization at the margins: Resources, benefactors, and the viability of homeless social movement organizations. *American Sociological Review,* 1089–1109.

Cross, T. L., et al. (1989). *Toward a culturally competent system of care: A monograph on effective services for minority children who are severely emotionally disturbed.* Washington, DC: ERIC Clearinghouse.

Crowfoot, J. E., & Chesler, M. A. (2003). White men's roles in multicultural coalitions. In M. S. Kimmel & A. L. Ferber (Eds.) (2003). *Privilege: A reader* (pp. 349–380). Boulder, CO: Westview Press.

Cudd, A.E. (2006). *Analyzing oppression.* New York, NY: Oxford University Press.

Dahrendorf, R. (1959). *Class and class conflict in industrial society* (Rev. ed.). Stanford, CA: Stanford University Press.

Dale, B. (2015). *Total quality management.* New York, NY: John Wiley & Sons.

Daley, J. M. (2002). An action guide for nonprofit board diversity. *Journal of Community Practice 10*(1), 33–54.

D'Amato, P. (2014). *The meaning of Marxism* (Rev. and updated ed.). Chicago, IL: Haymarket Books.

Danaher, K., & Mark, J. D. (2009). *Insurrection and the citizen challenge to corporate power.* London, UK: Routledge.

D'Angelo, P., & Kuypers, J. A. (Eds.). (2010). *Doing news framing analysis: Empirical and theoretical perspectives.* New York, NY: Routledge.

Dasgupta, P., & Serageldin, I. (Eds.) (2000). *Social capital: A multifaceted perspective.* Washington, DC: World Bank.

Day, P. R. (1981). *Social work and social control.* New York, NY: Tavistock Publications.

DeFilippis, J., Fisher, R., & Shragge, E. (2010). *Contesting community: The limits and potential of community organizing*. New Brunswick, NJ: Rutgers University Press.

DeFilippis, J., Fisher, R., & Shragge, E. (2009). What's left in the community? Oppositional politics in contemporary practice. *Community Development Journal, 44*(1), 38–52.

Delecta, P. (2011). Work life balance. *International Journal of Current Research, 3*(4), 186–189.

Delgado, G. (1994). *Beyond the politics of place: New directions in community organizing in the 1990s*. Oakland, CA: Applied Research Center.

Delgado, G. (1993). Building multiracial alliances: The case of people united for a better Oakland. In R. Fisher & J. Kling (Eds.), *Mobilizing the community* (pp. 103–127). Newbury Park, CA: Sage Publications.

Delgado, G. (1986). *Organizing the movement: The roots and growth of ACORN*. Philadelphia, PA: Temple University Press.

Delgado, M. (2000). *Community social work in an urban context: The potential of a capacity-enhancement perspective*. New York, NY: Oxford University Press.

Delgado, R., & Stefancic, J. (2017). *Critical race theory: An introduction*, 3rd ed. New York, NY: New York University Press.

Demopoulos, M. (2012). Patrick Leigh Fermor: We may just forget to die. *The Massachusetts Review, 53*(1), 42.

DeSario, J., & Langton, S. (Eds.) (1987). *Citizen participation in public decision making*. New York, NY: Greenwood Press.

Deutscher, P., & Lafont, C. (Eds.) (2017). *Critical theory in critical times: Transforming the global political and economic order*. New York, NY: Columbia University Press.

DeVita, C. J., & Roeger, K. L. (2010, March). *Measuring racial-ethnic diversity in the Baltimore-Washington region's nonprofit sector*. Washington, DC: The Urban Institute.

Dierenfield, D. J. (2013). *The civil rights movement* (Rev. ed.). New York, NY: Routledge.

Disch, L. J., & Hawkesworth, M. (Eds.) (2016). *The Oxford handbook of feminist theory*. New York, NY: Oxford University Press.

Djilas, M. (1957). *The new class*. Athens, Greece: Horizon.

Dobbie, D., & Richards-Schuster, K. (2008). Building solidarity through difference: A practice model for critical multicultural organizing. *Journal of Community Practice, 16*(3), 317–337.

Dolgoff, R., Harrington, D., & Loewenberg, F. M. (2012). *Ethical decisions for social work practice*, 9th ed. Belmont, CA: Thomson Brooks/Cole.

Dominelli, L. (2010). *Social work in a globalizing world*. Malden, MA: Polity Press.

Domhoff, G. W. (2003). *Changing the powers that be: How the left can stop losing and win*. Lanham, MD: Rowman and Littlefield.

Domhoff, G. W. (2010). *Who rules America? Challenges to corporate and class dominance*, 6th ed. Boston, MA: McGraw Hill Higher Education.

Dominelli, L. (2010). *Social work in a globalizing world*. Malden, MA: Polity Press.

Donaldson, L. (2001). *The contingency theory of organizations*. Thousand Oaks, CA: Sage Publications.

Dorfman, L., Wallack, L., & Woodruff, K. (2005). More than a message: framing public health advocacy to change corporate practices. *Health Education & Behavior, 32*(3), 320–336.

Douglass, F. (2013). *Frederick Douglass: A life in documents*. (Ed. by L. D. Barnes). Charlottesville, VA: University of Virginia Press.

Dropkin, M., Halpin, J., & La Touche, B. (2011). *The budget-building book for nonprofits: A step-by-step guide for managers and boards* (Vol. 5). New York, NY: John Wiley & Sons.

Drucker, P. F., with Maciarello, J. A. (2008). *Management* (Rev. ed.). New York, NY: Collins.

Duberman, M. B. (2014). *Hold tight gently: Michael Callen, Essex Hemphill, and the battlefield of AIDS*. New York, NY: The New Press.

Durkheim, E. (1972). *Selected writings* (Ed. & Trans. by A. Giddens). Cambridge, UK: Cambridge University Press.

Dworkin, G. (1972). Paternalism. *The Monist 56*, 64–84.

Dworkin, R. (1978). *Taking rights seriously*. Cambridge, MA: Harvard University Press.

Dyson, M. E. (2016). *Barack Obama and the politics of race in America*. Boston, MA: Houghton Mifflin Harcourt.

Dyson, M. E. (2017). *Tears we cannot stop: A sermon to white America*. New York, NY: St. Martin's Press.

Eagly, A. H., & Johannesen-Schmidt, M. C. (2001). The leadership styles of women and men. *Journal of Social Issues, 57*(4), 781–797.

Earl, L. M., & Timperley, H. (Eds.) (2009). Understanding how evidence and learning conversations work. In *Professional learning conversations: Challenges in using evidence for improvement* (pp. 1–12). Netherlands: Springer.

Edin, K. J., & Schaefer, H. L. (2015). *$2.00 a day: Living on almost nothing in America.* Boston, MA: Houghton Mifflin.

Edwards, B., & Foley, M. W. (1998). Civil society and social capital beyond Putnam. *American Behavioral Scientist, 42*(1), 124–139.

Edwards, H. R., & Hoefer, R. (2010). Are social work advocacy groups using Web 2.0 effectively? *Journal of Policy Practice, 9*(3-4), 220–239.

Eichler, M. (2007). *Consensus organizing: Building communities of mutual self-interest.* Thousand Oaks, CA: Sage Publications.

Ekman, J., & Amnå, E. (2012). Political participation and civic engagement: Towards a new typology. *Human affairs, 22*(3), 283–300.

Entman, R. M. (1993). Framing: Toward clarification of a fractured paradigm. *Journal of Communication, 43*(4), 51–58.

Ephross, P. H., Vassil, T. V., & Rose, S. R. (2017). Group work with working groups. In C. D. Garvin, L. M. Gutierrez, & M. J. Galinsky (Eds.), *Handbook of social work with groups* (pp. 510–524). New York, NY: The Guilford Press.

Epstein, I., & Tripodi, T. (1977). *Research techniques for program planning, monitoring, and evaluation.* New York, NY: Columbia University Press.

Epstein, L., & Walker, T. (2009). *Constitutional law for a changing America: Rights, liberties, and justice.* Washington, DC: CQ Press.

Estes, R. J. (2013). Global change and indicators of social development. In M. O. Weil, M. Reisch, & M. L. Ohmer (Eds.), *The handbook of community practice*, 2nd ed. (pp. 587–605). Thousand Oaks, CA: Sage Publications.

Etzioni, A. (1968). *The active society: A theory of societal and political processes.* New York, NY: Free Press.

Etzioni, A. (2004). *The common good.* Malden, MA: Polity Press.

Evans, S. D., Hanlin, C. E., & Prilleltensky, I. (2007). Blending ameliorative and transformative approaches in human service organizations: A case study. *Journal of Community Psychology, 35*(3), 329–346.

Ezell, M. (2001). *Advocacy in the human services.* Belmont, CA: Brooks/Cole.

Fabricant, M. B., & Burghardt, S. (1992). *The welfare state crisis and the transformation of social service work.* Armonk, NY: M. E. Sharpe.

Fairbanks R. P. (2009). *How it works: Recovering citizens in post-welfare Philadelphia.* Chicago, IL: University of Chicago Press.

Fanon, F. (2004). *The wretched of the Earth* (Trans. by R. Philcox). New York, NY: Grove Press.

Felchner, M. E. (Ed.) (2008). *Voting in America.* Westport, CT: Praeger.

Feld, A. (1987). Self-perceptions of power: Do social work and business students differ? *Social Work, 32*, 225–230.

Feldman, G., Strier, R., & Koreh, M. (2017). Liquid advocacy: Social welfare advocacy in neoliberal times. *International Journal of Social Welfare, 26*(3), 1–9.

Fellin, P. (2001). *The community and the social worker*, 3rd ed. Itasca, IL: F. E. Peacock Publishers.

Ferguson, I. (2008). *Reclaiming social work: Challenging neo-liberalism and promoting social justice.* London, UK: Sage Publications.

Ferguson, I., Lavalette, M., & Whitmore, E. (Eds.) (2005). *Globalisation, global justice, and social work.* London, UK, and New York, NY: Routledge.

Ferguson, I., & Woodward R. (2009). *Radical social work in practice: Making a difference.* Bristol, UK: The Polity Press.

Fertig, A. R., & Reingold, D. A. (2008). Homelessness among at-risk families with children in twenty American cities. *Social Service Review, 82*(3), 485–510.

Figart, D. M. (Ed.) (2004). *Living wage movements: Global perspectives.* New York, NY: Routledge.

Figueira-McDonough, J. (2001). *Community analysis and praxis: Toward a grounded civil society.* Philadelphia, PA: Brunner-Routledge.

Finch, J. B., Lurie, A., & Wrase, B. J. (1997). Student and staff training: Empowerment principles and parallels. *The Clinical Supervisor, 15*(1), 129–144.

Finn, J. (2016). *Just practice: A social justice approach to social work,* 3rd ed. New York, NY: Oxford University Press.

Fisher, B. (1994). *Let the people decide: Neighborhood organizing in America* (Updated ed.). New York, NY: Twayne Publishers.

Fisher, R. (2009). *The people shall rule: ACORN, community organizing, and the struggle for economic justice.* Nashville, TN: Vanderbilt University Press.

Fisher, R., & Corciullo, D. (2011). Rebuilding community organizing education in social work. *Journal of Community Practice, 19*(4), 355–368.

Fisher, R., & Fabricant, M. (2002). *Settlement houses under siege: The struggle to sustain community organizations in New York.* New York, NY: Columbia University Press.

Fisher, R., & Karger, H. J. (1997). *Social work and community in a private world: Getting out in public.* New York, NY: Longman.

Fisher, R. & Kling, J. (Eds.) (1993). *Mobilizing the community: Local politics in the era of the global city.* Newbury Park, CA: Sage Publications.

Fisher, R., Ury, W. L., & Patton, B. (2011). *Getting to yes: Negotiating agreement without giving in.* New York, NY: Penguin.

Fitzpatrick, J. L., Sanders, J. R., & Worthen, B. R. (2011). *Program evaluation: Alternative approaches and practical guidelines.* Upper Saddle River, NJ: Pearson Education.

Foner, E. (2015). *Gateway to freedom: The hidden history of the Underground Railroad.* New York, NY: W. W. Norton and Co.

Fook, J. (2014). Social justice and critical theory. In M. Reisch (Ed.), *The Routledge international handbook of social justice* (pp. 160–172). London, UK: Routledge.

Ford, J. D. (1999). Organizational change as shifting conversations. *Journal of Organizational Change Management, 12*(6), 480–500.

Ford, J. D., & Ford, L. W. (1995). The role of conversations in producing intentional change in organizations. *Academy of Management Review, 20*(3), 541–570.

Ford, J. D., Ford, L. W., & McNamara, R. T. (2002). Resistance and the background conversations of change. *Journal of Organizational Change Management, 15*(2), 105–121.

Formicola, A. J., & Hernandez-Cordero, L. (Eds.) (2011). *Mobilizing the community for health: What the rest of American can learn from Northern Manhattan.* New York, NY: Columbia University Press.

Foster, W. L., Kim, P., & Christiansen, B. (2009). Ten nonprofit funding models. *Stanford Social Innovation Review, 7*(2), 32–39.

Foucault, M. (1995). *Discipline and punish: The birth of the prison*, 2nd ed. (Trans. by A. Sheridan). New York, NY: Vintage Books.

Fox, J. (2001). Vertically integrated policy monitoring: A tool for civil society policy advocacy. *Nonprofit and Voluntary Sector Quarterly, 30*(3), 616–627.

Frank, N. (2017). *Awakening: How gays and lesbians brought marriage equality to America.* Cambridge, MA: The Belknap Press of Harvard University Press.

Frankel, A. J., & Gelman, S. R. (2004). *Case management: An introduction to concepts and skills*, 2nd ed. Chicago, IL: Lyceum.

Franklin, B. (1766, November 29). On the price of corn and management of the poor. *The London Chronicle.*

Freeman, R. (2005). Fighting for other folks' wages: The logic and illogic of living wage campaigns. *Industrial Relations: A Journal of Economy and Society, 44*(1), 14–31.

Freire, P. (1990). A critical understanding of social work. *Journal of Progressive Human Services, 1*(1), 3–9.

Freire, P. (1971). *Pedagogy of the oppressed.* New York, NY: Seabury.

Freire, P. (2013). The banking concept of education. In A.S. Canestrari & B.A. Marlowe (Eds.), *Educational foundations: An anthology of critical readings* (pp. 99–111). Thousand Oaks, CA: Sage Publications.

French, J., & Raven, B. (1968). The bases of social power. In D. Cartwright & A. Zander (Eds.), *Group dynamics*, 3rd ed. (pp. 259–269). New York, NY: Basic Books.

Fukuyama, F. (2014). *Political order and political decay: From the industrial revolution to the globalization of democracy.* New York, NY: Farrar, Straus, & Giroux.

Funnell, S. C., & Rogers, P. J. (2011). *Purposeful program theory: Effective use of theories of change and logic models* (Vol. 31). New York, NY: John Wiley & Sons.

Furman, R., & Gibelman, M. (2012). *Navigating human service organizations: Essential information for thriving and surviving in agencies.* Chicago, IL: Lyceum Books.

Galer-Unti, R. A. (2010). Advocacy 2.0: Advocating in the digital age. *Health promotion practice, 11*(6), 784–787.

Galer-Unti, R. A., Tappe, M. K., & Lachenmayr, S. (2004). Advocacy 101: Getting started in health education advocacy. *Health Promotion Practice, 5*(3), 280–288.

Galowitz, P. (1999). Collaboration between lawyers and social workers: Reexamining the nature and potential of the relationship. *Fordham Law Review, 67*, 2123–2154.

Gamble, D. N. (2013). Participatory methods in community practice. In M. O. Weil, M. Reisch, & M. L. Ohmer (Eds.), *The handbook of community practice*, 2nd ed. (pp. 327–344). Thousand Oaks, CA: Sage Publications.

Gamson, W. A. (1990). *The strategy of social protest*, 2nd ed. Belmont, CA: Wadsworth.

Gans, H. J. (1982). *The urban villagers: Group and class in the life of Italian-Americans* (Rev. and updated ed.). New York, NY: The Free Press.

Garrow, E. E., & Hasenfeld, Y. (2014). Institutional logics, moral frames, and advocacy: Explaining the purpose of advocacy among nonprofit human service organizations. *Nonprofit and Voluntary Sector Quarterly, 43*(1), 180–198.

Garvin, C. D, & Ortega, R. M. (2016). Socially just group work practice. In M. Reisch & C. D.

Garvin, *Social work and social justice: Concepts, challenges, and strategies* (pp. 166–197). New York, NY: Oxford University Press.

Garvin, C. D., & Tropman, J. E. (1992). *Social work in contemporary society.* Englewood Cliffs, NJ: Prentice Hall.

Gaylin, W., Glasser, I., Marcus, S., & Rothman, D. J. (1978). *Doing good: The limits of benevolence.* New York, NY: Pantheon Books.

Geertz, C. (2000). *The interpretation of cultures—Selected essays.* New York, NY: Basic Books.

Gerdes, L. I. (Ed.) (2010). *Political campaigns.* Detroit, MI: Greenhaven Press.

Gibelman, M. (2003). *Navigating human service organizations.* Chicago, IL: Lyceum Books.

Giddens, A. (1977). *Studies in social and political theory.* New York, NY: Basic Books.

Giddens, A. (2013). *The third way: The renewal of social democracy.* New York, NY: John Wiley & Sons.

Gil, D. C. (2013). *Confronting injustice and oppression: Concepts and strategies for social workers* (Updated ed.). New York, NY: Columbia University Press.

Gilligan, C. (1983). *In a different voice: Psychological theory and women's development.* Cambridge, MA: Harvard University Press.

Gitlin, T. (2012). *Occupy nation: The roots, the spirit, and the promise of Occupy Wall Street.* New York, NY: itbooks.

Gitlin, T. (2003, 1980). *The whole world is watching: Mass media in the making and unmaking of the New Left.* Berkeley, CA: University of California Press.

Gladwell, M. (2010). Small change. *The New Yorker, 4*(2010), 42–49.

Glisson, C. (2007). Assessing and changing organizational culture and climate for effective services. *Research on Social Work Practice, 17*(6), 736–747.

Glisson, C., & James, L. R. (2002). The cross-level effects of culture and climate in human service teams. *Journal of Organizational Behavior, 23*, 767–794.

Godwin, K., Ainsworth, S. H., & Godwin, E. (2013). *Lobbying and policymaking: The public pursuit of private interests.* Thousand Oaks, CA: Sage Publications/CQ Press.

Gorz, A. (1968). *Strategy for labor: A radical proposal* (Trans. by M. Nicolaus & V. Ortiz). Boston, MA: Beacon Press.

Gouldner, A. W. (1970). *The coming crisis of Western sociology.* New York, NY: Avon.

Gramsci, A. (1992). *Prison notebooks.* (Ed. by J. Buttigieg; Trans. By J. Buttigieg & A. Callari). New York, NY: Columbia University Press.

Grandori, A. (1984). A prescriptive contingency view of organizational decisionmaking. *Administrative Science Quarterly, 29*(2), 192–209.

Gray, W. B. (n.d.). Barriers in the way of organizing a community: Handout. San Francisco, CA: San Francisco State University, School of Social Work.

Gray Panthers (n.d.). *The Gray Panthers organizing manual*, Vol. 1. Author.

Green, J. (1998). *Cultural awareness in the human services: A multi-ethnic approach*, 3rd ed. Boston, MA: Allyn & Bacon.

Green, G. P., & Goetting, A. (2010). *Mobilizing communities: Asset building as a community development strategy*. Philadelphia, PA: Temple University Press.

Griswold, W. (2008). *Cultures and society in a changing world*, 3rd ed. Los Angeles, CA: Pine Forge Press.

Gronbjerg, K. A., & Salamon, L. M. (2002). Devolution, marketization, and the changing shape of government-nonprofit relations. *The state of nonprofit America* (pp. 447–470). Washington, DC: The Brookings Institution.

Gross, B. M. (1965). What are your organization's objectives? A general-systems approach to planning. *Human Relations*, *18*(3), 195–216.

Guerin, D. W., Oliver, P. H., Gottfried, A. W., Gottfried, A. E., Reichard, R. J., & Riggio, R. E. (2011). Childhood and adolescent antecedents of social skills and leadership potential in adulthood: Temperamental approach/withdrawal and extraversion. *The Leadership Quarterly*, *22*(3), 482–494.

Guerra, J. M., Martínez, I., Munduate, L., & Medina, F. J. (2005). A contingency perspective on the study of the consequences of conflict types: The role of organizational culture. *European Journal of Work and Organizational Psychology*, *14*(2), 157–176.

Gunitsky, S. (2015). Corrupting the cyber-commons: Social media as a tool of autocratic stability. *Perspectives on Politics*, *13*(1), 42–54.

Guo, B. (2006). Charity for profit? Exploring factors associated with the commercialization of human service nonprofits. *Nonprofit and Voluntary Sector Quarterly*, *35*(1), 123–138.

Guo, C., & Saxton, G. D. (2014). Tweeting social change: How social media are changing nonprofit advocacy. *Nonprofit and Voluntary Sector Quarterly*, *43*(1), 57–79.

Gutiérrez, L. M. (1997). Multicultural community organizing. In M. Reisch & E. Gambrill (Eds.), *Social work in the 21st century* (pp. 249–259). Thousand Oaks, CA: Pine Forge Press.

Gutierrez, L. M. (1995). Understanding the empowerment process: Does consciousness make a difference? *Social Work Research*, *19*(4), 229–237.

Gutierrez, L. M. (1990, March). Working with women of color: An empowerment perspective. *Social Work*, *35*(1), 149–153.

Gutierrez, L. M., & Lewis, E. (1998). A feminist perspective on organizing with women of color. In F. G. Rivera & J. Erlich (Eds.), *Community organizing in a diverse society*, 3rd ed. (pp. 97–116). Needham Heights, MA: Allyn & Bacon.

Gutierrez, L. M., Nagda, B., Raffoul, P. R., & McNeece, C.A. (1996). The multicultural imperative for human service organizations. In P. R. Raffoul & C. A. McNeece (Eds.), *Future issues for social work practice* (pp. 203–213). Boston, MA: Allyn & Bacon.

Gutierrez, L. M., Parsons, R. J., & Cox, E. O. (Eds.) (1998). *Empowerment in social work practice: A sourcebook*. Pacific Grove, CA: Brooks/Cole.

Gutierrez, L.M., & **Reisch, M.** (eds.) (2017). *Community practice in an increasingly diverse society: Essays in memory of Dr. Felix Rivera*. Special issue of the *Journal of Community Practice*, *25*(3–4).

Haedicke, M. A. (2012). 'Keeping our mission, changing our system': Translation and organizational change in natural foods co-ops. *The Sociological Quarterly*, *53*(1), 44–67.

Hall, P. D. (2016). Historical perspectives on nonprofit organizations in the United States. In D.O. Renz and R.D. Herman (Eds.), *The Jossey-Bass handbook of nonprofit leadership and management*, 4th ed. (pp. 3–41). Hoboken, NJ: Wiley Publishers.

Handler, J. F. (1992). Discretion: Power, quiescence, and trust. In K. Hawkins (Ed.) *The uses of discretion* (pp. 331–360). New York, NY: Oxford University Press.

Hanna, M. G., & Robinson, B. (1994). *Strategies for community empowerment: Direct action and transformative approaches to social change practice*. Lewiston, NY: Mellen.

Hardcastle, D., with Powers, P. R., & Wenocur, S. (2011). *Community practice: Theories and skills for social workers*, 3rd ed. New York, NY: Oxford University Press.

Hardcastle, D., & Powers, P. R., with Wenocur, S. (2004). *Community practice: Theories and skills for social workers*, 2nd ed. New York, NY: Oxford University Press.

Hardina, D. (2004). Guidelines for ethical practice in community organization. *Social Work*, *49*(4), 595–604.

Hardina, D. (2003). Linking citizen participation to empowerment practice: A historical overview. *Journal of Community Practice, 11*(4), 11–38.

Hardina, D. (2005). Ten characteristics of empowerment-oriented social service organizations. *Administration in Social Work, 29*(3), 23–41.

Hasenfeld, Y. (1972). People processing organizations: An exchange approach. *American Sociological Review, 37*(3), 256–263.

Hasenfeld, Y. (2010). Power in social work practice. In Y. Hasenfeld (Ed.) *Human services as complex organizations*, 2nd ed. (pp. 259–275). Thousand Oaks, CA: Sage Publications.

Hasenfeld, Y. (2015). What exactly is human services management? *Human Service Organizations: Management, Leadership, & Governance, 39*, 1–5.

Hasenfeld, Y., & Garrow, E. E. (2012). Nonprofit human service organizations, social rights, and advocacy in a neoliberal welfare state. *Social Service Review, 86*(2), 295–322.

Hasenfeld, Y., & Schmid, H. (1989). The life cycle of human service organizations: An administrative perspective. *Administration in Social Work, 13*(3–4), 243–269.

Hassan, A., & Wimpfheimer, S. (2014). *Human services management competencies: A guide for public managers*. Los Angeles, CA: The Network for Social Work Management.

Hayek, F. A. (1976). *The mirage of social justice*. Chicago, IL: University of Chicago Press.

Haynes, K. S., & Mickelson, J. S. (2010). *Affecting change: Social workers in the political arena*, 7th ed. Boston, MA: Allyn & Bacon.

Healey, P. (2003). Collaborative planning in perspective. *Planning theory, 2*(2), 101–123.

Healey, P. (2006). *Collaborative planning: Shaping places in fragmented societies*. New York, NY: Palgrave MacMillan.

Healy, K. (1999). Power and activist social work. In B. Pease & J. Fook (Eds.), *Transforming social work practice: Postmodern critical perspectives* (pp. 115–134). London, UK, and New York, NY: Routledge.

Healy, L. M. (2008). *International social work: Professional action in an interdependent world*, 2nd ed. New York, NY: Oxford University Press.

Healy, M., & Sofer, G. (2017). Policy advocacy at the federal level: A case study of AmeriCorps—How the little guys won. In M. Reisch, *Social policy and social justice: Meeting the challenges of a diverse society*, 2nd ed. (pp. 249–267). San Diego, CA: Cognella Academic Publishing.

Hibbert, P., Huxham, C., & Ring, P. S. (2008). Managing collaborative inter-organizational relations. In S. Cropper, C. Huxham, M. Ebers, and P. Smith Ring (Eds.), *The Oxford handbook of interorganizational relations*. New York: NY: Oxford University Press.

Hick, S., & McNutt, J. (Eds.) (2002). *Advocacy, activism, and the Internet*, Chicago, IL: Lyceum Books.

Hill Collins, P. (2009). *Black feminist thought: Knowledge, consciousness, and the politics of empowerment*. New York, NY: Routledge.

Hill Collins, P., & Bilge, S. (2016). *Intersectionality*. Cambridge, UK: Polity Press.

Hindsworth, M. F., & Lang, T. B. (Eds.) (2009). *Community participation and empowerment*. New York, NY: Nova Science Publishers.

Hirshleifer, J. (2001). *The dark side of the force: Economic foundations of conflict theory*. New York, NY: Cambridge University Press.

Hoefer, R. (2016). *Advocacy practice for social justice*, 3rd ed. Chicago, IL: Lyceum Books.

Hoefer, R. (2017). State and local policy advocacy. In M. Reisch, *Social policy and social justice: Meeting the challenges of a diverse society*, 2nd ed. (pp. 269–292). San Diego, CA: Cognella Academic Publishing.

Hoefer, R., & Ferguson, K. (2007). Moving the levers of power: How advocacy organizations affect the regulation-writing process. *Journal of Sociology and Social Welfare, 34*(1), 83–108.

Holcomb, S. H. (1995). *Managing to empower: The Grameen Bank's experience of poverty alleviation*. Atlantic Highlands, NJ: Zed Books.

Holland, T. P., & Jackson, D. K. (1998). Strengthening board performance. *Nonprofit Management and Leadership, 9*(2), 121–134.

Hollihan, T. A. (2009). *Uncivil wars: Political campaigns in a media age*. Boston, MA: Bedford/St. Martin's.

Holmstrom, N. C. L. (Ed.) (2002). *The socialist feminist project: A contemporary reader in theory and politics*. New York, NY: Monthly Review Press.

Holvino, E. (2008). *Developing multicultural organizations: A change model*. Chaos Management Ltd. Retrieved from: http://www.chaosmanagement.com/images/stories/pdfs/MCODmodel.pdf.

Homan, M. S. (2016). *Promoting community change: Making it happen in the real world*, 6th ed. Belmont, CA: Brooks/Cole.

Hopkins, B. R. (2012). *Starting and managing a nonprofit organization: A legal guide*, 7th ed. New York, NY: John Wiley & Sons.

Horwitt, S. (1992). *Let them call me rebel: Saul Alinsky, his life and legacy*. New York, NY: Vintage Books.

HoSang, D. M. (2010). *Racial propositions: Ballot initiatives and the making of postwar California*. Berkeley, CA: University of California Press.

Howard, R., & Steigerwalt, A. (2011). *Judging law and policy: Courts and policymaking in the American political system*. New York, NY: Routledge.

Hubbard, A. (1997). Face-to-face at arm's length: Conflict norms and extra-group relations in grassroots dialogue groups. *Human Organization, 56*(3), 265–274.

Huntington, S. P. (2011). *The clash of civilizations and the remaking of world order*. New York, NY: Simon & Schuster.

Hyde, C. (1989). A feminist model for macro-practice: Promises and problems. *Administration in Social Work, 13*(3–4), 145–181.

Hyde, C. (1996). A feminist response to Rothman's 'The interweaving of community intervention approaches.' *Journal of Community Practice, 3*(3–4), 127–145.

Hyde, C. A. (2012). Organizational change rationales: Exploring reasons for multicultural development in human service agencies. *Administration in Social Work, 36*(5), 436–456.

Hyde, C. A., & Hopkins, K. (2004). Assessing the diversity climate in human service agencies. *Journal of Ethnic & Cultural Diversity in Social Work, 13*(2), 25–43.

Hynes, H. P. (2017). *Community research in environmental health: Studies in science, advocacy and ethics*. New York, NY: Routledge.

Iglehart, A. P. (2012). Identity-based organizing. Paper presented at Symposium on "Interdisciplinary Scholarship for Community Practice in the 21st Century," University of Michigan, Ann Arbor, MI.

Iglehart, A. P., & Becerra, R. M. (2010). *Social services and the ethnic community: History and analysis*, 2nd ed. Long Grove, IL: Waveland Press.

Ife, J. (2010). *Human rights from below: Achieving human rights through community development*. New York, NY: Cambridge University Press.

Independent Sector (2016). *Giving and volunteering in the United States: Finding from a national survey*. Washington, DC: Author.

Independent Sector (2015). *Principles for good governance and ethical practice: A guide for charities and foundations*. Washington, DC: Author.

Ing. C. (2001). Culturally appropriate evaluations. In Y. A. Unrau, P. A. Gabor, and R. M. Grinnell (Eds.), *Evaluation in the human services* (pp. 285–303). Itasca, IL: F. E. Peacock Publishers.

Ingram, R. T. (2003). *The 10 basic responsibilities of nonprofit boards*. Washington, DC: BoardSource.

International Federation of Social Workers (2007). *International definition of the social work profession; Ethics in social work, statement of principles; Global standards for the education and training of the social work profession*. Geneva, Switzerland: Author.

Isaacs, W. N. (1996). The process and potential of dialogue in social change. *Educational Technology, 36*(1), 20–30.

Iscoe, I. (1974). Community psychology and the competent community. *American Psychologist, 29*(8), 607.

Israel, B. A., Coombe, C. M., Cheezum, R. R., Schulz, A. J., McGranaghan, R. J., Lichtenstein, R., & Burris, A. (2010). Community-based participatory research: A capacity-building approach for policy advocacy aimed at eliminating health disparities. *American Journal of Public Health, 100*(11), 2094–2102.

Iyengar, S., & McGrady, J. (2007). *Media politics: A citizen's guide*. New York, NY: W.W. Norton.

Jackson, B., & Holvino, E. (1988). Developing multicultural organizations. *Journal of Religion and Applied Behavioral Science, 9*, 14–19.

Jacobson, D. (2001). *Doing justice: Congregations and community organization*. Minneapolis, MN: Fortress Press.

Jani, J. S., & Reisch, M. (2011). Common human needs, uncommon solutions: Applying a critical framework to perspectives on human behavior. *Families in Society, 92*(1), 13–20.

Jansson, B. S. (2014). *Becoming an effective policy advocate: From policy practice to social justice*, 7th ed. Belmont, CA: Brooks/Cole.

Jansson, B. S., Heidemann, G., McCroskey, J., & Fertig, R. D. (2013). Eight models of policy practice. In M. O.Weil, M. Reisch, & M. L. Ohmer (Eds.), *The handbook of community practice*, 2nd ed. (pp. 403–420). Thousand Oaks, CA: Sage Publications.

Jaskyte, J. (2010). An exploratory examination of correlates of organizational culture. *Administration in Social Work, 34*(5), 423–441.

Jaskyte, J., & Dressler, W. W. (2005). Organizational culture and innovation in nonprofit human service organizations. *Administration in Social Work, 29*(2), 23–41.

Jernigan, D. H. (n.d.). Applying media advocacy to the reduction of college alcohol problems. Baltimore, MD: Johns Hopkins Bloomberg School of Public Health.

Jernigan, D. H., & Wright, P. A. (1996). Media advocacy: Lessons from community experiences. *Journal of Public Health Policy, 17*(3), 306–330.

Johnson, C. (2005). *Meeting the ethical challenges of leadership: Casting light or shadow*, 2nd ed. Thousand Oaks, CA: Sage Publications.

Johnson, J., Brotherhood of St Laurence, & Taylor, J. (2000). *Growing apart: A new look at poverty in Australia: The findings of the understanding poverty project of the Brotherhood of St. Laurence.* Melbourne, AU: Brotherhood of St. Laurence.

Johnson, R. A. (2003). *Whistleblowing—When it works and why.* Boulder, CO: L. Rienner Publishers.

Johnson, R. A., & Kraft, M. E. (1990). Bureaucratic whistleblowing and policy change. *Western Political Quarterly, 43*(4), 849–874.

Jost, J. T. (1995). Negative illusions: Conceptual clarification and psychological evidence concerning false consciousness. *Political Psychology, 16*(2), 397–424.

Kadushin, A., & Harkness, D. (2002). *Supervision in social work*, 4th ed. New York, NY: Columbia University Press.

Kagle, J. D., & Kopels, S. (1994). Confidentiality after Tarasoff. *Health & Social Work, 19*(3), 217–222.

Kahn, S. (2010). *Creative community organizing: A guide for rabble-rousers, activists, and quiet lovers of justice.* San Francisco, CA: Berrett Koehler.

Kahn, S. (1991). *Organizing: A guide for grassroots leaders* (Rev. ed.). Silver Spring, MD: National Association of Social Workers.

Kamber, V. (2003). *Poison politics: Are negative campaigns destroying democracy?* New York, NY: Basic Books.

Kamerman, S. B., & Kahn, A. J. (Eds.) (2014). *Privatization and the welfare state.* Princeton, NJ: Princeton University Press.

Kane, L. (2001*). Popular education and social change in Latin America.* London, UK: Latin American Bureau.

Kanter, B., & Fine, A. H. (2010). *The networked nonprofit: Connecting with social media to drive change.* San Francisco, CA: Jossey-Bass.

Kaplan, R. S. (2001). Strategic performance measurement and management in nonprofit organizations. *Nonprofit management and Leadership, 11*(3), 353–370.

Kaplan, S. A., & Garrett, K. E. (2005). The use of logic models by community-based initiatives. *Evaluation and Program Planning, 28*(2), 167–172.

Karim, L. (2008). Demystifying micro-credit: The Grameen Bank, NGOs, and neoliberalism in Bangladesh. *Cultural Dynamics, 20*(1), 5–29.

Karpf, D. (2012). *The MoveOn effect: The unexpected transformation of American political advocacy.* New York, NY: Oxford University Press.

Katz. M. B. (1996). *In the shadow of the poorhouse: A social history of welfare in America*, 10th anniversary ed. New York, NY: Basic Books.

Kazda, M. J., Beel, E. R., Villegas, D., Martinez, J. G., Patel, N., & Migala, W. (2009). Methodological complexities and the use of GIS in conducting a community needs assessment of a large US municipality. *Journal of Community Health, 34*(3), 210–215.

Keast, R., Mandell, M. P., & Agranoff, R. (Eds.) (2014). *Network theory in the public sector: Building new theoretical frameworks.* New York, NY: Routledge.

Kegler, M. C., Painter, J. E., Twiss, J. M., Aronson, R., & Norton, B. L. (2009). Evaluation findings on community participation in the California Healthy Cities and Communities program. *Health Promotion International*, dap036.

Kegler, M. C., Twiss, J. M., & Look, V. (2000). Assessing community change at multiple levels: The genesis of an evaluation framework for the California Healthy Cities Project. *Health Education & Behavior, 27*(6), 760–779.

Kemp, S. P. (2010). Place matters: Toward a rejuvenated theory of environment for direct social work practice. In W. Borden (Ed.), *Reshaping theory in contemporary social work: Toward a critical pluralism in clinical practice* (pp. 114–145). New York, NY: Columbia University Press.

Kennedy, L. (2015). Top 5 ways Citizens United harms democracy and top 5 ways we're fighting to take democracy back. New York, NY: Demos.

Kennedy, T. A. (2017). *Historicizing post-discourses: Post-feminism and post-racialism in United States culture.* Albany, NY: State University of New York Press.

Kernan, B., Freundlich, M., Lee, J. M., Brenner, E. (2012). Learning while doing in the human services: Becoming a learning organization through organizational change. *Administration in Social Work, 36*(3), 234–257.

Kim, H., & Stoner, M. (2008). Burnout and turnover intention among social workers: Effects of role stress, job autonomy and social support. *Administration in Social Work, 32*(3), 5–25.

Kimberlin, S. E. (2010). Advocacy by nonprofits: Roles and practices of core advocacy organizations and direct service agencies. *Journal of Policy Practice, 9*(3-4), 164–182.

King, B. G. (2011). The tactical disruptiveness of social movements: Sources of market and mediated disruption in corporate boycotts. *Social Problems, 58*(4), 491–517.

Kippenberger, T. (2002). *Leadership styles.* Oxford, UK: Capstone Publishing.

Kirk, G., & Okazawa-Rey, M. (1998). *Women's lives: Multicultural perspectives.* New York, NY: McGraw-Hill Humanities, Social Sciences & World Languages.

Kirkpatrick, S. A., & Locke, E. A. (1996). Direct and indirect effects of three core charismatic leadership components on performance and attitudes. *Journal of Applied Psychology, 81*(1), 36–51.

Kirkpatrick, S. A., & Locke, E. A. (1991). Leadership: Do traits matter? *The Executive, 5*(2), 48–60.

Klandermans, B. (2004). The demand and supply of participation: Social-psychological correlates of participation in social movements. *The Blackwell companion to social movements* (pp. 360–379). Cambridge, MA: Blackwell.

Knickmeyer, L., Hopkins, K., & Meyer, M. (2003). Exploring collaboration among urban neighborhood associations. *Journal of Community Practice, 11*(2), 13–25.

Kotter, J. P., Schlesinger, L. A., & Sathe, V. (1986). *Organization: Text, cases, and readings on the management of organizational design and change.* Homewood, IL: Irwin.

Kretzmann, J. P., & McKnight, J. L. (1993). *Building communities from the inside out: A path toward finding and mobilizing a community's assets.* Evanston, IL: Center for Urban Affairs and Policy Research, Northwestern University.

Kwon, S., Cha, M., Jung, K., Chen, W., & Wang, Y. (2013, December). Prominent features of rumor propagation in online social media. In *Data Mining (ICDM), 2013 IEEE 13th International Conference* (pp. 1103–1108).

Lake, C. C., with Harper, P. C. (1987). *Public opinion polling: A handbook for public interest and citizen advocacy groups.* Washington, DC: Island Press.

Lappe, F. M., & DuBois, P. M. (1994). *The quickening of America: Rebuilding our nation, remaking our lives.* San Francisco, CA: Jossey-Bass.

Lasch, C. (1991, 1979). *The culture of narcissism: American life in an age of diminishing expectations* (Rev. ed.). New York, NY: W. W. Norton.

Lassman, P. (2011). *Pluralism.* Malden, MA: Polity Press.

Lauffer, A. (2013). Fundraising and community practice: A stakeholder model. In M. O. Weil, M. Reisch, & M. L. Ohmer (Eds.), *The handbook of community practice*, 2nd ed. (pp. 773–788). Thousand Oaks, CA: Sage Publications.

Lauffer, A. (1978). *Social planning at the community level.* Englewood Cliffs, NJ: Prentice-Hall.

Lauffer, A. (1992). *Understanding your social agency*, 2nd ed. Thousand Oaks, CA: Sage Publications.

Laverack, G., & Labonte, R. (2000). A planning framework for community empowerment goals within health promotion. *Health policy and planning, 15*(3), 255–262.

Lee, J. (2001). The empowerment approach: A conceptual model. In J. Lee, *The empowerment approach to social work practice: Building the beloved community* (pp. 30–55). New York, NY: Columbia University Press.

Leighley, J. (2004). *Mass media and politics: A social science perspective.* Boston, MA: Houghton Mifflin.

Leighley, J. E., & Nagler, J. (2014). *Who votes now? Demographics, issues, inequality and turnout in the United States.* Princeton, NJ: Princeton University Press.

Leitner, H., & Strunk, C. (2014). Spaces of immigrant advocacy and liberal democratic citizenship.

Annals of the Association of American Geographers, 104(2), 348–356.

Lelieveldt, H., Dekker, K., Völker, B., & Torenvlied, R. (2009). Civic organizations as political actors: Mapping and predicting the involvement of civic organizations in neighborhood problem-solving and coproduction. *Urban Affairs Review, 45*(1), 3–24.

Lens, V. (2005). Advocacy and argumentation in the public arena: A guide for social workers. *Social Work, 50*(3), 231–238.

Lens, V. (2003). Reading between the lines: Analyzing the Supreme Court's views on gender discrimination in employment, 1971–1982. *Social Service Review, 77*(1), 25–50.

Lens, V. (2017). The judiciary and social policy. In M. Reisch, *Social policy and social justice: Meeting the challenges of a diverse society*, 2nd ed. (pp. 293–314). San Diego, CA: Cognella Academic Publishing.

LeRoux, K. (2007). Nonprofits as civic intermediaries: The role of community-based organizations in promoting political participation. *Urban Affairs, 42*(3), 410–422.

Lester, D. L., Parnell, J. A., & Carraher, S. (2003). Organizational life cycle: A five-stage empirical scale. *The International Journal of Organizational Analysis, 11*(4), 339–354.

Levitt, J. (2010). Confronting the impact of 'Citizens United.' *Yale Law & Policy Review, 29*(1), 217–234.

Levy, C. S. (1976). Personal versus professional values: The practitioner's dilemma. *Clinical Social Work Journal, 4*(2), 110–120.

Levy, C. S. (1976). *Social work ethics.* New York, NY: Human Sciences Press.

Lewicki, R. J., Tomlinson, E. C., & Gillespie, N. (2006). Models of interpersonal trust development: Theoretical approaches, empirical evidence, and future directions. *Journal of Management, 32*(6), 991–1022.

Lewin, K. (1997, 1948). *Resolving social conflicts & field theory in social science.* Washington, DC: American Psychological Association.

Lewis, H. (2003). Management in the nonprofit social service organization. In M. Reisch (Ed.), *For the common good: Essays of Harold Lewis* (pp.54–60). New York, NY: Brunner-Routledge.

Lewis, H. (1980). The battered helper. *Child Welfare, 59*(4), 195–201.

Lewis, H. (1982). *The intellectual base of social work practice: Tools of thought for a helping profession.* New York, NY: Haworth Press.

Lewis, H. (1985). The whistle blower and the whistle-blowing profession. *Child and Adolescent Social Work Journal, 2*(1), 3–12.

Lewis, J., Lewis, M., Packard, T., & Souflee, F. (2001). *Management of human service programs.* Belmont, CA: Brooks/Cole.

Li, W. D., Arvey, R. D., & Song, Z. (2011). The influence of general mental ability, self-esteem and family socioeconomic status on leadership role occupancy and leader advancement: The moderating role of gender. *The Leadership Quarterly, 22*(3), 520–534.

Lillie-Blanton, M., & Hoffman, S. C. (1995). Conducting an assessment of health needs and resources in a racial/ethnic minority community. *Health Services Research, 30*(1, Pt. 2), 225–236.

Littlejohn, S. W., & Foss, K. A. (2011). *Theories of human communication*, 10th ed. Long Grove, IL: Waveland Press.

Litwak, E. (1961). Voluntary association and neighborhood cohesion. *American Sociological Review, 26*(2), 258–271.

Litwak, E., & Meyer, H. (1974). *School, family, and neighborhood: The theory and practice of school-community relations.* New York, NY: Columbia University Press.

Locke, B., Garrison, R., & Winship, J. (1997). *Generalist social work practice.* Belmont, CA: Brooks/Cole Publishing.

London, S. (n.d.). *Collaboration and community.* A report prepared for the Pew Partnership for Civic Change. Washington, DC: Pew Charitable Trust.

Lott, C., & Fremont-Smith, M. (2017). Nonprofits and advocacy. In E. T. Boris & C. E. Steuerle (Eds.), *Nonprofits and government: Collaboration and conflict*, 3rd ed. Lanham, MD: Rowman & Littlefield.

Lovejoy, K., Waters, R. D., & Saxton, G. D. (2012). Engaging stakeholders through Twitter: How nonprofit organizations are getting more out of 140 characters or less. *Public Relations Review, 38*(2), 313–318.

Lubove, R. (1969). *The professional altruist: The emergence of social work as a career, 1880–1930.* New York, NY: Atheneum.

Lubove, R. (1986). *The struggle for Social Security, 1900–1935*, 2nd ed. Pittsburgh, PA: University of Pittsburgh Press.

Luckman, T. (1981). *Black and white styles in conflict.* Chicago, IL: University of Chicago Press.

Lum, D. (2004). *Social work practice and people of color: A process-stage approach*, 5th ed. Belmont, CA: Thomson, Brooks/Cole.

Maddox, D. C. (1999). *Budgeting for not-for-profit organizations.* New York, NY: Wiley.

Mahaffey, M. (1987). Political action in social work. *Encyclopedia of Social Work, 2,* (pp. 283–294). Washington, DC: National Association of Social Workers.

Mahon, J. F., & Waddock, S. A. (1992). Strategic issues management: An integration of issue life cycle perspectives. *Business & Society, 31*(1), 19–32.

Mandell, M. P., & Keast, R. (2009). A new look at leadership in collaborative networks: Process catalysts. In J.A. Raffel, P. Leisink, and A.E. Middlebrooks (Eds.), *Public sector leadership: International challenges and perspectives* (pp. 163–178). Northampton, MA: Edward Elgar Publishing.

Mandler, P. (1990). *The uses of charity: The poor on relief in the nineteenth-century metropolis* Philadelphia, PA: University of Pennsylvania Press.

Mann, F. C. (1965). Toward an understanding of the leadership role in formal organizations. In *Leadership and productivity* (pp. 68–103). San Francisco, CA: Chandler.

Manzo, L. C., & Perkins, D. D. (2006). Finding common ground: The importance of place attachment to community participation and planning. *Journal of Planning Literature, 20*(4), 335–350.

Marable, M. (2009). *Beyond black and white: Transforming African-American politics*, 2nd ed. New York, NY: Verso.

Marable, M. (2000). *How capitalism underdeveloped Black America: Problems in race, political economy, and society.* Cambridge, MA: South End Press.

Margolin, L. (1997). *Under the cover of kindness: The invention of social work.* Charlottesville, VA: University of Virginia Press.

Martinson, M., & Minkler, M. (2006). Civic engagement and older adults: A critical perspective, *The Gerontologist, 46*(3), 318–324.

Marx, J., & Davis, C. (2012). Nonprofit governance: Improving performance in troubled economic times. *Administration in Social Work, 36*, 40–52.

Marx, K., & Engels, F. (1959). *Basic writings on politics and philosophy* (Ed. by L.S. Feuer). Garden City, NY: Doubleday.

Marx, K., & Engels, F. (1848, 1932). *The Communist manifesto.* In M. Eastman (Ed.), *Capital, the Communist Manifesto, and other writings by Karl Marx.* New York, NY: Modern Library.

Mary, N. L. (2005). Transformational leadership in human service organizations. *Administration in Social Work, 29*(2) 105–119.

Maslow, A. H. (1968). *Toward a psychology of being*, 2nd ed. Princeton, NJ: Van Nostrand.

Massey, D. S., & Denton, N. (1993). *American apartheid: Segregation and the making of the underclass.* Cambridge, MA: Harvard University Press.

Massey, D. S., & Pren, K. A. (2012). Unintended consequences of U.S. immigration policy: Explaining the post-1965 surge from Latin America. *Population and Development Review, 38*(1), 1–29.

Mathie, A., & Cunningham, G. (2003). From clients to citizens: Asset-based community development as a strategy for community-driven development. *Development in Practice, 13*(5), 474–486.

May, R. (1969). *Love and will.* New York, NY: Norton.

Maybach, C. W. (1996). Investigating urban community needs: Service learning from a social justice perspective. *Education and Urban Society, 28*(2), 224–236.

Mayer, J. (2016). *Dark money: The hidden history of the billionaires behind the rise of the radical right.* New York, NY: Doubleday.

Mayer, R. B. (1972). *Social planning and social change.* Englewood Cliffs, NJ: Prentice-Hall.

McAfee, A., & K. T. McGuire (2007). Lawyers, justice and issue salience: When and how do legal arguments affect the U.S. Supreme Court, *Law and Society Review, 41*(2), 259–278.

McBeath, B. (2016). Re-envisioning macro social work practice. *Families in Society: The Journal of Contemporary Social Services, 97*(1), 5–14.

McCarthy, M. (1998). *The ethics of political advocacy and the democratic process.* Washington, DC: Woodstock Project on Ethics & Public Policy.

www.georgetown.edu/centers/Woodstock principles.

McCarty, N., Poole, K. T., & Rosenthal, H. (2016). *Polarized America: The dance of ideology and unequal riches*. Cambridge, MA: MIT Press.

McDavid, J. C., & Hawthorn, L. R. L. (2006). *Program evaluation and performance measurement: An introduction to practice*. Thousand Oaks, CA: Sage Publications.

McDonald, C., & Reisch, M. (2008). Social work in the workfare regime: A comparison of the U.S. and Australia. *Journal of Sociology and Social Welfare, 35*(1), 43–74.

McGary, H. (1999). *Race and social justice*. Malden, MA: Blackwell.

McGregor, D., & Cutcher-Gershenfeld, J. (2006). *The human side of enterprise*. New York, NY; McGraw Hill Professional.

McIntyre, A. (2007). *Participatory action research*. Thousand Oaks, CA Sage Publications.

McNamara, C. (2006). *Field guide to nonprofit program design, marketing and evaluation*. Minneapolis, MN: Authenticity Consulting.

McNulty, R. H. (1999). *Community empowerment manual: Accomplishing a place-based strategy for community revitalization*. Washington, DC: Partners for Livable Communities.

McNutt, J., & Boland, K. (2007). Astroturf, technology and the future of community mobilization: Implications for nonprofit theory, *Journal of Sociology and Social Welfare, 34*(3), 165–178.

McNutt, J., & Menon, G. (2008). The rise of cyber-activism: Implications for the future of advocacy in the human services. *Families in Society: The Journal of Contemporary Social Services, 89*(1), 33–38.

Medina, F. J., Munduate, L., Dorado, M. A., Martínez, I., & Guerra, J. M. (2005). Types of intra-group conflict and affective reactions. *Journal of Managerial Psychology, 20*(3/4), 219–230.

Meenaghan, T. M., & Gibbons, W. E. (2000). *Generalist practice in larger settings: Knowledge and skill concepts*. Chicago, IL: Lyceum.

Meenaghan, T. M., Gibbons, W. E., & McNutt, J. G. (2005). *Generalist practice in larger settings: Knowledge and skill concepts*, 2nd ed. Chicago, IL: Lyceum.

Meyerson, D. E., & Scully, M. A. (1995). Tempered radicalism and the politics of ambivalence and change. *Organization Science, 6*(5), 585–600.

Michels, R. (1915). *Political parties: A sociological study of the oligarchical tendencies of democracy* (Trans. by E. Paul & C. Paul). New York, NY: The Free Press.

Midgley, J., & Livermore, M. (1998). Social capital and local economic development: Implications for community social work practice. *Journal of Community Practice, 5*(1–2), 29–40.

Mill, J. S. (1859, 1910). *Utilitarianism, liberty, and representative government*. New York, NY: E. P. Dutton.

Mill, J. S. (2002). *The basic writings of John Stuart Mill: On liberty, the subjection of women, and utilitarianism*. New York, NY: Modern Library.

Miller, I. (2000). *The mystery of courage*. Cambridge, MA: Harvard University Press.

Miller, M. (2009). *A community organizer's tale: People and power in San Francisco*. Berkeley, CA: Heyday Books.

Mills, C. W. (1963). *Power, politics, and people: The collected essays of C. Wright Mills*. Oxford University Press.

Mills, C. W. (1956). *The power elite*. New York, NY: Oxford University Press.

Minkler, M. (Ed.) (2012). *Community organizing and community building for health and welfare*, 3rd ed. New Brunswick, NJ: Rutgers University Press.

Miranda v. Arizona (1966). 384 US 436.

Mizrahi, T. (2015). Community organizing principles and guidelines. In K. Corcoran & A. R. Roberts (Eds.), *Social workers' desk reference*, 3rd ed. (pp.194–206). New York, NY: Oxford University Press.

Mizrahi, T., & Morrison, J. (Eds.) (2013). *Community organization and social administration: Advances, trends, and emerging principles*. New York, NY: Routledge.

Mizrahi, T., & Rosenthal, B. (2001). Complexities of coalition building: Leaders' successes, strategies, and solutions, *Social Work, 46*(1), 63–78.

Molina, F., & Nelson, L. C. (2001). *The Neighborhood Jobs Initiative: An early report on the vision and challenges of bringing an employment focus to a community-building initiative*. Washington, DC: Manpower Demonstration Research Corporation.

Mondros, J. B., & Wilson, S. M. (1994). *Organizing for power and empowerment*. New York, NY: Columbia University Press.

Mor-Barak, M. E. (2005). *Managing diversity: Toward a globally inclusive workforce*. Thousand Oaks, CA: Sage Publications.

Morris, A. D. (1986). *The origins of the civil rights movement: Black communities organizing for change*. New York, NY: Free Press.

Morris, P. M. (2002). The capabilities perspective: A framework for social justice. *Families in Society: The Journal of Contemporary Human Services, 83*(4), 365–373.

Mosley, J. E. (2012). Keeping the lights on: How government funding concerns drive the agendas of nonprofit homeless service providers. *Journal of Public Administration Research and Theory, 22*, 841–866.

Mott, A. (2008). *Community learning project report on university education for social change*, 2nd ed. Retrieved from www.communitylearningpartnership.org/strategy.htm.

Moynihan, D. P. (1970). *Maximum feasible misunderstanding: Community action in the war on poverty*. New York, NY: Free Press.

Mullaly, R. (2010). *Challenging oppression and confronting privilege: A critical social work approach*, 2nd ed. Don Mills, ONT: Oxford University Press.

Mullen, E. J., & Magnabosco, J. L. (Eds.) (1997). *Outcomes measurement in the human services: Cross-cutting issues and methods*. Washington, DC: NASW Press.

Muller v. Oregon (1908). 208 U.S. 412.

Mulroy, E. A. (2003). Community as a factor in implementing interorganizational partnerships: Issues, constraints, and adaptations. *Nonprofit Management & Leadership, 14*(1), 47–65.

Mulroy, E. A. (2004). Theoretical perspectives on the social environment to guide management and community practice: An organization-in-environment approach. *Administration in Social Work, 28*(1), 77–96.

Murdach, A. (2011). Is social work a human rights profession? *Social Work, 56*(3), 281.

Nadler, E. (1971). Militant action and organizational development. Brooklyn, NY: Author.

Naples, N. A., & Desai, M. (Eds.) (2002). *Women's activism and globalization: Linking local struggles and transnational politics*. New York, NY: Routledge.

Narro, V. (2005). Impacting next wave organizing: Creative campaign strategies of the Los Angeles worker centers. *New York Law School Law Review, 50*, 465.

Nasir, N. I. S., & Al-Amin, J. (2006). Creating identity-safe spaces on college campuses for Muslim students. *Change: The Magazine of Higher Learning, 38*(2), 22–27.

National Association of Social Workers (2017). *Code of ethics* (Rev. ed.). Washington, DC: Author.

National Association of Social Workers (2015). *Achieving racial equity: A call to action*. Washington, DC: Author.

Nelson, N., & Wright, S. (1995). *Power and participatory development: Theory and practice*. ITDG Publishing.

Neruda, P. (1981). Injustice. (Translated by A. Reid). In K. Van den Heuvel (Ed.) *The Nation, 1865-1990: Selections from the independent magazine of politics and culture* (pp. 509–510). New York, NY: Thunder Mouth Press.

Netting, F. E., Kettner, P. M., & McMurty, S. L. (2004). *Social work macro practice*, 2nd ed. Englewood Cliffs, NJ: Prentice Hall.

Netting, F. E., Kettner, P. M., McMurty, S. L., & Thomas, M. L. (2012). *Social work macro practice*, 5th ed. Englewood Cliffs, NJ: Prentice Hall.

Neubauer, D. W., & Meinhold, S. S. (2016). *Judicial process: Law, courts, and politics in the United States*. Chicago, IL: Nelson Education.

Neubeck, K. J., & Cazenave, N. A. (2002). Welfare racism and its consequences: The demise of AFDC and the return of the states' rights era. In F. F. Piven, J. Acker, M. Hallock & S. Morgen (Eds.), *Work, welfare, and politics: Confronting poverty in the wake of welfare reform* (pp. 333–346). Eugene, OR: University of Oregon Press.

Newcomer, K. E., Hatry, H. P., & Wholey, J. S. (2015). *Handbook of practical program evaluation*. New York, NY: John Wiley & Sons.

Nicholls, W. (2013). *The DREAMers: How the undocumented youth movement transformed the immigrant rights debate*. Palo Alto, CA: Stanford University Press.

Nicholson-Crotty, J. (2011). Nonprofit organizations, bureaucratic agencies, and policy: Exploring the determinants of administrative advocacy. *The American Review of Public Administration, 41*(1), 61–74.

Nielsen, R. K. (2012). *Ground wars: Personalized communication in political campaigns*. Princeton, NJ: Princeton University Press.

Nielsen, R. K. (2011). Mundane internet tools, mobilizing practices, and the coproduction of citizenship in political campaigns. *New Media & Society, 13*(5), 755–771.

Nocon, A., & Qureshi, H. (1996). *Outcomes of community care for users and carers: A social service perspective*. Bristol, PA: Open University Press.

Nonprofit Finance Fund (2015). *A field in flux: 2015 state of the nonprofit sector survey*. Retrieved from http://nonprofitfinancefund.org/files/2015/2015survey_natl_summary.pdf.

Novak, W. J. (2016). *The pluralist state: The convergence of public and private power in America*. Chicago, IL: American Bar Association.

Nowell, B., & Boyd, N. M. (2014). Sense of community responsibility in community collaboratives: Advancing a theory of community as resource and responsibility. *American Journal of Community Psychology, 54*(3-4), 229–242.

Nowell, B., & Foster-Fishman, P. (2011). Examining multi-sector community collaboratives as vehicles for building organizational capacity. *American Journal of Community Psychology, 48*(3–4), 193–207.

Nozick, R. (1974). *Anarchy, state, and utopia*. New York, NY: Basic Books.

Nussbaum, M. C. (2014). *Capabilities, gender, equality.* Cambridge, MA: Cambridge University Press.

Nussbaum, M. C. (2011). *Creating capabilities: The human development approach*. Cambridge, MA: Belknap Press of Harvard University Press.

Nyerges, T. L., Couclelis, H., & McMaster, M. (Eds.) (2011). *The Sage handbook of GIS and society*. Los Angeles, CA: Sage Publications.

Nystrom, N. M., & Jones, T. C. (2003). Community building with aging and old lesbians. *American Journal of Community Psychology, 31*(3/4), 293–300.

Ohmer, M. L., & DeMasi, K. (2009). *Consensus organizing—A community development workbook: A comprehensive guide to designing, implementing, and evaluating community change initiatives*. Los Angeles, CA: Sage Publications.

Olson, C. (2013). Voices from the field: Social workers define and apply social justice. *Journal of Progressive Human Services, 24*(1), 23–42. doi: 10.1080/10428232.2013.740407.

Olson, L. R., & Green, J. C. (Eds.) (2009). *Beyond red state, blue state: Electoral gaps in the twenty-first century American electorate.* Upper Saddle River, NJ: Pearson/Prentice Hall.

Olson, M. (2009). *The logic of collective action.* Cambridge, MA: Harvard University Press.

Orslene, L. (2010). *Starting a nonprofit organization.* Morgantown, WV: U.S. Department of Labor, Office of Disability Employment Policy, Job Accommodation Network.

Ortega, R. M. (2017). Group work and socially just practice. In C. D. Garvin, L. M. Gutierrez, & M. J. Galinsky (Eds.), *Handbook of social work with groups* (pp. 93–110). New York, NY: The Guilford Press.

Ortega y Gasset, J. (1985). *The revolt of the masses.* New York, NY: W. W. Norton.

Ortiz, L., & Jani, J. S. (2010). Critical race theory: A transformational model for teaching diversity. *Journal of Social Work Education, 46*(2), 175–193.

Ostrom, E. (2014). Collective action and the evolution of social norms. *Journal of Natural Resources Policy Research, 6*(4), 235–252.

Ott, J. S., & Dick, L. A. (Eds.) (2012). *Understanding nonprofit organizations: Governance, leadership, and management.* Boulder, CO: Westview Press.

Ouchi, W. G., & Price, R. L. (1978). Hierarchies, clans, and theory Z: A new perspective on organization development. *Organizational Dynamics, 7*(2), 25–44.

Paley, J. (2001). *Marketing democracy: Power and social movements in post-dictatorship Chile.* Berkeley, CA: University of California Press.

Parenti, M. (2008). *Democracy for the few*, 8th ed. Boston, MA: Thomson-Wadsworth.

Parenti, M. (1978). *Power and the powerless.* New York, NY: St. Martin's Press.

Parsons, T. (1954). *Essays in sociological theory.* Glencoe, IL: Free Press.

Patti, R. (Ed.) (2008). *Handbook of human services management*, 2nd ed. Newbury Park, CA: Sage Publications.

Perlman, J. E. (1976). Grassrooting the system. *Social Policy, 7*(2), 4–20.

Perrault, E., McClelland, R., Austin, C., & Sieppert, J. (2011). Working together in collaborations:

Successful process factors for community collaboration. *Administration in Social Work, 35*(3), 282–298.

Peters, A. (2003). Isolation or inclusion: Creating safe spaces for lesbian and gay youth. *Families in Society: The Journal of Contemporary Social Services, 84*(3), 331–337.

Philip, D., & Reisch, M. (2015). Rethinking social work's interpretation of 'environmental justice': From local to global. *Social Work Education: An International Journal, 34*(5), 471–483.

Pimlott, J. P. (2010). *Women and the Democratic Party: The evolution of EMILY's List.* Amherst, NY: Cambria Press.

Piott, S. L. (2003). *Giving voters a voice: The origins of the initiative and referendum in America.* Columbia, MO: University of Missouri Press.

Piven, F. F., & Cloward, R. (1977). *Poor people's movements: How they succeed, why they fail.* New York, NY: Pantheon.

Plekhanov, G. V., & Fineman, J. (1940). *The role of the individual in history.* New York, NY: Foreign Languages Publishing House.

Polack, R. J. (2004). Social justice and the global economy: New challenges for social work in the 21st century. *Social Work, 49*(2), 281–290.

Polletta, F., & Jasper, J. M. (2001). Collective identity and social movements. *Annual Review of Sociology, 27*(1), 283–305.

Portney, K., & Berry, J. (1997). Mobilizing minority communities: Social capital and participation in urban neighborhoods, *American Behavioral Scientist, 40*(5), 632–645.

Powers, R. S., & Voegele, W. B. (Eds.) (1997). *Protest, power, and change: An encyclopedia of nonviolent action from ACT-UP to women's suffrage.* New York, NY: Garland Publishers.

Prilleltensky, I. (2001). Value-based praxis in community psychology: Moving toward social justice and social action. *American Journal of Community Psychology, 29*(5), 747–778.

Putnam, R. D. (2001). *Bowling alone: The collapse and revival of American community.* New York, NY: Touchstone.

Quinn, R. E., & Cameron, K. (1983). Organizational life cycles and shifting criteria of effectiveness: Some preliminary evidence. *Management Science, 29*(1), 33–51.

Quirion, H. (1972). Community organization and political action in Montreal. *Social Work, 17*(5), 85–90.

Quiroz, J., et al. (2014). *Echoing justice: Communications strategies for community organizing in the 21st century.* Oakland, CA: Center for Media Justice.

Raheim, S. (2003). Building organizational capacity for cultural competence. *International Journal of Diversity in Organisations, Communities and Nations, 3B*, 137–151.

Rahim, M. A. (2011). *Managing conflict in organizations*, 4th ed. New York, NY: Transaction Publishers.

Rahim, M. A. (2002). Toward a theory of managing organizational conflict. *International Journal of Conflict Management, 13*(3), 206–235.

Rank, M. R. (2014). Why poverty and inequality undermine justice in America. In M. Reisch (Ed.), *The Routledge international handbook of social justice* (pp. 436–447). London, UK: Routledge.

Rank, M. G., & Hutchison, W. S. (2000). An analysis of leadership within the social work profession. *Journal of Social Work Education, 36*(3), 487–502.

Rawls, J. (1999). *A theory of justice* (Rev. ed.). Cambridge, MA: Belknap Press of Harvard University Press.

Reamer, F. G. (1987). Ethics committees in social work. *Social Work, 32*(3), 188–192.

Reamer, F. G. (2013). *Social work values and ethics*, 2nd ed. New York, NY: Columbia University Press.

Reber, B. H., & Kim, J. K. (2006). How activist groups use websites in media relations: Evaluating online press rooms. *Journal of Public Relations Research, 18*(4), 313–333.

Reich, R. (2010). *Aftershock: The next economy and America's future.* New York, NY: Alfred A. Knopf.

Reichert, E. D. (Ed.) (2007). *Challenges in human rights: A social work perspective.* New York, NY: University Press.

Reichert, E. D. (2011). *Social work and human rights: A foundation for policy and practice*, 2nd ed. New York, NY: Columbia University Press.

Reid, W., & Turbide, J. (2012). Board/staff relationships in a growth crisis: Implications for nonprofit governance. *Nonprofit and Voluntary Sector Quarterly, 41*(1), 82–99.

Reisch, M. (2013a). Community practice challenges in the global economy. In M. O. Weil, M. Reisch, & M. L. Ohmer (Eds.), *Handbook of community practice*, 2nd ed. (pp. 47–71). Thousand Oaks, CA: Sage Publications.

Reisch, M. (2008a). *Die politik der soziale arbeit in zeiten der globalisierung*. (The politics of social work in the age of globalization). In F. Kessl & H.-U. Otto (Eds.), *Soziale arbeit ohne wohlfahrtsstaat? Zeitdiagnosen, problematisierungen und perspektiven* (pp. 223–244). Weinheim, Germany: Juventa.

Reisch, M. (2014b). Ethical practice in an unethical environment. In S. Banks, *Ethics* (pp. 45–49). Bristol, UK: Policy Press.

Reisch, M. (1987). From cause to case and back again: The reemergence of advocacy in social work. *Urban and Social Change Review, 19*, 20–24.

Reisch, M. (2008b). General themes in the evolution of human services administration. In R. Patti (Ed.), *Handbook of human services management*, 2nd ed. (pp. 920–927). Newbury Park, CA: Sage Publications.

Reisch, M. (2015d, May 5). How research in the social sciences has influenced American attitudes toward poverty. Unpublished invitational paper presented at SAGE Social Sciences Speakers Forum on Capitol Hill, Washington, DC.

Reisch, M. (2012a). Intervention with communities. In C. Glisson, C. N. Dulmus, & K. M. Sowers (Eds.), *Social work practice with groups, communities, and organizations: A foundation of social work* (pp. 81–130). Hoboken, NJ: Wiley Publishing.

Reisch, M. (2015a). Legislative advocacy to empower oppressed and vulnerable groups. In K. Corcoran (Ed.), *Social workers' desk reference*, 3rd ed. (pp. 920-927). New York, NY: Oxford University Press.

Reisch, M. (1990). Organizational structure and client advocacy: Lessons from the 1980s. *Social Work, 35*(1), 73–74.

Reisch, M. (2016b). Rethinking poverty. *Management Information Exchange Journal, 30*(2), 41–48.

Reisch, M. (2015b). Social justice. In R. Hugman & J. Carter (Eds.), *Ethics in social work* (pp. 33–48). London, UK: Palgrave/MacMillan.

Reisch, M. (2017). *Social policy and social justice: Meeting the challenges of a diverse society*, 2nd ed. San Diego, CA: Cognella Academic Publishing.

Reisch, M. (2013c). Social work education and the neoliberal challenge: The U.S. response to increasing global inequality. *Social Work Education, 32*(6), 217–233.

Reisch, M. (2014a). The boundaries of justice: Addressing the conflict between human rights and multiculturalism in social work practice and education. In K. Libal, L. Healy, M. Berthold, & R. Thomas (Eds.), *Advancing Human Rights in Social Work Education* (pp. 177–195). Alexandria, VA: Council on Social Work Education.

Reisch, M. (2012b). The challenges of health care reform for hospital social work in the U.S. *Social Work in Health Care, 51*(10), 873–893.

Reisch, M. (2008b). The democratic promise: The impact of German Jewish immigration on social work in the United States. *Yearbook of the Leo Baeck Institute* (pp. 169–190). London, UK: Leo Baeck Institute.

Reisch, M. (2014c, October). The end of social welfare history: Implications for social work education. Unpublished paper presented at the Annual Program Meeting, Council on Social Work Education, Tampa, FL.

Reisch, M. (2015c). U.S. social work and the working class: Coalition and conflict. *Zapruder* (Special issue, in Italian), C. DeVito & G. Strippoli (Eds.). Bologna, Italy.

Reisch, M. (2012c, January 16). Using oral history to understand leadership and leadership development. Unpublished paper presented at the Annual Conference of the Society for Social Work and Research, Washington, DC.

Reisch, M. (2013b). What is the future of social work? *Critical and Radical Social Work, 1*(1), 67–85.

Reisch, M. (2016a). Why macro practice matters. *Journal of Social Work Education 52*(3), 1–11.

Reisch, M., & Andrews, J. (2002). *The road not taken: A history of radical social work in the United States* (Rev. ed.). Philadelphia, PA: Brunner-Routledge.

Reisch, M., & Bischoff, U. M. (2002). Welfare reform and community-based organizations: The impact on family well-being in an urban neighborhood. In F. F. Piven, J. Acker, M. Hallock & S. Morgen (Eds.), *Work, welfare, and politics: Confronting poverty in the wake of welfare reform* (pp. 333–346). Eugene, OR: University of Oregon Press.

Reisch, M., & Garvin, C. (2016). *Social work and social justice: Concepts, challenges, and strategies.* New York, NY: Oxford University Press.

Reisch, M., & Guyet, D. (2007). Communities as 'big small groups': Culture and social capital. In R. Cnaan & C. Milofsky (Eds.), *The handbook of communities and organizations* (pp. 163–178). New York, NY: Springer.

Reisch, M., Ife, J., & Weil, M. O. (2012). Social justice, human rights, values, and community practice. In M. O. Weil, M. Reisch, & M. L. Ohmer (Eds.), *The handbook of community practice*, 2nd ed. (pp. 73–103). Thousand Oaks, CA: Sage Publications.

Reisch, M., & Jani, J. S. (2012). The new politics of social work practice: Understanding context to promote change. *British Journal of Social Work, 42*(6), 1132–1150.

Reisch, M., & Lowe, J. I. (2000). 'Of means and ends' revisited: Teaching ethical community organization in an unethical society. *Journal of Community Practice, 7(1)*, 19–38.

Reisch, M., & Rivera, F. (1999). Ethical and racial conflicts in urban-based action research. *Journal of Community Practice, 6(2)*, 49–62.

Reisch, M., & Sommerfeld, D. (2003b). Inter-organizational relationships among nonprofits in the aftermath of welfare reform. *Social Work, 48(3)*, 307–319.

Reisch, M., & Sommerfeld, D. (2002). Race, welfare reform, and nonprofit organizations. *Journal of Sociology and Social Welfare, 29(1)*, 155–177.

Reisch, M., & Sommerfeld, D. (2003a). Welfare reform and the future of nonprofit organizations. *Nonprofit Management and Leadership, 14(1)*, 19–46.

Reisch, M., Wenocur, S., & Sherman, W. (1981–1982). Empowerment, conscientization, and animation as core social work skills. *Social Development Issues, 5(2–3)*, 108–120.

Reitan, T. C. (1998). Theories of inter-organizational relations in the human services. *Social Service Review, 72*(3), 285–309.

Rhode, D. (2014). *What women want: An agenda for the women's movement.* New York, NY: Oxford University Press.

Richan, W. C. (2013). *Lobbying for social change*, 4th ed. New York, NY: Haworth Press.

Rickford, R. (2016). Black lives matter: Toward a modern practice of mass struggle. *New Labor Forum 25*(1), 34–42.

Rivera, F. G. (1995). Personal communication with author. San Francisco, CA: San Francisco State University.

Rivera, F. G. (1997). Personal communication with author. San Francisco, CA: San Francisco State University.

Rivera, F. G., & Erlich, J. (Eds.) (1997). *Community organizing in a diverse society*, 3rd ed. Needham Heights, MA: Allyn & Bacon.

Ryan, W. (1971). *Blaming the victim.* New York, NY: Pantheon Books.

Roberts, V. Z. (1994). The organization of work: Contributions from open systems theory. In *The unconscious at work* (pp. 28–38). London, UK: Routledge.

Robinson, B., & Hanna, M. G. (1994). Lessons for academics for grassroots community organizing: A case study—the Industrial Areas Foundation. *Journal of Community Practice, 1*(4), 63–94.

Robinson, T., & Robinson, G. (2006). The limits of interracial coalitions: *Méndez v. Westminster* reexamined. In N. De Genova (Ed.), *Racial Transformations: Latinos and Asians Remaking the United States* (pp. 93–119). Durham, NC: Duke University Press.

Rocha, C., Poe, B., & Thomas, V. (2010). Political activities of social workers: Addressing perceived barriers to political participation. *Social Work, 55*(4), 317–325.

Roe v. Wade (1973). 410 U.S. 113.

Rodrik. D. (2011). *The globalization paradox: Democracy and the future of the world economy.* New York, NY: W. W. Norton.

Rosanvallon, P., & Goldhammer, A. (2008). *Counter-democracy: Politics in an age of distrust.* Cambridge, MA: Cambridge University Press.

Rose, S. M. (1992). *Case management and social work practice.* New York, NY: Longman.

Rose, S. M. (1972). *The betrayal of the poor: The transformation of community action.* Cambridge, MA: Schenkman.

Rosenthal, A. (2006). Balance of power: The case of the budget, in R. A. Clucas (Ed.), *Readings and cases in state and local politics* (pp. 328–336). Boston, MA: Houghton Mifflin.

Rothman, J. R. (2013). *Education for macro intervention: A survey of problems and prospects.*

Los Angeles: Association of Community Organization and Social Administration (available online at www.acosa.org).

Rothman, J. R. (1968). Three models of community organization practice. *Social Work Practice, 25(1)*, 16–47.

Rothman, J. R. (Ed.) (1999). *Reflections on community organization: Enduring themes and critical issues*. Itasca, IL: F. E. Peacock.

Rothman J. R., & Mizrahi, T. (2014). Balancing micro and macro practice: A challenge for social work. *Social Work, 59*(1), 91–93.

Rothman, J. R., & Tropman, J. E. (1987). Models of community organization and macro practice perspectives: Their mixing and phasing. In F. Cox, et al. (Eds.), *Strategies of community organization*, 4th ed. (pp. 3–26). Itasca, IL: F. E. Peacock Publishers.

Rubin, H. J., & Rubin, I. S. (2008). *Community organizing and development*, 4th ed. Boston, MA: Pearson/Allyn & Bacon.

Rusk, D. (2013). *Cities without suburbs: A 2010 census perspective*. Baltimore, MD: Johns Hopkins University Press.

Rusk, D. (1999). *Inside game outside game: Winning strategies for saving urban America*. Washington, DC: Brookings Institution Press.

Ruvio, A., Rosenblatt, Z., & Hertz-Lazarowitz, R. (2010). Entrepreneurial leadership vision in nonprofit vs. for-profit organizations. *Leadership Quarterly, 21*(1), 144–158.

Ryan, W. (1981). *Equality*. New York, NY: Pantheon Books.

Said, E. W. (2003). *Orientalism*. London, UK: Penguin.

Salamon, L. M. (2012). *The state of nonprofit America*, 2nd ed. Washington, DC: Brookings Institution.

Saleeby, D. (2002). *The strengths perspective and social work practice*, 3rd ed. Boston, MA: Allyn & Bacon.

Sample, T. S. (1979). Paradigm on consensus and. conflict strategies. In F. M. Cox, J. L. Erlich, J. Rothman, & J.E. Tropman (Eds.), *Strategies of community organization*, 3rd ed. (pp. 475-477). Itasca, IL: F. E. Peacock Publishers.

Sampson, T. J. (1973). *Welfare: A handbook for friend and foe*. Philadelphia, PA: United Church Press.

Sandler, R., & Pezzullo, P. C. (Eds.) (2007). *Environmental justice and environmentalism: The social justice challenge to the environmental movement*. Cambridge, MA: MIT Press.

Sassen, S. (2006). *Cities in a world economy*, 3rd ed. Thousand Oaks, CA: Pine Forge Press.

Sathe, V. (1985). *Culture and related corporate realities: Texts, cases, and readings on organizational entry, establishment, and change*. Homewood, IL: R.D. Irwin.

Sathe, V. (1984). *Organizational culture: Some conceptual distinctions and managerial implications*. Boston, MA: Division of Research, Harvard Business School.

Schein, E. H. (1981). Does Japanese management style have a message for American managers? *Sloan Management Review 23*(1), 55–64.

Schein, E. H. (1993). On dialogue, culture, and organizational learning. *Organizational Dynamics, 22*(2), 40–51.

Scheider, H., & Libercier, M.-H. (Eds.) (1995). *Participatory development: From advocacy to action*. Washington, DC: OECD Publications and Information Center.

Schneider, R., & L. Lester (2001). *Social work advocacy: A new framework for action*. Belmont, CA: Wadsworth.

Schram, S. (2006). *Welfare discipline: Discourse, governance, and globalization*. Philadelphia, PA: Temple University Press.

Schulz, A. J., Israel, B. A., & Lantz, P. (2017). Assessing and strengthening characteristics of effective groups in community-based participatory research partnerships. In C. D. Garvin, L. M. Gutierrez, & M. J. Galinsky (Eds.), *Handbook of social work with groups* (pp. 433–453). New York, NY: The Guilford Press.

Schwartz, W. (1969). Private troubles and public issues: One social work job or two? *Social Welfare Forum, 1969*. New York, NY: Columbia University Press.

Seif, H. (2010). The civic life of Latina/o immigrant youth: Challenging boundaries and creating safe spaces. In L. R. Sherrod, J. Torney-Purta, & C. A. Flanagan (Eds.), *Handbook of research on civic engagement in youth* (pp. 445–470). Hoboken, NJ: Wiley.

Sen, A. (2009). *The idea of justice*. Cambridge, MA: Belknap Press of Harvard University Press.

Sen, R. (2013). New theory for new constituencies: Contemporary organizing in communities of color. In M. O. Weil, M. Reisch, & M. L. Ohmer (Eds.), *The handbook of community practice*, 2nd ed. (pp. 249–264). Thousand Oaks, CA: Sage Publications.

Senge, P. M. (2006). *The fifth discipline: The art and practice of the learning organization.* New York, NY: Doubleday.

Sharpe, T. L., & Boyas, J. (2011). We fall down: The African American experience of coping with the homicide of a loved one. *Journal of Black Studies, 42*(6), 855–873.

Shaw, R. (2013). *The activist's handbook: Winning social change in the 21st century.* Berkeley, CA: University of California Press.

Shields, G., King, W., Williams, M., Chard, S., & Lab, S. (2004). Evaluating media strategies in rural communities. In T. L. Scales & C. Streeter (Eds.), *Rural social work: Building and sustaining community assets* (pp. 317–327), Belmont, CA: Brooks/Cole.

Shier, M. L., & Graham, J. R. (2013). Identifying social service needs of Muslims living in a post 9/11 era: The role of community-based organizations. *Advances in Social Work, 14*(2), 379–394.

Shier, M. L., Graham, J. R., Deane, L., & Jones, M. E. (2013). Leadership in a Chinese advocacy focused non-profit organization: Adaptability to context for leadership success. *Social Development Issues, 35*(3), 96–108.

Shier, M. L., & Handy, F. (2016). Executive leadership and social innovation in direct-service nonprofits: Shaping the organizational culture to create social change. *Journal of Progressive Human Services, 27*(2), 111–130.

Shier, M. L., & Handy, F. (2015). From advocacy to social innovation: A typology of social change efforts by nonprofits. *Voluntas: International Journal of Voluntary and Nonprofit Organizations, 26*(6), 2581–2603. doi: 10.1007/s11266-014-9535-1.

Shier, M. L., & Handy, F. (2015). Social change efforts of direct-service nonprofits: The role of funding and collaborative networks in shaping social innovations. *Human Service Organizations: Management, Leadership & Governance, 39*(1), 6–24.

Shier, M. L., McDougle, L. M., & Handy, F. (2014). Nonprofits and the promotion of civic engagement: A conceptual framework for understanding the 'civic footprint' of nonprofits within local communities. *The Canadian Journal of Nonprofit and Social Economy Research, 5*(1), 57–75.

Shih, J. (2006). Circumventing discrimination: Gender and ethnic strategies in Silicon Valley. *Gender & Society, 20*(2), 177–206.

Shilts, R. (2007). *And the band played on: Politics, people, and the AIDS epidemic*, 20th anniversary ed. New York, NY: St. Martin's/Griffin.

Shulman, D. (2017). *The presentation of self in contemporary social life.* Los Angeles, CA: Sage Publications.

Simon, B. L. (1990). *The empowerment tradition in American social work.* New York, NY: Columbia University Press.

Skocpol, T., & Fiorina, M. P. (Eds.). (2004). *Civic engagement in American democracy.* Washington, DC: Brookings Institution Press.

Smith, M. M., & Powell, L. (2013). *Dark money, super PACs, and the 2012 election.* Lanham, MD: Lexington Books.

Smith, R., Bucchio, J., & Turnage, B. F. (2017). Social group work in a global context. In C. D. Garvin, L. M. Gutierrez, & M. J. Galinsky (Eds.), *Handbook of social work with groups* (pp. 43–54). New York, NY: The Guilford Press.

Smith, S. R. (2015). Managing human service organizations in the 21st century. *Human Service Organizations: Management, Leadership, & Governance, 39*(5), 407–411.

Smith, S. R. (1997). Partnerships, community building, and local government. *National Civil Review, 86*, 167–174.

Smucker, B. (2005). Nonprofit lobbying. In R. D. Herman & Associates (Eds.), *The Jossey-Bass handbook of nonprofit leadership and management* (pp. 230–253). San Francisco, CA: John Wiley.

Solomon, B. B. (1976). *Black empowerment: Social work in oppressed communities.* New York, NY: Columbia University Press.

Sommerfeld, D., & Reisch, M. (2003). Unintended consequences: The impact of welfare reform on nonprofit organizations. *Voluntas, 14(3),* 299–320.

Soss, J., Fording, R. C., & Schram, S. (2011). *Disciplining the poor: Neoliberal paternalism and the persistent power of race.* Chicago, IL: University of Chicago Press.

Specht, H., & Courtenay, M. (1994). *Unfaithful angels: How social work abandoned its mission.* New York, NY: Free Press.

Speer, P. W., Ontkush, M., Schmitt, B., Raman, P., Johnson, C., Rengert, K. M., and Peterson, N. A. (2003). The intentional exercise of power: Community organizing in Camden, New Jersey, *Journal of Community and Applied Social Psychology, 13*(5), 399–407.

Staggenborg, S. (2016). *Social movements*, 2nd ed. New York, NY: Oxford University Press.

Staller, K. M. (2017). Federal and state budget basics for social workers. In M. Reisch, *Social policy and social justice: Meeting the challenges of a diverse society*, 2nd ed. (pp. 227–247). San Diego, CA: Cognella Academic Publishing.

Starling, S. (2010). Monitoring and evaluating advocacy: Lessons from Oxfam GB's Climate Change campaign. *Development in Practice, 20*(2), 277–286.

Stern, M. J., & Axinn, J. (2012). *Social welfare: A history of the American response to need*, 8th ed. Boston, MA: Pearson Education.

Stienstra, D., Watzke, J., & Birch, G. E. (2007). A three-way dance: The global public good and accessibility in information technologies. *The Information Society, 23*(3), 149–158.

Stoesz, D. (2014). Conservatism and social justice. In M. Reisch (Ed.), *The Routledge international handbook of social justice* (pp. 147–159). London, UK: Routledge.

Stoesz, D., Karger, H. J., & Carrilio, T. (2010). *A dream deferred: How social work education lost its way and what can be done.* New Brunswick, NJ: Transaction Publishers.

Stone, C., Trisi, D., Sherman, A., & DeBot, B. (2015, July 15). *A guide to statistics on historical trends in income inequality.* Washington, DC: Center on Budget & Policy Priorities.

Stone, S. I., Austin, M. J., Berzin, S., & Taylor, S. (2007). Exploring the knowledge base of HB & SE using the concept of reciprocity. *Journal of Human Behavior and the Social Environment, 16*(3), 89–106.

Stoner, M. R. (1995). *The civil rights of homeless people: Law, social policy, and social work practice.* New York, NY: Aldine de Gruyter.

Stotzer, R. L., & Tropman, J. E. (2006). Profess-ionalizing social work at the national level: Women social work leaders, 1910-1982. *Affilia, 21*(1), 9–27.

Strom-Gottfried, K. (2007). *Straight talk about professional ethics.* Chicago, IL: Lyceum Books.

Sumner, W. G. (1883, 1982). *What social classes owe to each other.* Caldwell, ID: Caxton Printers.

Tan, Y., & Weaver, D. H. (2009). Local media, public opinion, and state legislative policies: Agenda setting at the state level. *The International Journal of Press/Politics, 14*(4), 454–476.

Tarrow, S. G. (2011). *Power in movement: Social movements and contentious politics.* Cambridge, MA: Cambridge University Press.

Taylor, F. W. (1911). *The principles of scientific management.* New York, NY: Harper & Brothers.

Teles, S., & Schmitt, M. (2011). The elusive craft of evaluating advocacy. *Stanford Social Innovation Review, 9*(3), 40–43.

Theiss-Morse, E., Hibbing, J. R. (2005). Citizenship and social engagement. *Annual Review of Political Science, 8*, 227–249.

Thomas, D. C. (December 1978). Training in medical ethics: An ethical workup. *Forum in Medicine, 1*(9), 33–36.

Thomas, R. R. (1991). *Beyond race and gender: Unleashing the power of your total work force by managing diversity.* New York, NY: AMACOM.

Thompson, N. (2002). Social movements, social justice and social work. *British Journal of Social Work, 32*(6), 711–722.

Thyer, B. A. (2007). Evidence-based practice in the U.S. In B. A. Thyer & M. A. F. Kazi (Eds.), *International perspectives on evidence-based practice in social work* (pp. 9–27). Birmingham, UK: Venture Press.

Tilly, C. (1978). *From mobilization to revolution.* Reading, MA: Addison-Wesley.

Ting-Toomey, S., & Chung, L. C. (2012). *Understanding intercultural communication*, 2nd ed. New York, NY: Oxford University Press.

Ting-Toomey, S., Gao, G., Trubisky, P., Yang, Z., Soo Kim, H., Lin, S. L., & Nishida, T. (1991). Culture, face maintenance, and styles of handling interpersonal conflict: A study in five cultures. *International Journal of Conflict Management, 2*(4), 275–296.

Todd, S. (2016). Social work ethics in community practice. In R. Hugman & J. Carter (Eds.),

Rethinking values & ethics in social work (pp. 164–179). New York, NY: Palgrave MacMillan.

Tolbert, C. J., & Smith, D. A. (2005). The educative effects of ballot initiatives on voter turnout. *American Politics Research, 33*(2), 283–309.

Tonnies, F. (1957). *Community and society* (Trans. & Ed. by C.P. Loomis). East Lansing, MI: Michigan State University Press.

Toseland, R. (2017). Group dynamics. In C. D. Garvin, L. M. Gutierrez, & M. J. Galinsky (Eds.), *Handbook of social work with groups* (pp. 9–27). New York, NY: The Guilford Press.

Tracy, B. (2014). *Leadership.* New York, NY: AMACOM.

Trapp, S. (1976). *Dynamics of organizing.* Chicago, IL: National Training and Information Center.

Tropman, J. E. (1996). *Effective meetings: Improving group decision making,* 2nd ed. Thousand Oaks, CA: Sage Publications.

Tropman, J. E. (1997). *Successful community leadership: A skills guide for volunteers and professionals.* Washington, DC: National Association of Social Workers.

Tsang, E. W. (1997). Organizational learning and the learning organization: a dichotomy between descriptive and prescriptive research. *Human Relations, 50*(1), 73–89.

Uldam, J., & Vestergaard, A. (Eds.) (2015). *Civic engagement and social media: Political participation beyond protest.* New York, NY: Palgrave MacMillan.

Ungar, M. (2001). Lesbian, gay, bisexual, and transgendered international alliances: The perils of success. In J. Bystydzienski and S. Schacht, (Eds.), *Forging radical alliances across difference: Coalition politics for the new millennium* (pp. 235–248), Lanham, MD: Rowman and Littlefield.

U.S. Bureau of the Census (2016). *Statistical abstract of the United States, 2015,* 135th ed., Washington, DC: U.S. Government Printing Office.

U.S. Department of Labor (2016). *Statistics on employment in the U.S.,* 2016. Washington, DC: U.S. Government Printing Office.

Waldman, D. A., De Luque, M. S., Washburn, N., House, R. J., Adetoun, B., Barrasa, A., & Dorfman, P. (2006). Cultural and leadership predictors of corporate social responsibility values of top management: A GLOBE study of 15 countries. *Journal of International Business Studies, 37*(6), 823–837.

Wallack, L., & Dorfman, L. (1996). Media advocacy: A strategy for advancing policy and promoting health. *Health Education Quarterly, 23*(3), 293–317.

Wallack, L. M., et al. (1999). *News for a change: An advocate's guide to working with the media.* Thousand Oaks, CA: Sage Publications.

Walls, N. E. (2012). Intersectionality: Thoughts on tensions and opportunities in identity-based politics. Unpublished paper presented at Symposium on "Interdisciplinary Scholarship for Community Practice in the 21st Century," University of Michigan, Ann Arbor, MI.

Warren, M. R. (2016). Creating a multiracial democratic community: A case study of the Texas Industrial Areas Foundation. *Civic Practices Network.* Washington, DC: Concern, Inc.

Warren, R. (1977). *Social change and human purpose: Toward understanding and action.* Chicago, IL: Rand McNally College Publishing Co.

Warren, R. (1978). *The community in America.* Chicago, IL: Rand McNally.

Warren, R. L. (1970). The good community—What would it be? *Journal of the Community Development Society, 1*(1), 14–24.

Warren, R. B., & Warren, D. I. (1977). *The neighborhood organizer's handbook.* South Bend, IN: University of Notre Dame Press.

Warwick, M. (2000). *The five strategies for fundraising success: A mission-based guide to achieving your goals.* San Francisco, CA: Jossey-Bass.

Weaver, H. N. (2014). Indigenous struggles for justice: Restoring balance within the context of Anglo settler societies. In M. Reisch (Ed.), *The Routledge international handbook of social justice* (pp. 111–122). London, UK: Routledge.

Weber, M. (1946). *From Max Weber: Essays in sociology* (Trans. & Ed. by H. H. Gerth & C. W. Mills). New York, NY: Oxford University Press.

Weil, M. O. (2013). Community-based social planning. In M. O.Weil, M. Reisch, & M. L. Ohmer (Eds.), *The handbook of community practice,* 2nd ed. (pp. 265–298). Thousand Oaks, CA: Sage Publications.

Weil, M. O. (1986). Women, community, and organizing. In N. Van Den Bergh & L. B. Cooper (Eds.), *Feminist visions for social work* (pp. 187–210). Silver Spring, MD: National Association of Social Workers.

Weil, M. O., Gamble, D. N., & Ohmer, M. L. (2013). Evolution, models, and the changing context of community practice. In M. O. Weil, M. Reisch, & M. L. Ohmer (Eds.), *The handbook of community practice*, 2nd ed. (pp. 167–193). Thousand Oaks, CA: Sage Publications.

Weil, M., & Sanchez, E. (1983). The impact of the Tarasoff decision on clinical social work practice. *Social Service Review, 57*(1), 112–124.

Weisbrod, B. A. (2000). *To profit or not to profit: The commercial transformation of the nonprofit sector*. New York, NY: Cambridge University Press.

Weissman, H. H., Epstein, I., & Savage, A. (1983). *Agency-based social work: Neglected aspects of clinical practice*. Philadelphia, PA: Temple University Press.

Wenocur, S., & Reisch, M. (1989). *From charity to enterprise: The development of American social work in a market economy*. Champaign, IL: University of Illinois Press.

Wenocur, S., & Soifer, S. (1997). Prospects for community organizing. In M. Reisch & E. Gambrill (Eds.), *Social work in the 21st century* (pp. 198–208). Thousand Oaks, CA: Pine Forge Press.

West, D. M. (2013). *Air wars: Television advertising and social media in election campaigns, 1952-2012*. Thousand Oaks, CA: Sage Publications.

Whitaker, T., & Arrington, P. (2008). *Social workers at work: NASW membership workforce study*. Washington, DC: National Association of Social Workers.

Whitzman, C. (2007). The loneliness of the long-distance runner: Long-term feminist planning initiatives in London, Melbourne, Montréal and Toronto. *Planning Theory & Practice, 8*(2), 205–227.

Wilks, T. (2012). *Advocacy and social work practice*. Maidenhead, MA: McGraw-Hill Education.

Wilson, S. (1980). *Confidentiality in social work: Issues and principles*. New York, NY: Free Press.

Wilson, W. J. (1976). *Power, racism, and privilege: Race relations in theoretical and historical perspectives*. New York, NY: Free Press.

Wolff, E. R. (1997). *Europe and the people without history: With a new preface*. Berkeley, CA: University of California Press.

Woloch, N. (1996). *Muller v. Oregon: A brief history with documents*. New York, NY: MacMillan.

Woo, L. C. (1980). *The campaign organizer's manual*. Durham, NC: Carolina Academic Press.

Woodford, M. R., & Preston, S. (2011). Developing a strategy to meaningfully engage stakeholders in program/policy planning: A guide for human services managers and practitioners. *Journal of Community Practice, 19*(2), 159–174.

Wronka, J. (2017). *Human rights and social justice: Social action and service for the helping and health professions*, 2nd ed. Thousand Oaks, CA: Sage Publications.

Yan, M. C., & Wong, Y. L. R. (2005). Rethinking self-awareness in cultural competence: Toward a dialogic self in cross-cultural social work. *Families in Society: The Journal of Contemporary Social Services, 86*(2), 181–188.

Yee, J. Y., Wong, H., & Schlabitz, (2014). Beyond inclusion training: Changing human service and public organizations. In M. B. Cohen & C. A. Hyde (Eds.), *Empowering workers and clients for organizational change* (pp. 135–155). Chicago, IL: Lyceum Books.

Yiftachel, O. (1998). Planning and social control: Exploring the dark side. *CPL bibliography, 12*(4), 395–406.

Yoder, J. D., & Kahn, A. S. (1992). Toward a feminist understanding of women and power. *Psychology of Women Quarterly, 16*, 381–388.

Young, D. R. (2006). Complementary, supplementary, or adversarial? Nonprofit-government relations. In E.T. Boris and C.E. Steuerle (Eds.), *Nonprofits and government: Collaboration and conflict* (pp. 37–80). Washington, DC: The Urban Institute.

Young, D. R., & Salamon, L. M. (2002). Commercialization, social ventures, and for-profit competition. In L.M. Salamon (Ed.), *The state of nonprofit America* (pp. 423–446), Washington, DC: Brookings Institution Press.

Young, I. M. (2011). *Justice and the politics of difference*. Princeton, NJ: Princeton University Press.

Young, I. M. (2008). Structural injustice and the politics of difference. In G. Craig, T. Burchardt, & D. Gordon (Eds.), *Social justice and public policy: Seeking fairness in diverse societies* (pp. 77–104). Bristol, UK: The Polity Press.

Young, J. C. (2017). *The age of charisma: Leaders, followers, and emotions in American society, 1870-1940.* New York, NY: Cambridge University Press.

Zimbalist, S. E. (1977). *Historic themes and landmarks in social welfare research.* New York, NY: Harper & Row.

Zúñiga, X., & Nagda, B. A. (1993). Dialogue groups: An innovative approach to multicultural learning. In D. Schoem, et al. (Eds.), *Multicultural teaching in the university* (pp. 233–248). Westport, CT: Praeger.

Index

A

D

J

K

L

O

P

Q

R

S

T

U

V

W

Y

CPSIA information can be obtained
at www.ICGtesting.com
Printed in the USA
LVHW062350201219
641263LV00002B/3/P